THE PUBLICATIONS

OF THE

𝕾𝖊𝖑𝖉𝖊𝖓 𝕾𝖔𝖈𝖎𝖊𝖙𝖞

περὶ παντὸς τὴν ἐλευθερίαν

VOLUME CXXV

FOR THE YEAR 2008

Henry Singleton as lord chief justice of the Common Pleas
© James Fennell, photographer

IRISH EXCHEQUER REPORTS

Reports of Cases in the
Courts of Exchequer and Chancery in Ireland
1716–1734

EDITED FOR

THE SELDEN SOCIETY

BY

ANDREW LYALL, Ph.D., (Lond.), LL.D., (Lond.)

of Gray's Inn, barrister

LONDON
SELDEN SOCIETY
2009

Printed on acid-free paper

ISBN 978 0 85423 126 3

Typeset by the author and Cambridge University Press.
Printed by Cambridge University Press

CONTENTS

PREFACE

It is always a pleasure to acknowledge the assistance of colleagues in bringing a work to publication. A special word of thanks is due in this case to Professor Sir John Baker, the Literary Director of the Selden Society, and to Dr Neil Jones, the Assistant Literary Director of the Society, for their detailed and helpful comments on earlier drafts. I am grateful to Professor Nial Osborough of University College Dublin for his extensive knowledge of sources of Irish legal history, and his willingness to share that knowledge, which provided many references. It was he who first brought the manuscript to my attention. Professor Joseph McMahon also generously gave his time to reading a draft of the Introduction. Conversations with Kevin Costello and John O'Dowd helped to clarify many issues. Norma Jessop of the Special Collections section of the Library in University College Dublin was always willing to assist with finding material as were Jonathan Armstrong, Librarian of King's Inns, Dublin, and his staff and the staff of Trinity College Dublin Early Printed Books. Dr Muriel McCarthy, Keeper, and Ms Ann Simmons, Deputy Keeper, Marsh's Library, helped with finding material and details of Henry Singleton's connection with the library. Whitney S. Bagnall, Librarian, Special Collections in Law at Columbia University, supplied useful information on the Singleton Collection and its acquisition by Columbia from her own research. Mr Andrew Mussell, Archivist, Gray's Inn, kindly supplied information on Cornelius Calaghan.

Dr Brendan Quigley, Dr Michael Mackey and Dr Wayne Sullivan of the Mathematics Department at University College Dublin introduced me to the wonders of the Linux operating system for computers and the LaTeX typesetting program.

Sir John Baker, Dr Nicholas Williams and Dr Michael Staunton generously provided Latin translations.

I should also like to thank the Revd Michael Graham of Drogheda and Ardee Unions of Parishes who kindly climbed up a ladder to transcribe the inscription on Henry Singleton's tomb in St Peter's Church, Drogheda.

A.B.L.
2008

LIST OF ILLUSTRATIONS

ABBREVIATIONS IN THE MANUSCRIPT

and old or idiosyncratic spelling
in the original manuscript

Notes: See J. H. Baker, 'Extract from Notes on English Legal Abbreviations (1971)' in W. H. Bryson, *Dictionary of Sigla and Abbreviations to and in Law Books before 1607*. Charlottsville: University Press of Virginia, 1975.

Spellings have been modernised, e.g. 'shew' to 'show', and some oddities also rendered in modern spelling, e.g. 'counsil' for 'counsel', and 'president' which is sometimes, but not always, used for precedent. Original abbreviations in the text for citations are retained, whether consistent or not.

'em = them

'emselves = themselves

'tis = it is

1t = first, 1st

accdts = accidents

accessary = accessory

acct = account

acctble = accountable

acquiesce = acquiescence

affirmce – affirmance

agt = against

answ^r = answer

antient = ancient

appellt = appellant

appt = appoint

ar^r = arbitrator

askd = asked

asš or asšš = assigns

attendce = attendance

atty = attorney

aug^t = August

behavr = behaviour

bloud = blood

BR = Banco Regis or Reginæ = King's, Queen's Bench

Canc. = Cancellaria = Chancery

CB = Common Bench, i.e. Common Pleas

certn = certain

cestuy q̃ trust = cestui que trust

consider^n = consideration

coud = could

complyed = complied

complt = complaint

comrs = commissioners

conseqce = consequence

conust = conusant = cognisant

covts = covenants

cred^r = creditor

custõ = custom

defce = defence

Deft = defendant

dem^r = demurrer

designd = designated

despight = despite

didñ = did not

differce = difference

dischargg = discharging

Dom. = Dominus, Lord (title)

draught = draft

ē = L. est

easie = easy

erĩtoire = escritoire

evidce = evidence

ex^{rs} = executors

feofmt = feoffment

feofment = feoffment

frõ = from

husbd = husband

indr̃e, indre = indenture

inferce = inference

inft = infant

inheritce = inheritance

iudgmt = judgment

joyntenants = joint tenants

Jño = John

J̃ tenants = joint tenants

Junr = junior

jture = jointure

Lõp = Lordship

Michmas =Michaelmas

mony = money

Mr = Master (in Chancery, etc.)

ñ = not

nev = never

ñpaymt = non-payment

of = off

paramt = paramount

p̃ = per

p^r añ = per annum

paup^r = pauper

Plt = plaintiff

poßn = possession

pow^r = power

prefermt = preferment

presid^t = precedent

prfected = perfected

prmes = premises

prop^r = proper

provg = proving

pson = person

ptial = partial

pticular = particular

pties = parties

pty = party

publicatn = publication

qn = question

q̃ = que, as in cestuy que trust

Quer = L. querens, plaintiff

Registr = register, registrar

rem^r = remainder

remrman = remainderman

replic^n = replication

residuũ = residuum

risq̃ = risque, i.e. risk

Scac. = L. Scaccarium, Exchequer

sd = said

seqrn = sequestration

Serjt = Serjeant

sen^r = senior

seperate = separate

servts = servants

shoud = should

showd = showed

spã = subpœna

ster̃ = sterling

strang^r = stranger

suffict = sufficient

sũ = sum

twards = towards

twoud = it would

tythe = tithe

ux or uxr = Lat. uxor, wife

warr^t = warrant

wast = waste

w^{ch} = which

wht = what

with^t = without

woud = would

y^e = the

y^n = then

y^r = your, sometimes, their

y^{re} = there

yreby = thereby

yrefore = therefore

yreof = thereof

y^s = this

yse = these

y^t = that

y^w = you

EDITOR'S ABBREVIATIONS

[. . .]	unreadable.
A.G.	Attorney General (not conventionally hyphenated in Ireland).
B.	Baron, of the Exchequer.
Baker *OHLE*	Sir John Baker, *Oxford History of the Laws of England*, vol. VI.
Bl. Com.	Blackstone's Commentaries.
BL	British Library.
B.P.P.	British Parliamentary Papers series, Irish Academic Press.
Cal. Pat. Rol. Ir.	Calendar of the Patent and Close Rolls of Chancery in Ireland.
C.B.	Chief baron.
C.J.	Chief justice.
C.P.	Common Pleas.
Co. Litt.	Coke on Littleton.
E.R.	English Reports.
HEL	Holdsworth, *History of English Law*.
Hist. Ir. Parlt.	E. M. Johnston-Liik, ed., *History of the Irish Parliament*.
HLRO	House of Lords Record Office (U.K.)
IMC	Irish Manuscripts Commission.
Inst.	Coke's *Institutes*.
J.	Justice.
J.Ir.H.C.	Journals of the Irish House of Commons.
J.Ir.H.L.	Journals of the Irish House of Lords.
K.B.	King's Bench.
KI	King's Inns, Dublin.
KI AP	E. Keane, P. B. Phair and T. U. Sadleir, eds. *King's Inns Admissions Papers 1607–1867* (IMC, 1982).
KI MS.	King's Inns Manuscript.
Kratz, *Hist. Cal.*	B. Kratz, *Historical Calendar of Western Europe A.D. 550 to 1970.* University of Kentucky, 1989. DOS freeware.
L.	Latin.

L.C.	Lord chancellor.
LF.	Law French.
L.K.	Lord keeper.
Lib. mun. pub. Hib.	*Liber munerum publicorum Hiberniæ 1152–1827*, ed. R. Lascelles, London, *c.* 1830–1852.
M.R.	Master of the Rolls.
N.A.I.	National Archives of Ireland.
ODNB	*Oxford Dictionary of National Biography.* Oxford: Oxford University Press, 2004.
OED	*Oxford English Dictionary.* 2nd edn. CD ROM version 3. Oxford: Oxford University Press, 2002.
P & M	Pollock and Maitland, *History of English Law.*
PRO	The National Archives: Public Record Office, Kew.
P.S.	Prime Serjeant.
RAGI	J. Foster, ed., *Register of the Admissions of Gray's Inn, 1521–1889* (1889).
RAMT	H. A. C. Sturgess, ed., *Register of the Admissions to Middle Temple*, vol. 1, *15th century to 1781*, (1889).
R.I.	Republic of Ireland.
Seld. Soc.	Selden Society.
S.G.	Solicitor General (not conventionally hyphenated in Ireland).
S.P.	State Papers.
St. Tr.	State Trials.
St. Realm	Statutes of the Realm.

JUDGES AND LAW OFFICERS

From: C. J. Smyth, *Chronicle of the Law Officers of Ireland*, and
F. E. Ball, *Judges in Ireland.*

Dates of appointment are those of the privy seal, where available.
Dates of patents are given in square brackets.

LORD CHANCELLORS

30 Sept. 1714 [11 Oct.] – 1725.	Alan Broderick, Viscount Midleton (1656–1728)
29 May 1725 [23 Jul.] – 1726.	Richard West (?–1726)
13 Dec. 1726 [21 Dec.] – 7 Sept. 1739	Thomas Wyndham, Baron Wyndham of Finglass (1681–1745)

CHIEF BARONS OF THE EXCHEQUER

1707–1714 [Superseded.]	Robert Rochfort (1652?–1727)
30 Sept. 1714 [14 Oct.] –	Joseph Deane (1674–1715)
16 Jun. 1715 [5 Jul.] – 18 May 1722.	Jeffrey Gilbert (1674–1726)
25 May 1722 [28 Jun.] – 1725.	Bernard Hale (1677–1729)
2 Sept. 1725 [17 Sept.] – 25 Jun. 1730.	Thomas Dalton (1682–1730)
29 Sept. 1730 [21 Oct.] – 1741.	Thomas Marlay (?–1756)

BARONS OF THE EXCHEQUER

8 Nov. 1714 [18 Jan. 1715.] – 1731.	John Pocklington (1658?–1731)
8 Nov. 1714 [18 Jan. 1715.] – 1741.	Sir John St Leger (1674–1743)
1 Jun. 1732 [26 Jun. 1732.] – 1741.	John Wainwright (1689–1741)

CHIEF JUSTICES OF THE KING'S BENCH

30 Sept. 1714 [14 Oct.] – 1727.	William Whitshed
3 Apr. 1727 [4 May] – 1741	John Rogerson

CHIEF JUSTICES OF THE COMMON PLEAS

30 Sept. 1714 [14 Oct.] – 1720.	John Forster
13 Oct. 1720 [5 Dec.] – 1724.	Sir Richard Levinge
22 Oct. 1724 [9 Nov.] – 1727.	Thomas Wyndham
23 Jan. 1727 [10 Feb.] – 1727.	William Whitshed
3 Nov. 1727 [24 Nov.] – 1740.	James Reynolds
11 May 1740 [30 May] – 1754.	Henry Singleton

PRIME SERJEANTS

1716 [23 Jun.] – 1724.	Robert Fitzgerald
1724 [26 Jan.] – 1726.	Francis Bernard
1726 [22 Jun.] – 1740.	Henry Singleton

ATTORNEYS GENERAL

8 Nov. 1714 [3 Dec.] – 1720.	George Gore
14 May 1720 [23 May] – 1727.	John Rogerson
1727 [5 May] – 1730.	Thomas Marlay
29 Sept. 1730 [22 Oct.] – 1739.	Robert Jocelyn

SOLICITORS GENERAL

8 Nov. 1714 [3 Dec.] – 1720.	John Rogerson
13 Oct. 1720 [26 Dec.] – 1727.	Thomas Marlay
5 Apr. 1727 [4 May] – 1730.	Robert Jocelyn
29 Sept. 1730 [23 Oct.] – 1739.	John Bowes

RECORDERS OF DUBLIN

From: J. Hill, *From Patriots to Unionists* (Oxford, 1997), appendix C.

1701–14	John Forster
1714–27	John Rogerson
1727–33	Francis Stoyte
1733–49	Eaton Stannard

CASES REPORTED

CASES CITED

in the text or footnotes

Year Books

UNREPORTED CASES

The list includes all those cases in the MS for which no report citations are given, including those few which are identified in the footnotes with a reported case. The bulk of them are therefore unreported Irish cases.

LIST OF STATUTES

Before 1801, (Ir.), (Eng.) or (G.B.) indicates the parliament which enacted the statute.
After 1800, all statutes were those of the then U.K. parliament and (Ir.), (Eng.), (G.B.)
or (U.K.) indicates to what part of the U.K. they applied.

INTRODUCTION

THE MANUSCRIPT

Provenance

The present reports are a transcription of manuscript No. 71 in the Singleton Collection in the possession of Columbia University, New York.

Columbia acquired the manuscript as part of a collection of manuscripts offered for sale by Myers and Co. of Bond Street, London, in 1937 'at the extremely low price of £120'.[1] They were advertised as the manuscript library of Henry Singleton (1682–1759), who was appointed prime serjeant in Ireland in 1726 and chief justice of the Irish court of Common Pleas in 1740. He also held the office of master of the rolls, which was not a judicial office in Ireland at the time. The arguments of Henry Singleton himself, as prime serjeant, are reported in some cases in the manuscript.

The catalogue does not explain how the manuscript came into the hands of Myers and Co., but it seems likely that it passed down through members of the Singleton family until the sale in 1937. Henry Singleton died unmarried and without issue, but one of his nephews, Sydenham Fowke (b. before 1732–1801)[2] changed his surname to Singleton. Henry Singleton had left land in his will to Sydenham on condition he changed his surname.[3] Sydenham Singleton's name also appears on the fly leaf of one of the volumes in the Singleton Collection,[4] and so it is possible that the collection came into his possession after his uncle's death.

Sydenham's eldest son, John, was born in 1759, the same year as the death of Henry Singleton, and so his surname changed to Singleton in the year of his birth. He moved to England and bought a house in Hazeley Heath, Hampshire. His daughter Patience Singleton married Lord Arthur Charles Hervey (1808–94), bishop of Bath and Wells, a son of the marquess of Bristol.[5] The Singleton collection may have passed to John Singleton and so came to England. The manuscript may, alternatively, have passed to the Revd James Sydenham Fowke Singleton, who was the grandson of a younger

---

[1] 'A Brief Catalogue of the manuscript English Law Library of the The Right Honourable Henry Singleton', October, 1937, Treasury Room, Columbia University, New York. The manuscripts were purchased by Miles Price, the law librarian at Columbia Law Library on the advice of Julius Goebel, Jnr., professor of legal history: Whitney S. Bagnall, 'History of the Columbia School of Law Library' (unpublished MS., Columbia Law Library), p. 27.

[2] E. M. Johnston-Liik, ed., *History of the Irish Parliament 1692–1800* (no. 1926) Singleton (Fowke), Sydenham. His mother was Patience Singleton, sister of Henry Singleton, both being children of Edward Singleton, *Hist. Ir. Parlt.* (no. 1922).

[3] P. B. Eustace, *Registry of Deeds, Dublin, Abstracts of Wills* (IMC, 1956–), vol. 2, 1746–85; KI AP, at p. 175.

[4] MS. 37 'Miscellaneous notes and definitions'. The flyleaf contains the inscription: 'Sydenham Fowke of the Inner Temple. Kew, June the 10th, 1742.' Sydenham was admitted to the Inner Temple in Trinity term 1740, and to KI in Hilary term 1745: KI AP, p. 175.

[5] W. Hunt, 'Hervey, Lord Arthur Charles (1808–1894)', rev. E. Clewlow, *ODNB*, <http://www.oxforddnb.com/view/article/13108>, accessed 26 April 2008. Their son was the Revd S. H. A. Hervey, the author of a parish magazine, the *Wedmore Chronicle, c.* 1800, 2 vols., vol. 2, ch. 12, 'Lord Arthur Charles Hervey', <http://www.tutton.org/wedchr12.html>, accessed 2 November 2007, from which this account of the later Singletons is taken.

son of Sydenham Singleton and who became vicar of Theale, a village near Wells, in 1879.[6]

The sale catalogue lists seventy-one manuscripts and they are still catalogued in Columbia with the same numbers as they appear in the 1937 sale catalogue. The manuscripts are also listed in J. H. Baker, *English Legal Manuscripts in the United States of America: a Descriptive List. Part. II, 1558–1902* (Selden Society, 1985–90). The present one is listed there as no. 334, p. 50.

The Singleton collection includes both Irish and English legal manuscripts and includes a number of manuscripts of the prolific English judge and legal writer Jeffrey (spelled variously Jeffray, or Geoffrey) Gilbert (1674–1726)[7] who was chief baron of the Irish court of Exchequer from 1715 to 1722, and later a puisne baron and then chief baron of the Exchequer in England.

The Singleton collection represents one of the most significant bodies of unpublished Irish legal material, and manuscript No. 71 is the largest known collection of surviving unpublished Irish cases before 1922, with the exception of some volumes in King's Inns[8] and Wainwright B.'s notes of cases in the British Library,[9] since the original records in the Public Record Office, housed in the Four Courts, were destroyed by fire in 1922. There is a sad irony in the comments of Gorges Edmond Howard,[10] the foremost expert on the practice of the Irish court of Exchequer in the 1760s and 1770s, when he lamented the fact that public records at that time were dispersed in various buildings round Dublin and called for them to be deposited in a single building which should be 'built in such a manner, as to be as safe from all accidents of fire, as human prudence can devise'.[11]

At present there is a large gap in published Irish reports between Davies' Reports of 1615[12] and the reports of the late eighteenth century, namely Ridgeway's Parliamentary Cases, Vernon and Scriven and the Irish Term Reports (also known as Ridgeway, Lapp and Schoales). Hopefully, this edition may inspire others to undertake work on the other surviving manuscript sources.

Description

The present manuscript consists of 495 bound folio-size pages of notes of cases mainly in the Irish court of Exchequer between the years 1716 and 1734. There are also a few judgments in the court of Chancery and an appeal before the revenue commissioners. The manuscript includes a contemporary subject index, which has

---

[6] *Kelly's Directory* (Theale, 1883).

[7] F. Elrington Ball, *Judges in Ireland, 1221–1921* (London, 1926, reprint by Round Hall, 1993), ii. 191; M. Macnair, 'Gilbert, Sir Jeffray (1674–1726)', *ODNB*, <http://www.oxforddnb.com/view/article/10688>, accessed 26 April 2008; Michael Macnair, 'Sir Jeffrey Gilbert and his Treatises' (1994) 15 *J. Leg. Hist.* 252–268.

[8] W. N. Osborough, 'Puzzles from Irish Law Reporting History' in Peter Birks, ed., *The Life of the Law: Proceedings of the 10th British Legal History Conference* (1993), at pp. 89–112.

[9] BL MSS Add. 19851–19858, *Notes of cases in the Irish Court of Exchequer, from Michaelmas Term 1732 to Easter Term 1740*, with index of names by another hand. Eight volumes. A note in volume 1 says that a volume containing most of the year 1734 is missing. The Museum bought the notebooks in the sale of Sir William Betham's MSS, on which see P. B. Phair (1972) 27 *Analectica Hibernica* 1, at 60. Phair says there were eleven volumes in the Betham Collection.

[10] See below, p. clxii.

[11] Howard, *A Compendious Treatise of the Rules and Practice of the Pleas Side of the Exchequer in Ireland As It Now Stands Between Party and Party* (2nd ed., 1793), preface, pp. xxxix–xl.

[12] *Le primer report des cases & matters en ley resolues & adiudges en les courts del Roy en Ireland. Collect et digest per Sr. Iohn Dauys Chiualer Atturney Generall del Roy en cest realme* (Dublin, John Franckton, printer to the king, 1615).

Fortunati Ambo.

GORGES EDMOND HOWARD

Figure 1: From the Calendar of the Ancient Records of Dublin

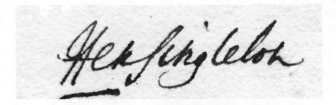

Figure 2: Henry Singleton's signature, King's Inns Library

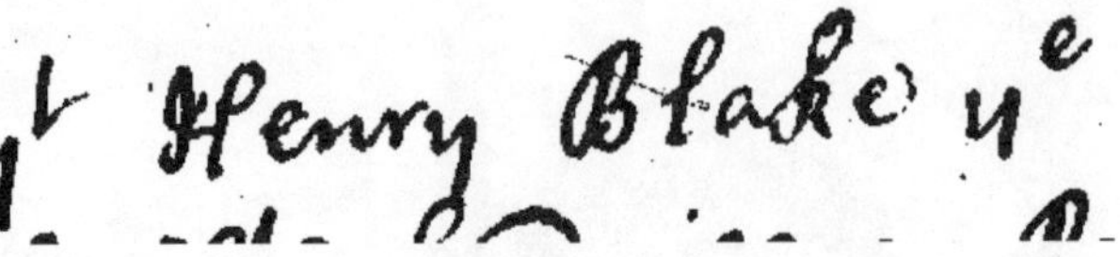

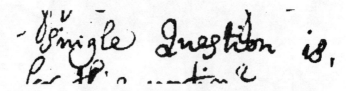

Figure 3: The word 'Henry' in MS. p. [6]

Figure 4: The word 'single' in MS. p. [184]

been transcribed. Modern indexes of people and places and of the subject matter have been supplied.

Unfortunately, the manuscript has no original title page. The first page bound with the manuscript in Columbia has the title 'Notebook of Cases Argued and adjudged in the High Court of Chancery and the Court of Exchequer in Ireland, Folio, 1716–34' written in pencil.

The author, or the person who commissioned the manuscript, remains a mystery at the present time. The handwriting is quite legible and varies little in style from the beginning to the end, suggesting that it may have been written at the end of the period from earlier notes. It does not seem to be the work of Henry Singleton himself. It is clear from a comparison of the handwriting of the manuscript and the signature of Henry Singleton in the records of the masters of the bench in King's Inns that they are not by the same hand.[13] Furthermore, Singleton's own arguments as prime serjeant are reported in the manuscript and he could hardly have spoken in court and written down his own words at the same time. It is possible that he kept rough or shorthand notes, but it seems more likely that the manuscript and the notes from which it was probably produced were the work of a secretary or scrivener[14] employed by whoever commissioned it, possibly Henry Singleton. The fact that the writer of the manuscript misheard 'Slade's Case' as 'Slane's Case' suggests that he

[13] See Figure 2, above Figure 3, above and Figure 4, above. Figure 2 is taken from King's Inns Library, Admission of Benchers, Mich. term 1727.

[14] The records of the Scriveners' Company in Guildhall Library, London, do not provide any signatures of members for this period, although there is a list of members.

may not have been a lawyer.[15] Wainwright B.'s notes in the British Library[16] are in a different handwriting, probably Wainwright's own.

Although it is correct to say that the range of years covered is 1716 to 1734, this is somewhat misleading. The last of three cases in 1716, on manuscript page [9],[17] is followed on page [10] by an undated case[18] and then on the same page by a case from 1728[19] and the rest of the manuscript is taken up by cases from that year to 1734. There is thus an unexplained gap of twelve years in the coverage from 1716 to 1728. There is, however, no physical gap in the manuscript at that point, which strengthens the view that the manuscript was written up from notes made earlier.

There is no reference in the manuscript to the controversy over appeals to the Irish House of Lords[20] which culminated in 'the Sixth of George the First',[21] also known as 'the Declaratory Act', which declared that the Irish House had no appellate jurisdiction, a position which was not to change until the end of the century.[22] The chronological gap in the manuscript between 1716 and 1728 spans the period of the controversy, but that may be pure coincidence. On the other hand, the gap might bear some relation to the careers of Jeffrey Gilbert and Henry Singleton. Jeffrey Gilbert became chief baron in 1715 and resigned in 1722. Singleton became prime serjeant in 1726. Singleton may have come by the notes of the earlier cases, possibly made by or at the direction of Gilbert, and then Singleton, or a secretary employed by him, resumed the note taking in 1728. It has already been mentioned that the Singleton Collection in Columbia University contains a number of manuscripts of Gilbert.

Marginal notes

The text also contains a number of marginal notes which seem to refer to records of cases which were probably destroyed in the fire of 1922. Some can nevertheless be traced to printed reports. 'MS͠S cas. in Canc.' obviously refers to Chancery cases in manuscript, but the cases in the main text to which such marginal notes refer can sometimes be traced to printed cases. For example, *Angier* v. *Angier* below on page 284 [369], which has the marginal note 'MS͠S cas. in Canc. D.93', is reported by

---

[15] See below, p. 57 n. 356 and below, p. 168 n. 883.

[16] See above, n. 9.

[17] *Hamilton* v. *Anonymous*. Note that page numbers in the MS. are inserted in these reports in italic between square brackets.

[18] *Terry, Lessee of the Sword Blades* v. *Donaldson*.

[19] *Digby* v. *Hanly*.

[20] The controversy arose as a result of the case of *Annesley* v. *Sherlock* in which appeals were taken to the Irish Lords, and then to the British Lords in a direct clash of jurisdiction. In 1717 Hester Sherlock appealed from the court of Exchequer to the Irish House of Lords in a case of forfeited lands, (1716) 2 *Ir. Lords J.* 541. As a result her opponent, Maurice Annesley, appealed to the British House of Lords, (1718) 21 *J. H. L. [Great Britain]* 55. The House of Lords at Westminster ruled that the Irish House of Lords could not act as an appeal court. The court of Exchequer in Ireland in another case followed the British Lords decision, which prompted the Irish Lords to dispatch a squad of soldiers under the authority of the Irish House and they placed three barons of the Irish Exchequer, Gilbert C.B., Pocklington B. and St Leger B., under house arrest. See further A. B. Lyall, 'The Irish House of Lords as a Judicial Body 1783–1800' (1993–95) 28–30 *Irish Jurist* 314–360; 'Proceedings against Jeffery Gilbert, Lord Chief Baron, John Pocklington, and Sir John St Leger' 15 St. Tr. 1301; M. Macnair, 'Gilbert, Sir Jeffray (1674–1726)', *ODNB*.

[21] 6 Geo. I, c. 5 (G.B.), 1719.

[22] By 'the Repealing Act', 22 Geo. III, c. 53 (G.B.), 1782 and 'the Renunciation Act', 23 Geo. III, c. 28 (G.B.), 1783. Ridgeway's Parliamentary Cases report cases before the Irish House of Lords in the later period from 1784 to 1796.

Gilbert as *Angier* v. *Angier* (1718) Gilb. 152, 25 E.R. 107,[23] since his reports contain some Irish cases from his time in Ireland. In other cases with the marginal notes, an appeal to the British House of Lords is reported. *Trevor* v. *Trevor*, 'MŜ cas. in Canc. C.24', below, on page 91 [*109*], is reported on appeal in the British House of Lords as *Trevor* v. *Trevor* (1719) 5 Bro. P.C. 2nd ed. 122, 2 E.R. 574.[24] Some marginal notes contain the abbreviation 'Mes App.' the meaning of which is unclear, but seems to refer to proceedings in Ireland. In some cases appeals to the British House of Lords can be traced to published reports or abridgments. In the case of *Mahon* v. *Lord Blany*[25] which has the marginal note 'Mes App. D.303' the appeal to the British House of Lords is reported in Brown's Parliamentary Cases, under the name *Lord Blaney* v. *Mahon* (1723) 4 Bro. P.C. 2nd ed. 76, 2 E.R. 52, and is noted at 2 Eq. Cas. Abr. 475, 22 E.R. 404, 2 Eq. Cas. Abr. 758, 22 E.R. 643, sub nom. *Blaney* v. *Mohon*.

Other examples are *Mammon* v. *Coote & Godsil*,[26] which has the marginal note 'Mes App. E.71.', which is mentioned as a decision in the Irish Exchequer and was affirmed on appeal to the House of Lords and reported as *Coote* v. *Mammon* (1724) 5 Bro. P.C. 2nd ed. 355, 2 E.R. 727, and *Lady Prendergast* v. *Sir Toby Butler*,[27] with the marginal note 'Mes App. D.193, E.851', the appeal to the British Lords being reported as *Butler* v. *Prendergast* (1720) 4 Bro. P.C. 2nd ed. 175, 2 E.R. 119. Some marginal notes refer to Gilbert's *Lex Prætoria*, which is manuscript No. 33 in the Singleton collection at Columbia,[28] and was published in 1758 as the second part of Gilbert's *History and Practice of the High Court of Chancery* and in *Two Treatises on the Proceedings in Equity*.[29]

ORIGIN OF THE IRISH EXCHEQUER

The earliest mention of the Irish Exchequer is in a charter of Henry III of 8 March 1221 cited in *Calvin's Case*.[30] The charter refers to the visit of King John to Ireland, probably about the twelfth year of his reign, which was 1210, when he declared that English law was to be applicable in Ireland:

> *Rex, &c. Baronibus, militibus, et omnibus libere tenentibus L. Salutem. Satis, ut credimus, vestra audivit discretio quod quando bonæ memoriæ Johannes, quondam rex Angliæ pater noster, venit in Hiberniam, ipse duxit secum, viros discretos et legis peritos, quorum communi consilio et ad instantiam Hiberniensium statuit et precepit leges Anglicanas in Hibernia, ita quod leges easdem, in scripturas redactas, reliquit sub sigillo suo ad scaccarium Dublin.*

[23] And see (1718) 2 Eq. Cas. Abr. 150, 22 E.R. 129.

[24] See also *Trevor* v. *Trevor* (1719) 1 Eq. Cas. Abr. 185, 21 E.R. 977. The marginal note 'MSŜ Cas. in BR, D.157, SC.', after the name *Leighton* v. *Leighton*, below, p. 328 [*416*] in an inserted note, is more puzzling. The English case of *Leighton* v. *Leighton* is reported in (1720) 1 P. Wms. 671, 24 E.R. 563, before the lord chancellor, affirmed on appeal to the British House of Lords and reported at (1720) 4 Bro. P.C. 2nd ed. 378, 2 E.R. 256. There were earlier trials at bar and the marginal note therefore seems to refer to a collection of English cases, or records, in the King's Bench.

[25] Below, p. 180 [*229*].

[26] Below, p. 106 [*129*].

[27] Below, p. 196 [*251*].

[28] Baker, *English MSS in USA*, no. 291.

[29] See below, 'Bibliography', Gilbert.

[30] (1608) 7 Co. Rep. 22b; Co. Litt. 141; Gorges Edmond Howard, *A Treatise of the Exchequer and Revenue of Ireland* (Dublin, 1776), i. 2. *Calvin's Case* appears to be the only source of the charter, which is not reproduced in H. F. Berry, ed., *Statutes and ordinances, and acts of the Parliament of Ireland* (Irish Record Office, 1907), and is not referred to by H. G. Richardson and G. O. Sayles, *The Administration of Ireland, 1172–1377* (IMC, 1963). There must therefore be some doubt as to its authenticity.

The King etc. to the barons, the knights and to all free tenants of Leinster, greetings. Sufficiently, as we believe, has your discretion heard, that when John of happy memory, one time King of England, our father, came into Ireland, he brought with him men discreet and learned in the law, by whose common counsel and at the instance of the Irish ordained and commended the laws of England in Ireland, and also left the same laws, drawn up in written documents under his seal in the Dublin Exchequer.

The Irish Exchequer was organised on similar lines to the English Exchequer, in that it was divided into two major parts, the Inferior Exchequer, also called the receipt of the Exchequer,[31] the administrative department concerned with the receipt of royal revenue and other debts due to the king, and the Superior Exchequer, the court of Exchequer, concerned at first with disputes as to royal revenue and debtors of the king.

Howard, citing Madox,[32] who wrote the definitive history of the English Exchequer, mentions that the Irish receipt of the Exchequer differed in one respect from its English counterpart:

And King Edw. I in the 21st year of his reign, commanded that for the future the accompts of Gascony and Ireland, should be rendered yearly at the Exchequer of England, before the treasurer and barons there: viz. the former by the constable of Bordeaux, and the latter by the treasurer of Ireland.

However, annual accounting was soon abandoned as impractical.[33] A statute of 1495[34] provided that the treasurer should account before the barons in Ireland and such members of the king's council as the chief governor should appoint, and the accounts would then be certified into England, avoiding an onerous annual journey to England by the treasurer.

The royal revenue in Ireland consisted of the 'hereditary revenue', the additional duties revenue voted by parliament for the support of the government, and the 'casual revenue'. The hereditary revenue consisted of crown rents,[35] quit rents,[36] composition rents,[37] and other dues from tenants in chief (also known as chiefries), port-corn rents,[38] customs outwards and inwards, import excise, duties on wines, ale, etc., lighthouse duties, licences relating to trade or merchandise, seizures and

---

[31] Howard, *Treatise*, i. 2.

[32] Thomas Madox, *The History and Antiquities of the Exchequer of the Kings of England* (2nd ed. 1711, reprinted, 1969), p. 633.

[33] P. Connolly, *Irish Exchequer Payments, 1270–1446* (IMC, 1998), p. ix. From 1360 on accounts were normally rendered for the whole term of office of the treasurer.

[34] 10 Hen. VII, c. 1 (Ir.), 1495.

[35] Most crown rents arose from lands formerly belonging to monasteries, abbeys, etc., before the dissolution of the monasteries. The next largest category was rents reserved on grants of the land in Ulster escheated or forfeited on the rebellion of the earl of Tyrone: Howard, *Treatise*, i. 32.

[36] 'Quit rent' in England meant a money rent by which the tenant went 'quit' of other services: G. Jacob and and T. E. Tomlins, *The Law–Dictionary Explaining the Rise, Progress, and Present State, of the English Law* (1797). In Ireland it had a more restricted meaning, namely, rents vested in the crown after the 1641 rebellion under the Acts of Settlement, by which forfeited lands were granted to adventurers, soldiers, and debenture holders, and on land returned to innocent Catholics. Howard, *Treatise*, i. 43.

[37] These were rents reserved to the crown in the reign of Elizabeth I on the surrender by lords and chieftains in Connaught, Munster and other counties in Ireland of their lands held by Irish, i.e., Brehon law titles, and re-grant to them of land by English tenure held from the English crown: Howard, *Treatise*, i. 38.

[38] Rents paid before the dissolution of the monasteries, by tenants of the monasteries and abbeys, by service or in kind.

forfeitures, etc., and hearth money.[39] Crown rents, quit rents and chiefries had been made inalienable by statute, and had to be used to maintain the government.[40]

The 'casual revenue' consisted of fines, forfeited recognizances, custodiam rents (rent from the leases of the land of outlaws and leases granted to recover crown debts),[41] waifs and estrays (stray animals), and the goods of felons.[42] The hereditary revenue was recovered by the commissioners of the revenue, whereas the casual revenue was recovered by 'the process of green wax', issued by the clerk of the estreats and carried out by the sheriffs.[43] The process was named after the green wax used to seal the documents issued by the Exchequer.[44] The first process of green wax was against goods only, in accordance with Magna Carta, which laid down that royal officials would not seize any land or rent to pay a debt so long as the debtor had chattels sufficient to satisfy it.[45] The summons of the green wax was issued by the clerk of the estreats, or as he was known in Ireland, the summonister.[46]

If this process failed to recover what was due, a second process, the process of the pipe, took place.[47] In England it too was against goods alone, but in Ireland it was against body, goods and lands.[48] Gilbert C.B. considered that the Irish process of the pipe was valid under Magna Carta because it had appeared on the first process that the debtor had no chattels.[49]

A third process, the second remembrancer's process, issued against body, goods and lands, and also heirs, executors and administrators.[50] Strictly, only the first process was properly called the green wax process, but Howard says that all three processes to recover the casual revenue were commonly so called.[51]

Definite evidence for the establishment of the Superior Exchequer in Ireland, that is, the court, comes later with the first appointment of a baron, William le Brun, in 1251.[52] In 1308 Walter de Islip was appointed baron and then in 1309, 'first baron', evidently referring to precedence, and so the first chief baron.[53] Walter was

[39] A tax under 14 & 15 Car. II, sess. 4, c. 17 (Ir.), 1662 and 17 & 18 Car. II, c. 18 (Ir.), 1665, which in Ireland remained in force until the Union. A similar tax in England had been repealed by 1 Will. & Mar., sess. 1, c. 10., 1688. See E. MacLysaght, *Seventeenth Century Hearth Money Rolls with Full Transcript for County Sligo* (IMC, 1967).

[40] Howard, *Treatise*, i. 29. 11 Will. III, c. 2 (Eng.), 1698. The Act specifically applied to forfeited states in Ireland.

[41] Howard, *Treatise*, preface, ix, i. 28–29, 137. Below, p. cxvi.

[42] Ibid., preface, pp. ix, 17, 29, chs. XIII, XIV.

[43] Howard, *Treatise*, i. 17.

[44] In the period 1308–09 eleven shillings were spent by the Exchequer on eleven pounds of green wax: P. Connolly, *Irish Exchequer Payments* (IMC, 1998), p. 209.

[45] Ibid., preface, p. ix.

[46] Howard, *Treatise*, i. 17.

[47] Pipe rolls were stiched together, head to head, and rolled up and so resembled a drainage pipe. The notion that the process was so-called because the 'streams' of revenue flowed into a single 'pipe', is a false etymology. *OED*.

[48] Ibid., p. 129, n. Howard comments that Gilbert, in his *Treatise on the Court of Exchequer* (1758), p. 133, considered the process of the pipe was unnecessary, since the sheriffs had already been given authority by the first process, but points out that, while that might be so in England, the reason did not hold good in Ireland, since the second process was not restricted to goods alone.

[49] Ibid.

[50] Ibid., p. 130.

[51] Ibid., preface, p. ix, p. 128. One of the points Howard made in his *Treatise* was that much additional revenue could be recovered, and there would be greater respect for the rule of law, if the process were more efficient: ibid., p. 126, 129, n.

[52] Ball, *Judges in Ireland*, i. 42, i. 48.

[53] Ibid., i. 41, i. 61. Walter appears several times in P. Connolly, *Irish Exchequer Payments, 1270–1446* (IMC, 1998). In 1346 he charged the Exchequer 'for rent of houses in which the king's pleas of the Exchequer and

a kinsman of Simon de Islip, archbishop of Canterbury and had become a canon of St Patrick's cathedral in 1306. Most of the early barons were ecclesiastics. Ball lists the chief barons from 1309 onwards, and puisne barons from 1251, including William de Moenes,[54] appointed in 1309, which effectively confirms that Walter de Islip had precedence as 'first' or chief baron. Ball[55] mentions that from 1309 there was 'a first and one or more puisne barons'. In 1495 a statute refers to 'the chief and secondary baron',[56] and as late as 1555 there is mention only of a chief baron and a second baron.[57] In 1566, under Elizabeth I, there is mention of a third baron,[58] and in 1613 even of a fourth.[59] The number seems to have varied from time to time according to the pressure of business. In 1783 the puisne judges of the common law courts were increased to three.[60]

As to the court of law, Howard[61] explains:

> The judicial or superior part of the Exchequer is conversant, especially, in the judicial hearing and deciding of all causes appertaining to the the King's coffers; and was anciently called *Scaccarium computorum.* And this part of the Exchequer is a court of law and equity.

Howard continues:[62]

> The court of law, or plea side, is held, after the course of the common law, before the Barons. And here the plaintiff ought to be farmer or debtor to the King, or some way accomptant to him. And in this Court the attorney general brings his information for any matter touching the King's revenue. And the leading process is either a writ of subpœna, or *quo minus.*[63]

> The court of equity is held before the treasurer, chancellor, and barons; but usually before the barons only. The proceedings are by English bill, and in a great measure agreeable to the practice of the High Court of Chancery. And the plaintiff must here likewise set forth that he is debtor or farmer to the King. In this Court the clergy usually exhibit bills for the recovery of their tithes. And here the attorney general brings bills for any matters concerning the revenue. And any person grieved in any cause prosecuted against him in behalf of the King, may bring his bill against the attorney general to be relieved in equity.

Dublin bench are held', ibid., p. 424. William Dwyer Ferguson, *A Treatise on the Practice of the Queen's Bench, Common Pleas, and Exchequer of Pleas, in Ireland, in Personal Actions and Ejectments* (1841), i. 8, states that the earliest patent of appointment specifically to the office of chief baron was in favour of Hugh de Burgh in 1346, but Ball lists several chief barons between Walter de Islip in 1309 and Hugh de Burgh, giving the date of the latter's appointment as 1344.

[54] Ball, *Judges in Ireland,* i. 58, says that the Dublin suburb of Rathmines, formerly known as Moenesrath, was named after him. De Moenes became chief baron in succession to Islip in 1311. The *Irish Times,* Monday, 24 Jan. 2000, p. 18, on the Rathmines place name, mentions William de Moenes as keeper of the timber to Queen Eleanor between 1289 and 1291, as having supplied timber from Ireland for the queen's castle at Haverford in Wales, and in 1294 as having been given money to buy wine and other victuals and crossbows for the provisioning of Dublin for the war of Leinster. In 1293 he was listed as chamberlain to the Exchequer. In 1399 a William Moenes, lord of Moenesrath, made a grant of land.

[55] Ball, *Judges in Ireland,* i. 16. He appears in P. Connolly, *Irish Exchequer Payments, 1270–1446.*

[56] 10 Hen. VII, c. 2 (Ir.), 1495.

[57] Ball, *Judges in Ireland,* i. 130.

[58] Ibid., i. 141.

[59] Ibid., i. 234.

[60] Peter Metge became fourth baron of the Exchequer: ibid., ii. 221; Constantine J. Smyth, *Chronicle of the Law Officers of Ireland* (1839), p. 255; Alexander Crookshank became fourth judge of Common Pleas: Ball, *Judges in Ireland,* ibid., Smyth, *Law Officers,* p. 256; and Sir Samuel Bradstreet became the fourth justice of the King's Bench: Ball, *Judges in Ireland,* ii. 221; Smyth, ibid.

[61] *Treatise,* i. 2.

[62] Ibid., i. 3.

[63] Below, p. lxix.

Howard uses 'Plea Side' here to refer to the court of law rather than equity, but he also uses the term 'law side' to refer to the common law side.[64] The phrase 'the chancery side of Exchequer' and 'the chancery of the court of Exchequer' is also found in Ireland in this period.[65] The term 'revenue side', referring to the court when dealing with the crown revenue directly, does not occur in these reports. Howard does, however, use the phrase in his *Treatise* on the revenue,[66] and appends an index of rules of court concerning the revenue.[67] It is clear from that work that what he means by 'the revenue side' is the court of Exchequer when hearing any case concerning the king's revenue. It is also clear from what he says of the 'court of law' and the 'court of equity', quoted above, that the court would sit on a revenue matter either as a court of law or of equity.[68] The 'revenue side' therefore seems to have referred to the common law side or the equity side when hearing a case actually concerning the king's revenue.[69] Howard notes that in the court of law, or pleas, the action was begun by an information, and on the equity side by bill. Coke wrote of the 'court of accounts' and the 'court of receipt',[70] but these are not mentioned by Howard. The process of sheriffs making their returns before the court is described in these reports, but had become obsolete by this time in Ireland. The phrase 'court of receipt' is not used to describe this procedure, although Coke's phrase may refer to it.

The relationship between the receipt of the Exchequer and the judicial side of the Exchequer in England was the subject of what became known as *The Banker's Case*.[71] Howard, writing in 1776, explains the effect of this case as follows:

> It was determined by Lord Somers,[72] on a writ of error brought in the Exchequer-chamber, on a judgment in the Exchequer in England, in the case of Hornby, &c. against the King, commonly called the bankers case (tho' contrary to the opinion of all the judges, except C. J. Treby)[73] that the Barons of the Exchequer could not, upon the prayer or petition of a grantee of any branch of the revenue to them immediately, order the treasurer or chamberlain to pay out of the receipts of the Exchequer the arrears or growing payments; but that such grantee must resort to his petition of right; for that their power over the King's treasure is only *in transitu* and that the law has intrusted the King himself only with his treasure when once it comes into his coffers.

The same point occurs in these reports and is discussed at great length in 1734 in *Lord Gage v. Attorney General*,[74] which also discusses the process of totting by sheriffs. The court decided to follow the *Banker's Case* in Ireland.

---

[64] *Pleas Side*, preface p. xxx.

[65] See KI MS. 50, p. 1; KI MS. 82, p. 1.

[66] Howard, *Treatise*, preface, pp. xxxviii, l, i. 112, 224.

[67] Ibid., ii. 425–434.

[68] Above, p. lxi. Howard, *Pleas Side*, i. 224, cites the case of *Attorney General* v. *Dillon*, Michaelmas Term 1751 'in the pleas office of the revenue side'. In his *A Treatise on the rules and practice of the Equity Side of the Exchequer in Ireland* (1760), i. 4, he cites the case of *Attorney General* v. *Carden, Gilborne and others*, Trinity Term, 1759, 'on an information for a forfeited estate in the nature of an English bill'. The latter case held that the attorney general could stop all other business before the court in order either to bring or defend an action, where the king's revenue was actually concerned, since the court was set up for the management of the royal revenue, and private persons could sue only on the *surmise* that the king's revenue was concerned.

[69] In Jones' Irish Exchequer Reports published in 1838, each case is headed 'Pleas side', 'Equity Exchequer' or 'Revenue side' and there are only a few 'revenue side' cases and they are brought under statutes.

[70] Inst., iv. 119.

[71] *The King* v. *Hornby* (1695) 5 Mod. 29, 87 E.R. 500; 14 S.T. at 105. Howard, *Treatise*, i. 8.

[72] John Somers, 1st Baron Somers (1651–1716), L.K., England, 1693–1697, L.C., England, 1697–1700.

[73] See *HEL*, i. 244 and below, p. lxxxiv n. 260.

[74] Below, p. 328 [*417*].

LORD TREASURER

Madox,[75] writing of England up to the end of the reign of Edward II, says of the role of the lord treasurer:

> It seems to have been the part or duty of the treasurer in ancient time, to act with the other barons at the Exchequer in the governance of the king's revenue, to examine and control accomptants, to direct the entries made in the great roll, to attest the writs issued for levying the King's revenue, to supervise the issuing and receiving of the king's treasure at the receipt of Exchequer, and, in a word, to provide for and take care of the king's profit.

There is no mention of any *judicial* role on the common law side, and Coke says that the barons alone were judges there,[76] and the same seems to have been true of Ireland. There is mention of a treasurer, or lord treasurer, in these reports in the case of *Costelo* v. *Costelo*, at p. 36, but Mr Daly says that 'the treasurer is no judge of law matters'. Below, at p. 39, Mr Costelo says that they have brought a new writ of error and that 'a new doubt arises with your lordship, whether it ought not to be directed to the treasurer and barons, for the barons to review', as if the formalities should be observed, although the treasurer would not in fact be present. Later, Mr Costelo says:

> I have heard say it was determined in Sir Constantine Phipps[77] his time that error in fact in this court was not examinable in the Exchequer Chamber, but in this court. This is directed to the barons, to review a record that is before them and the treasurer.

Certainly, there is no instance of a lord treasurer sitting on a case in these reports. The treasurer had been a judge on the equity side, but by statute in 1588 in England and in 1639 in Ireland the absence of the lord treasurer ceased to cause a discontinuance of the action.[78] By statute in 1727 in Ireland the attendance of the lord treasurer in Exchequer Chamber was made unnecessary,[79] and Howard mentions when he wrote in 1760 that cases in the court of Exchequer were 'usually' heard by the barons alone.[80] The office seems to have been a sinecure in the time of Burlington in 1731, who never set foot in Ireland.[81] The administrative work of the office was probably carried on by the vice-treasurer and deputy vice-treasurer.[82]

SHERIFFS' TOTTING

The following is an account of the system of collecting royal revenue as described in *Lord Gage* v. *Attorney General*[83] and in Howard's *Treatise*.

Until 1275, if the debtor to the king paid the sheriff, but the sheriff neglected to pay the money into the Exchequer, the debtor remained liable and the process of the pipe could be issued against him to recover the money all over again. To avoid this

---

[75] Madox, *The History and Antiquities of the Exchequer* (Matthews, 1711, reprinted, 1969), i. 80.

[76] Inst., iv. 109. Below, p. lxxvii.

[77] Lord chancellor, 1710–14. Ball, *Judges in Ireland*, ii. 70–71. He was an extreme Tory and a suspected Jacobite and was removed from office in 1714.

[78] Below, p. lxxxiii.

[79] Below, p. lxxxiv.

[80] *Treatise*, i. 3, and p. lxi.

[81] See below, pp. xci and 35.

[82] Howard, *Treatise*, i. 10, 21.

[83] Below, p. 328 [*417*].

injustice the o.ni. system,[84] was introduced by the Statute of Westminster I in 1275.[85] Thereafter, once a debtor to the king paid the sheriff, the debtor was discharged from liability and the sheriff became the debtor to the king instead.[86] He was 'oni'd', that is, he became liable until he discharged his liability by paying the money into the receipt of the Exchequer.

This system was perfected by the method of totting introduced by statute in 1368.[87] When the debtor paid the sheriff, the sheriff 'totted', that is, marked, the amount in his record and the debtor was thereby discharged. The sheriff then had to pay the money into the Exchequer or pay treble damages.

Once the money was paid into the receipt of the Exchequer it was beyond the jurisdiction of the court and the debtor, if he had overpaid, had to claim against the crown by petition of right.[88] In *Lord Gage* v. *Attorney General*[89] Marlay C.B. remarks that: 'The sheriffs formerly brought their tots into court in bags, and tendered it in court, which Mr Harrison remembers.' Harrison later says:[90] 'The sheriffs formerly brought the tots in bags sealed, and they remained with the Clerk of the Pipe, who kept a chest in court to deposit them.' This is evidence that the practice continued within the living memory of a practitioner in 1734. There is no barrister of the name of 'Harrison' listed in the printed King's Inns admission papers (which are admittedly incomplete) who would fit according to the dates. The only 'Harrison' is an attorney, Joseph Harrison, entered as master of an apprentice on 11 February 1719.[91] It seems most likely that the statement is made by him. Harrison is not arguing the case before the court, but commenting on the practice of the Exchequer, apparently at the invitation of the judge.

St Leger B. refers to a picture of this procedure when he says:[92] 'in old Magna Charta[93] there is a picture of the Exchequer, where the several officers are seated round the Cheque,[94] looking at the tots in the sheriff's bags'. St Leger seems to

---

[84] An abbreviation of the Latin words *oneratur, nisi habeat sufficientem exonerationem*, 'he is charged, or legally responsible, unless he have a sufficient discharge'. It was also used as a verb: Gilbert, *Treatise on the Court of Exchequer* (1758), p. 13: 'The Sheriff was o'ni'd on his Account, and shewed the Book of the Clerk of the Pells in his Discharge.' *OED*. Howard uses both 'oni'd' and 'onying': *Treatise*, i. 129, 175, 183.

[85] 3 Edw. I, c. 19 (Eng.), confirmed as to Ireland, 13 Edw. II, c. 2 (Ir.), 1320; Berry, *Statutes, Ireland*, p. 281.

[86] Below, p. 331 [*420*], Inst., iv. 116, and *Attorney-General* v. *Beston* (1666) Hard. 424, 145 E.R. 529.

[87] 42 Edw. III, c. 9 (Eng.), probably applied by Poynings' Law in 1495, below, p. cli, but confirmed by 11 Ann. c. 8 (Ir.).

[88] Howard, *Treatise*, i. 8.

[89] Below, p. 333 [*423*].

[90] Ibid.

[91] KI AP, p. 215.

[92] Below, p. 334 [*425*].

[93] There was a copy of Magna Carta, known as *Magna Carta Hiberniæ* in the Red Book of the Irish Exchequer, which was destroyed with the public records in the Four Courts in 1922, but the charter is reproduced in Berry, *Statutes, Ireland*. See R. Dudley Edwards, '*Magna Carta Hiberniæ*' in Ryan, ed., *Essays and Studies Presented to Professor Eoin MacNeill* (1940), pp. 307–318; H. G. Richardson, 'Magna Carta Hiberniæ' (1942–43) 3 *Irish Historical Studies* 31–33; Seán Ó Domhnaill, 'Magna Carta Hiberniæ' (Historical Revision, 5), ibid., 31–38. *Magna Carta Hiberniæ* cannot be traced further back than the early fourteenth century when it was copied into the Red Book. Apart from minor variations and mistakes, it follows the charter issued by Henry III on 12 November 1216. The only differences are in clauses in which Ireland is substituted for England, the Liffey for the Thames and Medway, and references to the Cinque Ports and Wales are omitted. The charter of liberties sent to Ireland on 6 February 1217 was that granted to England. Richardson notes that 'there is no hint, and no probability, that the text was then adapted in any way to Irish conditions or that any clause was omitted', ibid, p. 33.

[94] The chequered table used in the Exchequer, and from which it derived its name, for counting money, before the introduction of Arabic, or Indian, numerals facilitated counting. The word derives from the game of

refer to the picture from the Red Book of the Irish Exchequer described by James Ferguson[95] and shown as Figure 6 on page lxvi. The Red Book is depicted in the middle of the table next to a bag of writs. The sheriff, sitting at the bottom of the picture wearing a large hood and with his back to the observer, is totting. On his right is a suitor shown full length with a large sleeve, saying 'chalange'. The clerk of the pipe, the third from the left at the top, is writing a writ beginning with the words 'Henricus dei gra...', balancing it on his knee with his foot on the table. The figure next to him holding the Exchequer roll and examining his pen, appears to be the Chief Remembrancer. The figures on the left apparently are the barons, for the figure second up from the bottom is saying 'Voyr dire'. The words are clear in the Mason version of the picture.[96] In the top right corner the court crier is saying 'A demayn', 'until tomorrow', calling an end to the day's proceedings. According to Ferguson, in the nineteenth century the day's business in the court of Exchequer was brought to an end with the cry 'Tomorrow, God save the Queen!'

JURISDICTION OF THE EXCHEQUER

The judicial side of the Exchequer was originally instituted to allow the King to sue to recover the various kinds of revenue to which he was entitled.[97] Originally its jurisdiction was therefore quite limited, but in the course of time the court extended its jurisdiction, partly because the judges and clerks in the medieval period received fees in connection with suits, in addition to their salaries, and an increased jurisdiction would augment their income, and also perhaps in response to a demand on the part of litigants.

---

chess, and the word check, or cheque, from the Persian *shāh*, 'king', hence checkmate, in Arabic from Persian, *shāh māt*, 'the king is dead', *OED*. The operation of the table is described in *The Dialogue of the Exchequer*, written about 1179 by Richard FitzNigel, treasurer of the Exchequer and bishop of London. It now forms part of the English Black Book of the Exchequer. It describes the English Exchequer. No illustration exists of the English Exchequer table at the time. The Irish one must have operated in a similar fashion. The operation is also described in Hubert Hall, *Antiquities and Curiosities of the Exchequer* (1891), where there is a diagram. The columns, from right to left, represent pence, shillings, pounds, scores (twenties of pounds), hundreds and thousands, and occasionally, tens of thousands. Payments were represented in the rows. The counters were foreign currency gold coins.

[95] 'A View of the Court of Exchequer, Engraved from an Original Sketch drawn in the Reign of Henry IVth which is in the Red Book in the Chief Remembrancer's Office, Four Courts, Dublin.', opposite p. 46 in James F. Ferguson, 'A Calendar of the Contents of the Red Book of the Irish Exchequer' (1854–55) 3 *Proceedings and Transactions of the Kilkenny and South-East of Ireland Archæological Society* 35–52. There is an earlier reproduction of the picture in H. J. Monck Mason, 'A Description of an Ancient Drawing in the Red Book of the Exchequer in Ireland' (1820) 13 *Transactions of the Royal Irish Academy*, Polite Literature, p. 181. There are minor differences between the pictures. In Monck Mason's version the figure at the top left, and the one at the top middle, holding up the pen, have spectacles, probably an anachronism, and Mason concludes they were added later, since they were also in a different coloured ink. A word at the bottom left, near the figure with the forked beard, is missing from Ferguson's version, and is difficult to make out in Mason's. The figure on the right wearing the sword, on his right-hand side, is holding his left thumb between his right thumb and forefinger in a rude gesture, according to Ferguson, the sign of the fig. In the Monck Mason version the fingers are in an incorrect position, apparently bowdlerized, perhaps out of deference to the Royal Irish Academy's category of 'polite literature', although the pieces of text in Mason's picture are clearer. The actual page from the Red Book is reproduced by a photographic process called a 'photozincograph' in J. T. Gilbert, ed., *Facsimiles of National Manuscripts of Ireland* (*HMSO*, 1879), part III, no. 37, but is less clear than Ferguson's drawing.

[96] Above, n. 95.

[97] Howard, *Pleas Side*.

A VIEW of the COURT of EXCHEQUER

Engraved from an Original Sketch drawn in the Reign of Henry IVth which is in the Red Book in the Chief Remembrancers Office.

—— FOUR COURTS, DUBLIN. ——

Figure 5: Ferguson's Drawing of the Irish Court of Exchequer

The 'official' or 'minister' fiction

There is good reason to believe that the fiction of *quo minus* was preceded by an earlier fiction which may have been an earlier attempt to extend the jurisdiction of the Exchequer.

In England the Statute of Rutland, 1281[98] provided that no plea should be held in the Exchequer unless it specially concerned the king or his ministers. In Ireland a writ of Edward III in 1356,[99] recited in a statute of 1460,[100] prohibited all those who were not ministers or servants of ministers of the court from bringing actions in the Exchequer. The Latin is awkward, but is worth quoting in full:

> *Edwardus Dei gratia, Rex Angliæ & Franciæ, et dominus Hiberniæ thesaurario et baronibus suis de scaccario suo Dublin salutem.*

> *Cum secundum legem & consuetudinem terræ nostræ Hiberniæ communia placita coram vobis ad scaccarium placitari non debeant, nisi placita illa nos vel aliquem ministrorum nostrorum ejusdem scaccarii specialiter tangent:*

> *Ac jam ex parte hominum libertatis Midiæ in terra prædicta nobis est graviter conquerendo monstratum quod vosipsos homines ad sectam quorundam asserentium se val[ide el]ectos ministrorum dicti saccarii existere, qui ministri nostri in scaccario prædicto deservientes non existunt, ad respondendum coram vobis in scaccario prædicto, in placitis de transgressionibus, tractibus, debitis & compotis distringi facitis, contra leges & consuetudines supradictas:*

> *Nos nolentes ipsos homines indebite prægravari vobis mandamus, quod homines libertatis prædictæ, seu alios homines terræ nostræ prædictæ, ad respondendum coram vobis in scaccario prædicto de hujusmodi transgressionibus, convencionibus, contradictibus [sic], debitis, seu compotis, nisi tangant nos vel aliquos ministrorum nostrorum scacarii præd[icti] qui in eodem scaccario deserviens fuerit nullatenus compellat[u]s, seu compelli faciatis contra legem & consuetudinem supradictam. Teste meipso apud Westm[inisterio] vicesimo die Octobris anno regni nostri Angliæ 30. Regni nostri Franciæ decimo septimo.*

Edward by the grace of God, King of England and France, and lord of Ireland to his treasurer and his Exchequer barons in Dublin, greeting.

Whereas according to the law and the custom of our land of Ireland common pleas before you should not[101] come to the Exchequer of Pleas, unless those pleas are of special importance to us or any of our ministers of the same Exchequer:

But now on behalf of the men of the liberty of Meath in the aforementioned country by our gravely inquiring it has been shown to us that you very people belong to a group which asserts that they themselves have been properly chosen of the ministers of the same Exchequer, which ministers of ours serving in the aforementioned Exchequer do not exist, for answering among you in the aforesaid Exchequer, in pleas concerning trespass, contracts, debts and accounts you cause them [to] be engaged against the above mentioned laws and customs.

Since we do not wish that the same people be greatly oppressed, we command that the men of the aforementioned liberty or other men of our aforementioned land, for the purpose of answering cases among you in the said Exchequer in trespasses of this kind, in covenants, contracts, debts or accounts, unless they touch us or others of our ministers of the aforesaid Exchequer, whoever serving in the same Exchequer will have been compelled or you will make to be compelled against the law and above mentioned custom. Witnessed by me in Westminster 20 October in the thirtieth year of our reign in England, the seventeenth year of our reign in France.

---

[98]   12 Edw. I (10 Edw. I in Ruffhead), 1281 (Eng.), Statute of Rutland.

[99]   30 Edw. III, 20 October 1356.

[100]   38 Hen. VI, c. 1. See n. 103.

[101]   Lit. 'ought not'.

What is described is hardly a general fiction, and seems to have been an abuse, perhaps a favour for some influential litigants, but it did involve a fiction and might have developed further. At any rate, the writ of 1356 seems to have had little effect, for a statute of 1449[102] enacted that the Exchequer was not to issue writs of privilege directed to officers of liberties, or elsewhere, but only for the ministers, servants or 'yeomen' of the court. A further statute of 1460[103] recited that the earlier writ of 1356 had apparently been ignored and that 'men of the liberty of [Meath]' had been subjected to writs of *capias*[104] and distress issued by the Irish Exchequer at the suit of persons claiming to be 'yeomen or ministers' of the court, but who were not so in fact. The statute prohibited, under penalty, the beginning of any action by *capias* or distress from the Exchequer to answer any plea of trespass, contract, debt, or account at the suit of persons who were not ministers of the Exchequer.[105]

Although the English statute does not say why it was necessary to enact the statute, the recital in the Irish Act makes it clear. The court was evidently extending its jurisdiction by allowing persons who were not ministers of the court to bring actions. There is a suggestion that the barons may have acquiesced in persons claiming to be ministers or servants of the court who were not in fact so. On the other hand, it is not clear whether this process was entirely under the control of the judges. If ministers did not object to persons falsely claiming to be their servants, then the barons might not have been able to discover the falsehood. At any rate, it seems clear that this was the first, if limited, extension of the jurisdiction of the Exchequer by the use of a fiction.

The statutes probably eventually put an end to the 'minister' fiction, but another fiction developed in its place: the fiction of *quo minus*, discussed below. It is interesting to note that the writ of 1356 seems to anticipate *quo minus*, by the statement that 'you should not come to the Exchequer for pleading, unless those pleas are of special importance to us'. This may have suggested to some lawyers at the time that if they could allege that the king's revenue was indeed affected, they could get their pleas into the Exchequer.

It is also a matter of speculation as to why lawyers or litigants at the time wanted to bring actions in the Exchequer rather than in the Common Pleas; but it may have been that there was greater expertise in matters such as debt and accounts in the Exchequer, or that the procedure was quicker, or both, or because wager of law was not available in *quo minus*.[106] Also, the weight of opinion is that *quo minus* in

---

[102] 28 Hen. VI, c. 4 (Ir.); Howard, *Pleas Side*, ii. 252.

[103] 38 Hen. VI, c. 1, 1460, Parliament of Drogheda.

[104] L. 'you may take, seize', sing. A writ or process commanding the officer to take the body of the person named in it, that is, to arrest him. The term *capias* included writs of various kinds; *capias ad respondendum*, to enforce attendance at court; *capias ad satisfaciendum*, after judgment, to imprison the defendant, until the plaintiff's claim was satisfied; *capias utlagatum*, to arrest an outlawed person; *capias in withernam*, to seize the cattle or goods of any one who has made an unlawful distraint, although note that in this case it was against goods.

[105] Ferguson, *Treatise*. i. 12.

[106] Baker, *OHLE*, p. 167. On England, see Harold Wurzel, 'The Origin and Development of Quo Minus', (1939) 49 *Yale Law Journal* 39–64, at pp. 51, 55; *The Reports of Sir John Spelman*, part 2 (J. H. Baker, ed.), 94 Seld. Soc. (for 1977), at p. 63; Sir John Baker, *Oxford History of the Laws of England*. vol. 6. *1483–1558* (2003), at p. 167; Bl.Com., iii. 345. Blackstone says wager of law was only available in debt on a simple contract; for an amercement in detinue; in account, 'where the debt may have been paid, the goods restored, or the account balanced, without any evidence of either'; and in real actions where the tenant alleged he was not legally summoned. Howard, *Pleas Side*, i. 98, says that 'the old way was to lay it in debt, but then the defendant could wage his law . . . therefore to avoid this, plaintiffs do now generally declare in case. See *Slade's* Case 4 Co. 92 to 94. Where it is said on a *quominus* in the Exchequer, that a defendant cannot wage his law in that court, because the plaintiff surmises that he is the king's debtor.' If the reference to case is to *assumpsit*, then wager

the Exchequer had never been started by original writ, but by judicial writs such as *capias* or *venire*. This might also have been a reason for preferring the Exchequer, on ground of cost, or to avoid the pitfalls of original writs.

The privilege of those who were actually ministers or officials of the court continued and was reasserted in 1686.[107] Officers of the revenue had seized silk goods in the possession of certain merchants of Limerick and condemned them. The revenue officers had then been arrested under writs obtained by the merchants from the court of Common Pleas. On 15 November 1686 Rice B.,[108] by order of the barons, had attended before the Common Pleas, taking with him the Black Book of the Exchequer,[109] 'according to the ancient practice'[110] and in the name of the court had demanded the privilege for some of the officers of the revenue who were recorded as officers of the Exchequer, but who had been impleaded in the Common Pleas. 'After some debate' the privilege was allowed. The next day, Mr. Macnamara, one of the Limerick merchants, went to the commissioners of the revenue in the Custom House and said 'he came to tell them, that he intended to have a trial at law for those silks, which were condemned at Limerick', to which the commissioners replied, 'that he might take his course'.

The fiction of quo minus

By the fiction of *quo minus* the king's 'farmers', also called fermors, to whom the right to collect taxes or other dues owed to the king had been 'farmed out', came to be accorded the right to sue in the court, and so too did the king's debtors. The latter became more numerous after *Quia Emptores*, 1290, which produced a decline in mesne lordships and therefore more freeholders would have come to hold land directly from the crown and so to owe rent to the king. The development of taxation would have had a similar effect, so that in the course of time there would have been many 'debtors of the king' who were not fermors and who did not hold any specific appointment as accountants to the king. Private litigants came to be allowed to sue in the Exchequer in order to recover debts or other sums due to them on the

of law was not available in that action, and from the 1520s it could be brought in the King's Bench for money (Baker, *OHLE*, p. 168), which removed that particular advantage of suing in *quo minus* in the Exchequer from then on. Wager of law was abolished in England in 1833 by 3 & 4 Will. IV, c. 42, s. 13 and in Ireland in 1840 by 3 & 4 Vict., c. 105 (Ir.), s. 42.

[107] Earl of Clarendon to earl of Rochester, 20 November 1686 in Henry Hyde, *The Correspondence of Henry Hyde, Earl of Clarendon, and his brother Laurence Hyde, Earl of Rochester* (S. W. Singer, ed., Colburn, 1828), i. 69–70.

[108] Sir Stephen Rice (?–1715). Ball, *Judges in Ireland*, i. 362–363. A Catholic, he was appointed third baron in the spring of 1686, and so was probably given the unpleasant task of attending the Common Pleas since he was the most junior baron, although he also had connections with Limerick. He became C.B. the following year. He was appointed Baron Monteagle by King James II. He had been given the benefit of the Treaty of Limerick and restored to his estate. He also argued before parliament against the penal Bill of 1703, one of only two members to do so. *Stone* v. *Rice* (1720) Howard, *Popery Cases*, p. 71, concerns his will, which is a puzzle, because he left his property on a settlement which he must have known would have been nullified by the penal law he had opposed and spoken against. Perhaps he expected the statute to be only a temporary measure and to be repealed before his death. See N.A.I. T13736 (will); T. P. O'Neill, 'The Rices of Mountrice: solicitors' records of an epigonal family' (1996–97) 18 *Journal of the County Kildare Archaeological Society*, 351–366.

[109] King's Inns MS. No. 35 is listed as a copy of the Black Book, dated 1899.

[110] See W. H. Bryson, *The Equity Side of the Exchequer* (1975), p. 29. Bryson there describes the practice in relation to the King's Bench. A *supersedeas* could not be used in the King's Bench to remove the record into the Exchequer because the King's Bench was *coram rege* and one could not therefore bring a *supersedeas* against the king directly. What is not clear here is why in Ireland the officers of the revenue did not bring a *supersedeas* in the Common Pleas.

'mere surmise or suggestion'[111] that because the defendant owed them the money, they were thereby less (*quo minus*) able to pay the king the debts they owed to him. Howard[112] explained it as follows:

> But now, by a fiction all kinds of personal actions may be prosecuted by any person in this court. For as all the officers and ministers of this court have, like those of other superior courts, the privilege of suing and being sued only in their own courts, so also the King's debtors and farmers, and all accomptants of the Exchequer, are privileged to, sue and implead all manner of persons in the same court that they themselves are called into. So that by the suggestion of privilege, any person may be admitted to sue in the Exchequer as well as the King's accomptant; and the surmise of being the King's debtor is become mere matter of form and not traversable. And the same holds with regard to the equity side of the court; for there any person may file a bill against another upon a bare suggestion that he is the King's accomptant.

Whether the suggestion was true in fact, or not, it was not traversable, that is, it could not be contradicted in pleadings by the other side, and so it was a pure fiction.

The new fiction was at least a more plausible basis for jurisdiction than the earlier fiction of being servants of Exchequer officials. An assertion based on the notion of protecting the royal revenue was more likely to appeal to the king, or the barons, than one based on private people pretending to have some official capacity, when they did not.

The statutes concerning the earlier fiction are interesting as to what they suggest. The English one suggests that *quo minus* did not begin until after 1281, and the Irish measures suggest both that the 'official' fiction operated in Ireland from some time before 1356 and continued to be used until 1460, and also that *quo minus*, whether fictional or otherwise, did not begin to be used in Ireland until after that date.

The weight of opinion is that in England *quo minus* did not emerge fully as a fiction until much later than these dates, until the Commonwealth or the reign of Charles II.[113] The emergence of the fiction is also related to other issues affecting the Exchequer, namely, as to whether actions were ever started in the Exchequer by original writ and as to whether outlawry was ever allowed in the Exchequer, since outlawry was only obtainable if an original writ had been issued.[114]

Jenkinson, writing of England, did not find an instance of *quo minus* in his extensive study of the plea rolls and files of writs of the thirteenth century[115] and concluded that it was the product of a later age. Wurzel, also writing of England, found the earliest example of the phrase in an administrative writ of 1230[116] and concluded that, although it was unclear as to when it began to be used in court proceedings, there were instances of its use in the early to mid-fourteenth century.[117] Nevertheless, this does not imply that it had become a fiction by then. Baker notes that *quo minus* suits were common in England in the early Tudor period, without implying that this was novel, and considers that the fiction had certainly developed by 1660.[118] Ball found English examples in Mary's reign.[119]

---

[111] Ferguson, *Treatise*, i. 12.

[112] *Treatise*, i. 4; and see Howard, *Equity Side*, i. 213.

[113] Wurzel, 'Quo Minus', 55.

[114] Jacob, *Law Dictionary*, 'Outlawry.'; Ferguson, *Treatise*, i. 121.

[115] *Select Cases in the Exchequer of Pleas* (H. Jenkinson and B. Fermoy, eds), 48 Seld. Soc. (for 1931), xcix.

[116] Wurzel, 'Quo Minus', 42–47.

[117] Ibid., at pp. 48–49. He cites Brooke, *La Graunde Abridgement* (1586), 'Quo minus', no. 5, referring to FitzHerbert, *La Graunde Abridgement* (1565), 'Ley', no. 66.

[118] Sir John Baker, *OHEL*, p. 167.

[119] R. M. Ball, 'Exchequer of Pleas, Bills and Writs' (1988) *Journal of Legal History* 308 at p. 317.

The assertion of *quo minus* consisted in fact of two distinct assertions: 1. that the plaintiff was a debtor or accountant of the king, and 2. that, because of the debt owed to him by the defendant, the plaintiff was thereby less able to pay his debt to the king. Early suits may not have been fictional. If a claimant owed considerable sums to the king, the king would have a direct interest in the claimant's recovering his own debts. Also, if the assertion was taken literally, it would have been necessary to establish as a fact that the debtor was less able to pay the king's debt, and proof might be difficult. The transition to a fiction in the case of the second assertion might therefore have been brought about as much by practical considerations of proof as the desire of the court of Exchequer, or litigants, to extend its jurisdiction.

Furthermore, the two branches of the fiction may not have developed at the same time. The available evidence suggests that fiction 2 may have developed sometime before fiction 1.

As to fiction 1 in England, *Bellamy's Case*[120] in 1605 states that 'if the King's fermor brings *quo minus* in the Exchequer, he ought to alledge that he is the King's fermor to enable him to sue there; but he need not shew it to the court, for that is merely collateral to the action'.[121] However, the case does not state, or necessarily imply, that if the allegation were untrue the plaintiff would not be liable for deceit in another court. Wurzel says that while the assertion of being an accountant was originally an assertion of privilege, it had become recognized by the 1670s that the assertion of being the king's debtor had ceased to be so.[122] Sheppard, writing in the 1670s, states that the plaintiff had actually to *be* a debtor to the king, but he does not say that the debtor had to assert that he was a fermor. Nor does he mention the issue of proof, perhaps deliberately.

Further, he says that if the plaintiff asserted he was the king's debtor, then he 'may surmise' that he was less able to pay the king.[123] This suggests that fiction 2 had been established in England by then, that there remained some doubt about fiction 1, but that fiction 1 had at least dropped the requirement that the debtor allege that he was a fermor.

The final act in the transformation of the *quo minus* clause into a fiction only took place when an allegation could no longer be denied by the other party in pleadings. Bryson notes that, while the formula of alleging that the plaintiff was 'debtor and accountant' to the king was used occasionally during the last years of Charles I, it appeared in most bills after 1649, and he continues: 'The evidence of the records thus points with some precision to the year 1649 for the introduction of the wider jurisdiction based on the fictitious and non-traversable allegation of indebtedness to the crown [or Commonwealth].'[124] This would therefore date this final development earlier than Sheppard's statement, or earlier than Sheppard was prepared to admit. It may be that Sheppard, writing after the Restoration, was reluctant openly to recognize fiction 1, since it had been established during the Commonwealth, even if it was being followed in practice in Sheppard's time.

As to Ireland, the earliest example discovered to date of a refusal to allow a traverse of the assertion that the plaintiff was a debtor of the king comes from a manuscript in

---

[120] (1605) 6 Co. Rep. 38a, 77 E.R. 309.
[121] Ibid., at 6 Co. Rep. 39a.
[122] Wurzel, 'Quo Minus', at p. 58.
[123] Sheppard, *Grand Abridgement* (1675), p. 126; Wurzel, 'Quo Minus', p. 59.
[124] Bryson, *The Equity Side of the Exchequer*, p. 25.

King's Inns, Dublin.[125] The manuscript contains a note stating that: 'In the Booke of Orders in the yeare 1637 by an order 21 May: plea to a bill that the plaintiff was not the king's debtor overruled for that the plaintiff by the bill ownes it.'[126] This is evidence that fiction 1 had become untraversable in Ireland slightly earlier than in England (at least on current English evidence). Nevertheless, as late as 1695 a committee of the Irish House of Lords questioned the use of *quo minus* as a fiction and was instructed by the House to consider means of preventing 'persons making use of the King's prerogative in suing in the court of Exchequer as His Majesty's debtors and farmers' unless they 'make it appear that they really are debtors of the King'.[127] It is noted below that the peers of the Irish House of Lords were attempting to assert greater legal privileges for themselves in this period.[128] It seems that they were also jealous of privileges being extended to commoners. In any case, the intervention seems to have had no effect.

As to the present reports, in *Dawson* v. *Spiers*[129] the chief baron, apparently referring to the *quo minus* jurisdiction, says: 'This is a prerogative process. 'Tis only the suggestion of His Majesty's debtor and farmer that gives us a jurisdiction.'

Ferguson, writing in the 1840s, says that in Ireland it was not the practice even to include the *quo minus* clause in the *capias*, although the correct practice was to include the fiction in the plaintiff's declaration.[130] Nevertheless, earlier case law did not insist even on this.[131] In the nineteenth century in Ireland the courts even went beyond this and eliminated the requirement in pleadings altogether. In *Keogh* v. *Murray*[132] in 1843 it was held that a declaration that did not include the *quo minus* clause, but did state that the plaintiff was a debtor of the Queen, was good. In *Knox* v. *Ingram*[133] the court held that a declaration that included neither the *quo minus* clause nor a statement that the plaintiff was a debtor of the Queen was still good.[134] Brady C.B. noted that it had long been the case in Ireland that the omission of the *quo minus* clause was not an objection to a declaration and further cited Burton's *Exchequer Practice*[135] to the effect that 'all his Majesty's subjects are his debtors and as such are equally privileged with accountants to sue and are equally liable to be sued in the Office of Pleas'. It remained the case that a plaintiff who was actually, and not fictionally, a 'minister, or accountant' of the crown could sue or be sued in the court. The special demurrer in the present case did not also allege that the plaintiff lacked the character of a minister or accountant of the Queen, and if he was, the court would have jurisdiction. The demurrer was therefore deficient, and the court did not find it necessary to decide whether the defendant had that character or not.

The final issue is whether *quo minus* was ever an original writ. In the eighteenth century *quo minus* was certainly started in the Exchequer by *capias quo minus*. The *capias* was a judicial writ, issued not by Chancery but by the court in which the action

---

[125] KI MS. No. 108.

[126] I am grateful to Professor Sir John Baker for this reference.

[127] J.Ir.H.L., i. 508, 1 September 1695. I am grateful to Professor W. N. Osborough for this reference.

[128] Below, p. xcviii.

[129] Below, p. 294.

[130] Ferguson, *Treatise*, i. 124.

[131] In *Higgins* v. *McClenaghan* (1794) Ir. Term Rep. 253, Yelverton C.B. dismissed a demurrer objecting to the absence of a *quo minus* clause in the plaintiff's declaration with the one sentence: 'That is a great objection to be sure!'

[132] (1843) 6 Ir. L.R. 237.

[133] (1843) 6 Ir. L.R. 250.

[134] Ibid., p. 256.

[135] Philip Burton, *Practice of the Office of Pleas, in the Court of Exchequer* (1791), i. 31.

was to take place.[136] It followed that there was no outlawry in the Exchequer. Wurzel says so[137] and this is repeated as to Ireland by Ferguson writing in 1841.[138] Howard is quite clear on the point:[139]

> nor are there any original writs in it [the Exchequer]; neither is any process of outlawry sued forth here upon any actions.

Howard was the leading practitioner in the Irish Exchequer in the middle of the eighteenth century and his opinion must represent not only the understanding at the time but also the practice.[140]

There is indeed evidence that *quo minus* was never an original writ in England. Wurzel[141] cites Y.B. Hil. 32 Hen. VI, fo. 24a pl. 7 in 1454. It concerned one form of *quo minus* which enabled a grantee of a royal franchise to redress infringement. The report adds: *et cest briefe issist hors del Eschequer*, that is, the writ issued from the Exchequer, and Wurzel notes that it 'thereby removes any doubt that the writ of *quo minus* then was issued as a judicial writ by the court of Exchequer, not as an original writ issuing from Chancery',[142] and he quotes Price as pointing out that 'the reason [was] . . . that the Exchequer of Pleas was never recognized as an open king's court for the holding of common pleas'.[143] There is at least one example of a 'writ of debt' apparently brought in the Exchequer, although whether it was an original or a *capias* is not clear.[144] Ball,[145] speaking of *quo minus* in England, says that:

> There is no distinct writ of *quominus* in the middle ages: the formula may be used in any writ, of *venire facias*, of *distringas* or of *capias*. The *quominus* writ of the modern period is distinguished by two peculiarities: the plaintiff is by a fiction styled *debitor domini Regis*, and the writ is a *capias* in the first instance. In this sense the writ of *quominus* first appears about the beginning of Mary's reign.

The *venire facias*, *distringas* and *capias* were, of course, judicial writs, not originals.

Overlapping jurisdictions

Common law

The competition between the courts naturally led to overlapping jurisdictions, and by the early eighteenth century rules had developed which, while they did not eliminate the problem, allocated certain causes of action among the different courts.

Howard[146] says that 'this court has greatly enlarged its jurisdiction and power, most actions being now allowed to be brought therein; as *debt, detinue, trover and conversion, trespass, covenant, case, ejectment, waste, prohibition, actions on penal statutes,*

---

[136] See below, p. lxxxvi.
[137] Wurzel, 'Quo Minus', at p. 55;
[138] Ferguson, *Treatise*, i. 123.
[139] *Pleas Side* pp. 2–3.
[140] See also Bl. Com., iii, appendix iii, sec. 4. Blackstone's example of the writ of *quo minus* in his time appears to be a *capias* and returnable by *cepi corpus*.
[141] 'Quo Minus', at p. 51, n. 47.
[142] Ibid.
[143] (1933) 11 *Publications of the Pipe Roll Society* (n.s.) 14; Wurzel, 'Quo Minus', p. 51 n. 47.
[144] Y.B. Mich. 8 Hen. V, fo. 10b pl. 19, Baker & Milsom, *Sources of English Legal History*, p. 428.
[145] At p. 317, see above, p. lxx, n. 119.
[146] *Pleas Side*, i. 1–2.

&c.'[147] 'Case', i.e. actions on the special case, included *assumpsit*.[148] Ejectment was permitted in the Exchequer because a small amount of damages for trespass was claimed.

The remarkable inclusion of prohibition, normally a prerogative writ, was the result of the case of *Carey* against a judge of the consistory court of Cloyne and Forster, 19 and 20 June 1750, cited in Howard.[149] It was decided in the Exchequer after full debate that an order of prohibition could 'issue from the court'. Howard adds that 'this jurisdiction is taken up by the court, under the notion or surmise that the party is debtor to the king'.[150]

At an earlier period there was an advantage in bringing debt in the Exchequer rather than in Common Pleas, in that, as already noted, wager of law was not allowed in *quo minus*, although this had probably ceased be a factor by the time of these reports[151] and wager of law is not mentioned in them.

Any action which involved the king's revenue or property had also to be brought in the Exchequer, or if started elsewhere, it had to be removed to the Exchequer. So if someone had been outlawed in a civil action and his lands forfeited to the crown, but a third party then claimed that some of the lands were in fact his and had wrongfully been included in the forfeiture, the third party had to bring his action in the Exchequer.[152]

There was one disadvantage of bringing an action in the Exchequer. Howard notes:[153]

> as there is no original writ in this court, (the first proceeding here being merely a compulsory process to the bring the defendant into court) therefore no cause can be said to be in court until the defendant appears; wherefore when any action is limited by any law, as to the time of bringing it . . . the better way will be to sue forth a writ from some of the other courts of record, where the writ is an original, for in such a case only, the plaintiff may be said to have brought his action.

Howard says that: 'actions in *replevin, dower, quare impedit*,[154] etc. and all real actions' were excluded from the Exchequer.[155] KI MS. 82 adds that 'all other writs issued out of Chancery and returnable into a court of common law cannot be returnable into this court',[156] Moreover, we have seen that no original writ was issued to begin an action in the Exchequer and, since outlawry could only be obtained on an original writ, no outlawry could be obtained in an action in the Exchequer.[157] For this reason the Exchequer remedy against someone who was in contempt by failure to appear, or resisting enforcement of decrees, was attachment (arrest by the sheriff or bail)

---

[147] KI MS. 82, p. 97, on the pleas side, states that the actions were: 'Actions of debt, trover and conversion, ejectment, trespasses, actions on penal statutes and covenants, etc.'

[148] See in these reports, for example, *Anonymous* v. *Administrators of Cogan* at p. 12 and *Hind* v. *Lynch* at p. 72, below.

[149] *Pleas Side*, i. 3.

[150] Ibid.

[151] Above, p. lxviii.

[152] Howard, *Treatise*, i. 4.

[153] *Pleas Side*, i. 14.

[154] L. 'why he hinders'. An action by which a person whose right to a benefice had been obstructed recovered the presentation, and also an action to try a disputed title to an advowson.

[155] Howard, *Pleas Side*, i. 1–2; Ferguson, *Treatise*, i. 12; KI MS. 82, p. 98.

[156] At p. 98.

[157] Above, p. lxxiii.

and commission of rebellion.[158] Commission of rebellion was a procedure in use in England and Ireland until the early nineteenth century, where the action was started by *capias*, or by common law[159] or equitable[160] subpœna.[161]

In 1759 in *Pippard* v. *Mayor of Drogheda*[162] it was held that *quo warranto*[163] did not issue from the Exchequer. The writ in *Pippard* had been issued in 1686 against the corporation of Drogheda in order to invalidate its charter; James II used the writ to invalidate the charters of a number of Irish cities. He then granted new charters favouring Catholics. The new charters were declared void on the accession of William and Mary.[164] *Pippard* itself concerned the validity of a lease granted by the new corporation in 1678. The lease was held void. Howard,[165] notes that a Rule of 13 June 1664 had provided for the issue of *quo warranto* from the Exchequer, but this must have been anomalous and *Pippard* settled the issue. There is no mention of it in Howard's *Pleas Side* nor in KI MS. 82.

Later in the century, in *Maingay* v. *Gahan*[166] it was held by the Exchequer Chamber that the court of Exchequer had no jurisdiction in a case challenging the validity of a decision of the sub-commissioners of excise, affirmed by the commissioners of appeal, in a *qui tam* action in which the commissioners had seized excisable goods as forfeited for failure to pay duty.[167] The Exchequer Chamber held that the *qui tam* procedure, an action by informer, was a special jurisdiction set up under statute conferring exclusive power on the commissioners. There are examples of *qui tam* procedure in the present reports earlier in the century in *Foord qui tam* v. *Sullivan and Orpin*[168] and *Coleman qui tam &c* v. *White*,[169] although these were under the Navigation Acts.

---

[158] Below, p. xcvi.

[159] KI MS. 82, p. 98; Ferguson, *Treatise*, i. 13; First Report of Commissioners on Courts of Common Law, 1829, ix. 87, B.P.P., Legal Administration, 1829, i. 87.

[160] Gorges Edmond Howard, *A Treatise on the rules and practice of the Equity Side of the Exchequer in Ireland* (Dublin, 1760), ii. 753.

[161] The subpœna was once thought to have been invented by John de Waltham, keeper of the rolls and later bishop of Salisbury and lord treasurer of England: Foss, *Judges of England* (London, 1857), iv. 110; Rot. Parlt. 5 Ric. II p. 1 m. 22; Howard, *Equity Side*, ii. 729; but P. Tucker, 'The Early History of the Court of Chancery: A Comparative Study', (2000) 115 *English Historical Review* 791, at 801, has shown this to be false, and that the subpœna pre-dated Waltham.

[162] (1759) 2 Bro. P. C. 2nd ed. 321, 1 E.R. 971.

[163] L. A writ that lay for the king against anyone who claimed or usurped any office, or liberty, to inquire *by what authority* they supported their claim, in order to test their right to do so.

[164] 1 Will. & Mar. sess. 2, c. 9 (Eng.), 1688, s. 2.

[165] *Treatise*, ii. 425.

[166] (1793) Ir. Term Rep. 1. See also the note of the case in 1 Ridg. P.C. at 43–44 and corrective advertisement in 2 Ridg. P.C. at p. v.

[167] The plaintiff merchants had sought to get the matter before a jury by bringing trespass *vi et armis* against the officers of the revenue. The case was first tried at Cork (1 Ridg. P.C. 43–44) before Crookshank J. who directed the jury to find for the defendant. The jury found for the plaintiff (2 Ridg. P.C. v.) and the verdict was set aside in Exchequer. The case was tried again before Hamilton B. and the jury found a special verdict, finding irregularities in the judgments of the sub-commissioners of revenue. The jury indicated that, if the court had jurisdiction to review the decisions of the revenue commissioners, they would find for the plaintiffs. There seemed little ground on the facts for impugning the action of the excise officers, so the plaintiffs' evident view that a jury would be likely to find for them and against the revenue despite the facts was sound. The question of the jurisdiction of the ordinary courts then went to Exchequer and subsequently to Exchequer Chamber. Yelverton C.B., Power, Hamilton and Metge BB. held in favour of the jurisdiction of the Exchequer to review the revenue commissioners, but they were reversed in Exchequer Chamber where the case was heard by Lord Clonmell, Lord Carleton and Viscount Fitzgibbon L.C. See also n. 748 on p. cxxxiii, below.

[168] Below, p. 164.

[169] Below, p. 66.

Real actions, that is, the writ of right, the possessory assizes of novel disseisin, mort d'ancestor, etc., and writs of entry, were in England within the exclusive jurisdiction of the court of Common Pleas, as were fines and recoveries,[170] and the same was true of the Irish court of Common Pleas.[171] Real actions were the actions by which freeholders had recovered their land, but it is doubtful whether they were of much significance by the eighteenth century. The action of ejectment was the means by which leaseholders and their grantors enforced their titles to land, and since it was a more recent action, it was not attended by the complexities and expense of the real actions at common law. In Ireland ejectment took two main forms, ejectment on title, in which the plaintiff claimed a superior title to the defendant, and ejectment for non-payment of rent, in which a landlord sought to eject a tenant who had failed to pay the rent.[172]

Freeholders naturally wished to avail themselves of the action. In England a fictional form of the action was invented to enable them to do so. This involved the fictional plaintiff John Doe.[173] The principal fiction was that the freeholder had granted a lease to John Doe, who was the nominal plaintiff. No actual lease was granted, and there was no actual ouster by the defendant. The sole purpose was to test the title of the defendant.[174] As Howard explains it:[175]

> The party who claims the title, feigns a lease and in the name of the feigned lessee, delivers a declaration to the tenant in possession, in the name of the casual ejector, who is also now some feigned person.

In the non-fictional form the action was brought against the tenant or a 'casual ejector'. It was a rule of ejectment, however, that notice had to be given to the defendant/lessor in order that he should not lose his right to possession without an opportunity to defend it. In the fictional form, the casual ejector was fictitious, but notice was still given to the defendant/'lessor', so that his title was then in issue.

The name 'John Doe' was not in fact used in Ireland, where the phrase 'The Lessee of [freeholder]' was used instead, as shown in these reports, as for example in *Lessee of Burk* v. *Blake*.[176] In Ireland in the nineteenth century there is an example of a more imaginative choice of fictional plaintiff.[177] In England the name of the fictional defendant was often given as 'Richard Roe', or 'William Stiles', but in Ireland the name usually given in the pleadings was 'John Thrustout'[178] and in the name of the case as 'the Casual Ejector', as in *Lessee of Ram* v. *The Casual Ejector*.[179]

These reports provide evidence that ejectment had largely replaced the real actions in Ireland by this time, as they had done in England. In *Costello* v. *Costello*[180] it is argued that repeated actions in ejectment in respect of the same land could

---

[170] Inst., iv. 99.

[171] Ferguson, *Treatise*, i. 11.

[172] Howard, *Pleas Side*, ii. 41.

[173] It has been attributed to the ingenuity of Chief Justice Rolle, C.J. of the Upper Bench during the Commonwealth: Jacob, *Law Dictionary*, 'Ejectment'; *HEL*, vii. 10.

[174] Jacob, *Law Dictionary*, 'Ejectment'.

[175] *Pleas Side*, ii. 36, and generally see *Pleas Side*, ii. 36–59. Howard cites rules of court in 1663 and 1665.

[176] Below, p. 7 [6].

[177] *Barnaby Rudge, Lessee of Hull* v. *McCarthy* (1841) 4 Ir. L. R. 157. Dickens had published his novel, *Barnaby Rudge*, in 1841.

[178] Howard, *Pleas Side*, ii. 37.

[179] Below, p. 25 [30].

[180] Below, p. 328 [416].

be restrained by injunctions, just as they could be in the case of 'verdicts in disseisin . . . since ejectments are substituted in the room of real actions'.[181]

Thus the exclusive jurisdiction of the Common Pleas in real actions was of reduced significance by the early eighteenth century and gave it less of an advantage over the Exchequer in terms of business, although its jurisdiction in fines and common recoveries, used to bar entails, and its jurisdiction over unassigned dower, which could not be leased, would have been significant. Nevertheless, when, on the death of Whitshed in 1727,[182] John Rogerson sought a transfer from his post of chief justice of the King's Bench to that of the Common Pleas, Archbishop Boulter described the latter post as 'almost a sinecure'.[183] Boulter may, however, have exaggerated, since he opposed the move on the ground that Rogerson was seeking not only lighter duties but also to prevent the appointment of an English lawyer. Common Pleas had, in theory, concurrent jurisdiction with the Exchequer in ejectment, the main form in which actions over land and titles were tried.

Equity

The jurisdiction of the equity side of the Exchequer in England was in theory just as extensive as that of the court of Chancery.[184]

The judges of the equity side of the Exchequer were originally the lord treasurer, the lord chancellor and the barons of the Exchequer.[185] On the common law side the barons alone were judges, although the treasurer may have been present, as keeper of the records.[186] Of the court of law, Coke says that:[187] 'All judiciall procedings according to law in the exchequer, are *coram baronibus*, and not *coram thesaurario et baronibus*: but the court of equity holden in the exchequer chamber [i.e. the equity side], is holden before the lord treasurer, chancelor, and barons.' However, we have seen that the presence of the lord treasurer on the equity side had long since ceased to be necessary in England or in Ireland by the time of these reports.[188] Procedure was by English bill.[189]

The question as to why, by the eighteenth century, there were two superior courts with equity jurisdiction, is probably answered by the fact that in Chancery the only judge was the lord chancellor and with the growth of equity suits up to the end of the seventeenth century there was simply a need for another equity court. What is more difficult is to identify the practical considerations which might have influenced the decision to choose one court rather than the other, what today is known as 'forum shopping'. In Exchequer there were three judges, so there would be a majority vote, which might have been a factor. Experience of financial matters might have been another. The available evidence from the present reports shows a full range of equity issues before the court in Ireland, although with a certain financial flavour in many cases. Examples of bills and issues before the court include: bills for redemption of a

---

[181] Below, p. 328 [*416*].
[182] Whitshed had been C.J.K.B. from 1714 to 1727 but stepped down in 1727 to become C.J.C.P. shortly before his death.
[183] *Hist. Ir. Parlt.* Rogerson (no. 1812), at p. 188.
[184] Inst., iv. 118; Bryson, *The Equity Side of the Exchequer*, at p. 11.
[185] Inst., iv. 118.
[186] Ibid., iv. 105.
[187] Ibid., iv. 109.
[188] Above, p. lxiii, below, p. lxxxiii; Howard, *Treatise*, i. 3, and p. lxi;
[189] Howard, *Treatise*, i. 3; *Equity Side*, i. 205; *Sir Thomas Cecil's Case* (1597) 7 Co. Rep. 18b, 77 E.R. 440.

mortgage with an account for sums due,[190] and for foreclosure with account,[191] for account of various other kinds, including for sums due by a tenant holding over,[192] for interest due,[193] and account in a partition action by tenants in common.[194] Other actions include a bill against an executor for discovery of assets;[195] the enforcement in equity of a conditional bond;[196] the enforcement of an equitable charge;[197] specific performance of an agreement for a lease;[198] part performance of a contract of sale of land;[199] bills to set aside a conveyance of land for misrepresentation;[200] bills to compel a tenant to execute a counterpart of a lease;[201] consideration in equity;[202] notice in equity;[203] whether interest on interest was allowable, in the case of a portion;[204] and an injunction to restrain repeated common law actions.[205]

MASTER OF THE ROLLS

There is occasional mention in these reports of the master of the rolls and Henry Singleton held the office after he resigned from the bench, so it would be as well to consider briefly the history of the office in Ireland.

Two questions may be considered in relation to the history of the office in Ireland. Did it, at any time, have a judicial function? At what time did it become a sinecure? What follows is an approximately chronological account taking note of these issues.

Ball lists the first appointment of a clerk, or keeper of the rolls as that of Edmund de Grymesby in 1333,[206] in the same year that it became a patent office.[207] In the 1520s the office was still known as keeper of the rolls,[208] but by the 1550s the title 'master of the rolls' began to be used.[209]

A statute of 1495 had laid down that a person or persons 'that have ministration of justice, that is for to say, the chancellor, the treasurer, judges of the king's bench and common place, the chief and secondary baron of the Exchequer, the clerk or the master of the rolls', were to hold office at pleasure, and not for life.[210] The following

---

[190] *Geoghegan* v. *Chevers*, below, p. 1, *Lewis* v. *Delarue*, below, p. 295.

[191] *Tuthill* v. *The Bishop of Killala*, below, p. 54.

[192] *Dowdal* v. *Cusack*, below, p. 37, and see Index, 'Account'.

[193] *Boyd* v. *Montgomery*, below, p. 276.

[194] *Waller* v. *White*, below, p. 170.

[195] *Blackhall* v. *Blackhall*, below, p. 343.

[196] *Hodson* v. *Rowley*, below, p. 122, *Ivers* v. *Ivers*, below, p. 188.

[197] *Ridge* v. *Hurley*, below, p. 182.

[198] *Hodson* v. *Rowley*, below, p. 235.

[199] *Manly & Baily* v. *Shimmin & Purfield*, below, p. 110.

[200] Ibid.

[201] *Lord Ranelagh* v. *Fitzgerald*, below, p. 230.

[202] *Ridge* v. *Hurley*, below, p. 182.

[203] *Barlow* v. *Harris & Barlow Esqr*, below, p. 203, *Hodson* v. *Rowley*, below, p. 235, and see Index, 'Equity: notice'.

[204] *Whitlow* v. *Gore*, below, p. 179.

[205] *Costello* v. *Costello*, below, pp. 327, 342.

[206] Ball, *Judges in Ireland*, i. 36.

[207] Ibid., i. 33. The duty of the clerk, or keeper, of the rolls was to enrol all patents before they were delivered to the parties concerned and to keep the records, ibid., i. 94.

[208] Ibid., i. 115, 1520, Thomas Rochfort; 1524, John Ricard, both being dean of St Patrick's cathedral, Dublin.

[209] Ibid., i. 130.

[210] 10 Hen. VII, c. 2 (Ir.), 1495.

may be inferred from the statute: (a) that it did not *require* that the master of the rolls have judicial power; (b) but if he were to be granted such power, then he should only hold office at pleasure; that (c) an appointment for life could still be made after the Act, and some were, but it should not then grant the judicial power; and (d) if a grant for life remained silent as to the judicial power, it would necessarily be construed as excluding it, since it would be presumed to conform to the law. Any grant for life which expressly conferred the judicial power can only then be explained as an exercise of the dispensing power,[211] but that raises a further question. If the statute could be so avoided, then what was the purpose of the statute in the first place, since it only referred to appointments made by the crown?

Edward VI appointed Patrick Barnewall in 1550, for life,[212] nevertheless, the patent included the power 'to hear, discuss, and determine all causes and complaints in court, in the absence of the chancellor, or vacancy of his office; to grant injunctions in the chancellor's absence'. This could only be explained as an exercise of the dispensing power.

On Barnewall's death, the king appointed John Parker for life.[213] In 1553 Queen Mary issued a commission to Parker with power to proceed to parts of Ireland then under English control, to 'hear, examine, and take order for all matters in controversy . . . betwixt party and party' and even charged him with the 'punishment of all malefactors, as well enemies, Irishmen, or subjects, as thieves and vagabonds', in other words, with a criminal, or possibly even a military, commission.[214] There is no evidence that Mary I granted a new patent reappointing Parker, but perhaps the commission was thought to be sufficient recognition, or continuation. The commission did not refer to the tenure, so if it was a continuation for life, it must have been an example of the dispensing power.

The patent of Edward FitzSymon, 1578,[215] by Elizabeth I, expressly conferred power 'to sit in our said High Court of Chancery, and there to hear, decide, order, decree, and determine such cause and causes'. He was appointed at pleasure. This clearly complied with the statute of 1495 and it was evidently intended that the master of the rolls should actually exercise judicial functions.

Between 1614 and 1617 under the influence of Sir John Davies,[216] five circuits, covering the whole of Ireland, were mapped out and Ball relates that at that time the judges were insufficient to supply each of the circuits with two, 'although the master of the rolls rode regularly as justice of assize, and the number had to be made good by the employment of the law officers'.[217] The master of the rolls at the time

---

[211] Below, p. cxxii.

[212] Patent, 1 October 1550, Smyth, *Law Officers*, p. 55–57; Cal. Pat. Rol. Ir., Hen. VIII to Eliz. I, p. 208–209, no. 99; Lib. mun. pub. Hib., vol. 1, Part 2, p. 18. The patent mentioned that the records of the Chancery were kept in the tower in Dublin Castle which was both ruinous and distant from the courts, which were situated near St Patrick's cathedral, and that the records should be moved to the library of the cathedral.

[213] Patent, December 1552, Smyth, *Law Officers*, p. 57; Lib. mun. pub. Hib., vol. 1, Part 2, p. 18; but Cal. Pat. Rol. Edw. VI vol 5, p. 79 has privy seal, 9 June 1553.

[214] Commission, 6 July 1553, Smyth, *Law Officers*, p. 57–58; Cal. Pat. Rol. Ir., Hen. VIII to Eliz. I, p. 319–320, no. 80; Lib. mun. pub. Hib., vol. 1, Part 2, p. 18.

[215] Ibid., p. 62.

[216] (1569–1626), S.G., 1603, A.G., 1606–1619, see also H. S. Pawlisch, *Sir John Davies and the conquest of Ireland: a study in legal imperialism* (1985), A. R. Hart, *A History of the King's Serjeants at Law in Ireland* (Four Courts Press for Irish Legal History Society, 2000), 48–49.

[217] Ball, *Judges in Ireland*, i. 233.

was Sir Francis Aungier.[218] Grants for life were made by Charles I, to Christopher Wandesforde[219] and to Sir John Temple.[220]

Grants of the office were also made in reversion to take effect after the death of a life recipient. In 1644 the office was granted by Charles I to Sir Maurice Eustace in reversion[221] after Sir John Temple. The patent expressly excepted the judicial power, presumably to avoid the statute of 1495. Again, this may also indicate that the office was granted as a sinecure.

In 1659 Richard Cromwell, the lord protector, gave Sir John a licence to visit England for a year or more, indicating that, for that time at least, the office became a sinecure.[222] In 1664, under the Restoration, the office was granted by Charles II in reversion to Sir William Temple, after the deaths or surrenders of his father and Eustace.[223] When Sir John died in 1677, Ball writes that the office passed accordingly 'to his distinguished son, Sir William Temple . . . [and] although he was given the fullest judicial as well as ministerial power, the office became a sinecure', and worth £2,000 a year.[224] In fact the patent of 1664, granting the office in reversion, during Sir John's life, had only granted 'the ministerial part' of the office.[225] Ralph Wallis, 'who lately executed the office' under Sir John, was appointed deputy and took an oath to that effect. When Sir John died in 1677, a new appointment was made in Sir William's favour, first, as was customary, by an order under the privy seal and then by patent. The order under the privy seal recited that Sir William was abroad on the king's business,[226] and that, while the king had granted the office in reversion to Sir William, 'with an exemption and reservation of all judicial power', the king had resolved, both Sir Maurice Eustace and Sir John being dead, to grant Sir William 'as well the said judicial power and authority as the ministerial part power' and that a patent be granted for life. Since Sir William was in fact absent from Ireland, Ralph Wallis was 'again to execute the office of clerk and keeper of the rolls'. The new patent was issued.[227] Since it carried with it the judicial power, and was for life, the grant was in breach of the 1495 statute. Again, it can only be explained as an exercise of the dispensing power.

Temple was removed in 1689 by James II and replaced by Sir William Talbot, who was to hold at pleasure. This appointment was not recognized under William III. In

---

[218] (1558–1632), Smyth, *Law Officers*, p. 63–64; M.R., patent, 1609, continued, 1625; cr. Baron Aungier of Longford, 1621, Cokayne, *Complete Peerage*, viii. 118, 'Longford and Aungier of Longford'.

[219] Patent, 22 March 1633: Smyth, *Law Officers*, p. 64; there had been a partial destruction of the public records, a few years before 1635, when, as Lord Strafford noted, the rolls were kept in the house of the master of the rolls 'as now most records here are'. (Smyth, *Law Officers*, p. 66, Lord Strafford to Coke, 24 March 1635). The letter merely indicates that 'many' records were destroyed, and some embezzled, on that occasion. The master of the rolls at the time was probably Christopher Wandesforde, appointed 1633, or possibly Sir Francis Aungier. Buildings were erected in 1639 to house the records. When Sir William Temple was master of the rolls, i.e. 1677–89, the 'the rolls office of the kingdom' was said to be in King's Inns: Ball, *Judges in Ireland*, ii. 16, citing John Dunton, a visitor to Ireland. King's Inns were then situated on the east side of Church Street, on the north side of the Liffey on part of the site now occupied by the Four Courts: Colum Kenny, *King's Inns and the Kingdom of Ireland* (Dublin, 1992), pp. 218–19. The buildings still existed in 1760, but were in a 'crazy condition' and supported by props: Smyth, *Law Officers*, p. 67.

[220] Patent, 20 February 1640, Smyth, *Law Officers*, p. 67.

[221] Smyth, *Law Officers*, p. 67, privy seal, Oxford, 22 June 1644.

[222] Ibid., p. 67.

[223] Ibid., p. 68.

[224] Ball, *Judges in Ireland*, i. 294.

[225] Patent, Dublin, 10 May 1664; Smyth, *Law Officers*, p. 69–70.

[226] Privy seal, 23 November 1677; ibid., p. 70–71.

[227] Patent, Dublin, 8 Dec 1677; ibid., p. 70–71.

1696 Sir William Temple 'surrendered' and the office was conferred on his nephew, the Hon. William Berkeley, who succeeded in 1697 to the title of Lord Berkeley of Stratton, again for life, as if it had become a form of family property.[228] The patent did not expressly reserve judicial power, although that might be implied from the fact it was for life, and there was no dispensing power by that time.[229] A deputy was appointed.

Deputy keepers were regularly appointed from then on, and when Thomas Carter was appointed in 1731, he had four deputies.[230]

The office was still probably a sinecure when it was conferred on Henry Singleton[231] after he resigned from the bench in 1752, as he did so on health grounds. Singleton had only one deputy, John Lodge. Lodge was appointed clerk of the rolls during the vacancy when Singleton died in 1759.[232] Some weeks went by before George II appointed Richard Rigby.[233] The appointment was for life, the office to be carried out by the grantee or his deputy, so, again, it seems to have been a sinecure. Rigby appointed Lodge his deputy, and they were both sworn together at Lord Chancellor Bowes's house in Henrietta Street, Dublin. Singleton, who was Irish, had been replaced, belatedly, by an Englishman who was an absentee. The incident gave rise to adverse comment in Ireland.[234] In 1761 George III issued a new patent to Rigby. Again it was for life, and again to be executed by the grantee or his deputy, but the patent did expressly except all administration of justice.[235]

In the negotiations leading up to the Act of Union, it was agreed to give the master of the rolls judicial functions by statute, as a judge in Chancery, with appeal to the lord chancellor.[236] This was done in 1801 and the holder of the office was given the same tenure as other judges.[237]

In *Ex parte Shaw*[238] Hart L.C. held that, while the master of the rolls in England had inherent jurisdiction by prescription, that was not so as to the office in Ireland. Although finding that there was no inherent jurisdiction associated with the office in Ireland, he recognized that the Irish master of the rolls 'occasionally exercised equitable jurisdiction; and on one occasion, a judgment appears to have been given by him on a pure legal principle'.[239] He also commended the valuable research of counsel for the petitioner, who found that from the reign of Henry VIII to Charles II, sixty-one decrees had been pronounced by Irish masters of the rolls.[240]

From 1801 there was indeed a Rolls Court in Ireland, but there is no indication that one existed under that name before then. There are a number of references in the present reports to cases in the Rolls Court, but all but one can be identified as references to the English court of that name. There is a reference to *Creagh* v. *Willis*[241] 'in Trin. 1729 at the Rolls' and there is also a marginal note 'MSS cas. in Canc. A.276'

[228] Ball, *Judges in Ireland*, ii. 16 (does not mention Talbot); Smyth, *Law Officers*, p. 71–72.
[229] Below, p. cxxii.
[230] Ibid., p. 72.
[231] Patent, 24 April 1754, ibid., p. 73.
[232] Ibid., p. 73. Singleton died on 9 November 1759.
[233] Patent, 20 November 1759; ibid., p. 74; Lib. mun. pub. Hib., vol.1, part 2, p. 20.
[234] Ibid., at p. 310.
[235] Patent, 21 February 1761, Smyth, *Law Officers*, p. 74; Lib. mun. pub. Hib., vol. 1, part 3, p. 61.
[236] Ball, *Judges in Ireland*, ii. 238.
[237] Master of the Rolls (Ireland) Act, 1801, 41 Geo. III, c. 25.
[238] (1827) Beatty 24.
[239] Ibid., at p. 39.
[240] Ibid., at p. 25.
[241] Below, p. 256 [*331*].

but the case is reported as *Cray* v. *Willis*[242] and is an English case. Similarly, in *Astle* v. *Richardson*[243] there is a reference to a decision of the master of the rolls in *Staniforth* v. *Staniforth*, but that case is reported at 2 Vern. 460, 23 E.R. 895 and is likewise an English case. The only reference that has not been traced is *Piggot* v. *Foley*,[244] said to be decided 'in 1727 at the Rolls', but this probably also refers to the English Rolls Court.

EXCHEQUER CHAMBER

Coke, writing of England, said there were seven different courts held in the Exchequer.[245] The first three he mentions, the court of pleas, the court of accounts and the court of receipt, have either been dealt with previously, or are not mentioned as such in these reports. The other four courts which he mentions are:

1. the assembly of all the judges of England for settling matters of law;

2. the court for errors in the court of Exchequer, under 31 Edw. III, st. 1, c. 12[246] and 31 Eliz. I, c. 1;

3. the court for errors in the King's Bench, under 27 Eliz. I, c. 8 and 31 Eliz. I, c. 1. This will not be dealt with here;

4. the court of equity in the Exchequer Chamber, as Coke calls it, which is synonymous with what later became known as the equity side of the Exchequer, and does not therefore require further discussion in this section.

The assembly of all the judges

This court in England was apparently the most ancient and grew up as a matter of practice.[247] In fact it was hardly a court at all, in that proceedings were not started by writ, or by the parties. It simply became the practice for any of the common law courts to adjourn proceedings, if a sufficiently difficult point of law arose, and wait until the assembly of judges, meeting in a room near the Exchequer, had resolved the issue. Judgment was then given by the court in which the issue had arisen. Moreover, theoretically the assembly was purely advisory, and so it was unlike other courts in this respect also.

The common law judges in Ireland, unlike those in England, actually had to attend the sittings of the Irish House of Lords, but could not speak unless and until called upon to give their opinion on a point of law. The procedure was provided for in standing orders of the House adopted in 1692.[248]

There is no instance in these reports of this assembly.

The court for errors in the court of Exchequer

It is this court which is referred to in these reports in the case of *Costelo* v. *Costelo*[249] by counsel, Frank Blake, when he says: 'Error [in fact] in the Exchequer before the

---

[242] (1729) 1 Eq. Cas. Abr. 243, 21 E.R. 1020; 2 Eq. Cas. Abr. 537, 22 E.R. 453; (1729) 2 P. Wms. 529, 24 E.R. 847.

[243] Below, p. 147 [*184*]

[244] Below, p. 217 [*280*].

[245] Inst., iv. 119.

[246] c. 8 in Coke.

[247] *Select Cases in the Exchequer Chamber* (M. Hemmant, ed.) 51 Seld. Soc. (for 1933), xix.

[248] 'Rules and Orders of the Upper House' (1692) *Ir. Lords J.* p. 470, 'Concerning the Judges'.

[249] Below, p. 40.

31 Ed. 3 which erected the Exchequer Chamber was redressed by special commissioners.'

Reports of cases in the court may possibly occur in these reports, although the name 'Exchequer Chamber' is not used at the heading of any report, and it seems more likely that the cases mentioned below are instances of the lord chancellor sitting in Chancery and being assisted by other judges.[250]

The court, usually known as Exchequer Chamber, was strictly the 'Chamber of Council', or the 'court of Council Chamber'. It was a court in the true sense, in that proceedings were begun by writ of error, which in theory was a separate proceeding from the original action which gave rise to the alleged error.[251] The court was established in 1357 by the statute 31 Edw. III, st. 1, c. 12 (Eng.).[252] The statute is not mentioned by Donaldson[253] as having been expressly applied to Ireland, but it would have applied through Poynings' Law, 1495.[254] The statute of 1357 provided that 'the chancellor and treasurer shall cause to come before them in any chamber of council nigh the Exchequer the record of process out of the Exchequer taking to them the justices and other sage persons such as to them seemeth to be taken . . . and if any error be found they shall correct and amend the rolls'.

As to the composition of the court, there was a related issue as to the office of lord keeper. In England, by the statute 5 Eliz. I, c. 18 in 1562, the lord keeper was given the same powers as the lord chancellor. Jacob[255] maintains that there were instances before this of the offices being vested in different people at the same time, citing Coke.[256] Coke relates that a doubt had arisen on this point since King Henry V had two great seals made, one of gold and one of silver, and had given the gold one to the bishop of Durham, making him chancellor, and the silver one to the bishop of London 'to keep'. He gives no other example. Coke continues:[257]

> But all questions are now taken away by the said act of 5 Eliz. and at this day there being one great seale, there cannot be both a lord chancellor and a lord keeper of the great seale at one time, because both these are but one office, as it is declared by the said act.

In the reign of Queen Elizabeth and from then until the latter part of the eighteenth century the title of lord keeper seems to have been preferred in some appointments.[258]

In England a statute of 1588[259] first recited that the lord chancellor and lord treasurer, 'being great officers of the realm', were often suddenly called away, causing a discontinuance in the court of Council Chamber, and then, to prevent such a thing happening in future, provided that if either one of them, or if both chief justices, were present, there should be no discontinuance. However, no judgment could be

---

[250] See Inst., iv. 84. Baker, *OHLE*, vi. 172, n. 13.

[251] This meant, among other things, that originally there was no set time within which a writ of error had to be brought. 6 Geo. I, c. 6 (Ir.), 1719 s. 3 laid down a generous 20 years. See also 5 Geo. I, c. 13 (Eng.), 1718.

[252] St. Realm i. 351.

[253] A. G. Donaldson, 'The Application in Ireland of English and British Legislation Made Before 1801', (unpublished Ph.D. thesis, Queen's University, Belfast, 1952).

[254] Below, p. cli.

[255] *Dictionary*, 'Chancellor'.

[256] Inst., iv. 88.

[257] Ibid.

[258] There were four lord keepers in England in the eighteenth century, the last being Sir Robert Henley L.K., afterwards 1st earl of Northington who became L.C. in 1761 having been L.K. since 1757.

[259] 31 Eliz. I, c. 1 (Eng.); and see also 16 Car. II, c. 2 (Eng.), 1664.

given unless both were present. In 1668 the vacancy in the office of lord treasurer made it necessary to enact that the judgment of the court could be given by either the lord chancellor or the lord keeper.[260] It was this provision that persuaded the court in *The Banker's Case, The King* v. *Hornby*[261] that the other judges present were merely 'assistants' and so in that case that Lord Keeper Somers could reverse the court of Exchequer contrary to the opinion of the majority of the judges.

In Ireland the composition of the court of Exchequer Chamber was amended in 1639[262] by adding the vice-treasurer as an alternative to the lord treasurer and by providing that if one of the three (lord chancellor, lord treasurer, or vice-treasurer), or both chief justices, appeared on the day of adjournment, it would prevent a discontinuance. It also provided that judgment was to be given by the lord chancellor and lord treasurer 'in the presence and by advice of both the chief justices'. A further amendment in 1727[263] provided that the lord chancellor, in the absence of the treasurer and vice-treasurer, could give judgment, 'in the presence and by the advice of both or either of the said chief justices'. There was no mention of a lord keeper.[264]

Astle v. *Richardson*[265] and *Stepney* v. *Rowson*[266] were two cases decided together in 1734. They both involved closely related points as to jointures in family settlements. The report says they were 'reheard by the lord chancellor assisted by the same judges which had formerly given opinions'.[267] In these two cases those present were in fact the lord chancellor, Marlay C.B. and Rogerson C.J.K.B. The statute of 1727 specifically allowed *either* of the two chief justices, of the Common Pleas or the King's Bench, but the presence of Marlay C.B. would be odd, unless he were allowed as a 'sage person' under the statute of 1357, if indeed that category survived the statutes of 1639 and 1727 mentioned above. It seems more likely to be an instance of a rehearing in Chancery in which the lord chancellor was assisted by other judges, the same judges also having been present at the original hearing.[268]

In *Hussy* v. *Sheehy*[269] in 1730 there again is some doubt as to what court is constituted. The manuscript states that the proceedings are 'in Chancery', and they are not by a writ of error, but by a demurrer. The judges are Wyndham L.C., Marlay C.B. and Bernard J.C.P. The issue was whether errors in law and in fact could be assigned in the same bill of review. Both Marlay C.B. and Bernard J. give opinions and then, in a section headed 'Curia', the conclusion is stated that 'we are all of opinion [that] matters of fact and law may be assigned for errors in a bill of review', but continues 'and therefore I allow the demurrers', and so it is evidently the opinion of Wyndham L.C. It seems again to be a decision in Chancery, the lord chancellor availing himself of the assistance of the two other judges.

---

[260] 19 & 20 Car. II, c. 9 (Eng.), 1668; *HEL*, i. 244. The statute actually says 'lord keeper', but necessarily implied by then that it included lord chancellor if there was one.

[261] (1695) 5 Mod. 29, 87 E.R. 500; 14 S.T. at 105.

[262] 15 Car. I, c. 5 (Ir.).

[263] 1 Geo. II, c. 17 (Ir.).

[264] There are only two instances of a lord keeper being appointed in Ireland, both in the sixteenth century. Ball, *Judges in Ireland*, i. 155 mentions Thomas Cusake in 1546 and Adam Loftus, archbishop (1533/4–1605) (ibid., i. 155–56, 215–17) in 1573 and again in 1577, 1579 and 1581. Loftus was appointed L.C. in 1581.

[265] Below, pp. 147, 324.

[266] Below, pp. 154, 324.

[267] Below, p. 324.

[268] See above, p. lxxxiii n. 250.

[269] Below, p. 14.

Finally, an unreported case is cited, *Matthews* v. *Richardson*,[270] in which 'lord chief justices Levinz [*sic*] and Whitshed[271] assisted the lord chancellor'. 'Levinz' seems to be an error for Sir Richard Levinge.[272] This might also be a case in Chancery.

PROCEDURE

Starting an action at common law

It is necessary to give some account of the process of starting an action at common law as it had developed by the early eighteenth century. The following is an account from English sources. Irish sources are considered later in the section.

The medieval procedure had been based on the writ system which had many pitfalls for litigants and often led to the failure of an action on technical grounds alone. Original writs issued out of the common law side of Chancery.[273]

By the end of the sixteenth century a stage of abstraction had been reached whereby the medieval system of separate writs was seen as an expression of separate *forms* of action,[274] each with its own characteristics but also retaining its own technical pitfalls. Original writs could fail simply by some minor defect or by the wrong writ being issued. The response to this on the part of the judiciary was to create a number of conventions and fictions by which the technicalities of original writs were avoided, but at the price of great complexity and artificiality.

The complexity had three main causes:[275] 1. avoiding the expense and pitfalls of the original writ; 2. the King's Bench and Exchequer encroaching on the jurisdiction of the Common Pleas; and 3. the privilege allowed to attorneys and other officers of courts of suing and being sued in the court to which they were attached.

The overall result was that, before the reforms of the early nineteenth century, there were five ways of starting an action in the King's Bench, five in the Common Pleas, and six different ways of starting an action in the Exchequer.[276]

As far as the Exchequer was concerned, actions were not started there by private persons by original writ, and seemingly never had been. In the other common law courts the method of starting an action had developed by the eighteenth century as follows. If a defendant did not appear in response to an original writ, the next step in enforcing an appearance had been to issue a further writ called the *capias ad respondendum*. The courts of Common Pleas and King's Bench avoided the pitfalls of

---

[270] Below, p. 130.

[271] C.J.K.B., 1714–27.

[272] C.J.C.P., 1720–24, below, p. clxv.

[273] The Petty Bag Office was an office of the common law courts in Chancery from which issued all writs in which the crown was interested. Such writs and the returns to them were kept in small bags. Writs between subject and subject were kept in a hamper, or hanaper (hence, the Hanaper Office, Clerk of the Hanaper). The Petty Bag and the Hanaper Office together constituted the common law side of Chancery. Bl. Com., iii. 49; Jacob, *Law Dictionary*, 'Writ'; Brown, *Law Dictionary*, 'Hanaper', 'Petty Bag Office'. The common law side could also hear pleas of *scire facias*, challenging the validity of a record. Ferguson, *Treatise*, i. 16, writing of Ireland in 1841, says: 'The petty bag jurisdiction of the lord chancellor to hold pleas of *scire facias*, is a common law authority, in which, when an issue is joined, the record is delivered into the King's Bench by mittimus, to be tried by a jury at the sittings or at bar . . . and when tried, the record is returned to the chancellor, who may then give judgment and award execution; and the court of law may do so also. But in exercising this jurisdiction, the chancellor acts entirely in analogy to the rules and principles of the common law courts.'

[274] *HEL*, ix. 248–50.

[275] First Report of Commissioners on Courts of Common Law, Parlt. Papers, 1829, ix. 77; *HEL*, ix. 250.

[276] First Report of Commissioners on Courts of Common Law, Parlt. Papers 1829, ix. 74; *HEL*, ix. 249–250.

the original writ by adopting the convention that the plaintiff could start the action in most cases by issuing a *capias*,[277] and the original was never issued, or only fictionally. Blackstone, writing of the Common Pleas in England, says that 'a fictitious original is drawn up . . . in order to give the proceedings a colour of regularity'.[278] The *capias*, in distinction to an original writ, was a judicial writ, issued by the court in which the action was brought and theoretically after it had begun.

The convention of starting an action by *capias* in the Common Pleas and King's Bench seems to date from the latter part of the sixteenth century[279] but may have begun earlier.

It also seems that, in common law courts other than the Exchequer, the defendant could still insist that the original writ be issued. But such a course had its own risks, since among other things, an outlawry could only later be obtained against the defendant if an original writ had been issued in the first place.[280] According to Ferguson, writing in 1841, an original writ was never in fact issued in Ireland unless the process was to proceed to outlawry.[281]

Moreover, Holdsworth,[282] citing Stephen[283] on the Common Pleas, says that starting by *capias* was not possible in real or mixed actions, and that an original writ was still necessary in some personal actions where *capias* did not lie.[284]

Ferguson,[285] writing in 1841, points out that the original writ was abolished in England by 2 & 3 Will. IV, c. 39, 1832, but was then still part of the legal system in Ireland, 'although in most cases obsolete'. The original writ was abolished in Ireland by 13 & 14 Vict., c. 18 (Ir.), 1850, s. 1.[286] From what has been said earlier, however, it would seem that, since actions had long been started in the Exchequer only by *capias*, or *venire*, etc., and for entirely different reasons, the defendant could not insist on an original writ in the Exchequer even in personal actions or if he did, that the action would have had to be transferred to another court.

It may also be that the procedure in the Exchequer of starting an action by *capias* was the origin of the device in the other common law courts, described above, of avoiding the technicalities of the medieval original writs by issuing the judicial writs of *capias* or *venire* instead.[287]

---

[277] Bl. Com., iii. 281–282; See Anstey's ingenious poem, inspired by Pope's mock-heroic couplets: John Surrebutter [John Anstey], *The Pleader's Guide, A Didactic Poem* (1796), Lecture 4, pp. 40–41:

> A *Capias* is conceiv'd and born
> Ere yet th'ORIGINAL is drawn,
>
> . . . .
>
> And thus, by ways and means unknown
> To all but Heroes of the Gown
> A Victory full oft is won
> Ere Battle fairly is begun;

[278] Bl. Com., iii. 282–284.

[279] Bl. Com., iii. 282; *HEL*, ix. 250; Reeves, *History of English Law*, iii. 757–758.

[280] Above, p. lxx n. 114.

[281] *Treatise*, i. 11. He also states, as we have seen, that there was no outlawry in the Exchequer. Ferguson, *Treatise*, i. 12–13.

[282] *HEL*, ix. 251.

[283] H. J. Stephen, *A treatise on the principles of Pleading in Civil Actions* (London, 1824), at p. 27.

[284] As where the defendant was privileged against, arrest, see below, p. xcii, and actions on the case, when the original was necessary to specify the precise facts on which the case was based.

[285] *Treatise*, i. 123.

[286] (Personal actions started by writ of summons), and repeated by 16 & 17 Vict., c. 113 (Ir.), 1853, s. 6.

[287] Above, p. lxxxv.

The methods of starting an action on the common law side of the Exchequer were as follows:

1. Subpœna ad Respondendum
2. Capias Quo minus
3. Venire ad Respondendum
4. Venire of Privilege
5. Capias of Privilege
6. Bill, in the case of peers and members of parliament
7. A letter missive and subpœna, in the case of peers only.

1. Ferguson[288] says simply that the *subpœna ad respondendum* was another method of commencing a suit in the Exchequer, 'which would also appear, from analogy of proceedings on the equity side of the court, to have been founded upon a bill previously filed in the court in a plea of debt'. King's Inns MS. 82, which seems to date from the early eighteenth century, and is in the form of a catechism, contains the following questions and answers on the point:[289]

> Q. What is a common law subpœna?
> A. It is a process directed to the defendant requiring him personally to be and appear before the barons, (who alone are judges at law of this court) at a certain day and under certain pain therein to be limited to answer such matters as shall be objected against him and the parties name[d] as indorsed thereon.
> Q. Is this way of proceeding frequently used?
> A. Yes, and in many cases is more convenient than proceeding by *capias quominus*.
> Q. Why?
> A. For four different reasons namely, first, because you can compel the defendant to appear in a much shorter time than you can proceed against the sheriff to oblige him to return his writ or bring in the defendant's body; secondly you don't thereby affront or expose the defendants by arrest as you do by *capias*; thirdly, if the defendant be obstinate and stands out process of contempt you can compel him to give bail as soon as on a *capias quominus* observing the rules hereafter mentioned; fourthly, if the defendant stands out to a commission of rebellion he must give bail 'though the sum demanded be less than £10 which you can never oblige him to do by *capias quominus*.

Howard also states that the subpœna was used in preference to a *capias quominus* and gives a similar but not identical list of reasons.[290] He adds to the second reason above that if the person was 'of credit and substance' it did not expose him to the ignominy of arrest, and that an action against an executor or administrator was started by subpœna because an executor or administrator was not to be arrested for the debt of the testator or intestate.[291]

It follows from what else has been said that the subpœna was the process by which the crown began an action.[292] It also seems clear that when brought by a party other

---

[288] *Treatise*, i. 124.
[289] KI MS. 82, p. 98–99.
[290] *Pleas Side*, p. 69, 'Of Common Law Subpœna, and Process of Contempt'.
[291] The similarity between Howard's text and KI MS. 82 suggests either that Howard may have used it in writing his book, or possibly that he was the author of KI MS. 82, although the MS. may be too early for that.
[292] See Howard, *Treatise*, i. 3, above, p. lxi; William Tidd, *The Practice of the Courts of King's Bench and Common Pleas in Personal Actions* (7th ed., London, 1821), i. 177. See Dickens, *David Copperfield*, ch. 16: 'I am improving my legal knowledge, Master Copperfield,' said Uriah. 'I am going through Tidd's *Practice*. Oh, what a writer Mr. Tidd is, Master Copperfield!'

than the crown, it must have been based, as Ferguson suggests, on the fiction of *quo minus*, whether stated or not.

There are references in these reports to subpœnas on both the equity and common law sides,[293] although it would seem that on the equity side subpœnas[294] were part of mesne process, properly so called, actions always being started by English[295] bill.[296]

2. The *Quo minus capias* was the fiction, as already noted, by which private litigants were permitted to start an action in the Exchequer.[297] In *Allen* v. *Mandevil*[298] in these reports an issue was whether a *quo minus* gave authority to 'break open doors' in order to serve the *capias* on a defendant. It is there mentioned, with reference to a case that is not cited, that at the time of Gilbert C.B. it had been held that it did, but that the court had subsequently decided that it did not, because 'then it would be done every day'.[299]

3., 4. & 5. A *venire* was a writ directed to the sheriff to impanel a jury to try an issue and was therefore the method to begin an action on the common law side where a jury trial was to take place. By the eighteenth century an original writ does not seem to have been issued, or only fictionally.

The *venire* of privilege and *capias* of privilege were the methods to begin an action where an attorney or other officer of the court had the privilege of suing, or being sued, in the court to which he was attached. This seems to occur in these reports in *Prendergast, one of the attorneys* v. *Green*,[300] one of the cases on a Kerry bond.[301] Howard gives the reason for the privilege that, if it were otherwise, the business of the court where the attorney was required to attend would be prejudiced.[302] The privilege did not apply if the crown proceeded against the attorney,[303] nor where the attorney sued as trustee or executor, for it was personal privilege and extended only to suits in which the attorney was concerned in his own right.[304] The attorney could not be compelled to appear by arrest or subpœna.[305] There was no privilege between attorneys. If an attorney privileged in one court sued another attached to another court, the one sued had no privilege, since there was no privilege between equals.[306] Neither barristers nor serjeants were privileged,[307] as they were not officers of the court.

---

[293] See *His Majesty* v. *Sir William Courtney* below, p. 267, *Dawson* v. *Spiers* below, p. 293.

[294] *McCarthy* v. *Kelly*, KI MS. 50, p. 2 (equity side: Dalton C.B.: subpœna could be made returnable at any time). *Higginbottom* v. *Cheevers*, KI MS. 50, p. 7 (equity side: Gilbert C.B.: service of subpœna could be made in the afternoon, because it was not certain how long the court sits).

[295] I.e., in the English language.

[296] Howard, *Treatise*, i. 3.

[297] Strictly, therefore, in Exchequer there was only mesne process and final process, although by the nineteenth century, even though *quominus* was a *capias* and so a judicial writ, it was sometimes referred to as 'first process', the writs subsequent to *quominus* being referred to as mesne process, e.g. Jacob, *Law Dictionary* (1811), 'Process, I', v. 305.

[298] Below, p. 138.

[299] Below, p. 139.

[300] Below, p. 317.

[301] Below, p. cxxiii.

[302] Howard, *Pleas Side*, ii. 246.

[303] Ibid.

[304] Ibid.

[305] Ibid., ii. 247.

[306] Ibid., ii. 249.

[307] Ibid., ii. 250.

In Ireland the privilege may be traced back to the writ of 1356[308] and the statutes of 1449[309] and 1460.[310]

6. A statute of 1700[311] allowed actions against peers or members of parliament to be brought by bill at common law and a similar provision was made in Ireland in 1727.[312]

7. In the case of peers and privy counsellors, a letter missive and subpœna was an alternative method of proceeding.[313]

The next step was for the plaintiff to file a declaration, stating his cause of action.[314] The defendant then put in an answer, which was a plea of one kind or another. Howard[315] says that 'pleas are either general or special: general, to the declaration, as in debt, or on contract,[316] *nihil debet per patriam*; in debt on bond, *non est factum*; in an action of the case upon a promise; *non assumpsit*, in trespass, etc., not guilty, in covenant, *performance of covenants*, etc.' The defendant might also enter a demurrer, denying that the facts, even if proved by the plaintiff, disclosed a cause of action. A special plea would be that he had acted under duress, or in trespass, that he admitted the fact, but pleaded justification. The plaintiff might then enter a replication, objecting to some aspect of the defendant's plea. This in turn to could give rise to a rejoinder on the part of the defendant, a sur-rejoinder by the plaintiff, a rebutter by the defendant, and even a sur-rebutter by the plaintiff.[317] The purpose of pleadings was thus to produce an issue of law to be decided by the court or of fact to be decided by a jury.

Procedure on the equity side

A bill and subpœna was the method of starting an action on the equity side.[318] It also applied in cases of privilege.[319] In the case of peers and privy counsellors, the bill was followed by a letter missive to the defendant.[320]

As Howard notes, a bill in the Exchequer was necessarily based on the same *quo minus* fiction as on the common law side.[321] The plaintiff had to 'surmise' that he was debtor to the king in his bill, otherwise the defendant had a demurrer,[322] even though the allegation was not traversable.

In addition to original bills, there were also bills of revivor, bills of discovery of evidence, bills of discovery on the Popery Acts, cross bills, amended bills, supplemental bills, bills of interpleader, bills to quiet possession of titles, also called possessory bills,

---

[308] Above, p. lxvii n. 99.

[309] Above, p. lxviii n. 102,

[310] Above, p. lxviii n. 103.

[311] 12 & 13 Will. III, c. 3 (Eng.); Jacob, *Law Dictionary*, 'Privilege III'.

[312] 1 Geo. II, c. 8 (Ir.).

[313] Howard, *Pleas Side*, i. 83–88.

[314] Ibid., i. 113.

[315] Ibid., i. 114.

[316] This seems to refer to debt on a contract.

[317] Ibid., i. 113–162.

[318] Howard, *Equity Side*, i. 205.

[319] Ibid., i. 119.

[320] Ibid., ii. 629–634. Howard mentions that in Ireland the practice had been for many years to issue the letter missive and the subpœna at the same time.

[321] Howard, *Treatise*, i. 3, see above, p. lxi.

[322] Ibid., i. 213.

injunction bills (to halt proceedings at law, or stay equitable waste, etc.), and bills of review and reversal.[323]

Howard[324] says the bill was derived from the *libel* of canon law. The bill was in the form of a petition to the chancellor, or the judges where the action was to be heard. It set out the facts, how the plaintiff was aggrieved, why he or she was without a remedy except in equity, and prayed such relief as was suitable and a subpœna or other process to compel the defendant to answer the allegations. It also framed interrogatories for the defendant to answer.[325] After the bill was engrossed on parchment, signed by counsel and attorney and filed in the chief remembrancer's office, the plaintiff could then issue a subpœna to compel the attendance of the defendant.[326]

The defendant was then to put in a sworn answer[327] contesting the facts alleged; or a demurrer, alleging that no cause of action was disclosed by the facts, or that the proper remedy was available at law; or a plea, such as that the cause had already been decided, or that the plaintiff was outlawed, or of purchase for consideration without notice, etc.[328] The defendant might put in both an answer and a demurrer.[329] Quakers could affirm[330] and Jews could swear on the Pentateuch.[331] If the defendant lived twenty miles or more from Dublin, he was entitled to a *dedimus*,[332] giving authority for the answer to be taken by commission, that is, by commissioners appointed to take it.[333] The commissioners, having taken the answer, would have it engrossed and then had to fill in the caption at the foot which stated that they had taken it at a certain place and they then signed their names.[334]

Further pleadings might then follow. The plaintiff could put in a replication and the defendant a rejoinder, etc.[335]

Either party could put in exceptions to pleadings, as where the plaintiff alleged the answer was 'short', that is, inadequate, and requiring a better answer.[336] The party could then obtain an order for reference to a baron for his report.[337] This was heard either in the baron's chambers, or sometimes in the Exchequer chamber.[338] The baron would then hear both parties and deliver his opinion in a written report.[339] He could, for example, order a new answer or other pleading.[340] If no fault was found, then the party seeking the baron's report would be liable for costs. Howard[341] comments that the baron seemed to be acting in a ministerial rather than a judicial

---

[323] Howard, *Equity Side*, i. 207–8; KI MS. 82, p. 3.

[324] *Equity Side*, i. 205.

[325] Ibid., ii. 206.

[326] Ibid., i. 208.

[327] Ibid., i. 68–90.

[328] Ibid., i. 103–105.

[329] Ibid., i. 86, *Blake* v. *Lynch*.

[330] Howard, *Equity Side*, i. 89–90, and below, p. cxli.

[331] Ibid., i. 90.

[332] *Dedimus potestatem*, 'we have given the power'. Howard, *Equity Side*, i. 73–76, Rule 16 of the rules of the Exchequer.

[333] See also below, p. ciii. In *Hoonahan* v. *Lord Orrey*, ibid., i. 76, a *dedimus* was granted into England.

[334] Howard, *Equity Side*, i. 77–83.

[335] Ibid., ii. 808–809.

[336] Ibid., i. 434, 441.

[337] Ibid., i. 444, ii. 798.

[338] Ibid., i. 444.

[339] Ibid., i. 446.

[340] Ibid., i. 443–44.

[341] Ibid., i. 453.

capacity for that purpose since either party could appeal from the report to the court, by way of exceptions to the baron's report.[342] Pleadings could also be referred for impertinence, where they contained long digressions, or for prolixity or for scandal, where they contained scandalous allegations not material to the point at issue.[343] Pleadings had to be signed by counsel 'allowed to practice'[344] and Howard mentions a case which he refers to as *Woogan* v. *Jones*, in Exchequer, 31 May 1731, in which he says that an answer and plea were sworn before Lord Treasurer Burlington[345] in England, signed by an English barrister, sealed, and 'brought over here', where an objection was successfully made that they were not properly signed by a barrister entitled to practise in Ireland.[346] There is a report of the case in the present reports.[347] Burlington never visited Ireland,[348] so it is not surprising that he was unfamiliar with the rules of the Irish Exchequer. The office appears to have become a sinecure in his time.

Evidence was taken from witnesses by written interrogatories, described in the section 'Trials by Leading Order' below,[349] and the witnesses responded by written depositions.[350] Evidence might also be taken by commission if the defendant lived twenty miles or more from Dublin.[351] Commissioners had to be impartial.[352]

An order for publication, when copies of the pleadings would be made and distributed, marked the end of the process of pleading and a date would then be set for hearing the action.[353]

At the hearing before the barons, the plaintiff's counsel presented the bill, the defendant's counsel presented the answer and the case on each side was stated and argued, and the proofs were read.[354] If some issue on the evidence could not be

[342] Ibid.

[343] Ibid., ii. 704–708.

[344] Ibid., ii. 706. Rule 10 of the Exchequer: Howard reproduces some of what he refers to as the standing rules of the Exchequer in the appendix to vol. 2 of his *Equity Side*.

[345] Richard Boyle (1694–1753), 3rd earl of Burlington (Eng.), 4th earl of Cork (Ir.), made lord treasurer of Ireland in 1715, at the age of twenty-one, sworn of the Irish privy council, and made governor of Co. Cork and vice-admiral of York, 1715–33, lord lieutenant, East Riding 1715–21, and West Riding, 1715–33. P.C. (Eng.), 15 May 1729. K.G., installed 18 June 1730. Known as an amateur architect and prolific collector of paintings. The famous portico of Burlington House, Piccadilly, London, is not thought to be his design, he being only twenty-three when it was erected. It was extended in the nineteenth century and is now the home of the Royal Academy. He built a villa at Chiswick, Middlesex, which was his own design. It was said to be 'too small to live in and too large to hang a watch'. He is represented in Hogarth's 'Man of Taste', as a mason climbing up a ladder, and is also satirised, with his friends, in Hogarth's 'Taste of the Town'. Cokayne, *Complete Peerage*, i. 432–33. He nevertheless made a significant contribution to architecture in his own right, was a patron of William Kent and of a number of poets including Pope and Gay. See P. D. Kingsbury, 'Boyle, Richard, third earl of Burlington and fourth earl of Cork (1694–1753)', *ODNB*, <http://www.oxforddnb.com/view/article/3136>, accessed 26 April 2008.

[346] Ibid.

[347] *Wogan* v. *Jones*, below, p. 35.

[348] The income from his Irish estates nevertheless funded his expensive tastes and architectural activities. He owned Lismore House, Co. Waterford (which had been bought by Richard, the first earl of Cork, from Sir Walter Raleigh in 1602) and its vast estates, some 42,000 acres. He lived at Burlington House, at Chiswick House, and at his house at Londesborough in the East Riding of Yorkshire. Lord Burlington is listed as an absentee in Thomas Prior, *A list of the absentees of Ireland, and the yearly value of their estates and incomes spent abroad* (3rd ed., 1730), at p. 10.

[349] Below, p. ciii.

[350] Howard, *Equity Side*, ii. 570–77.

[351] Above, p. xc, and below, p. ciii; ibid., ii. 573–77.

[352] Ibid., ii. 573.

[353] Ibid., ii. 613, 469–473.

[354] Ibid., ii. 472–73.

resolved, the court could refer an issue for trial on a leading order by the common law side before a jury. This procedure is described below.[355]

Compelling appearance by the defendant

It was a principle of the common law that an action could not proceed against a defendant in his or her absence. One of the principal problems, possibly the main problem, of the legal process at the time was the difficulty in compelling a defendant to appear and answer the action brought by a plaintiff. What process was used depended on the court in which the plaintiff had brought the action, how the action was started, and the person who was the defendant.[356]

Members of parliament,[357] peers and privy councillors[358] were privileged against arrest, as were females who were noble by marriage or descent.[359] In equity, there was no process of contempt against peers.[360] After the bill was issued the lord chancellor wrote a letter missive to the peer and in Ireland a subpœna was issued at the same time.[361] If an answer was not then put in, an order was issued to show cause why a sequestration should not issue, and if there was still no answer, the sequestration would be granted.[362] The process was the same against a member of parliament, except for the letter missive.

Attorneys and officers of the court were also privileged from arrest on mesne process in all civil actions, because it was presumed that they were required to be in attendance at court.[363]

Subject to such personal privilege, there were three basic methods of compelling appearance:[364] 1. *distringas* (distraint on the goods of the defendant), 2. *capias* (arrest of the defendant), and 3. *subpœna* (attachment and commission of rebellion). Which of these could be employed depended on how the action was started. In the Exchequer they were as follows:[365]

1. On a *venire* or summons of a person entitled to privilege of parliament, only a *distringas* was available.

---

[355] Below, p. ciii.

[356] Howard, *Pleas Side*, i. 73; *HEL*, ix. 253.

[357] They were privileged against suits being brought against them until 'after' the parliament had ended by 3 Edw. IV, c. 1 (Ir.), 1463: Howard, *Equity Side*, ii. 713–15; Howard, *Pleas Side*, i. 17. But due to the uncertainty of the word 'after', 6 Ann., c. 8 (Ir.), s. 1, laid down that the privilege began 40 days before until 40 days after the sessions or prorogations, and during the sittings. By 1 Geo. II, c. 8 (Ir.), 1727 although the person of a member of parliament was privileged against arrest during that period, suits could be begun up to 14 days before and from 14 days after: Howard, *Equity Side*, ii. 714–15.

[358] KI MS. 90, p. 5.

[359] Howard, *Pleas Side*, i. 16. Privilege extended to widows of peers who subsequently married commoners after their husband's death, unless they were commoners before marriage: *Mead* v. *Pearse and Lady Barrymore*, KI MS. 50, p. 3, St Leger B., KI MS. 90, p. 5 (equity side). The Lady Barrymore referred to was probably Katharine (bap. 9 May 1663), da. of Richard, 2nd Baron Barry of Santry, and therefore was noble by birth. Her husband, Laurence (Barry), earl of Barrymore, died on 17 April 1699 and Katherine in the same year married Francis Gash, one of the Revenue Commissioners. St Leger B. held she was still entitled to privilege. Cokayne, *Complete Peerage*, i. 444. KI MS. 90 p. 5 notes that the privilege did not extend to women who were commoners before marriage to a peer if they married a commoner after the peer's death. See also Howard, *Pleas Side*, i. 16: 'that which is gained by marriage may also be lost by marriage'.

[360] Jacob, *Law Dictionary*, 'Chancery'.

[361] Howard, *Equity Side*, ii. 629–632; KI MS. 90, p. 5.

[362] Ibid., ii. 629–632.

[363] Ibid.

[364] Howard, *Pleas Side*, i. 15; *HEL*, ix. 253.

[365] Howard, *Pleas Side*, i. 73; *HEL*, ix. 253, and n. 4. First Report of the Commissioners on Courts of Common Law, Parlt. Papers, 1829, ix. 86.

2. On an attachment of privilege, in the case of suits by attorneys and officers of the court, the defendant was liable to arrest.[366] A higher amount of bail was to be taken from the defendant in such a case.[367]

3. On a subpœna, process was by attachment and commission of rebellion.[368] This was essentially process of contempt of court, and could go eventually to the serjeant at arms acting for the court, against whom the defendant was held to be in contempt. If there was no response to the first writ, in which case the sheriff of the county in which the defendant lived when the action was started made a return to the writ of *non est inventus,* that the defendant could not be found, a second writ, called *alias,*[369] was issued, and if with the same result, a third writ, called *pluries,*[370] was issued and if with the same result, then a proclamation of rebellion, followed by attachment, under the serjeant at arms, as the court's own officer, and then, if necessary, a commission of rebellion.[371] *Beaumont* v. *Jessop*[372] in these reports mentions both *alias* and *pluries.*

On the equity side the method was by subpœna and attachment. Howard sets out the successive writs as follows: 1. attachment, 2. *alias* attachment, 3. *pluries* attachment, 4. proclamation, 5. commission of rebellion, 6. serjeant at arms, 7. sequestration.[373]

4. On a *capias,* which in the Exchequer was the *capias quo minus,* the writ authorised the sheriff to arrest the defendant and bring him to court. In cases where the defendant was willing to attend court, it was not necessary to arrest him, and he could give bail for his appearance instead.

Cowel, writing of England, explains with his usual precision of language the difference between common bail, special bail and mainprise:[374]

> It [bail] is used in our common law properly for the freeing or setting at liberty of one arrested or imprisoned upon action, either civil or criminal, under surety taken for his appearance at a day and place certainly assigned . . . The reason why it is called bail, is because by this means the party restrained is delivered into the hands of those that bind themselves for his forthcoming: there is both common and special bail; common bail is in actions of small concernment, and is called common, because any sureties in that case are taken; whereas, upon causes of greater weight, or apparent speciality, special bail or surety must be taken, as subsidy-men at the least, and that to the value . . . He that is mainprised, is always said to be at large . . . until the day of his appearance . . . but where a man is let to bail . . . he is always accounted by the law to be in their ward and custody for the time: and they may, if they will, keep him in prison or ward during that time.

Bail took two main forms: 'bail below' (or 'bail to the sheriff'), which the defendant had to give to the sheriff who had made the arrest, for his appearance in court, and 'bail above' (or 'bail to the action'), which was bail which the defendant had to give

---

[366] Howard, *Pleas Side,* i. 14, 68.

[367] ibid., i. 68.

[368] Howard, *Pleas Side,* i. 69–81.

[369] So-called from the words *Sicut alias præcipimus* L.'as we on another occasion commanded', which occurred in it.

[370] So-called from the phrase *pluries capias* occurring in the first clause, late L. '(you may take) several times'. *OED.*

[371] Howard, *Pleas Side,* i. 73.

[372] Below, p. 69 [*81*].

[373] Howard, *Equity Side,* ii. 753. A fourth writ before proclamation, called *exigent,* occurred in courts other than the Exchequer where outlawry was sought. Jacob, *Law Dictionary,* 'Exigent'.

[374] Cowel, *Interpreter* 'Bail'. The spelling has been modernized; Bl. Com., iii. 290.

to the court, that he would satisfy judgment.[375] As to bail below, normally not more than two persons, typically friends of the defendant, stood bail for the defendant and were responsible for his appearance in court. Common bail could be any persons, not of any particular standing, whereas special bail had to be substantial bondsmen. Blackstone mentions that in England before the time he wrote, in the 1760s, common bail were fictitious persons, and indicates that bail below was by then always special bail.[376] The defendant was legally in the custody of the bail bondsmen, who could actually confine him if they wished, but were answerable for his appearance in court in any case. The defendant would give a bail bond to the sheriff naming the persons. The sheriff was obliged by statute[377] to take reasonable bail from a defendant whom he arrested, otherwise an action on the case lay against him.[378] No person was obliged to give bail exceeding £40 unless the cause of action was stated in the initial process.[379]

If the person accepted by the sheriff as bail below were insolvent, the plaintiff could call on the sheriff to produce the defendant, and if the sheriff then failed to secure sufficient bail above, the sheriff was personally liable to the plaintiff.[380]

On taking the defendant into custody or taking bail, the sheriff then returned *cepi corpus* on the writ and was then responsible for the custody of the defendant until he appeared in court.[381] As Cowel and Howard[382] indicate, the sheriff did not necessarily have to confine the defendant, but could let him be 'at large', but was in any case answerable for producing him in court.

On taking a bond, the sheriff had then to assign it to the plaintiff.[383] If the plaintiff refused the assignment, because he distrusted the security, the sheriff had to produce the defendant at once to the court.[384] If he did not, the court would amerce him.[385] In *Anderson* v. *Eustace*,[386] after the period of these reports, it was decided that the

---

[375] *HEL*, i. 253; Bl. Com., iii. 290–291.

[376] Bl. Com., iii. 290. Dickens in *Pickwick Papers*, the first part of which was published in 1836, describes 'sham bail', a group of men who made a living by standing bail for anyone, for a consideration. 'Bail you to any amount, and only charge half-a-crown. Curious trade, isn't it?' said Perker . . . 'What! Am I to understand that these men earn a livelihood by waiting about here, to perjure themselves before the judges of the land, at the rate of half-a-crown a crime!' exclaimed Mr Pickwick, quite aghast at the disclosure. 'Why I don't exactly know about perjury, my dear sir', replied the little gentleman. 'Harsh word, my dear sir, very harsh word indeed. It's a legal fiction, my dear sir, nothing more'. Dickens, *Pickwick Papers*; *HEL*, ix. 254.

[377] 23 Hen. VI, c. 9 (Eng.), 1444; applicable to Ireland through Poynings' Law, confirmed, 7 Will. III, c. 25 (Ir.), 1695–96; Howard, *Pleas Side*, i. 40 (refers to 'c. 10').

[378] Howard, *Pleas Side*, i. 40

[379] 7 Will. III, c. 25 (Ir.), 1695–96. The statute applied to any 'writ, bill or process'. In the case of original writs, the cause of action would necessarily be expressed in the writ. Howard, *Pleas Side*, i. 41; see the English statute 13 Car. II, st. 2, c. 2, 1661.

[380] Bl. Com., iii. 291; J. Anstey, *Pleader's Guide* (1796), Lecture V, p. 49–50:

The bond assign'd, the Debtor fled,
Himself Defendant in his stead,
Be doom'd with curses to bewail
The horrors of insolvent Bail.

[381] Howard, *Pleas Side*, i. 31, 45, 48, 51.

[382] Ibid., i. 51 n.

[383] 6 Ann., c. 10 (Ir.), 1707.

[384] Howard, *Pleas Side*, i. 41.

[385] Howard, *Pleas Side*, i. 42. Amercement, also spelled 'amerciament', was a penalty left to the 'mercy' of the inflicter; hence the imposition of an arbitrary fine (originally lighter in amount than fines fixed for specific offences). *OED*.

[386] Exchequer, Trinity Term, 1745. Cited in Howard, *Pleas Side*, i. 45–46.

plaintiff could not be compelled to take an assignment of a bail bond. The plaintiff's remedy was to compel the sheriff to produce the defendant by fines.

'Bail above' was bail given in court as earnest that the defendant would attend and satisfy the judgment, if it went against him. On acceptance of bail above, bail below was vacated and any bail bond discharged.[387] If the defendant could not raise bail above, the next step on a *capias* was usually that the court would commit him to the 'marshalsea or gaol of the four courts'.[388]

From 1733 in Ireland in Chancery or Exchequer on any bill, if there was proof that a subpœna had been served on the defendant personally and that, through neglect, there had been no response up to the point of sequestration, either by the defendant or his or her attorney or agent, the court could enter an appearance as if the defendant had actually appeared,[389] and the plaintiff could then proceed to judgment and execution. This was known as the 'parliamentary appearance'.[390] In 1781, long after these reports, the same procedure was recognized for the common law side of Exchequer, in the case of a common law subpœna.[391]

So long as personal service of the writ was required, the defendant had the opportunity of knowing that an action had been begun against him. At the beginning of the nineteenth century, however, substituted service was introduced, which Ferguson says was 'in great measure peculiar to Ireland'.[392] Under that provision, where personal service was 'impossible',[393] service could be made at the dwelling house of the defendant, or to his or her spouse, son, daughter or to a servant.[394] There was no express requirement that the plaintiff swear an affidavit that the defendant was aware of the writ or was wilfully avoiding service, as there was later in nineteenth century statutes.[395] The danger of the 'parliamentary appearance', when substituted service was introduced, meant that the defendant might not in fact be aware that an action had been started against him or her until it proceeded to judgment, which was an obvious injustice and cause of oppression. A reform that was intended to aid the plaintiff had gone much too far in the opposite direction. However, during the period of these reports, the system would not seem to have been as open to oppression as it later became.

However, in the period of these reports, in courts in Ireland other than the Exchequer, there was a similar problem in relation to secret outlawries. Statutes in 1612[396] and 1707[397] attempted to prevent secret outlawries by providing that a public

---

[387] Howard, *Pleas Side*, i. 42.

[388] Ibid., i. 46.

[389] 7 Geo. II, c. 14 (Ir.), 1733, s. 7, and 13 Geo. II, c. 9 (Ir.), 1739; a similar change had been introduced in England in 1725 by 12 Geo. I, c. 29 (Eng.); and extended by 45 Geo. III, c. 124 (Eng.), 1805, s. 3 and 7 & 8 Geo. IV, c. 71 (Eng.), 1827, s. 5; *HEL*, ix. 253; First Report of Commissioners on Courts of Common Law, 1829, ix. 85–86, B.P.P., Legal Administration, 1829, i. 85–86.

[390] Ferguson, *Treatise*, i. 213–217. See *Sheehy* v. *Professional Life-Assurance Company* (1857) 2 C.B. (n.s.) 211, 140 E.R. 395.

[391] 21 & 22 Geo. III, c. 18 (Ir.), 1781–82, s. 3.

[392] Ferguson, *Treatise*, i. 137.

[393] 43 Geo. III, c. 53 (Ir.), 1803, s. 8, (Process (Ireland) Act, 1803). Ferguson, ibid., cites the statute incorrectly as c. 46. Section 8 allowed the courts in Ireland to regulate substituted service by rules of court.

[394] Ferguson, *Treatise*, i. 138.

[395] See 16 & 17 Vict., c. 113 (Common Law Procedure Amendment Act (Ireland), 1853), s. 32.; 15 & 16 Vict., c. 76 (Eng.) (Common Law Procedure Act, 1852), s. 17.

[396] 11 Jac. I, c. 8 (Ir.), 1612.

[397] 6 Ann., c. 15 (Ir.), 1707.

proclamation should be made, in terms set out in the Acts.[398] According to Howard, writing in 1759, these measures were not entirely effective because sub-sheriffs were being bribed so that proclamations were 'transacted... in so private and secret a manner, that it was impossible the defendants should have ever heard of them'.[399] The problem still existed in England in 1829 when the Commissioners presented their report on the courts of common law.[400] The proclamation did not necessarily prevent the problem, unless the defendant was living in the parish at the time the proclamation was made, or in the vicinity, but he might have gone abroad, or be in England, and his place of abode there unknown.[401]

Another oppressive feature of procedure at the time of these reports was that where a person was liable to arrest in a civil case, and could not post bail, they could be imprisoned before the action proceeded to proof, as mentioned earlier. This most commonly occurred in cases of debt. Civil arrest was ameliorated in Ireland in 1803[402] when arrest for actions on sums of less than £10 was replaced by personal service of the writ. This became known as 'serviceable process', as opposed to 'bailable process', where arrest or bail was still required.[403] The reform of civil arrest began much earlier in England, in 1725, when arrest was dispensed with in actions claiming sums of less than £10.[404]

Arrest on mesne process was abolished for most civil actions in England in 1838[405] and in Ireland in 1840,[406] and for all actions in England in 1869[407] and in Ireland in 1872.[408] The remaining problem of civil imprisonment was imprisonment in final process, that is, in the enforcement of judgments; this is dealt with below under 'Execution of Judgments', at page cvii.

Commissions of rebellion

A commission of rebellion was the ultimate method of forcing a defendant to attend and answer in the court of Exchequer. On the law side, if a defendant did not respond to the *capias quo minus*, the next step was to issue an *alias*, and so on. The order of writs in the Exchequer was as follows: 1. *capias quo minus*, 2. *alias*, 3. *pluries*,

---

[398] I.e. after the writ of *exigent* was issued, which was the last chance for the defendant to respond, and before the issue of the *quinto exactus* which brought the outlawry into effect

[399] *Pleas Side*, preface, xxxi.

[400] First Report of Commissioners on Courts of Common Law, 1829, ix. 93–94, B.P.P., Legal Administration, 1829, i. 93–94:

> The defendant against whom judgment of outlawry passes, has therefore in general had no previous notice that the suit has been commenced, and may probably have had no opportunity of becoming acquainted with that fact; and it is quite possible that even his property may be seized and sold, and the proceeds paid over to the plaintiff, before he is aware that any action is pending against him.

[401] Ibid., at 93.

[402] 43 Geo. III, c. 53, (G.B.), 1803, (Process (Ireland) Act, 1803). Ferguson, *Treatise*, ch. 6.

[403] Ferguson, *Treatise*, ch. 6, 7 (Ireland); Tidd, *Practice*, ch. 8 (England); First Report of Commissioners on Courts of Common Law, 1829, ix. 85, B.P.P., Legal Administration, 1829, i. 85. Even the commissioners did not set out the notoriously complex law on this topic in full detail, referring readers to Tidd, who did.

[404] 12 Geo. I, c. 29 (Eng.), 1725; am. by 5 Geo. II, c. 27 (Eng.), 1731; made perpetual by 21 Geo. II, c. 3 (Eng.), 1747; extended to inferior courts by 19 Geo. III, c. 70 (Eng.), 1779. Tidd, *Practice*, i. 166, ch. 8.

[405] 1 & 2 Vict., c. 110 (Eng.).

[406] 3 & 4 Vict., c. 105 (Ir.).

[407] Debtors Act, 1869, 32 & 33 Vict., c. 62 (Eng.), s. 6.

[408] Debtors Act (Ireland), 1872, 35 & 36 Vict., c. 57 (Ir.), s. 7.

4. proclamation, 5. commission of rebellion, 6. serjeant at arms, 7. sequestration.[409] A recalcitrant party, by persistently refusing to attend court under earlier writs, was taken to be in rebellion against the crown. Howard says that the reason the court did not appoint the sheriff was that it would not entrust 'so great a power' to a deputy nominated by the sheriff and therefore appointed 'its own commissioners, who were trusted to do every thing very carefully'.[410] The commission authorised those named in it to go and apprehend the recalcitrant party and bring him or her to court, by force if necessary.[411] Commissioners of rebellion could break into houses[412] and call upon other subjects of the crown to assist them.[413] The commissioners were 'generally four private persons'.[414] They were 'not entitled to any certain fixed fee, but shall be paid for their trouble as they deserve'.[415] They could take bail for the defendant's appearance, unless the process issued after a decree, in which case they had to bring the prisoner to the Four Courts Marshalsea.[416] But who were the commissioners? Apart from the party himself, were they friends, or hired for the purpose? Howard's comment, that commissioners were not entitled to fees but only to expenses, and that the court trusted them more than sheriff's deputies, suggests they were not ruffians.[417]

Commissions of rebellion were abolished in the Irish Chancery before 1835.[418] Howard, writing of the equity side of Exchequer in Ireland in 1760, mentions in a footnote that the commission of rebellion was rarely resorted to as it was regarded as oppressive. The practice then was to go to the serjeant at arms.[419]

There are many examples of commissions of rebellion in the English Reports. The great case in the nineteenth century is *Miller* v. *Knox*,[420] an appeal from the Irish court of Exchequer, where the law is fully discussed.[421]

[409] Howard, *Equity Side*, ii. 753 lists the stages of 'process of contempt' on the equity side as: 1. attachment, 2. *alias* attachment, 3. *pluries* attachment, 4. proclamation, 5. commission of rebellion, 6. serjeant at arms 7. sequestration.

[410] Howard, *Equity Side*, ii. 764.

[411] KI MS. No. 82, p. 103 (common law).

[412] Howard, *Equity Side*, ii. 764. KI MS. 82, p. 22 (equity).

[413] Ibid., ii. 765.

[414] Ibid., ii. 761; C. Barton, *An Historical Treatise of a Suit in Equity* (London, 1796), p. 82–85.

[415] Howard, *Equity Side*, ii. 765; KI MS. No. 82, p. 21 (equity side: 'They have no set fees but are to be paid for their trouble.')

[416] Howard, *Equity Side*, ii. 765; KI MS. No. 28, p. 10, Rule 18.

[417] In England in 1829 they were said to be usually 'bailiffs and neighbouring gaolers': First Report of Commissioners on Courts of Common Law, 1829, ix. 88, B.P.P., Legal Administration, 1829, i. 88.

[418] *Knox* v. *Gavan* (1835) Jo. Ir. Ex. 190 counsel at 198, citing Rule 37; see W. F. Darley, *General Orders of the Court of Chancery in Ireland* (Dublin, 1843), p. 26. Rule 29 declares writs of proclamation, commissions of rebellion and *distringas* to be abolished.

[419] *Equity Side*, ii. 765. In the text he mentions the case of *Gibbons* v. *Leary* Trinity Term 1757, *Equity Side*, ii. 762, in which a proclamation of rebellion was issued, and the defendant then entered an appearance without giving notice to the other side or tendering the costs of the process. The plaintiff's attorney then entered a commission of rebellion and obtained an order giving liberty to proceed with the process despite the appearance. Defendant's counsel then made a motion to set aside the order as the commission was issued after the defendant had appeared, but after debate the court refused to rule on the motion, as the defendant had failed to give notice or costs.

[420] (1838) 4 Bing. N.C. 574, 132 E.R. 910.

[421] Proceedings in the Irish court of Exchequer are reported as *Knox* v. *Gavan* (1835) Jo. Ir. Ex. 190. It arose out of the Tithe War at the time. The plaintiff was a Church of Ireland clergyman seeking to enforce a tithe against a Catholic, who, like other Catholics at the time, objected to paying for the maintenance of a church to which he did not belong. Forms of writs on both the law and equity sides, which are virtually the same, are set out in the report. Forms of the English writs are set out in C. Barton, *An Historical Treatise of a Suit in Equity* (London, 1796), pp. 83–85. On English cases see also *Studd* v. *Acton* (1790) 1 Black. H. 468, 126 E.R. 271; *Hull*

The abolition of arrest on mesne process for most civil actions in Ireland in 1840[422] would seem to have seen the end of commissions of rebellion in the Exchequer.

There are a several references to commissions of rebellion in the manuscript. Although they do not add greatly to our knowledge of how they operated in practice, given the dearth of material on the subject, they do at least confirm that they were in use in this period.

In one case, process proceeded to a commission of rebellion after the defendant had made appearance and answered, but because he made further delay,[423] and in another case a commission followed after a bill for discovery.[424]

Kerry bonds were a general form of bond used for many purposes in Ireland and as such are described below,[425] but there are two instances in the reports of their being used by the serjeant at arms instead of his immediately placing a defendant under arrest. These instances are also considered below.

Answers by peers

The Irish House of Lords adopted a rule in 1692 asserting that peers were to put in answers to bills in actions in court upon honour only, and not upon oath.[426]

In 1695 the bishop of Waterford complained to the committee of privileges of the Irish House of Lords that Echlin B.,[427] in a suit in the court of Exchequer, had refused to take the bishop's answer on his honour, and had required him to be sworn.[428] The committee resolved that it was a breach of privilege and called Echlin B. to bring precedents of the court to show whether it was the practice of the court, and if so, for how long. Echlin B. duly appeared a week later with his precedents. The committee was unimpressed. It 'excused' the judge, but ruled that in future it should not be the practice of any court or person to require a peer to answer on oath.[429]

There is no definite indication in the present reports as to whether peers were required to put in answers or give evidence on oath or not. The case of *The Executors of Sir Patrick Dun* v. *Mitchel and the College of Physicians* is cited in which the lord chancellor 'suffered the archbishop of Dublin to be examined to a fact in his own knowledge' but does not say whether he was sworn or not,[430] and in *King* v. *Burgh* it is mentioned that the same archbishop made a deposition, which would normally be sworn, but again there is no indication if an exception was made in his case.[431] Nevertheless, Howard,[432] writing in 1760, states that peers were allowed to put in answers to bills upon honour only. If they answered falsely, they were not liable for

---

v. *Mackay* (1828) 2 Y. & J. 472, 148 E.R. 1003; *In re Clarke* (1842) 2 Q.B. 619, 114 E.R. 243; *Cobbett* v. *Shallowman* (1854) 9 Exch. 633, 156 E.R. 270.

[422] 3 & 4 Vict., c. 105.

[423] *Costello* v. *Costello* at p. 342.

[424] *Pomeroy* v. *Steadman*, below, p. 109.

[425] Below, p. cxxiii.

[426] Rules and Orders of the House of Lords, 1790, rule 49, dated 2 November, p. 46.

[427] Below, p. cliv.

[428] J.Ir.H.L. i. 508, 21 September 1695.

[429] J.Ir.H.L. i. 514.

[430] Below, p. 309.

[431] Below, p. 34.

[432] *Equity Side*, i. 63–64.

perjury, but only a misdemeanour.[433] Nevertheless, where they were examined as witnesses, on interrogatories or otherwise, they had to be sworn.[434]

He also mentions the case of a peeress who was allowed to produce deeds, in answer to a bill for discovery, on honour, since that was supplementary to her answer.[435] The Rules and Orders of the House of Lords of 1790 state the privilege as to answers alone.[436]

There are other examples of the Irish House of Lords at the end of the seventeenth century attempting to interfere with or influence the procedure of the courts. One was the instance of *quo minus*[437] and there are at least two examples of the House of Lords attempting to charge commoners with breach of privilege in land disputes with peers.[438]

TRIALS

Nisi prius

In England, after the royal courts settled at Westminster, witnesses and jury members had the onerous duty, when a trial was to take place, of travelling to Westminster for the hearing of all causes, no matter what part of the country they had originated in. Moreover a trial at Westminster was cumbersome since it was a trial at bar before all three judges of the court concerned and the jury.

Nisi prius jurisdiction was established[439] by the Statute of Westminster II, 1285, which was extended to Ireland.[440] A *venire facias* would command the sheriff to impanel a jury to hear the case at Westminster (or in Ireland, Dublin) before the judges there on a given date in the following term, unless before (*nisi prius*) that date the case should be decided before a jury and the justices of assize in the county in which the issue arose.[441] This eliminated the need for juries to travel to Westminster. It seems that in Ireland, 'Westminster' was interpreted to mean 'Dublin'. It was only in 1665 that the judges at the Four Courts in Dublin were given *nisi prius* jurisdiction of their own.[442] This also permitted cases to be heard before a single judge and jury. The statute of 1665 permitted the chief justices of the King's Bench or Common Pleas or the chief baron of the Exchequer, or in default of them, the puisne judges or barons of the courts, to hear cases as justices of *nisi prius* for the city or county of Dublin. The *nisi prius* trial was to have same effect as a trial at bar in the court from which the issue was joined.[443]

---

[433] Ibid., ii. 723. If they answered upon their honour they could not be charged with perjury, since it required an oath on holy scripture, by 28 Eliz. I, c. 1 (Ir.), 1586.

[434] Howard, *Equity Side*, ii. 722.

[435] *Duke of Hamilton et Ux. v. Lady Gerard*, Howard, *Equity Side* i. 63–64.

[436] Rule 49.

[437] Above, p. lxxii.

[438] J.Ir.H.L. i. 519 (Lord Loftus of Ely), ibid., i. 533 (Lord Londondery).

[439] There were instances of *nisi prius* jurisdiction as early as 1225: P & M, i. 202, n. 5.

[440] 13 Edw. I, c. 30 (Eng.) (justices of *nisi prius*). Extended to Ireland by writ in 1285, confirmed by 13 Edw. II, c. 2 (Ir.), 1320; Berry, *Statutes, Ireland*, p. 281.

[441] Howard, *Pleas Side*, i. 185; Blackstone, *Commentaries* (1768), iii. 59. The full phrase was *nisi prius justitiarii ad assisas capiendas venerint.*

[442] 17 & 18 Car. II, c. 20 (Ir.), 1665 (*nisi prius* in Dublin).

[443] Ibid., s. 1.

However, a doubt had arisen as to whether puisne barons in Ireland were qualified generally to hear cases as justices of assize or of *nisi prius*. An English statute of 1340[444] had allowed all justices of the Common Pleas and King's Bench to act as justices of *nisi prius* and also the chief baron of the Exchequer, if he was a serjeant, plus the king's serjeant. This would have been extended to Ireland by Poynings' Law[445] and would have meant that all of them were *ex officio* qualified to take *nisi prius* cases. But the statute did not refer to puisne barons and so would have left it in doubt as to whether they were qualified, if they had not been a king's serjeant.

A statute of 1721[446] extended the system of *nisi prius* and resolved the doubt as to whether puisne barons not 'sworn as serjeants' were qualified to hear *nisi prius* cases.

In England, where there was an order of serjeants at law, the judges of the King's Bench and Common Pleas had long been chosen from among the serjeants, but it had only been the practice in the case of the court of Exchequer from about 1580.[447]

In Ireland, unlike England, there was no order of serjeants at law. King Charles I, 'in order to encourage the judges and serjeants-at-law' in 1639 had instructed the lord deputy to raise them to 'the dignity of the coif' and also instructed that in future all persons appointed to be judges or serjeants should also be appointed 'serjeants of the coif'.[448] It must have been doubtful also as to whether such an instruction could have been followed so as to create such an order in Ireland. The instruction contemplated letters patent being issued to all existing and future serjeants and judges, but no such patents are known. The statute of 1721 itself seems to indicate that such patents were not issued, hence the doubt as to puisne barons who had not been king's serjeants. In Ireland there was a king's, or prime, serjeant, and later, a second[449] and a third serjeant,[450] who were law officers.[451] It does not appear that barons in Ireland, including the chief baron, were required to hold the office of one of the king's serjeants before being raised to the bench and indeed there is no evidence that even judges of the other common law courts were either.[452] Nevertheless, the statute of 1721 implies that puisne barons who had been sworn as king's serjeants continued in some sense to be serjeants even after they were

[444]   14 Edw. III, st. 1, c. 16.

[445]   10 Hen. VII, c. 22 (Ir.), 1495. See below, p. cli.

[446]   8 Geo. I, c. 6 (Ir.), 1721 (expiring laws, *nisi prius* and assizes); Howard, *Pleas Side*, i. 188.

[447]   Bryson, *Equity Side of the Exchequer*, pp. 22, 48–51. J. H. Baker, *The Order of Serjeants at Law* (Selden Society, 1984) at p. 57, n. 8.

[448]   Cal. St. Pap. Ir. 1633–1647, p. 224, King to the Lord Deputy, 7 Oct. 1639.

[449]   The first person to hold the office of 2nd serjeant was Nathaniel Catelyn, the recorder of Dublin, appointed in 1627: Smyth, *Law Officers*, p. 193.

[450]   The first person to hold the office of 3rd serjeant was John Lyndon, appointed in 1682: Smyth, *Law Officers*, p. 194; Ball, *Judges in Ireland*, i. 359. But the office was not apparently regularly filled until Jocelyn was appointed in 1726: Ferguson, *Treatise*, i. 18.

[451]   Ferguson, *Treatise*, i. 17–18.

[452]   Of those barons featuring in these reports, Geoffrey Gilbert had not been a king's serjeant in Ireland when he was appointed J.K.B. in 1714: Smyth, *Law Officers*; Ball, *Judges in Ireland*. He was appointed C.B. the following year. After he resigned as C.B. in Ireland, on 18 May 1722, Gilbert became a serjeant in England on 7 June 1722 shortly before taking his seat as puisne baron of the English Exchequer on 9 June 1722. M. Macnair, 'Gilbert, Sir Jeffray (1674–1726)', *ODNB*; Marlay C.B. was not a king's serjeant, but had been appointed S.G. in 1720 and A.G. in 1727. Of the puisne barons, neither Pocklington, St Leger, nor Wainwright had held the office of king's serjeant before appointment. As to the King's Bench, Rogerson was appointed S.G. in 1714 and A.G. in 1720 and in 1727 became C.J.K.B., but had not held the office of king's serjeant.

appointed to the bench and so the appointment as king's serjeant may have been regarded as conferring something more than simply an office.

Interestingly, there are several examples of Marlay C.B. and one of St Leger B. in these reports referring to other judges as 'brother'.[453] In England it was the practice for judges to refer to each other as 'brother', as fellow members of the order of the coif, and even to other serjeants in court.[454] Swift lampooned Serjeant Bettesworth for referring to Singleton, the prime serjeant, as 'brother'.[455] However, this practice does not in itself establish anything significant as to serjeants in Ireland, or that judges who had not been king's serjeants had been 'raised to the dignity of the coif'.

The statute of 1721 declared the puisne barons to have *nisi prius* and assize jurisdiction, and extended the jurisdiction to the prime serjeant, the attorney and solicitor general, and to king's counsel,[456] which may indicate that there was a serious backlog of cases waiting to be heard. In England, the five-hundred-year-old rule that only serjeants could be commissioners of assize was only abolished in 1850.[457] The jurisdiction at the same time was extended to queen's counsel. In Ireland the similar change had therefore occurred nearly 130 years earlier, due to the absence of an order of serjeants in Ireland. The extension of the jurisdiction in Ireland also indicates the growth of business in the courts about this time.

The commissions of *nisi prius* under which judges on circuit heard civil pleas were annexed to the assizes by the Statute of Westminster II, 1285.[458] The other civil branch of the assizes was that hearing writs of assize, using the term in its other sense as meaning the possessory assizes such as novel disseisin, mort d'ancestor,[459] and thirdly, civil bill jurisdiction. Barons of the Exchequer in Ireland carried out the criminal commissions of oyer and terminer (to hear and to determine) and gaol delivery. Wainwright B. went on assizes in Munster in 1741[460] and, together with Attorney General Bowes, dealt with several hundred criminal cases.[461] The assizes were in fact the cause of Wainwright's death and that of Serjeant Bettesworth, from the same outbreak of jail fever.[462] The assizes could bring death by more than one means, and to lawyers as well as prisoners.

After every trial at *nisi prius*, or on assizes, where either a verdict or a nonsuit had been obtained, the clerk endorsed on the record an account in Latin of the proceedings at trial known as the *postea*,[463] which was then returned to the court from which the *nisi prius* issued. The case of *Lessee of Bull* v. *Lord Darnley*[464] concerns proceedings in arrest of judgment on a *postea*, in ejectment on a lease. The question was whether the verdict of the jury was sufficiently certain to justify execution on the

---

[453] See Marlay C.B., below, pp. 176, 214, 217, 222, 232, 265, 265 and St Leger B., below, p. 334.

[454] An example is provided by *Spincer* v. *Spincer* (1841) 5 Jur. (o.s.) 100 at 102. Megarry, *Miscellany at Law*, p. 47.

[455] Below p. clvii.

[456] King's counsel had been established in Ireland from about 1613: Ferguson, *Treatise*, i. 18.

[457] Baker, *The Order of Serjeants at Law*, p. 125; 13 & 14 Vict., c. 25 (Eng.).

[458] Ferguson, *Treatise*, i. 15.

[459] Jacob, *Law Dictionary*, 'assize'.

[460] Smyth, *Law Officers*, p. 246 says 1740.

[461] Ball, *Judges in Ireland*, i. 131, letter, Jocelyn to Hardwicke, BL MSS Add. 35586, fo. 335.

[462] I.e. typhus, probably the epidemic form, spread by the human body louse (*Pediculus humanus corporis*). Below, p. clix n. 935 and p. clxxiv n. 1026. It was an aftermath of the famine of 1740: Ball, *Judges in Ireland*, ii. 181, and see below, p. clxviii. Rogerson C.J.K.B. also possibly died from the same cause, though not on the same assizes: see p. clxxiv n. 1027.

[463] L. 'afterwards'. Howard, *Pleas Side*, i. 287.

[464] Below, p. 341.

judgment. The report ends inconclusively with argument by Stannard, and if there were further proceedings they do not appear in these reports.

Civil bills

Civil bill jurisdiction in Ireland, the hearing of small civil claims, can be traced to a statute of 1697[465] but it became obsolete[466] and civil bill jurisdiction was put on a permanent basis by the Act of 1716.[467] Judges of assize could hear minor disputes by English bill in debt, assumpsit, *insimul computassent*,[468] trover, *quantum meruit*, trespass and detinue, in all cases provided that title to land was not in issue. The system was designed to be cheap, if not cheerful. Perjury was punishable by the pillory rather than imprisonment,[469] and the offender was to stay in the pillory for an hour and 'have his ears nailed thereto'.[470] A jury could be impanelled from those in the area of the court if required.[471] Appeal lay to the assizes.[472] Jurisdiction was extended to Dublin, before the recorder, in 1757.[473]

Henry Singleton[474] heard civil bills while on assize, apparently after 1740 when he was chief justice of the Common Pleas.

An interesting feature of civil bill jurisdiction is that although the jurisdiction extended only to common law actions, the defendant had the benefit 'of all matters in his defence, that he might have had, if he had been sued in the ordinary forms of the common law, or in any court of equity: and the said judge or judges ... shall have full power and authority' and they could award interest where it would have been awarded in equity.[475] There was therefore a partial merger of law and equity, in this limited context, as early as 1715.

Trials at bar

Trials at bar, the most formal kind of trial, were held in Dublin in the common law courts before, in theory at least, a full court of three judges, and a jury.[476] If on the day of the trial a full jury did not appear, or if they did appear, but fell short through challenges, the plaintiff could 'pray a *tales*', that is, ask for the court to issue a writ to the sheriff commanding him to impanel *such* (*tales*) men, that is, men of similar standing to the panel, until the jury of twelve was made up.[477] The writ would be for

---

[465] 9 Will. III, c. 15 (Ir.), 1697 (small debts; civil bill). The statute only deals with small debts.
[466] According to the preamble to the 1716 Act.
[467] 2 Geo. I, c. 11 (Ir.), 1715 (small debts; civil bill); 1 Geo. II, c. 14 (Ir.), 1727 (small debts; civil bill; Act to amend 2 Geo. I, c. 11) 19 & 20 Geo. III, c. 26 (Ir.), 1779–80 (civil bill amendment). There was a temporary Act in 1703: 2 Ann., c. 18 (Ir.) which was originally to last for three years (s. 13) but was renewed for a further three years in 1707: 6 Ann., c. 5 (Ir.); see Greer, 'The Development of Civil Bill Procedure in Ireland' in *The Common Law Tradition: Essays in Irish Legal History* (McEldowney and O'Higgins, eds., 1990).
[468] L. 'they had settled their accounts together', a type of assumpsit in which the plaintiff and defendant had settled their accounts and the defendant had agreed to pay the balance, but, it was alleged, had failed to do so.
[469] 2 Geo. I, c. 11 (Ir.), 1715, s. 7.
[470] Ibid.
[471] 2 Geo. I, c. 11 (Ir.), s. 1.
[472] Section 5.
[473] 31 Geo. II, c. 16 (Ir.), 1757.
[474] See p. clxviii.
[475] Ibid.
[476] Ferguson, *Treatise*, i. 300. At the end of the century it was, in theory, before the four judges: see p. lxi n. 60.
[477] Howard, *Pleas Side*, i. 223, 238. Howard cites the case of *Damer* v. *Mahony*, Exchequer, Easter Term 1742, in which this occurred.

decem tales, or *octo tales* ('ten such', or 'eight such'), depending on how many were required, and the procedure was allowed at common law.

In the case of assizes or *nisi prius* trials, a less formal method was introduced to make up deficiencies in the jury. By the statute 10 Car. I sess. 2, c. 13 (Ir.), 1634[478] the court would grant a *tales de circumstantibus* by which the sheriff was to impanel such bystanders as appeared to be of similar standing to the freeholders who made up a jury.[479]

Howard says that 'on a trial at bar the court gives judgment immediately, unless a day be prayed, and it is seldom granted'.[480]

There are several examples of trials at bar in these reports, most usually on the issue of ejectment on title to land. In *Ryley* v. *Weseley*[481] the chief baron refused to order a new trial after a trial at bar in ejectment because 'the old opinion was not to grant a new one after a trial at bar, because the court may have the assistance of the judges and counsel who are generally better prepared and furnished with evidence than at *nisi prius*'.

Special juries

According to Jacob[482] and Tidd[483] the practice of impanelling special juries began in England in trials at bar without specific statutory authority.[484] Howard mentions special juries in Ireland, but does not give details as to their qualifications, apart from their having to be freeholders.[485] A panel of forty-eight freeholders was made up, from which each side could strike off twelve, leaving a jury of twenty-four.[486] In England a statute of 1729[487] gave parties the right to a special jury either in trials at bar or at assizes. In Ireland the practice does not appear to have been given statutory recognition until the 1770s.[488] A doubt had arisen as to whether special juries could be impanelled without the consent of the parties, and so the statute declared trials with special juries to be valid 'as special juries have been and are usually struck in such courts respectively upon trials at bar to be had in the same courts'.[489]

There is no mention of special juries in these reports, although that does not of course mean that they were not in use at the time.

Trials by leading order: feigned actions at law

Proof in Chancery and the equity side of Exchequer was based more on the Civilian or Roman law model than on that of the common law.[490] Sworn written depositions were taken from witnesses in answer to written interrogatories, usually before the

---

[478] In England by 35 Hen. VIII, c. 6, 1543 and subsequent statutes. Jacob, *Law Dictionary*, 'Jury I'.

[479] Howard, *Pleas Side*, i. 238–39.

[480] Howard, *Pleas Side*, i. 223.

[481] Below, p. 24.

[482] *Law Dictionary*, 'Jury: special juries'.

[483] Tidd's *Practice*, p. 825.

[484] See James Oldham, 'The Origin of the Special Jury' (1983) 50 *U. Chi. L. Rev.* 137–221; and see James Oldham, *Trial by Jury: The Seventh Amendment and Anglo-American Special Juries* (New York, 2006).

[485] *Pleas Side*, i. 264, ii. 392.

[486] Howard, *Pleas Side*, i. 264-65.

[487] 3 Geo. II, c. 25. (G.B.), 1729.

[488] 17 & 18 Geo. III, c. 45 (Ir.), 1777–78, s. 3 (outlawries, special juries). Howard, *Pleas Side*, i. 265.

[489] 17 & 18 Geo. III, c. 45 (Ir.), s. 3.

[490] See, on England, M. R. T. Macnair, *The Law of Proof in Early Modern Equity* (Berlin, 1999).

oral hearing.[491] 'Examination' on the equity side referred to this procedure.[492] Cross-examination took place through cross-interrogatories.[493] If necessary, evidence was taken by commission.[494] The questions in the interrogatories had to anticipate what the other side would later say in the depositions, and were therefore far less satisfactory in getting the facts before the court than oral direct examination and cross-examination. The depositions were taken down by the examiner or commissioner and were in his words in the third person and not in the direct words of the witness. However, where the evidence was contradictory a trial before a jury could be directed on the common law side, or, in the case of Chancery, before a common law court. In the latter case all the instances in these reports are to the court of Common Pleas. Howard[495] describes this in the following terms:

> This trial is upon a feigned action commenced in the pleas side of this court, in pursuance of an order for that purpose made in the equity side.

> And this order is usually granted when the court upon the hearing of the cause doubts of some material intervening fact, which often happens when the proofs relating to such fact are opposite and contradictory, or uncertain, or when the plaintiff goes into a court of equity for damages which are uncertain, and not to be settled but by a jury, and the defendant answers and contests without demurring, in such and the like cases, the court will direct an issue at law to try the fact or the *quantum* of the damages . . . and this is called a leading order.

The issue of damages could arise in equity as follows.[496] Suppose that A sued B at law for damages for breach of covenant. B then filed a bill in equity for an injunction, on the suggestion that the covenant had been obtained by fraud. If A filed a cross bill in equity for relief on the covenant, the court would retain it, because the validity of the covenant was disputed in the court of equity and on a ground valid there. If the court then found the covenant to be valid, the court would direct an issue to be tried on the common law side to fix the *quantum* of damages, 'because the damages cannot be ascertained by the conscience of the chancellor, and therefore must be settled by a jury at law'.[497] If, however, the covenant were to pay a specific sum, and A brought a bill in equity for relief, and the defendant demurred on the ground that relief could be sought at law, the court of equity would dismiss the case on that ground, and leave the plaintiff to his remedy at law. On the other hand, if the defendant did not demur to the relief, but put in an answer, denying the validity of the deed, then, if the deed were proved by two witnesses, the court of equity would decree for the plaintiff for the specific sum.[498] If it were proved by only one witness,

---

[491]   Howard, *Equity Side*, ii. 570–72.

[492]   Howard, *Equity Side*, ii. 570.

[493]   Ibid., ii. 570–571.

[494]   In Ireland a special order had to be obtained if evidence was to be taken by commission in Dublin or within 12 miles of the city: 'Rules in the Chancery Side of His Majesty's Court of Exchequer in Ireland.', Harvard Law School Library, MS. 505, rule 33; Howard, *Equity Side*, ii. 573. Taking evidence by commission provided a source of income for the most junior barristers, as it still does when evidence by commission is taken today. In *Archdekin* [*sic*] v. *Horan* cited in King's Inns MS. No. 90, 'Rules of the Court of Exchequer in Ireland with notes and observations', *c.* 1734, at p. 73, it was held that if a witness refused to give evidence by commission, the commissioners should report it to the court and the court could then attach the witness or oblige him to come to the court at his own expense and give evidence before an Examiner. See also *Horan* v. *Archdeckne* in these reports, below, p. 135.

[495]   *Pleas Side*, i. 232–233, 'Trial by Leading Order'; see also *Equity Side*, ii. 662 et seq., 'Of Leading Orders'.

[496]   Howard, *Equity Side*, i. 231–232.

[497]   Ibid., i. 230.

[498]   Ibid., p. 232.

which was insufficent, then the court would grant a leading order to try the validity of the deed at law.

The phrase 'leading order' is not used in these reports although there are references in Exchequer and Chancery to the court ordering a trial at law, and which are detailed below. The phrase is not used in English sources and so seems to be a term peculiar to Ireland.[499]

In *Lynch* v. *Kirwan*,[500] on a leading order, Chief Baron Gilbert held that if at law the plaintiff made use of an answer, it could be read through and should be evidence for the defendant as well as the plaintiff, but not conclusive evidence for the defendant.

The feigned action at law in England was described by Blackstone in the following terms:[501]

> this court is so sensible of the deficiency of trial by written depositions, that it will not bind the parties thereby, but usually directs the matter to be tried by jury; especially such important facts as the validity of a will, or whether A is the heir at law to B . . . But, as no jury can be summoned to attend this court, the fact is usually directed to be tried at the bar of the court of king's bench or at the assises, upon a *feigned issue*. For, (in order to bring it there, and have the point in dispute, and that only, put in issue) an action is feigned to be brought, wherein the pretended plaintiff declares, that he laid a wager of £5 with the defendant, that A was heir at law to B; and then avers that he is so; and brings his action for the £5. The defendant allows the wager, but avers that A is not the heir to B; and thereupon that issue is joined, which is directed out of chancery to be tried: and thus the verdict of the jurors at law determines the fact in the court of equity.

Howard, cited above, also speaks of a feigned issue and so the procedure in Ireland was probably by such a wager as described by Blackstone. The use of a feigned wager would not have been effective unless an action on a real wager were possible, of course. Wagering contracts are dealt with below.[502]

The trial by leading order on a feigned issue was still part of procedure when Ferguson wrote in 1841.[503] He comments that in the case of the equity side of the Exchequer, the court not only had the power to direct a trial at the bar of its own court sitting at law, but that it was often desirable that it should, 'in order to avoid the inconvenience too often felt to arise from the judge at law not being apprised of the view with which the issue was directed; so that when the case comes before the jury, the question sent to them happens to be wide of the point which the court of

---

[499] An early occurrence in Ireland is in the *Directions* of 1622: G. J. Hand and V. W. Treadwell, eds., 'His Majesty's Directions for the Irish Courts, 1622' 26 *Analecta Hibernica* 177–212, Direction X, 'Limiting of forreyne tryalls.' The section refers to the problem of trials directed to try title to land and 'forreyne' is contrasted with 'the proper countie where the land lyeth', and so 'forreyne' evidently refers to a county other than that in which the land lay, and so 'leading order' refers to an order for such a trial. The phrase is not mentioned by Jacob in his *Dictionary*, under 'Trials', nor by *HEL*, ix. 357, nor by Tidd, *Practice*. Tidd refers to the procedure as 'trial on a feigned issue', but the phrase 'leading order' is used both by Howard and Ferguson, in the sense in the text above. See also Sir Marmaduke Coghill, *Letters of Marmaduke Coghill 1722–1738*, (D.W. Hayton, ed., IMC, 2005), p. 70, n. 242. It also occurs three times in the E.R., in that sense, but they are all Irish cases: *Bandon* v. *Belcher* [1835] 9 Bli. N.S. 532, 5 E.R. 1388 ('By a leading order . . . made in this cause, it it was ordered that the Respondent should commence a feigned action in his Majesty's Court of King's Bench in Ireland against the Appellant, for the trial by a special jury in the county of Cork'); *Collins* v. *Hare* [1828] 1 D. & C. 139, 6 E.R. 476; *Boyse* v. *Rossborough* [1856–57] 6 H.L.C. 1, 10 E.R. 1192.

[500] Howard, *Equity Side*, i. 86.

[501] Blackstone, *Commentaries*, iii. 452–3. See also Holdsworth, *Dickens as a Legal Historian*, p. 96.

[502] At p. cxxxvii.

[503] *Treatise*, i. 246, 321; ch. 38, 'Issues from Courts of Equity', ii. 851–856.

equity wished to have determined'.[504] He also comments that the order 'in general directs the case to be tried before a special jury'.[505]

In *Hodson* v. *Rowley*[506] the attorney general says that 'If any doubt arise on the words of a deposition, the court will inform themselves by trial' and St Leger B. in the same case confirms this when he refers to the answer being short and evasive and says 'I don't like his answer, but we can direct a trial.'

In *Franks* v. *Isaac*[507] the chief baron contrasts the procedure in the Exchequer with the spiritual courts and says:

> it was frequent in the spiritual court to examine to the credit of a witness, because their [*sic*] trials were by witnesses, but that it was sparingly granted by courts of equity, because if they had any reason to suspect their credit, they could send the matter to a trial.

In that case the chief baron instead granted a commission to examine the proof of the articles, where a witness had 'swore she would pursue her [a party] to hell for revenge'.

There are several instances of the chancellor ordering a trial in the Common Pleas, and Chancery seems to have used the Common Pleas fairly frequently for this purpose.

In *Hussy* v. *Sheehy*[508] in these reports in Chancery counsel argues that the court ought to direct a trial at law to try the validity of a letter of attorney.[509] In *Dillon* v. *Edgworth* in 1731[510] an 'issue was directed out of Chancery' to the Common Pleas to try whether a deed was executed by the father of the defendant. The jury found that he did not execute the deed, and the defendant then moved in Chancery for a new trial on the ground that evidence had been improperly presented to the jury. The lord chancellor, Wyndham, says first that 'I shall consider the case as I think it would be at law, and then in equity', concludes that there is no ground for a new trial, and then comments intriguingly that:[511]

> as this was a trial to satisfy my own conscience, the verdict must stand; and the judges of the Common Pleas assured me they were very well satisfied with this verdict, and not dissatisfied with any one circumstance.

Trials on a feigned issue were abolished by the Gaming Act, 1845, which applied to Ireland.[512]

---

[504] Citing as an example *Webb* v. *Rorke* (1806) 2 Sch. & Lef. 661. See Lord Redesdale L.C. at 667. The lord chancellor directed two issues to be tried. The judge at common law considered that only the second need be tried because it determined the first. Redesdale comments that that was not his intention, and that he thought the first issue the determining one.

[505] As in *Bandon* v. *Belcher* [1835] 9 Bli. N.S. 532, 5 E.R. 1388.

[506] Below, p. 237 [*306*].

[507] Below, p. 282 [*366*].

[508] Below, p. 15 [*14*].

[509] See also *Byrn* v. *Rathborne*, below, p. 283 [*367*]: in an action of account, where the defendant trustee entered an exception to the master's report as to the value of the land, and where the trustee was in breach of trust but over 80 years of age, the chancellor refused to grant a trial unless the defendant gave security to pay the balance.

[510] Below, p. 70 [*82*].

[511] Below, pp. 71, [*84–85*].

[512] 8 & 9 Vict., c. 109, (U.K.), s. 19 and 2nd schedule. The trial on the issue was to be directed by summons before the courts of Queen's Bench, Common Pleas or Exchequer as appropriate.

Other relations between equity and law

In one case the court of Exchequer even contemplated common law and equity proceedings taking place together, although there is no evidence that it in fact happened. In *[Anonymous]* v. *Administrators of Cogan*[513] in 1729 a bill was brought against an administrator of a deceased's estate to discover assets and for money due by *assumpsit*.

Discovery of assets was an equity proceeding, whereas *assumpsit* was a common law action. The plaintiff had elected to proceed in equity for a discovery of assets, apparently before the answer had been entered.[514] We are not told why: perhaps the answer was late in coming. In her answer, when it did come, the defendant 'confessed assets', but denied the *assumpsit*. The defendant's admission of sufficient assets had therefore made the proceeding on discovery in equity unnecessary. The report then goes on:

> The demurrer was overruled by Mr Baron St Leger, for that the plaintiff was brought into equity to discover assets and therefore shall not be sent to law but may proceed to prove the assumpsit in equity.

However, there remained the problem that equity proceedings were conducted by deposition. The report ends with the question as to whether the plaintiff should not therefore have the issue tried before a jury, but nothing more is said on the point.

In the early seventeenth century a litigant would have been sent back to common law in such a situation, but by the mid-seventeenth century in England, equity declared that it had a jurisdiction to reduce the multiplicity of suits[515] and in such a case would hear the common law action itself. St Leger's comment therefore shows that the Irish court by this time had adopted a similar procedure.

EXECUTION OF JUDGMENTS

Execution was the obtaining of actual possession of whatever a judgment declared was due to the plaintiff.[516] It was part of final process, as opposed to mesne process which continued only until judgment was given. It was therefore distinct from an action which ended with judgment, so that a release of all actions was no bar to execution of a judgment.[517]

According to Howard, in the Irish Exchequer there were four forms of execution: 1. the writ of *fieri facias* for seizure of the chattels of the judgment debtor, 2. the writ of *elegit*, 3. the writ of *capias ad satisfaciendum* against the person of the judgment debtor, and 4. a writ of *habere facias possessionem* in *ejectione firmæ*, giving possession of land in ejectment.[518]

---

[513] Below, p. 12 [*12*].

[514] In *Nesbit* v. *Nesbit*, below at p. [*412*], the point is made that a plaintiff was not bound to elect whether to proceed at law or in equity until the defendant had answered, and the case of *Tillotson* v. *Ganson* (1682) 1 Vern. 103, 23 E.R. 344 cited for that.

[515] *Cases Concerning Equity and the Courts of Equity, 1550–1660*, vol. 1 (W. H. Bryson, ed.) 117 Seld. Soc. (for 2000), 71, 77; ibid, vol. 2, 118 Seld. Soc. (for 2001), 304, 391.

[516] Howard, *Pleas Side*, ii. 107.

[517] Ibid.; Co. Litt. 289.

[518] Howard, *Pleas Side*, ii. 107.

1. On a writ of *fieri facias* (called 'fi. fa.' for short) the sheriff was not to deliver the goods of the defendant to the plaintiff in satisfaction of the judgment, but had to sell them and pay the money into court.[519] The sheriff could not grant freehold estates in the land of the debtor, but could grant leases, since they were considered mere chattel interests.[520] If the sheriff made a return on the writ that the defendant had insufficient goods to satisfy the judgment, then the plaintiff had either another *fieri facias* for the residue, or an elegit, giving rights over the debtor's freehold land, or a *capias* against his body.[521] But once the plaintiff took the body of the defendant he could neither have another *fieri facias* nor an elegit, since the law considered the body to be the greatest satisfaction apart from the money.[522] It also followed that a plaintiff could not have a *fieri facias* and a *capias* at the same time, and this is held in these reports in *Allen* v. *Mandevil*.[523] If the defendant died after execution granted but before it was served, it could still be served against his goods in the hands of his executors.[524]

2. The writ of *elegit* ('he has chosen') was established by the Statute of Westminster II, 1285, c. 18[525] to enable execution against the lands, or rather, the freehold estates, of a debtor, against which there was no execution at common law.[526] The plaintiff could choose it in preference to a *fieri facias*. The sheriff was to impanel a jury to appraise the goods and lands of the debtor and the sheriff was then to deliver goods of the debtor, other than beasts of the plough, or if the goods were insufficient,[527] up to half[528] his land to the plaintiff. The sheriff had to hold an inquiry into the elegit on receiving it in the main town of the county and give notice the plaintiff.[529] It was the sheriff's task to mark out the half of the land. If there were no lands and the goods were insufficient, the plaintiff could obtain a *capias* for the residue.[530]

3. The writ of *capias ad satisfaciendum* (called 'ca. sa.' for short)[531] lay where the action was personal, as for 'debt, damages, detinue, etc.'.[532] It commanded the sheriff to take the body of the debtor and detain him in prison until he made satisfaction. The sheriff could not take bail on this writ, for the purpose was to apprehend the debtor, and for this the sheriff had the *posse comitatus*, the 'power of the county', the power given to the sheriff, and other king's officers, by the Statute of Westminster II 1285, c. 39,[533] of calling upon men of the county of the age of fifteen or over to

---

[519] Howard, *Pleas Side*, ii. 109.

[520] Ibid., ii. 108; Bacon's Abr., ii. 351.

[521] The point is made by the prime serjeant in *Allen* v. *Mandevil*, below, at p. 139.

[522] Howard, *Pleas Side*, ii. 111.

[523] Below, p. 140.

[524] Ibid., ii. 110.

[525] Extended to Ireland by writ in 1285, confirmed by 13 Edw. II, c. 2 (Ir.), 1320; ibid., ii. 281; Berry, *Statutes, Ireland*, pp. 47, 105–177; Thomas Lefroy, *Observations on the proceedings by Elegit, for recovery of Judgment debts* (Dublin, 1802), KI Law Tracts.

[526] Howard, *Pleas Side*, ii. 121.

[527] Inst., ii. 59, 395.

[528] By 13 Edw. I, c. 18.; Howard, *Pleas Side*, ii. 121 (where cited as '31 Edw. I'); 1 & 2 Vict., c. 110 (Eng.), 1838 extended it to all lands: Brown, *Dictionary*, and this was enacted for Ireland by 3 & 4 Vict., c. 105 (Ir.), 1840, Ferguson, *Treatise*, i. 424.

[529] 6 Ann., c. 7 (Ir.).

[530] Howard, *Pleas Side*, ii. 124.

[531] J. Anstey, *Pleader's Guide* (1796), Lecture 6, p. 55.

[532] Howard, *Pleas Side*, ii. 137–8.

[533] '*Assumpto secum posse comitatus sui est [vicecomes] in propria persona*', 'taking with him the power of the county, he shall go in proper person'. See also the Statute of Winchester, 13 Edw. I, 1285. Stat. Wynton., St. Realm, i. 96 under which men were bound to have arms and armour for that purpose: Jacob, *Law Dictionary*,

assist him in arresting the object of the writ. Although literally referring to the legal power, the phrase came to be associated with the body of men so constituted. The sheriff had to keep the prisoner in 'safe and close custody'.[534] If the sheriff let him go free before satisfaction was made under the judgment, the plaintiff would have an action of debt, or an action on the case, against the sheriff.[535] The sheriff had no power to break into a house to execute the writ, except in the case of a real action or ejectment where the judgment was to deliver possession.[536]

At one time there was a difference of judicial opinion in the case of a person dying while in custody on a *capias*. The weight of opinion was that the plaintiff had no further remedy, because he had chosen the *capias* and a remedy that deprived a person of his liberty was strictly construed,[537] but a case in Coke's Reports held otherwise.[538] This point was resolved in Ireland by 10 Car. I sess. 3, c. 9 (Ir.) which enacted that a new execution could be brought against the lands and goods of the defendant's estate, except as to land sold *bona fide* after the judgment by the defendant for payment of his creditors.[539]

As to civil imprisonment, some steps had been taken to prevent abuses and to allieviate the situation of persons imprisoned for debt, both on mesne and final process, but they had only a minor effect.[540]

Imprisonment in final process, that is, civil imprisonment, which in practice was mostly for debt, was abolished in England in 1869, with some exceptions for fraudulent debtors.[541] It was not abolished in Ireland by the Debtors Act (Ireland) 1872: section 6 specifically saved the power of committal for small debts, with imprisonment for up to six weeks.[542]

4. The writ of *habere facias possessionem* applied only in the case of ejectment and was authority to obtain possession of the property.

In courts other than the Exchequer, final process could also result in outlawry,[543] until 1835.[544]

---

and general defence. Howard, *Pleas Side*, ii. 138; KI MS. No. 82, p. 161; 1 Roll. Abr. 904. The power was restated as to England in the Sheriffs Act, 1887 (Eng.), s. 8, *HEL*, i. 68.

[534] Howard, *Pleas Side*, ii. 139, '*salva et arcta custodia*'.

[535] Ibid., ii. 139.

[536] Ibid.; *Semayne's Case* (1604) 5 Co. Rep. 91a, 77 E.R. 194: 'The house of every one is his castle . . . It is not lawful for the sheriff . . . at the suit of a common person, to break the defendant's house, *scil.* to execute any process at the suit of a subject.' See Coke, *Third Part of the Institutes of the Laws of England* (1628), ch. 73, p. 162: 'For a man's house is his castle, *et domus sua cuique est tutissimum refugium* [and each man's home is his safest refuge].'

[537] Ibid., ii. 139; *Williams* v. *Cutteris* (1601) Cro. Jac. 136, 79 E.R. 118; Cro. Jac. 143, 79 E.R. 125; 1 Roll. Abr. 903.

[538] *Case of Executions* (1596) 5 Co. Rep. 86, 77 E.R. 185 (plaintiff could obtain *elegit* or *fi. fa.*).

[539] Howard, *Pleas Side*, ii. 140.

[540] On England, see *HEL*, xi. 595–596. In Ireland the statute 7 Geo. III, c. 25 (Ir.), of 1767 for the relief of debtors had been repealed in 1771 by 11 Geo. III, c. 8 (Ir.). It was replaced by the Act of 1793, 33 Geo. III, c. 42 (Ir.) but those provisions were only temporary except for section 28 which provided for execution against goods or lands even if a person was detained under a ca. sa.

[541] Debtors Act, 1869, s. 4.

[542] The Debtors Act (Ireland) 1872 was repealed in the Republic by the Statute Law Revision Act, 2007. The Enforcement of Court Orders Act, 1940, R.I., s. 6, amended the Enforcement of Court Orders Act, 1926, s. 18, by providing that imprisonment for civil debt applied only in case of wilful refusal. The Debtors Act (Ireland) 1872 is still in force in Northern Ireland, but section 6 has been repealed. Article 1 of the Fourth Protocol of the European Convention on Human Rights and Fundamental Freedoms guarantees freedom from imprisonment merely on the ground of inability to fulfil a contactual obligation.

[543] Ferguson, *Treatise*, iii. 1053

[544] Below, p. cxvi n. 630.

Judgments which had not been executed within a year had to be revived by a writ of *scire facias*.[545]

Assignment

In Ireland, judgments were made assignable at law in 1735,[546] but no similar measure was passed in England.[547] The Irish legislation gave assignees the right to enforce or revive such judgments in their own names.[548] Before the legislation judgments had been recognized as assignable in equity and were thus a form of equitable security.[549] Assignment of judgments is mentioned in *Sanderson* v. *Rose McCain, and Nichols*,[550] and in *His Majesty* v. *Garret Bourke*.[551]

Writs of error

If after judgment an unsuccessful party wished to dispute a matter afresh, he or she might bring a writ of error, which was issued out of Chancery addressed to the court in which judgment had been given, commanding them either to examine the record themselves or to send it to a court of competent jurisdiction. A writ of error was in theory a separate action until 1852 in England,[552] and until 1853 in Ireland.[553] The writ might concern a matter of fact or law.

1. The matter of *fact* must not have been one found by a jury, in which case the only mode of reconsidering it was by a motion for a new trial.[554] If it was, for example, the fact that the plaintiff was a minor and appeared by attorney instead of by his guardian, or that the plaintiff was a married woman and appeared without her husband, then in such a case and similar cases affecting the validity of the proceedings, a writ of error *coram nobis* in the King's Bench, or *coram vobis* in the Common Pleas and Exchequer,[555] was available, being a writ of error to be tried before the same judges, on the theory that the reversal of the error was not a reversal of the judgment of those judges, but the correction of something which had not previously been brought to their attention.[556]

---

[545] L. 'that you make known'. A writ founded on a matter of record, and requiring the person against whom it is issued to show cause why the party bringing it should not have the advantage of the record, or in the case of a *scire facias* to repeal letters patent, why the record should not be annulled. If execution of a judgment was not obtained within the time set, the court would issue *scire facias*, which stated the judgment recovered by the plaintiff, that execution remained outstanding, and commanded the sheriff that he should instruct the defendant to be in court on the return day to show cause why the plaintiff ought not to have execution against him or her. The writ was introduced by 13 Edw. I, c. 45, Statute of Westminster II, 1285; Ferguson, *Treatise*, i. 440.

[546] By 9 Geo. II, c. 5 (Ir.), 1735, as amended by 25 Geo. II, c. 14 (Ir.), 1751, revived and continued by 11 Geo. III, c. 1 (Ir.), 1771 and made permanent by 11 & 12 Geo. III, c. 19 (Ir.), 1771–72.

[547] Ferguson, *Treatise*, i. 413.

[548] 9 Geo. II, c. 5 (Ir.), 1735, s. 2; 25 Geo. II, c. 14 (Ir.), 1751.

[549] T. Lefroy, *Observations on the Proceedings by Elegit*, preface: 'The practice of borrowing money upon bond with a warrant of attorney for confessing judgment, having so long existed in this country, it is not surprizing, that judgments should have become a very prevailing species of private security.' Ferguson, *Treatise*, i. 413.

[550] Below, p. 140.

[551] Below, p. 292.

[552] Common Law Procedure Amendment Act, 1852 (Eng.), s. 148.

[553] Common Law Procedure Amendment Act (Ireland), 1853, s. 169.

[554] Brown, *Law Dictionary*.

[555] Ferguson, *Treatise*, i. 486. A writ of error *coram vobis*, L. 'before you', called upon the court to review its own decision in the light of some matter not considered in the original hearing. In the court of King's Bench the same procedure was known as *coram nobis*, 'before us'.

[556] Ferguson, *Treatise*, i. 486; Brown, *Law Dictionary*.

2. A writ of error of *law* lay where the judges had made an error of law on the face of the record, and in that case the remedy was a writ of error generally, and not *coram nobis,* or *vobis.* It consisted of a *certiorari* to remove the record, or a transcript, to the higher court.[557]

Although Ferguson[558] treats the matter as settled, it does not seem to have been settled in 1731 that a writ of error *coram vobis* could be brought in the Exchequer at all, for in *Costelo* v. *Costelo*[559] Mr Daly, opening the case, says: 'the question is, whether an error in fact in this court can be remedied by a writ of error *coram vobis*?' The case comes before the court for argument several times in these reports, and we do not have the ultimate decision. In a later hearing the issue seems to be a narrower one: whether a writ of error, if it is not general, that is, not by *certiorari,* and is as to fact, can be brought without a commission from the king, and also whether in such a case it should be directed to the treasurer and barons, or, as it was here, to the barons alone.[560] In the last hearing reported in these reports,[561] the chief baron, apparently referring to error *coram vobis,* comments that:[562]

> King's Bench have had this power time out of mind, though it is not natural for a court to correct their own mistakes without a commission from the King. This court has stood above 600 years, and yet there is no precedent.

Argument continued by counsel and the report ends without the final decision.

There are two other interesting comments in the case, this time by counsel, Mr. Costelo. He states, without contradiction by the court, that 'error of fact in petty bag can be amended by *scire facias*', and also that the first precedent of error in fact brought in King's Bench *coram nobis*[563] was Y.B. Mich. 2 Ric. III, fo. 1.

OUTLAWRY AND ATTAINDER

As we have seen, outlawry was not a consequence that could follow from failure to appear and answer a claim in the Exchequer, so the question of outlawry only arises indirectly in these reports, and usually in the context of someone having reversed their outlawry and bringing an action in the Exchequer to recover their land, or sue for a settlement under their parents' marriage articles. Outlawry could be reversed by writ of error. In one or two cases in the present reports, reversal was brought about by obtaining a private British Act of parliament.

Attainder

In England, attainder at common law was the consequence of a sentence of death pronounced after a person confessed to, or was found guilty of, a capital crime.[564] A person attainted could not act as a witness nor carry out other legal functions, since, as Coke chillingly puts it, he was already dead in law.[565] It was not conviction which

---

[557] Ferguson, *Treatise,* i. 486.
[558] *Treatise,* i. 486.
[559] Below, p. 36.
[560] Below, p. 39.
[561] Below, p. 52.
[562] Below, p. 53.
[563] The MS. reads '*vobis*', but appears to be an error for '*nobis*'.
[564] Bl. Com., iv. 373; Jacob, *Law Dictionary,* 'attainder'.
[565] Inst., iii. 213; Bl. Com., iv. 373–74.

brought about attainder, but judgment of death, so that if a person was convicted, but died before sentence was passed, forfeiture or escheat of property did not follow.[566] Attainder also followed in circumstances equivalent to judgment of death, as in the case of a judgment of outlawry on a capital crime, when the person had fled from justice, which was taken as a tacit confession of guilt.[567] A person could also be attainted by Act of parliament, which avoided the necessity, and inconvenience, of a trial and conviction. This violation of the right proclaimed in Magna Carta to trial by one's peers, had begun during the Wars of the Roses and continued under the Tudors and Stuarts,[568] including William III.[569]

The consequences of attainder were forfeiture of property, the crown's right of 'year, day and waste', escheat and corruption of blood. These concepts had developed independently but came to converge in the case of crime. Forfeiture was the prerogative right of the crown to all lands of a person convicted of high treason,[570] and, as Blackstone noted,[571] had nothing to do with feudal tenure. Escheat was an aspect of medieval land tenure, and corruption of blood was an early theory which, confusingly, overlapped with escheat in some respects.

Loss of real property, under these various doctrines, occurred in the cases of treason, felony, misprision of treason, *præmunire,* drawing a weapon on a judge, or striking anyone in the presence of the king's courts and, in Ireland, under the Popery Acts imposing penalties on Catholics. Forfeiture, as a distinct royal prerogative, applied only in the case of high treason.

In the case of high treason, at common law a traitor forfeited all his or her lands and tenements of inheritance, whether held in fee simple or fee tail, and all rights of entry, and they vested permanently in the crown.[572] At a time when intermediate tenures still existed, forfeiture destroyed all tenures between the traitor and the king.[573] However, the statute *De Donis,* 1285[574] was held to give estates tail immunity from forfeiture beyond the life of the traitor,[575] so that the next heir in tail would take the estate, but this immunity was removed in the reign of Henry VIII.[576]

In the case of petit treason, misprision of treason and felony, the crown was entitled to the profits of freehold land under the right of 'year, day and waste',[577]

---

[566] Bl. Com., iv. 374; Jacob, *Law Dictionary,* 'forfeiture', II 1.

[567] Ibid.

[568] T. F. T. Plucknett, *Concise History of the Common Law* (5th ed., 1956), p. 205.

[569] 7 & 8 Will. III, c. 3 (Eng.), 1695 (Sir John Fenwick); Jacob, *Law Dictionary,* 'attainder'.

[570] *HEL,* iii. 70; P & M, i. 332.

[571] Bl. Com., ii. 271; *HEL,* iii. 70. The technical distinction was that land forfeited, if granted out again by the crown, was held *ut de corona,* whereas land escheated for felony, if granted out again, was held *ut de honore.*

[572] Jacob, *Law Dictionary* 'forfeiture II 1; Ferguson, *Treatise,* iii. 1045.

[573] P & M, ii. 500; Hale, *Pleas of the Crown,* i. 254. Mesne lords' rights were extinguished, but Hale adds that if the king granted it out again, he had to revive the former tenure, for which there lay a petition of right under 46 Edw. III, c. 19.

[574] Applied by writ, Berry, *Statutes, Ireland,* pp. 47, 105–77; confirmed, 13 Edw. II, c. 2 (Ir.), 1320; Berry, ibid., p. 281.

[575] Bl. Com., ii. 116–118. Nor did it involve corruption of blood as to the heirs of the body, R. P. Gadd, *Peerage Law* (Bristol, 1985), p. 117.

[576] Ibid.; 26 Hen. VIII, c. 13 (Eng.), 1534, (high treason). 28 Hen. VIII, c. 7, s. 4 (Ir.), 1537, applied to 'estates of inheritance'. Before it was held that the tenant in tail could bar the issue in tail by fines and recoveries, the view was that since the tenant in tail could not alienate, he should not be liable for forfeiture either: *Brown* v. *White* (1677) 2 Mod. 130, 86 E.R. 982. 27 Eliz. I, c. 1, s. 9 (Ir.), 1584, extended forfeiture to treasons at common law or by Act of attainder after the statute and also applied it to all other 'rights, entries and conditions' relating to land.

[577] See the history of this in Bl. Com., iv. 378–79.

although by the time of Blackstone this was usually compounded for.[578] The king could reasonably have claimed the land permanently, since a felony was a threat to royal authority, and so the crown's right of 'year, day and waste' was the result of a compromise between the claim of the crown and the rights of feudal lords arising from tenure, namely, their right to escheat. A fee simple would have escheated to the lord of the tenure under the feudal law.

Corruption of blood at the time of Bracton[579] explained why heirs were thus deprived at a time when they were regarded as otherwise having a right to inherit the fee simple.[580] Then *Quia Emptores*, 1290, gave to tenants in fee simple the right of free alienation and heirs lost the 'right' to inherit. Corruption of blood then became redundant as a theory to explain the escheat of a fee simple. Later, corruption of blood still provided an explanation for the cancellation of peerages. Corruption of blood was abolished by the Inheritance Act, 1833.[581] By the eighteenth century mesne lordships were rare and so the crown would have taken the fee simple of a felon by escheat. It had no reason to deprive the wife and children of the felon of their support. In 1800 the practice of restoring the land to the families was recognized[582] and this had evidently become the practice from at least the end of the seventeenth century.[583]

As to a fee tail, escheat for felony only affected the tenant in tail and the land passed to the next heir of the body. Under the statute *De Donis*, 1285, a gift 'to A and the heirs of his body' was to take effect '*secundum formam doni*', 'according to the form of the gift', and descent of the fee tail was traced from A. Thus, if A's eldest son, B, committed a felony, B's eldest son, C, took the fee tail as heir of the body of A, who had committed no felony, and not as heir of the body of his father B.[584] Corruption of blood never provided an adequate explanation for this.

Confiscation of real property did not follow on *suicide*, since there was no sentence and so no attainder.[585]

Confiscation of *personal property* followed on conviction, not on sentence. It applied in all the higher offences, of treason, petit treason, misprision of treason, and felonies of all kinds.[586] It also applied in the case of striking in the presence of the king's courts, and where the jury found *flight* on an accusation of treason, felony, or even petty larceny, whether the person was found guilty or acquitted, because it was an attempt to evade the course of justice. Confiscation of personal property did apply in the case of suicide,[587] because the law reflected the religious condemnation of the

---

[578] Bl. Com., iv. 378.

[579] *Bracton*, iii. 313.

[580] He did not have a right, however, to inherit the same services as had been due to the father. If a father subinfeudated in fee simple in his lifetime with a warranty which barred his heir, the heir would inherit the fee simple in the new seignory. Assuming the father had been the freeholder at the bottom of the feudal pyramid before he subinfeudated, the father would have been entitled to the services due on the old seignory, i.e. the services due from the villeins who held from him on unfree tenure.

[581] 3 & 4 Will. IV, c. 106 (U.K.), 1833, s. 10.

[582] 39 & 40 Geo. III, c. 88 (U.K.), 1800, s. 12; explained and amended by 47 Geo. III, sess. 2, c. 24, 1807; 59 Geo. III, c. 94, 1819; extended to leaseholds by 6 Geo. IV, c. 17, 1825.; J. Williams, *Real Property* (11th ed., 1875), p. 126 n. b;

[583] It occurred in Ireland in 1686 in the case of William Aston, below, p. cxiv.

[584] *Dowtie's Case* 3 Co. Rep. 9b at 10b n. (E), 76 E.R. 643 at 645; *Digby's Case* 8 Co. Rep. 165b at 166a, 77 E.R. 725; J. Williams, *Real Property* (11th ed., 1875), p. 57–58.

[585] Bl. Com., iv. 379; Inst., iii. 55.

[586] Jacob, *Law Dictionary*, 'forfeiture II 1'.

[587] Ibid.

taking of life, even one's own,[588] and also probably for the more practical reason, when it followed an accusation of treason or felony, that it was regarded as a form of flight.

Jacob notes that the jury rarely found flight, since forfeiture was looked upon 'since the vast increase in personal property, as too large a penalty for an offence to which a man is prompted by the natural love of liberty'. However, it did mean that in the case of outlawry for treason and felony, although lands were only confiscated by judgment, personal property was confiscated on the issue of *exigent* without waiting for the final judgment of outlawry, for, as Jacob puts it, 'the secreting of himself so long from justice is construed a flight in law'.

In Ireland these rules were modified in one important respect. Under the draconian statute of 1495[589] murder was treated as treason in Ireland, and so real property was indeed *forfeited* in Ireland in the case of murder, rather than escheated.[590] This continued to be the case until the statute was repealed in 1791.[591] Nevertheless, from the early seventeenth century, in some cases at least, it was the practice to return the land to the family, since the wife and children of the murderer might be left destitute. In 1686, in the reign of James II, William Aston, the son of Mr Justice Aston,[592] was convicted of the murder of a Mr Keating, after an altercation on the quays in Dublin in which, so Aston alleged, Keating had insulted his wife and children. Aston drew his sword, intending, he said, only to wound Keating, but ran him through. Aston was convicted, sentenced to death and executed.[593] Two of the judges at his trial in the King's Bench, Lyndon[594] and Nugent,[595] interceded[596] and requested the crown to restore his lands to his widow and children after his death and this was granted.[597] There was no appeal to the crown to exercise the prerogative of mercy to prevent his execution, for reasons that remain obscure. One reason might be that Aston had little to say in his own defence and, until 1836,[598] a defendant in felony had no right to have counsel address the jury on his behalf,[599] although it was allowed informally before then.

A further instance of forfeiture in cases of murder in Ireland occurred in August 1738 when Lord Barry of Santry[600] was tried before the Irish House of Lords, and convicted, of the murder of Laughlin Murphy, a footman whom he had stabbed in 'a fit of passion'.[601] Barry, who was probably suffering from mental illness, was condemned to death on 27 April 1739 and attainted, and his estates were thereby

---

[588] C. S. Kenny, *Outlines of Criminal Law* (18th ed. by J. W. C. Turner, 1962), para. 127.

[589] 10 Hen. VII, c. 21 (Ir.), 1495. Under 9 Ann., c. 4 (Ir.), 1710 an appeal was not barred; Henry Hyde, *Correspondence*, i. 377.

[590] Ibid., i. 377.

[591] 31 Geo. III, c. 17 (Ir.), 1791.

[592] Sir William Aston (d. end 1670, or early 1671). Ball, *Judges in Ireland*, i. 346.

[593] On 4 June 1686: Henry Hyde, *Correspondence*, i. 426.

[594] Sir John Lyndon (d. 1699), Ball, *Judges in Ireland*, i. 359–60.

[595] Thomas Nugent, 1st Baron Nugent of Riverston (created after James II landed in Ireland in 1689), appointed puisne judge of King's Bench in the spring of 1686, appointed chief justice of King's Bench in autumn 1687: Ball, *Judges in Ireland*, i. 361–62. Below, p. 81.

[596] Henry Hyde, *Correspondence*, i. 397. Chief Justice Davys was ill with gout.

[597] Ibid., i. 491.

[598] 6 & 7 Will. IV, c. 114 (Eng., Ir.);

[599] Allyson N. May, *The Bar and the Old Bailey, 1750–1850* (2003).

[600] Born 1710. Colloquially known as 'Lord Santry'.

[601] Cokayne, *Complete Peerage*, i. 448; F. G. James, *Lords of the Ascendancy: the Irish House of Lords and its Members, 1600–1800* (1995), at p. 152.

forfeited. The effect of attainder on his peerage, however, was that it was forfeited only for his own life.[602] The peerage descended in the same way as an entail and under the statute *De Donis*, 1285, it was held that the forfeiture did not affect heirs to the peerage.[603] He obtained a pardon in June 1740 and so survived his attainder. His estates were restored, by regrant, in 1741, but not his title. He died without issue in March 1750/1 in Nottingham and the peerage probably became extinct.

Since the reign of Henry VIII many statutes creating new felonies had not imposed corruption of blood.[604] In the time of Queen Elizabeth I, it had been dispensed with in England in a number of instances,[605] and there had been some exemptions in Ireland.[606] By the eighteenth century this was coming to be regarded as outmoded and exceptions had become more frequent.[607]

In Ireland attainder also followed outlawry under the statute against foreign education, discussed below.

Outlawry

Outlawry, in its civil context, was punishment for contempt, in refusing to be amenable to a court which had authority to call the defendant to appear. Refusal to attend court was an act of rebellion against the state or community of which the person was a member.[608] In the ancient common law a male was 'sworn of the law' by taking an oath of allegiance to the king in the court leet at the age of twelve or over.[609] Hence he could not be outlawed, or put out of the law's protection, below the age of twelve.[610] Females were never sworn of the law and so could not strictly be outlawed, but a similar proceeding called *waiver* applied in their case.[611] An example of a woman being waived of the law occurs in these reports in *Lessee of Ogara v. Fleming*.[612]

Outlawry involved attainder, the consequences of which were so severe that until some time after the Conquest outlawry applied only to felony. By the time of Bracton it had been applied to all actions *vi et armis*[613] and since then, by a number of statutes, to account, debt, detinue and other civil actions.[614]

There were three types of outlawry in Ireland at the time of these reports: 1. Criminal outlawry applied in the case of treason and felony;[615] 2. Civil outlawry

---

[602] Cokayne, *Complete Peerage*, i. 448 n. c.

[603] The statutes of Henry VIII and Elizabeth I as to the removal of the immunity of fees tail in *land* did not expressly apply to peerages: see above, n. 576, but the position was far from clear. Some precedents held that a peerage, being an office of trust and confidence, was forfeited for breach of a condition tacitly attached to it: Gadd, *Peerage Law*, pp. 117–119. An Act of attainder could forfeit the dignity outright, in which case the crown could not reinstate it. Reinstatement would require another statute. Ibid. p. 119.

[604] Jacob, *Law Dictionary*, 'attainder'.

[605] 5 Eliz. I, c. 1 (Eng.), 1562 (treasons in respect of papal supremacy); 5 Eliz. I, c. 11 (Eng.), 1562 (coinage).

[606] 28 Eliz. I, c. 3 (Ir.), s. 7, 1586 (forging of evidence); 10 Car. I, sess. 2, c. 21 (Ir.), s. 4, 1634 (bigamy); 10 Car. I, sess. 3, c. 20 (Ir.), s. 2, 1634 (levying fines, etc. in the name of another); 7 Will. III, c. 3 (Ir.), s. 3, 1695 (attainders under James II's Parliament).

[607] Jacob, *Law Dictionary*, 'attainder'.

[608] Ferguson, *Treatise*, ch. 53. Co. Litt. 128; Christopher St German, *Doctor and Student*, dial. 2 cap. 3; Bl. Com., iii. 283–84; Jacob, *Law Dictionary*, 'outlawry'.

[609] Jacob, ibid.

[610] Ibid.; Co. Litt. 128a.

[611] Jacob, ibid; Litt. 186; Co. Litt. 122b.

[612] Below, p. 251 and see p. 251 n. 1160 and Appendix B.

[613] *Bracton*, v. 425; Ferguson, *Treatise*, iii. 1045.

[614] Ferguson, *Treatise*, p. 1045; Jacob, *Law Dictionary*, 'outlawry'.

[615] Ferguson, *Treatise*, iii. 1045.

applied where a person refused to attend court in response to a writ in a civil action;[616] 3. Outlawry also applied under the Irish Act against foreign education.[617]

1. Criminal outlawry originally meant that the outlaw could be killed on sight, as one might kill a wolf,[618] but by the time of Hale, writing in the mid to late seventeenth century, it had become murder to kill an outlaw, unless it happened in an attempt to apprehend him.[619]

2. Civil outlawry originally meant that the outlaw was incapable of bringing actions,[620] could be imprisoned, and forfeited his personal and real property: personal property immediately upon outlawry and his leaseholds and the profits of real property when found by inquisition.[621]

In *Executors of Morris* v. *Cairnes*[622] Marlay C.B. says that: 'Where a man is outlawed he is considered in law as dead'[623] and Daly, counsel in *Morris* v. *Henery*,[624] says that 'On an outlawry the party forfeits all his goods and chattels, and he can't appear, but is considered as a dead person.'

This was only partly true, however. Civil outlawry did not necessarily result in a permanent forfeiture of real property, but the profits vested in the crown while the outlawry was in force.[625] The crown, not having any interest in the direct management of such land, would let it out on a *custodiam* lease.[626] Outlawry could be reversed by writ of error, or on motion,[627] or by Act of parliament. If a civil outlawry was reversed, the former outlaw recovered his land, but lost the profits which had accrued in the meantime, unless it was by Act of parliament and the statute provided otherwise.

Outlawry in courts other than the Exchequer could be resorted to not only in mesne process, when the defendant failed to appear, but in final process, when the defendant failed to satisfy the judgment, in which case the plaintiff could apply to the Revenue Exchequer for the *custodiam* lease to be made in his favour in order to recover the debt, or for a sale of the personal property.[628] The practice of granting *custodiam* leases was ended in Ireland in 1835,[629] after which there was no point in seeking outlawry in final process.[630] The plaintiff could still apply for the sale of the personal property of the outlaw, and this was more frequently done than in England when Ferguson wrote in 1841.[631]

Howard,[632] writing in the middle of the eighteenth century, strongly criticised civil outlawry as far too drastic a remedy, since those who held mortgages and other

[616] Ibid., ch. 53.
[617] 7 Will. III, c. 4 (Ir.), 1695.
[618] Jacob, *Law Dictionary*, 'outlawry I'.
[619] Ibid.; *Bracton*, fo. 125; Hale, *Pleas of the Crown*, i. 497; *Hawkins* v. *Hall* (1838) 1 Beav. 74, 48 E.R. 866.
[620] *Wallis* v. *Scott*, KI MS. 50, p. 55 (Chancery: defendant pleaded outlawry of plaintiff, and swore that person in the *capias utlagatum* was the same person who preferred the bill); *Aldridge* v. *Buller* (1837) 2 M. & W. 412, 150 E.R. 818.
[621] Jacob, *Law Dictionary*, 'outlawry I'; Ferguson, *Treatise*, iii. 1045.
[622] Below, p. 221.
[623] Below, p. 222.
[624] Below, p. 220.
[625] Ferguson, *Treatise*, iii. 1045.
[626] See Howard, *Treatise*, ch. 30; Conroy's Custodiam Reports, 1652–1788.
[627] Jacob, *Law Dictionary*, 'outlawry V'. The outlaw had to appear in person. The statute 4 & 5 Will. & Mar., c. 18 (Eng.) (appearance by attorney), allowing, by section 9, appearance by attorney, except in cases of treason and felony, did not apply to Ireland: Ferguson, *Treatise*, iii. 1054.
[628] Ferguson, *Treatise*, iii. 1045.
[629] 5 & 6 Will. 4, c. 55 (Ir.), s. 31.
[630] Ferguson, *Treatise*, iii. 1053–54.
[631] Ibid., iii. 1046.
[632] *Treatise*, introduction.

securities over the land would lose their rights on its becoming vested in the crown. Innocent third parties were injured by it, and commerce damaged.

Civil outlawry was curtailed in Ireland in 1840[633] and it was finally abolished throughout the then United Kingdom by the Civil Procedure Acts Repeal Act, 1879.[634]

3. The Act against foreign education,[635] an Act of the Irish parliament in 1695, created a novel form of outlawry in Ireland. The Act not only made it an offence resulting in outlawry for any person to send a child out of Ireland to be educated as a Catholic: it also made it an offence for 'persons', in other words, the children, 'being sent'. Extraordinarily, it punished the child, who was capable neither of forming the intent to do the act, in many cases, nor of resisting being sent abroad. The purpose of this measure was probably to prevent the children inheriting their parents' lands. It was repealed in 1792.[636]

Note on forfeited estates

Several cases in these reports concern the forfeited estates of James II and his followers, including the first case, *Geoghegan* v. *Chevers*, which is discussed in the next section. The following note therefore sets out the background to the treatment of these estates.

William III had rewarded his followers by distributing among them the lands of James II in Ireland and those of his followers which had been forfeited. Parliament, however, did not accept this assertion of royal patronage and took steps to place the estates under statutory control. The private estates in Ireland of James II and those of his followers who had been outlawed and attainted,[637] were vested by the Act of 1698, 11 Will. III, c. 2. (Eng.)[638] variously called the Resumption Act, the Trustee Act, or the Statute of Trustees, in the Trustees for Forfeited Estates.[639] Anyone claiming that their land had been wrongfully designated as forfeited could make a claim against the trustees but the Act stated that the decision of the trustees 'shall be in all courts allowed as a sufficient evidence of the allowance of any such claim' and that it should 'never afterwards be impeached, avoided or called in question' by the king or anyone deriving title from him, by the trustees or by any person purchasing or having any estate, right or interest 'by, from or under' them.[640] The trustees were to sell the estates to purchasers who were required to be Protestant.[641]

In *Annesley* v. *Dixon*[642] it was argued that the jurisdiction of the trustees to determine claims was exclusive and could not be challenged in the ordinary courts. A proprietor took a writ of error against the decision of the trustees denying his claim. The trustees had already purported to sell the estate to a purchaser. The case went

---

[633] 3 & 4 Vict., c. 105 (Ir.), 1840; Ferguson, *Treatise*, iii. 1047.

[634] 42 & 43 Vict., c. 59. (G.B.), s. 3.

[635] 7 Will. III, c. 4 (Ir.), 1695.

[636] 32 Geo. III, c. 21 (Ir.), 1792 s. 14.

[637] It included only persons outlawed before 1701, below, p. cxx.

[638] 11 & 12 Will. III in Ruffhead.

[639] The trustees were named in the Act, 11 Will. III, c. 2 (Eng.), 1698, s. 1, as Sir Cyril Wyche, Francis Annesley, James Hamilton, John Baggs, John Trenchard, John Isham, John Cary, Sir Henry Sheeres, Thomas Harrison, William Fellowes and Thomas Rawlins. The names of Henry Langford and James Hooper were written into the roll later, having apparently been originally omitted by mistake: St. Realm. vii. 545 n.

[640] 11 Will. III, c. 2 (Eng.), 1698, s. 16.

[641] 1 Ann., c. 6 (Eng.), 1702 ss. 133–34. 1 Ann., st. 2, c. 18 (Eng.), 1702 (c. 21 in Ruffhead).

[642] (1706) Holt 372, 377, 388, 90 E.R. 1106, 1108, 1114; 11 Mod. 104, 88 E.R. 925 (Eng. Q. B.). 7 Bro. P. C. 2nd ed. 213, 3 E.R. 139 (G.B. HL).

from the Irish Queen's Bench by writ of error to the English Queen's Bench, and thence by writ of error to the British House of Lords. In the English Queen's Bench, Holt C.J. held that recourse to the ordinary courts had not been excluded. What estates were or were not forfeited was a matter for the ordinary courts of law. The Act had vested in the trustees only such land as was vested in James II and other persons whose land had been properly forfeited and their jurisdiction was limited to such land. He described the alternative view as a 'mad construction'[643] and that 'to say, that the trustees had a power to say an innocent person's estate should be liable etc., would be a hellish construction, and such as the parliament of England could never intend'.[644] In support of Holt's view, it should be noted that section 16 of the Act of 1698 declaring the trustees' decision to be final, referred to the *allowance* of such a claim and not its denial and so its purpose was apparently to protect an innocent claimant, whose title had been upheld by the trustees, from a subsequent challenge by a purchaser in the ordinary courts. It in fact implied that a *denial* of a claim by a proprietor, who alleged that the land had been improperly forfeited, could still be challenged by the proprietor.

In 1707 the British parliament passed what was known as the Statute of Periods, or Act of Periods,[645] which limited the time within which persons should have lodged a claim to land from the trustees to two years from 24 June 1708.[646] Furthermore, nothing was to prejudice the title of a person who was in actual possession of any lands, estates or interests sold by the trustees.[647] In other words, even if a claim was made within the period, it was to be denied if the trustees in the meantime had sold the land to a purchaser.

There seems little doubt that the Act was in response to *Annesley* v. *Dixon*. According to the preamble to the Act:

> divers actions and suits have been brought against several purchasers of estates under the said Acts of parliament, and the title to the same, under the said Trustees, hath been called into question, and several judgments have been given in Ireland against some of the said purchasers, and one of those judgments hath been affirmed on a writ of error in her Majesty's Court of Queen's Bench in England, and also in the House of Peers in England, whereby the said purchasers are in danger of having their titles to the estates and interests, so by them purchased, further called into question and disputed.

Claims could be brought in any court of record, but then, as if to contradict Holt's confidence expressed in *Annesley* in the liberal instincts of the legislature, the time limit was imposed and also the restriction that if the land had been sold to a purchaser, claims were to be denied.

Error in outlawry: Edward Chevers

Geoghegan v. *Chevers*[648] in 1716 is part of the complicated litigation over the estates of Edward Chevers. Further litigation, and an appeal from a decree in the Irish court of Exchequer, followed in 1720 and is reported in Brown P.C. as *Chevers* v. *Geoghegan*.[649]

---

[643] Holt 393, 90 E.R. 1117.
[644] 11 Mod. 105, 88 E.R. 927.
[645] 6 Ann., c. 61 (G.B.).
[646] Ibid., s. 1.
[647] Ibid., s. 4.
[648] Below, p. 1.
[649] (1720) 6 Bro. P.C. 2nd ed. 12, 2 E.R. 900.

What follows is an account taken from the facts in Brown's report, and the printed pleadings.[650]

John Chevers 'of Turpanmore',[651] or Macetown,[652] had four sons by his wife Joan: Edward, the eldest, Andrew, Christopher and John.[653] In 1656 John Chevers the elder created a lease for 99 years of some of his land in favour of trustees in trust for his wife and children. He retained other land for his own use. In 1697 the residue of this term became vested[654] in Christopher Chevers and Andrew Crosby.

In 1682 John Chevers borrowed money from Nicholas Netterville and made a mortgage in his favour of part of the lands subject to the trust, plus other land, with the concurrence of the trustees, and his sons Edward and Andrew. He retaining possession of the lands, and the equity of redemption.

John died soon after, leaving his four sons, but Edward died without issue before the litigation mentioned here. According to Cokayne[655] Edward died in 1693 in France and the report in this manuscript states that he was outlawed for treason in 1695.[656] Nevertheless, one of the main issues in both cases was that this outlawry was in the name of 'Christopher Chevers, commonly called Lord Mount-Leinster'. A mistake had been made as to the Christian name.

It should be mentioned at this point that Edward Chevers had married Ann, the daughter of Patrick Sarsfield, who was created earl of Lucan by James II, and that Edward Chevers had joined with his relatives in the cause of James II in Ireland and was his aide-de-camp at the Battle of the Boyne. James II created him Baron Bano, or Bannow and Viscount Mount-Leinster in 1689.[657] He was also present at the siege of Limerick, was included as one of the officers in the Articles[658] but accompanied

---

[650] Lincoln's Inn, 'House of Lords Printed Cases' 1720–23. vol. 6, fo. 91; the printed pleading is not among those in Trinity College Dublin Library. The standing orders of the British House of Lords in 1698 had recognized the practice of parties issuing printed pleadings and required them to be signed by counsel who attended the hearing in the court below, to avoid the many 'scandalous and frivolous' printed cases: *Standing Orders of the House of Lords relative to Writs of Error and Appeals* (London, 1843), no. 59. The Irish House adopted the same practice: see the Rules of the Irish House of Lords reproduced in 1 Ridg. P.C. xxii, rule 81.

[651] 6 Bro. P.C. 12.

[652] Cokayne, *Complete Peerage*, ix. 354.

[653] Ibid., ix. 354 expressed doubt as to whether Joan was the mother of the mentioned sons, or whether they were the sons of John's first wife, but (1720) 6 Bro. P.C. 12, 2 E.R. 900 states that Joan was the mother. The seniority of the sons is given in 6 Bro. P.C. 12, 2 E.R. 900.

[654] By an asignment of 1667 by the surviving original trustee and by an appointment by Joan in 1697.

[655] Cokayne, *Complete Peerage*, ix. 354.

[656] In 6 Bro. P.C. 15, 2 E.R. 902 it is stated that an outlawry produced in the Irish court of Chancery was promulgated in 1696.

[657] Cokayne, *Complete Peerage*, ix. 354.

[658] Ibid. The Treaty of Limerick, 1691, ended the Siege of Limerick and the Williamite war in Ireland. It contained articles guaranteeing certain rights to followers of James II. Jacobite soldiers had the option to leave for France and to continue to serve under James II, or they could join the Williamite army, or they could return home. Those who chose to remain in Ireland, most of whom were Catholics, were to retain their property if they swore allegiance to William and Mary, and were guaranteed the same rights 'as they did enjoy in the reign of King Charles the Second' (Article 1, 3 October 1691), which did not debar them from sitting or voting in parliament, if otherwise qualified. The English parliament broke the Treaty in the same year by 3 Will. & Mar., c. 2, (Eng.), 1691, which introduced oaths of allegiance, supremacy and abjuration before any person took a seat in either house of the Irish parliament or practised at the Bar. Section 11 contained a limited exception, as to the practice of law or medicine, for those who had taken the oath under the Treaty of Limerick. The Act was complied with in Ireland. In 1695 the Irish parliament enacted 7 Will. III, c. 4 (Ir.) against foreign education, aimed against Catholics, (see above, p. cxvii) and 9 Will. III, c. 2 (Ir.), 1697, 'confirming' the Treaty, also encroached on the rights guaranteed by it. The Articles are reproduced in Henry Parnell, *A History of the Penal Laws against the Irish Catholics* (Dublin, 1808), pp. 7–24. The Articles dated 3 October 1691, art. 4, mention 'Chieveas of Maystown, commonly called Mount-Leinster'.

King James into exile in France and apparently died there in 1693 without issue.[659]

With the death of John Chevers, the father, and his eldest son Edward, the equity of redemption in the mortgaged lands descended to Andrew Chevers, who continued in possession for nineteen years. Andrew and the younger son, John, also remained in possession of the leased lands after their mother's death in about 1701.

In 1700, the mortgagee, Nicholas Netterville, fearing that the mortgagors, or some of them, might be subject to forfeiture, and fearing that his security might also thereby be lost, entered a cautionary claim with the trustees of forfeited estates in Ireland,[660] claiming the benefit of the mortgage, and Christopher Chevers and Andrew Crosby claimed the benefit of the term of 99 years. The trustees, however, sold the reversion of the term, and the equity of redemption, as forfeited estates, 'on a presumption' that the outlawry intended to be against Edward was valid despite the mistake as to the name. It appears that Christopher and Andrew Crosby's interest was not affected, since they did not claim through Edward, the alleged outlaw.

The trustees for forfeited estates sold the interest of Andrew, being the equity of redemption in the mortgaged lands and the reversion on the leased lands, to the Governor and Company for Making Hollow Sword-Blades in England, a corporation incorporated by charter in 1691 to establish the manufacture in Cumberland of swords for the army in the French war. It had been taken over by London merchants since its charter permitted it to purchase land.[661] The company is referred to in the present report variously as as the 'Hollow Blades', or the 'Sword Blades'. The company in turn sold these interests to Geoghegan, who had acted as solicitor for Christopher and Andrew Crosby.

In an apparent attempt to overcome the objection to the outlawry of 1695, Geoghegan in 1710 tried to obtain a new outlawry against Edward Chevers by alleging 'foreign treason' on his part committed against the government of Queen Anne after he arrived in France, and he obtained an indictment by a grand jury in Dublin. This was odd, since Edward Chevers had evidently died before the return of the writ,[662] but Geoghegan did not attempt to rely on this dubious outlawry either in *Geoghegan* v. *Chevers* in this manuscript or in *Chevers* v. *Geoghegan* reported in Brown, apparently because it became clear to him that under the Statute of Trustees, 1698,[663] the only land vested in the trustees of forfeited estates was that of persons outlawed before 1701.[664] He relied instead on the argument that the outlawry of 1695 was valid despite the mistake.

In 1710, as reported in Brown, Geoghegan brought a bill in the Irish court of Exchequer claiming an account and redemption of the mortgaged land against Andrew Chevers and Netterville, the original mortgagee. The result of a series of hearings was that the Irish court granted possession of some of the lands to Geoghegan, apparently on the arguments that Andrew should have lodged a claim challenging the sale by the trustees of forfeited estates and was precluded from doing so by 1710 by the Statute of Periods,[665] which had limited the time within which persons could

---

[659] Cokayne, *Complete Peerage*, ix. 354.

[660] 11 Will. III, c. 2. (11 & 12 Will. III in Ruffhead) (Eng.), 1698.

[661] See J. G. Simms, *The Williamite Confiscation in Ireland, 1690–1703* (1956), p. 151 et seq. On the history of the purchase of company charters, including the Sword Blades, see *HEL*, viii. 213–215.

[662] 6 Bro. P.C. 13, 2 E.R. 901.

[663] Above, n. 639.

[664] 6 Bro. P.C. 18, 2 E.R. 904; 11 Will. III, c. 2 (Eng.), 1698, s. 1.

[665] 6 Ann., c. 61 (G.B.), 1707 Statute of Periods, Act of Periods.

claim land from trustees of forfeited estates in Ireland to two years from 24 June 1708.[666] This was despite the fact that Andrew had actually remained in possession of the land and would have had to claim the 'return' not of the land itself but of the equity of redemption. The Irish court also had little sympathy for the view that the outlawry of Edward was invalid.

In 1720, after various other proceedings, Andrew Chevers appealed to the British House of Lords,[667] the proceedings in which are reported in Brown. His appeal was on the ground that he had not been given notice of Geoghegan's amended bill which was the basis of the decision of the Irish court. The British House of Lords reversed the decision of the Irish court and gave liberty to Geoghegan to bring another action in the Irish Court of Exchequer. This latter hearing does not appear in the manuscript and so unfortunately we do not learn the end of the story. The fire in the Public Record Office in 1922 may have deprived us of this, or perhaps it may eventually come to light from other sources.

Geoghegan v. *Chevers* in 1716 in these reports appears to be one hearing in the series which took place in the Irish court of Exchequer prior to the appeal reported in Brown. The report is in note form and is not easy to follow. There is much debate between counsel on whether or not a 'misnomer' was fatal to the outlawry of Edward Chevers, but Gilbert C.B. gives no opinion on the issue. He ends the hearing with the single sentence: 'The Statute of Periods is conclusive, where enjoyment has been under the conveyance of the trustees.'

Foreign education: Hyacinthus Nugent

Attorney General v. *Nugent*[668] concerns Hyacinthus Richard Nugent,[669] known as Baron Nugent of Riverston, or Lord Riverston, who had been outlawed under the Act against foreign education. He was the son of Thomas Nugent (d. 1715) who had been appointed chief justice of the King's Bench in 1687 by King James II, who also created him Baron Nugent of Riverston.[670] The report states that Hyacinthus was seven years old when he was attainted and outlawed. The evidence as to his age at the time of his outlawry is conflicting. According to Cokayne he was outlawed in 1694 when under the age of ten. At common law a male could not be outlawed

---

[666] Section 1.

[667] The headnote in 6 Bro. P.C. 12, 2 E.R. 900, suggests that the appeal was from the Irish court of Chancery, but the body of the report indicates that the appeal was from the decretal order of 30 April 1719 of the court of Exchequer, in which case it is not explained why a writ of error was not first brought in the Irish court of Exchequer Chamber.

[668] Below, p. 80.

[669] (c. 1687–1738). Cokayne, *Complete Peerage*, ix. 796–98, where he appears as Hyacinth Richard Nugent.

[670] Above, n. 595. The appointments and peerage had been made after James II had been declared to have 'vacated' the throne. Cokayne, *Complete Peerage*, i. 480, appendix F, makes the point that the English parliament declared James to have vacated the English throne on 11 December 1688, but that no similar declaration was made in Scotland until 4 April 1689, and that he remained *de facto* King of Ireland thereafter, and the sole *de facto* authority until the landing of General Schomberg in Ulster in August 1689. The title of King of Ireland had been adopted by Henry VIII in 1542 by the statute 33 Hen. VIII, c. 1 (Ir.) which declared that the King of England was also to be King of Ireland. If, therefore, James II had ceased to be King of England, then under the statute he had also ceased to be *de jure* King of Ireland, but his *de facto* authority was nevertheless accorded some recognition. Cokayne, *Complete Peerage*, ix. 796, notes that Thomas Nugent was referred to by General de Ginkell, commander in chief of King William's forces, in his letter of protection of 5 October 1691, as 'The Right Hon. Thomas, Lord Riverston', and by the commissioners of Irish forfeitures in an order of 5 July 1701, as 'The Lord Riverston'. Cokayne also notes that in 1839 the title 'Nugent of Riverston' was the only remaining such Jacobite peerage, the others having become extinct or merged. In that year a claim to it was made, but no decision pronounced. Assuming it existed, it merged in 1871 with the earldom of Westmeath.

under the age of twelve.[671] The Irish statute[672] did not specifically dispense with the age restriction in cases within the Act, but nor did it mention any age restriction in relation to the child. The preamble to the British Act of parliament obtained by his wife Susanna Catherina Nugent[673] says that Hyacinthus was outlawed at the age of thirteen, presumably on his return from France. In his petition of 23 February 1705 for reversal of his outlawry he stated that his father sent him to France at the age of five to be educated.[674] His wife in her petition of 16 June 1710 to the Irish parliament alleged that when she married him in 1703 he had conformed to the established Church of Ireland, but that 'he returned back to Popery, and is now in the actual service of the French King'.[675] She obtained an Irish Act[676] but later also obtained a private Act from the British parliament allowing her to sue for a jointure despite his outlawry.[677]

Hyacinthus did not get an Act reversing his outlawry from the Irish parliament, but he must have persuaded the British parliament that his conformity was genuine, because he applied successfully for a private Act from the British parliament in 1727.[678] The preamble to the British Act expresses some disapproval of the Irish Act in so far as it penalised children. It states that Hyacinthus was 'an infant of so tender years as made it impossible for him to be guilty of such treason or to use any endeavours to prevent his outlawry and the ill consequences thereof'.

THE DISPENSING POWER

The Act reversing the outlawry in Ireland of Hyacinthus Nugent, Lord Riverston, had the effect of exempting him from the Irish Act against foreign education. This seems to be evidence that it was no longer constitutionally acceptable to obtain a royal dispensation from the Irish Act. The dispensing power had been prohibited in England by the Bill of Rights. Although no similar Act had been passed in Ireland[679] the dispensing power in Ireland nevertheless appears to have been regarded as a dead letter after the end of James II's reign. It was certainly regarded as obsolete by the nineteenth century.[680] Further evidence comes from the end of the eighteenth century with the passing of the statute 32 Geo. III, c. 31 (Ir.), in 1792, the long title of which is *An Act to empower His Majesty to grant licences to alien lands in Mortmain*. The word 'empower' clearly implies that, without a statute, the king had no such power.

---

[671] Jacob, *Law Dictionary*; Co. Litt. 128a.

[672] 7 Will. III, c. 4 (Ir.), 1695.

[673] See Appendix A, below, p. 383.

[674] Cokayne, *Complete Peerage*, ix. 796; J.Ir.H.C. vol. 2, pt. 1, p. 432.

[675] Cokayne, *Complete Peerage*, ix. 796; J.Ir.H.C. vol. 2, pt. 1, p. 661. Sometime after his marriage he had gone to Spain and was later made a cornet in Lord Peterborough's Dragoons.

[676] For relief of Susanna-Catherina Nugent, 10 Ann. c. 4 (Ir.)(private), 1711–12, listed in vol. 8 of Irish *Statutes at Large*.

[677] 'An Act to enable Susanna Catherina Nugent to sue for, recover and hold the Portion of fourteen hundred Pounds, provided for her out of her Father's Estate, notwithstanding her Coverture and the Outlawry of her Husband Hyacinthus Nugent Esquire', Private Act, 1716, 3 Geo. I, c. 10, *HLRO*, Original Act, 3 Geo. I, no. 16. See Appendix A.

[678] 'An Act for Relief of Hyacinthus Richard Nugent, 1727', Private Act, 1 Geo. II, st. 2, c. 23, *HLRO*, Original Act, 1 Geo. II, st. 2, no. 46. See Appendix C.

[679] A Bill had been drafted but never enacted: W. N. Osborough, 'The Failure to Enact an Irish Bill of Rights: a Gap in Irish Constitutional History' (1998) 33 *Irish Jurist (n.s.)* 392–416.

[680] That was the view expressed in *Verschoyle* v. *Perkins* (1847) 13 Ir. Eq. R. 72. I am grateful to Prof. W. N. Osborough for this point.

The Act exempting Hyacinthus Nugent is further evidence that this was the position from the early eighteenth century.

The eschewing of the dispensing power in Ireland can in be traced back to the Irish Act of 1697[681] 'to hinder the reversal of outlawries' imposed after the siege of Limerick, in which provisos were inserted permitting specific individuals to petition the king for permission to bring writs of error seeking the reversal of their outlawries. In one case, that of Henry Crofton, a lord justice, Sir Charles Porter, petitioned the king and the Irish privy council for the proviso to be inserted, which was done.[682] There are also examples during the reign of Queen Anne of outlawries being reversed by writs of error, by way of exemptions from the Irish statute, brought under powers specifically granted to the Queen by private Acts of the British of parliament.[683] In other words, powers to provide for the reversal of outlawries under the Irish statute were specifically granted to William III and Anne by parliament.

KERRY BONDS

A Kerry bond was a bond, usually conditional, with a warrant of attorney incorporated within the bond itself.[684] It is not known how the name came about. Later, the treatment at common law and in equity of conditions in bonds will be dealt with,[685] but the present section is concerned with the peculiar characteristics of the Kerry bond and the warrant of attorney.

The warrant of attorney gave authority to an attorney to confess judgment on behalf of the promisor of the bond or to suffer judgment to be entered by default.[686] In other words, if the promisee sued to enforce the bond, the promisor had given up in advance the right to defend the action and the promisee could obtain judgment forthwith. It was thus a dangerous instrument for the promisor.

Bonds, conditional and otherwise, were common in England[687] and Ireland in the early eighteenth century and remained so until the nineteenth century when oral contracts became prevalent. Conditional bonds were enforced by the action of debt on an obligation.[688] Some conditional bonds were given in conjunction with a warrant of attorney, but the distinct feature of the Kerry bond was that the warrant was contained in the same document as the bond.[689] This would have some advantages

---

[681] 9 Will. III, c. 5 (Ir.) (to hinder reversal of outlawries).

[682] SP, Domestic, William III, vol. 1698, p. 347–348, 10 July.

[683] SP, Domestic, Anne, vol. 1702–03, pp. 99–100. Petition of John Mapas of Rochestown. The petition alleges he was outlawed at the age of seven, that the Irish Act (9 Will. III, c. 5 (Ir.), 1697) made the outlawry irreversible, that a clause had been added to a bill then going through parliament for the relief of Thomas Plunket, in similar terms, 'empowering Your Majesty to pardon the petitioner', and that he now petitions to bring writs of error to reverse the outlawry. See ibid., p. 400, which refers to the Act of parliament relating to Thomas and Catherine Plunket, Private Act, 1 Ann., c. 74, 1702, 'An Act for the Relief of Thomas Plunket Gentleman, and Katharine his Wife, with relation to the forfeited Estates in Ireland, and for empowering Her Majesty to grant Writs of Error for reversing the Outlawries against John Mapas and Lawrence Fitzgerald.'

[684] Ferguson, *Treatise*, iii. 1151–52.

[685] Below, p. cxxvii.

[686] See 3 & 4 Vict., c. 105 (Ir.), 1840, s. 10, which indicates that bonds with warrant of attorney were still in use in Ireland at the time, and provided that warrants of attorney were to be executed in the presence of an attorney except where collateral to a bond.

[687] See J. H. Baker, *An Introduction to English Legal History* (4th ed., 2002), pp. 323–26.

[688] Ibid.

[689] Ferguson, *Treatise*, iii. 1151; See, for example, the English cases of *Ivye* v. *Ashe* (1702) Colles 267, 1 E.R. 280 and *Stafford* v. *Southwick* (1692) 2 Vern 265, 23 E.R. 771 in which the bond and the warrant are clearly separate documents.

for the promisee. The warrant could not become separated from the bond among the promisee's papers. Also, there would never be an issue as to whether the warrant referred to that bond or to a different one. It had one disadvantage and that was that when judgment was about to entered upon it, the bond had to be filed with the warrant.[690] The promisee would therefore have to surrender his security to the court.

Howard noted that bonds with warrants of attorney were witnessed, filed with the court, and verified by the original witness when filed, since they were tantamount to judgments.[691] He pointed out the possibility of fraud and advised that great care should be taken when accepting them for filing. Ferguson writing in 1841 noted that Kerry bonds were commonly used in Ireland as a collateral security to a mortgage, covenant or debt.[692] In Ireland a statute of 1721[693] provided that after twenty years the defendant could plead payment in bar to an action on the bond. By 1823 the practice of the King's Bench in Ireland was that judgment could be entered on a bond within twenty years of the bond being issued without the leave of the court. After twenty years from the date of the warrant, however, judgment could not be entered on the bond without the leave of the court. If it were otherwise, the plaintiff, by delaying entry of the judgment for many years after the date of the bond, could deprive the defendant of the benefit of the statute.

By the early nineteenth century the courts construed Kerry bonds with great strictness.[694] The usefulness of such bonds was also limited by the necessity to hand them over to the court to be filed.[695]

Duffy v. *Bath*[696] in these reports is an instance of a bond with a warrant of attorney given to secure an account for the profits of the woods of Mellifont, and was probably a Kerry bond although it is not specifically stated to be so.

In *Marney* v. *Frissel*[697] a bond 'with warrant of attorney' was used as a promise to pay wages, and was also probably a Kerry bond, since that seems to have been the general form of bonds with warrants of attorney in Ireland at the time.[698] The case

---

[690] Ferguson, *Treatise*, iii. 1151–52.

[691] *Pleas Side*, preface, xxxvi. He does not use the phrase 'Kerry bond', but refers to bonds with warrants of attorney.

[692] Ferguson, *Treatise*, iii. 1140.

[693] 8 Geo. I, c. 4 (Ir.). See *Archer* v. *Carroll* (1823) 2 Fox & Sm. 43 at 44 n. (a).

[694] Per Bushe C.J., in *Archer* v. *Carroll* (1823) 2 Fox & Sm. 43; Practice directions (1830) 4 Law Rec. 1st ser. 156, (1834) 1 Glascock 54 (judgment could not be entered against the executor or administrator of the obligee unless they were specifically named in the warrant of attorney). *Anonymous* (1838) 1 Craw. & Dix Abr. Cas. 450, Queen's Bench (bond and warrant to obligee only, held insufficient to enter judgment against administrator of obligee), Practice direction (1830) 4 Law Rec. 1st series 186. *Anon.* 4 Law Rec. 1st series 94, Common Pleas (warrant to enter judgment against obligor held no authority to enter judgment against personal representative). *Executors of Bell* v. *Auchinleck and Woods* (1833) 1 Hay & Jo. 350, and other cases cited by Ferguson, *Treatise*, at iii. 1152, n. r, (judgment could only be entered at suit of person named in warrant and not in favour of the executors of the plaintiff unless they were expressly named, even if bond itself was in favour of the plaintiff and his executors and administrators). A late example of such a warrant of attorney seems to be *London Finance and Discount Company Ltd* v. *Butler* [1929] I.R. 90 (by a moneylender registered in Northern Ireland, held unenforceable).

[695] *Executors of Cinnamon* v. *McQuinlan* (1834) 2 Law Rec. 2nd series 120, Mr Andrews: 'in this case the warrant is included in the bond, it being what is generally called a Kerry bond, and the plaintiff did not wish to part with his security by filing it'. Court: 'We cannot alter the rule. He must file the bond and warrant; as they cannot be separated in this bond, they must both be filed. They will be safe in the office.'

[696] Below, p. 306.

[697] Below, p. 326.

[698] The phrase in the case, 'with warrant of attorney', rather than 'with *a* warrant of attorney' suggests that the latter was not a separate document.

also illustrates that relief could be obtained in equity from what appears to be an oppressive form by way of an action of account. In *Marney* the plaintiff, an old man of eighty, employed the defendant to write his letters for him. The defendant brought him a bond, in the form of a letter, to pay £120 with a penalty of £240, and with a warrant of attorney, and the old man signed it. The defendant got two persons in the house to witness it, which they did when they saw the old man's signature. The defendant later took out execution on the bond against the plaintiff's property, which mainly consisted of some 'gabbarts', the word used for lighters or barges, 'the working [of] them being his only subsistence', in the words of the judgment.[699] The plaintiff claimed an account on the basis that the bond was only given for the balance of wages due. The court granted him relief, from the suggestion of fraud, and exempted the gabbarts from the execution, 'on his giving security for the sum and costs', and in view of his being 'very poor', did not require him to pay the money into court.

There are two cases in these reports concerning Kerry bonds taken as bail bonds by the serjeant at arms, and one issue was as to the propriety of such an action. In each case the serjeant at arms, Richard Povey,[700] had been dispatched to arrest a defendant for contempt of court in failing to appear in court. Instead of taking the defendant into custody, the serjeant at arms had taken a Kerry bond from the defendant as a bail bond to secure his appearance in court. One issue seems to have been whether such a procedure was to be countenanced, since it was arguable that the serjeant at arms should not have taken the bond at all, but should have proceeded to arrest the defendant and place him in custody. The serjeant at arms was not, after all, in the position of a local sheriff who was required by statute to take a bail bond. The reports show that the courts were persuaded to allow these bonds because of the practical problem that there were no places available in civil jails, and even if there were, the defendant would face the appalling prospect of spending the summer in jail during the long vacation before he could appear in court in the new law term.

In *Higgins* v. *Butler*[701] the bond is stated to have a warrant of attorney 'in the body of it'. Singleton, the prime serjeant, says:

> When the party is apprehended, the serjeant has no gaol to lay him in, and the gaolers do, and may refuse him, so that taking this bond for his appearance is not only of necessity for the officer, but of great ease to the defendant, and if he don't think fit to execute it, he may go with the officer. This was the original design of these bonds, and this is usual practice, and the bond of itself is not irregular. If the officer must arrest, 'tis not unreasonable he should take bond for his security, or at least till the return of the writ, nor is it against law, there being no Act of Parliament to the contrary.

Later the recorder of Dublin says:[702] 'The taking [of] these bonds is an advantage to the party, for otherwise if he is attached in the beginning of the long vacation, he must lie in close custody all the summer.'

---

[699] One should explain that at this time, before Gandon's Custom House, completed in 1791, was built further down the Liffey, Thomas Burgh's Custom House of 1707 stood on the present Wellington Quay in the centre of the city, which made it necessary for ships to stand out at anchor and cargoes to be loaded onto lighters, or 'gabbarts', which had a shallow enough draught to be brought up the river to the Custom House.

[700] Povey is mentioned in a poem by Swift: Jonathan Swift, *Poetical Works*, (H. Davis, ed., 1967), at p. 592, 'An Epigram Inscribed to the Honourable Serjeant Kite'.

[701] Below, p. 318 [*404*].

[702] Below, p. 321.

In *Prendergast, one of the attorneys* v. *Green*,[703] in 1734 the bond is expressly said to be a 'Kerry bond'. Wainwright B. clearly had his doubts about the propriety of such a bond as a bail bond:[704]

> the original of the serjeant at arms was, that where the party had stood long in contempt, the court sent their own officer to bring him in immediately, but as they proceed now, justice instead of being furthered, is greatly delayed by them, to the expense and vexation of the suitor. If the defendant is rich, the serjeant will not return his writ till the plaintiff force him by several fines, and an attachment, and when he has returned a *cepi*,[705] if the defendant is able to indemnify him, he will not bring in the body, till he is compelled by the same methods.

But concludes: 'The court perhaps may connive at these bonds, which are really a great ease to the party in a long vacation . . . on these bonds they suffer him to go at large.'

The second issue before the court in *Higgins* v. *Butler*[706] was whether the serjeant at arms should have cashed in part of the bond to recoup his expenses in travelling to Clare, and, rather more dubiously, his 'day fees' which were allowed as the cost of keeping the defendant in custody before appearance. The report states:[707]

> In September Butler was taken, and executed a bail bond in the penalty of £1,500 with a warrant in the body of it to confess judgment, and the serjeant returned a *cepi corpus*,[708] and took out execution on the bond for £136, his day fees, and £15 his expenses in travelling to the county of Clare, and his 12 days stay there.

In the same case Bowes, the solicitor general, rejects the suggestion that the serjeant at arms should be treated by analogy as subject to the same rules as applied under the Act[709] requiring a sheriff to take bail, or regulating sheriffs in relation to writs:[710]

> It has been a constant practice in all the courts where attachments have issued to take these bonds for appearance, &c, and the courts have never censured them, because of their necessity, for the sheriffs are not obliged to take persons into custody who are attach[ed] on contempts of your courts. And as very many be taken up, and there is no public gaol for them, it was not the design of the court they should be close confined till they gave particular orders, for which there are frequent motions.

> But 'tis said, when these bonds lie for a great while, 'tis an oppression to sue for the whole sum. By the condition of the bond he is only to be paid his due fees, & the swelling the sum is not the act of the officer but of the party. He knew he ought to appear and discharge his contempts, and he might have put an end to them.

The position was complicated by subsidiary issues. Should the serjeant at arms have tried to recover his fees before the defendant actually appeared, or even before some of them were proved to be due, such as the day fees? Should he have done so before

---

[703] Below, p. 317 [*403*].
[704] Below, p. 318 [*404*].
[705] L. perfect of *capio*, i.e. I have taken, or seized.
[706] Below, p. 318 [*404*].
[707] Below, p. 318.
[708] L. I have taken the body.
[709] Above, n. 377.
[710] 6 Ann. c. 7 (Ir.), 1707, below, p. 320.

he was pressed by the plaintiff to enforce the bond? The petition of the serjeant at arms put the problem from his point of view. He and his assistant, the pursuivant:

> were often at great expense in searching for those against whom attachments issued, and could not take them, and that the party after issued a *supersedeas*[711] without paying them their fees.

This was clearly a serious issue which the serjeant at arms was seeking to resolve. There is a suggestion that it is a test case. The court orders that in future 'when an attachment issued to the serjeant, or pursuivant, no discharge from the attorney should hinder execution, unless their fees were first paid, and that no *supersedeas* should issue till they were first paid, and that they may renew the attachments till their fees were paid'.

As to the issue whether the serjeant should be subject to the same rules as a sheriff, Wainwright B. and Marlay C.B. refuse to resolve the issue on motion. They also express their doubts as to the propriety of the serjeant's action. The report ends by stating that the serjeant at arms had noted the doubts of the court and had reached agreement with the parties.[712]

EQUITY

Finding agreements in equity

In the first section below on conditional bonds there is an example of equity showing a willingness to find and enforce an agreement where in the past it would have left the plaintiff to the remedy at common law, and in the second section to spell out an agreement from a transaction which was void at common law, which may have been novel. This may suggest a more general movement of ideas in this direction.

Conditional bonds and substantive agreements

In this section we examine the change in the attitude of equity towards conditions in bonds and the growth of a willingness to treat them as giving rise to obligations.

In the centuries before the eighteenth century the common method of entering into an important written agreement was for one or both parties to enter into a conditional bond. Suppose A's daughter was to marry B's son. A agreed that he would settle land of a certain value on the couple. If he failed to do so, a lump sum would be payable as a penalty. However, the bond which gave legal expression to this agreement took a rather curious form. The bond (or obligation), was a document under seal in the form that A acknowledged that he owed B a sum of money, the penalty, as a present debt,[713] but that the obligation to pay this money would become void if A performed the condition, in this example, settling the land on the couple.[714] The condition set out the terms of the agreement (to settle the land, etc.) or referred to more detailed terms set out in an indenture. The advantage, over a covenant, was that a liquidated sum, fixed in advance, could be obtained, as a

---

[711] L. 'you shall desist'. A writ which lay in various cases to supersede or to stay proceedings as improper for some reason, and used to stay proceedings in a lower court, or to remove them from one court to another.

[712] Below, p. 323.

[713] In the example, the acknowledgement of a present debt was therefore a fiction.

[714] Baker, *Introduction*, p. 323–24; A. W. B. Simpson, *A History of the Common Law of Contract: The Rise of the Action of Assumpsit* (1975), at pp. 90–117.

debt, for non-performance of the condition.[715] The penalty, or liquidated sum, was not, strictly speaking, damages, but in practice the parties set the amount so that it was in effect a pre-estimate of loss. The common law was content to recognize, as the form of the bond itself set out, that there was only one obligation, the obligation to pay the penalty. The significance of the condition was simply that performance of it was a defence to an action on the bond. By the eighteenth century it is true that the common law, partly assisted by statute, had come to recognize that there was an obligation behind the condition, and to treat the liquidated sum as an estimate of damages, which it could therefore modify, but that was the extent of its remedy.[716]

As to equity, in the past it had been content in such a case to leave B to his common law remedy.[717] It is, however, clear from these reports that in the early eighteenth century, equity took a different approach. Now, equity looked beyond the form to recognize the agreement that lay behind it. It was prepared, in suitable cases, to recognize that there were two alternative obligations: (a) to pay the sum, and (b) to perform the agreement represented in the form of the condition. Furthermore, equity came to regard (b) as the primary obligation. Equity had the means to enforce the performance of the agreement, by specific performance, and not merely to award damages for non-performance. Equity came to recognize, in other words, that the conditional bond took the form that it did, not because that reflected the actual agreement between the parties, but because it took into account the limited remedies available at common law. It was the only way at common law that the promissor could be indirectly induced to perform the agreement.

This new attitude in equity is evident in the 1733 case of *Ivers* v. *Ivers*.[718] John Ivers had married Helen Fitzgerald in 1692 and there were four sons and five daughters of the marriage. By marriage articles of 1692 he was constrained by certain covenants. Helen died, and John married Jane (the report does not give her maiden name) in 1718. He evidently mistreated his eldest son, Henry, who was his son by his first marriage, for St Leger B. says of Henry that 'his father bred him up in poverty and obscurity, and from the beginning he intended to ruin him, for he sold £10,000 worth of the estate before he came of age'.[719] In order to provide for Jane, John Ivers induced Henry to release him, John, from the covenants in the articles of 1692 in consideration for entering into a settlement, dated 1718, to settle his real estate on his sons, but subject to a *power* to grant any part of the real estate in favour of any wife he, or his sons, might marry. Although the power included the sons, the evident intent was that it would enable John Ivers to provide for his second wife. This he did by entering into a bond with Jephson, described as Jane's counsel,[720] under which he would, after marriage and on the request of Jephson, settle land to the value of £200 a year on his second wife for life as her jointure, or pay a penalty of £2,000. Jane was not a party to the bond. John drew up a draft of the jointure deed, but never executed it. Jephson never requested the settlement on Jane. John Ivers lived another eleven years. Some time before his death he had given his children part

---

[715] Baker, ibid.

[716] See the *Prendergast* case below, p. cxxx and n. 732.

[717] Although it had given relief against forfeiture of the penalty in a growing number of instances in England since at least the time of Elizabeth I: Simpson, *History of Contract*, pp. 118–119.

[718] Below, p. 188 [*240*].

[719] Below, p. 199 [*255*].

[720] St Leger B., below, p. 200 [*256*], and p. 200 n. 985.

of his personal estate. A few days before his death he made a will leaving the rest of his personal estate and all his real estate to his children. Hasset, the attorney or barrister[721] called to draw up the will, asked to see the marriage articles of 1718. The eldest son, Henry brought the articles and other documents and the draft jointure deed was among them. Hasset suggested that, in the interests of Jane, John should execute it. John said he would do so the following Monday, some four days hence. On the following Monday, John died without executing the deed.

Jane in the present case filed a bill claiming either, 1. that Henry, the eldest son, should be compelled execute a settlement in terms of the condition of the bond which she alleged 'is in nature of an agreement to settle £200 a year according to his power' or, 2. that if the bond was not to be taken as an agreement to settle, or an execution of his power, it should be satisfied out of the personal assets of John's estate.

The prime serjeant, Singleton, for the plaintiff, notes a change in the attitude of equity:[722]

> Formerly I allow courts of equity turned the obligee to law, but now they proceed on another foot, that the condition is an agreement to settle, and she has the choice of two remedies, and to fix her to one, to confine her to law, is to destroy that election.

It is also mentioned in the report that there could be no action at law, because Jephson never requested John to settle the jointure.[723]

The court accepted that the plaintiff was a 'purchaser', at least under the settlement of 1718, without notice of any impropriety in the way it was obtained. The court also accepted that although in the past the plaintiff would have been confined to the penalty at law, the attitude of equity had changed. Wainwright B. said:[724]

> By the old resolutions indeed the parties to these bonds have been left to law to the remedy they had provided for themselves by the penalty, but the modern authorities run otherwise, and the court has considered them as contracts or agreements, and carried them into execution.

The chief baron agreed:[725]

> This contract then to settle is what in justice he ought to perform, and it don't appear that he can do it otherwise. Whatever it may have been formerly, it is not the present opinion that the party is bound up by[726] what they have held themselves to, and this was the opinion of the Lords in the case of *Sir Thomas Prendergast* v. *Sir Toby Butler*[727] on an appeal from a decree of the court of Chancery in Ireland.

As to the case at hand, Jane could not sue at law on the bond since she was not a party to it, and John Ivers was dead. Jane therefore sought specific performance of the power which Henry had under the settlement of 1718. The court held that land to the value in the bond should be settled on Jane and the arrears since John's death

---

[721] Counsel by the name of Hasset addresses the court in *Blenerhasset* v. *Babington*, below, p. 224.

[722] Below, p. 195 [*250*].

[723] Wainwright B., below p. 190.

[724] Below, p. 199 [*255*].

[725] Below, p. 201 [*258*].

[726] I.e. limited to.

[727] *Butler* v. *Prendergast* (1720) 4 Bro. P.C. 2nd ed. 175, 2 E.R. 119, from the Irish Chancery. The Irish proceedings are cited at p. 196 [*251*] as *Lady Prendergast* v. *Sir Toby Butler*, with the marginal note 'Mes App. D.193, E.851.'

made a charge on the land. The court was faced with two relatively innocent parties. As for Henry, he was treated unfairly by his father, and was not a party to the bond, but he was a party to the settlement of 1718 and therefore to the agreement on which the bond was based. He had also obtained a benefit under the settlement of 1718: an annual allowance and a life estate after his father, albeit subject to the provisions for the younger children and an estate burdened by debt. Wainwright B. dismissed the suggestion of fraud in the following terms:[728] 'Whatever fraud or hardship appears on the son, the plaintiff not being accessory to it, cannot be affected by it, and she is a purchaser not only from the father, but from Henry the son, who joined in creating this power, the day she was married, and [the day] that John executed the bond.' The decision of the court seems harsh in relation to Henry, but Jane was an entirely innocent party who would be left with nothing from the marriage if the settlement was not made on her. Jane had agreed to the marriage in reliance on the arrangements for her future security. St Leger B., however, dissented, regarding the fraud on Henry as more significant, as well as the fact that Jane was a witness to the settlement and Jephson was present.

One final point: John Ivers does not seem to have been unusual in his treatment of his second wife. Malone, one of the counsel in the case, comments that:[729] 'nothing is more common in this kingdom than not to make a provision for a second wife, or her issue, but leave them to the father's industry'.

In *Butler* v. *Prendergast* equity also found a way of awarding damages for breach of the agreement in a suitable case. Butler had induced Prendergast to sell valuable woods on his land to Ryan, who was Butler's servant. The sale exempted saplings of a certain size. Butler and Ryan entered into a bond with Prendergast to that effect, but only Ryan, and not Butler, was made a party to the condition. This was held to be a fraud on Prendergast. The penalty in the condition was to pay a fixed amount for each sapling wrongly cut down. Butler proceeded to cut down most of the saplings. Ryan disappeared. Prendergast could not sue at law to recover the penalty, since he was not a party to the condition. In the Irish Chancery Lord Midleton L.C., assisted by Whitshed C.J.C.P. and Dolbin J., held that Prendergast could maintain an action in equity and ordered that the plaintiff could proceed by feigned action at law to have the amount of damages tried by a jury.[730] The House of Lords upheld this with a minor variation as to the method of assessing damages.

By the early eighteenth century a similar development had occurred in the common law courts.[731] In cases on a penal bonds, they had begun to leave to a jury the issue of the actual damages for non-performance.[732] The common law had begun to recognize the obligation that lay behind the penalty.

---

[728] Below, p. 199.

[729] Below, p. 193 [*246*].

[730] *Butler* v. *Prendergast* (1720) 2 E.R. 119 at 121.

[731] Simpson, *History of Contract*, p. 122, dates the adoption by the common law courts of the principle in equity to the 1670s.

[732] By the 1670s judgment could be entered for the whole penalty, but the defendant could only recover the damages assessed by the jury. The action would be stayed on payment of these damages and costs: Simpson, *History of Contract*, p. 122. The English statute 8 & 9 Will. III, c. 11 (Eng.), 1696, s. 8, recited this and allowed the party alleging breaches to specify them. It was then the duty of the jury to assess damages for each breach. The statute 4 & 5 Ann., c. 3 (Eng.), 1705 (c. 16 in Ruffhead) authorized the court to discharge an obligor who brought into court the principal, interest and costs due on a money bond, and reversed the common law rule by allowing payment to be pleaded in bar to an action on a bond without acquittance by deed. The same was provided in Ireland by 9 Will. III, c. 10 (Ir.), 1697 and 6 Ann. c. 10 (Ir.), 1707 s. 13.

These developments meant that the conditional bond had come to have little, if any, advantage over covenant.[733] As Calaghan put it in argument in *Ivers*: 'Now a bond in equity is the same as covenant.'[734] They must also account for the use, or increased use, in some cases at least, of the conditional bond with warrant of attorney, and the special form of it in Ireland, the Kerry bond.[735] By that means the promisee could obtain, in effect, judgment on the penalty in advance, and so avoid the risk that a jury would award a lower amount as damages. However, it would be unwise for anyone to agree to such a bond if the penalty was much in excess of the value of the performance, and so they were probably used in more limited circumstances than the older bonds.

Transactions void at law, agreement in equity

The second instance of the growing willingness of equity to recognize and enforce an agreement is in the case of leases which failed as legal leases for want of a formality. This is an early attempt at the doctrine which is more familiar to modern property lawyers in the English cases of *Parker* v. *Taswell*[736] and *Walsh* v. *Lonsdale*.[737] The doctrine of those cases is that where there is a failed lease equity may consider it to be an agreement to make a new lease, and if it is a contract of which equity would grant specific performance, then the court will do so, and in the meantime, under the doctrine that equity regards as done that which ought to be done, it will treat the agreement as creating a lease in equity. That position is not fully reached in these reports but there are preliminary steps in that direction.

In *Hodson* v. *Rowley*[738] in 1733 the purported lease was void at law because it had only been made in the name of the attorney and signed by him.[739] The case in fact concerns whether there was sufficient evidence of the lease at all. Calaghan, counsel in the case, makes the point that acceptance of rent by the lessor does not confirm a lease which is void, and cites Lord Midleton L.C. in an unreported Irish case, *Butler* v. *Worth* for this proposition. The chief baron then comments: 'But Lord Midleton said it might amount to a new agreement.' Calaghan responds that 'it would not amount to a new agreement, because he was a tenant at will'. This was a correct statement of the *common law* position: if a person went into possession under a void lease, the common law ignored the lease and looked at the objective facts. It held him to be a tenant at will, until he paid rent and then to be a tenant from year to year if the rent was paid quarterly, etc. The argument then moves on. The case is resumed at a later hearing.[740] While Marlay C.B. is delivering judgment counsel, possibly Lindsay, interrupts and objects:[741] 'though an interest which is void at law can't be confirmed by a subsequent act, yet such an act may in equity amount to a new agreement'. Marlay C.B. does not reject the point, but decides that there is insufficient evidence of the lease in any case.

---

[733] There could still be procedural benefits. Judgment entered for a penal sum could be drawn against should further loss be incurred, avoiding the need for a new action. See Baker, *Introduction*, pp. 325–26.

[734] Below, p. 196.

[735] Above, p. cxxiii.

[736] (1858) 2 De G. & J. 559, 44 E.R. 1106.

[737] (1882) 21 Ch. D. 9.

[738] Below, p. 122 [*149*].

[739] Calaghan, below, p. 123 [*151*].

[740] Below, p. 125 [*161*].

[741] Below, p. 132 [*163*].

Proprietary estoppel: an early instinctive example

Nowland v. *Bagget*[742] is a brief report of an otherwise unreported decision of Lord Midleton L.C. The plaintiff, Nowland, was granted a lease by the defendant's father. Later, the father offered Nowland a lease for lives, which was more advantageous to Nowland. He agreed and surrendered his existing lease. Unknown to him, the father had no power under his marriage settlement to make a lease for lives. The father died, and his son, the defendant, brought an ejectment at common law to evict Nowland. Nowland then brought a bill in equity to reinstate the surrendered lease. Lord Midleton L.C. granted the decree, and an account for the difference in rent in the meantime.

There was no question here of treating the purported lease as a new agreement because the father had no power to grant the lease in the first place. But would it be right for the son to insist on his strict legal rights and evict Nowland? The note of the decision is brief and does not make the reason explicit, but there is no doubt as to its correctness. If the son, who was in a better position than Nowland to know his father's powers under the marriage settlement, wanted to insist on the invalidity of the new lease, he could not ignore the fact that Nowland was induced to surrender a perfectly good lease in order to get the new one. If the agreement cannot be performed, there must be restitution. The son must put Nowland back in the position he was in before the agreement was made. It is a pity that we do not have Midleton's judgment, because the decision is an early example of what today would be called proprietary estoppel. The reasons would be articulated in terms of detrimental reliance: Nowland, by surrendering a valid lease, relied on the assurance, express or implied, of the father that the new lease would be valid, and Nowland would suffer a detriment if he were then to be evicted from the land. This raised an equity in his favour and the obvious remedy to satisfy it is to grant what the plaintiff asks, the restoration of the original lease.

Registration of deeds and access to case reports

The Registration of Deeds Act, 1707, provided that all deeds concerning land executed after 25 March 1708 should be registered, and if not, they were declared to be 'fraudulent and void'.[743] In 1715, Arthur, earl of Granard, granted a lease of part of his estate called Drumceele, to Deniston. Deniston 'who lived in the remotest part of Ireland'[744] was unaware of the statute and failed to register the deed. In 1717, the earl being seriously in debt, his son, Lord Forbes, agreed to pay his father's debts in consideration of his father assigning his life estate under the family settlement to trustees for Lord Forbes. Lord Forbes looked into the estate and found that the lease to Deniston had been let at a considerable under-value, and since the document setting it out was unregistered, he brought ejectment against Deniston. He obtained a verdict in his favour at the assizes in 1719, and judgment was given in his favour by the court of King's Bench in 1720. Deniston then filed a bill in the court of Chancery in Ireland, arguing that the trustees for Forbes had actual notice of the unregistered deed when he obtained his father's life estate, and should be bound in equity by the

---

[742] Below, p. 230 [297].

[743] 6 Ann. c. 2 (Ir.), 1707. A memorial of the deed, setting out its essential details, was registered, rather than the deed itself. The statute at first included wills, but these were later excluded. At the time of writing, the statute is still in force, and in use, in the Republic.

[744] 13 and 19 Vin. Abr.; 2 Eq. Cas. Abr.

lease, despite the words of the statute. The lord chancellor, Lord Midleton, held that the trustees had indeed had actual notice of the unregistered lease, and that therefore the purchase by the trustees was fraudulent. He granted a perpetual injunction preventing the trustees of Forbes taking any further proceedings at law during the term of the lease. Forbes and the trustees appealed against this to the British House of Lords, which, in 1722, reversed the court of Chancery in Ireland but only on the point that the lease was binding on Forbes only during the life of the earl, since the lease was created out of his life estate. The main point was upheld, that actual notice bound a purchaser in equity despite the clear words of the Act, because, it was argued, the Act was intended to prevent fraud and so could not itself be used as a means of it.[745]

The point of interest here is that the same point is alluded to briefly by counsel, Calaghan, in the present reports in *Blenershasset* v. *Babington*[746] in 1733. He mentions that Gilbert C.B., in a case identified only as *Costegan*,[747] had decided that at common law actual notice was irrelevant but that 'it may be otherwise in equity'. In other words, Calaghan, who was a leading member of the Irish bar at the time and whose instincts were correct, was nevertheless unaware of the decision, eleven years before, of the British House of Lords . This must say something about the availability at the time, or lack of it, of British precedents in Ireland, even those on appeal from Ireland. *Forbes* v. *Deniston* is reported by Brown, but the first edition of Brown's *Parliamentary Cases* was only published towards the end of the century in 1779.[748]

Interestingly, earlier in the present reports, in 1731, Calaghan cites the case of *Cusack*[749] v. *Cusack* decided in 1714 in the Irish Chancery before Sir Constantine Phipps L.C., and Calaghan then notes that the British House of Lords had reversed the Irish Chancery. This judgment was later reported in 5 Bro. 2nd ed. 116, 2 E.R. 570, but it seems that some British House of Lords judgments were available to him at the time of the present reports.

A 'TREATY OF CONCUBINAGE'

Marriage, in the case of the gentry and aristocracy in the eighteenth century, was often more a matter of property agreements between the groom and the father of the bride than a romantic relationship between the man and the woman concerned. Love was therefore often found outside marriage. Just as marriage was in a sense debased by property concerns, so was there a corresponding tolerance of extra-marital sexual relationships. In *Cromwell Price* v. *Sophy Hamilton*[750] in the Exchequer in 1732 the plaintiff had entered into what is described as a 'treaty of concubinage'

---

[745] *Forbes* v. *Deniston* (1722) 4 Bro. P.C. 189, 2 E.R. 129. The point is still valid in Ireland: *Re Fuller* [1982] I.R. 161. After the Judicature Act, 1877 (Ir.), the rule in equity of course prevails.

[746] Below, p. 223.

[747] Below, p. 224.

[748] See also *Maingay* v. *Gahan* (1793) Ir. Term Rep. 1, at the end of the century in which Yelverton C.B., Power, Hamilton and Metge BB. in Exchequer relied on the case of *Henshaw* v. *Pleasance* (1778) 2 Black. W. 1174, 96 E.R. 612, but in Exchequer Chamber where the case was heard by Lord Clonmell, Lord Carleton and Viscount Fitzgibbon L.C., Fitzgibbon mentions (at p. 79) that on a visit to Westminster he had discussed the issue with a judge of the King's Bench there, who told him that the general view was that *Henshaw* v. *Pleasance* was not regarded as good law and would be overruled if it came before the courts again.

[749] Below, p. 43.

[750] Below, p. 140.

with the defendant. He alleged that she had represented herself to be a woman of virtue, and that she had prevailed on him, while under the influence of alcohol, to settle an annuity of £30 a year on her. It was to be increased to £40 after the death of his father, or she was to have £240. He also alleged that Sophy was in the habit of ensnaring young heirs in this way and sought an injunction to stay a trial at law.

Sophy, in her disarming answer, denied that she had ever represented herself to be a woman of virtue, asserted that the plaintiff voluntarily executed the deed of annuity 'after a night's deliberation', and that the consideration was 'agreeable favours'. She added that if the agreement was immoral or illegal, then the plaintiff was as guilty as she was.

St Leger B. refused the injunction 'because the deed was voluntary and the provision small, and the plaintiff was not imposed on by the defendant'. He notably did not treat the agreement as tainted by immorality.

POPERY ACTS, NATURAL RIGHTS, AND LAWYER–CLIENT PRIVILEGE

The disabilities and penalties imposed on Catholics by the Popery Acts, part of what are now known as the Penal Laws,[751] seem to have been applied, on the evidence of these reports, in a way which undermined further the common law's own protection of natural rights, in the form of lawyer/client privilege, and the privilege against self-incrimination. The judiciary seem to have been well aware of this, and somewhat uneasy about it, but that does not appear to have inhibited them.

First, the main provisions of the Popery Acts will be outlined as they applied to property.

Any Catholic who did not conform to the Church of Ireland by the prescribed oaths suffered the penalties and disabilities under the statutes of Queen Anne. The oaths had to be sworn and the conformity made before a Church of Ireland congregation. The provisions as to property were briefly as follows.

Under 'An act to prevent the further growth of popery',[752] section 3, if the eldest son of a Catholic became a member of the Church of Ireland during his father's lifetime, then any land of which the Catholic parent had been seised in fee tail or fee simple would from then on vest in the parent for a life estate only, the remainder vesting in interest in the son.

Under section 7 any Catholic who took property by devise, descent at common law, gift, remainder or trust had six months in which to conform to the established church. If he did not do so, then he retained only a life interest and the remainder vested in his nearest Protestant relative.

Under section 6, a Catholic could not purchase land in his or her own name, or in the name of any other person to his or her own use, or in trust for him or her,

---

[751] A point needs to be made as to terminology. Part of what are known today as the Penal Laws were known at the time of these reports, at least by those in authority, as the Popery Acts. The term is to be rejected today as sectarian, but it has been retained in this introduction, partly because it is the term used in these reports and it therefore avoids possible confusion, and also because the Popery Acts were mainly concerned with property and were only a part of a larger body of legislation which came to be known collectively as the Penal Laws.

[752] The statute 2 Ann., c. 6 (Ir.), 1703. On the Popery Acts as to property generally, see W. N. Osborough 'Catholics, Land and the Popery Acts of Anne' in Wheelan and Power, eds., *Endurance and Emergence: Catholics in Ireland in the Eighteenth Century* and in W. N. Osborough, *Studies in Irish Legal History* (Dublin 1999).

other than a lease not exceeding 31 years where the rent was not less than two thirds of the improved yearly value.

Under the 'Gavelkind Clause',[753] section 10 of the 1703 Act, land held by a Catholic in fee simple or fee tail was considered to be 'in the nature of gavelkind' and was to be divided among the sons of the landowner on the landowner's death. The provisions of the Act overrode a gift in a will of real property.[754] The section was repealed by the Catholic Relief Act, 1778, s. 1[755] and the estates of Catholics after that date descended as before at common law.

Under a further proviso in the Act, if at the Catholic father's death the eldest son was or became a Protestant, the son took the fee simple or fee tail as heir at common law.[756]

A court had power to provide maintenance for a Protestant child out of the estate of a Catholic parent[757] and to make a jointure for a conforming wife of a Catholic, but not exceeding his power to do so, normally circumscribed by his marriage articles.[758]

The Act of 1709, 8 Ann., c. 3 (Ir.), 'An Act for explaining and amending an act intituled, an Act to prevent the further growth of popery', introduced the Protestant 'discoveror' as a feature of the Popery Acts.[759] Under section 27 of the Act any Protestant was given *locus standi* to challenge the legality of a conveyance prohibited to Catholics. The reward for a successful challenge was that the Protestant discoveror could keep the land for the period of the estate purported to be conveyed, a huge incentive. The legal device was not an innovation: common informers had previously been rewarded with part of the penalty imposed on a convicted person, under the *qui tam* procedure, but the reward was enormously increased in the case of the successful Protestant discoveror.

In two of the cases, *Digby* v. *Hanly* and *Green* v. *Ryland*, the issue was whether an attorney or barrister could be compelled to give evidence as to his knowledge of his client's affairs. In all three of the cases the allegation was that the challenge by the ostensible Protestant discoveror was a sham, that it was a collusive action whereby the discoveror, if successful, would hold the land in trust for the Catholic, whom he or she had apparently displaced. First, the two cases on lawyer/client privilege will be dealt with.

In *Digby* v. *Hanly*[760] the attorney objected that any knowledge of the matters alleged came to him as agent of his client. The court decided on the narrow ground that he did not allege that the knowledge came to him *only* as agent of his client. This therefore avoided a decision on the privilege issue, but such a case does occur later

---

[753] In Ireland 'gavelkind' was used to refer to the Brehon law of succession whereby land was divided among all the sons. The practice continued in some families until the 1590s: Nicholls, 'Some Documents on Irish Law and Custom in the Sixteenth Century' (1970) 26 *Analecta Hibernica* 105, at 106. The name was given to it by the Anglo-Normans because it reminded them of English gavelkind, an Anglo-Saxon form of succession in Kent recognized by the Normans after the Conquest.

[754] *Burke* v. *Morgan* (1717) 5 Bro. P. C. 2nd ed. 365; 2 E.R. 734.

[755] 17 & 18 Geo. III, c. 49 (Ir.), 1777–78; Co.Litt., 18th ed., 176a n. 1.

[756] 1703 Act, s. 12.

[757] Under s. 3 of the 1703 Act.

[758] Under s. 14 of the 1709 Act.

[759] An earlier Act had in fact introduced the Protestant discoveror for a limited purpose. The Act 11 Will. III, c. 2 (Eng.), 1698 vested forfeited estates in Ireland in trustees. 1 Ann., c. 6 (Eng.), 1702, ss. 133–34, provided that trustees could only sell them to Protestants, and introduced the discoveror.

[760] Below, p. 11 [*11*].

in *Green* v. *Ryland* in 1733,[761] where Mr Baron Wainwright notes at the beginning of his judgment that several cases await the result of the judgment.

In *Green* the allegation was that Fitzgerald, a Catholic, had bought lands in breach of the Acts, and that when challenged by a real Protestant discoveror, Gernon, he had then arranged with his attorney, Hiffernam, to buy off Gernon and to set up instead a false Protestant discoveror, Ryland, who would if successful, have held the land in trust for Fitzgerald. The attorney, Hiffernam, when called upon to appear as a witness against Fitzgerald, objected that to force him to answer would be to make him break his oath and that even in cases of 'treason, or felony, an attorney or barrister is not to disclose what they know as counsel'. There was nothing in the Act creating an exception to the normal rule of lawyer/client privilege. Nevertheless, the court decided he was compellable against his client. Wainwright B.[762] noted first that 'The statute was made to establish lands in the hands of Protestants, and is one of the pillars of the government.' He goes on to make the point that the privilege is that of the client, not of the lawyer, decides that the Act expressly removes it, but in doing so takes away a 'natural right' of the client:[763]

> what the defendant insists on as the privilege of the attorney, is really the privilege of the client, and since the client is barred by the statute from pleading or demurring, his attorney who is privileged only on his account, shall answer and discover as well as he, and the Act takes this natural right from the party himself, so it must be understood to do from the attorney, who is privileged only in regard to his client.

The 'natural right' here is not merely the right against self-incrimination as to a criminal offence, which if that alone were the reason, might not have been conceded, but the prejudice the client might suffer in the pursuit even of his legitimate rights, were his confidences to be disclosed. Wainwright is quite open about the purpose of the Popery Acts and describes them as a 'pillar of the government', but gives no indication of how he reconciles that with the contradiction that they, in his view, take away natural rights.

Marlay C.B., on the other hand, is not prepared to concede the point about natural rights in the case before him:

> 'Tis no injury or contrary to the law of nature to discover an unlawful confidence, but on the contrary the party is obliged to discover it, for confidence is grounded on a presumption that the transaction is fair . . . nobody can have a natural right to do a thing unlawful.

The real distinction would seem to be that, if the attorney was the passive recipient of the information, then the privilege would have applied at common law, but the attorney could not then continue to represent the client. If the attorney knew, but continued to represent him, then he would be a party to a conspiracy to deceive the court. If there was evidence of that from another source, the attorney would then be liable. But Marlay's point as to the privilege involves a circular argument: what the attorney knew could only be discovered if he was himself compellable to give evidence, and that is the point at issue.

In other cases, the ostensible Protestant discoveror was a son or daughter of the Catholic landowner, the son or daughter having converted and brought the action for discovery against his or her own parent. The suspicion was that the conversion was

---

[761] Below, p. 211 [*273*] and p. 356.
[762] Below, p. 213 [*274*].
[763] Below, p. 214.

not genuine and that the purpose of the action was to prevent any genuine Protestant discoveror from bringing a discovery. In a number of cases the courts responded to the suspicion by examining the reality of the conformity, holding that someone who had apparently conformed to the Church of Ireland was still in reality a Catholic. Under a statute of 1697 a Protestant man who married a Catholic woman was deemed to be a Catholic.[764] The courts extended this concept of 'constructive papist'.

In *Roderick* v. *Osborn*[765] the court engages in the less certain exercise of drawing an inference from the facts. Osborn was a Catholic and indebted to Chily. Chily filed a bill of discovery. Osborn's daughter, Helen, then conformed and filed her own bill, as a discoveror against her own father. She petitioned to be allowed to do so as a pauper and to defend the suit against Chily. St Leger B., however, did not accept that Helen's conformity was genuine. In his view, she had pretended to conform in order to protect her father's property and to forestall Chily, the real discoveror:

> It don't appear that Helen is a real Protestant discoveror, because her conforming was approved of by her father as a proper means to bring this bill of discovery for the maintenance of the family, whereas all friendship is generally broke off where there is a real conformity and discovery, and the daughter is more to be suspected as a discoveror for the family than a creditor.

It remains a matter of speculation as to how frequent these collusive actions by sham discoverors were and how effective the courts were in countering them. The courts' treatment of them might also have introduced a degree of uncertainty into conveyancing which could have caused problems for the system as whole.

COMMERCIAL LAW AND TRADE

A theme that occurs many times in the reports is the importance attached to encouraging trade and commerce and there is concern that decisions of the courts should not hamper their development and might even promote it.

Before dealing with some points of detail it is necessary to set the context by discussing the status of wagering contracts at the time.

Wagering contracts

Wagering contracts were not void at common law, since they satisfied the technical tests of a contract,[766] and so the winner could sue the loser for the money won. But there were numerous grounds on which they would not be enforced, as, for example, if the subject matter was immoral or against the interests or feelings of third parties.[767] The suppression of wagering contracts by statute was in pursuit of public policy, but that policy varied considerably from time to time. In the medieval period, a fascination with games of chance or skill was seen as detracting from archery practice, which was compulsory, and hence as endangering the defence

---

[764] 9 Will. III, c. 3 (Ir.), s. 2. If his wife converted within a year, the disabilities ceased: s. 2. Disabilities under the Act also applied to Protestant women who married Catholic men. Under 2 Ann. c. 6 (Ir.), 1703, there had to be a conviction before the penalties applied. Howard, *Equity Side*, i. 259, mentions two cases on the point, *Babe* v. *O'Neil* and *Dobbins* v. *Purcel* in the time of West L.C.

[765] Below, p. 78 [92].

[766] Such as consideration, etc. See Fletcher Moulton L.J. in *Moulis* v. *Owen* [1907] 1 K.B. 746, at 758 et seq.

[767] G. H. Treitel, *The Law of Contract* (11th ed., 2003) p. 519; Brown, *Law Dictionary* 'Wagering'; *Thackoorsey-dass* v. *Dhondmull* (1848) 4 Moo. Ind. App. 339.

of the country.[768] In the seventeenth century in England games of chance were suppressed as interfering with religious observance.[769] By the eighteenth century the objection was to the more general effect on society and its class structure which was seen as part of the natural order. The preamble to the Irish Deceitful Gaming Act, 1698,[770] amply illustrates the attitude:

> Whereas all lawful games and exercises should not be otherwise than used than as innocent and moderate recreations, and not as constant trades and callings to gain a living and make unlawful advantages thereby... and whereas by the immoderate use of them many mischiefs and inconveniences do arise and are daily found to the maintaining and encouraging of sundry idle, loose, and disorderly persons in their dishonest, lewd, and dissolute course of life and to the circumventing, deceiving... and debauching [of] many of the younger sort, both of the nobility and gentry and others, to the loss of their time, and the utter ruin of their estates and fortunes... [be it therefore enacted...]

In 1718 the lord chancellor, Lord Midleton, told Alan, the son of his second marriage, that he wished him to be 'bred up virtuously according to my best wishes' and took him to Newmarket to 'make you hate gaming, cockfighting and its attendant vices... and that you see that horse racing is an introduction to cheating, sharping, hypocrisy, and lying, and ends in the ruin of men's estates as well as the loss of their characters gradually'.[771] Blackstone at the end of the century had no doubt that the law should prohibit gaming as destructive of the social order:[772]

> taken in any light, it is an offence of the most alarming nature; tending to promote... debauchery among those of a lower class: and, among persons of a superior rank, it hath frequently been attended with the sudden ruin and desolation of antient and opulent families, an abandoned prostitution of every principle of honour and virtue, and too often hath ended in self-murder.

Gaming, or wagers on the outcome of games, had been regulated by a statute in England in 1664[773] and 1710,[774] and in Ireland in 1698[775] and 1712.[776]

---

[768] *HEL*, ii. 466; 12 Ric. II, c. 6 (Eng.), 1388 (archery); 11 Hen. IV, c. 4 (Eng.), 1409; 17 Edw. IV, c. 3 (Eng.), 1477 (unlawful games); 10 Hen. VII, c. 9 (Ir.), 1495: every subject having goods and cattle to value of four pounds was to have a bow and a sheaf of arrows, and freeholders, lords, knights and esquires were to have helmets, bows and arrows for their servants By section 3, practice was to be held every holy day. By section 4, each parish was to have butts to practice at, and anyone failing to appear without reasonable cause was to be amerced and the amercements presented to the barons of the Exchequer as the king's revenue.

[769] *HEL*, vi. 404. Similar legislation in Ireland was enacted by 7 Will. III, c. 17 (Ir.), 1695 (lord's day observance), which banned hurling and football on Sundays, as well as other games and pastimes.

[770] 10 Will. III, c. 11 (Ir.), 1698 (deceitful gaming).

[771] *Hist. Ir. Parlt.* (no. 0237) Broderick, Alan.

[772] Bl. Com., iv. 171. In Ireland there was one spectacular example of the ruin of estates through gambling, although it comes from the early nineteenth century. In 1831 John Scott Vandeleur, an Irish landlord and also an idealistic socialist, set up an agricultural commune on his estate at Ralahine, Co. Clare based on Robert Owen's socialist principles: E. T. Craig, *An Irish Commune: The Experiment at Ralahine County Clare 1831–1833* (Dublin, 1983). The experiment aroused the hostility of local landowners not only because of its radical political principles but also, and perhaps more so, because the members of the commune refused to allow foxhunting on the estate. However, after only two years the scheme collapsed when Vandeleur gambled his fortune away at his club. He fled the country rather than face both ruin and dishonour. The debts were later honourably discharged by his son, after his return from the Crimean war, but he had to mortgage the estate to do it. The whole incident has been described as 'a drama so poignant with quiet heroism and tragedy that it resembles a nineteenth century Russian novel' (foreword by T. O'Brien).

[773] 16 Car. II, c. 7 (Eng.), 1664 (Gaming). *HEL*, xi. 539–543. Lotteries were declared public nuisances by 10 Will. III, c. 23 (Eng.), 1698, and 6 Ann., c. 17 (Ir.), 1707.

[774] 9 Ann., c. 14 (Eng.), 1710 (excessive and deceitful gaming).

[775] 10 Will. III, c. 11 (Ir.), 1698 (deceitful gaming).

[776] 11 Ann., c. 5 (Ir.), 1712 (excessive and deceitful gaming).

In England the Act of 1664 was not aimed against gaming in general, but only against unfair or excessive gaming. Those who acquired money or property by *fraud* in playing at cards, dice, cockfighting, horseracing, foot races 'or other pastimes game or games whatsoever' were liable to forfeit treble the amount of the winnings.[777] Contracts to pay bets over £100 on games were void, and all securities given for such bets were also void. The winner of bets over £100 was liable to the treble penalty.[778] Betting on games for ready money to any amount was not prohibited, and the winner could keep the winnings.[779] It also followed that a loser could go to the limit of £100 on credit and still be liable to have the debt enforced against him by action.

The statute of 1710[780] went much further. It enacted that if a person lost £10 or more at play, or in betting on players, at a sitting, and paid the winner, he could recover the money if he sued within three months.[781] If he did not do so, anyone else could sue the winner for treble the value.[782] The Act thus not only reduced the limit to £10, but penalised play above that limit and even for ready money. By a rather curious exception it allowed a gaming table to be held in the palaces of the Queen when she was actually resident. It was a public gaming table held by the groom-porter, an official of the royal household.[783]

The Irish Act of 1698 was in similar terms to the English statute of 1664 but the ban on bets on credit was not limited to bets exceeding £100: it made all gaming bets on credit void.[784] As in the English Act, the winner was subject to the treble penalty.

The Irish Act of 1712 reinforced the earlier Act by providing that all securities given for gambling debts were void.[785] It is this provision which was in issue in these reports in *Blenerhasset* v. *Babington*, considered in the next section below. It also, like the English Act of 1710, removed the requirement of fraud.[786] The Act did, however, exempt debts under £10,[787] as in the English Act of 1710.[788] The curious exemption in the English Act of 1707 of the groom-porter's table was also permitted in Ireland.[789]

---

[777] The penalty to be divided between the plaintiff, who was the loser, or in default, anyone, and the king. 16 Car. II, c. 7 (Eng.), s. 1.

[778] Section 2.

[779] Ibid.; see *Moulis* v. *Owen* [1907] 1 K.B. 746, per Fletcher Moulton L.J. at 760.

[780] 9 Ann., c. 14 (Eng.), 1710 (gaming).

[781] Section 2.

[782] Ibid. Half the amount was to go to the person suing and half to the poor of the parish.

[783] His main function from the sixteenth century was to regulate gaming within the precincts of the court, supply dice or cards and decide disputes. *OED*, 'Judge', Selden, *Table Talk*, p. 94, 'Though there be false dice brought in at the Groom-Porters, and cheating offered, yet unless he allow the cheating, and judge the dice to be good, there may be hopes of fair play.'

[784] 10 Will. III, c. 11 (Ir.), s. 2.

[785] 11 Ann., c. 5 (Ir.), s. 1. It was held in the eighteenth century that it was still possible to recover money lent for the purpose of gaming, since the Act of Anne had only made void the security and not the debt created by the loan: *HEL*, xi. 541; *Barjeau* v. *Walmesley* (1746) 2 Str. 1249, 93 E.R. 1161; *Robinson* v. *Bland* (1760) 1 Wm. Bl. 256 at 260, 96 E.R. 141 at 142.

[786] Section 1.

[787] Section 4.

[788] In the case of Ireland this actually introduced an exemption not found in the earlier Irish Act.

[789] In this case held in Dublin Castle, or any other house, when the lord lieutenant was actually resident there. 6 Ann., c. 17 (Ir.), s. 1; 11 Ann., c. 5 (Ir.), s. 10. An Act of 1739 attempted to strengthen the earlier provisions by banning gaming houses: 13 Geo. II, c. 8 (Ir.), 1739. It also attempted to regulate horse racing, since suppressing it had proved impossible. Horse races had to be for a prize of at least £20, a more liberal limit than the £50 required in England, no doubt taking into account the less affluent conditions in Ireland. 13 Geo. II, c. 19 (Eng.) ss. 2, 3 and 5. 13 Geo. II, c. 8 (Ir.), 1739, s. 12.

The effect of this legislation was that, in England and Ireland, the winner could sue for an amount less than £10 won fairly at play.[790] Wagers other than gaming ones made void by legislation were still lawful, provided they were a contract in law, so that, for example, one could still sue to enforce a wager that A had purchased a waggon from B.[791]

As Holdsworth pointed out, the legislature could not have rendered all wagers void without a reform of the machinery of the courts, because the feigned action, dealt with above, would have been rendered impossible.[792]

Gambling and negotiability

One issue that arose in these reports was whether the statute of 1712 made a promissory note originally given for a gambling debt void in the hands of an innocent third party who had given value for it.

In *Blenerhasset* v. *Babington*[793] a promissory note was given to settle a gambling debt. The promissory note had then been passed for value to a third party who said he was unaware of the original consideration, although there was disagreement on the point. A statute of 1709 made promissory notes endorsable[794] while, as we have seen, contracts for gambling debts of £10 or more were void[795] but the statute made no mention of innocent third parties. There were precedents on the English statute of Charles II,[796] but none on the Irish statutes. There were two principles in conflict, and no clear legal rule to decide between them. The court had to decide which principle was more important. On the one hand, the will of parliament in suppressing gambling should be carried out, while on the other, the court saw it as a principle of statutory interpretation that the innocent should not be punished, and decided in favour of the innocent third party, but the court did so in the belief that this also had the happy consequence of encouraging, or not discouraging, commerce. Wall for the plaintiff argued that: 'innocence would be punished, and trade discouraged, and if the endorsee must enquire into the consideration, that would elude the Act, and put a stop to trade'. Wainwright B. saw the dilemma that whichever way the case was decided the policy behind one statute or the other would be frustrated:

> But however we determine this point, the mischief designed to be prevented by one or other of the statutes will be evaded. If we adjudge the demurrer good, the good of the public and trade which was considered by making notes negotiable, will be evaded, and if we shall judge it not good, the good and welfare of private families, which the statute designed to promote, will be evaded.

The court came down on the side of trade. The welfare of families was held to be of lesser value.

---

[790] *Bulling* v. *Frost* (1794) 1 Esp. 235, 170 E.R. 341; *Quarrier* v. *Colston* 1 Ph. 147, 41 E.R. 587 per Lord Lyndhurst.

[791] *Good* v. *Elliot* (1790) 3 T.R. 693, 100 E.R. 808, and the cases there cited by Lord Kenyon.

[792] *HEL*, xi. 542. Wagering contracts, with some exceptions, were later made null and void by the Gaming Act, 1845, 8 & 9 Vict., c. 109, which applied to Ireland. The exceptions were in 16 & 17 Vict., c. 119, 1853 (U.K.).

[793] Below, p. 223 [*288*].

[794] 8 Ann., c. 11 (Ir.), 1709.

[795] 11 Ann., c. 5 (Ir.), 1712 (for the better preventing of excessive and deceitful gaming). Above, p. cxxxviii.

[796] 16 Car. II, c. 7 (Eng.), 1664 (Gaming).

Quakers

The statute 1 Geo. II, c. 5 (Ir.), 1727 provided that in giving evidence Quakers were permitted to affirm rather than to take an oath, which they refused to do on religious grounds.[797] The Act of 1727 replaced an earlier, temporary statute, 10 Geo. I., c. 8 (Ir.), 1723. Under the 1727 statute a person claiming to be a Quaker had to produce a certificate verifying that fact by six members of his or her own congregation. Since the statute merely required a certificate one would have thought that it was clear that oaths were not required, because otherwise there would have been no point to the statute. Nevertheless, in at least one instance, a court had apparently required the certificate to be sworn, which, if that had been allowed to stand, would indeed have rendered the statute pointless.

The issue came before the court of Exchequer in *Underhill Lessee of Galway* v. *Echlin*.[798] The point had apparently arisen many times in lower courts. The recorder of Dublin[799] noted that certificates had been admitted on affirmation more than forty times on circuit. On the other hand, the late recorder, Mr Stoyte, in the Dublin Tolsel court, had refused to allow a certificate without oaths.[800] This would have made a nonsense of the Act and the court had little trouble in deciding that the certificate need not be sworn. Yet the decision had as much to do with the concern over trade as it had with religious toleration. Marlay C.B. certainly expressed a sympathy for the beliefs of Quakers that contrasts starkly with the prevailing attitude to Catholics:

> Quakers have the same belief of their word, because every word is spoke in the presence of God. But I think this ought to be the opinion of everyman.

He also noted that Quakers would be liable for perjury in the same way as other witnesses. It is not surprising that Marlay favoured a decision rendering the Act effective, since it was he when attorney general who had introduced the Bill in parliament.[801] But the motive behind the Act was not principally religious toleration. He pointed out that:

> the Act says it was necessary to carry on trade to give the Quakers this liberty, and if their testimony was taken away the sole witness in a cause might pretend to be a Quaker; by this Act Quakers are allowed to affirm instead of swear except in criminal cases.

The preamble to the temporary Act of 1723 began: 'Whereas for the more easie carrying on of trade and commerce'. The later Act of 1727 also notes that Quakers supported the Protestant succession to the crown, the linch-pin of the constitution, and so the concession was also a reward for loyalty. But exception of criminal cases reinforces the view that it was the encouragement of trade that was foremost in the minds of the legislators. So also does the enumeration of the several specific commercial transactions in the Act where an oath was normally required but where Quakers were in future to be able to affirm instead. The list gives an indication of the extent to which Quakers were involved in commerce at the time:

> making entries, invoicing of ships or goods, obtaining debentures at the Custom-house, in all and every other case where an oath is required in the way of trade before any

---

[797] See Howard, *Equity Side*, i. 59, 'Affidavits', i. 89–90.
[798] Below, p. 313 [*400*].
[799] Below, p. 313 [*400*].
[800] Carlton, below, p. 314 [*401*].
[801] *Hist. Ir. Parlt.* (no. 1344) Marlay.

person . . . concerned in the management of His Majesties revenue . . . recovering small debts
in a summary way by civil bill . . . proving their book debts for any sum not exceeding one
hundred pounds, . . . recovering of rent and arrears of rent due to any quaker, where the title
to land doth not come into question, and in ejectments, to be brought where the lessor of the
plaintiff is a quaker, upon the several acts made to prevent frauds committed by tenants . . . in
taking out administrations, proving of wills . . . returning inventories . . . in obtaining freedoms
in cities and other towns corporate, and upon attachments, and foreign attachments in inferior
courts.

Partnership and co-ownership

The encouragement or otherwise of commerce was also a policy concern of the court
in the case of *Digby* v. *Clerk*.[802] The father, James Clerk, was a silk merchant and had
two sons, Luke and Augustine. In his will their father devised them a yard on which
his merchandise was stored as tenants in common, but appointed them executors
of his will as joint tenants at law. He made other provisions for all his children and
grandchildren, but left a large residue of personal estate, mostly the merchandise
of his business, undisposed of. This vested in the sons as executors. By the early
eighteenth century executors had become accountable for any surplus to the next
of kin, but this was not the main point in issue.[803] Luke made a will and left a legacy
to his daughter Ann. After Luke's death, Ann brought a bill against the executors
of Luke and against Augustine. The issue was whether Luke and Augustine took the
residue in equity as joint tenants or tenants in common.

If they had taken as joint tenants, then on Luke's death his interest would have
ceased and Augustine would have become entitled to the whole on the principle of
survivorship. Luke left insufficient property of his own to satisfy the legacy. If they
had taken as tenants in common, Luke's share would have survived for the benefit
of his estate and have been available to satisfy the legacy of Ann. Luke and Augustine
had made no division of the residue during their lifetime, but had traded with it as
merchants.

In Wainwright B.'s view, a severance had taken place before Luke's death:

> the father was a merchant, and bred his sons Luke and Augustine merchants . . . and he seems
> to have nominated them executors to encourage them to go on with the business, having
> devised to them the yard wherein his merchandises stood, and he knew they must trade with
> the assets, and they had been joint factors in his life. He devises the yard to them as tenants
> in common, but makes them joint executors, because he knew as they were merchants, they
> would trade with the surplus, and therefore it would not survive.

Wainwright B. suggested here that the father made them joint executors because he
knew that there would be severance in equity. Apart from the intention of the father,
Wainwright B. concluded that survivorship did not occur because by trading with
the surplus, Luke and Augustine caused a severance in equity before Luke's death.
Hence, half passed to Luke's estate and therefore Ann got her legacy.

The other judges agreed.[804] Marlay C.B. saw that in this situation, where merchants
were also brothers, the interests of the family coincided with the normal position of

---

[802] Below, p. 255 [*330*].

[803] Wainwright B. gives a long and useful account in his judgment of the changes in the law of succession
as to personal estate.

[804] Oddly, St Leger B. makes a short comment and the report does not indicate his decision, but Marlay
C.B. says he agrees with 'his brothers'.

partners' assets being held as tenants in common. A brother/partner who died first might die poor and his family be left unprovided for: 'there is no survivorship in trade, because it is necessary to be carried on in partnership, and the ruin of a family might be risked by it'. Unfortunately for Ann, despite the evident good sense of this, there was an appeal to the British House of Lords which reversed the decision,[805] on the ground that trading with part of the residue did not produce a severance of the whole.

The Navigation Acts

A number of English measures in the seventeenth century had discriminated against Irish goods, particularly wool[806] and cattle,[807] the latter effectively preventing the development of a cattle industry in Ireland. Both these measures caused great resentment in Ireland and can be seen as the point at which the sentiment took hold in Ireland that Great Britain did not have Ireland's interests at heart when they were seen to conflict with those of Great Britain.

Nevertheless, by the eighteenth century the principal measure which discriminated against Ireland in commercial matters was the body of legislation known as the Navigation Acts. At first they were designed to force the development of an English merchant navy, and did not discriminate against Ireland, but they later came to implement other policies, particularly protecting English trade and manufacturing against foreign and colonial competition in an age of mercantilism. As Calaghan pointed out in *Foord qui tam v. Sullivan and Orpin*,[808] the seventeenth-century legislation was aimed against the Dutch, England's greatest commercial rival at the time. It was found, to the consternation of the government, that English goods were being transported from one English port to another in Dutch ships.

The policy of the Navigation Acts can be traced back to 1381.[809] The measure which first created a general scheme of protection and became the basis of the Navigation Acts as in force in the eighteenth century was the Act of the Commonwealth parliament of 9 October 1651.[810] Neither it, nor earlier legislation, had made any distinction between England and Ireland.[811]

The 1651 Act distinguished between goods imported from European countries, which could be brought in either English (or Irish) ships or ships of the country of origin, and goods brought from Asia, Africa, or America, which could travel to England, Ireland, or any English colony only in ships from England (or Ireland) or the particular colony. Certain fish imports and exports were entirely reserved to English (or Irish) shipping, as was the English coastal trade.

The Act of 1660[812] after the Restoration re-enacted the Act of 1651 with only a few alterations. It also introduced the practice of 'enumerating' certain colonial products, which could be shipped directly only to England, Ireland, or another

---

[805] *Digby* v. *Hall* (1735) 4 Bro. P. C. 1st ed. 524; 4 Bro. P.C. 2nd ed. 577, 2 E.R. 393. Augustine died intestate and his administrator, Hall, revived the appeal to the House of Lords.

[806] J.G. Simms, 'The Establishment of Protestant Ascendancy, 1691–1714', ch. 1, pp. 13–15 in T. W. Moody and W. E. Vaughan, eds., *A New History of Ireland: IV Eighteenth-Century Ireland 1691–1800* (Oxford, 1986).

[807] Carolyn A. Edie, *The Irish Cattle Bills: A Study in Restoration Politics* (Philadelphia, 1970).

[808] Below, p. 164.

[809] A. E. Murray, *A History of the Commercial and Financial Relations between England and Ireland from the period of the Restoration* (New York, 1903, reprinted, 1970), pp. 6–8.

[810] Jacob and Tomlins, *Law Dictionary*, 'Navigation Acts', 'Ireland'.

[811] Murray, *History*, at pp.6–8.

[812] 12 Car. II, c. 18 (Eng.), 1660.

English colony. Non-enumerated goods could go in English or Irish ships from English colonies directly to foreign ports.

From 1664 English colonies could receive European goods only via England. Scotland was treated as a foreign country until the Act of Union 1707 after which it was generally treated in the same way as England, but discrimination against direct landing of goods in Scotland was applied by the Act of 1670 cited below. The first statute to discriminate against Ireland was that of 1670 and it lasted until 1780.

Jacob in his *Law Dictionary* sets out the effect of the Navigation Acts in a series of rules. What follows is a version of those rules as they applied in the early eighteenth century and with emphasis as to how they affected Ireland. The numbers used by Jacob have been retained for the sake of comparison with his work.

Rule 1. No goods or commodities could be imported into, or exported from, any British colony or plantation in Asia, Africa or America except in British, or Irish, ships owned by British, or Irish, subjects and of which the master and three quarters of the crew were British, or Irish, or in prize ships.[813]

The prime serjeant, Singleton, notes the inclusion of Ireland in this rule in *Foord qui tam* v. *Sullivan and Orpin.*[814]

Rule 2. No enumerated goods of the growth, production or manufacture of any British plantation in Asia, Africa or America could be transported into any place whatever other than to some British plantation or to Great Britain. This was so even if Rule 1 was satisfied. 'America' included the West Indies.[815]

The enumerated goods were sugar (until 1739), cotton, wool, indigo, ginger, and fustic[816] or other dying woods.[817] Rice and molasses were added in 1703.[818] Copper ore was added in 1721,[819] and coffee, pimento, cocoa nuts, whale fins, raw silk, hides or skins, pot or pearl ashes, iron, and lumber were added in 1763.[820]

The prohibition applied to Ireland from 1670[821] until 1780.[822] Singleton noted the prohibition against Ireland in the 1670 Act.[823]

One problem of interpretation bore particularly heavily on Ireland. There was some doubt as to the effects of the statutes of 1670 and 1695. One view was that the Act of 1695 had prohibited the importation directly into Ireland of any goods at all, whether enumerated or not, from the 'the American plantations or colonies', including the West Indies. The 1695 Act was ambiguous, using the word 'goods' without limiting the word to enumerated goods. All goods from 'America' would have to be imported into Great Britain first, and then re-exported to Ireland, incurring

[813] 12 Car. II, c. 18 (Eng.), 1680, ss. 1, 3; the word 'England' included Ireland, Wales and Berwick on Tweed, and the plantations, and 14 Car. II, c. 11 (Eng.) (Customs) s. 5 made it clear that 'English' had the same meaning; *HEL,* vi. 317. The expression 'British-built ships' was given a more precise definition by 26 Geo. III, c. 60 (G.B.), 1786 (Shipping), but it still included Irish.

[814] Below, p. 166.

[815] See, for example, *Coleman qui tam &c* v. *White* where this is assumed.

[816] The name of a kind of wood *Cladrastis (Chlorophora, Maclura) tinctoria* of America and the West Indies used for dying things yellow. It is also sometimes called 'old fustic' to distinguish it from a different species of wood, the Venetian sumach (*Rhus Cotinus*) used for the same purpose, which is called 'young' or 'Zante' fustic. *OED.*

[817] 12 Car. II, c. 18 (Eng.), 1660 (Navigation), s. 18; 25 Car. II, c. 7 (Eng.), 1672, s. 5; 7 & 8 Will. III, c. 22 (Eng.), 1695 (Plantation Trade), s. 7.

[818] 2 & 3 Ann., c. 6 (Eng.), 1703 (Navigation).

[819] 8 Geo. I, c. 18 (G.B.), 1721 (Customs).

[820] 4 Geo. III, c. 15 (G.B.), 1763 (Customs duties).

[821] 22 & 23 Car. II, c. 26 (Eng.), 1670 (plantation trade).

[822] 20 Geo. III, c. 10. (G.B.), 1780 (Trade); 33 Geo. III, c. 63 (G.B.), 1793 (Importation).

[823] In *Coleman qui tam &c* v. *White,* below, p. 67.

customs duty twice. That view of the law in that period prevailed in *Coleman*, discussed more fully below. This may well not have been the intention of the 1695 Act and it was probably a mistake in the drafting. The law was mitigated as to this point in 1731 to allow the direct importation of non-enumerated goods.[824]

Rule 3. All other goods not so enumerated, being of the growth, production or manufacture of any British colony or plantation in Asia, Africa or America could be transported to any place whatsoever, except East Indies goods, which had to be brought to the port of London.[825] Furthermore, all hops imported into Ireland had to be from Great Britain and of British growth.[826]

As Singleton puts it, the purpose was 'to oblige subjects to go for the East India goods themselves'.[827]

This rule had the major qualification, specifically in relation to Ireland, noted in Rule 2 above.

Rule 4. No goods of the growth, production or manufacture of Europe could be imported into any British territory in Asia, Africa or America unless shipped in Great Britain.[828] Ireland was subject to this discrimination until 1780.[829]

The prohibition in Rules 2 and 3 of course meant that such goods were much more expensive, not only because of additional transport costs, but also because British customs duty would have to be paid first, and then Irish customs duty when they were landed in Ireland. British and Irish customs were not amalgamated until 1826.[830]

Rule 11. No goods or commodities of the growth, production or manufacture of Asia, Africa or America could be brought from any place or country except from those of their growth, production or manufacture, or from the only ports where they could be first shipped.[831]

There are two cases in these reports on the Navigation Acts and the plantation trade.

In *Coleman qui tam &c* v. *White*,[832] a ship arrived at Dublin with a cargo of rum, sweetmeats and staves and lay at anchor off the port. The report makes no mention of enumerated goods, but states that the relevant goods, the rum, sweetmeats and staves, were non-enumerated. The goods were entered as coming from St Lucia in the West Indies, the duty was paid, and a warrant issued authorising them to be brought ashore. While some were still on board, and some in gabbarts, or lighters,[833] they were seized under a warrant from the commissioners of revenue, on the information of the informer, Coleman, claiming that they were goods directly imported from Barbados,[834] contrary to the statute 7 & 8 Will. III, c. 22 (Eng.), 1695,[835] under Rule 2 above. The goods in *Coleman* were landed on the orders of the

---

[824] 4 Geo. II, c. 15 (G.B.), 1731.

[825] 7 Geo. I st. 1, c. 21 (G.B.), 1721 (Trade to the East Indies), s. 9.

[826] 5 Geo. II, c. 9. (G.B.), 1731 (Importation). Murray, *History*, p.82–83.

[827] In *Foord qui tam* v. *Sullivan and Orpin*, below, p. 166.

[828] 15 Car. II, c. 7 (Eng.), 1663 (Encouragement of Trade), s. 6.

[829] 20 Geo. III, c. 6 (G.B.), 1780 (Trade); 20 Geo. III, c. 7 (G.B.), 1780 (Customs); 20 Geo. III, c. 10 (G.B.), 1780 (Trade).

[830] Murray, *History*, at pp. 345, 379.

[831] 12 Car. II, c. 18 (Eng.), 1680, s. 4; 7 Geo. I, st. 1, c. 21 (G.B.), 1721 (Trade to the East Indies) s. 9.

[832] Below, p. 66 [*76*].

[833] See above, p. cxxv n. 699.

[834] Nothing was made in the case of the discrepancy between St Lucia and Barbados.

[835] Above, p. cxliv.

commissioners of revenue and put in the king's stores. If the seizure was valid, the ship and goods would be forfeit and the proceeds divided between the crown and the informer.

It also seems clear from the arguments, that the facts occurred just before 4 Geo. II, c. 15 of 1731 came into force, which made legal a landing of goods in a similar case to that which was alleged in *Coleman*. If the ship and goods were to be forfeited in *Coleman*, it would be under a law which had already been repealed by the time the case got to court, which would seem, and no doubt would have seemed then, particularly harsh.

The first issue was whether the Act of 1695 extended to goods not enumerated under the earlier Navigation Acts of Charles II and so prohibited their landing.

Section 13 of the Act recited that several vessels carrying enumerated goods from American plantations had landed in Scotland or Ireland contrary to the earlier Acts under the pretence of bad weather or lack of provisions, and provided that from 1696 it should be unlawful 'on any pretence whatever' to put in to ports in Scotland or Ireland to land goods 'of the growth or product of any of His Majesties plantations aforesaid' unless they had been landed in England, Wales or Berwick upon Tweed[836] and paid duties there first, under penalty of forfeiture of the ship and goods, three quarters of the value to go to the crown and a quarter to the informer. However, section 14 made a concession to Ireland alone, that in genuine case of bad weather a ship could put in to a port in Ireland, but land goods in the customs store which could then be put on another ship to England. The words in the recital in section 13 mentioned enumerated goods and so the section could be seen as limited to such goods, but the general words in the operative part, 'of the growth or product of any of His Majesties plantations aforesaid', did not mention any distinction between enumerated or non-enumerated goods and so it could also be argued that the section applied to non-enumerated goods as well.

Counsel for the defendants argued that the Act of 1731 was declaratory of the law and had merely resolved an ambiguity in the meaning of the statutes of 1670 and 1695. Singleton's argument, for the government, was that the 1731 Act repealed those of 1670 and 1695 and assumed therefore that the earlier Acts included non-enumerated goods in the prohibition. Singleton's argument prevailed:

> The 22 and 23 s. 2[837] first prohibited Ireland, the design of which was to preventing breaking bulk anywhere but in England, and was a total prohibition of the direct trade to Ireland, which might easily have been ended by putting on board some goods that were enumerated and some that were not, and so breaking bulk in this kingdom under pretence of the goods that were not enumerated only; and the Act 4 Geo. II[838] says the construction was always so, which supposes it right, and enacts it as a new law for the future, and is a repeal *pro tanto* of that statute of W. 3,

---

[836] Berwick-upon-Tweed is situated on the north bank of the River Tweed, long held to be the nominal border between Scotland and England. The town consequently changed hands no fewer than 14 times in warfare in the two centuries up to 1482. It was finally captured by Henry VII in 1482, but that did not simplify matters. Under the Treaty of Perpetual Peace between Henry VII of England and James IV of Scotland in 1502, Berwick was given a special status as being 'of' the Kingdom of England but not 'in' it. Eleven years later, when war broke out between England and France, James IV, caught between his alliance with France and the treaty of 1502, invaded England in breach of the treaty. The Scottish army and nobility were heavily defeated by the English at the Battle of Flodden. The Wales and Berwick Act 1746, 20 Geo. II, c. 42 (Eng.), s. 3, provided that where England was mentioned in any existing or future Act of Parliament, it was to include Wales and Berwick-upon-Tweed. The Act did not annexe Berwick to England.

[837] 22 & 23 Car. II, c. 26 (Eng.), 1670; *Chalmers* v. *Bell* (1804) 3 Bos. & Pul. 604, 127 E.R. 326.

[838] 4 Geo. II, c. 15 (Eng.), 1731 (plantation trade).

and don't say, that the former judgments were illegal, so the old construction is the best rule for Your Lordship to go by, and is not a declaratory law, but a law of repeal, and the forfeiture is the same by 22 & 23 Ca. 2[839] as by the 7 & 8 W. 3,[840] so that statute would be nugatory, unless the general words are of force.

The statute 4 Geo. II, c. 15 recited the doubts that had existed as to the effect of earlier Acts, that they had prohibited the direct landing even of non-enumerated goods into Ireland, and by section 1 provided that in future it should be lawful to import all except enumerated goods from 'America' directly to Ireland.[841] In Singleton's emphasis on the change of the law and the repeal of the Act under which the present action was brought, one might read a certain sense of the injustice if the case were to succeed, but the argument was properly made on behalf of his client.

The second issue, which turned out to be crucial in the case, was whether the goods had been 'landed' at all within the meaning of the Acts. The defence argued that it was not the merchant who had landed the goods, since he had only put some into the lighters[842] at the point when they were seised. It was the king's officers who had landed the goods and put them in the king's stores. Nor could it be argued that the king's officers were acting as agents of the merchant. The argument impressed Marley C.B. To punish the merchant on these facts would be to impose a penalty not for what he had done, but for what he might have been intending to do, which was contrary to a fundamental principle of law:

> The lord chief baron said that the great difficulty was, that a man who was going to do an illegal act might repent of it, and mentioned the case of *Reniger* v. *Fogassa*[843] in the Commentaries.

Marlay asked cogently: 'Might not he have kept them on board till he had an order to re-export them to England?' He refused to hold as a 'construction of law' that a landing by the king's officers was to be considered as a landing by the merchant, and left it to the jury to decide. The jury held for the defendant and neither the goods nor the ship were forfeited.

Foord qui tam v. *Sullivan and Orpin*[844] concerned East Indies goods imported directly from Nantes in France to Waterford, contrary to 7 Geo. I, c. 21, i.e. Rule 3. above. The ship, the *Mary Magdalene*, and the goods were claimed to be forfeited. Calaghan for the defendants argued that the information was deficient. It only alleged that the goods were shipped at Nantes. They might have come via London, or have been sent from London first to Nantes, which was not against the Act. Singleton for the crown argued that the information was sufficient, but in putting the case revealed a possible contradiction in the statutes. On the one hand, East Indies goods had to be brought 'from the place of their growth, or manufacture, or from the place where they were generally brought'. On the other, under 7 Geo. I, c. 21, East Indies goods had to be imported into Great Britain before they were transported elsewhere. If read in the context of Ireland, this would involve the contradiction that, on the one

---

[839] 22 & 23 Car. II, c. 26 (Eng.), 1670 (plantation trade).

[840] 7 & 8 Will. III, c. 22 (Eng.), 1695.

[841] The Act did not mention Asia or Africa. Its passing had been brought about as a result of a petition by Dublin merchants who had the support of the lord lieutenant: see the memorial of the Dublin Guild of Merchants, 1729, reproduced in Cal. Anc. Rec. Dublin, vii. 610, 'Petition of Trade between Ireland and English Plantations in America, Asia and Africa' addressed to Lord Carteret, the lord lieutenant, and Carteret's letter to the duke of Newcastle, 23 February 1730, ibid., p. 612.

[842] See above, p. cxxv n. 699.

[843] (1550) 1 Plow. 1, 75 E.R. 1.

[844] Below, p. 164 [*211*].

hand, East Indies goods could be brought only from the place of their production, which would mean *not* Great Britain, whereas under 21 Geo. I, c. 21 they could *only* be imported from Great Britain. Marlay C.B. seised on the point:[845]

> If the Act of Navigation said, you should not bring them from Great Britain, and the 7 Geo. I. that you should bring them only from Great Britain, would that not be an inconsistency?

Singleton seems aware of this, though he argues against it.

> But one says you shan't bring them from France, and the other says you shall bring them from Great Britain only, is not that a proclamation too against bringing them from France?

The argument turned to procedure. As Singleton pointed out, the statutes gave an election to the informer to proceed *in rem* against the ship or for its value. Here, he had elected to proceed *in rem* and in such a case there was no necessity to name a person against whom the action was brought. If anyone challenged the information, they made themselves defendants. Marlay C.B. decided that in such a case, a new information should be laid and the case was adjourned. There is no further report of the case. The point raised by Marlay was not resolved, although it seemed a fanciful one, since it would strain the interpretation of the English Act to hold that it prohibited export *from* England.

FATHERS' DEBTS AND MINOR HEIRS

A recurrent problem was as follows. A father had run up large debts. In order to pay them off he needed to grant leases. But the father only had a life estate. His son was his heir and would take an estate in remainder. The leases would only bind the son if he joined with the father to grant them. But the son and heir was a minor and could repudiate them on coming of age. Prospective tenants would not be willing to take such leases. The expensive way to deal with the problem was to obtain a private Act of parliament which would override the heir's right at common law to repudiate the leases on coming of age. This was done in *Hodson* v. *Rowley* in these reports.[846] A less creditable alternative by a selfish father, where some of his lands were not held in settlement, was to sell off the fee simple in those lands, thus depriving his heir of part of his inheritance. This was John Ivers's solution, as described above in *Ivers* v. *Ivers*,[847] where it is said that John, the father, sold off £10,000 worth of the estate before his son came of age. In the infamous *Annesley case*,[848] which inspired Robert Louis Stevenson's novel *Kidnapped*, the uncle found an even more drastic and vicious method: he sold his nephew into slavery in America.

THE DONERAILE CASE

The extraordinary facts of *Donerail* v. *Donerail*[849] make it worthy of mention. The report in the present volume is of the proceedings in the Irish Chancery for specific performance of a deed providing for pin money by Lady Doneraile, the second wife

---

[845] Below, p. 167.

[846] Below, p. 235 [*302*].

[847] Above, p. cxxviii and below, p. 188 [*255*].

[848] Andrew Lang, ed., *The Annesley Case* [Notable British Trials] (1913).

[849] See p. 283. The name is so spelled in the manuscript. The original grant of the peerage spelled it 'Downerayle': Cokayne, *Complete Peerage*, iv. 395, where it is spelled 'Doneraile', as it is in the report of the case in the British House of Lords, see below, n. 853.

of Arthur St Leger, the 2nd Viscount Doneraile,[850] a nephew of the half-blood of St Leger B.[851] Lord Doneraile married his second wife, Catherine Sarah Conyngham, in 1725. The lord chancellor, Wyndham, notes that the defendant attempted to cast doubt on the validity of the marriage, since the 'courtship and marriage were in one day', and that he was drunk for several days both before and after the marriage and 'he don't know if he ever married her'. It was even alleged in the printed pleadings before the House of Lords[852] that James and Standish Barry[853] had got Arthur continually drunk before the marriage and prevailed on him to marry Catherine and to settle £300 on her by executing the deed. None of Arthur's friends or relatives were present at the marriage, or at the execution of the deed. The marriage was alleged to be in a private house attended only by the bride's father, mother and brother. However, Catherine alleged that Arthur had represented her to his relations and friends as being his wife and had introduced her to the lord lieutenant, Lord Carteret, as such. After Arthur signed the deed, Catherine left him and he advertised that he was not married to her and was not liable for her debts.[854]

The lord chancellor did not find the denial of the marriage sustainable, as there were other witnesses, and there was proof that he had acknowledged her as his wife. However, there was ample reason to deny specific performance of the deed. It was in consideration of her good behaviour and there was ample evidence of her mistreatment of Lord Doneraile. The pleadings in the appeal to the British House of Lords[855] on his behalf alleged that she had constantly abused him, used foul language to him, calling him 'a poor mean-spirited rascal, an ideot, eunuch' and other scandalous names, and had even 'laid violent hands on him' for refusing to sign the deed. For her part, she alleged that 'being a weak man and a sot, his relatives have him entirely in their keeping in the Isle of Man, where, for £200 a year, he may have his dose of brandy and claret twice a day'.[856] Wyndham refused relief, having concluded that the deed was not fairly obtained.

Rather surprisingly, Lady Doneraile appealed successfully to the British House of Lords.[857] The report notes that although there was only one law peer present, it was Lord Chancellor Talbot.[858] The House of Lords noted that it was pointed out in Lady Doneraile's printed pleadings, which had been drafted by Sir Dudley Ryder and Fazakerley, 'a very eminent practitioner', that the lord chancellor of Ireland had improperly allowed an allegation of adultery with Captain Barry,[859] to be admitted as part of the deposition in Chancery, whereas the allegation should have been put to a trial at common law. Lady Doneraile in her bill in the Irish court of Chancery had alleged that she had always behaved with 'duty, tenderness, and affection, towards her lord'. Lord Doneraile in his original answer responded that the plaintiff 'had not

---

[850]   *Hist. Ir. Parlt.*, no.1853; Cokayne, *Complete Peerage*, iv. 395–96.

[851]   St Leger B., Sir John St Leger, *Hist. Ir. Parlt.*, no. 1858, was the son of John St Leger (no. 1857) and his second wife, Afra. John's eldest son, with his first wife, was Arthur (no. 1852), who was created Viscount Doneraile in 1703, and Arthur (no. 1853) was his eldest son.

[852]   King's Inns, 'House of Lords Appeals', 1734, vol. 11, fo. 180; Trinity College Dublin Library, 'Appeals to the House of Lords', 1711–39, 202 r. 35, fo. 51–52; Lincoln's Inn, 'Cases in the House of Lords', vol. 12, 1733–36, 24 February 1734, fo. 214 at 218.

[853]   It appears from *Doneraile (Viscountess* v. *Doneraile (Viscount)* (1734) 1 Coop. t. Cott. 534, 47 E.R. 987, at p. 988, that Captain James Barry was probably her lover.

[854]   Lincoln's Inn, 'Cases', vol. 12, fo. 214–15.

[855]   Lincoln's Inn, 'Cases', vol. 12, fo. 219. *Hist. Ir. Parlt.* (no. 1853).

[856]   Cokayne, *Complete Peerage*, iv. 396.

[857]   *Doneraile* v. *Doneraile* (1734) 1 Coop. t. Cott. 534, 47 E.R. 987.

[858]   Ibid., 47 E.R. at p. 989.

[859]   Ibid., 47 E.R. at p. 988.

behaved herself with that duty, tenderness, and affection as became a virtuous woman, much less his wife', but did not specifically allege adultery. Nevertheless, he had been allowed to examine witnesses to prove adultery.[860] The House of Lords ordered an account to be taken of the profits of the estate on which the annuity was charged in order that Lady Doneraile might have it paid to her. The court also considered the deed to be voluntary. Lord Doneraile died in the Isle of Man in 1734.[861]

TITHES IN WATERFORD

In the penultimate case in the manuscript, *Dean and Chapter of Waterford* v. *Congreve*,[862] the dean and chapter claimed tithes of fish in Waterford. Singleton appears for the plaintiffs, and cites as evidence a book by 'Balusius' published in Paris in 1682.[863] The book is *Epistolarum Innocentii III* (*Letters of Pope Innocent III*) by Étienne Baluze (1630–1718), also known as Stephanus Baluzius, a canon lawyer. The reference is to a decretal espistle of Pope Innocent granting tithes to the then dean and canons. Marsh's Library, Dublin, contains a number of the works of Baluze, including a copy of the *Epistolarum Innocentii III* (Paris, 1682).[864] The letter is in volume 2 at page 461 and is reproduced in Appendix E.

In 1670, Baluze was appointed professor of canon law at the Collège de France, of which he became director in 1707. He began a study of the history of Auvergne just at the time when cardinal de Bouillon was trying to prove his descent from the hereditary counts of Auvergne in the ninth century. Associates of the cardinal produced forged documents to prove the case and they succeeded in deceiving many leading scholars, including Baluze. Encouraged and financially supported by the cardinal, Baluze published his *Histoire généalogique de la maison d'Auvergne* (Paris, 1708), containing 'proofs', among which were found many deeds which were subsequently shown to be spurious. The cardinal fled abroad and Baluze was dismissed from his post and exiled from Paris. He was later recalled, but not to his post. He died in Paris in 1718 still refusing to acknowledge the error. He nevertheless collected a large number of genuine ancient documents, published in other works, which have been of great value to later scholars.[865] The objections which apply to his genealogical history of Auvergne do not apply to these other works, including the *Epistolarum*.

The prime serjeant felt obliged to point out that canon law was no authority in the court, but that the letter of the Pope 'is a strong proof, and may be given in evidence

---

[860] See also Hardwicke L.C.'s remarks on the case in *Clark* v. *Peryam* (1741) 9 Mod 340, at p. 345, 88 E.R. 493 at p. 497, also sub nom. *Clarke* v. *Periam* (1741) 2 Atk. 333, 26 E.R. 603. He mentioned that he was not present in the House of Lords to hear the case, and based his views on the printed pleadings. His view was that a general allegation of lewdness was enough to let in particular proofs of it, for to require specific allegations in bills and answers 'would tend to great indecency'. The reason for the decision in the House of Lords, in his view, was that no evidence of her misconduct had been properly proved by trial. Proof of misconduct, even falling short of adultery, such as cruelty, would have been enough to disentitle her to relief in equity.

[861] Cokayne, *Complete Peerage*, iv. 396.

[862] Below, p. 348.

[863] Below, p. 353, and n. 1587.

[864] The records of Marsh's Library show that, at a later period, between 1740 and 1753, when Henry Singleton, as chief justice of the Common Pleas, was a governor of the library, he attended meetings of the governors there. The meetings always took place in October and Singleton is recorded as having attended the meetings of 1740, 1745, 1746, 1749 and 1751.

[865] *Dictionnaire de Biographie Française* (Paris, 1933–); *Encyclopedia Britannica Online (academic edition)* <http://www.search.eb.com>; *Catholic Encyclopedia* (London, 1907–1912).

as an ancient history'. There is much discussion of the nature of tithes, especially tithes of fish, and their acquisition, and of moduses. The court upholds the claim, but only as against the defendants.

STATUTE LAW

Confusingly, there were two statutes of the Irish parliament commonly known in Ireland as 'Poynings' Law', both enacted when Sir Edward Poynings[866] was lord deputy under Henry VII.

10 Hen. VII, c. 22 (Ir.), 1495, (Poynings' Law, English statutes) was a reception clause which applied a body of English statute law to Ireland. It is discussed briefly in the first sub-section below, which however is mainly concerned with the issue of whether there was a theory in the eighteenth century that English or British statutes enacted after 1495 could apply to Ireland without express words in the Act. The present reports cast some light on this issue.

10 Hen. VII, c. 4 (Ir.), 1495, (Poynings' Law, Irish parliament) was the statute which made the Irish parliament dependent upon the British administration, and is discussed briefly in the second sub-section below.

English/British statutes

The statute 10 Hen. VII, c. 22 (Ir.), 1495, applied statute law 'late made' in England 'concerning or belonging to the common and publique weal' to Ireland. Whatever these somewhat equivocal phrases meant,[867] it was clearly confined to English statutes made before the date of the Act. Despite this, there seems to have been a theory in the eighteenth century in Ireland that English or British statutes made *after* the Act applied to Ireland, even if they did not expressly say so, if they satisfied a test of general public benefit, or some such test. Edward Bullingbrooke, writing on ecclesiastical law[868] at the end of the century, seems to have thought so, for he made liberal use of British statutes, without discussing whether they expressly applied or not. He was criticised by Finlay[869] in the nineteenth century for doing so.

From the evidence in these reports, there appear to be a few English or British statutes after Poynings' Law which were applied in this way. All but one affect two areas: the legal system itself, and the constitution.

In *Roderick* v. *Osborn*,[870] reference is made to 'the Pauper Act' which seems to refer to 11 Hen. VII, c. 12 (Eng.), 1495, which was enacted just after Poynings' Law.[871]

In *Costelo* v. *Costelo*[872] Frank Blake, counsel in the case, says:

---

[866] Steven G. Ellis, 'Poynings, Sir Edward (1459–1521)', *ODNB*, <http://www.oxforddnb.com/view/article/22683>, accessed 2 June 2008.

[867] See D. B. Quinn, 'The Early Interpretation of Poynings' Law, 1494–1534' (1941) 2:7 *Irish Historical Studies* 241–254; A. G. Donaldson, 'The Application in Ireland of English and British Legislation Made Before 1801', pp. 174–84. Donaldson's work contains an appendix listing English statutes, 1236–1800, and their applicability to Ireland.

[868] *Ecclesiastical Law* (Dublin, 1770).

[869] John Finlay, *A Treatise on the Law of Tithes in Ireland, and Ecclesiastical Law Connected Therewith* (Dublin, 1828).

[870] Below, p. 80 [*94*].

[871] 10 Hen. VII, c. 22 (Ir.).

[872] Below, p. 41 [*48*].

When the Statute of Elizabeth,[873] gave a power to the Exchequer Chamber to redress the judgments of King's Bench, it appears from the preamble it only designed to give them a jurisdiction in lieu of the House of Lords, and not to try an error in fact, but by the 31 Ed. 3 error in fact may be brought in the Exchequer Chamber.

The Act of Elizabeth is cited as if it had the same effect in Ireland, and there is no objection by the other side, nor an intervention by the judges.

In *Geoghegan* v. *Chevers*[874] Sir Richard Levinge cites 29 Eliz. I, c. 2. (Eng.), 1586, on errors in attainders, again as if it applied in Ireland.

In *Hussy* v. *Sheehy*[875] Blake makes the point that:[876]

by the 16 Car. I, c. 10 [(Eng.), 1640 (abolition of Star Chamber)] it is enacted that neither the King nor his privy council have or ought to have any right or jurisdiction to determine property by English bill, or otherwise, that the same ought to be tried by the ordinary courts of the law,

and seems to assume that it had the same effect in Ireland. Star Chamber had its equivalent in Ireland in the court of Castle Chamber.[877] There was never an Act in Ireland to abolish Castle Chamber, but the statement is not challenged by the other barristers nor by the judges, and so it seems to indicate that the equivalent jurisdiction in Ireland was also regarded as having become redundant by this time.[878]

The one instance in these reports of a statute outside the categories of the legal system and the constitution, is the English Statute of Bankrupts, 1542,[879] which St Leger B., at the end of *Digby and Ann his wife* v. *Clerk*,[880] seems to have assumed applied in Ireland

The evidence for any general theory at this time in favour of the application of English or British statutes of general utility to Ireland enacted after Poynings' Law (English statutes), and without an express provision, is slight. The evidence from these reports is that there was such a theory, but that it was limited to a few statutes which concerned the legal system itself or the constitution. When changes to the court system had been introduced in England and a similar change in Ireland would have been uncontroversial, but the Irish parliament had not yet enacted a similar statute, the courts were willing to treat the English Act as applying. It is also clear that a number of English statutes which might be thought to be of general benefit were clearly *not* regarded as applying, such as the Statute of Uses, 1536, the Statute of Wills, 1540 and the Statute of Frauds, 1677, because special Irish versions were enacted later by the Irish parliament.[881] Wills continued to be executed in the old form in Ireland until the Irish Statute of 1634.[882]

---

[873] 27 Eliz. I, c. 8 (Eng.), 1585, (error from Q.B.).

[874] Below, p. 1 [*1*].

[875] Below, p. 14 [*14*].

[876] Below, p. 15 [*16*].

[877] Jon G. Crawford, *A Star Chamber Court in Ireland: the Court of Castle Chamber 1571–1641* (Dublin, 2005).

[878] See Crawford, *The Court of Castle Chamber*, p. 415. The author states that there is no evidence of proceedings before the court after 1641.

[879] 34 & 35 Hen. VIII, c. 4 (Eng.), 1542.

[880] Below, p. 261.

[881] Statute of Uses (Ireland), 1634 , 10 Car. I, sess. 2, c. 1 (Ir.); Statute of Wills (Ireland), 1634, 10 Car. I, sess. 2, c. 2 (Ir.); Statute of Frauds (Ireland), 1695, 7 Will. III, c. 12 (Ir.).

[882] See for example the will of Richard Netterville (1545–1607). He made his will in Ireland in the old form, used in England before the English Statute of Wills, 1540, by a conveyance to uses, dated 16 June 1606 followed by a declaration of uses, dated 11 April 1607: *Calendar of Exchequer Inquisitions*, County Dublin, i. 353.

The Irish parliament

Under 10 Hen. VII, c. 4 (Ir.), 1495, (Poynings' Law, Irish parliament) no parliament could be held in Ireland until the 'king's lieutenant' and council, i.e. the Irish privy council, should certify under the great seal of Ireland, the 'causes and considerations and all such acts' as seemed to them should be passed by the Irish parliament. Only when these had been approved by the king and the English/British council would the king grant a licence to hold a parliament in Ireland under the great seal of England. Taken literally, this would have meant that the Irish parliament had no role in initiating legislation at all, since it assumed that an Irish parliament did not exist until the licence had been obtained in the first place.[883]

Fortunately it was not taken literally, at least after Lord Strafford's[884] time as lord deputy. It came to be accepted that bills could be proposed during a session, by the Irish council, but it was only at the end of the seventeenth century that the Irish parliament won the right to initiate bills itself. A faction in the Irish parliament, led by Alan Broderick,[885] had demanded the sole right to initiate money bills. Under the compromise of 1695, brought about principally by Henry Capell,[886] the Irish parliament was to have the right to initiate draft legislation, including money bills, but not the sole right. The term 'bills' came to be used for bills initiated by the Irish council. Draft legislation initiated by the Irish parliament itself came to be referred to as 'heads of bills', an expression still used in Ireland today. The Irish or British privy councils could still initiate bills at this time.

Heads of bills required the approval of both the Irish and the British councils and the seal of Great Britain. The Irish parliament could then either pass them unamended, or reject the bills outright. If it amended them, the amended bill would have to be approved in the foregoing manner.

In the eighteenth century, before the constitutional changes brought about by 'Grattan's parliament', heads of bills were regularly proposed by the Irish parliament and went through the process of amendment or rejection by the Irish and British councils.

The Irish parliament achieved greater powers under Yelverton's Act, 1782, the key element in 'Grattan's Parliament'.[887] Bills passed by both houses of the Irish parliament were still to be sent to England and were to be returned with the great seal of Great Britain attached, but 'without addition, diminution or alteration whatsoever', and no other bills. In theory, the royal assent could still be refused, but it was clear to all that this would be exercised only in rare cases.

TENURE OF JUDGES

Before 1700 English judges had generally lacked security of tenure.[888] One exception was the chief baron of the Exchequer, and the other barons, of whom Coke says:[889]

---

[883] See generally, James Kelly, *Poynings' Law and the Making of Law in Ireland, 1660–1800* (Four Courts, and Irish Legal History Society, 2007).

[884] Thomas Wentworth, earl of Strafford (1593–1641).

[885] Below, p. clix.

[886] 1st Baron Capell of Tewkesbury, appointed lord deputy by William III in 1695.

[887] 21 & 22 Geo. III, c. 47 (Ir.).

[888] See Baker, *Introduction*, at pp. 167–68, for a fuller treatment of the subject in England.

[889] Inst., iv. 117.

The chief baron is created by letters patents, and the office is granted to him *quamdiu se bene gesserit* [during good behaviour], wherein he hath more fixed estate (it being an estate for life) then [*sic*] the justices of either bench, who have their offices but at will . . . And in like manner are the rest of the barons of the exchequer constituted.

This practice as to barons in England was not guaranteed by statute, but the majority of them were given such tenure from 1450 until the reign of Charles I.[890] William III had in fact appointed all his judges in England during good behaviour and this was guaranteed by the Act of Settlement, 1700, which required that judges' patents so appoint them.[891] Thereafter they could be removed only on an address to both houses of parliament.[892] Even so, judges' tenure ceased automatically on a demise of the crown until a statute of 1760 secured their continuation in office.[893]

Irish judges had no security of tenure until 1781. First, they held office only during the king's pleasure, by an Irish statute of 1495,[894] and secondly, their commissions ended on a demise of the crown. The exception as to barons specifically did not apply in Ireland under the statute of 1495.[895] Judges in Ireland could thus be superseded and in some cases were, generally because of their political views rather than personal failings. James Macartney (1651–1727), appointed 2nd J.K.B., 1701, was superseded in 1711 with the change of administrations,[896] at the same time that Alan Broderick (1656–1728), later Lord Midleton, was removed as chief justice of the Queen's Bench by the Tory lord lieutenant, the duke of Ormonde.[897] Sir Henry Echlin,[898] a judge of the King's Bench and later baron of the Exchequer was superseded on the accession of George I, as was the chief baron of the Exchequer, Rochfort,[899] when the Tory administration gave way to the Whigs. Sir Constantine Phipps (1656–1723) was superseded as L.C. at the same time.[900] The vulnerability of the Irish judiciary to changes in the British political administration was one of the ways in which Ireland, a 'sister kingdom', was subordinated to British control, as was also the case in North America, the lack of security of tenure of judges there being one of the grievances set out by Jefferson in the *Declaration of Independence* of 1776.

The first judicial officer in Ireland to be appointed 'during good behaviour' was the recorder of Dublin in 1759.[901] Up to that time he had been elected by the city

---

[890]   Baker, *Introduction*, at p. 167.

[891]   12 & 13 Will. III, c. 2 (Eng.).

[892]   Section 3; Lemmings, 'The Independence of the Judiciary in Eighteenth-Century England' in P. Birks, ed., *Life of the Law: Proceedings of the Tenth British Legal History Conference* (London, 1993).

[893]   1 Geo. III, c. 23 (Eng.).

[894]   See 10 Hen. VII, c. 2 (Ir.), 1495, including the lord chancellor, the chief and second baron of the Exchequer, and the master and clerk of the rolls (in the case of the master of the rolls, only if he had been granted the judicial power: see p. lxxviii).

[895]   The fact that they were superseded in practice is shown by the cases of Rochfort and Echlin mentioned below.

[896]   Below, p. 120.

[897]   James Butler, 2nd duke of Ormonde, (1665–1745), lord lieutenant, 1703–1707, 1710–1713, Cokayne, *Complete Peerage*, x. 157; Stuart Handley, 'Butler, James, second duke of Ormond (1665–1745)', *ODNB*, <http://www.oxforddnb.com/view/article/4193>, accessed 14 July 2008.

[898]   Sir Henry Echlin (1652–1725) was the second son of Robert Echlin of Ardquin in Co. Down, was B. of the Exchequer in 1690, J.K.B. in 1692, reappointed to the Exchequer in 1693, was a justice of assize in Ulster and was superseded on the accession of George I: Ball, *Judges in Ireland*, ii. 56–57. See also *Tasburgh* v. *Echlin* (1733) 2 Bro. P.C. 2nd ed. 265, 1 E.R. 934.

[899]   Ball, *Judges in Ireland* ii. 69. He was appointed C.B. in 1707 and superseded in 1714.

[900]   Ibid., ii. 71.

[901]   33 Geo. II, c. 16 (Ir.), 1759, s. 20.

corporation, and held office at the pleasure of the city. From 1759 he was removable, by the city, on promotion to the bench of the superior courts. There had been great agitation in the years before 1759 at the state of law and order in the City, and the failure of the City corporation to control it. This in turn was attributed to the constitution of the corporation which allowed a small group of people to elect the officers of the City, including the recorder, thus weakening the authority of the magistrates.[902]

An early mention of tenure 'during good behaviour' occurred in relation to commissioners of customs and of excise, although they continued to hold office at pleasure. By a statute of 1662 commissioners of excise were to be appointed by the lord lieutenant and to be commissioned under the great seal 'during their good behaviour'.[903] Under a customs statute enacted in the same year commissioners of customs were to be appointed by the lord lieutenant and the privy council 'during pleasure'.[904] In 1721 the king by letters patent appointed five new commissioners of excise and two other commissioners of the customs 'during pleasure' and by letter under the sign manual dated 7 March 1721 authorized the lords justices to issue the new commission, determining the former commissioners' appointments and appointing the new ones, 'during pleasure'. The question arose as to whether the letter was sufficient to authorize the appointment. Thomas Marlay S.G. gave his opinion that the appointment was valid as there were no words expressly limiting the royal prerogative which would have prevented the king appointing the commissioners during pleasure.[905] A statute of 1760[906] enacted that commissioners of customs and of excise were to be appointed from then on either during good behaviour, or at pleasure, but they apparently continued to be appointed during pleasure only. By statute in 1823 officers of customs or of excise in England, Scotland or Ireland were to hold office at pleasure.[907]

Irish judges of the superior courts came to be appointed 'during good behaviour' in 1781,[908] and removable only on an address to both houses of the Irish parliament. Thereafter their commissions did not end on a demise of the crown either. Thurlow, as British attorney general, had reported against the change, on the ground that the resolution would not be subject to the procedure under Poynings' Law.[909] The change was nevertheless made. There were several attempts to impeach Irish judges in the nineteenth century.[910]

---

[902] See also Irish Parliament, Commons, 'Heads of a Bill for better Regulating the Elections of the Lord Mayor, Aldermen, Sheriffs, Commons and other Officers of the City of Dublin, and for Preserving Peace, Order and Good Government in the said City' (Dublin, 1759), and an earlier version, 1758. See generally J. R. Hill, *From Patriots to Unionists: Dublin civic politics and Irish protestant patriotism, 1660–1840*, (Oxford, 1997). Appendix C is a list of recorders of Dublin from 1660 to 1841. Gorges Edmond Howard took part in the controversy: below, p. clxiv.

[903] 14 & 15 Car. II, c. 8 (Ir.), 1662, s. 42.

[904] 14 & 15 Car. II, c. 9 (Ir.), 1662, s. 57.

[905] 'Opinion of Solicitor General, Thomas Marlay, concerning the legality of the New Commission of Excise, 1721', 19 March 1721, Marsh's Library.

[906] 1 Geo. III, c. 7 (Ir.), 1760, s. 18.

[907] 4 Geo. IV, c. 23 (U.K.), 1823.

[908] 21 & 22 Geo. III, c. 50 (Ir.), 1781–82, s. 1; Ferguson, *Treatise*, i. 16.

[909] 10 Hen. VII, c. 4 (Ir.), 1495 (Poynings' Law, Irish Parliament), above, pp. cli, cliii; 'Report of the Attorney and Solicitor General on an Irish bill, the Judges' Commission Bill', 28 Feb. 1776, PRO PC 1/11/9.

[910] In 1804 a complaint was made, to the Union parliament, against Fox J. of the Irish court of Common Pleas. At the time there was much criticism of the Irish administration for failing to take sufficient measures against the rising led by Robert Emmet in 1803. There was also alarm at the prospect of a French invasion and concern at the adequacy of measures taken to prevent such an event. Fox J., while on the north-west circuit,

BARRISTERS

The barristers who made most appearances in these reports, or most often addressed the court, were Cornelius Calaghan,[911] 'Mr Daly', and 'Mr Malone'. 'Mr Daly' is almost certainly Peter Daly,[912] prominent at the bar at the time.

The 'Mr Malone' mentioned on the first page of the reports is probably Richard Malone, who was called to the bar by King's Inns in Trinity term, 1703 and died in 1744. Anthony Malone,[913] who was prime serjeant from 1740 to 1754, and prominent in Irish politics in the period after these reports, is first identified by his full name on page 88, below, in 1731. He was not admitted to King's Inns until Easter term, 1726,[914] and so is certainly not the earlier Malone. It may be that Anthony is the Malone referred to from page 88 on, and he was certainly the most prominent barrister of that name at that later period, but the fact that he is also mentioned much later by his first name[915] and that by contrast 'Mr Malone' without the first name is referred to in several places after 1731 suggests otherwise.[916] Richard Malone is referred to as 'old Dick Malone' in the verse 'A View of the Bar', suggesting that he was still prominent at that time, or at least more senior, in age, than Anthony.[917]

Both Peter Daly[918] and Cornelius Calaghan[919] were converts to the Church of Ireland, but there is no evidence as to Richard Malone.[920]

---

had apparently gone so far as to recommend the grand jury in Longford to petition the crown to remove the Irish executive, and at Enniskillen he recommended the commander of the yeomanry to do the same. He had also levied fines against the earl of Enniskillen The 1804 attempt was abortive, but another one in 1805 caused a committee of the House or Lords to consider whether to present an address to the crown. The judge was present and represented by counsel. After protracted hearings the House accepted a motion by Lord Granville which brought the proceedings to an end. His view was that it was undesirable for such a petition to originate in the House of Lords, since the House of Commons might wish to institute proceedings for impeachment, which would have to be heard by the House of Lords. The judge duly resumed his seat on the bench and remained in office until he resigned some ten years later. R. E. Megarry, *Miscellany at Law* (1969), pp. 15–17, Ball, *Judges in Ireland*, ii. 245. Unsuccessful attempts to present petitions were made against McClelland B., in 1819 (for corruption), O'Grady C.B. in 1821 (for unjustly increasing his fees), and Smith B. in 1834 (for introducing politics into his charges to grand juries). All were attacked in the House of Commons, but in each case the House refused to present petitions. Megarry, ibid., p. 16.

911 See below p. clxii.

912 Below, p. 14 n. 72.

913 (1700–76), *Hist. Ir. Parlt.* (no. 1336). See below, p. 88.

914 KI AP, p. 325.

915 Below, p. 207 and p. 310.

916 E.g. below, pp. 124, 133, 141, 149, 161, 171, 179, 182.

917 Ball, *Judges in Ireland*, ii. 112.

918 E. O'Byrne and Fr. W. Clare, *Convert Rolls: the Calendar of the Convert Rolls, 1703-1838* (IMC, 1981; 2nd ed., A. Chamney, 2005), at p. 61; certificate, 22 Oct. 1716, conformity 21 Oct. 1716, and see below, p. 14 n. 72.

919 Ibid., at p. 317. He is not listed in the Calendar of the Convert Rolls, and so is not in the 1st ed. of this work, but appears in the 2nd ed. in Appendix II, in Fr. Clare's list of 'Converts having taken the oaths', at p. 275, and in his Notes, n. 186, at p. 317, and see below, p. clxii.

920 If the 'Mr Malone' referred to was named Richard, it depends upon which person of that name he was. The most likely seems to be Richard Malone, s. of Anthony Malone, of Ballyconey, Co. Westmeath, admitted to Middle Temple, 28 Nov. 1699; admitted KI, Trinity term, 1703: KI AP, p. 325, d. 6 Jan. 1744. See below, p. 1. He does not appear in the *Convert Rolls*. Richard Malone, of Dublin, s. and heir of Edmond Malone of Ballynahown, Co. Westmeath is in the *Convert Rolls*: pp. 176 (spelled 'Ballyneowen'), certificate, enrolled 30 May 1704; 394, n. 811, ('Ballynahown') but is not mentioned as a barrister in n. 811, and does not seem to be the same person as the Richard Malone, s. and heir of Edmund Malone, of Dublin, in KI AP, p. 325, who in any case was not admitted to KI until Hilary term, 1767.

ATTORNEYS

There are two instances in these reports of attorneys addressing the court, evidently not in the formal sense under a right of audience, but apparently as called upon by the barons to advise them on points of history or practice. The instance of Mr Harrison, who was probably Joseph Harrison, mentioned as master of an apprentice in 1719, relating how he remembered the sheriffs bringing their bags into court,[921] has already been mentioned. Mr Flack, probably one of three James Flacks who were attorneys during the period,[922] addresses the court on receiving pleas, on execution in ejectment and on Quakers' certificates.[923]

BIOGRAPHICAL NOTES

The main sources of the biographies of Irish lawyers have depended until recently on Ball's *Judges in Ireland*, which was useful if they had become judges, Cokayne's *Complete Peerage*, if they had obtained peerages, and such other sources as O'Flanagan's *Lives of the Lord Chancellors of Ireland*. These have now been considerably augmented by the six-volume *History of the Irish Parliament 1692–1800*, edited by Johnston-Liik, which, despite its name, covers only the Irish House of Commons. To these has now been added the sixty-volume *Oxford Dictionary of National Biography* which covers Irish lives to a greater extent than its predecessor, the *Dictionary of National Biography*. These notes are intended mainly to supplement these sources. The titles or appointments following the names are those held at about the time of these reports. The entries are in alphabetical order.

Richard Bettesworth (1689–1741), second serjeant

Richard Bettesworth was the son of Richard Bettesworth and Catherine Foulke. After school in Drogheda, Bettesworth entered Trinity College Dublin in 1705, the Middle Temple in 1710 and was called to the Irish bar in 1716. He was M.P. for Thomastown 1721–27 and Midleton 1727–41. He became second serjeant on 29 April 1732.[924]

Bettesworth's character is revealed in the incident involving Swift and Swift's lampoon of him. Swift was infuriated at Bettesworth's habit of voting against the established church. A bill was promoted in the Irish House of Commons for encouraging the growth of flax. It contained a clause for commuting the tithe on the crop, which would cause a loss of income to the established Church. Bettesworth strongly supported the bill. He also voted for the repeal of penalties against Dissenters' marriage contracts.[925] There is no doubt as to Bettesworth's dissenting sympathies. In 1733 a bill had been promoted to repeal the Sacramental Test Act,[926] and Bettesworth

---

[921] Below, p. 333.

[922] Below, p. 316.

[923] Below, pp. 303, 303, 316, 318, 318.

[924] *Hist. Ir. Parlt.* (no. 0130) Bettesworth; Smyth, *Law Officers*, p. 197. Smyth says 3rd serjeant, but on the same page has Robert Marshall replacing Bettesworth as 2nd serjeant on Bettesworth's death in 1741.

[925] 11 Geo. II, c. 10 (Ir.), 1737, s. 3.

[926] 2 Ann. c. 6 (Ir.), 1703, s. 16. Under the Act, any person holding a civil or military office under the crown had not only to take the customary oaths and the declaration against transubstantiation, but also had to produce a certificate within three months of appointment stating that they had received the sacrament of the Lord's supper 'according to the usage of the church of Ireland' in a public church on a Sunday. Any person failing to do so was '*ipso facto* adjudged incapable and disabled in law' from occupying the offices specified.

supported the repeal. Swift responded with a lampoon, issued anonymously, 'On the Words Brother Protestants'.[927] The title suggests that Swift took Bettesworth's use of the word 'brother' to refer to Protestants, possibly in parliamentary debate, but in the body of the poem it is Bettesworth's use of the word in his professional role which is the subject of Swift's invective:

> Thus at the Bar that Booby Bettesworth,
> Tho' Half a Crown o'er-pays his Sweat's Worth;
> Who knows in Law, nor Text, nor Margent,
> Calls Singleton his Brother Serjeant.

Bettesworth's fault, if anything, was professional pomposity, and what would today be called a 'colonial mentality', in blindly following an English practice even though it had no basis in Ireland. English serjeants addressed each other as 'brother', in recognition that they were members of the 'order of the coif'.[928] But there was no order of serjeants in Ireland.

Bettesworth vowed revenge, and, according to Sheridan, swore to cut off Swift's ears with a penknife.[929] The punishment for criminal libel could be the cutting off of ears, at the discretion of the court.[930] So the implication was that Bettesworth was threating to administer, as it were, an appropriate sentence himself.

Swift's own account of the incident is worth setting out in his own words:[931]

> On Monday last week, toward evening, there came to the Deanry one Mr. Bettesworth; who, being told by the servants that I was gone to a friend's house, went thither to enquire for me, and was admitted into the street-parlour. I left my company in the backroom, and went to him. He began with asking me, whether I were the author of certain verses, wherein he was reflected on. The singularity of the man in his countenance, manner, action, style and tone of voice, made me call to mind that I had once seen him, about two or three years ago, at Mr. Ludlow's country-house. But I could not recollect his name, and of what calling he might be I had never heard. I therefore desired to know who, and what he was; said I had heard of some such verses, but knew no more. He then signified to me, that he was a serjeant-at-law, and a member of Parliament. After which, he repeated the lines that concerned him with great emphasis; said, I was mistaken in one thing, for he assured me he was no booby, but

---

The test clause had been added in England. In 1715 there was alarm at the prospect of an invasion by the 'old pretender', Prince James Francis Edward, and a rebellion by his Catholic supporters in Ireland. It was felt that the army would be weakened if dissenting officers were forced to resign, and this led to the passing of the Toleration Act in 1719, 6 Geo. I, c. 5 (Ir.). Although the test remained until 1779, Protestant Dissenters were relieved of various penalties if they took a series of oaths: an oath of allegiance, an oath of abjuration of the papal power to depose sovereigns (oddly), an oath of abjuration of the pretender, and a declaration against transubstantiation and other Catholic doctrines (also, oddly). If they did so, then they were no longer liable to the penalties for non-attendance at parish churches under the Elizabethan Act of Uniformity, and they could not be prosecuted for mere non-conformity. If such a Dissenter qualified after a prosecution had begun, it was to be stopped at once. A long series of indemnity Acts from 1719 onwards laid down additional time limits within which to comply with the test. See J. C. Beckett, *Protestant Dissent in Ireland 1687–1780* (London, 1948), pp. 43–46. The appendix to ch. 7 contains a list of the indemnity Acts. The test was repealed by 19 & 20 Geo. III, c. 6 (Ir.), 1779.

[927] 'On the Words Brother Protestants, and Fellow Christians, so familiarly used by Advocates of the Repeal of the Test Act in Ireland, 1733', *Swift: Poetical Works* (H. Davis, ed., 1967), p. 587–89.

[928] See above, p. ci n. 454.

[929] *The Correspondence of Jonathan Swift* (H. Williams, ed., 1965), iv. 219.

[930] Jacob, *Law Dictionary*, 'Libel' IV. In *Wrennum's Case* (1618) Pop. 135, 79 E.R. 1237 an information laid by the A.G. in the court of Star Chamber alleged that Wrennum had libelled Sir Francis Bacon L.C. Wrennum was sentenced to a fine of £1,000, to ride a horse with his face to the tail from the Fleet to Westminster, to stand in the pillory and to have one of his ears cut off at Westminster and the other at Cheapside.

[931] Swift to the duke of Dorset, Jan. 1733–34; *Correspondence of Jonathan Swift*, ed. Williams, iv. 220–21.

owned himself to be a coxcomb. However, that being a point of controversy wherein I had no concern, I let it drop. As to the verses, he insisted that by his taste, and skill in poetry, he was as sure I writ them as if he had seen them fall from my pen. But I found the chief weight of his argument lay upon two words that rhymed to his name, which he knew could come from none but me. He then told me, That since I would not own the verses, and that since he could not get satisfaction by any course of law, he would get it by his pen, and shew the world what a man I was. When he began to grow over-warm and eloquent, I called in the gentleman of the house, from the room adjoining; and the Serjeant, going on with less turbulence, went away. He had a footman in the hall during all his talk, who was to have opened the door for one or more fellows, as he hath since reported; and, likewise, that he had a sharp knife in his pocket, ready to stab or maim me. But the Master and Mistress of the house, who knew his character, and could hear every word from the room they were in, had prepared a sufficient defence in such a case, as they afterward told me. He hath since related, to five hundred persons of all ranks, above five hundred falsehoods of this conversation, of my fears and his own brutalities, against all probability as well as fact; and some of them, as I have been assured, even in the presence of your Grace. His meanings and his movements were indeed peevish enough, but his words were not. He threatened me with nothing but his pen, yet owned he had no pretence to wit. And indeed I am heartily glad, for his own sake, that he proceeded no further; for, the least uproar would have called his nearest neighbours, first to my assistance, and next to the manifest danger of his life. And I would not willingly have even a dog killed upon my account. Ever since, he hath amused himself with declaring, in all companies, especially before bishops, and lords, and members of parliament, his resolutions for vengeance, and the several manners by which he will put it in execution.

A satirical verse, possibly by Swift, rubbed salt into the wound by supposing that Bettesworth celebrated the fact that he would be remembered in future as having been the subject of the lampoon, implying that that would be the only reason.[932]

An entry in the *The Grub Steet Journal* stated that Bettesworth had declared, before an audience of several hundred people in Dublin, his intention to assault Swift, and that some thirty-one of them had signed a paper stating their intention to defend the Dean's life and limb if necessary.[933]

Whether Bettesworth really had a knife in his pocket, or had ever intended to use it, seems unlikely, and his reaction seems boorish, but one should also note that Swift's attack on his professional competence had been vicious. According to his own account, Bettesworth's income from his practice fell by £1,200 a year as a result.[934]

Serjeant Bettesworth died on 31 March 1741 of jail fever (typhus) contracted at the Munster assizes of that year, in the same outbreak that caused the death of Wainwright B.[935]

Alan Broderick (1656–1728), Viscount Midleton L.C.

Alan Broderick (or Brodrick) was one of the most significant political and legal figures in the early eighteenth century in Ireland. However, since he resigned as lord chancellor in 1725, his decisions are not reported in this manuscript, but it is the

---

[932] 'Bettesworth's Exultation upon hearing that his name would be transmitted to posterity in Dr Swift's Works', Jonathan Swift, *Poems of Jonathan Swift D.D.* (W. E. Browning, ed., 1910), ii. 254. The poem is not included in Davis's edition, *Swift: Poetical Works.*

[933] *The Grub Steet Journal* No. 189, 9 August 1724, noted in 'The Yahoo's Overthrow', Jonathan Swift, *Poems* (Browning, ed.), at p. 256, and n. 1.

[934] *Hist. Ir. Parlt.*, (no. 0130) Bettesworth.

[935] Ball, *Judges in Ireland* ii. 131; Gent. Mag. 1743 p. 275.

only source at this time of his legal opinions, some of them being cited in argument in cases which are reported here.

He was born in Co. Cork in 1656, the second son of Sir St John Broderick of Ballyanon in Co. Cork; his mother Alice, was the daughter of Randal Clayton of Thelwall in Cheshire.

He developed a powerful political base in Cork. He was a convinced Whig and Hanoverian, but in the earlier part of his career his Irish roots led him into conflict with the British administration. He first achieved office in 1690 when he was elected recorder of Cork, and became third serjeant about the same time, his career benefiting from his having actively supported William of Orange and having been attainted by James II's parliament. He nevertheless supported the notion, propounded by Patrick Darcy among others,[936] that no statute was valid in Ireland until it had been enacted by the Irish parliament. He had given legal expression to this view in 1692, before Molyneux's famous study, *The Case of Ireland's Being Bound by Acts of Parliament in England Stated*, and this probably accounts for his being removed from the office of third serjeant in 1692. Another factor was his leadership of the faction which pressed for the Irish Commons to have the sole right to initiate money bills.[937]

Broderick supported the Popery Acts of 1695, and had himself strong dissenting religious opinions. He supported Dissenters in their attempt to obtain the repeal of the Sacramental Test Act imposed on them by the Popery Acts of 1703 and 1709, and his reward was to be removed from the office of solicitor general in 1704, to which he had been appointed in 1695. He had become speaker of the House of Commons in 1703.[938]

The Whig lord lieutenant Wharton appointed him chief justice of the Queen's Bench in 1710, but was he was superseded in 1711 when the Tory Ormonde became lord lieutenant. He was elected as M.P. for Co. Cork in 1713 and again elected Speaker of the House. After the accession of George I in 1715 he was appointed lord chancellor, at the age of fifty-nine, in succession to the Tory and suspected Jacobite, Sir Constantine Phipps. He was created Baron Broderick in the same year, and Viscount Midleton in 1717.

Two incidents in his later career seem to show a lessening in his radicalism, or a greater support for the Hanoverian government rather than 'pro-Irish' positions if they came into conflict with the former. Although he was opposed to Wood's patent, when lord chancellor he was in favour of prosecuting Swift over the affair of the *The Drapier's Letters*. Wood, an English manufacturer, had obtained a patent, it was said through bribery, giving him the right to produce half-penny coins for Ireland. The patent had been granted without any reference to the parliament of Ireland or the commissioners of the revenue in Dublin and was widely opposed in Ireland, not only as giving an unwarranted preference to English manufacture, but also because it might destabilise the Irish currency by an increase in the money supply. The allegation of bribery had been communicated to Alan Broderick, the second son of Midleton, and relayed by him to friends in Dublin.[939] *The Drapier's Letters*, a series of letters ostensibly written by a draper in Dublin, but which were generally known to be written by Swift, lampooned the proposal. Chief Justice Whitshed was in favour

---

[936] *Hist. Ir. Parlt.* (no. 0237) Broderick, Alan.

[937] Above, p. cliii.

[938] He was M.P. for Cork, city, from 1692 to 1710, and M.P. for Co. Cork, 1713–14.

[939] Cox, *Memoirs of Walpole* (London, 1798), cited by Davis, introduction, p. x to Jonathan Swift, *The Drapier's Letters and other Works 1724–1725, The Prose Works of Jonathan Swift*, vol. 7., ed. Davis (Oxford, 1966).

of prosecuting Swift, but a prosecution could only be authorised by a grand jury. Midleton not only turned down Swift's offer of dedicating the *Letters* to him, but also favoured his prosecution. Swift wrote him a long letter, full of legal references, making the case against Wood's patent and its unpopularity in Ireland, defending the author of *The Drapier's Letters*, while carefully not admitting to being the author himself.[940] Swift implored Midleton not to support the prosecution, but failed to change his mind. Ultimately the grand jury was discharged by Whitshed, and Wood surrendered his patent.

Midleton also incurred the displeasure of the Irish Lords in the constitutional crisis provoked by the *Annesley* v. *Sherlock*[941] case in which the Irish lords had attempted to establish the ultimate appellate jurisdiction of the Irish house. In 1725 he resigned, aged seventy, after a resolution critical of him was passed by the Irish House of Lords. By the end of his career he had achieved the distinction of being sacked by the British for being too pro-Irish and by the Irish for being too pro-British. He was the last Irish-born lord chancellor until John Fitzgibbon in 1789.[942]

From the meagre evidence in these reports, Midleton's judicial pronouncements show him to have been an original and instinctive equity lawyer and more puritanical in sexual matters than other judges in Ireland at the time. *Nowland* v. *Bagget*,[943] already considered, is evidence of his creative grasp of equitable principles. In *Delap* v. *Richardson*[944] Midleton decided a point on notice in equity which is now the earliest recorded precedent on the point in Ireland. Richardson had a lease from Trinity College Dublin and granted leases to sub-tenants with covenants of renewal. The sub-tenants evidently went into possession. Richardson then sold his head lease to Archdekne, Hamilton and Matthews. When the sub-tenants brought a bill for renewal, Archdekne, Hamilton and Matthews pleaded that they were purchasers without notice of the covenants for renewal and so should not be bound by them. Midleton held that the lack of notice was their own fault 'because they might have seen and known, though they had no actual notice'. They 'might have gone to the

---

[940] 'A Letter to the Lord Chancellor Middleton [*sic*]' in Jonathan Swift, *The Drapier's Letters* (Davis, ed.), pp. 99–115. A study has yet to be made of Swift's relations with the law and lawyers. Swift wrote, with an ironic reference to lawyers which he might have been wiser to suppress: 'I sent these Papers to an eminent Lawyer (and yet a Man of Virtue and Learning into the Bargain), who, after many Alterations returned them back, with assuring me, that they are perfectly innocent.' In his letter to the earl of Oxford, 6 January 1734/35, *Correspondence of Jonathan Swift*, ed. Williams, iv. 283, he refers to 'An eminent Person in the law here, and an intimate friend of mine upon the score of Virtue learning and superior Knowledge in his own Profession'. Davis says his adviser in that letter was Robert Lindsay (1679–1743), who was appointed legal adviser to the chapter of St Patrick's cathedral on 15 February 1721–22 and seneschal on 13 January 1723–24. He was Henry Singleton's brother-in-law, having married his sister Elizabeth in 1707. He was the son of Robert Lindsay, or Lindsey, of Loohry, Co. Tyrone, was called to the bar at King's Inns in 1709 (KI AP, p. 280), and was appointed a puisne judge of the C.P. in 1733 (Swift to earl of Oxford, 6 January 1734-35, n. 2. Ball, *Judges in Ireland*, ii. 203). Davis also states as a fact that he was Swift's adviser when writing the *The Drapier's Letters*. Henry Singleton, although an intimate of Swift, was probably too busy by this time. Swift also wrote two letters to Whitshed on his treatment of the grand jury: *The Drapier's Letters* p. 156 et seq. In the letter to Midleton, Swift reveals that he knew Lord Somers ('the greatest Man I ever knew of your Robe') and probably Holt C.J. ('I have heard the late Chief Justice Holt affirm'). Swift also dined in London at the house of Robert Harley (1st earl of Oxford and Earl Mortimer, 1661–1724), on several occasions in the company of Lord Keeper Harcourt (Simon Harcourt, 1st Viscount Harcourt, *c.* 1661–1727): J. Swift, 'Memoirs, relating to that Change which happened in the Queen's Ministry in the Year 1710', in H. Davis and I. Ehrenpreis, eds., J. Swift, *Political Tracts, 1713–1719* (1964). Swift refers to Harley several times as 'first minister'.

[941] See above, p. lvii.

[942] *Hist. Ir. Parlt.* (no. 0749).

[943] Above, p. cxxxii and below, p. 230.

[944] Below, p. 127. See also *Delap* v. *Hamilton*, below, p. 248.

tenants, and known how they held'.[945] The notion that purchasers have constructive notice of the rights of those in actual occupation of land was held in the later cases of *Hamilton* v. *Lyster*[946] in Ireland and *Hunt* v. *Luck*[947] in England.

Sanderson v. *Rose McCain, and Nichols*,[948] cited in *Cromwell Price* v. *Sophy Hamilton*[949] provides some evidence of Midleton's attitude on sexual morality. It concerned a contract or bond obtained in return for sexual favours and the plaintiff sought an injunction to prevent a trial at law. Broderick refused to consider the case since there was no fraud, but also because he considered it below the dignity of a court of equity.

Cornelius Calaghan (c. 1680–1742), barrister

Cornelius Calaghan, or Callaghan, or O'Callaghan, was the eldest son of Timothy O'Callaghan of Bantyre, Co. Cork.[950] He was admitted to Gray's Inn in 1701[951] and to King's Inns in 1705.[952] He conformed to the Church of Ireland in 1709.[953]

In 1709 he married Elizabeth (or Mary? or Maria?)[954] daughter of Robert Jolly of Knockelly, Co. Tipperary with whom he had seven sons and eight daughters, all but three sons dying young. He was briefly an M.P., being returned for Fethard for the second parliament of Queen Anne in 1713, which was prorogued in December 1713 and dissolved automatically on the Queen's death on 1 August 1714. Calaghan had Tory sympathies and signed an address supporting Sir Constantine Phipps, who was shortly to be superseded as lord chancellor. He was ordered to attend parliament in 1715 to answer for his conduct in supporting Phipps and taken into custody, but was released the next day on expressing his regret and asking for pardon. He was recorder of Fethard from 1713 to 1735, when he resigned in favour of his son, Robert, who was then elected.

Calaghan made a considerable fortune as a lawyer. When asked by his future mother-in-law, Mrs Jolly, as to where his estates lay, he is said to have stuck out his tongue and pointed to it.[955] He died on 4 January 1740.[956]

Gorges Edmond Howard (1715–86), attorney and writer

Howard was the son of Francis Howard, a captain of dragoons, and his wife, Elizabeth Jackson.[957] His mother was a descendant of Dudley Loftus (1619–95), the antiquarian

---

945 See also *Matthews* v. *Richardson* at p. 130, where the same point is decided by the lord chancellor and the two chief justices.

946 (1844) 7 Ir. Eq. R. 560.

947 [1902] 1 Ch. 428.

948 Below, p. 140.

949 Above, p. cxxxiii, and below, p. 140.

950 O'Byrne and Clare, *Convert Rolls*, p. 317; KI AP, p. 71. H. F. Cusack, *A History of the City and County of Cork* (1875), mentions a lease of 21 Jan. 1722, whereby Cornelius Callaghan, Bantyre, made over to John Wrixon, the lands of Gurteenbaghs & Coolenaghan, barony of Duhallow, for 99 years; vol. 6, 'Historical and Generalogical Items Relating To North Cork And East Kerry.'

951 RAGI vol. 1, p. 352, fo. 1371, 24 Dec. 1701, 'Cornelius Callaghan'; *Hist. Ir. Parlt.* (no. 1560).

952 KI AP, p. 71.

953 Above, p. clvi, n. 919.

954 O'Byrne and Clare, *Convert Rolls*, p. 317 gives the name as Maria. *Hist. Ir. Parlt.* (no. 1560), p. 377, gives it as 'Elizabeth (Mary?)'.

955 *Hist. Ir. Parlt.* (no. 1560); See also Ball, *Judges in Ireland*, ii. 112.

956 KI AP, p. 71.

957 T. Barnard, 'Howard, Gorges Edmond (1715–1786)', *ODNB*, <http://www.oxforddnb.com/view/article/13903>, accessed 26 April 2008.

and orientalist. In his *Treatise* on the revenue in Ireland, Howard relates how some of Loftus's manuscripts had come into the hands of his mother, mainly concerning the 'Acts of settlement and explanation' and the events of of 1688, but that she 'having married a gentleman in the army, and they not knowing the value of them, the whole, except for one volume, was used as waste paper upon all occasions in the house'. The one suviving volume was in his possession and he used some of the information as to the Acts of settlement in his book.[958]

Howard was born at Coleraine, Co. Londonderry, on 28 August 1715. He was educated at the Dublin school of Thomas Sheridan, the most famous in Ireland at the time, and apparently entered Trinity College Dublin, although his name is not included in surviving lists of undergraduates or graduates, suggesting that if he did attend the college he did so only briefly. Howard himself attributed the frustration of his early hopes of academic success to his relative poverty at the time and this circumstance led him to become apprenticed to an attorney practising in the court of Exchequer in Dublin, which proved to be the foundation of his later career and the considerable fortune he had amassed by the time of his death. Nevertheless, he seems to have been dissatisfied with the work at first and had ambitions to excel in other areas of life. He joined General Otway's foot regiment, but within a year had returned to practice in the Exchequer. His practice flourished due in part to connections through his wife to the influential Parry family and he secured many briefs concerning landed estates in Ireland. In 1743 he was appointed solicitor for the king's rents in Ireland and also held an established post in the quit rent office, quit rents being the name in Ireland for land rent owed to the crown. He also became legal counsel for the revenue commission in Dublin and registrar to the trustees for the creditors of the failed Burton's Bank.

Our knowledge of the Irish Exchequer in the eighteenth century is almost entirely due to Howard's writings. The major works are his *Treatise* on the royal revenue of the Exchequer,[959] and his volumes on both the common law[960] and equity sides[961] of the court. Many of the cases he cites only survive in his work and his insights into the failings of the system are equally invaluable. Howard argued for the reform of his own profession of attorney, particularly by controlling entry more strictly and so reducing numbers. His criticisms, probably since they favoured those already in the profession, did not prevent him becoming president of the Society of Attorneys in Dublin. He also published volumes on the rules of the court of Chancery.[962] In 1765, when he retired, he valued his practice at £1,600 per annum.

His knowledge of the revenue proved useful to successive administrations. However, his defence (in *A Short Account*) of the unpopular one of the duke of Dorset[963]

---

[958]   Howard, *Treatise*, preface, p. iii.

[959]   Gorges Edmond Howard, *A Treatise of the Exchequer and Revenue of Ireland* (Dublin, 1776).

[960]   Gorges Edmond Howard, *A Compendious Treatise of the Rules and Practice of the Pleas Side of the Exchequer in Ireland As It Now Stands Between Party and Party* (Dublin, 1759; 2nd ed. Dublin, 1793).

[961]   Gorges Edmond Howard, *A Treatise on the rules and practice of the Equity Side of the Exchequer in Ireland* (Dublin, 1760).

[962]   Gorges Edmond Howard, *The rules and practice of the High Court of Chancery in Ireland, with the several statutes relative thereto.* (1772); Howard, *A supplement to the rules and practice of the High Court of Chancery in Ireland, lately published.* (1774).

[963]   Lord lieutenant, 1731–1737, 1751–1755. See Robert E. Burns, 'Sackville, Lionel Cranfield, first duke of Dorset (1688–1765)', *ODNB*, <http://www.oxforddnb.com/view/article/24446>, accessed 3 June 2008.

in the crisis of 1753,[964] made him enemies and saw him attacked as 'a mercenary court scribbler'.[965] M.P.s prevented his salary being increased by £300. Lords lieutenant, however, were appreciative of his support and in the 1770s Lord Harcourt,[966] the lord lieutenant, made him solicitor for the revenue of Ireland, reputedly worth £1,200 a year.

Howard was nevertheless more complex than this account suggests. On the one hand he supported the unpopular administration of Lord Townshend[967] and the corporation of Dublin in their opposition to reinstating a wider franchise. On the other, he showed independence and a taste for reform in supporting the relief of Irish Catholics from the Penal Laws. In 1761 he drafted a bill to free Catholics from the law which restricted them from acquiring land for more than leases for thirty-one years. The bill was suppressed in England.[968] Howard's collection of Popery Cases was compiled in pursuit of the same cause. Grateful Catholics presented him with a silver epergne inscribed 'for his candour and humanity in endeavouring to obtain a relaxation of the Popery laws'.[969] He also wrote on Poynings' Law.[970] Howard supported schemes for the physical improvement of Dublin, was made a freeman of the Dublin guild of merchants in 1766 and became a member of the Dublin Society in the same year. Despite his professional achievements, Howard was ambitious for recognition in the realm of literature. His play, *The Siege of Tamor*, celebrated Irish resistance to the Vikings and his *Almeyda* had a similar theme of the struggle for liberty. He states that he sought the help of his acquaintance Edmund Burke to have them staged, but without success, and seems to have contacted Sheridan (presumably Thomas, the son) and Garrick,[971] with no greater success, and, although he hinted at their favour, it all came to nothing. His stubborn refusal to accept defeat led to him being attacked in an ironic *Epistle* by one Faulkner published in the *Dublin Mercury* and in other anonymous satirical verses. Howard was unwise enough to respond by publishing at his own expense a bitter pamphlet[972] which actually repeated some the scurrilous verses in order apparently to rebut them, together with verses in his support by his friends, who had likewise been attacked. The verses of his friends were equally extravagant, comparing his efforts to Shakespeare. In the pamphlet he describes Faulkner as 'that paultry animal' and a 'reptile'. Some anonymous verses were more vicious than the Epistle but Howard apparently rejected legal action on

[964] The crisis concerned the expenditure of surplus revenue. Crown lawyers argued that since the surplus had arisen from hereditary revenues of the crown, the crown's consent was necessary to approve how it was to be applied. The Irish House of Commons insisted on its right to dispose of the surplus without royal consent. A consent provision had been inserted in the money bill by Westminster. The Irish House rejected the bill. Dorset then recommended that George II order under his sign manual the appropriation of the revenue surplus to the same purposes intended by the rejected money bill, and the king did so, but the ensuing public outcry in Ireland forced Dorset's removal. See Burns, above, n. 963.

[965] G. E. Howard, *The Miscellaneous Works, in Verse and Prose* (1782), i. xxxiii.

[966] Lord lieutenant, 1772–1777. See Martyn J. Powell, 'Harcourt, Simon, first Earl Harcourt (1714–1777)', *ODNB*, <http://www.oxforddnb.com/view/article/12245>, accessed 3 June 2008.

[967] Lord lieutenant, 1767–1772. See Martyn J. Powell, 'Townshend, George, first Marquess Townshend (1724–1807)', *ODNB*, <http://www.oxforddnb.com/view/article/27624>, accessed 3 June 2008.

[968] See also Kelly, *Poynings' Law*, pp. 270–71.

[969] Howard, ibid., i. lii.

[970] 10 Hen. VII, c. 4 (Ir.) (Poynings' Law, Irish Parliament), James Kelly, *Henry Flood* (Dublin, 1998), p. 145. Above, p. cli.

[971] *A Candid Appeal to the Public, &c*, at p. 8. Howard's play *The Female Gamester*, is still in print.

[972] Ibid.

the ground that whereas he had strong suspicions as to the identity of the authors it 'may not amount to a legal proof in a court of judicature'. He suspected a political motive behind the attacks, and defended his support of Lord Townshend 'however this may be taken by fanatics and true-blues, whom I have always opposed at the hazard of my life and fortune'.

Howard died in Dublin in June 1786. His plays and verses have long sunk into obscurity, as have the enemies who lampooned him. 'His enduring legacy', Barnard writes, 'remains his detailed analyses of law, revenue, and administrative practice in mid-eighteenth-century Ireland.'[973]

Sir Richard Levinge (1656–1724), barrister

Sir Richard Levinge[974] appears only in the first case in these reports in the period between his being dismissed as solicitor general in 1709 and being appointed chief justice of the Common Pleas in 1720.

He was born on 2 May 1656, the second son of Richard Levinge (d. 1691) of Parwich, Ashborne, Derbyshire, and his wife, Anne, the daughter of George Parker of Park Hill, Staffordshire. He was educated at Audlem School, Derbyshire, and matriculated at St John's College, Cambridge in 1671. He entered the Inner Temple in September of the same year and was called to the bar in November 1678. In 1680 he married Mary, the daughter of Sir Gawen Corbyn. He became recorder of Chester in 1686 under the royal charter of James II which controversially restricted municipal voting rights.

Levinge was appointed solicitor general for Ireland in 1690 and was knighted on 23 September 1692. In the same year he was elected M.P. for both Belfast and Blessington and chose to sit for the latter constituency in the Irish House of Commons. On 5 October of the same year he was unanimously chosen as speaker of the Irish Commons in the short first parliament of William III. He at first declined the office due to 'the sense of my own imperfections'. He had 'ever studied rather to do than to speak or write well'. However, he accepted the post, and remained speaker throughout that parliament. In 1695 he was elected by Bangor and Longford, and sat for the latter.

He was chosen by the English House of Commons in April 1699 as a commissioner to inquire into forfeited land in Ireland but he questioned the legality of including James II's private estates in the forfeiture for treason. He was summoned before parliament on 16 January 1700 to explain himself, but spoke ill of his fellow commissioners and was committed to the Tower until 13 April. A victim of Whig politics, he received only £500 for his services, while those commissioners who accepted the forfeiture of King James's estates received £1,000.

Levinge was re-elected M.P. for Longford in 1703, and on 13 April 1704 was created a baronet. He was again appointed solicitor general for Ireland in 1704 but in 1709 was sacked by the Whig lord lieutenant, Thomas Wharton,[975] who

[973] T. Barnard, 'Howard, Gorges Edmond (1715–1786)', ODNB.

[974] T. Venning, 'Levinge, Sir Richard, first baronet (1656–1724)', ODNB, <http://www.oxforddnb.com/view/article/16552>, accessed 26 April 2008; Hist. Ir. Parl. (no. 1230).

[975] Lord lieutenant, 1708–1710. See J. Kent Clark, 'Wharton, Thomas, first marquess of Wharton, first marquess of Malmesbury, and first marquess of Catherlough (1648–1715)', ODNB, <http://www.oxforddnb.com/view/article/29175>, accessed 3 June 2008.

suspected him of passing information to Jonathan Swift, who for his part believed that Levinge's reluctance to provide information against Wharton prevented the latter's impeachment. In 1710 he was elected M.P. for Derby in the English parliament, and in the following year was promoted to be attorney general for Ireland. In 1713 he was elected for Gowran and Kilkenny and sat for the latter. He lost the contest for speaker to Alan Broderick.

On the Hanoverian succession he was dismissed as attorney general in November 1714, but in 1720 was made chief justice of the Common Pleas through the influence of his friend Archbishop King of Dublin. In the same year his wife died.

In 1723 he married Mary Johnson, the daughter of a political colleague, Robert Johnson, baron of the Irish Exchequer. Levinge died on 13 July 1724.

Thomas Marlay (c. 1678–1756), chief baron

Thomas Marlay was born about 1678 in Drogheda, the son of Anthony Marlay of Newcastle-on-Tyne and Co. Longford and of Elizabeth, daughter of Robert Morgan. He was the grandson of Sir John Marlay (1590–1673) who was mayor of Newcastle-upon-Tyne and sat as M.P. for that city in the English parliament of 1661. Thomas was in turn the grandfather of Henry Grattan.[976] His daughter Mary married James Grattan, recorder of Dublin.[977] He entered Trinity College Dublin in 1695, and graduated as bachelor of arts in 1697. He entered the Middle Temple in the same year. He married Mary, the daughter of Charles de Laune of Dublin in 1707. He became king's counsel in 1715, solicitor general in 1720 and attorney general on 4 May 1727. He was M.P. for Newtown Limavady from 1717 to 1730 and was appointed chief baron of the Exchequer on 21 October 1730. He became chief justice of the King's Bench on 14 January 1742 and retired in 1751. He lived in Dublin in Henry Street and in Celbridge Abbey, Co. Kildare, some eleven miles from Dublin, which he bought in 1723 from the executors of Esther Van Homrigh, Swift's 'Vanessa', on her death.[978] Mrs Delany[979] in her letters mentions having breakfast with Marlay and his daughter in law, after he had become chief justice, though later records that Marlay had accused her husband of being the author of an attack on Lord Orrery.[980]

Marlay's son became bishop of Clonfert and later of Waterford. Marlay retired from the bench in 1751 on health grounds and died in in 1756 in Chief Justice Singleton's house in Drogheda when visiting him there.[981]

[976]   *Hist. Ir. Parlt.* (no. 1344) Marlay, (0895) Grattan.
[977]   *Hist. Ir. Parlt.* (no. 0896).
[978]   Celbridge Abbey was built by Bartholomew Van Homrigh, lord mayor of Dublin, in 1697. His daughter, Esther Van Homrigh was Swift's 'Vanessa' and Swift visited her there regularly. The deed, dated 6 July 1723, was made between Alderman John Pearson and Peter Partinton, executors of Bartholomew Van Homrigh, and the Revd George Berkeley (see below, p. clxx) and Robert Marshall, (see below, p. 133) executors of Esther Van Homrigh and Thomas Marlay (then S.G.); Sir John R. O'Connell, *Celbridge Abbey: its History and Traditions* (Dublin, 1913?), p. 26. Marlay's son, the bishop of Waterford, remodelled the Abbey in the Gothic style and Marlay's grandson, Henry Grattan, lived there for a time.
[979]   Mary Granville (Mrs Delany), *The Autobiography and Correspondence of Mary Granville, Mrs Delany* (Lady Llanover, ed., 1861), 1st Series, Mrs Delany to Mrs Dewes, 16 June 1750, iii. 154.
[980]   Ibid., iii. 282.
[981]   Ball, *Judges in Ireland*, ii. 201.

As to his judicial attitudes as shown in these reports, Marlay's sympathy for Quakers has already been noted[982] and by contrast his antagonism to Catholics is shown in *Green* v. *Ryland* in 1733,[983] where he refused to concede that lawyer/client privilege applied to an attorney representing a client accused under the Popery Acts, thus being prepared to create an exception in such a case to the normal protection of natural rights developed by the common law. In other contexts, however, he was quite prepared to insist on strict compliance with common law tests, as in the case of the Navigation Acts,[984] where he refused to punish the merchant for 'landing' goods on proof that goods had been unloaded from the ship into the lighter, upholding the principle that the law would not punish a person for a mere intention and refusing to regard the seisure by the revenue officers as a 'landing' attributable to the merchant. This strictness in applying the Acts may also show a sympathy for Irish trade when restricted by British legislation. In relation to trade generally he indicated a favourable attitude to its encouragement, as in *Blenerhasset* v. *Babington*[985] where, in upholding the right of the innocent purchaser, he refered to 'a statute calculated to promote credit, and for the benefit of trade, and the public advantage of the kingdom'.[986]

Sir John St Leger (1674–1743), baron

St Leger B. was the son of John St Leger,[987] who had served as captain in a company of foot in 1661 and who became high sheriff of Co. Cork in 1695 and deputy governor in 1699, and his second wife, Afra.

He was at Westminster School and entered Christ Church, Oxford in 1692 aged eighteen. He was a member of the English bar, was knighted in 1701, at the age of twenty-seven, and called to the Irish bar in 1707. On the Hanoverian succession he was appointed second baron of the Exchequer a position which he held until his death in 1743. He attributed his early promotion to his friendship with Lord Chancellor Cowper and Lord Macclesfield, the chief justice of the King's Bench.[988] In 1702/3 he bought land from the Commissioners for Sale of the Forfeited Estates in Co. Cork.

In 1719 he was involved, with Gilbert C.B. and Pocklington B., in the conflict of jurisdiction in the famous case of *Annesley* v. *Sherlock*[989] when the Irish House of Lords reversed a decision in favour of Annesley and the British House of Lords held in his favour. The Irish House ordered the barons of the Irish Exchequer to restore Annesley to the possession of the lands which were the subject of the case and instructed the barons of the Irish Exchequer to follow their ruling. Gilbert C.B. took a strong line, declared that he was not answerable to the Irish House in

---

[982] Above, p. cxli.

[983] Above, p. cxxxvi.

[984] Above, p. cxlvii.

[985] Above, p. cxl and below, p. 223.

[986] Below, p. 228.

[987] *Hist. Ir. Parlt.* (no. 1857).

[988] Thomas Parker, 1st earl of Macclesfield (1667–1732), appointed C.J.K.B. in 1710, following the death of Sir John Holt. At the time, the C.J.K.B. was known informally as the 'lord chief justice of England'. Created Baron Parker of Macclesfield, 1716. Appointed L.C. on 12 May 1718. Created earl of Macclesfield in 1721. A. A. Hanham, 'Parker, Thomas, first earl of Macclesfield (1667–1732)', *ODNB*, <http://www.oxforddnb.com/view/article/21341>, accessed 26 April 2008.

[989] Above, p. lvii.

proceedings involving the British Lords, but Pocklington and St Leger took a more cautious approach, saying that they were placed in an impossible position. This failed to impress the Irish peers. A committee of the Irish House held that the barons had broken their oath of office which was to support the royal prerogative and the powers of the chief governor and council of Ireland. They ordered that the barons be taken into custody, which seems to have taken the form of house arrest during the summer recess.[990] St Leger and others believed that the Irish peers' action was influenced by Molyneux's book asserting the legislative independence of Ireland.[991] The result was the Declaratory Act of 1719.[992]

From the evidence in these reports, St Leger was a strong supporter of the Popery Acts at the time. It has been noted that in *Roderick* v. *Osborn*[993] he was prepared to extend the concept of 'constructive papist', more on supposition than on firm evidence, to a daughter who sued her father, ostensibly as a Protestant discoveror.

Henry Singleton (1682–1759), prime serjeant

Henry Singleton[994] was born in Drogheda in 1682, the son of Edward Singleton,[995] an alderman of the town, and Catherine Newtown also of Drogheda. He entered Trinity College Dublin in 1698, aged sixteen, entered the Inner Temple in 1702 and was called to the Irish bar in 1707. He was a friend of the Foster family of Drogheda and his early career seems to have benefited from their patronage in giving him a start in practice before the consistory court there.[996] He entered parliament as M.P. for Drogheda in 1713. He was regarded as a Tory and so when the Queen died on 1 August 1714 his career seemed unlikely to advance. He was returned for Drogheda again in 1715 and 1719. In 1738–39 he was mayor of Drogheda. He was appointed prime serjeant in 1726 and in 1740 became chief justice of the Common Pleas. He was sworn of the privy council in 1740. He retired from the bench in 1752 due to ill-health and was appointed master of the rolls, which was not a judicial office in Ireland at that time.

Singleton displayed a sympathy for the ordinary people which is difficult to detect in either Marlay or St Leger. Unlike many of his contemporaries, his religion was seemingly not a mere matter of form. He was active in several charities In 1729 he introduced an Act[997] 'for the encouragement of Tillage and the better employment of the Poor'. Landowners had increasingly introduced pastoral farming to the detriment of tillage which had led an increase in rural unemployment and poverty. Shortly after being raised to the bench Singleton contributed over £400, a considerable sum, for the purchase of oatmeal for the inhabitants of Drogheda to relieve the famine which was affecting the people of the town as well as the rest of Ireland

[990] 'Proceedings of the House of Lords in Ireland against Jeffery Gilbert, esq. Lord Chief Baron, John Pocklington, Esq. and Sir John St Leger, knt. Barons of the Exchequer there, for issuing Process in the Cause of Annesley and Sherlock, in opposition to an Order of that House' (1719) 15 St. Tr. 1302.

[991] Above, p. clx and *Hist. Ir. Parlt.* (no. 1858).

[992] Above, p. lvii.

[993] See above p. cxxxvii and below, p. 78.

[994] *Hist. Ir. Parlt.* (no. 1924); Andrew Lyall, 'Singleton, Henry (1682–1759)', *ODNB*, <http://www.oxforddnb.com/view/article/68109>, accessed 3 May 2008.

[995] *Hist. Ir. Parlt.* (no. 1922).

[996] A. P. W. Malcomson, *John Foster: The Politics of the Anglo-Irish Ascendancy* (Oxford, 1978), pp. 10–11.

[997] 3 Geo. II, c. 3 (Ir.), 1729.

at the time.[998] The fact that this was done after his promotion is further to his credit, in showing that it was not done to ingratiate.

Mary Granville, Mrs Delany, who had a wide circle of friends and acquaintances and left an autobiography and remarkable collection of letters, described a dinner at Singleton's in June 1750:[999]

> Yesterday we dined at Lord Chief Justice Singleton's, at Drumcondra, a mile off. Our company were his brother and sister Fowkes (who keeps his house, for he is a bachelor) and their son and daughter, Mr and Mrs Foster, and the *grand connoisseur*, Mr Bristowe... [the] Lord Chief Justice is very busy adding to his house and altering his gardens.

Mrs Delany seems to have been a frequent visitor at the time, for the following day she wrote:[1000]

> today we dine at Lord Chief Justice Singleton's at Drumcondra. He has given Mr Bristowe *full dominion* over house and gardens, and like a conceited connoisseur he is doing *strange things*, building an absurd room, turning fine wild evergreens *out of the garden, cutting down* full grown elms and *planting twigs!*... I shall be under some difficulty today to know *how* to commend *anything*.

The house at Drumcondra was Belvedere House which Singleton leased from Sir Marmaduke Coghill (1673–1738), a judge of the prerogative court and later chancellor of the Exchequer. Singleton leased the house from Coghill sometime before Coghill's death in 1738 and lived there until his own death in 1759.[1001] It is now the main house of St Patrick's College, Drumcondra. It is also Coghill who provides the best portrait of Henry Singleton's character in a letter to Southwell:[1002]

> Some are of opinion of his being very proud and haughty, and this notion they take up from outward appearance, he having something in his carriage that may make him suspected to be of such a temper, but his conduct and behaviour in his publick and private capacity shew how greatly those are mistaken who impute either pride or haughtinesse to him.

A story about Singleton that attests to his sense of duty was related by Secretary of State John Hely-Hutchinson in a debate in 1786 in the Irish House of Commons. He was speaking on a bill that sought to protect vicars who had been subjected to physical assaults in their parishes. The procedure was to be by civil bill. Hely-Hutchinson commented:[1003]

> It had been said that judges were generally in so much haste, that civil bills were seldom tried with that deliberation that was due to justice. He hoped it was not so... He remembered when civil bills were tried with as much solemnity as ever the cause of Hume and Loftus[1004] had been... He remembered a circumstance of that able and honest lawyer, Judge Singleton,

---

[998] Ball, *Judges in Ireland*, ii. 131; *Dublin Evening Post*, 14 June 1740.

[999] Mary Granville (Mrs Delany), *Correspondence*, ii. 555, see above, p. clxvi n. 979.

[1000] Ibid., ii. 557, Mrs Delany to B. Granville, 17 June 1750.

[1001] Revd John P. Campbell, 'Two Memorable Dublin Houses' (1940) 2 *Dublin Historical Record* 141.

[1002] Coghill to Edward Southwell, jr, 15 March 1732[/3], Dublin. BL MSS Add. 21123, ff. 267; Sir Marmaduke Coghill, *Letters of Marmaduke Coghill 1722–1738* (D.W. Hayton, ed., IMC, 2005).

[1003] *The Parliamentary Register*, Debate, Monday, 3 April 1786, vi. 431.

[1004] The allusion here is to the extensive litigation concerning the will of Sir Gustavus Hume who died in 1731, and the mental capacity of the earl of Ely. See *Hume* v. *Earl of Ely* (1775) 7 Bro. P.C. 2nd ed. 469, 3 E.R. 305; See also *Hume* v. *Burton* (1784) 1 Ridg. P.C. 16, 204, 554; *Rochfort* v. *Ely* (1768) 1 Bro. P.C. 2nd ed. 450, 1 E.R. 682; 1 Ridg. P.C. 524, 528, 551. The headnote in the report of *Hume* v. *Earl of Ely* states that: 'Where the validity of a will is impeached by a suit in the ecclesiastical court, as to the personal estate, and another in the court of Chancery, as to the real estate, and the will is established by a sentence of the ecclesiastical court, the bill in Chancery ought to be dismissed.'

which was so much to his honour, and so good an example to others, that he could not refrain from relating it.— The learned judge had sat in court, at an assize, till between four and five o'clock in the morning trying civil bills; just as the court broke up, and he was coming out, he heard a poor woman lamenting that she must be ruined by a bill for three or four pounds which was left untried; he immediately turned back, and with equal patience and humanity sat attentively to hear every thing that could be offered on either side, and then made his decision.

Singleton died in 1759, so it is interesting to note that Hely-Hutchinson was relating a story which dated from at least thirty years earlier. Presumably it had become part of oral tradition over that time.

Singleton was a friend of Jonathan Swift and Bishop Berkeley[1005] and advised Archbishop Bolton on personal matters.[1006] Swift expressed his high opinion of the prime serjeant in a letter to Barber:[1007]

> Mr. Singleton, the King's prime serjeant here, is one of the first among the worthiest persons in this kingdom; of great honour, justice, truth, good-sense, good-nature, and knowledge in his faculty: this gentleman, whom I have the honour to know, although his business be too great to allow me the happiness of seeing him as often as I desire, hath commanded me to recommend the bearer, Mr. Richardson,[1008] agent to the Derry Society, whereof you are a member. From such a recommendation as the Prime Serjeant's, I will engage that Mr. Richardson is a very deserving man, and that whatever he desires of you will be perfectly just and reasonable.

Swift also records that Singleton called at his house in 1737 on his way to visit France.[1009]

Singleton also had a house in Lawrence Street, Drogheda, which became Drogheda Grammar School.[1010]

In 1754, after he had retired from the bench, Singleton was described by Archbishop Stone as 'wasted very much' and 'when he speaks is with difficulty to be understood', suggesting he may have had a stroke. Nevertheless, he survived a trip to Bath and lasted another six years.[1011] He was buried in St Peter's church, Drogheda. Singleton's fine marble monument in the church was made in 1787 in London by John Hickey (1756–95), an Irishman and sculptor to the Prince of Wales.[1012] The inscription reads:

[1005] George Berkeley (1685–1753), Church of Ireland bishop of Cloyne and philosopher. Berkeley wrote to a friend who had raised the issue of how many justices of the peace were available in Northern Ireland and whether they could only be augmented by appointing Dissenters: 'The prime serjeant, Singleton, may probably be a means of assisting you to get light in these particulars.' Berkeley, *Works*, viii. 216.

[1006] Bolton to Swift, 5 May 1735; *Correspondence of Jonathan Swift* (Williams, ed.) iv. 330.

[1007] Swift to John Barber 1 March 1734/35, *Correspondence of Jonathan Swift* (Williams, ed.), iv. 300.

[1008] *Correspondence of Jonathan Swift* (Williams, ed.), iv. 300 n. 3: William Richardson of Summerseat, near Coleraine, Co. Londonderry, was a brother of the Revd John Richardson whose life's work was the printing and distribution of Bibles and prayer books in the Irish language.

[1009] Swift to Richardson, 30 April 1737, *Correspondence of Jonathan Swift* (Williams, ed.), v. 114.

[1010] In 1989, despite its being a listed building, the building was demolished illegally by an unscrupulous developer. The development company was later prosecuted and subsequently Lardner J. ordered that the parts of the demolished building be preserved so that the house might be reconstructed at some time in the future: *Irish Times*, 24 Aug. 1989; Andrew Lyall, 'Singleton, Henry (1682–1759)', *ODNB*, <http://www.oxforddnb.com/view/article/68109>, accessed 26 April 2008.

[1011] *Hist. Ir. Parlt.* (no. 1924).

[1012] Potterton, *Irish Church Monuments 1570–1880* (1975); *Freeman's Journal*, 3 Jul.– 2 Aug. 1787.

Plate 1. Henry Singleton, formerly prime serjeant, lord chief justice of the Common Pleas. Monument in St Peter's church, Drogheda.

Justissimus unus Qui fuit in Teucris & Servantissimus Aequi[1013]
To the Memory
OF THE
RT HON HENRY SINGLETON
who was chosen in early life
RECORDER OF DROGHEDA
And its Representative in Parliament
Eminently qualified
To sustain the Dignity of the Profession
he was successively appointed
PRIME SERJEANT and LORD CHIEF JUSTICE
of the COMMON PLEAS
And a MEMBER of the Most Honourable the PRIVY COUNCIL
Which high & important Duties he discharged with distinguished
WISDOM and INTEGRITY
And finally evinced a noble Spirit & Moderation
By retiring from Office without increasing the Burdens of his Country
He was afterwards solicited to accept
THE
MASTERSHIP OF THE ROLLS
And in that exalted Station
he departed this transitory life
AD 1760[1014] AE 78
The Excellence of his publick Character
was happily supported by an ardent
ZEAL for RELIGION
And by the extensive Benevolence of his private life
In grateful Esteem to his memory, his Nephew
SYDENHAM SINGLETON Esq.
Caused this Monument to be Erected.

Henry Singleton died on 9 November 1759 and was buried in St Peter's graveyard on 12 November 1759.

Eaton Stannard (1685–1755), recorder of Dublin

Eaton Stannard was the second son of George Stannard of Co. Cork. He entered Trinity College Dublin in 1702 aged seventeen, was a Scholar in 1704, and graduated with a BA in 1706. He was called to the bar by the Middle Temple in 1710 and to the Irish bar in 1714. He was elected recorder of Cork in 1728 but did not accept. He was appointed King's Counsel in 1726, and was M.P. for Midleton from 1727 to 1755. His appointment as recorder of Dublin in 1733 was said to be due to the influence of Swift. When Francis Stoyte, the recorder of Dublin, died in 1733[1015] there were a number of candidates to fill the office, including Forbes, the alderman's son, and Eaton Stannard, a 'zealous patriot'. Jonathan Swift supported Stannard's candidature in the rather oblique pamphlet 'Some Considerations...'[1016] which

---

[1013] 'He was the most just of Trojans and a true servant of the law.' Virgil, *Aeneid*, bk. 2, lines 426, 427.
[1014] This is an error for 1759.
[1015] d. 30 January 1733, *Dublin Journal*, 3 Feb. 1733.
[1016] 'Some Considerations Humbly offered to the Right Honourable the Lord Mayor, the Court of Aldermen, and Common Council of the Honourable City of Dublin, in the Choice of a Recorder', *Correspondence of Jonathan Swift* (Williams, ed.), xiii. 69.

does not mention Stannard by name. However, it was said that everyone knew who he had in mind.[1017] Stannard succeeded to the office. He was a member of Swift's lunacy commission and an executor of his will.

Eaton Stannard served on a number of charity boards, and was justice of Assize for North East Ulster in the summer of 1741.

Stannard was well regarded for his integrity and ability as a lawyer.[1018] An incident in his earlier career may explain why he was not appointed to a higher judicial position than recorder. In 1729 there was a controversy over the shortage of currency, and Archbishop Boulter blamed Swift and his protégé Stannard. Boulter complained to this effect in a letter to Lord Lieutenant Carteret on 13 May 1729. In December 1753 Primate Stone wrote to the duke of Newcastle that 'Mr Stannard is at the head of his profession at the bar, and always reputed in the House of Commons to have carried great weight and credit with him.' His fortunes had turned, but rather too late. He replaced Anthony Malone as prime serjeant in 24 January 1754, but died 'of a fever' at his house in St Stephen's Green, Dublin, in 1755.

John Wainwright (1689–1741), baron

John Wainwright was the son of Thomas Wainwright, chancellor of the diocese of Chester, and Rebecca, née Jackson. He was born in 1689, was at Westminster School in 1703, matriculated at Christ Church, Oxford University, and graduated a BA in 1712. He was called to the bar by the Inner Temple in 1716, and became a member of Lincoln's Inn in 1720. He appears as clerk to the Prince of Wales' council.

Wainwright appears to have had an early association in England with Gilbert, since he says in quoting him in *Coventry* v. *Coventry*[1019] that he 'expressed himself in these words, as I took them from his own mouth'. Wainwright's comment also identifies Gilbert as delivering the judgment in the case, which does not appear from the report. He came to Ireland in 1732 as baron of the Exchequer in succession to Pocklington.

In *Green* v. *Ryland*,[1020] the case concerning lawyer/client privilege and the Popery Acts, he demonstrated a greater degree of integrity than Marlay did in recognizing that the Popery Acts set up a conflict with natural rights. In expressing approval of the policy to 'establish lands in the hands of Protestants' and calling it 'one of the pillars of the government', he takes the side of power rather than justice. But he nevertheless concedes that the statute took away the 'natural right' of the accused against self-incrimination, a point Marlay refused to recognize.[1021] There is an element of using the declaratory theory as an excuse, in that it is arguably his interpretation of the statute rather than the statute itself which reaches this result, but he does recognize the conflict.

His attitude to statutory interpretation in a different context is well illustrated by his judgment in *Blenerhasset* v. *Babington*:[1022]

[1017]   Ibid., iv. 128 and n.

[1018]   *Hist. Ir. Parlt.* (no. 1981).

[1019]   Gilb. 160, 25 E.R. 112, and 9 Mod. 12, 88 E.R. 284. Gilbert there appears in Chancery assisting the lord chancellor, Lord Macclesfield, with Sir Joseph Jekyll M.R., and Price B.

[1020]   Below, pp. 211 and 356.

[1021]   Below, p. 213.

[1022]   Below, p. 227.

The first rule to construe statutes by is laid down in 1 Inst. 381b, that a statute is to be construed in suppression of the mischief, and advancement of the remedy designed by the statute.

Another rule is also in 1 Inst. 11, that a statute is not to be so interpreted, as to injure an innocent person.

To make all notes, bills &c. for money won at play void, would tend to suppress the mischief, and advance the remedy designed by the 11 Anne; but then what would become of innocent persons who have paid money for these notes, and taken an endorsement of them on the credit [of] 8 Anne?

The second rule is a breach of natural justice, and ought always to be observed, the first is only to be observed *sub modo*, and qualified.

In this context, where the policy behind the statute is in conflict with a natural right, he sees the natural right as the trump card, resolving the conflict between two principles of statutory interpretation by assigning a greater weight to one of them on the basis of a more fundamental value derived from a theory of natural rights.

In *Blenerhasset* Wainwright B. decided in favour of the principle of negotiability as essential to the development of commerce, which is the first recorded case on the point in Ireland, and in *Digby* v. *Clerk*[1023] he delivered a significant judgment on the principle of survivorship in relation to partners in trade.

Wainwright left a collection of notebooks, now in the British Library, of cases in the Irish court of Exchequer[1024] and some from his time England.[1025]

Wainwright contracted typhus at the Munster assizes in the spring of 1741. He was brought back to his house at Mount Merrion, Dublin, and died there a few days later.[1026] The same outbreak caused the death of Serjeant Bettesworth and probably Chief Justice Rogerson.[1027] Lord Chancellor Jocelyn wrote to Hardwicke on 19 March:[1028]

Mr Baron Wainwright, Mr Attorney Bowes, and Mr Serjeant Bettesworth went to Munster. By the account I had yesterday from the baron, I am afraid that the serjeant is before this dead, and we have sent a fourth person to finish the business of that circuit. The baron and attorney are worn down, and no wonder since in the county of Cork they have had upwards of four hundred criminals. I am in great pain for them. One of the baron's expressions is that they are grievously offended daily with miserable spectacles, expiring wretches and noisome smells. The attorney made it his choice to go that circuit, but the baron undertook it out of good nature, to obviate some difficulties, which must otherwise arise.

Wainwright was buried at Chester in Trinity Church.

Thomas Wyndham (1681–1745), Baron Wyndham L.C.

Thomas Wyndham was the fourth and youngest, but eldest surviving, son of John Wyndham of Norrington, a colonel in the army and M.P. for Salisbury in 1681 and 1685, and his wife Alice, daughter of Thomas Fownes.[1029] His grandfather,

---

[1023] Below, p. 255.
[1024] Above, p. liv n. 9.
[1025] BL MS. 19847–50. 1720–30.
[1026] Ball, *Judges in Ireland*, ii. 131, 203.
[1027] Ibid., ii. 131. See above, p. ci n. 462.
[1028] Ibid.; BL MSS Add. 35586, fo. 335.
[1029] Andrew Lyall, 'Wyndham, Thomas, Baron Wyndham (1681–1745)', *ODNB*, <http://www.oxforddnb.com/view/article/30147>, accessed 3 June 2008.

Sir Wadham Wyndham, one of the justices of the English King's Bench (1660–68),[1030] was the grandson of John Wyndham and Florence, sister of Nicholas Wadham, founder of Wadham College, Oxford. Thomas was educated at the cathedral school, Salisbury, and matriculated at Wadham College, Oxford in 1698 at the age of sixteen. He does not appear to have taken a degree, but he was admitted to Lincoln's Inn in 1698, and called to the bar on 9 May 1705. He was appointed recorder of Sarum in 1706, and in 1724 was appointed chief justice of the court of Common Pleas in Ireland, an 'easy post' according to Archbishop Boulter, in succession to Sir Richard Levinge. He was elected a bencher of Lincoln's Inn and sworn of the Irish privy council in 9 December 1724.

On the death of Lord Chancellor West in November 1726, Wyndham was appointed to succeed him. He was recommended by Boulter, who was opposed to native Irish being appointed to such posts. Boulter also successfully sought the appointment of his protégé, the poet Ambrose Philips, to be Wyndham's secretary,[1031] prompting Alexander Pope, a Catholic, to pen the line: 'Still to one bishop Philips seem[s] a wit?'[1032]

On 3 February 1729 Wyndham laid the foundation stone of the Irish Parliament House in College Green. He was appointed one of the lords justices of Ireland, who exercised authority in the absence of the lord lieutenant, in 1728 and served in that capacity on eight occasions.

In 1730 Daniel Kimberly, an attorney, was sentenced to death for abduction. Petitions seeking to invoke the prerogative of mercy were presented to the lords justices, to the lord lieutenant, then in London, and to the king, on a technical ground. The matter was referred to the lord lieutenant who agreed with the lords justices that the petitions should be denied. Wyndham convened the Irish privy council which then rejected the petitions after taking the oral opinion of the judges and later the written opinion of the law officers, being the prime serjeant, Singleton, the attorney general, Marlay, the solicitor general, Jocelyn, and Serjeant Bowes.[1033] The incident established that petitions to invoke the Irish prerogative of mercy should not thereafter be sent to England.[1034]

Thomas Wyndham was created Baron Wyndham of Finglass, Co. Dublin in 1731. He presided over six sessions of the Irish parliament as speaker of the House of Lords.

As lord high steward he presided over the trial of Lord Barry of Santry (1710–51) for murder.[1035] Wyndham recites in his will that this was the first trial of a peer before the Irish lords. Barry was found guilty on 27 April 1739 and Wyndham sentenced him to death. The stress of the trial affected Wyndham's health, as he says in his will, and he resigned the chancellorship on 7 September 1739, sailing for England the following day. He died in Wiltshire on 24 November 1745, aged sixty-three, and was buried in Salisbury Cathedral, where there is a fine marble monument to him by Rysbrack on the south side of the west door. He was unmarried, and the title became extinct on his death.

[1030] Foss, *Judges of England*, vii. 198.

[1031] H. Boulter, *Letters written by His Excellency Hugh Boulter, D.D., Lord Primate of All Ireland* (George Faulkner and James Williams, eds., 1770), i. 88, n.

[1032] *Epistle to Dr Arbuthnot*, line 100. Philips's verses gave rise to the epithet 'namby pamby'. *OED*.

[1033] J. R. O'Flanagan, *Lives of the Lord Chancellors and Keepers of the Great Seal of Ireland* (1870), ii. 59–62.

[1034] Boulter, *Letters*, ii. 17.

[1035] Above, p. cxiv.

The present reports unfortunately contain only two judgments of Wyndham and so there is little to suggest a pattern in his judicial thinking. In *Hussy* v. *Sheehy*[1036] he decided a technical point as to bills of review, deciding that matters of fact and law may be included, and in *Bishop [of] Elphin* v. *Leigh*[1037] he dealt with an arbitration case in which nineteen grounds to challenge the award were set out. He first decided the point of law that the arbitration legislation applied to the court of Chancery. One of the challenges was a suggestion of bias in that the arbitrators who drew up the award did so not in the old Custom House, where one of the arbitrators had his office, but in a private house belonging to the agent of the plaintiffs. Wyndham rejected this, noting that the old Custom House was not suitable for such work over several days, which says something about the state of its accommodation.

[1036] Below, p. 14.
[1037] Below, p. 44.

THE REPORTS

[*1*][1]

GEOGHEGAN v. CHEVERS[2]

In Exchequer

Michaelmas 1716

Mr Malone pro Defendant[3]

In 1656 John Chevers made a lease of part of these lands for 99 years, in trust for the wife of John and his children.

In 1672 the trustees assign to Sutton and Veal[4] and letters patent passed to the assignees subject to the trust in the lease. A patent passed of the rest of the land to John Chevers to his own use. The assignees mortgage part of the trust lands for £400 to Nettervil in fee, and the mortgagors were to enjoy paying £40 a year. That [*sic*] the equity of redemption and interest of all the lands came to Edward Chevers. That in the year 1695 Edward Chevers was outlawed of treason, by the name of Christopher Chevers of Killany, commonly called Lord Mount Leinster.[5] That the mortgagee and lessee have continued always in possession and paid the rent to the defendant Andrew Chevers, who is heir to Edward. The late trustees[6] upon the attainder of Christopher sell the equity of redemption to the Hollow Blades[7] who convey to the plaintiff. That this bill is to redeem and call the defendant Andrew to an account for the mesne profits. To which the defendant pleads that the attainder of Christopher Chevers no ways affects the estate of Edward.

---

[1] Page numbers in the MS. are inserted in these reports in italic between square brackets.

[2] See above p. cxviii. See also *Chevers* v. *Geoghegan* (1720) 6 Bro. P.C. 2nd ed. 12, 2 E.R. 900, an appeal from the Irish court of Chancery concerning the same litigation.

[3] Probably Richard Malone, s. and heir of Anthony Malone, Balliconey, Co. Westmeath, admitted, Middle Temple, 28 Nov. 1699, RAMT, vol 1, p. 246. admitted KI, Trinity term, 1703, d. 6 Jan. 1744. Above, p. clvi.

[4] *Sic.* It appears from the report cited in n. 2 above that the name was Wall.

[5] The peerage was created by James II in 1689. Edward Chevers, the elder, was created Baron Bannow in Co. Wexford and Viscount Mount-Leinster in Co. Carlow on 23 August 1689. He died in 1693. Cokayne, *Complete Peerage*, vol. 1, appendix F and ix. 354. Above, p. cxviii.

[6] The trustees of forfeited estates in Ireland. Below, p. 2 n. 19.

[7] The 'Governor and Company for Making Hollow Sword-Blades in England'. Above, p. cxx. See also *Hollow Sword Blade Company* v. *Dempsey* (1731) Fitzg. 201, 94 E.R. 719; *Anderton* v. *Magawley* (1726) 3 Bro. P.C. 2nd ed. 588, 1 E.R. 1515; *Bernard* v. *Woodley* (1753) 5 Bro. P.C. 2nd ed. 407, 2 E.R. 761; *Ellis* v. *Segrave* (1760) 7 Bro. P.C. 2nd ed. 331, 3 E.R. 214.

Sir Richard Levinge pro Quer.[8]

Insists that by the Act 9 Wm.[9] all outlawries are irreversible and no misnomer shall make them void, Ed. 4 *Sir John Paston's Case*,[10] 7 H. 4. 41 pl. 7 Misnomer,[11] 4 Ed. 4 fol. 41,[12] Moyl. Entr. 404, Shower 392,[13] Keilw.19.[14] 5 Co. 111.[15] 29 El. ch. 2.[16] 10 & 11 Ca. 1. 31,[17] 3 Inst. 21, Cook's reading on the aforesaid statute. [2] See the Statute of Periods in England 6 Ann.[18] for limiting persons to claim the lands vested in the trustees.[19]

The lands were sold by the trustees, where this was litigated and of which they had cognisance and no claim according to the Statute of Periods.

Mr Bernard pro Quer.[20]

Misnomers in Indictments makes [*sic*] them only voidable by the persons appearing and pleading or by writ of error after judgment, Lit. Rep. 182,[21] judgment voidable by error. Indictment is good against a peer by his Christian name and dignity.

The Act 9 W.[22] fixes the outlawry.

Trustees adjudication who were to judge of identities or persons and validity of outlawries.

Mr Butler pro Defendant[23]

As to the Act of Periods, we are in possession, and the Act does not extend to persons in possession.[24]

---

[8]　L. *querens*, plaintiff, from *quero*, to ask, seek.

[9]　9 Will. III, c. 5 (Ir.), 1697 (to hinder reversal of outlawries).

[10]　*Paston's Case* (1472), cited in Parliament 13 Co. Rep. 63 at 64, 77 E.R. 1473 at 1474: 'And in 12 E. 4. 2. in *Sir John Paston's Case*, it is holden, that every Court shall determine and decide the privileges and customs of the same Court, etc.' See also note in *Stockdale* v. *Hansard* (1839) 9 Ad. & El. 1 at 59, 112 E.R. 1112 at 1135: 'In *Sir J. Paston's Case*, there is a case cited from the Year-Book, where it is held that every Court shall determine of the privilege of that Court' and note (b): 'in 13 Rep. 64, Coke cites case as *Sir John Paston's*. The reference is to P 12 Ed. 4, 2: perhaps Y.B. Hil. 4 Edw. IV, fo. 43a, pl. 4, is meant.'

[11]　Y.B. Pasch. 2nd 7 Hen. IV, fo. 41, pl. 7.

[12]　Y.B. Hil. 4 Edw. IV. fo. 41, pl. 3.

[13]　*Rex* v. *Lord Dover* (1692) 1 Show. K.B. 392, 89 E.R. 660.

[14]　Keil. 19, 72 E.R. 174, 12 Hen. VII.

[15]　*Mallory's Case* (1601) 5 Co. Rep. 111b, 77 E.R. 228.

[16]　29 Eliz. I, c. 2 (Eng.), 1586 (errors in attainders).

[17]　The reference has not been not traced. 10 & 11 Car. I in Irish *Statutes at Large* ends at c. 19. There are no English statutes between 3 Car. I (1627) and 16 Car. I (1640).

[18]　6 Ann., c. 61 (G.B.), 1707, Statute of Periods, Act of Periods (limiting a time to persons to claim from trustees of forfeited estates in Ireland).

[19]　Under 11 Will. III, c. 2. (11 & 12 Will. III in Ruffhead) (Eng.), 1698, Trustee Act, Resumption Act (forfeited estates in Ireland vested in trustees).

[20]　This is probably a son of Bernard J., who was Francis Bernard, s. and heir of Francis, Castle Malone, Co. Cork, and Elizabeth Freke; b. 1662, ed. Trinity College Dublin and Middle Temple, 14 Dec. 1683. C.J. of palatinate of Tipperary, 1704. S.G., 1711, superseded 1714, P.S., 1724, J.C.P., 1726 (Ball, *Judges in Ireland*, ii. 199, KI AP, p. 34). Francis Bernard may have been his first son, KI, Hilary term, 1724, KI AP, p. 34. Stephen Bernard was his second son, KI, Michaelmas term, 1727, KI AP, p. 34.

[21]　*Countee de Pembroke* v. *Green and Bostocke* (1629) Lit. 181, 124 E.R. 197.

[22]　9 Will. III, c. 5 (Ir.), 1697 (to hinder reversal of outlawries).

[23]　There are two possible barristers called Butler in KI AP for the period: Thomas, of Kilveleaghier, Co. Tipperary, Grays's Inn, 28 May 1700, KI, Hilary term, 1704; and Thomas, *c.* 1734. KI AP, p. 68.

[24]　6 Ann., c. 61 (G.B.), 1707, s. 4.

1. H. 5[25] the proper name of the party, Christopher is in the proper name of Edward.

That Christopher could not appear by the name of Edward, therefore not to be outlawed. Commonly called Lord Mount Leinster, superfluity, which can neither vitiate nor make good the indictment, 2 Inst. 295, 599.

Mr Gore Attorney General pro Defendant

The Act 9 W. 3 does not extend to make a new outlawry, and so stands upon Christopher Chevers, who is the person outlawed.

In the Act of Periods a saving for persons in actual possession.[26]

Edward Chevers is not attainted, is an innocent person, the mortgagee of the innocent person claims his interest and then the trustees sell the equity of redemption.

That the possession of the mortgagee was the only possession he could have, and it would be very hard [3] to turn it into a right, and to transfer it to the purchasers under the trust.

That he had no way to claim under the Act of Periods.

Mr Malone

That if it were a good record against Edward it would also be good against Christopher, and so one record against two. If Edward was brought to the bar instead of Christopher, the court would discharge him. 2 Cro. 650 *The Case of Outlawry*.[27]

In 1708 the Act of Periods [was] passed.[28]

The trustees convey by bargain and sale.

The possession of the mortgagee and lessee is the possession of him who has the inheritance. But this Act says actual possession.

That we had no action or suit against anyone holding under the trustees, being always in actual possession, therefore we may now say, that the lands were never vested.

Mr Calaghan pro Quer.[29]

It appears that Andrew who claims the inheritance is in possession but of part, and only under the lease and mortgage claimed and decreed by the trustees, therefore possession goes with the purchase of the trust.

---

[25]   Y.B. Pasch. 1 Hen. V, fo. 4 pl. 6. Below, p. 5 n. 32.

[26]   6 Ann., c. 61 (G.B.), 1707, s. 4.

[27]   The page reference may be an error: *Archer* v. *Dalby* (1623) Cro. Jac. 660, 79 E.R. 571 is a case on outlawry. Croke published the volumes Cro. Jac. and Cro. Car. before he published Cro. Eliz., so '2 Cro.' was originally Cro. Car. There is no p. 650 in Cro. Car. The volumes were subsequently numbered chronologically. See Glaville L. Williams, 'Addendum to the Table of English Reports' (1939–1941) 7 *Cambridge Law Journal* 261 at 262. In the later printing '2 Cro.' would therefore be Cro. Jac. The case at Cro. Jac. 650 is *Savile* v. *Thornton* (1622) 79 E.R. 561, which does not seem relevant. There is no relevant case at Cro. Eliz. 650. See also *Ive* v. *Ambrey* (1595) Cro. Eliz. 268, 78 E.R. 615. Note that the reference '3 Cro. 133', below, at p. 341 [435] is to Cro. Eliz. 133, 78 E.R. 390.

[28]   6 Ann., c. 61 (G.B.), 1707, Act of Periods (limiting a time to persons to claim from trustees of forfeited estates in Ireland).

[29]   Above, p. clxii.

Plate 2. Cornelius Callaghan, councillor at law (d. 1741).

If the defendant had not been within the Statute of Periods, he might have brought his bill to redeem.

If the misnomer did not operate a mere nullity, he ought to have claimed.

1. Inst. 359b, that this is reversible only by plea, or writ of error. 33 H. 6 fol. 40,[30] that misnomer is an error in fact, therefore a writ of error is to be brought and now too late. Rast. Entr. 296, 399. They cannot say that this is an erroneous outlawry till the judgment is reversed.

Mr French pro Quer.[31]

That the trustees were judges of the outlawry against Edward Chevers.

That the trustees determined it upon the claim of the mortgagee.

1 H. 5 fol. 4,[32] 22 Ed. 4, 34,[33] Dy. 88 Oldcastle's Case,[34] if you come in upon outlawry, you cannot plead misnomer, but must bring a writ of error, or *identitate nominis*.[35] That this is no nullity, 21 Ed. 3, 7.[36] 19 Ed. 4, 24.[37] [4] Bro. Misnomer 40,[38] *Doctr[ina] Placitandi*; misnomer must be pleaded in bar. Palmer 44[39]

If only voidable by writ of error, 9 Wm. 3[40] cuts them off.

Sir Richard Levinge pro Quer.

That the mortgagor being in by the covenant of the mortgagee, it is a tenancy at will, and determinable on the death of the mortgagee.

Lord Chief Baron

If the heir or executor of the mortgagee accepts the rent, it revives the tenancy at will.

Sir Richard Levinge

The trustees having sold only the equity of redemption no actual possession could be, and the Act must be understood *secundum subjectam materiam*,[41] as if a reversion were sold, it must be understood of such a possession as by law they could have, or the nature of the thing admits.

[30] Y.B. Mich. 33 Hen. VI, fo. 40, pl. 17.
[31] This is presumably not Patrick French, who is mentioned by that name below, p. 86. The only other barrister of that surname mentioned by KI AP, p. 179, in the period is Richard French, admitted to KI, Michaelams term, 1708.
[32] Y.B. Pasch. 1 Hen. V, fo. 4, pl. 6.
[33] Y.B. Mich. 22 Edw. IV, fo. 34, pl. 12.
[34] *Allington* v. *Oldcastel* (1553) 1 Dy. 88a, 73 E.R. 191.
[35] An ancient and, according to Jacob and Tomlins, by the end of the eighteenth century, obsolete writ brought by a person claiming that they were wrongly committed to prison in a personal action as a result of mistaken identity.
[36] Y.B. Hil. 21 Edw. III, fo. 7, pl. 18.
[37] Possibly Y.B. Hil. 19 Edw. IV, fo. 7b, pl. 7.
[38] Brooke's Abridgement, 'Misnomer', 40.
[39] *Taylor's Case* (1619) Palm. 44, 81 E.R. 970.
[40] 9 Will. III, c. 5 (Ir.), 1697 (to hinder reversal of outlawries).
[41] L. according to the subject matter.

Such a bill admits the title of the mortgagee.

Chevers having nothing but an equity of redemption, ought by the Statute of Periods to have brought his bill to redeem within two years.

Mr Bernard

That the Statute of Trustees[42] vests the lands where there was an equity of redemption, or a reversion, and where they sell the vendee is in actual possession, and he who claims the mortgage takes the possession out of the trustees, and the equity only remained in them.

By the Statute of Periods[43] whatever was purchased was intended to be preserved, see the Act, 'whosoever has any incumbrance or demand in law or equity shall claim in two years or be barred', and then comes the exception, that the possession mentioned in the exception is a possession in his own right, and not a tenancy at will, and a right to redeem.

Mr Calaghan

Geoghegan having purchased the equity under the Sword blades,[44] comes here to redeem. [5]

The Act of Periods excludes the plea of saying the lands are not vested. Here can be no actual possession being an equity of redemption.

All purchasers enrolling their deeds shall be deemed to be in actual seisin.

See the Trustee Act fol. 41. That this clause divests the possession, and turning it to a right on the other side, and he is limited by the statute.

That the Act intended at least to give an actual possession to those who purchased under the Act. [The] lease [was granted] in 1656 to John Chevers the father in trust for his wife and children. In 1682 [he] mortgages subject to the lease. Edward [was] outlawed, and the second brother claims the land. John claims the lease lands.

Andrew got possession of some of the lease lands, and John holds the rest of the lease lands.

Mr Geoghegan pro Quer

That a tenancy at will is not an actual possession not even to bring trespass.

Mr Attorney General

Upon the Trustee Act it could not be that the sale of lands not vested should put the owner to a bare right.

---

[42] 11 Will. III, c. 2. (11 & 12 Will. III in Ruffhead) (Eng.), 1698, Trustee Act, Resumption Act (forfeited estates in Ireland vested in trustees).

[43] 6 Ann., c. 61 (G.B.), 1707, Act of Periods.

[44] I.e. the Hollow Blades. Above, p. 1 n. 7.

Mr Malone

Neither the trustees [n]or the plaintiff were ever in possession. A conveyance of a man out of possession shan't divest. That all the Act of Trustees is relative, shall be in possession of estate so sold, is of lands vested and the clause of the Statute of Periods shows, that the actual possession did not go with the sale, because it supposes others to be in possession.

That the conveyances shan't go beyond the vesting clause, to dis-seize or turn to a right.

The possession of the mortgagee and the lessee is the possession of him in reversion, or of him that has the right of redemption.

That the defendant was in possession of what he could be in possession of.

The Statute of Periods must be construed as the Statute of Fines,[45] that is, where the parties interest is turned to a right, and the equity is not divested by the trustees conveyance, the estate not being vested.

Lord Chief Baron

The Statute of Periods is conclusive, where enjoyment [6] has been under the conveyance of the trustees.   Mes App. F. 591.

LESSEE OF BURK v. BLAKE

In Exchequer

Easter 1716

On a Special Verdict

Mr Malone pro Quer

The jury find that Henry Blake the grandfather of the lessor of the plaintiff had issue Patrick his first son, who had issue the lessor of the plaintiff, and John his second son.

That 26 January 1702 Henry the grandfather made his will, and devises the lands in question to Anthony Brown, in trust for Catherine during her life, with power to make leases for seven years only, and after her decease to John his second son for life, with remainder to the heirs of John in tail, with remainders over, and devises [£]200 to the lessor of the plaintiff, and that if he set up any title to the estate, this legacy should be void.

Several endorsements on the will, in one there is mention of a codicil.

The jury further find an Act made the 21 September 1703, intitled, An Act to prevent the further growth of Popery.[46]

---

[45] 4 Hen. VII, c. 24 (Eng.), 1488 (fines); 10 Car. I, sess. 2, c. 8 (Ir.), 1634 (Act for the exposition of 4 Hen. VII, c. 24).

[46] 2 Ann., c. 6 (Ir.), 1703 (to prevent the further growth of popery).

Find a clause for maintenance of any Popish child that shall become Protestant.

Find another clause in the same Act, where the eldest son becoming Protestant, makes the popish parent tenant for life of his real estate in fee and fee tail.

Finds another clause that disables any Papist to purchase lands.

Find the Gavelkind clause,[47] whereby the estates of all Papists shall descend in Gavelkind.

Find another clause, that if any son of a Papist shall become Protestant, he shall succeed according to the common law.

Find a clause, that no person shall take benefit but [7] who shall take oaths etc.

Find the second Act 6 May 1709[48] to explain the Gavelkind Clause and find that by the second Act that clause should be in force from the 21 of September 1703.

Find another clause, that all sales made after the 21 September 1703 to the 25 of March 1704 for good consideration are saved.[49]

Find another clause, that no person conforming on the first Act should have the benefit of it, unless he took the oaths, and filed a certificate in 6 months.

Find that Henry Blake died seised 3 March 1703, and was a Papist.

That Patrick was a Papist in his lifetime, and is dead.

That John was and is a Papist.

That the lessor of the plaintiff 15 July the twelfth of the Queen[50] became a Protestant, that he filed a certificate in the Rolls Office 6 of August 1713 *in hæc verba*, that he took the oaths of *abjuram* and subscribed the declaration and conformed himself as the several Acts require.

Find that the lessor of the plaintiff was twenty at the finding.

Find that this ejectment was brought in Michaelmas 1713.

First objection, that the will being made before the 21 of September is good.

Second objection, that the lessor of the plaintiff not being of the age of 21 years when he filed his certificate he is not entitled.

That Henry Blake being found seised 3 March 1703 sets the first objection out of doors notwithstanding the will.

That Henry could have disposed of it at any time before his death and that the Act is in nature of a conveyance.

That as to the second objection, it cannot be denied if the lessor of the plaintiff had a been a Protestant at the death of Henry, but that he should have all.

Mr Nutley pro Defendant[51]

That if the Acts had not been made the will had been good to pass the lands. [8] That the Act does not take away the effect of the will, it being made 26 January 1702.

That lands in Gavelkind may be disposed of by deed or will.

That all deeds and wills made before the Act are not controlled by the Act, the Act being, [*sic*] notwithstanding any disposal by deed or will which shall be made.

---

[47] Ibid., s. 10. ('Gavelkind Act').
[48] 8 Ann., c. 3 (Ir.), 1709 (popery: Protestant discoverors).
[49] Ibid., s. 14.
[50] I.e. the regnal year 12 Anne.
[51] Either William Nutley or Richard Nutley, who were brothers. William was s. and heir of William, one of the masters of the Utter Bar, decd. William was admitted to Middle Temple, 25 July 1685, called, 26 May 1693. KI, Michaelmas term, 1701. Richard was 2nd son, admitted to Middle Temple, 2 July 1695, called, 3 June 1698. KI, Trinity term, 1700. KI AP, p. 368.

That Henry dying after the beginning of the session they would have it he had not made any disposal till his death, but in pleading we say, he did such a day *facere et condere* his will, and such a day he died.

That the making of a will is legally and properly said to be when it bears date, Plow. 343.[52] If A devises all his lands, and has but 10 acres, and before he dies he purchases twelve more, none but the first ten pass by the will.

A feme covert[53] makes a will, the husband dies, and after she dies the will is void.

A bargain and sale made; the enrolment makes it consummate; it takes its effect at the date of the bargain and sale.[54]

An infant makes a will; after dies of full age; the will is void.

Co. Lit. 186: an attornment is necessary to the grant of a reversion, yet the date of the grant takes effect.

Statute 7 Wm. 3:[55] Witnesses [are] necessary to make a will, yet a will made before the statute according to the law I think is good. But *quære* that.

Mr Nutley

The second Act confirming all conveyances made before 21 September 1703.

All explanatory Acts explain all matters omitted in the first.

A deed made with a power of revocation before the Act would certainly be a good deed to pass the lands.

As to the second point, that the plaintiff has not performed the requisites to entitle him to the benefit of the Act:

That the heir is under 21 at the death of the testator, he is to file a certificate within a year after he comes of age.

The clause is to be construed strictly and literally. [9]

That he is not within the words of the Act, so neither is he within the meaning of it, that the law makers designed that the convert should be of mature age to judge of religion.

Lord Chief Baron

The words in the Act are, 'notwithstanding any disposition by deed or will'. The will is made at the time of making, but not consummate till after the death of the testator. No disposition is made till the death of the testator, the estate is not vested in the devisee, and therefore no disposition. The reason that the second clause did not take notice of the wills made is because the first clause had taken hold of it. As to the second point, the words are, that, if the heir at law be a Papist, and an infant, if he within one year after he comes of age shall conform, etc., he shall inherit. I think he may conform at any time from the death of the testator to the age of 22 years, and

---

[52] *Brett* v. *Rigden* (1568) 1 Plow. 343, 75 E.R. 520. This was the law until the Wills Act, 1837.

[53] LF. married woman.

[54] A reference to the Statute of Uses (Ireland), 1634, s. 17. Before the statute a bargain and sale, i.e. a contract to convey land, raised a use in favour of the purchaser, i.e. an equitable interest. The statute of 1634 would have 'executed' the use giving the purchaser the legal estate, which would have made every contract to convey land a conveyance in itself, which was not an intended consequence of the statute, so s. 17 provided that the use was not executed unless the indenture of bargain and sale was enrolled in the king's court in Dublin. The Statute of Enrolments, 1536 had been to the same effect in England.

[55] 7 Will. III, c. 12 (Ir.), 1695 (wills).

the bishop is to judge of the sincerity of the person conforming. It would be hard if the heir at law being of age should have no time to conform.

Curia

Judgment pro Quer.

No writ of error was brought in the Exchequer Chamber, and judgment affirmed and a new writ of error brought to England and on 22 of June 1717 it was adjudged by the Lords, that the heir of a Papist may file his certificate before his age of 21, for the Act was only meant as an encouragement for persons to renounce popery. *Burk* v. *Morgan.* SC.[56]

HAMILTON v. [ANONYMOUS]

In Exchequer

Trinity 1716

A clause in a lease of lives that the lessee should pay all taxes, country charges and impositions whatsoever imposed on the premises. *Quære* whether by the above words the lessee is obliged to pay the quit rent. [*10*]

Lord Chief Baron

Modern Reports *Brueston* v. *Kitchin*,[57] whether the parliamentary taxes after the demise are chargeable on the lessee. By the better opinion they are, but 'tis clear all the taxes before the demise must be paid by the lessee.

Mr Malone

It was ruled in the Chancery this term, that in the words 'taxes, charges, and impositions', the quit rent was not included.

Mr Baron St Leger

I think the words 'taxes and country charges' do not comprehend the quit rent. Suppose the tenant of a freehold[58] should set[59] his freehold to an undertenant, he paying the rent and all taxes and country charges, I don't think the lessee shall pay the lord of the fee.[60]

---

[56] *Burke* v. *Morgan* (1717) 5 Bro. P.C. 2nd ed. 365, 2 E.R. 734.
[57] *Brewster* v. *Kitchin* (1697) 1 Raym. Ld. 317, 91 E.R. 1108.
[58] I.e. a fee simple.
[59] *OED*, 57 a: to let at lease, lease, let. Now local. 1710 Swift, *Jrnl. to Stella* 26 Oct., 'I have had also a letter from Parvisol, with an account how my livings are set; and that they are fallen, since last year, sixty pounds.' 1788 Burke *Sp. agst. W. Hastings*, Works. XIII. 233, 'By setting the rest to farmers at rents and under hopes, which could never be realized'.
[60] A lease for lives is strictly a freehold. If the holder of a fee simple granted a lease for lives, that would create freehold tenure between the grantor and grantee. St Leger's point is that if the lessee undertook to pay 'taxes and country charges', he would not be liable to pay the quit rent to the lord of the grantor's tenure.

Lord Chief Baron

The quit rent being a reservation on a patent, is a tax within the letter of the law. Impositions comprehend a rent.

Mr Baron Pocklington

Clear rent over and above all taxes and country charges, I think the quit rent comes within the word charges.

TERRY, LESSEE OF THE SWORD BLADES[61]

v.

JOHN DONALDSON

On a trial at bar in Ejectment.

The plaintiff produced an inquisition taken in 1693 as an evidence of a lease for years found without commencement, but that 498 years of the term continued. There was an endorsement on the back of the inquisition that was returned in 1705, but the endorsement was not signed by any officer. The court allowed the inquisition as evidence. [*11*] The defendant offered the memorial of a deed out of the Registry office as evidence that the lessor of the plaintiff sold to Edwards before the commencement of the plaintiff's lease, but denied by the court upon which two points the counsel for the defendants prayed a bill of exceptions[62] might be allowed which was done accordingly.

DIGBY v. HANLY ET AL.[63]

In Exchequer

7 May 1728

On a plea by Mr Keon[64] the attorney to interrogatories exhibited to him.

The plaintiff's bill is on the Popery Acts to be decreed to the benefit of a decree had in Chancery by one Moreton against the defendant Hanly on the Acts, that decree having been in trust for the defendant.

---

[61] Above, p. 1 n. 7.

[62] At common law a writ of error lay for an error of law where it appeared on the face of the record and for an error of fact where either party died before judgment. No writ of error was available where an error of law did not appear on the record, as where a judge ruled evidence inadmissible. A bill of exceptions to evidence was allowed by the Statute of Westminster II, 13 Edw. I, c. 31. The bill stated the exceptions taken to the judge's rulings and was signed by the judge and both counsel. The bill was in the nature of an appeal and examinable by writ of error in the court immediately superior. Jacob, *Law Dictionary*.

[63] Below, p. 213.

[64] Ambrose Keon, attorney of the Exchequer, *c.* 1734, d. 6 July 1752. KI AP, p. 266. His first name is mentioned below, p. 213.

Mr Keon was agent to Hanly in the cause of Moreton and is made a party for discovery in this. He answered and confessed that the bill of Moreton was in trust for Hanly. The cause being at issue, Keon is struck out of the bill and interrogatories exhibited to him in behalf of the plaintiff but as to the interrogatories which relate to the proceedings on the decree of Moreton he pleads he came to the knowledge of them as agent to Hanly and therefore insists he is not obliged to discover them.

Lord Chief Baron

The plea is wrong, for he does not swear he came to the knowledge of the facts only as agent for Hanly which he ought to have done. We will not determine the point whether an attorney is obliged on the Popery Acts to answer interrogatories till that point comes regularly before the courts, but apprehend it would be absurd that though he must answer a bill, he need not answer the interrogatories.

Post 272.

Curia

Overrule the plea and Keon to answer the interrogatories.

[*12*] N.B. Publication was past in the cause before the plea was set down and yet Keon ordered to be examined to the interrogatory pleaded to and after he was examined, plaintiff was obliged to move the rules for publication *de novo*.

[ANONYMOUS] v. ADMINISTRATORS OF COGAN

In Exchequer

Michaelmas 1729

The bill was brought against an administratrix to discover assets and be decreed to money due by assumpsit. The defendant answered and demurred. In her answer she confessed assets, but denied the assumpsit. The demurrer was overruled by Mr Baron St Leger, for that the plaintiff was brought into equity to discover assets and therefore shall not be sent to law but may proceed to prove the assumpsit in equity, and the case of *Mead*[65] was cited, where a bond creditor having brought a bill to discover assets and the defendant having confessed assets, and the bond, demurred to the relief and the court overruled the demurrer and decreed plaintiff to his money.

The difference between that case and this I think is this, in *Mead's case* the bond was confessed and therefore no occasion to try it at law, but in the principal case the assumpsit being denied, *quære* if plaintiff ought not to have this matter tried by a jury?

MSS̃ cas. in Canc. D. 350.[66]

---

[65] No citation given. Possibly *Mead* v. *Hide* (1690) 2 Vern. 120, 23 E.R. 687, and sub nom. *Gower* v. *Mead* (1689) Prec. Ch. 2, 24 E.R. 1.

[66] The marginal note at this point appears to refer to *Mead's Case*.

LESSEE OF LORD ORRERY v. ONAGHAN

In Exchequer

15 November 1729

On two points saved by the judges at Nisi Prius on an ejectment brought for non-payment of rent. First point was, that on the trial a bill filed by the defendant against the plaintiff was produced, which set forth [*13*] that the plaintiff had demised the lands to the defendant but did not mention that any clause of re-entry was contained therein, on which evidence plaintiff obtained a verdict.

Second point, that part of the lands demised lay in the county of Cork, and part in the county of Limerick.

Adjudged by the whole court, that by the statute 4 Geo. [I][67] no clause of re-entry was necessary to support the action. And that although the demised lands lie in several counties, yet the ejectment may be brought for the lands in either county.

WESTBY v. BUTLER

In Exchequer

27 November 1729

In Arrest of Judgment

The case on the record was that the plaintiff's father being seized in fee of some lands in County Clare, he in the year 1711 demised them to one Butler for a term of years, excepting thereout all timber and timber trees; the lessee covenants for himself and his assigns to preserve the timber trees. The lessor dies and the plaintiff as his son and heir became seized of the rent and reversion of the demised premises. The lessee in 1717 assigns the term to the defendant and he having suffered some trees to be cut down, the plaintiff brought an action of covenant against him on the lease, and the defendant having pleaded no trees were cut, issue was joined thereon, and a verdict for the plaintiff with £50 damages.

The defendant's counsel insisted, that the trees being excepted out of the lease did not pass, and that therefore the covenant to preserve them was a collateral covenant, and did not bind the assignee of the term. But agreed that it would have been otherwise if the trees had not been excepted out of the lease.[68] [*14*] After several arguments the court were agreed to arrest the judgment, but on motion of the plaintiff's counsel he had liberty to discontinue paying costs.

---

[67]   4 Geo. I, c. 5 (Ir.), 1717 (ejectment for non payment of rent).
[68]   If the trees had been demised with the land the covenant would have 'touched and concerned' the land and the burden would therefore have passed to the assignee of the lease.

BRACE, WEBBER AND CANE v. FRENCH

2 December 1729

In Exchequer

A lease was made by the ancestor of the defendant to the assignor of the Plaintiff for 31 years in 1699, and a covenant in the lease, that the lessor should at the end of the term make a new lease for 31 years with the same clauses, covenants and reservations as in the former.

The Plaintiff insisted that in the new lease there should be a covenant for renewal as in the old lease.

But decreed otherwise.

But it was adjudged in the House of Lords that the new lease should likewise be with covenants to renew. *Bridge* v. *Hitchcock* 24 June 1716.[69]

HUSSY v. SHEEHY

Michaelmas 4to Geo 2di [1730][70]

In Chancery

In court: Wyndham, Lord Chancellor
                                   Marlay, Chief Baron
                                   Bernard, J.C.B.[71]

Mr Daly[72]

The question on this demurrer before the court is, if, in a bill of review, errors at law and in fact may be assigned in the same bill.

The errors at law assigned were that the lease decreed to be set aside was so decreed to be set aside by a bill filed against the cestui que trust [15] without making

---

[69] *Bridges* v. *Hitchcock* (1715) 5 Bro P.C. 2nd ed. 6, 2 E.R. 498. The date in E.R. is 24 June 1715. Also in 1 Bro. P.C. 1st ed. 522, and so cited in Bridgman's *Index* (2nd ed. 1813), Landl. & Ten., ii. 131. The E.R. reproduces the 2nd ed. of Bro. P.C. by Tomlins. Some cases in the 1st ed. of Bro. P.C. do not appear in the 2nd and therefore are not in E.R. Bridgman's *Index* uses the first edition of Brown's *Parliamentary Cases* in folio, but has a table of the 1st and 2nd ed. of Bro. P. C. in vol. 3, p. 779.

[70] The 4 Geo. II was from 11 June 1730 to 10 June 1731.

[71] Judge of the Common Bench, i.e. Common Pleas. See Ball, *Judges in Ireland*, ii. 199.

[72] There are two barristers of that name and of that period listed in KI AP. This is almost certainly Peter Daly, admitted, KI, Michaelmas term, 1716, KI AP, p. 119, d. 27 Feb. 1757. He was prominent at the Bar in 1730. Ball, *Judges in Ireland*, ii. 110–12 quotes a poem, 'A View of the Bar' published in Dublin in 1730 which mentions Peter Daly. He is probably the same person as Peter Daly, s. of Denis, Carownekelly, Co. Galway, admitted to Gray's Inn, 3 May 1710: RAGI at p. 357, fo. 1388. Peter Daly, of Carownekelly, Co. Galway, is also listed in the O'Byrne and Clare, eds., *Convert Rolls* (see above p. clvi), certificate, 22 Oct. 1716, conformity 21 Oct. 1716, and this coincides in date with the Peter Daly in KI AP. There is also Denis Daly, KI, Michaelmas term, 1710; KI AP, p. 118.

the trustee in such lease any party to the suit, on pretence that the lease was made by a forged letter of attorney.

Secondly, that this court ought to direct a trial at law to try the validity of that letter of attorney, before the same was, or should be construed in this court, which with the want of proper parties above-mentioned were the errors at law.

The error in fact assigned is, that the court on hearing being persuaded that the letter of attorney was actually forged, directed a prosecution in the King's Bench against the plaintiff, and that such prosecution since making the degree the plaintiff Hussy was on a fair trial acquitted, on which trial he fully proved the perfection of the said letter of attorney, and therefore ought now to be at liberty to give that new matter that happened since the decree in evidence on this bill of review.

And that errors in law and in fact may be assigned in a bill of review where the fact is matter of evidence that came to a man's knowledge after the decree made, and relative to the thing in issue in the original cause, he cited Hardr. 57,[73] 174,[74] 1 Chan. Cas. 43,[75] 44,[76] 61, 62, 63, 64;[77] 1 Vern. 135,[78] 166,[79] and in Lord Bacon's *Works* 4 vol, 146,[80] therein in the very order made by him which recites the method and causes for admitting bills of review to be filed, in which order this is admitted a good ground for such bill, and it explaining what new matter is allowable to be assigned for error in a bill of review and reversal. For these bills of review and reversal are but a modern invention or practice for formerly the King sometimes appointed others to assist my lord chancellor, and those chiefly of his Privy Council, as his secretaries, etc. as 27 H. 8 14b 15.[81]

But by the 16 Car. I, c. 10[82] it is enacted that neither [*16*] the King nor his Privy Council have or ought to have any right or jurisdiction to determine property by English bill, or otherwise, that the same ought to be tried by the ordinary courts of the law and since that time bills of review have been found necessary. And till of late it was a question whether this court could ever examine into any matter after judgment at law, as Cro. Ja. 335;[83] 2 Bulstr. 197,[84] 215;[85] 3 Buls. 118;[86] 2 And. 162,[87] and till of late appeals from decrees in Chancery to Parliament were not known, wherefore it was thought a præmunire to impeach a judgment at law by bill in equity and that the courts of equity ought to be prohibited, because there was no method to impeach these decrees, and my Lord Coke[88] went so far as to say courts of equity were not courts of record. But now that the courts of Chancery of late days enlarged this power, this method of examining their own decrees was established, and that as well for errors in fact as at law, and that in one and the same bill of review, because

[73] *Walsingham* v. *Baker* (1655) Hard. 49 at 51, 145 E.R. 375.
[74] *Fanshaw* v. *Anonymous* (1660) Hard. 174, 145 E.R. 438.
[75] *Curtis* v. *Smallridge* (1664) 1 Ch. Cas. 43, 22 E.R. 685.
[76] *Read* v. *Hamby* (1664) 1 Ch. Cas. 44, 22 E.R. 686.
[77] *Cocker* v. *Bevis* (1665) 1 Ch. Cas. 61, 22 E.R. 695.
[78] *Price* v. *Keyte* (1682) 1 Vern. 135, 23 E.R. 369.
[79] *Mellish* v. *Williams* (1683) 1 Vern. 166, 23 E.R. 390.
[80] *The Works of Francis Bacon*, 4 vols. (London, 1730), iv. 146.
[81] Y.B. Trin. 27 Hen. VIII, fo. 14b–15 pl. 6 (Thomas Cromwell assisting Audley L.C.).
[82] 16 Car. I, c. 10 (Eng.), 1640 (abolition of Star Chamber).
[83] *Heath* v. *Rydley* (1613) Cro. Jac. 335, 79 E.R. 286.
[84] Note, Coke C.J., 2 Bulst. 197, 80 E.R. 1064.
[85] Note, Coke C.J., 2 Bulst. 215, 80 E.R. 1078.
[86] *Vaudry* v. *Pannel* (1615) 3 Bulst. 116 at 118, 81 E.R. 99 at 101.
[87] *Sir Moyle Finch's Case* (1606) 2 And. 162, 123 E.R. 600.
[88] *Sic.* Sir Edward Coke.

otherwise a great inconvenience may ensue, for that a man can never have a second bill of review, be the errors of the decree ever so flagrant.

And even in a writ of error at law a man may assign errors in law and errors in fact and all is good unless taken advantage of by demurrer and much more so in a bill of review, where a man shall never have a second bill.

'Twas argued on the other side, that the demurrer ought to be allowed and said that the decree consisted of several particulars and the only part now complained of is the setting aside of a lease made under colour of a letter of attorney not proved on the hearing.

And as the demurrer stands now before the court it consists of four points or questions. The first is, whether the present bill as a bill of [17] review be properly before the court or not? The second, if the errors in law assigned in this bill of review are sufficient to reverse the decree? The third, if the new facts charged as errors in fact in this bill, though true in every particular, would be sufficient cause to reverse the decree? The fourth, if the default of the defendants in not taking due advantage by special demurrer of the irregularity of filing this bill hath totally dispensed with the irregularity, so as your Lordship cannot take any notice of it now?

And as to the first, 'tis clear this bill of review is not properly before the court, for no man is entitled to file a bill of review without performing the decree, unless it be where such performance would extinguish his right, as by his perfecting a conveyance, or release, levying a fine, or the like; or a special order made by the court to dispense with the non-performance of the decree upon reasonable suggestions, 1 Chan. Cas. 42,[89] and also giving sufficient bail if the decree being a penal matter not only for the costs but for the matter in demand; 'tis true in decrees in the realty 'tis sufficient to give bail for the costs only, but even this rule may be dispensed with, where the party swears he is not able to procure bail, nor has he sufficient to answer the same.

But no bill of review can ever be filed for a new matter without the plaintiff makes affidavit that such new matter came to his knowledge after the decree, and that such new matter is true and that the petition to admit a man to file such bill and affidavit and order are part of the bill of review, which pro tanto is a new bill. 'Tis true errors in law and in fact may be in one bill of review.

As to the second, 'tis part of the original jurisdiction of a court of equity to suppress forged deeds. As is said in the case of *Lord Macclesfield* v. *Fitton*, 1 Vern.,[90] so this court need not direct a trial at law [18] and as for want of parties 'tis a different thing to make a decree for want of parties and to reverse a decree already made for want of parties where the court will presume every thing done right.

And on this decree it appears the bill was brought to set aside a lease charged to be made to Dom. Rice,[91] or to somebody in trust for him by the plaintiff Hussy, and Hussy and Rice in their answers confess such lease was made in trust for Rice, and that Rice enjoyed, so that till hearing it did not appear who the trustee was, or that Hanly had any concern in it; besides it appears that Rice was the person for whose use such lease was made and was in the actual possession of the lands and to be supposed by assignment from the trustee; besides this decree cannot end his right

[89]   *Savil* v. *Darcey* (1663) 1 Ch. Cas. 42, 22 E.R. 685.
[90]   *Macclesfield (Earl)* v. *Fitton* (1683) 1 Vern. 168, 23 E.R. 399, and see *Fitton* v. *Macclesfield* (1684) 1 Vern. 287 at 292, 23 E.R. 459 at 476.
[91]   Perhaps L. *dominus*, Lord, possibly refers to Sir Stephen Rice, Baron Monteagle, but may be an abbreviation of Dominic, or Dominick.

and this bill seeks only to set aside this decree as far as it is relative to the interest of the plaintiffs and not his.

As to the third, supposing all the new matter true as charged in this bill, it cannot be a cause to reverse this decree for no want of evidence or bare supplemental parol proof can ever be introduced as a cause to reverse a decree as Hard. 51,[92] 174;[93] 1 Chan Cas. 54.[94] And this man's acquittal of the forgery cannot be a cause of reversal, for this letter of attorney may be forged though not by him, or supposing it had been really perfected, yet if he failed of proving it, sure he cannot now assign it as a cause to reverse this decree, yet he can prove it now in the same court and cause.

As to the fourth, the demurrer here, though not so accurately drawn, plainly distinguishes the errors at law from the errors in fact, and is applied to them, and the answer cannot overrule it as to the errors in law; and though the demurrer is taken to the whole bill, yet if it be proper to any part of it, 'tis for so much good, and ought to be allowed pro tanto, and that your lordship will at this [19] day take as much notice of your not complying with the orders of the court on this demurrer as if we specially demurred for that reason.

Mr Justice Bernard

Said, that the errors in law for want of parties etc. were immaterial on this bill, being it complains of such part of the decree as relates to the plaintiff; beside it appears in the decree that [the] lease was in trust for Dom. Rice which may be by assignment.

Nor can it be a cause for a bill of review and reversal, that you did not prove the perfection of this letter of attorney before the hearing, and you aver nothing according to the course of the court, and though you have had an answer, yet shall the person that answered and denied the suggestions of your bill be in a worse condition as to the course of the court, than you that averred nothing according to the course of the court?

Errors in law and of fact may be assigned in a writ of error, Sid. 147;[95] 1 Lev. 76,[96] 105,[97] and though that is a doubleness, yet if the parties do not take advantage of it by special demurrer 'tis good, and the courts at law ought to be delayed until the fact is tried, least [sic] the court should make contradictory decrees. And these errors in fact must arise from matters known after the decree, and relative to the matters in issue before the decree, and both errors must necessarily be in the same bill, because being the suitor cannot have a second bill of review, he should otherwise be in a bad condition. As to the errors in fact which are fact and matters of record blended together, the court ought to be apprised of the same before the bill was filed, and to have an affidavit of the truth of the same, otherwise they don't come properly before the court, and had they been properly before the court, still they are things not relative [20] to the thing in issue, as the forgery and acquittal, or things that could be proved before making the decree, as the perfection of the letter of attorney, so that either way there is no cause to reverse the decree assigned. And this is a bad

---

[92] *Walsingham* v. *Baker* (1655) Hard. 49 at 51, 145 E.R. 375.
[93] *Fanshaw* v. *Anonymous* (1660) Hard. 174, 145 E.R. 438.
[94] *Combs* v. *Proud* (1664) 1 Ch. Cas. 54, 22 E.R. 691.
[95] *Smith* v. *Smith* (1663) 1 Sid. 147, 82 E.R. 1023.
[96] *Molins* v. *Werby* (1662) 1 Lev. 76, 83 E.R. 305.
[97] *Slaughter* v. *Tucker* (1663) 1 Lev. 105, 83 E.R. 320.

bill, not being filed according to the rule of the court, nor the decree performed nor bail given, and done by fraud on the court, so should be set aside on motion.

Lord Chief Baron

As to the point if errors at law and in fact may be assigned in the same bill of review, 'tis clear they may, as *Swift* v. *Lightborn*[98] in Chief Baron Gilbert's time in the Exchequer, and so it was resolved in the Chancery of England in 1713 in Lord Chancellor Harcourt's[99] time. There a man petitioned for liberty to file a bill of review in order to prove a partnership, on affidavit that he met with or found a letter in his brother's box that would fully prove the partnership which he knew nothing of until after the decree, though he had the box before; but [the] lord chancellor rejected it, and said he would not make so dangerous a precedent, but on approval the House of Lords adjudged it otherwise. And I am of the opinion there are no errors in fact sufficiently before the court for want of the proper affidavit, and giving security, or performing the decree, and yet though the defendant by answer put such fact in issue, yet the court ought not to admit it in breach of the rule of the court. I am also of opinion that the plaintiffs have no reason to assign the want of parties for error, the prayer of your bill being to be relieved against the decree as far as it relates to them.

Curia

We are all of opinion [that] matters of fact and law [*21*] may be assigned for errors in a bill of review, and so are the precedents, though if it were *res integra*[100] I should much doubt it from the inconvenience, for though it may be done in a writ of error yet that is in a superior court, and errors in fact are only assignable in a writ of error *coram vobis*, but it may be done in a bill of review, because the court can impose reasonable terms on the plaintiff before they admit him to file his bill, and that he can never have a second bill of review. I think this bill is not properly before the court as to the errors in fact, it being filed in defiance of the rules of the court, nor are the facts assigned sufficient to reverse the decree, though they were true, for the decree is to set aside the lease it being made by virtue of a letter of attorney not proved, but the contrary, and suppose it were proved now, I do not think it should be admitted as a cause to reverse the decree.

And it fully appears that at the time of the decree Dom. Rice appeared to be cestui que trust, so that as to the error at law the demurrer is good and therefore I allow the same.

And as to the errors in fact they are not before the court, however, I must dispose of it as it now stands in the paper before me, nor do I think I can dispose of it by motion as Mr Justice Bernard proposes, nay I can never dispose of it by motion unless there is such a motion made; which ought to be made before it be put down to be heard and therefore I allow the demurrers as to the errors at law and dismiss the bill as to the errors in fact.

---

[98] No citation given.

[99] Simon Harcourt (*c.* 1661–1727), first Viscount Harcourt L.C.; L.K. from October 1710 and became L.C. in April 1713. *ODNB*.

[100] A point governed neither by any decision nor by any rule of law, which must therefore be decided upon principle. Jowitt, *Dictionary*.

RYLEY LESSEE OF LADY MARY COOLEY, MOTHER AND GUARDIAN TO HER TWO DAUGHTERS

v.

RICHARD WESELEY [101]

Hilary Term 1730 [/1731], [102]

Friday, January 29,

In Exchequer

Marley [103]

Lord Chief Baron

Pocklington, St Leger, Barons

[22] On ejectment brought for non payment of rent on the 8 Geo. 1, c. 2 [104] and defence taken by Mr Graten the tenant and by Mr Weseley separately by order of court.

Dudley Cooley the great grandfather of the minors in 1673 made a lease for three lives of certain lands to the Grattens [sic] whereof one is still in being, and in 1674 on the marriage of his son Henry he made a settlement of all his estate on Henry for life, remainder to his first and every other son in tail male: Henry had two sons, Henry and the defendant Richard. Henry the son intermarries with Lady Mary and levies a fine and suffers a recovery of the manors of Carbery and Castle Carbery by name, and dies leaving two daughters and the great question was, whether the reversion and rent due on the lease for lives belongs to the daughters as heirs of their father or to the defendant Richard as heir in tail under the settlement in 1674? And the jury found for the defendant Richard, that these lands were not parcel of the manor and consequently not barred by the recovery, which made the question at law, which the court would have reserved for the defendant in case the verdict had gone for the plaintiff, needless. The plaintiffs gave in evidence the counterpart of the lease which was found by a sister of the defendant Richard among the papers of the family left in her hands by Lady Mary, without proving the execution or attestation of it, or that the witnesses were dead.

And at first they could only prove the possession of the rent by Henry the grandfather, who died about 12 years before, which the lord chief baron thought

---

[101] Resumed on p. 24.

[102] 29 January was a Friday in 1731 (Julian), Kratz, *Hist. Cal.* See date immediately below. The British statute 24 Geo. II, c. 23, 1750 (also known as Chesterfield's Act, after Philip Stanhope, 4th earl of Chesterfield) provided that 2 September 1752 (Julian) was to be followed by 14 September 1752 (Gregorian), thus omitting the eleven days, 3 to 13 September, and that the change was to apply 'throughout all His Majesty's dominions and countries in Europe, Asia, Africa and America, belonging or subject to the crown of Great Britain'. Years inserted in square brackets in the text are given in modern style, i.e. the year beginning on 1 January.

[103] [Sic] i.e. Marlay C.B.

[104] 8 Geo. I, c. 2 (Ir.), 1721.

sufficient, if they could prove a seisin within 19 years, though they after proved payment of the rent to Henry the younger, and that this was sufficient [23] to make out their title by the words of the statute (or show any other sufficient title).

The defendant Weseley, to show his title to the rent, produced the settlement in 1674, whereby he claimed as heir male.

The plaintiffs produced fines and recoveries, whereby the estates in tail were barred.

The defendant Weseley insisted that these lands were not mentioned by name in the recovery, but only the manors of Carbery and Castle Carbery, that they were not manors, nor the lease parcel of them, and insisted that if they were, by law they could not pass for want of a tenant to the *præcipe*,[105] the freehold being then in the lessee for lives.[106]

The plaintiffs gave in evidence that it was a manor by reputation, though never made one by charter and that the lands in lease for 60 years had been reputed parcel of this manor, and that the tenant in the lease had expressly covenanted to do suit and service to the manor for these lands; the defendant produced no evidence.

'Twas said that where no defence is taken, but judgment goes by default, the rent may be ascertained by the affidavit of the plaintiffs, but not where defence is taken, and that Lord Orrery who was in England was non-suited for this reason; but this distinction was not allowed by Baron St Leger, who said his oath should be taken in both cases.

As to the point of law, the defendants counsel insisted that here was no tenant to the *præcipe* of these lands, and so they could not pass by the fine and recovery according to *Moyle Finche's Case*,[107] for though the manor is recovered, yet it don't follow that all passes, for the lord might sell or alien the freehold of part for life, and then for want of a proper tenant this part would not pass, and that this is clear by the late Act[108] which would have been [24] otherwise made to no purpose.

Mr Prime Serjeant for the plaintiffs

The lease for life did not sever the reversion and rent from the manor, therefore they would pass by a grant of it, Co. Lit. 324b, 325a. By the grant of a manor an advowson appendant[109] passes, though not said *cum pertinentiis*[110] and a *præcipe* lies of a manor,

---

[105] L. imper. of *præcipere*, to admonish, enjoin, from the first words of the writ: *præcipe quod reddat*, 'you shall enjoin him/her that he/she render'. The 'tenant to the præcipe' was a party to a common recovery, the action developed at common law for barring entails and involving a number of complex fictions. For an explanation of common recoveries see A. W. B. Simpson, *A History of the Land Law* (2nd ed., 1986), 125 ff.

[106] Below, n. 108.

[107] *Sir Moyle Finch's Case* (1606) 6 Co. Rep. 63a, 77 E.R. 348.

[108] 8 Geo. I, c. 6 (Ir.), 1721, s. 10 (common recoveries, tenant to the præcipe where lease for lives). Tenants in tail, unless they suffered a common recovery, could only grant an estate for their own life. They were given power to grant leases for three lives or 31 years, which would therefore bind the issue in tail etc., in Ireland by 10 Car. I, sess. 3, c. 6 (Ir.), 1634. Where a tenant in tail subsequently suffered a recovery to bar the entail there was a problem if a lease for lives had been granted. The lease for lives being freehold, the lessee for lives had the seisin and the tenant in tail did not, and so the latter was not a proper tenant to the præcipe of the writ. The recovery would be ineffective to bar the entail. The statute 8 Geo. I, c. 6 provided that the recovery should therefore be effective as if the lease for lives had not been granted. A similar Act was passed in England in 1740: 14 Geo. II, c. 20 (Eng.). The reason that the English Act was nearly 20 years after the Irish Act is probably because leases for lives were more common in Ireland.

[109] I.e. an advowson attached to the manor.

[110] L. with the appurtenances.

and if a *præcipe* is brought for a manor and also for Blackacre part of [the] manor, the count must be abridged, or it will abate as *bis petitum*[111] and *Sir Moyle Finche's Case*[112] is an authority for us: if a tenancy escheats it becomes part of the manor again, while it continued the services were in lieu of the land, when those cease, the land returns again.

And it was adjudged in England in the case of *Lord Derby*[113] that a recovery suffered of a manor would pass those parts of the manor that were in lease for life.

It was also determined so on a reference to the greatest men in England in the case of the *Earl of Pembroke* and *Lord Windsor*,[114] for if these lands are not severed, they must pass to the conusee of the fine, who has a freehold of the whole manor in him, though not of all the lands.

Mr Lindsay[115]

A manor is *unum Ens*,[116] may be entailed, and has a freehold, and if a *præcipe* is brought for a manor, no particulars are to be denominated, 36 H. 6, 11a[117] and [if] a fine of it is levied, no lands are to be mentioned, 36 H. 6, 12,[118] and the question is, if by a recovery the reversion on a lease for life will pass? Dyer 234,[119] 5 Co. [25]

Mr Daly

The reversion is part of the manor, though the lands were lease[d] for life, Cro. Eliz. 522,[120] Plowd. 104, a, b.[121] Co. 47b,[122] 50a,[123] 6 Co. 56a,[124] 66b[125] if the whole manor is in lease, the lessee is *dominus pro tempore*,[126] but while an acre remains, he owns the whole manor. If the reversion don't pass by the recovery, it would amount to a severance of these lands from the manor, contrary to the intent of the parties; a manor may be demanded by a *præcipe* and then all the parts pass.

And the judges seemed to be of this opinion. Post 28.

---

[111] L. demanded twice.

[112] *Sir Moyle Finch's Case* (1606) 6 Co. Rep. 63a, 77 E.R. 348.

[113] See *Sodor & Man (Bishop)* v. *Derby (Earl)* (1751) 2 Ves. Sen. 340, 28 E.R. 217 (*De Donis* did not extend to the Isle of Man).

[114] Perhaps *Earl of Pembroke's Case* (1690) Carth. 111, 90 E.R. 669.

[115] Above, p. clxi n. 940. The Columbia Singleton MS. No. 6 is entitled 'Notes of cases taken in court 1708–1710 by Robt Lindsay.' The flyleaf has the inscription: 'Robt Lindsay esq Aug 30th 1718'.

[116] L. a single thing, a unity.

[117] Y.B. 36 Hen. VI, fo. 11a pl. 5.

[118] Y.B. 36 Hen. VI, fo. 12 pl. 5.

[119] *Dorset* v. *Lane* (1564) 2 Dy. 234b, 73 E.R. 518.

[120] *Ive* v. *Sams* (1596) Cro. Eliz. 522, 78 E.R. 770.

[121] *Fulmerston* v. *Steward* (1554) 1 Plow. 104, 75 E.R. 163 (opinion of the judges on Statute of Dissolutions of Abbeys, 31 Hen. VIII, c. 13 (Eng.), 1539). Note that this was preceded by the Irish statute providing for the dissolution of Irish monasteries: 28 Hen. VIII, c. 16 (Ir.), 1537. See Donaldson, 'The Application in Ireland of English and British Legislation Made Before 1801' (unpublished PhD thesis, Queen's University, Belfast, 1952), i. 196. Donaldson cites P. Rogers, 'The policy of Henry VIII regarding the Religious Houses in Ireland' (unpublished PhD thesis, Queen's University, Belfast, 1928).

[122] *Attorney-General* v. *Bushopp* (1600) 1 Co. Rep. 40b at 47b, 76 E.R. 89 at 108.

[123] Ibid., at 113.

[124] *Duke of Chandos's Case* (1606) 6 Co. Rep. 54b at 56a, 77 E.R. 336.

[125] *Sir Moyle Finch's Case* (1606) 6 Co. Rep. 63a at 66b, 77 E.R. 348 at 355.

[126] L. lord for the time being.

'Twas determined in Chancery in the case of *O'Neal* v. *O'Hara*,[127] and affirmed on appeal by the House of Lords[128] that a Roman Catholic may bring a bill for a specific execution of an agreement for a lease, & c.

Post 79.

Michaelmas 1730, in Chancery; *Burke* v. *Lady Roscommon*,[129] if a mortgagee on payment of principal and interest assigns, the assignee shall not have interest for the interest.

Mr Calaghan said, a decree is equal to a judgment, and that the courts of equity had made this distinction, that if the decree was merely personal, and for a duty which did not bind the heir, it would not affect the heir after the death of the ancestor, unless carried into execution by a sequestration in the lifetime of the ancestor, and then it would bind his heirs and assigns, but where the lien bound the heir, it would bind the lands also after the death of the father. [*26*]

Quære, whether by the Registry Act 6 Ann.[130] a deed enrolled shall be void against a decree? The words being only of creditors by judgment, etc., made, confessed, and acknowledged and not the words, or otherwise; but by the letter of W. 2[131] bills of exceptions extend only to the Common Bench,[132] but by the equity of it to all the courts.

In the case of *French* v. *Staunton*[133] in Chancery, a bill was brought to have the benefit of the trust of a lease. The defendant denied the trust, and the plaintiff fully proved it, yet the Statute of Frauds and Perjuries[134] being insisted on at the hearing, though not in the cause, Lord Midleton[135] dismissed the bill. The plaintiff after found a letter that declared the trust, and on a rehearing had a decree in his favour.

In Exchequer

[continued]

A question was, whether a bill filed by the defendant's father in 1699 for an injunction against ejectment should be read in evidence against the defendant, who produced the register's notes, whereby it appeared that an order was made to dismiss the bill, for being filed without the knowledge or privity of the plaintiff.

The plaintiffs in this cause insisted, that the bill was marked pauper, whereas no one is admitted as such who does not make an affidavit of his circumstances, and that the contents of his petition are true; besides he obtained an injunction on this bill, and the same attorney who filed it, took on him the defence in the ejectment, that no affidavit appeared, that it was [*27*] filed without his privity, and if it appeared to be so, the court would not have made an order to dismiss the bill, but to take it of[f] the file.

---

[127]   No citation given.
[128]   *O'Hara* v. *O'Neill* (1717) 7 Bro. P.C. 2nd ed. 227, esp. 230, 3 E.R. 148 at 150.
[129]   No citation given.
[130]   Registration of Deeds Act, 1707, 6 Ann., c. 2 (Ir.).
[131]   Statute of Westminster II, 1285, 13 Edw. I, c. 31 (Eng.) (bills of exceptions). See Donaldson, ii. 385. The statute introduced bills of exceptions.
[132]   I.e. Common Pleas.
[133]   No citation given.
[134]   Statute of Frauds, 1695, 7 Will. III, c. 12 (Ir.).
[135]   Spelled 'Middleton' in the MS. Alan Broderick, Viscount Midleton PC (1656–1728), appointed C.J.Q.B., 1709, superseded, 1711, L.C., 1714, on accession of George I, created viscount, 1717. Ball, *Judges in Ireland*, ii. 69–70, 85, 186. Above, p. clix.

The counsel for the defendant insisted, that this was *objectio ejusd[em] rei cujus petit[u]r dissolutio.*[136] We say the bill so marked pauper was without the consent of our father (and there is no affidavit of his being admitted pauper) so that its being marked pauper is no more an objection than the bill itself, and it appears by Chan. Rep. 65,[137] that it is incumbent on those who produce the bill, to show it was filed by the privity of the plaintiff. The bill was filed in June 1699, and dismissed in February following, and the parties did not complain till 1708.

Lord Chief Baron

This bill must be read from the presumption that it was filed with consent. The plaintiff in that cause had the benefit of it by injunction, he was admitted pauper, which must be on affidavit not only of his poverty, but that the contents of his petition were true, and there is no objection to this but the order of dismission. No order appears, but only short notes which are the allegations of the counsel, and which if the matter had been contested would not have been obtained, and if it had appeared to the court that the bill was filed without the plaintiff's privity, they would have ordered it to be taken off the file, and examined the attorney.

SIR WALTER BLAKE v. KIRWIN & STAUNTON

Wednesday, February 3 [1731][138]

In Exchequer

Cross examination don't make a man a good witness if he appears to be concerned in interest, plainly not, if on the first cross interrogation he [*28*] denies his being interested, and it appears in the course of his examination he is, and then he is examined no further, and this far my lord chancellor Midleton[139] went, because on a voir dire[140] at law, if a witness denies that he wins or loses by the event of the cause, yet if it after appears he is concerned in interest, the court will not suffer his evidence to go to the jury. But the court here were of opinion that the examining of him after he appeared to be interested should not be taken as a consent of the party to his being examined, though it would be so before a jury, if they went on to examine him after he had owned himself [interested], or he appeared to be concerned in interest, because by the practice of courts of equity a whole set of interrogatories is at once delivered to the examiner or commissioners, and therefore if they go on with interrogatories after the witness has owned himself interested, that should not so far be construed the act of the party, as if he waived taking the advantage of it, and admitted his being a good evidence.

---

[136] L. objection to that of which the dissolution is sought.

[137] Perhaps *Woollet v. Roberts* (1665) 1 Ch. Cas. 64 at 65, 22 E.R. 697.

[138] 3 February was a Wednesday in 1731 (Julian), Kratz, *Hist. Cal.*

[139] Above, n. 135.

[140] LF. to speak the truth. LF. *voier* from L. *verus*, Baker *Manual of Law French*. An oath to speak the truth when examined. Also an investigation, or 'trial within a trial', to determine the truth or admissibility of evidence. Howard, *Pleas Side*, ii. 851.

RYLEY v. WESELEY[141]

Saturday, February the 6 [1731][142]

In Exchequer

The counsel for the plaintiffs moved to set aside the verdict, as being against the evidence they had offered, and which was not confronted by any on the defendant's side.

They insisted that verdicts had been often set aside on trials at bar, Styl. 154.[143] *The Queen* v. *Bendley* in Shropshire, 11 Q. Ann. on an information in King's Bench, where the question was, whether Smyth was well chosen burgess or not? And there on motion to set aside the verdict, Lord Parker consulted all the judges in England, who [29] all agreed (except Powel) that the verdict might be set aside, and that the party should not be in a worse condition than if the trial had been at nisi prius. And Easter 10 Geo. 1, *Sir Christopher Musgrave* v. *Nevil*,[144] on an action on the case for a false return the verdict was set aside on the authority of *Bendley's Case*, and of *Tyley* v. *Roberts*[145] in Common Bench, where the issue was *non compos*[146] or not.

That though this trial in ejectment was not conclusive, yet the verdict would be evidence to a jury on a second trial.

That this motion was in lieu of an attaint, and that lay as well on a verdict in ejectment, as any other action.

The defendant's counsel insisted, that new trials were never granted, but where the verdicts were conclusive, and that this court had denied it in the case of *Kelly* v. *Prendergast*,[147] that there was nothing in their objection, that in that case there was evidence on both sides, and here only one, because the jury may know them selves.

Lord Chief Baron

There is no precedent[148] of a verdict being set aside on a trial at bar in ejectment. The old opinion was not to grant a new one after a trial at bar, because the court may have the assistance of the judges and counsel who are generally better prepared and furnished with evidence than at *nisi prius*.

Though the defendant gave no evidence of this not being a reputed manor, or that the lands were not parcel of it, yet the plaintiffs did not offer the best evidence, that this was constituted a manor by letters patents, and this being an ejectment according to the precedent[149] of *Kelly* v. *Prendergast* we must deny the motion. [30]

---

141 Continued from p. 19
142 6 February was a Saturday in 1731 (Julian), Kratz, *Hist. Cal.*
143 Mich. 24 Car. I, Style 154, 82 E.R. 605, 606, Rolle C.J.
144 No citation given.
145 No citation given.
146 I.e. *non compos mentis*, not of sound mind.
147 No citation given.
148 The original says 'president'.
149 The original says 'precedt' (abbreviated).

LYNCH v. BLAKE

Wednesday, February the 10th [1731][150]

In Exchequer

The question was, whether the depositions were right filed, two of the defendants being left out. And they were allowed to be read, because though process was prayed against them, no subpœna had been taken out, and so there was no *lis pendens* as to them; so a defendant may be examined without leave of the court, who is never served with process.

And this distinction was allowed in Chancery in the case of *Moor* v. *More*,[151] where the depositions were titled in a cause between one plaintiff and defendant, and they had proceeded to issue against several.

MSS̃ ord. Canc. 87.
MS cas. in Canc.
D.334.

Post 36.

LESSEE OF RAM v. THE CASUAL EJECTOR[152]

Thursday, February the 11 [1731][153]

In Exchequer

A judgment of Michaelmas term was now set aside after *habere facias* etc. delivered to the sheriff, but not returned, on payment of all the costs and consenting to appear gratis at the next assizes, on the head of accident, upon affidavit that Counsellor Purdon[154] who was agent for Mr Clayton had been wounded by Mr Lewis, so that he could not manage his affairs.[155]

And the court said, it was frequent to set aside judgments in ejectments in a subsequent term for fraud or surprise even after execution executed.

And the attorney general said, that it was laid down as a rule in Salkeld, always to do it where they could put the plaintiff in as good a case as he was before. [*31*]

---

[150] 10 February was a Wednesday in 1731 (Julian), Kratz, *Hist. Cal.*

[151] No citation given.

[152] That is, the fictional defendant in the form of ejectment used by freeholders. See above, p. lxxvi.

[153] 11 February was a Thursday in 1731 (Julian), Kratz, *Hist. Cal.*

[154] Spelled 'Councelor' in MS. Henry Purdon (?–1737). Son and heir of Adam Purdon, of Mallow, Co. Cork: KI AP, p. 412. Henry entered Middle Temple in 1707, became K.C. in 1716 and 3rd serjeant on 23 October 1730. According to Smyth, *Law Officers*, he d. March 1737, but KI AP, p. 412 states he d. 9 December 1737. See also Hart, *King's Serjeants at Law in Ireland* (Dublin, 2000).

[155] The comment here seems to imply that Purdon had been wounded in a duel with Lewis. James Kelly, '*That Damn'd Thing Called Honour': Duelling in Ireland 1570–1860* (Cork, 1995), at p. 54, mentions a Charles Lewis, a stock officer, who was killed in a duel in 1740 with John Lynch, a Galway merchant. Lynch was convicted of manslaughter and ordered to be burnt in the hand. It is not known whether it was the same Lewis. It is interesting to note that the court accepts Purdon's temporary incapacity as a ground for setting aside the judgment in ejectment even after execution and permits him to appear in defence later. Purdon recovered and appears below, p. 191, as serjeant in 1733. The incident is also mentioned below, at p. 303.

RYLEY v. AYLMER

Eodem die

In Exchequer

Moved that the sheriff might amend his return on a *fieri facias*, or be attached.

And the court resolved, that without consent of the parties the sheriff could not employ an auctioneer to sell the goods, for that might be elusive of the statute, which has settled his fee, and he is auctioneer in law, and cannot increase his own fees, and he might make one of his bailiffs auctioneer, or be confederate with him.

Secondly, that without consent he can sell upon trust, but must have *nummus paratus*.[156]

[ANON.]

Eodem die

In Exchequer

On an habeas corpus *cum causa* it was moved that the plaintiff might show cause of bail.

But the court denied the motion, because he had showed cause below, and therefore the defendant ought to offer some very good reason why he should show cause here, and was in a suit where bail was requited below, would take away the jurisdiction of the courts below, and was contrary to the statute.

They insisted that the action was vexatious, a subpœna having been taken out in this court to which they appeared, and were after sued in the court below. But they did no go on in the first action. 1 Salk. 98,[157] 101;[158] 6 Mod. 242[159] 2 Lev. 104,[160] *Sir John Lawrence's Case* Sir Tho. Jon. 82.[161]

WOLF v. MADDEN

Friday, February the 12, [1731][162]

In Exchequer

'Twas moved that the executors might plead one plea, but denied as being without precedent, one pleaded not assumpsit, and *plene administravit*,[163] and the two others joined in a plea of *plene administravit*.[164] [*32*]

---

[156] L. ready money.

[157] *Williams* v. *Williams* (1696) 1 Salk. 98, 91 E.R. 90.

[158] *Anon.* (1695) 1 Salk. 101, 91 E.R. 93.

[159] *Denham* v. *Stevenson* (1704) 6 Mod. 242, 87 E.R. 990, per Holt C.J.;

[160] *Saltonstall's Case* (1674) 2 Lev. 104, 83 E.R. 470.

[161] *Lawrence* v. *Bligh* (1677) Jones T. 82, 84 E.R. 1157.

[162] 12 of February was a Friday in 1731 (Julian), Kratz, *Hist. Cal.*

[163] A plea by an executor or administrator that he or she had administered the estate of the deceased fully and faithfully before the action brought against him or her.

[164] *Sic,* for *plene administraverunt.*

[ANON.]

Eodem die

In Exchequer

'Twas moved to change the venue, on affidavit that if the plaintiff had any cause of action it arose in that county.

And it was said, that the court would grant such motion, unless the plaintiff would consent to enter into a rule not to give evidence out of the county where he had laid his action and that this was the constant practice in England.

But the court denied it and said they would change the venue if the plaintiff (as he did here) would not enter into a rule to show some cause of action (as here of a conversion) in the county where he had laid his action, and not that he should be confined to no other evidence.

MSŜ Cas. in BR.
B.78. A.27.

[ANON.]

Eodem die

In Exchequer

An estrepement[165] was granted on a writ of error in ejectment, though the writ was prayed by one who claimed only a sixth as coparcener.[166] Moor 622.[167]

CONOLLY ET UX. v. SHERIDAN

Eodem die

In Exchequer

The action was brought by the husband and wife as administratrix, and judgment, and execution taken out, and between the *teste*[168] and delivery to the sheriff the wife died, the sheriff seizes a term on the *fieri facias*, and sells it, and it was now moved in behalf of the administrator *de bonis non*[169] to set aside this execution, that he ought to bring a *scire facias* on the judgment, and that the husband had no title to it, that the goods were not bound till [*33*] the delivery of the execution to the sheriff, and that the wife being dead before that time the writ was abated; though they allowed it was otherwise in case the defendant died. Cro. Ca. 227.[170]

---

[165] A writ of waste, whereby a reversioner alleged that the tenant for life had damaged the land or timber, etc., which damage would still be apparent when the reversion fell in.

[166] When a freehold tenant died without a male heir all the daughters took in a form of co-ownership called coparcenary. The daughters took as if they were a single heir.

[167] *Holland* v. *Jackson* (1599) Moo. K.B. 622, 72 E.R. 798.

[168] L. witness. The part of a writ that begins 'witness'. Generally the report uses *teste* to refer to an event or point in time.

[169] L. with no goods.

[170] *Beaumont* v. *Long* (1631) Cro. Car. 227, 79 E.R. 798.

For the plaintiffs it was observed that the question was not, who should have the money, but whether the execution was not good?

And it was insisted, that the writ was *teste* before the death of the wife, from which time the goods were bound as between the parties, though not as to strangers, by the Statute of Frauds and Perjuries.[171]

That after the judgment executed, the writ could not abate, for neither side had a day in court, and the sheriff might bring the money into court, and was not bound to take notice of the death of either of the plaintiff or defendant, but must execute his writ by sale, 2 Vern. 218,[172] and though he is out of his office, he must go on with his sale, Cro. Ja. 73,[173] and that though the money did not belong to him, they had a right to the costs marked on the execution.

Lord Chief Baron

There can be no abatement after execution taken out, for the cause is out of court, and neither side can make this motion, but the sheriff only is before the court after execution executed, and may bring the money into court.

At law the execution takes place from the *teste*, and does so until as to the parties, though the statute of frauds makes it void as to strangers till the delivery.

Motion denied.

[HATFIELD v. SUTTON][174]

Eodem die

In Exchequer
Post 48, 392.

The court were of opinion that in an action on the Statute of Usury[175] the party should not be held to bail (here by affidavit £400 was due) and that it was never done in penal statutes only in a *scandalum magnatum*,[176] because of the great injury [which] might arise to the party through spleen or malice. Mr Bradstreet[177] quoted Yelv. 53,[178] and said that it was so adjudged in Common Pleas last Michaelmas [term

---

171   Statute of Frauds, 1695, 7 Will. III, c. 12 (Ir.).

172   *Aspinwall* v. *Leigh* (1690) 2 Vern. 218, 23 E.R. 741.

173   *Style* v. *Hearing* (1605) Cro. Jac. 73, 79 E.R. 62.

174   Below, p. 306 [393].

175   10 Car. I, sess. 2, c. 22 (Ir.), 1634 (against usury); 2 Ann., c. 16 (Ir.), 1703 (to reduce rate of interest on money to 8 per cent); 8 Geo. I, c. 13 (Ir.), 1721 (to reduce rate of interest on money to 7 per cent); 5 Geo. II, c. 7 (Ir.), 1731 (to reduce rate of interest on money to 6 per cent).

176   Derogatory words spoken of a peer, a judge, or another great officer of state, which, though not actionable if spoken of an ordinary person, were the subject of an action on the case. It had its origin in the Statute of Westminster I, 3 Edw. I, c. 34., Jacob, *Law Dictionary*, 1797, although actions on the statute are not known before the 15th century.

177   Probably Simon Bradstreet, s. of Simon, Kilkenny; ed. Trinity College Dublin May 1720, d. 23 April 1762. KI AP, p. 50.

178   *St George's Case* (1604) Yelv. 53, 80 E.R. 38.

in the case of *Hand* v. *Davis*,[179] that by 2 Geo. 2 ch. 10[180] a prosecution on a penal statute ought to be within a year, whereas [if] supported by their own affidavit not to be within 6. But the court would not enter into that, but left them to plead it.][181]
[*34*]

BURROUGHS v. MUSHET

In Exchequer

Thursday, February the 18th, [1731][182]
one of the 8 days after Hilary term.

The bill was brought to set aside deeds of purchase executed by the father of the plaintiff to the defendant.

The plaintiff's father being on the death of his father entitled to certain lands in the neighbourhood of the defendant, whose sister he had married, and serving a cure in a distant part of the country, entrusted the defendant to receive the rents, and sell the estate, who purchased it from him for 4d, for which he gave his bond. The father died, and the son went clerk to the defendant (who practised for many years as an attorney, and after was admitted to the bar)[183] who received him very kindly till he came of age, when the defendant pressed him by letters and otherwise to levy a fine, and desired him to keep it secret, which he refusing, he turned him out of his house, prevailed on another gentleman who had received him to do the like, and on his laundress to arrest him, and said, the only way to force him to a compliance, was to distress him.

The defendant by his answer set forth, that as to one part of the lands about the yearly value of £25, they were worth £400, that he computed £360 was due on a mortgage, and that the other £40 was the full value of them: that as to the two other denominations he owned he paid nothing for them, because they were mortgaged for more than they were worth, and he said the whole estate was about the yearly value of £60.

Lord Chief Baron

This purchase must be set aside being [*35*] gained by a misrepresentation of the defendant who was agent and employed by the plaintiff's father to sell: as to one

---

[179] No citation given.

[180] *Sic.* There are no statutes in 2 Geo. II in the Irish statutes. 2 Geo. II, c. 10 in the English statutes concerned a parish. 2 Geo. I, c. 20 (Ir.), 1715 ss. 3, 4 (penal statutes) provided that where a forfeiture was given to the king only, the action was to be brought within two years, where to the king and an informer, by the informer within one year, and by the king in default within two years after that expired, but within a shorter time if so limited by a particular Act. 28 Hen. VIII, c. 21 (Ir.), 1537 provided that where an action lay by common informer only, it was to brought within one year, and by the king in default in three years.

[181] The passage in square brackets is inserted in the margin in the MS.

[182] 18 February was a Thursday in 1731 (Julian), Kratz, *Hist. Cal.*

[183] There is one entry for the name of William Mushet, in KI AP, p. 359: listed as attorney, 25 Nov. 1727, as master of an apprentice; and one entry for William Mushett (with two 't's), as barrister, Middle Temple, 19 Apr. 1721, KI, Michaelmas, 1727, s. and heir of [Revd] William, of Magherafelt, Co. Londonderry, clerk.

parcel he gave the mortgagee nothing, paid him no money, nay by the proofs in the cause he was overpaid, so that he would be a gainer by the account of the profits. By the deed of conveyance the father covenants to warranty the land against all men, so that if the mortgage was subsisting, he covenants against that also, and there is sufficient in his answer to set aside these deeds for he says the mortgage money was the consideration, whereas the deed appears to be an absolute purchase of the lands, and not of the equity of redemption, for 'tis plain this defence must be an afterthought; and he has the two other denominations for nothing, so he must reconvey, and account for the profits, and the deeds must be lodged in court.

Mr Baron St Leger

The defendant was agent, friend and relation to the plaintiff's father. He lays down as the consideration of his purchase the mortgage that was standing out, which he ought to have shown, and that he paid it off and did not deceive his brother, whereas the evidence shows it to be paid at that time, for in 1694 the mortgage was made by way of demise and redemise for 3 years, and in 1698 a bill for foreclosure is filed, and by his account in 1725 he computes the whole to be due for principal and interest, whereas some payments appear to have been made, and it is not probable that the mortgagee who brought his bill so early, would have acquiesced, if he had not been satisfied .

If the defendant consents to appear *gratis* etc, yet the plaintiff must serve his attorney with a [*36*] subpœna to have judgment by way of notice, unless he further consents to waive all service and the officer certified the practice to be so.

WARREN v. CAULFIELD

Monday, February the 22d [1731][184]

In Exchequer

The depositions were titled 'Warren v. Caulfield et al.', who were defendants against whom process was prayed, but none served on them, nor did they ever appear; and these depositions could not be read; and the case of *Stafford & ux.*[185] v. *Crofts*[186] last Hilary Term in Chancery was mentioned, where the depositions were taken in a cause between Stafford and Crofts omitting *uxor*,[187] and the objection was allowed

Ante 30. to be fatal.

---

[184] 22 February was a Monday in 1731 (Julian), Kratz, *Hist. Cal.*
[185] *Uxor*, wife.
[186] No citation given.
[187] Above, n. 185.

BAKER v. BARRY, ET AL.,

Eodem die

In Exchequer

The bill was to set aside a decree against the now plaintiff obtained in his minority, and set forth, that the plaintiff was entitled to the lands in question in tail charged with legacies to the defendants, who filed their bill for payment and satisfaction, that Spranger who had married their sister in combination with them pretended to have received the rents as guardian to the plaintiff's father, whereas he really received them as trustee for the legatees, and that therefore the estate having once born its burden ought to be discharged.

The defendants pleaded the decree enrolled, which was allowed in this case, because there had been a rehearing, and a trial at bar, whether Stranger [*sic*] received any and what money out of the estate for the plaintiff's use? Whereby the fact [*37*] he suggested must have come under consideration, though the lord chief baron allowed such a bill to be proper; and the plaintiff's counsel quoted the case of *Lord Dunsany* v. *Shaw*,[188] where the defendant a minor put in a plea which was overruled, and after when he came of age he applied by petition, and obtained liberty to amend, and put in a new plea.

MSŜ cas. in Canc.
A.105, 301, 452, 462.

1 Vern. 295[189] (288)
2 Vern. 224[190] (206)
342[191] 429[192] (391)
479[193] (474)
Mes App. E.953.

Tuesday, February the 23d, [1731][194]

In Exchequer

A certificate of commissioners may be read, not of referees, but they must make affidavit, but when they are armed with a commission, as to what they do by virtue of that they are considered as officers of the court.

BEGG v. FOWNES, AND È CONTRA[195]

Eodem die

In Exchequer

Begg filed a bill to be relieved against a distress for rent, on an allegation that Sir William Fownes had promised him an abatement. Sir William by his cross bill allowed the promise, but that it was to continue only during the war,[196] and said, that it would

---

[188] No citation given.

[189] *Booth* v. *Rich* (1684) 1 Vern. 295, 23 E.R. 478.

[190] *Earl of Salisbury* v. *Bennet* (1691) 2 Vern. 223, 23 E.R. 744 at 745.

[191] *Lord Falkland* v. *Bertie* (1696) 2 Vern. 333 at 342, 23 E.R. 814 at 817.

[192] *Cooke* v. *Parsons* (1701) 2 Vern. 429, 23 E.R. 875.

[193] *Gundry* v. *Baynard* (1704) 2 Vern. 479, 23 E.R. 907.

[194] 23 of February was a Tuesday in 1731 (Julian), Kratz, *Hist. Cal.*

[195] L. from a contrary position, in opposition. The defendant enters a cross bill.

[196] This seems to refer to the War of Spanish Succession (1701–14). Note the similarity between the facts alleged and the English case of *Central London Property Trust* v. *High Trees House Ltd* [1947] K.B. 130, which established the doctrine of promissory estoppel. Unfortunately the issue as to estoppel did not arise here.

appear to be so by receipts which he had since given him for the whole rent, which he desired him to set forth *in hæc verba*,[197] or bring them before the proper officer, and prays a *duces tecum*;[198] the defendant accepts the alternative, and submits to produce them before the proper officer, which the plaintiff now moved he might do, and though this was to cover an insufficient answer, the court would not grant the motion, but said he must pray a *duces tecum*, and that the other side would have an opportunity to show cause before a baron.

You may have a *duces tecum* for deeds, if you have an interest in them, though they are the defendant's title. [*38*]

Post 90.

CLAYTON v. LYSHAT[199]

Eodem die

In Exchequer

Mr Baron St Leger delivered it as the practice of the court, that no time is fixed for taking exceptions to a Baron's Report, but that in order to quicken the other side, 'tis usual to move to confirm the report *nisi*[200] the other side shows cause, that is, files exceptions within four days after the order is served.

JOHNSON, VIDUA[201]

v.

MARY GRAVE AND DAVID JOHNSON

Wednesday, February the 24, [1731][202]

In Exchequer

The bill was for a legacy of £500 devised to the plaintiff by her husband, who made Mary Grave and Edward Johnson his brother executors and an account was decreed, and £3,000 assets appeared to be in their hands, whereof Edward had 318. He dies, and makes the defendant David his executor, against whom the suit is revived. Mary Grave for non-performance of the decree is taken on an attachment, and lies in gaol, and on the return of a serjeant at arms a sequestration issued against David, and it was now moved for the plaintiff, that a sequestration might go against Mary notwithstanding her body was in custody, according to *Plunket* v. *Welsh*[203] in Chancery, where a creditor taken on an attachment, and choosing rather to lie in prison than

---

197   L. in these (following) words.

198   L. more fully *subpœna duces tecum*, under penalty you shall bring with you. A writ commanding a person to produce in court specified documents or other things which are in his or her custody, and are required as evidence.

199   *Sic*, for Lysaght?

200   L. unless.

201   L. widow.

202   24 February was a Wednesday in 1731 (Julian), Kratz, *Hist. Cal.*

203   No citation given.

pay the money decreed, a sequestration was granted against his goods, and that an MSŜ Ord. in Canc. 49. 185. attachment might be revived against David notwithstanding the sequestration.

But the court denied the motion, 1. Because [39] Mary had lodged the mortgages and other securities which were the bulk of the assets in court, and was not to blame that David the other defendant, in whose name most of the securities were taken, opposed the sale of them. 2. Because all the assets in the hands of Edward which came to David were taken on the sequestration.

Mr Baron St Leger said, he thought it reasonable a sequestration should go at one who would obstinately lie in gaol, but not to revive an attachment against him whose effects had been sequestered for no-performance of a decree; for they went upon very different reasons: the person who lies in gaol is still in contempt, and more so by his persisting to lie there, than if he had avoided the officer abroad, and therefore this court will stretch their process according to the ingenuity of the person who endeavours to avoid it, that their decrees may not be eluded.

But when all the parties goods and lands are under a sequestration, he is punished for his contempt, the one has gone the whole length of the process, and the other has expatiated his crime.

The chief baron said, he thought an attachment ought not to be revived after a sequestration, unless the party himself endeavoured to elude the process, by con- MSŜ cas. in Canc. A.364. cealing his effects, or the like.

KING v. BURGH

Eodem die

In Exchequer

Lord Chief Baron

This cause stands for the judgment of the court.

The plaintiff as executrix of her late husband files her bill against the defendant to have the benefit of lease. The trustees of the charity schools of Erasmus Smyth in 1702 made a lease to Mr King the plaintiff's late husband for 21 years, reserving a rent of £450 a year. Several differences arose and bills were filed between the said trustees and Mr King, not only about the arrears of the rent, but the bounds of the said lands, upon which they complained that Mr King having lands contiguous [40] had encroached, and the said causes being ready for hearing, Mr King wrote to Mr Burgh who was his relation, to come to an agreement with the trustees on his behalf for the arrears, an abatement of his rent in respect of a deficiency of the acres demised to him, and as to the bounds, and a new lease, which Mr Burgh carried on for a long time as agent to Mr King, but after Mr Burgh's return from England in 1721, the trustees refused to continue Mr King [as] tenant, or to make any agreement with him for a new lease, but offered on Mr King's surrender and paying his arrears to make a new lease to Mr Burgh, and these matters being referred to the archbishop of Dublin and others, they awarded, that a new lease should be made to Mr Burgh, (which was accordingly done in 1721) if a map of the lands were annexed to the lease, and signed by Mr King, which he did and released to the trustees all demands, for which he was to have an abatement of £1,000 arrears, and Mr Burgh enjoyed this lease for 7 months in the lifetime of Mr King.

And if this lease was taken in trust for Mr King, it must either be by operation of law, or by writing; but I am of opinion that first this is not a trust by operation of law. Such trusts stand as they did before witness Statute of Frauds and Perjuries, and may arise and be destroyed by witness parol declaration of witness parties, as to Post 88. which I ground myself on the authority of *Lady Bellasis* v. *Compton*,[204] 2 Vern. 294. Here there is no resulting trust, for it appears by the deposition of the archbishop of Dublin and Mr Coghill, that Mr King has as much renounced and declared there was no resulting trust for him, [*41*] as my Lord Bellasis did, and here is no trust in writing, for by Mr Burgh's letter which they have made use of as evidence against him it appears, that he was for some time a trustee, but that afterwards declared he took the lease for himself. But if he had taken the lease before he had made this declaration, he would have been a trustee by writing, and if Mr King was to have a benefit by his release, it don't appear plain enough to deprive the defendant of what belongs to him by law. So the bill must be dismissed.

PAYZANT v. LAMAIGUANET È CONTRA[205]

Eodem die

In Exchequer

Lord Chief Baron

We are unanimous of opinion that the executors are not entitled to the residue undisposed of but that it belongs to the plaintiffs as next of kin, because the executors are no way related to the testator, and have a ring expressly devised to them by way of acknowledgement for their trouble, and therefore we think they are not entitled MSS cas. in Canc. to the residue, not only for Lord Macclesfield's reason, that it would be absurd to a.5. 31. 66. 74. 425. suppose the testator designated them a part and the whole, but because it looks as if so much was designated them as a recompense for their trouble and that an executor was never considered in ours as he is in the civil law as *hæres*,[206] but as one who is seised only *in auter droit*,[207] who is never looked upon as person that has an interest; and that spiritual courts in superstitious times always made him distribute the surplus in pious uses, and the personal estates in the time of the feudal tenures being very small, little care was taken to check the churchmen who then had the command of every thing in their hand; afterwards the executors thought, that as wills were governed by the civil law, they ought to be heirs to the personal estate not actually disposed of from them. In the case of *Lady Rachel Manners* v. *Duke of Rutland*,[208] [*42*]

---

204   *Lady Bellasis* v. *Compton* (1693) 2 Vern. 294, 23 E.R. 790.
205   By cross bill, by counter claim.
206   L. heir.
207   LF. in the right of another.
208   *Duke of Rutland* v. *Duchess of Rutland* (1723) 2 P. Wms. 210 at 213, 24 E.R. 703 at 704 per Lord Macclesfield L.C.

Lord Macclesfield declared that executors succeeded *in jure alieno*,[209] and therefore should not have the surplus where there was not a plain intention of the testator appearing, as there was in that case, for she had left legacies to all her next of kin, and begged the duke's pardon for leaving £300 from him; and parol proof was admitted for her intention.

Lex Præt.[210] 109, 10, 11, 18.

Easter Term, 1731. Tuesday, May the 18.[211]

In Exchequer

A motion was made for the sheriff, that the plaintiff might be obliged to take an assignment of the bail bond, but denied, because though the party may compel the sheriff if he refuses to assign it, yet he is not obliged by the statute to accept it. But the court said the proper motion was to stop the fines for the sheriff not his return, for they would not fine him where he had pursued the statute by taking a sufficient security.

WOGAN v. JONES

Eodem die

In Exchequer

The bill was brought to foreclose the mortgage of a custodia[m]. The defendant was served with process in this kingdom, prayed time to answer, goes to England, puts in a plea and answer which was sworn before the lord treasurer Burlington,[212] and signed by an English barrister, and filed after he was in contempt. The plaintiff for want of an answer goes on with the process to a serjeant at arms, for every answer is to be signed by counsel at this bar, who was answerable to the court.

And it was moved to put counsel's name to the plea and answer, which was granted on their [43] giving security to abide the decree which the plaintiff was entitled to on a [process to a] serjeant at arms, for the defendant should have made this motion sooner.

---

[209] L. in the right of another.

[210] The reference is to Gilbert's *Lex Prætoria*, of which there is a copy in MS. 33 in the Singleton collection at Columbia (see J. H. Baker, *English Legal Manuscripts in the United States of America: a Descriptive List* (Selden Society, 1985–1990), no. 292), printed in Sir Geoffrey Gilbert, *Two treatises on the proceedings in equity: and the jurisdiction of that court. In two volumes . . . The second entitled, Lex prætoria: or, the Prætorian law* (Dublin, 1756–58), at p. 59.

[211] 18 May was a Tuesday in 1731 (Julian), Kratz, *Hist. Cal.*

[212] Above, p. xci.

COSTELO v. COSTELO[213]

Eodem die

In Exchequer

Mr Daly

The question is, whether an error in fact in this court can be remedied by a writ of error *coram vobis*?

MSŠ Cas. in BR
D.67.

We think not. Before the 13 Ed. 3 when the Parliament was not sitting error in fact in this court was to be tried by particular commissioners Mo. 566,[214] 4 Inst. 105. And 'tis particular to King's Bench to try error in their own judgments, and the Exchequer Chamber would not try error in fact in King's Bench, 2 Lev. 38,[215] 1 Ventr. 207.[216]

But by this writ of error the treasurer and barons are to amend the error if any, and in this the writ is wrong, because the treasurer is no judge of law matters.

Mr Costelo[217]

It appears by the case of *Dawkes* v. *Peyton* in Stil. Rep.[218] that when the case in Moor was determined, it was not settled that error in fact lay *coram vobis* in King's Bench. If the writ of error is bad, they should demur, 2 Keb. 507, [219] 8 Co. *Blackmore's Case*,[220] and this is within the 6 Geo. 1.[221]

Mr Daly

If 'tis variant from the record it may be amended by the court, but it appears by every day's practice, that if a writ of error is not regular, the court will quash it after allowance, as *Dunkellin* v. *Morgan*,[222] where a writ of error on a *quare impedit*[223] was quashed five terms after allowance.

Curia

We ought not to have allowed this writ, but since [*44*] we have, we shall now quash
Post 46, 49, 61, 68.   it for the objection to the word 'treasurer'.

---

[213] Resumed on p. 39.
[214] *Agar* v. *Candish* (1468) Moo. K.B. 564, 72 E.R. 761.
[215] *Baddington* v. *Freeman* (1672) 2 Lev. 38, 83 E.R. 442.
[216] *Prior* v. *Anonymous* (1672) 1 Vent. 207, 86 E.R. 140.
[217] Possibly Edmund Costello, 2nd s. of Charles, Tullaghane, Co. Mayo. Middle Temple, 26 July 1721. KI, Michaelmas term, 1727, d. Dec. 1769. KI AP, p. 102.
[218] *Dawkes* v. *Payton* (1650) Sty. 216, 82 E.R. 657; Sty. 218, 82 E.R. 659 (error to reverse a judgment in Upper Bench upon an issue directed out of Chancery).
[219] *Alow* v. *Moor* (1669) 2 Keb. 507, 84 E.R. 319.
[220] *Blackamore's Case* (1611) 8 Co. Rep. 156a, 77 E.R. 710.
[221] 6 Geo. I, c. 6 (Ir.) (writs of error).
[222] No citation given.
[223] L. why he hinders. An action by which a person whose right to a benefice had been obstructed recovered the presentation, and also an action to try a disputed title to an advowson.

DOWDAL v. CUSACK

Thursday, May 20 [1731][224]

In Exchequer

Lord Chief Baron

Allowed the evidence to be read of Tandis plaintiff, guardian, and trustee to Lord Darnley, for though the defendant might have filed a cross bill against him, yet his answer could have been read against himself only, but his examination is good   Post 141. against all the defendants.

The bill was brought against the defendant as a tenant holding over to account for the full value of the lands, he insisted there was a covenant for renewal in his lease, and an issue was directed to try, whether there was any such covenant, and 'twas moved for a second issue as to the value of the lands, but denied, as never done till the officer has reported he could not ascertain it, for then it would be time enough to put the party to the expense.

DR ST GEORGE v. BRADSHAW

Eodem die

In Exchequer

The bill was for the tithe of barren cattle not employed in the plough, or used for the pail, and the officer was directed by the decree to take an account of what dry and barren cattle were agisted, and the value of such agistment,[225] though this is properly the business of a jury.

LESSEE OF ROWLEY v. BURKIT

Eodem die

In Exchequer

On an ejectment. The certificate of the judge under seal that letters of administration were granted was allowed as evidence, being the [45] judicial act exemplified, and is stronger evidence than the book which has been allowed to be read, 1 Lev. 25.[226]

Here was great variety of evidence to the possession, and the court being inclined for the plaintiff, that it was good evidence to go to a jury, the defendants counsel said they would demur to the evidence, and then Mr Daly insisted there ought to be no verdict, for by their demurrer they allowed the evidence to be true like a special verdict.

---

[224] 20 May was a Thursday in 1731 (Julian), Kratz, *Hist. Cal.*
[225] A licence or contract to use land for pastoral purposes.
[226] *Garrett* v. *Lister* (1661) 1 Lev. 25, 83 E.R. 279.

Lord Chief Baron

This is in nature a bill of exceptions. We think this evidence ought to go to a jury, for there are some presumptive proofs which they only can judge of.

Mr Prime Serjeant

If their demurrer should be overruled, and no verdict given, what are we the better for the trial?

MORRISON v. LEY

Wednesday, May the 19 [1731][227]

In Exchequer

Nels. Fol. Rep. in Canc. 457.[228] 1 Vern. 196.[229] 193) 2 Vern. 744[230] 652), 548[231] (498). If money out at interest is paid voluntarily the executor shall be allowed a reasonable time to put it out again before he shall be charged with interest, otherwise if he calls it in without occasion. 2 Chan. Cas. 21,[232] 35,[233] 152,[234] 235.[235]

Lord Chief Baron

Post 87, 278. 'Tis no reason why an executor should not pay interest, because he lends the principal at his own risk, for he may lay it out by the direction of the court, but where the sum is small, it would not be worth while.

---

[227] 19 May was a Wednesday in 1731 (Julian), Kratz, *Hist. Cal.*

[228] *Haslewood* v. *Baldwin* (1680) Cas. t. Finch 457, 23 E.R. 248 (money placed out at interest and called in by executor without cause, executor shall pay interest on it).

[229] *Ratcliffe* v. *Graves* (1683) 1 Vern. 196 at 197, 23 E.R. 409 at 410.

[230] *Bird* v. *Lockey* (1716) 2 Vern. 743, 23 E.R. 1086.

[231] *Lee* v. *Lee* (1706) 2 Vern. 548, 23 E.R. 955.

[232] *Grosvenor* v. *Cartwright* (1679) 2 Ch. Cas. 21, 22 E.R. 827.

[233] *Linch* v. *Cappy* (1680) 2 Ch. Cas. 35, 22 E.R. 834.

[234] *Ratcliff* v. *Graves* (1683) 2 Ch. Cas. 152, 22 E.R. 890.

[235] *Hilliard* v. *Gorge* (1677) 2 Ch. Cas. 235, 22 E.R. 924.

LODGE v. LEY

Eodem die

In Exchequer

Lord Chief Baron

[*46*] If any part of an answer is given in evidence at law, the defendant may read the rest. 'Tis his evidence, and it is like cross-examining a witness, and the evidence that may be trusted to a jury may sure much sooner [be trusted] to this court; besides when an answer is made use of in another cause, the defendant don't know what use will be made of it, and so can't fence against it as he may in the same cause; and the party who produces it sees first whether it is for his purpose or not; but I won't introduce new evidence since Mr Baron St Leger (who was only in court) was of another opinion.

Mr Baron St Leger

If the whole might be read it would render the end of an answer useless, and the defendant might add anything, and I was of this opinion in the time of Lord Chief Baron Gilbert, who allowed it, and said it was done every day in England.

COSTELO v. COSTELO[236]

Friday, May the 21 [1731][237]

In Exchequer

Mr Costelo

We have brought a new writ of error directed to the barons, for the barons to review Ante 43. and redress, and a new doubt arises with your lordship, whether it ought not to be directed to the treasurer and barons, for the barons to review. Where they are directed in the writ of error to remove the record into the Exchequer Chamber, there is a *certiorari* in the body of the writ, but this is only a commission, and need not be directed to the treasurer and barons, because the writ is not to be removed.[238]

Lord Chief Baron

Is the direction of the writ of error to King's Bench when [*47*] *coram vobis* [*sic*], the same as when to remove into Parliament?

---

[236] Continued from p. 36. Resumed on p. 42.
[237] 21 May was a Friday in 1731 (Julian), Kratz, *Hist. Cal.*
[238] *Sic.* Presumably meaning the record is not to be removed.

Mr Costelo

As to the question, whether the writ lies? Error in fact in every court may be redressed in the same or a superior court, otherwise there would be a failure of justice, Hard. 51.[239] A bill of review lies of an error in fact: error in fact in the Petty Bag[240] may be amended by *scire facias*, 42 Ass. Ed. 3 pl. 22, Bro. Tit. Error 131, Fitz Ass. 349. If two patents, one may be reversed by *scire facias*, 7 H. 6 fol. 14,[241] Bro. Tit. Patent 23.[242] The first precedent of error in fact being brought in King's Bench *coram vobis* [*sic*] is 2 Rich. 3 fol. 1,[243] and after the erection of the Exchequer Chamber opinions were different, Cro. El. 731,[244] Cro. Ja. 5 pl. 5,[245] Cro. Car. 514,[246] Styl. 216,[247] 218,[248] and the first case determined that it would lie after that statute is 1 Sid. 147.[249]

Error in fact in an inferior court or Common Pleas may be tried in the same or some other court, Fitz Nat. Brev. fol. 20 E.[250]

31 Ed. 3 ch. 12[251] gives power to the Exchequer Chamber only to correct errors in law; and the 15 Ca. 1[252] gives no new jurisdiction, but is only to prevent the abatement of writs of error, 1 Lev. 149.[253] King's Bench may correct errors in law in criminal cases, Dy. 195, 196.[254] Error in fact in King's Bench in Ireland lies to King's Bench in England, 3 Keb. 384,[255] the case in Moor[256] only says that error in law before the 31 Ed. 3[257] in the Exchequer was to be corrected by special commissioners, and 4 Inst. has nothing about it.

Mr Frank Blake contra[258]

As to the reason drawn from the failure of justice, the question is, whether this court has such a jurisdiction, and not whether it ought to have, and if it has not, it must be submitted to like other inconveniences till they are redressed by [*48*] Parliament.

Error in the Exchequer before the 31 Ed. 3 which erected the Exchequer Chamber was redressed by special commissioners, so they may bring a writ of error and try it before commissioners, who may direct a *nisi prius* appears by later authorities. When

---

[239]　*Walsingham* v. *Baker* (1655) Hard. 49 at 51, 145 E.R. 375.
[240]　Above, p. lxxxv.
[241]　Y.B. Mich. 7 Hen. VI, fo. 14 pl. 21.
[242]　Brooke's *Abridgement*.
[243]　Y.B. Mich. 2 Ric. III, fo. 1 pl. 1.
[244]　*Price's Case* (1599) Cro. Eliz. 731, 78 E.R. 964.
[245]　*Rew* v. *Long* (1600) Cro. Jac. 4 at 5, 79 E.R. 4.
[246]　*Fitzherbert* v. *Leach* (1638) Cro. Car. 514, 79 E.R. 1043.
[247]　*Dawkes* v. *Payton* (1650) Sty. 216, 82 E.R. 657.
[248]　*Dawkes* v. *Payton* (1650) Sty. at 218, 82 E.R. at 659.
[249]　*Smith* v. *Smith* (1663) 1 Sid. 147, 82 E.R. 1023.
[250]　Fitzherbert's *New Natura Brevium* (1534).
[251]　31 Edw. III, st. 1, c. 12 (Eng.), 1357 (Exchequer Chamber).
[252]　15 Car. I, c. 5 (Ir.), 1639 (against discontinuance of writs of error in Exchequer, Exchequer Chamber). See also 1 Geo. II, c. 17 (Ir.), s. 3, 1727 (chancellor, in absence of treasurer and vice-treasurer, may in presence of both or either of chief justices, give judgment on writ of error).
[253]　*Cornhill's Case* (1664) 1 Lev. 149, 83 E.R. 342.
[254]　*Debenham* v. *Bateman* (1561) 2 Dy. 195b, 73 E.R. 430 at 431.
[255]　*Duke of Albermarle* v. *Keneday* (1650) 3 Keb. 384, 84 E.R. 780 (error of judgment in Ireland in ejectment).
[256]　*Holland* v. *Jackson* (1599) Moo. 622, 72 E.R. 798.
[257]　31 Edw. III, St 1, c. 12 (Eng.), 1357 (Exchequer Chamber)
[258]　Francis Blake, 2nd son of Patrick, Corbally, near Galway, KI, Hilary 1727, KI AP, p. 39, see below, p. 186
[*237*].

the Statute of Elizabeth[259] gave a power to the Exchequer Chamber to redress the judgments of King's Bench, it appears from the preamble it only designed to give them a jurisdiction in lieu of the House of Lords, and not to try an error in fact, but by the 31 Ed. 3 error in fact may be brought in the Exchequer Chamber, and the difference arises from the different pennings of the two Acts, that error in fact will lie from the Exchequer to the Exchequer Chamber, but not from King's Bench to the Exchequer Chamber. Fitz. Nat. Brev. 219.[260] Writs of error depend upon custom, but there is no instance of one being ever brought in this case.

As to the direction, all writs should be directed to those who have the custody of the records. If error is brought to reverse a fine, it is directed to the Chirographer, because he has custody.

Lord Chief Baron

But that is to remove a fine. If error in fact can't be brought the party is not remediless, because this ejectment is not conclusive.

Mr Blake

'Tis no difference, whether the writ is to remove the record, or bring it before you, because you only have the custody.

Post 49, 61, 68.

WELLINGTON v. NOWLAND

Eodem die

In Exchequer

An action was brought for treble damages on the statute 8 Q. Ann.[261] for wrong Ante 33. Post 392. marking a writ, and the question was, whether the defendant should give bail.

And the court were of opinion that an action [49] lay at common law, and that the statute only gave increase of damages, that here the informer was really damaged, though not in a threefold injury; and that therefore bail ought to be given, though they would consider what; that in St George's Case[262] in Yelverton and on [an]other penal statute the informer was not injured.

---

[259] 27 Eliz. I, c. 8 (Eng.), 1584 (error from Queen's Bench).
[260] Fitzherbert's *New Natura Brevium* (1534).
[261] Error for 6 Ann., c. 7 (Ir.), 1707 (sheriffs; treble damages for wrongly marking writs).
[262] *St George's Case* (1604) Yelv. 53, 80 E.R. 38.

EXECUTORS OF CREAGH
v.
THE EXECUTORS OF MAXWELL

Monday, May the 31 [1731][263]

In Exchequer

Mr Daly moved that the coroner might amend his return of *nulla bona*,[264] the action being brought against an executor, who if he had no goods he ought to have pleaded Post 69, 71. so, but now it is a *devastavit*, Salk. 310,[265] and it was ordered accordingly.

LESSEE OF BIRMINGHAM v. THE CASUAL EJECTOR

Eodem die

In Exchequer

Mr Daly said, that if the defendant in ejectment died within a year and the day, a *scire facias* lay by the common law for the damages, but not for the realty, 1 Sid. 351.[266]

But this case is denied for law in the case of *Withers* v. *Harris*[267] in Salkeld.

COSTELO v. COSTELO[268]

Eodem die

Mr Daly

Ante 43, 46. No writ of error lies to the barons, but error in fact must be taken advantage of by plea, or be brought before special commissioners, and this writ is not well directed. There is no precedent[269] [50] of this writ, and non user is the strongest authority, for such errors must have often happened, Moo. 566,[270] 1 Buls. 5, & 7.[271] Errors in fact can't be taken advantage of by writ of error, where there was an opportunity of

---

263 31 May was a Monday in 1731 (Julian), Kratz, *Hist. Cal.*
264 L. no goods.
265 *Rock* v. *Leighton* (1700) 1 Salk. 310, 91 E.R. 273.
266 *Okey* v. *Viccars* (1668) 1 Sid. 351, 82 E.R. 1151.
267 *Withers* v. *Harris* (1702) 1 Salk. 258, 91 E.R. 226.
268 Continued from p. 39. Resumed on p. 52.
269 Spelled 'president' in MS.
270 *Agar* v. *Candish* (1468) Moo. K.B. 564 at 566, 72 E.R. 761 at 762.
271 *Earl of Shrewsbury* v. *Earl of Rutland* (1610) 1 Buls. 4 at 5, 7; 80 E.R. 710 at 711, 712.

pleading to them, and 2 Lev. 38,[272] 1 Ventr. 207[273] says, that it is peculiar to King's Bench to try error in fact *coram vobis*.

And it is no inconvenience to the party if no such writ lies, because he may take advantage of it in the proceedings *puis darrein continuance*,[274] (which if he neglects he may blame himself) as he may suggest the death of the party, or the like on the roll.

But if such a writ lay, this is misdirected, for then this is in [the] nature of a special commission to the barons, and the writ ought to be directed to the keepers of the records. If they are commissioners 'tis a new authority, and they are a new court, and it must be directed to the treasurer etc. to deliver it over. It can't be brought into another court without their joint consent, and if 'tis directed to them as commissioners, then the record is to be removed into another court.

Lord Chief Baron

The words in Savil[e] 39[275] are, that every writ of error to remove the records (which are part of the King's treasure) must be directed to the keepers.

Savil 36[276]

Mr Costelo

If the defendant is an infant, or feme covert,[277] he may bring a writ of error, though they might take advantage of it by plea.

I have heard say it was determined in Sir Constantine Phipps[278] his time that error in fact in this court was not examinable in the Exchequer Chamber, but in this court. This is directed to the barons, to review a record [51] that is before them and the treasurer.

Post 61, 68.

Mr Calaghan quoted the case of *Cusack* v. *Cusack*[279] adjudged in Chancery by Sir Constantine Phipps.

Mr Cusack[280] by articles of intermarriage covenants to convey his lands to the use of himself and the heirs males [*sic*] of the marriage, the wife dies, and by articles previous to his second marriage he recites the first articles, that he was thereby tenant in tail, and had a power to provide for the daughters of that marriage, and then settles [it to other uses] etc. Afterwards in a cause between the son of the first venter[281] and the daughters of the second Sir Constantine Phipps adjudged in favour

---

[272] *Hopkins* v. *Weigglesworth* (1671) 2 Lev. 38, 83 E.R. 443.

[273] *Prior* v. *Anonymous* (1672) 1 Vent. 207, 86 E.R. 140.

[274] LF. [matter pleaded] after the last continuance.

[275] Error in Camera Scacc', Sav. 39, 123 E.R. 1000.

[276] Error in Camera Scacc', Sav. 35 at 36, 123 E.R. 998.

[277] LF. married woman.

[278] L.C., 1710–1714; Ball, *Judges in Ireland*, ii. 70–71. He was an extreme Tory and a suspected Jacobite and was removed from office in 1714.

[279] The House of Lords judgment is reported in (1714) 5 Bro. 2nd ed. 116, 2 E.R. 570. Brown was not published until the end of century. Below, p. 44 n. 283.

[280] Robert Cusack, to whom the land was given under a deed by his relative, Adam Cusack, a judge of the Irish court of Common Pleas, as is noted in 2 E.R. 570. Adam was appointed in 1672 and died in 1681: see Ball, *Judges in Ireland*, i. 286–7, 295, 310, i. 353. The appellant was the only son of the first marriage.

[281] L. womb.

of the daughters. But this decree was [reversed][282] in the House of Lords,[283] where it was adjudged, that the father by the first articles was only a tenant for life, and that the recital was sufficient notice of them, though they are misdirected.

Post 94, 128.

Friday, June the 4th [1731][284]

BISHOP [OF] ELPHIN v. LEIGH

In Chancery

Thomas Wyndham Esq, lord chancellor

The bishop of Elphin and his wife (who is the daughter of the defendant Mrs Leigh by her former husband Mr Bulloign,) exhibited their bill in this court against the defendants Mr Leigh and his wife for an account of the profits of her estate during her minority which they received as guardians; this dispute was submitted to the award of Mr Fowkes and Mr Bailey, who were [52] to choose an umpire, and the submission was made an order of this court pursuant to the statute 9 Wm. 3.[285] The arbitrators made their award that £3,000 and upwards were due to the plaintiffs; Mr Leigh being served with notice to show cause why the order should not be made absolute, has taken by his counsel 21 objections to this award, one goes to the whole, seven to the body, to the recitals, three to the judicial part, and ten to collateral matters, which relate to the behaviour of the referees.

The first objection is that the Court of Chancery is not within the Act.

If this was *res integra*[286] I don't know what weight it might be of, for the Act seems to be restrained to the courts of law, and this court having originally exercised this power, they seem not to have been within the intention of the legislature; but they having ever since the Act assumed this power, 'tis now too late to controvert it.

As to the objections made to the body of the award, I think the court is not at liberty to inquire into them, nor can examine into the foundation of the award without having the same matters laid before them the arbitrators had, but this must be left to their integrity, unless there was proof of their having rejected any evidence that was offered.

The first objection is, that the referees had ascertained the rent from a view they took of the lands in 1730, which was a bad method to judge the rent by for 35 years before.

If this was a bad reason, and stood singly, I would not inquire into it, because they might have other reasons, and which indeed they have given, as that they had the leases laid before them. [53]

[282] Original word obliterated.

[283] *Cusack* v. *Cusack* (1714) 1 Bro. P.C. 470; 5 Bro. 2nd ed. 116, 2 E.R. 570. The House of Lords held that the appellant, Robert's only son by the first marriage, was entitled to specific performance of the marriage articles entered into on the first marriage.

[284] 4 June was a Friday in 1731, Kratz, *Hist. Cal.*

[285] The regnal year suggests the reference is to 9 Will. III, c. 15 (Eng.), 1697 (arbitration), but see the Irish statute 10 Will. III, c. 14 (Ir.), 1698 (arbitration).

[286] See above, p. 18 n. 100.

The second objection is, that they charge him for rent before he entered, which was in May. But it is plain he received the profits before that time.

The third objection is to the law charges and repairs, which receives the general answer.

The fourth is, that they might have staid till the debts were made out.

The fifth, that they valued the stock by guess.

But what better judgment could they make of the worth of it, than by considering the market price at the time, or who knew the contrary, and if they knew it to be better or worse than ordinary, they should have showed it to be so, or the arbitrators are justified.

The sixth, that at all events there ought to have been an examination of witnesses, because the arbitrators by the order were armed with a commission.

But this was not an order on them to examine, but leaves it to their discretion, and only if they thought it necessary, saves them the trouble of applying to the court for a power.

The seventh, that they have allowed too much interest. The arbitrators sure are clear judges of this, unless the fact plainly appears.

The eighth, that they did not examine witnesses. If witnesses had been tendered and they had refused to examine them, this would have been an undue practice, but no proof has been made that any were produced.

The ninth: that they gave no copy of the award before they published it. This was not necessary to be done, and they deny that Mr Leigh ever asked it.

The tenth, that they would not examine his [54] wife. His wife could not be examined but by consent and there is no proof that she was tendered to be examined.

The eleventh, that it was obtained by surprise, and that neither the defendant, nor his agent were there. They were not there indeed, but yet here was no surprise. There were sixteen attendances, Mr Leigh went to Drogheda within twenty miles of the town, never had any settled agent, the referees gave him notice, and his withdrawing from his attendance or giving evidence when he thought the account would come out against him, is no corruption or undue means in the referees.

The twelfth: there was a month's time left to have chose an umpire, and they should have staid that time out. This objection is of no weight, if the award is well made.

The thirteenth: the next evidence of corruption is, that the bishop gave twenty guineas to Mr Bailey the referee of Mr Leigh. Mr Bailey who has an office in the Custom House[287] declared as he was a stranger to both parties he would not undertake the reference without a consideration, and I think the time it took him up was well worth it. They spent about five hours a day for sixteen days. Mr Fowkes was related to both sides, and therefore was willing to undertake it out of friendship.

The fourteenth: Mr Leigh was not apprised they would go on with their award at that time, because they informed him by letter, they resolved if possible to make their award by such a day, and desired him to send them the papers they wanted. They did not know what these papers were [55] and it was his fault if he thought them material he did not bring them up, for they told him they would make their award by such a time if possibly they could.

---

[287] This is not Gandon's Custom House, which was not completed until 1791, but the old Custom House designed by Thomas Burgh in 1707 and which stood on the south bank of the Liffey on arcades back from the quayside on the present Wellington Quay, beside Essex Bridge, renamed Grattan Bridge in 1874: see J. O'Brien and G. Guinness, *Dublin: A Grand Tour* (London, 1994), p. 174.

Plate 3. The Old Custom House, Wellington Quay, Dublin, and Essex Bridge.

The fifteenth objection is the change of place, that they removed from the Custom House[288] to Mr Williams's, who was the plaintiff's agent. I can't say this was a prudent step, but then it must be considered with all its circumstance. The Custom House was a proper place to meet in for four or five hours, but when the award was to be made up which was a work of time a public office would not serve the purpose, and as to their going to the plaintiff's agent, who was to get them a house? The referees themselves sure were not obliged to find one, and the plaintiffs were not all this while in town, but indeed if any irregularity had followed from hence, this would have been an undue practice, but it is plain he had nothing to do with drawing up the award.

The sixteenth: they gave Leigh notice he should come up the twenty-ninth to see what objections he could make to the award, whereas they finished their award on the twenty-fourth. They had agreed indeed at that time on their award, but did not sign it till four or five days after, in which time Mr Leigh might have objected to it.

The first objection to the judicial part of the award is, that they have awarded some deeds to be delivered up which is out of the submission. But if this award is sufficient to end all the differences submitted, I shan't think the doing this which is not legal, sufficient to vitiate the whole award.

The second, that they have awarded that the defendant's wife should give a release. [56] This was right because she was a defendant to the bill, and therefore it was good for conformity, but surely to order an unnecessary thing won't vitiate the award, for then it would be necessary for a referee to be the best judge of law, and they must do nothing simple, which would overturn all awards if there was any mistake in the judgment, though there was sufficient to answer the purpose of the reference.

The third objection is, that they were to give such a release as counsel should advise: though giving advice is a judicial act in the counsel, 'tis a ministerial one in respect of the arbitrators: Styl. 217.[289]

The fourth objection is to the accounts, which they made up arbitrarily, because they had not matters clearly before them. If each party had it in their power to lay matters equally before them this would be of weight, but this was only in Mr Leigh's power, who was guardian to the lady almost from her birth and was not called to account till 13 years after she came of age. She had none, he all the papers in his hands. The guardian avoids laying them before the referees, then they were in the right to go on in the best manner they could: if an account is referred to an arbitrator, and one side won't attend, he will make a report ex parte; and otherwise, there could never have been an account made up, the plaintiffs being strangers.

It would have been unnecessary and useless in the legislature to have passed this Act if this court might overhaul the proceedings. It appears from Salkeld,[290] that Lord Chief Justice Holt once went into the inquiry, whether the arbitrators had done right or no, and costs being afterwards moved for and denied, Mr Justice Powel said, [']I never will go into the account if the [57] party after all is not to have his costs[']. This Act meant no court should have power over an award, but for apparent corruption and unfair practice.

[288]   Above, n. 287.

[289]   *Cater* v. *Startute* (1650) Sty. 217 at 218, 82 E.R. 659.

[290]   There appear to be four cases in Salkeld decided by Holt C.J. concerning arbitrators: *Freeman* v. *Bernard* (1696) 1 Salk. 69, 91 E.R. 64; *Bacon* v. *Dubarry* (1697) 1 Salk. 70, 91 E.R. 65; *Anonymous* (1700) 1 Salk. 71, 91 E.R. 66; *Simon* v. *Gavil* (1703) 1 Salk. 74, 91 E.R. 70. The most likely one referred to is *Anonymous* (1700) 1 Salk. 71, 91 E.R. 66.

Mr Fowkes is a common relation of both parties, and each of the referees is a man of a fair and undeniable character, which is an answer to that objection that the plaintiffs' agent drew the award. Suppose he did, if indeed it was never after revised by the referees this would be sufficient to set it aside, but their revising and reviewing it after by their notes, and signing it makes it their award. But this was not the case here. They gave Williams their notes to draw it by, and perused with caution the draught and engrossment.

As to the case quoted of *Burton* v. *Knight*[291] 2 Vern. 514, of an award being set aside because it was drawn by the plaintiff's attorney, it was not set aside for that reason, but for other malpractices.

The difficulty then in this case is what ought to be done. I am positive the award ought not to be set aside, but the Act says nothing of confirming it: but I must make this my decree, and then it may be said, I make it for the good as well as the bad. But it has been held in many cases that an award may be good in part and bad in part, and when an action is brought on the bond, I assign a breach in the good part, if I do in a part that is bad, the other side has an opportunity to dispute it. So I may here make it part of the order, that no process shall issue to execute any part of this decretal order without special application to the court, as is done at law on the bond; but this is a new judgment, and therefore if any of you gentlemen can think of a better way I'll hear it.

But on the objection of counsel the last order was made absolute, and the decree was to be made up, for the six clerks[292] said it was the practice to [*58*] apply for an attachment or other process on a particular part of a decree.

Monday June the 14 [1731][293]

The Essoin day of Trinity Term

In Chancery

RICE v. TISDAL

Post 140. By the standing rules of the court no plea or demurrer can be put in after a commission of rebellion returned unless on motion, and pleas in bar in such cases are generally granted, but not dilatory pleas, as a plea of outlawry at the suit of others was refused in this case.

There were five outlawries against the plaintiff.

---

[291] *Burton* v. *Knight* (1705) 2 Vern. 414, 23 E.R. 929.
[292] Officers of the court of Chancery whose duties consisted of receiving and filing all bills, answers and other records on the equity side of the court.
[293] 14 June was a Monday in 1731, Kratz, *Hist. Cal.*

RYAN v. CUMMIN

Wednesday, June the 22[294]

In Exchequer

If an infant brings a bill by his prochein amy, and has a decree, and reaps the benefit of it after he comes of age, this shall be evidence against him, at least the material charges. 2 Vern. *Cecil* v. *Salisbury*[295]

A bill is the slightest evidence, drawn by counsel from the papers that are laid before him, and frequently not seen by the party. 1 Sid. 221.[296]   Post 113.

The lord chief baron said he was of opinion that though the defendant in his answer did not insist on the length of his possession, he might take advantage of it on the hearing, and the plaintiff in equity, as well as at law must recover by his own strength, and mentioned the case of *St John*[297] in Chancery where barely on his motion the bill was dismissed without a demurrer, because it appeared thereby that the defendant was 109 years in possession. [*59*]   Post 144.

LESSEE OF FOWKES v. BUTLER[298]

Saturday, June the 25th [1731][299]

In Exchequer

Upon a Trial at bar in Ejectment.

The question was, whether the copy of the parish book in England should be read in evidence to prove the death of Sir Richard Ingoldsby.[300]

Objection, that the copy of a record only had been allowed evidence, that in the case of *Digby* v. *Marlay*[301] last term in the Common Pleas the copy of a presentation was not suffered to be read, the register of Kildare not being a record.

That possibly the copy might be good evidence, if they had showed the book was lost, and that this evidence was disallowed in this court in the case of *Draycot* v. *Talbot*.[302]

---

[294] 22 June was a Tuesday in 1731 (Julian), Kratz, *Hist. Cal.*, but the year still seems to be 1731 from the previous dates.

[295] *Cecil* v. *Earl of Salisbury* (1691) 2 Vern. 224, 23 E.R. 745.

[296] *Snow* v. *Phillips* (1664) 1 Sid. 220 at 221, 82 E.R. 1069.

[297] *Overand* v. *St John*, no citation given, below, p. 118.

[298] Resumed on p. 64.

[299] 25 June was a Friday in 1731 (Julian), Kratz, *Hist. Cal.*, but the year still seems to be 1731. It was a Thursday in 1730 and a Sunday in 1732.

[300] The C.B. mentions below, p. 50, that he died 45 years before the case, and so refers to Sir Richard Ingoldsby (bap. 10 August 1617, d. 1685), army officer and regicide, the second son of Sir Richard Ingoldsby (d. 1656) of Lenborough, Buckinghamshire, and Elizabeth (d. 1666), daughter of Sir Oliver Cromwell, the uncle of the future lord protector. Ingoldsby survived the Restoration by claiming that he had been forced to sign the death warrant of Charles I by Cromwell, and Charles II chose to believe him: Timothy Venning, 'Ingoldsby, Sir Richard, appointed Lord Ingoldsby under the protectorate (bap. 1617, d. 1685)', *ODNB*, <http://www.oxforddnb.com/view/article/14411>, accessed 14 May 2008.

[301] No citation given.

[302] No citation given.

Mr Prime Serjeant contra

Copies of records are allowed evidence because they are not to be removed, and so of books that are appropriated, and belong to no particular persons; what method have we by law to get this book out of the custody of the parish?

Lord Chief Baron

Why the Register book is carried from Assize to Assize.

Mr Prime Sergeant

This was allowed as evidence at a *nisi prius* in the Common Pleas for the County of Middlesex in the case of *Stapleton* v. *Stalow*,[303] and otherwise what must become of the subjects in Ireland, and this is the best evidence we can give.

In the case of *Digby* v. *Marley*[304] the register was in court, and the counsel[305] did not oppose the reading [of] the copy, but Mr Barnard asked for the original Book.

In the case of *Carteret* v. *Gore*[306] in the King's Bench in [*60*] England, the certificate of the Register of Paris where he died was allowed to be read to prove the death of Dean Greenville.

Things of a public have been always distinguished from those of a private nature, and the copies of the former have been allowed, because the originals are to be exposed to no hazards, so many being interested in them. It is also always considered, whether the evidence is in the power of the party, or the process of the court and therefore the Acts of foreign admiralties may be certified, because they are in the power of the suitor, or the process of the court.

Lord Chief Baron

Sir Richard Ingoldsby has been dead but 45 years, so this is not the best evidence you can give. You may prove it by living witnesses.

Mr Prime Sergeant

If there are several witnesses to a deed, and all are dead but one, and he is abroad, his hand may be proved as well as those that are dead, because he is amenable.

Lord Chief Baron

MSS̄ Cas. in BR
A.239.
Palmr 326.[307]

I think this copy must be read, though I don't know that it has ever been determined it may. These registers in England are kept with great exactness and regularity. We are to take the best evidence. He died in England 45 years ago, so 'tis very difficult to

---

[303] No citation given. No case of that name in E.R.
[304] No citation given.
[305] Spelled 'council' in MS.
[306] No citation given. No case of that name in E.R.
[307] *Heylor* v. *Hall* (1623) Palm. 325, at 326, 81 E.R. 1105.

prove his death by living witnesses. This then is the best evidence. We can't compel them to produce the book, or if we could, it would not be reasonable for the perils of the sea.

But the counsel[308] waived the giving this evidence of the death of Sir Charles Ingoldsby, because he had been in this kingdom, and he died not above 24 years before. [*61*]

In this case the patent migrated the lands by placing them in a wrong barony, and it was said the first description vitiates, not otherwise, 3 Co. *Doughtie's Case*,[309] and the *non obstante*[310] in the patent notwithstanding the misnaming or not naming of any barony won't help, because the law says, where the first description is wrong, the patent is void, and the King's saying so won't amend it, but this saving is agreeable to law, for there are several mistakes in patents that are not fatal.

LESSEE OF HILL v. THE CASUAL EJECTOR

Friday, June the 24th [1731][311]

Mr Steward[312] for the plaintiff moved, that the tenant in possession who had been served, or somebody concerned in interest might be obliged to take the defence, on affidavit, that Ryley who had taken the defence was a person unknown, and so if they should recover they had nobody against whom to pray costs, and so it was so resolved in Comberbatch.[313]

On the other side was mentioned a case in Levinz[314] whereby it appeared that there was no occasion for this motion, because the attorney if he did not produce the defendant would be liable to the costs.

The chief baron ordered the tenant to take the defence, or security to be given to pay the costs, though at first he was of opinion, that the Act of Parliament[315] saying that on an ejectment for not payment of rent the tenant should not let any other take the defence, implied that he might on any other ejectment.

But a person was named to take the defence the plaintiff approved of.

---

[308] Spelled 'council' in MS.

[309] *Attorney General* v. *Dowtie* (1584) 3 Co. Rep. 9b, 76 E.R. 643. The case held that where the first description is wrong, the patent is void, even if there is a later description that is correct, but that if the first description is correct, the patent is valid even if there is a later description that is wrong.

[310] L. notwithstanding.

[311] 24 June was a Thursday in 1731 (Julian), Kratz, *Hist. Cal.*, but the year still seems to be 1731.

[312] Charles Steward, or Stewart, is listed in KI AP, as a barrister, *c.* 1734. KI AP, p. 464.

[313] Presumably Comberbach's Reports, King's Bench, 1685–99.

[314] Perhaps *Henloe* v. *Peters and Buck* (1672) 2 Lev. 66, 83 E.R. 452.

[315] 8 Geo. I, c. 2 (Ir.) (ejectment) s. 1.

COSTELO v. COSTELO[316]

Friday, July the 2d [1731] [317]

Mr Nat[hanie]l Blake[318]

Ante 43, 46, 49.   I shall endeavour to prove this writ of error lies.

First, from the nature, and constitution of this court. [62] Secondly, from necessity. Thirdly, from maxims of the law. Fourthly, from Acts of Parliament.

As to the first, when any doubts arise on the nature of courts, 'tis necessary to consider the ends for which they were erected: Regr 187,[319] 2 Inst. 551. This court was originally established for the King's debts and revenue, and by the 11 of Magna Charta, which is an affirmance of the common law, the end is the speedy execution of them, and as error in fact may be in the proceedings for them, they must have of necessity a power to redress it. The King in King's Bench can reverse error in fact between subject and subject, and why not in his own suit? And whoever is drawn in here by prerogatives ought to have the same remedy, and these debts being of public concern ought to have more expedition than private suits.

In the 22 Ed. 3[320] there was a petition in Parliament that error in fact in this court might be reversed in King's Bench, but denied, which they would not have rejected, if the court had not full power before.

31 Ed. 3[321] was only to reverse errors in law, and they would certainly have given them this power to reverse errors in fact, if they had not thought the court had it in itself. 33 H. 8 ch. 39 paragraph 11,[322] this court has a twofold jurisdiction as the Court of Chancery has. No appeals from the decrees of either court but to Parliament. Errors in fact are reversible in Chancery, and so must [be] in this court, which has as high a jurisdiction as King's Bench, and is generated out of both courts for the King's debts, there is no authority against it, and the reason is the same as for King's Bench.

Secondly, from necessity. Fleta B 6 ch. 36 in his Jurisdiction of Courts says, necessity was the mother of them, and upon this reason courts enlarge their jurisdiction, 4 Inst. 213, Magna Charta 10, so your Lordships may assume this jurisdiction out of necessity, 2 Salk. 511.[323] King's Bench redress errors [63] in fact because it is below the dignity of the House of Lords, and there, and there is the same reason here, and necessity made a writ of entry of an advowson necessary.

---

[316]   Continued from p. 42. Resumed on p. 57.

[317]   2 July was a Friday in 1731, Kratz, *Hist. Cal.*

[318]   Not listed in KI AP, which are incomplete: see KI AP, p. viii.

[319]   Rastell, *Registrum Omnium Brevium*, 1531–1687, p. 187, cited at 2 Inst. 551.

[320]   1348/9.

[321]   31 Edw. III, St 1, c. 12 (Eng.), 1357 (Exchequer Chamber).

[322]   33 Hen. VIII, c. 39 (Eng.), 1542 (crown debts).

[323]   *Rex* v. *Knollys* (1694) 2 Salk. 509 at 511, 91 E.R. 434 at 436. Holt C.J.: 'The House of Lords has no jurisdiction over an original cause mixed with matter of fact; because, 1st, That Supreme Court is the *dernier resort*; besides that, for the most part, original causes are mixed with matter of fact, and it is below the dignity of so supreme a judicature to try a matter of fact. It is for this reason, error in fact, in the Court of King's Bench, must of necessity be redressed before the Judges of this Court. 2dly, If the Parliament should take cognizance of original causes, the subject would lose his appeal, so much indulged by the common law in all cases. Causes come not thither, till they have tried all other judicatures.'

Thirdly, from maxims.

1. *Quod necessarium justa est,* a private person by this rule may justify what could not otherwise, and then courts sure[ly] more [so].

2. *Boni judicis est ampliare jurisdictionem.*[324]

3. *Curia non debet deficere in justitia.*[325]

Fourthly, as to acts, on a new offence an action on the case lies, and courts are not circumscribed. Sir William Jones 83,[326] Cro. Car. 15,[327] the action was adjudged to lie though no precedent.[328]

1 Saund. 74,[329] nothing shall be presumed out of the jurisdiction of sovereign courts.

The usage and practice of King's Bench is similar to this, not of the Common Pleas, because that[330] court has no original jurisdiction, and errors in fact may be reversed in King's Bench.

Lord Chief Baron

What we go upon is this. The King can't erect a court without an Act of Parliament to control any of the four supreme courts. The court to redress this error is not the same which gave the judgment, but the writ is a new commission. King's Bench have had this power time out of mind, though it is not natural for a court to correct their own mistakes without a commission from the King. This court has stood above 600 years, and yet there is no precedent.[331]

Mr Fr. Blake[332]

The Lord Coke[333] says errors in this court were reversible by special commissioners before 31 Ed. 3,[334] and since the law is proved once to be so, they must show when it was altered, for writs of error depend upon usage and custom. Dy. 376[335] (23).   Post 68.

---

[324] 'A good judge will extend the limits of his jurisdiction.' The maxim has been criticised as erroneous. Lord Mansfield always said that *justitiam* (justice) should be substituted: *Rex* v. *Philips* (1757) 1 Keny. 531 at 541, 96 E.R. 1081 at 1084; *In re Bombay Justices* [1829] 1 Kn. A.C. 1 at 39, 12 E.R. 222 at 236.

[325] L. a court ought not to be deficient in justice.

[326] *Blakestons Case* (1625) Jones W. 82, 82 E.R. 44.

[327] *Smith* v. *Crashaw Ward and Ford* (1626) Cro. Car. 15, 79 E.R. 618.

[328] Original says 'presidt'.

[329] *Peacock* v. *Bell and Kendal* (1667) 1 Wms. Saund. 73, 85 E.R. 84.

[330] This seems to refer to King's Bench, i.e. that the Exchequer, like the King's Bench, had no original jurisdiction in common pleas, although in the case of the Exchequer that had been avoided by the fiction of *quo minus.*

[331] Original says 'presidt'.

[332] See Francis Blake, below, p. 186.

[333] *Sic.* Sir Edward Coke.

[334] 31 Edw. III, St 1, c. 12 (Eng.), 1357 (Exchequer Chamber).

[335] *Knoles' Case* (1581) 3 Dy. 375b at 376a (23), 73 E.R. 841 at 843.

TUTHILL v. THE BISHOP OF KILLALA

Saturday, July the 3d, [1731][336]

In Exchequer

[*64*] The bishop brought a bill of foreclosure and an account being decreed, it appeared to the officer on examining the parties on personal interrogatories, that only £1,020 was originally lent, and that by frequent stating accounts of what was due for principal and interest, and turning the interest into principal, there was now due on the mortgage £5,000, and this bill being brought in aid of the account, the court ordered the report to stay, till the bishop had put in a full answer for further insight and view of the securities.

LEADBETER v. LEADBETER[337]

Eodem die

In Exchequer

Moved to set aside depositions taken at Sheffield because they were not signed.

The chief baron suspected them, because they would have their own set aside too.

Post 180.   The registrar said there was no such rule. It is not required by law, but by some courts of equity for the more easy conviction of the offender if guilty of perjury.

The counsel said, the minutes were signed, though not the transcript.

And an order was made, that the commissioners should hereafter return the diminicals[338] of the commission.

CALLAN v. BARRY

Eodem die

In Exchequer

A subpœna to hear judgment returnable on a *dies non*[339] was held good, because the Exchequer, both on the law and equity side, is always open to do the King's business.

Mr Daly said, that such a subpœna returnable the first day of term was disallowed in Chancery, that day by the custom of the court being a day for motions, and not for hearing causes. [*65*] In the case of *Hely* v. *Macarty*[340] a subpœna *teste* on a *dies non* was held good.

---

[336] 3 July was a Saturday in 1731, Kratz, *Hist. Cal.*

[337] Resumed on p. 105.

[338] Perhaps for 'dominical'. It is used in the sense of the returns of a commission to take evidence in KI MS. 90, p. 73. *OED*: 'dominical II. 3 in legal use, belonging to a demesne or domain [med. L. *dominicum*]; domanial'.

[339] I.e. not a legal day.

[340] No citation given.

But Mr Daly said he allowed that case, because till the Statute process might have been served on a Sunday.

In the case of *Macarty* v. *Sandys*[341] the same subpœna was allowed by Lord Chief Baron Dalton.[342]

AUDLEY v. SAVAGE AND COWPER

Monday, July the 5th, [1731][343]

In Exchequer

Lord Bellamont in 1714 executed a minute to the plaintiff to make him a lease for three lives of certain lands except the woods, but no lives were nominated.

In 1718 the plaintiff filed a bill against Lord Bellamont for a specific execution of the minute, but no lives were mentioned in his bill, and in 1719 there was a decree for an execution. Afterwards Lord Bellamont conveys the fee to Cowper, in trust for Savage. In 1725 the plaintiff applied to Savage for a lease, but he insisted that the woodlands were excepted. And this bill is brought to have the decree against Lord Bellamont made good by his assignee.

'Twas insisted on for the defendants, that the court is not obliged to execute such an agreement in favour of the plaintiff, who hoped by fraud to gain an advantage for himself, and that if he might after 17 years declining it, nominate lives. All that time would be clear gains to him, and if so, he might nominate at any time, and he don't now name the lives in his bill, and to decree him now a lease for 3 lives is more than he agreed for, for a life by the Act of Parliament[344] is estimated at seven years, for a lessee[345] abroad at the end of seven years is supposed [66] to be dead, if he is not proved to be alive; and in bishop's leases three lives and 21 years are considered the same.

Lord Chief Baron

Why did not you spur him on by bringing an ejectment? He has received a benefit by his own fault, but the question is if you have not been to blame too. He is limited to no time to name the lives, therefore he may at any time in his life, unless hastened by request.

It was further argued for the defendants, that a lease except the woods passes the soil, 5 Co. *Ivy's Case*,[346] that this was a young wood, which further explains my Lord's intention to reserve the young growth from being destroyed by the plaintiff's cattle. The decree is silent as to the woodlands, and only says the agreement shall be carried

---

[341] No citation given.

[342] Thomas Dalton (1682–1730), appointed C.B. 1725, died 1730: Ball, *Judges in Ireland*, ii. 198–199.

[343] 5 July was a Monday in 1731 (Julian), Kratz, *Hist. Cal.*

[344] 7 Will. III, c. 8 (Ir.) 1695 (life estates, cestuis que vie). Where a cestui que vie was 'absent or beyond the seas' for seven years or more without proof that he or she was still alive, the Act created a presumption that he or she had died.

[345] The Act only specifically refers to cestuis que vie.

[346] *Ive's Case* (1597) 5 Co. Rep. 11a, 77 E.R. 64.

into execution. In the case of *Newton* v. *Chamberlain*[347] in Chancery, a meadow left out of the articles was decreed by Sir Constantine Phipps to be inserted.

So if more is mentioned than the parties designed, the court will strike it out. But a deed executed without any surprise is to be construed according to law. In the case of *Blake* v. *Blake*[348] the House of Lords determined woods to mean woodlands.

Lord Chief Baron

'Twill be sufficient to decree a lease for three lives in being in 1714,[349] or won't the true way be to see what three lives are worth, and to subduct the years he has neglected, and give him a lease for the residue?

It was argued for the plaintiffs, that in the case of *Doyle* v. *Lindsay*,[350] Lindsay was trustee for Dalyel's children, and 14 or 15 years were passed and he insisted that they should be subtracted from the lives, but it was disallowed by the court.

Lord Chief Baron

But there Lindsay would have taken advantage [67] of his own fault, for he insisted that the minute was void.

It was further argued for the plaintiff, that Lord Bellamont gave possession of the woodlands, and 3d a year for entering, and paid for grazing of cattle; that the rent reserved explained the nature of the agreement, which is more than the lands are worth, unless the soil of the woods pass.

Savage insisted the woodlands were excepted, so that his litigating the operation of the agreement, is the same with Lindsay's litigating the minute; that the lives need not be named in the bill, but may at the hearing.

Lord Chief Baron

Savage allows he had notice of the minute, but how should he know by that Lord Bellamont's intention to reserve only the timber, and not the soil?

It was further insisted on for the plaintiff, that the lessee was entitled to name three lives in being in 1714, and his own one of them, for if tenant in fee makes a lease for life, that shall be construed to mean the life of the lessee, as most advantageous to him; but if [a] tenant in tail makes a lease for life, that must be understood of his own life, because he can make no greater lease. This will be no inconvenience for here is no fine for renewal; but all the lives are in being at once; and Savage bought nothing but the rent, so that is the measure of his purchase.

---

[347] No citation given.

[348] *Blake* v. *Blake* (1724) 5 Bro. P.C. 2nd ed. 384–391, 2 E.R. 747 (Protestant discoverer, Thomas Blake, was the son of respondent, Sir Walter Blake, and succeeded in the claim against his father).

[349] This a good piece of problem solving. The chief baron sees that, so long as the plaintiff names lives which were in existence when the agreement was entered into, the plaintiff would not gain any advantage from his delay.

[350] No citation given.

Lord Chief Baron

I must decree a lease. Where there has been a long delay which has been for the benefit of the lessee, the court ought to take some rule in it, or dismiss the bill, and whatever term is adequate to three lives take off the years he delayed.

In the case between the plaintiff and Lord Bellamont no advantage was taken of the lives not being named in the bill, but the decree was only to execute a lease. [*68*] Now you say that the word 'woods' though they may include lands don't in this agreement, because Lord Bellamont put you in possession of the soil. If he had put you in possession of the distinct woodlands it would have bound him, but I don't think the evidence good, and that the equity is the less against the purchaser. He had notice indeed of the minute, which imports a demise of lands with an exception of the woodlands. This is all the notice he had, and the decree implies no further notice. 'Tis said 'tis stronger against him because there is no consideration for the woods in the purchase. In purchases in England there is often no consideration for the buildings, but they are thrown in, and for that reason shall the lessee come and throw down the timber. I therefore decree a lease pursuant to the agreement, and the plaintiff, if he disputes it, may try that point at law.

COSTELO v. COSTELO[351]

Tuesday July the 6th [1731]

Mr Darcy[352]

Your Lordship will receive information what this writ of error is. Errors in fact are allowed by law to be a grievance, and then by Magna Charta there must be a remedy. Ante 43, 46, 49, 61. The Court of Exchequer is as high in esteem as any other court, and Mr Maddox[353] [*sic*] in his *History of the Exchequer* observes the King has sat there as well as in King's Bench, and their judgment is impeachable only in Parliament.

For 200 years scarce any writ of error was brought in the Exchequer, Savil 31,[354] and where there is no precedent,[355] reason and the rule of law is to take place, 4 Co. 94, *Slane's Case*,[356] and though we can't produce an authority, they can't show that on application it was ever denied, and 'tis as reasonable it should be so in this court as in King's Bench, which in civil cases can try only error in fact, but in criminal cases error both in law and fact. [*69*]

---

[351] Continued from p. 52.

[352] Probably Nicholas Darcy, listed in KI AP as a member, KI, 1710, d. May 1740. KI AP, p. 121.

[353] Thomas Madox, *The History and Antiquities of the Exchequer of the Kings of England* (2nd ed. 1711, reprinted, 1969).

[354] Error in Exchequer Chamber. Sav. 31, 123 E.R. 995.

[355] Spelled 'presidt' in MS.

[356] The reference is to *Slade's Case* (1602) 4 Co. Rep. 92b, 76 E.R. 1074. See also below, p. 168 n. 883. The name seems to have been misheard by the person who wrote the original notes in court, possibly by confusion with the Irish village and castle of Slane near Dublin.

27 Eliz.[357] gave a writ of error in law into the Exchequer Chamber, 2 Lev. 38,[358] Cro. El. 105, 106.[359] Error in fact is what never was in judgment before the court till now, and there is the same reason to give judgment on this as on the other part of the record.

Before 31 Ed. 3[360] judgments in this court were not to be impeached but by Parliament or special commissioners, 2 Inst. 105, and it is not known that errors in fact were ever examined by that Act. They were before inquireable by the court itself, or the legislature would have remedied this defect too. This writ is a commission under the Great Seal, and this is a proper court, and can issue a *venire*, and may come in under the reason of the case in 2 Inst. 105.

THE EXECUTORS OF CREAGH

v.

THE EXECUTORS OF MAXWELL[361]

Eodem die

Ante 49. Mr Attorney General moved to set aside the rule.

Though this was a judgment by default, which is a confession of assets by the executor, yet they ought to make affidavit, that they laid this matter before the sheriff, who then might have returned a *devastavit*, and it don't appear of itself how the judgment was obtained. It does indeed on a *scire facias*, but not on an execution. (And the officer being consulted said the execution did not mention whether the judgment was by default or how otherwise) and the court never will oblige the officer to amend his return. But where he is in some default, they ought to have carried down a copy of the judgment, and told the sheriff he must return a *devastavit*, is he [*sic*] obliged to get a copy of the judgment.

On the other side was quoted Cro. Eliz. 102,[362] 2 Salk. 310, *Lock* v. *Leighton*.[363]

Lord Chief Baron

If the law says he ought to return a *devastavit* [70] it will be no punishment on him Post 71. to amend his return. Let the officer attend with the record that this may appear.

[357] 27 Eliz. I, c. 8 (Eng.), 1584 (error from Queen's Bench).
[358] *Hopkins* v. *Weigglesworth* (1671) 2 Lev. 38, 83 E.R. 443.
[359] 78 E.R. 421. It is unclear to which case this refers.
[360] 31 Edw. III, c. 12 (Eng.), 1357 (Exchequer Chamber).
[361] Continued from p. 42.
[362] *Lacy* v. *Smith* (1588) Cro. Eliz., 78 E.R. 360.
[363] *Rock* v. *Leighton* (1700) 1 Salk. 310, 91 E.R. 273. The error in the name in the MS probably indicates the writer of the MS, or of original notes, took the name down from speech. Note that the pagination of Salkeld's reports is continuous in the edition in E.R, and the reference is to 1 Salk. not 2 Salk.

Plate 4. Robert Jocelyn (1688–1756), Baron Newport, as lord chancellor of Ireland.

THE EXECUTORS OF CHARLES BALDWIN
v.
THE HEIR AND TERTENANTS OF NEVE

Eodem die

In Exchequer

Mr Sutton[364]

The judgment was against Neve Michaelmas 12 An. On *scire facias* against the heir and tertenants[365] of Neve, the return was 'no heir or tertenants', upon which a *testatum scire facias* went to the sheriff of Longford, who returned, no heir, and that he had summoned several tenants, who put in several pleas, that Neve was not seised, *prout*,[366] and conclude *petit judicium de brevi*,[367] to which we have demurred. And this plea is bad in substance, because it contradicts the sheriff's return, which is matter of record, and can't be contradicted by averment or plea; and for this reason the general plea of non tenure[368] is always disallowed, 3 Lev. 205, *Barret* v. *Trotman*,[369] 1 Salk. 601,[370] and the plea begins in chief and ends in abatement.

Lord Chief Baron

In the case of *Hamilton* v. *O'Brien*[371] non tenure was determined in this court last Hilary term to be no plea, so final judgment was granted.

---

[364] Joseph Sutton, 3rd s. of Arnold, Bollenekill, Co. Wicklow. Middle Temple, 14 Dec. 1720, KI, Hilary term, 1725. KI AP, p. 470.

[365] More usually, terre-tenant [LF. holding land]. One who has the actual possession or occupation of land,

[366] L. as [the plaintiff has alleged].

[367] L. prays judgment of the writ.

[368] A plea of *non tenet* by the defendant, i.e. a plea that the defendant did not hold land in freehold tenure from the plaintiff. Reeves, *History of English Law* (1787), i.475.

[369] *Barret* v. *Trotman* (1684) 3 Lev. 205, 83 E.R. 652.

[370] *Adams* v. *Tertenants of Savage* (1704) 1 Salk. 40, 91 E.R. 41, 2 Salk. 601, 91 E.R. 510. Note that pagination of Salkeld's reports is continuous in the edition in E.R.

[371] No citation given.

SIMMS v. BRIEN

Eodem die

In Exchequer

Mr Sutton

One covenants to build a bridge, and to sustain secure and uphold it when built for 20 years, and on covenant the breach assigned is, that he suffered it to tumble down.

The defendant pleads *actio non*,[372] because on the 1 January [*71*] it was thrown down by a sudden tempest, and we have demurred generally.

And this is no plea in law, because it is a covenant to support it in all events, and for 20 years, and by their plea they admit they have not upheld it. This bridge is over a great water which in its own nature is apt to rise and fall.

Lord Chief Baron

The demurrer must be allowed. The defendant is in nature of a public insurer, the bridge is built with public money, and they confess it fell down.

THE EXECUTORS OF CREAGH

v.

THE EXECUTORS OF MAXWELL[373]

Lord Chief Baron

Ante 49, 69.

The case in 1 Salk. won't serve for the use you would make of it. It is only that the sheriff may return a *devastavit* at his peril, so the rule must be set aside on the reason of that case, for if the sheriff may return a *devastavit* at his peril, he may [return] *nulla bona*[374] if he pleases at his peril too, but we won't oblige him, but leave you to your action.

Mr Attorney General

Though the judgment by default is a confession of assets by the executor, they may be in another country, so the officer may safely return *nulla bona* in that country.

---

[372] A plea in bar, i.e. no good cause of action.
[373] Continued from p. 58.
[374] L. no goods.

Mr Prime Serjeant

If the executor suffers judgment to go by default, or demurs, he has estopped himself to say no assets. If he pleased he might have pleaded judgments. Here then is uncontrollable evidence he has assets, so the sheriff can run no risk by returning a *devastavit*, and need not make a *scire facias*, for if on such enquiry the jury should find *nulla bona*, would that bar us, or excuse the sheriff or executor [72] when assets appear on record, so that such an enquiry would be superfluous.

Lord Chief Baron

Though the court will oblige him in plain cases to amend his return, they won't where only by one construction of law he may be justified, and by another not.

Mr Daly

In the case of *Andrews* v. *Doolittle*,[375] the executor pleaded no assets, and the jury found assets, the sheriff returned *nulla bona*, and the Lord Chief Baron Dalton[376] obliged the sheriff to amend his return, and he paid the money himself. So in that case the court took judicial notice of the record.

Lord Chief Baron

We think that if the sheriff injures you, you have an adequate remedy against him, and [we] shan't take judicial notice of the record of the judgment, but only of the return; and won't oblige the sheriff to amend it on pain of attachment, but where he plainly abuses the court, and not where you would make it out by construction of law, for attachments are never granted in such cases, to construe a man out of his liberty; so the rule must be set aside.

Quære for the counsel seemed dissatisfied.

---

[375] No citation given.
[376] See above p. 55 n. 342.

HAMILTON ET UXOR v. THE HEIR AND TERTENANTS OF O'BRIEN

Eodem die

In Exchequer

Upon a *respondeas ouster* no plea can be admitted till the costs are paid.

LESSEE OF LORD MAZARINE v. THE CASUAL EJECTOR

Eodem die

In Exchequer

Lord Mazarine[377] made a lease for 3 lives [73] and brought an ejectment on the statute[378] for non payment of the rent, and on judgment by *nil dicit*,[379] and affidavit of the agreement, execution was granted and the sheriff delivered possession the 19 December Michaelmas term, and on the 17 of June a tender was made of the rent, costs etc., to the agent, and on affidavit of the tender, a motion was made to supersede the *Habere*, and to have restitution. And the question is, whether the statute is to be understood of lunar or calendar months.

Mr Prime Serjeant

When the law speaks of months, they are to be understood lunar, 6 Co. 62, *Catesbie's Case*[380] otherwise on the statute W. 2, which must be explained by the church law, and the words are *tempus semestre*.[381] And the most beneficial construction is to be made, because this Act benefits the landlord, and prejudices the tenant more than they were at law.

The tender must be to the lessor himself, and not to the agent.

The Act having made a distinction between calendar and lunar months, and having said calendar shall be sufficient in one case, but not in the other, is in our favour, 4 Geo. 1 ch. 5;[382] which is an explanation of the 11 Q. Ann. ch. 2.[383] The statute of Queen Anne in case of no distress gave an ejectment for 6 month's rent, the fourth of the King[384] for a twelve month's, so the time here ought to be taken more strictly.

---

[377] Below, p. 126 n. 698.
[378] 4 Geo. I, c. 5 (Ir.), 1717 (distress for rent).
[379] L. he or she says nothing, i.e. by default.
[380] *Catesby's Case* (1606) 6 Co. Rep. 61b, 77 E.R. 346.
[381] L. translated as 'a half year or six months' in *Catesby's Case*, above, n. 380.
[382] 4 Geo. I, c. 5 (Ir.), 1717 (distress for rent).
[383] 11 Ann., c. 2 (Ir.), 1712 (distress for rent, frauds by tenants).
[384] Above, n. 382.

Mr Malone

In the case of bargain and sale the months are calendar, and always in remedial or penal laws as in taking the oaths, Shower's Reports.[385] The word 'months' in the several provisos [74] of the Act must be explained as the Act has once expressed itself, for that is an explanation of their mind. This is a remedial law to the landlord, and penal to the tenant to deprive him of his freehold, and why should less time be given him, than is mentioned in the other clauses.

Mr Calaghan

Here are two Acts about the same matter, one is the best explainer of the other, and one clause of the other. Shall the rescuer, one that has broke the law, have more time than the tenant? Acts against common right are to be explained most favourably for him whose right is taken away. 'Months' in the Act are to be understood as they are by tenants, and such as they pay their rents by.

Lord Chief Baron

We must construe this by law, and not by equity. This is a constant rule, that where a statute takes away a right, 'tis to be taken strictly, and that explanatory Act of the King[386] is to be understood in the same sense with the 11 of the queen,[387] which speaks of calendar months, so I think he has come in time. The agent here made affidavit of the rent, so that this is a tender to the lessor, to one who he has appointed to receive it; and rents being reserved half yearly, they give this remedy before the other rent accrued. So this must be meant of calendar months, and therefore let there be a *supersedeas*.

LESSEE OF FOWKE v. BUTLER[388]

Eodem die

In Exchequer

An injunction for waste was granted without [75] affidavit, there being a special verdict.

---

[385] No clear reference; possibly *Morley* v. *Jones* (1698) Show. P.C. 140, 1 E.R. 96.
[386] Above, n. 382.
[387] Above, n. 383.
[388] Continued from p. 49.

KELLY v. BIERS

Eodem die

In Exchequer

A rule was made on motion, for one who had taken the defence in ejectment to give security, on an affidavit of his poverty, and living in Scotland; and this rule was now discharged on motion on an affidavit of his being in possession.

LESSEE OF MOLAND AND UXOR v. ORPIN

Eodem die

In Exchequer

This was an ejectment for non-payment of rent, and Mr Bradstreet moved in arrest of judgment, that the declaration was uncertain, that no county was mentioned, so what sheriff could give possession? *Qu[od]d[am] agru[m] vel qu[an]da[m] pecia[m] terræ cont[inentem] 4a plant[am] mens[alem]*,[389] and don't mention the quality of the land, 11 Co. 55a, *Savil's Case*,[390] Salk. 254, *Knight* v. *Symms*,[391] and that case affirmed for law, Carth. 204,[392] 4 Mod. 98,[393] 1 Show. 338,[394] Comber 198 SC,[395] and an ejectment won't lie for *quand[am]* or *una[m] peciam ter[ræ]*.[396] Hetl. 176,[397] Sir Wm Jon. 400.[398]

Mr Forbes[399]

The words in *Savil's Case* was *claus[um] terræ*,[400] which might contain lands of a different nature, and they were contradictory, *terre contin̄ arab et past̄*.[401] An ejectment won't lie for *peciam terræ*,[402] but when the bounds are set out, and it is shown how many acres it contains, this is sufficient certainty for an *habere facias possessionem*.[403]

---

[389] L. a certain field or a certain piece of land. The rest is unclear, but may mean 'including a quarter [or cartron] of mensal land'. A cartron is an Irish measure: a 'quarter' is a quarter of a townland and a cartron a fourth part of a quarter. Below, p. 389 n. 1625.

[390] *Savel's Case* (1614) 11 Co. Rep. 55a, 77 E.R. 1221 (in ejectment, it is not enough to state the name of the field or 'close'. The number of acres and usage, i.e. arable, pastoral etc., must be stated.)

[391] *Knight* v. *Syms* (1692) 1 Salk. 254, 91 E.R. 223.

[392] *Bishop of Lincoln* v. *Allen* (1669) Cart. 204, 124 E.R. 918.

[393] *Knight* v. *Syms* (1692) 4 Mod. 98, 87 E.R. 284 (ejectment: quantity of each type of land to be specified).

[394] *Knight* v. *Symmes* (1692) 1 Show. K.B. 338, 89 E.R. 610.

[395] *Knight* v. *Symms* (1692) Comb. 198, 90 E.R. 426.

[396] L. A certain or single piece of land.

[397] *Darlyes Case* (1631) Hetl. 175 at 176, 124 E.R. 433.

[398] *Anonymous* (1637) Jones W. 400, 82 E.R. 210.

[399] There are three possible barristers, all called John Forbes, in this period: John Forbes, s. and heir of George, alderman of Dublin city. Middle Temple, 19 May 1715, KI, Hilary term, 1721, d. 15 May 1737; John Forbes, s. and heir of the Revd Arthur, Newstown, Meath, ed. Trinity College Dublin, Middle Temple, 26 Nov. 1725, KI, Michaelmas term, 1731, d. July 1759; and John Forbes, jnr. *c.* 1734; KI AP, p. 173.

[400] I.e.? a 'close', a piece of land.

[401] LF.? '*terre contient arable et pasture*, 'land' includes both arable and pasture.

[402] L. A portion of land, i.e. without specifying further.

[403] L. that you make to have possession. The writ enforcing an ejectment.

Mr Attorney General

In libertat[ibus] civit[atis] Dublin[ensis] p[r]ed[ictæ][404] is sufficient, for *p[r]edict[æ]* alludes to the margin, where the county is named. [*76*]

Lord Chief Baron

Here is sufficient certainty for the sheriff to execute an *habere* etc. *Pecia[m] terræ*[405] is not certain enough, but here it is said to lie in a city, and to be so bounded. An ejectment will lie for a boilery. So I won't arrest the judgment, but the defendant, if he thinks proper, may bring a writ of error.

COLEMAN QUI TAM[406] ETC. v. WHITE

Friday, July 9th [1731]

In Exchequer

The information was for bringing rum, sweetmeats, staves, etc. directly from Barbados and landing them on Batchelors walk without calling first at some port in England, contrary to the statute 7 & 8 Wm. 3.[407] The goods were entered as come from St Lucia and the duty paid and the warrant given for bringing them ashore and some were in the gabbart[408] and some in the ship when they were seised by a warrant from the commissioners by virtue of this Act, landed, and put in the King's Stores.

And the first question was, whether this Act would extend to goods not enumerated by the former Acts of Ca. 2,[409] the rum and the other goods not being any of those enumerated.

And the counsel for the defendants insisted that although in 7 & 8 of Wm. 3[410] there are the general words, 'not of the growth or produce' etc. yet the 4 Geo. 2[411] saying, that the construction always was that the not enumerated were included, and enacting that the goods not enumerated shall not be included, is an evidence the goods not enumerated are not to be included. [*77*]

But Mr Prime Serjeant for the information said: It was allowed these goods were within the general words, but it was argued they were not within the meaning of the Act, because the former Acts were recited; but I think the construction is otherwise. The 12 of Ca: 2[412] equally prohibited England and Ireland. The 22 and 23[413] first

---

[404] L. in the liberties of the said city of Dublin.

[405] L. a piece of land.

[406] L. *qui tam pro domino rege, quam pro se ipso hac parte sequitur*, who sues as well for our lord the king as for himself. A kind of popular action in which part of the penalty was given to the crown, to the poor, or to some public use, and the other part to the informer or prosecutor.

[407] 7 & 8 Will. III, c. 22 (Eng.), 1695 (plantation trade).

[408] I.e. barge, lighter.

[409] 12 Car. II, c. 18 (Eng.), 1660 (Navigation Act, enumerated goods).

[410] 7 & 8 Will. III, c. 22 (Eng.), 1695–96 (plantation trade, ships not to enter port in Ireland, unless bad weather).

[411] 4 Geo. II, c. 15 (G.B.), 1730 (plantation trade).

[412] 12 Car. II, c. 18 (Eng.), 1660 (Navigation Act).

[413] 22 & 23 Car. II, c. 26 (Eng.), 1670 (plantation trade), s. 2. See *Chalmers* v. *Bell* (1804) 3 Bos. & Pul. 604, 127 E.R. 326.

prohibited Ireland, the design of which was to preventing breaking bulk anywhere but in England, and was a total prohibition of the direct trade to Ireland, which might easily have been ended by putting on board some goods that were enumerated and some that were not, and so breaking bulk in this kingdom under pretence of the goods that were not enumerated only; and the Act 4 Geo. 2[414] says the construction was always so, which supposes it right, and enacts it as a new law for the future, and is a repeal *pro tanto* of that statute of W. 3, and don't say, that the former judgments were illegal, so the old construction is the best rule for Your Lordship to go by, and is not a declaratory law, but a law of repeal, and the forfeiture is the same by 22 & 23 Ca. 2[415] as by the 7 & 8 W. 3,[416] so that statute would be nugatory, unless the general words are of force (N.B. but they restrain Scotland too).

And the court were of the same opinion.

The second question was, whether these goods were landed within the meaning of the Act. For the putting of them on shore made the forfeiture.

And 'twas insisted on for the defendant, that they were not, that it was the landing made the crime. The officers of the revenue land them as seised, shall they create the crime? And though it is probable from the invoice and the entry that the defendant designed [78] to land them, he was guilty of no crime till he had landed them and they should have waited till that time.

The lord chief baron said that the great difficulty was, that a man who was going to do an illegal act might repent of it, and mentioned the case of *Reniger* v. *Fogassa*[417] in the Commentaries.

Mr Prime Serjeant

After the duty is paid to the Collector, the merchant has a right to demand his warrant and the trader must land the goods and can't re-export them without landing, and the Collector's warrant is the authority to the inferior officers and the possession of them is in the law till they have gone through the examination. The merchant can't employ anyone to land them. The officer is concerned in the landing [of] them, which shows the merchant can't demand them till search and when they are landed, he can't take them away, but they must be viewed and inspected, for if he has entered different denominations they are forfeited, so the collector's warrant is the authority to bring them ashore and examine them; and this must be looked on as an authority from the merchant and a duty in the officer.

Mr Attorney General

The 54 hogsheads were put in the gabbart by virtue of the invoice, but they were landed as well by the warrant as by the seizure. The defendant has done that act which empowers the officer to do the rest and which he could not countermand. 'Tis the act of the defendant. The search shows whether he has truly paid the duty, and till then it can't be known, so that they must be landed and examined after entry and payment of duty. [79]

---

[414] 4 Geo. II, c. 15 (Eng.), 1731 (plantation trade).
[415] 22 & 23 Car. II, c. 26 (Eng.), 1670 (plantation trade).
[416] 7 & 8 Will. III, c. 22 (Eng.), 1695.
[417] *Reniger* v. *Fogossa* (1550) 1 Plow. 1, 75 E.R. 1.

Lord Chief Baron

I think the evidence don't support a landing within the Act, but if the counsel for the information insists on it, this point shall be found specially. The question is, whether by construction of law the seizure of these goods before they were landed and the landing [of] them by order of the King's officers shall be considered as the landing of the merchant? Might not he have kept them on board till he had an order to re-export them to England? If they had been landed indeed by any other person but the officers, however hard it might have been, this would have been considered as a landing by the merchant; may not the officer too search for goods on board, and let them go when he is certified the entry is fair? Is the merchant obliged in any time after the duty is paid to land them?

But the jury brought in a general verdict for the defendant.

Mr Attorney General quoted the case of *Madden* v. *Webber*[418] decreed by Lord Chief Baron Gilbert. The bill was brought for a specific execution of an article for a lease of three lives. The defendant insisted that the estate was void by the Popery Acts. But his Lordship decreed specific execution against the contractor for the benefit of a Protestant discoveror.

Ante 25.

But *quære* if good as to the creditors of the plaintiff, or others?

The defendant after answer can't refer a bill for scandal but as an *amicus*,[419] but then he shall have no costs; but a stranger may. [*80*]

BLOND v. BIAGDELL

Tuesday, July the 13, [1731]

In Exchequer

The plaintiff having married without consent the daughter of Hugh Baigdell, who was very old and infirm, procures a reconcilement and afterwards a lease of his estate of the yearly value of 12d from the said Hugh Baigdell, paying a certain rent during the life of the said Hugh and Hannah his wife, and after their deaths £40 a year, and after the plaintiff persuades Hugh to make a will and to make him executor thereof and to leave one moiety of his personal estate to his wife, and the other to the plaintiff, by which means the defendant the only son of the said Hugh Baigdell was wholly disinherited. The defendant when his father lay a dying endeavoured to procure letters of administration to him, but failing in that he broke open the doors, and entered in a forcible manner. The father dies, and the plaintiff brought his possessory bill against the defendant.

But the court dismissed the plaintiff's bill, and left him to be redressed by King's Bench, or the justices of the peace, his title being fraudulent, which appeared on the cross bill, though a plain force at midnight was fully proved.

---

[418] No citation given.

[419] L. *amicus curiæ*, a friend of the court. Someone not a party to the action but who is permitted to take some part in the proceedings.

LYNAM v. GORGE

Eodem die

In Exchequer

An account was decreed, the decree passed and signed, and revived by *scire facias*, and they proceeded before the officer for two years, and a [*81*] charge and discharge was brought in. Though the proceedings should have been revived by bill, and not by *scire facias*, because the decree was not enrolled, yet the defendant having acquiesced for two years, the Lord Chief Baron would not discharge it on motion and the special report of the officer, to whom the regularity had been referred, but left the party to his bill of review.

BEAUMONT v. JESSOP

Friday, July the 16, [1731]

In Exchequer

Ordin. MSŜ Canc. 117.
Post 399, 326.
Mes App. D.361.

A decree was made for payment of a sum of money, on affidavit of the defendant's absconding, serving the attorney with the decree was allowed good service, and non-performance a sequestration was granted without any intermediate process.

    But then it was observed for the defendant, that neither the *alias*[420] [n]or *pluries*[421] was taken away.

MSŜ Ordin. Canc. 49, 117, 133, 135.

WEBB v. CHARPLIS

Eodem die

In Exchequer

Mr Charplis by will devised £200 to his son then supposed in the East Indies if he returned in two years, if not to the plaintiff. The two years being expired, the plaintiff brought this bill for the legacy, and on motion obtained an order to bring this cause to a hearing without the son, but the court said they would not decree the money without the plaintiff's giving security to refund in case the son returned, 2 Vern. 487, *Hitchcock* v. *Ward*.[422] [*82*]

---

[420] Above, p. xciii.
[421] Above, p. xciii.
[422] The case at 2 Vern. 487 is *Clifton* v. *Jackson* (1704) 2 Vern. 486, 23 E.R. 912. There is no case by the name of *Hitchcock* v. *Ward* in E.R.

DILLON v. EDGWORTH

Monday, July the 19th, [1731]

In Chancery

An issue was directed out of Chancery to Common Bench,[423] to try whether a deed was executed by Robert Edgworth the father of the defendant, and the jury found that he did not execute the deed, and now the defendant Edgworth moved for a new trial, on affidavit that Packington Edgworth, his brother, who acted for the plaintiff handed up to the jury a letter and draft of a deed which was given them to see for a particular purpose only, and that they took them out though they were not sealed.

Mr Attorney General

'Tis agreed that the jury took a letter and the instructions for drawing the settlement with them, that they were produced by Packington Edgworth for the plaintiff, and not read through in court, but handed up to the jury as evidence only of a similitude of hands, and of the manner of spelling 'sonne'. The court would only suffer the jury to inspect this in court, not to take it out with them, and the defendant never consented they should, 2 Rol. Ab. 514 Tit. Trial,[424] is not so strong as this case. Here it was handed up to the jury for this particular purpose only, and therefore it is not material, whether they delivered it again, and it was handed back to them by Packington Edgworth, or whether they never returned it, but took it out with them. [83]

Mr Lindsey [sic]

In the letter the father used several severe expressions on the defendant his son, and therefore the court did not think it proper evidence for the jury, least it might influence them against the defendant, but this opprobrious part was folded down, that they might not inspect it, and they were only to look at the similitude of hands, and the manner of spelling the word 'sonne'. In the case in Roll[e']s[425] he is called agent only for proving the depositions, but here Packington Edgworth furnishes the evidence, and is more active than a clerk at the Rolls, or the like.

Lord Chancellor

I shall consider the case as I think it would be at law, and then in equity. At first these affidavits are not a sufficient ground for a new trial at law. Two reasons are assigned why this verdict should be set aside:

1. Because the court declared these papers to be no evidence to be given to the jury.

2. On the authority of the case in Roll[e']s,[426] because they were given them by the agent for the plaintiff.

[423] I.e. Common Pleas.
[424] Rolle's *Abridgement.*
[425] Ibid.
[426] Ibid.

But Packington Edgworth by his affidavit has expressly denied he was agent for the plaintiff.

It is agreed that this paper was given up the jury by the direction of the court, so it came regularly to their hands, but the misfortune is, that they took it out with them which they should not have done. [84] It is said it was given them folded down and so is within the reason of the case in Roll[e']s,[427] that part was read, and part not.

But this don't appear, nor anything more than that it was given to the jury in open court with the knowledge of all parties to compare the hands, and see how the word 'sonne' was spelled, and as bare reading it was not sufficient for that purpose, it was natural for them to say we'll take it out only to see and examine the spelling and manner of writing.

But this is not a foundation to set aside a verdict, for though every verdict is to be set aside for the misbehaviour of the party, 'tis not for that of the jury, for if they receive evidence of the part of the plaintiff, that shall only set it aside if they give a verdict for the plaintiff, but not *e converso*: so that it is the act of the party that infects the verdict.

I was not satisfied with the state of the case in Roll[']s, but looked into the report of it in Styl. 383, *Taylor* v. *Webb*,[428] where it is said, the agent delivered a state of the case to the jury, and depositions are very different from this letter, every part of which is proper to prove the handwriting of Richard Edgworth, but every deposition is a new evidence from a new witness, whereas the whole letter was equal proof of the similitude of hands; so that considering the agent denies he delivered it to the jury, and it is sworn it was handed up to them by the court, and no management is proved to make it evidence, and as this [85] was a trial to satisfy my own conscience, the verdict must stand; and the judges of the Common Pleas assured me they were very well satisfied with this verdict, and not dissatisfied with any one circumstance, 1 Inst. 227b, Cro. Eliz. 411,[429] 616,[430] 2 Salk. 645,[431] Moor 546 (728), *Drove* v. *Sharp*,[432] 451 (615), *Gibbon* v. *Bowyer*[433] Lit. Rep. 69.[434]

[427] Ibid.
[428] *Tayler* v. *Webb* (1653) Sty. 383, 82 E.R. 797.
[429] *Vicary* v. *Farthing* (1595) Cro. Eliz. 411, 78 E.R. 653, (616) Moore 451, 72 E.R. 688 (parish-books and registers are good evidence to prove births and marriages).
[430] *Graves* v. *Short* (1598) Cro. Eliz. 616, 78 E.R. 857.
[431] *Dent* v. *Hundred of Hertford* (1696) 2 Salk. 645, 91 E.R. 546 (new trial granted upon affidavit swearing that the foreman said the plaintiff should never have a verdict whatever witnesses he produced).
[432] *Drove* v. *Short* (1598) Moo. K.B. 546, 72 E.R. 748.
[433] *Gybon* v. *Bowyer* (1596) Moo. K.B. 451, 72 E.R. 688.
[434] *Sir George Trenchards Case* (1627) Lit. Rep. 65 at 69; 124 E.R. 139 at 141.

HIND v. LYNCH

Michaelmas Term

Friday, November the 19th, [1731]

In Exchequer

This is an *indebitatus assumpsit* for carrying 562 barrels of oats, and 168 barrels of wheat from Waterford to Dublin at 1s per barrel, and a *quantum meruit*[435] for so many barrels carried and delivered.

The evidence was of the carriage of 168 barrels of oats, and a bill of exceptions was taken to the evidence, that it did not support the declaration, and that the contract was with Doyle the master, and the defendant was owner. An *indebitatis assumpsit* ought to be as certain as debt, in which the evidence can't vary from the declaration, and so in a *quantum meruit,* if he had said generally in consideration he had carried etc., would have been good, but here he says he had carried so much, which evidence varies from the contract mentioned in the declaration, 1 Sid. 225, 226.[436]

And there was not only a contract in law with Doyle, but an express contract by signing the bill of lading. [*86*]

Mr Darcy pro Quer

3 Cro. 83,[437] 3 Buls. 271,[438] a contract with the servant is a contract with the master.
Curia advisare vult.[439]

ANON.

Tuesday, November the 16 [1731]

In Exchequer

You may demur to a plea in abatement after imparlance, 1 Lutw. 22, *Bartlot v. Bur ton,*[440] 2 Lut. 16,[441] 39,[442] 2 Lev. 190,[443] Raym. 34.[444]

---

[435] L. as much as he deserved. A claim for restitution, for money not specifically agreed in a contract, but reasonably to be expected in return for labour or services provided.

[436] *Game* v. *Gunston* (1664) 1 Sid. 225, 82 E.R. 1072.

[437] *Robsert* v. *Andrews and Cocket* (1580) Cro. Eliz. 82 at 83, 78 E.R. 341 at 342.

[438] *Robinson* v. *Walter* (1616) 3 Buls. 269 at 272, 81 E.R. 227 at 229.

[439] The case does not appear again in these reports.

[440] *Bartelot* v. *Burton* (1687) 1 Lutw. 22, 125 E.R. 12.

[441] *Papworth* v. *Stacy* (1686) 1 Lutw. 15 at 16, 125 E.R. 8 at 9.

[442] *Draycote* v. *Curzon* (1699) 1 Lutw. 39, 125 E.R. 21.

[443] *Granwell* v. *Sibly* (1677) 2 Lev. 190, 83 E.R. 512.

[444] *Barrington* v. *Venables* (1661) Raym. Sir T. 34, 83 E.R. 19.

KANE v. HAMILTON

Eodem die

In Exchequer

The plaintiff for cause of bail produced a note of £1,000 under the hand of the defendant for value received.

'Twas allowed no money was received, but that it was given for favours, so the recompense must lie in damages. The defendant is only an officer of the revenue.

Lord Chief Baron

Here is no probable cause of bail, when the defendant is only a surveyor.

Sir John St Leger

We can't examine the damages. That is only the business of a jury, and the defendant don't deny he perfected the note. Let him give £1,000 bail.

HOLMES v. THE EXECUTORS OF WEBB

Wednesday, November the 17th [1731]

In Exchequer

The plaintiff was bound to Webb,[445] an attorney, for four years, gave £100 for his fee, and served him two years and four months. Webb died, and the plaintiff after his death gave [87] £50 to another attorney.

Curia

Let it be referred to the officer to see how much an attorney of good credit deserves with a clerk so far qualified as the plaintiff.

---

[445] From KI AP, possibly Daniel Webb, Dublin city, attorney, 27 Oct. 1711, listed as master of an apprentice; James Webb, attorney of the Exchequer, *c.* 1734; James Webb, attorney, 1 Feb. 1726, 5 Feb. 1727, as master of an apprentice. KI AP, p. 504.

BLAKE v. KIRWIN

Thursday, November the 18, [1731]

In Exchequer

Ante 45.
Post 278.
On the special report of the officer, the executor was adjudged to pay interest for the assets from a year after the death of the testator, and it was said to have been so resolved in the case of *Grace* v. *Haines*.[446]

Sir John Kirwin by articles previous to the marriage of his son covenanted to settle and convey at any time on demand to the trustees therein named several lands in trust etc., provided always, and it is the true intent and meaning of these presents and of all parties thereto, that the said Sir John Kirwin may by any deed executed in his lifetime, or by his last will and testament attested by two or three credible witnesses charge and encumber all and singular the lands or any part thereof with any sum or sums of money, he thinks fit not exceeding in the whole £500, with the interest thereof from the time of his death.

Nels. 8vo Rep. in
Canc. 132.[447]
Curia

A power in favour of creditors is assets if there prove a deficiency, and as Sir John Kirwin ought to have executed it for his creditors, the court will do it for him. 1 Vern. 144.[448]

No counsel appeared for the defendant.

BRISAC v. CLERK

Saturday, December the 10, [1731][449]

In Exchequer.

The last of the eight days

[*88*] Where an account is decreed the defendant is in all cases entitled to examine the plaintiff on personal interrogatories, even after a report, for he may file a cross bill against him for a discovery.

Lord Chief Baron Dalton[450] thought it necessary the officer should certify there was occasion, but 'tis done of course in Chancery.

---

[446] No citation given.

[447] See *Naylor* v. *Baldwin* (1639) 1 Ch. Rep. 130 at 132, 21 E.R. 528 (bill to relieve creditors.).

[448] *Palmer* v. *Jones* (1682) 1 Vern. 144, 23 E.R. 376, does not seem particularly relevant. There are several cases on creditors in Vernon's Reports.

[449] 10 December was a Friday in 1731 (Julian), Kratz, *Hist.Cal.*, but the year still seems to be 1731, from the dates above and below.

[450] See above p. 55 n. 342.

DELAUNE v. DELAUNE

Saturday, December the 18, [1731] [451]

In Exchequer

Quære whether in case of a resulting trust parol proof may be made of the payment of Ante 40. the money? 2 Ventr. 361.[452] 1 Vern. 167.[453] 2 Vern. 294.[454] Cestuy que use at common law might maintain a suit at his own costs. 2 Lev. 17.[455]

BARRY v. OGARA

Eodem die

In Exchequer

An answer is evidence against the vendor and those claiming under him, but not Post 97. against the vendee, 1 Salk. 286, *Ford* v. *Grey*.[456] An objection was made to the reading a letter of Fleming in evidence against the purchaser.

Lord Chancellor

Any act of the ancestor is evidence against the heir. Answers have sometimes been allowed in this court to have been read against purchasers which were put in by the vendee before the sale, but that goes on another foot; an answer is on oath, and upon record, and it appears when it came in, and no sale being then in view, the defendant could not design to deceive by it, but this is not a general rule. And recitals are sometimes allowed in evidence [*89*] because the time of the execution of the deed may be proved by witnesses. But a letter is dangerous evidence, and in this case it is only proved to be his handwriting, which it is whenever it was wrote, and the time of writing it is not proved, and it is likely it was wrote to serve a turn, to help Mrs Ogara to procure this Act,[457] who was then under an attainder.

[ANON.]

In Exchequer

A counsel has a right to make the opposite side open the purport of any deed before they prove it, but has no right to see it. In the case of *Stanley* v. *Stanley*[458] it was ruled Post 220.

---

451 18 December was a Saturday in 1731 (Julian), Kratz, *Hist. Cal.*
452 *Anonymous* (1683) 2 Vent. 361, 86 E.R. 486.
453 *Vermuden* v. *Read* (1683) 1 Vern. 167, 23 E.R. 391.
454 *Lady Bellasis* v. *Compton* (1693) 2 Vern. 294, 23 E.R. 790.
455 *Freake* v. *Clarke* (1650) 2 Lev. 17, 83 E.R. 432.
456 *Ford* v. *Lord Grey* (1704) 1 Salk. 285 at 286, 91 E.R. 253.
457 Below, p. 251 n. 1161.
458 Below, p. 172 [*221*].

upon debate, that a deed may be proved by one who was present at the execution
of it, though it has witnesses to it, as where the witness is a party concerned, etc. A

Post 168, 169. deed may be proved as an exhibit, when there is no subscribing witness to it. You
may prove the hands of the witnesses to an old deed without first proving them dead,
and if the court has any doubt they may send it to a trial.

[ANON.]

In Exchequer

If the defendant files a cross bill before issue is joined in the original cause, he has
a right stop the proceedings that both causes may be brought to a hearing together,
Post 145. but if the bill is not filed till after issue, he is only entitled to an answer before the
original cause comes to a hearing. [*90*]

HEDGES v. CARMODY

Saturday, November the 6th [1731][459]

In Exchequer

A plea was allowed, and the plaintiff moved to dismiss his bill paying costs, and before
the payment thereof files the same bill in Chancery. The defendant moved that his
bill in the Exchequer might be retained that he might plead the decretal order to the
bill in Chancery. But the motion was denied because he might plead the dismission.

DALY v. DEVENISH

Monday, November the 8th [1731][460]

In Exchequer

Mr Dillon made a settlement of certain lands to the use of himself for life, remainder
to James for life, remainder to his first and every other son in tail, remainder to his
three daughters in tail. James soon after the settlement turned Protestant, and died
in 1712 without issue. The plaintiff who was the son of one of the daughters and the
next Protestant heir being entitled to the lands until till their conformity, brought
an ejectment, and a bill for the deed of settlement to prove his title, which was in
the hands of the two other daughters, who were in the possession of the estate by
survivorship for life, with several inheritances in tail, and now moved to have the
deed brought in by *duces tecum*, and on a reference to a baron, he was of opinion
that it ought not to be brought in and the report on exception was now confirmed
by the court.

---

[459] 6 November was a Saturday in 1731 (Julian), Kratz, *Hist. Cal.* Note that the date is earlier than the
previous date.
[460] 8 November was a Monday in 1731 (Julian), Kratz, *Hist. Cal.*

Lord Chief Baron

If we should allow the exception the plaintiff would [*91*] have the event and end of his bill as effectually as on a decree. A plaintiff has no right to a *duces tecum*, but Ante 37. where the defendant confesses his title, and denies that he has any. Otherwise it is not proper to have the deed brought in but on a decree, though the interest of the defendant be ever so small, and the plaintiffs ever so considerable; besides here is a term still standing out of 61 years to raise portions for daughters.

DESPARD v. BARRY

Tuesday, December the 4th[461]

In Exchequer

Richard Cockram in 1689 settled lands to the use of himself for life, remainder to his wife for her jointure, remainder to his first and every other son in tail male, remainder to his daughters in tail, and after died without issue male leaving two daughters, one died leaving the plaintiff her son. The defendant Susannah Vicars the other daughter who was entitled to the whole by survivorship, with her husband made a mortgage in fee, which by mesne assignments came to the defendant Barry, to whom they levied a fine. The plaintiff as remainderman in tail brought an eject-ment, and afterwards a bill for a discovery of what estate the said Susannah and the defendant Vicars her husband had in the lands at the time they levied the fine, and if to prevent a forfeiture they did not pretend to have made a lease of 99 years, etc. whether the same was not antedated, and whether they did not set up such lease in bar of his ejectment, and for a discovery of the settlement and to have the title deeds delivered up to him. To this bill the defendant demurred.

Mr Daly for the defendant

The whole bill tends to a discovery of the forfeiture [*92*] 2 Chan. Rep. 68, *Monyns* v. *Monyns*,[462] and the plaintiff ought to offer to confirm our estate for life, a jointuress may retain the deeds till the heir confirms her jointure.

Lord Chief Baron

The demurrer must be allowed. In other cases the plaintiff may have a right to a discovery of the settlement, but in this the court ought not to aid him, because the very ground of his equity is to enable him to recover at law on this forfeiture, and therefore since he has not offered to waive the benefit of it, he has no right to a discovery.

---

461 4 December in 1731 (Julian) was a Saturday, Kratz, *Hist. Cal.*, but the year still seems to be 1731.
462 *Monnins* v. *Monnins* (1672) 2 Chan. Rep. 68, 21 E.R. 618.

Mr Attorney General

This would establish a fraud. The tenant for life has no right to the deeds, but if he may cover himself in this manner, he has an advantage by the forfeiture. Sure the plaintiff has an equity for a discovery of the deed under which he is claiming?

Lord Chief Baron

A demurrer to the whole is not favoured but in case of a forfeiture, and combination need not be denied, but a plea must stand on the new matter it introduces.

RODERICK v. OSBORN

Tuesday, November the 16, [1731][463]

In Exchequer

Mr Stannard

Roderick a Protestant, married to the eldest daughter of the defendant, who conformed within three days after the 6 months required by the [93] Act, filed a bill on the Popery Acts against the defendant his father in law to be decreed to the benefit of a lease for three lives. Reeves filed an amicable bill against Roderick and Osborn, setting forth, that Roderick was son in law to Osborn, and was a constructive Papist by marrying a Papist, and the court was of this opinion. April 1730 Chily as a creditor of Osborn for £200 filed a bill of discovery against Osborn, Roderick and Reeves. June 1720 Helen Osborn, one of the daughters of the defendant Osborn who had conformed, filed her bill, and petitions to be admitted a pauper to prosecute her own suit and to defend the suit against Chily, and the usual order was made *nisi*, etc.

And I am now to show your Lordship cause why Helen should not be admitted a pauper. No person ought to be admitted to prosecute a popular or penal action as a pauper, especially against a defendant who has sworn himself to be a real discoveror, as Chily has by his answer. A popular action is not within the 11 H. 7 ch. 10,[464] which must be meant of private rights, and not of informations. Helen had no right when Chily exhibited his bill, but conformed after. In Acts of Parliament popular actions are always distinguished from private, and the court won't suffer a pauper to worry a real discoveror to discourage and frighten him with the expense, and he is not liable to costs, which would weaken the Popery Acts, and discountenance discoverors, which the court who have a discretionary power will not suffer. She was set up as a discoveror by her father and mother, and supported by them, and conformed to this very purpose to defeat Chily as creditor.

---

[463] 16 November was a Tuesday in 1731 (Julian), Kratz, *Hist. Cal.* Note that the date is earlier than the previous case.

[464] 11 Hen. VII, c. 10 (Eng.), 1495 (taxation).

Plate 5. Eaton Stannard (d. 1755), recorder of Dublin.

Mr Attorney General

If a pauper can't prosecute a real suit, a sham [*94*] discoveror will run away with the benefit. These Acts which are made for the safety of the kingdom are more to be regarded than a private right. A pauper is not exempted by the Acts, which would lessen the Protestant interest, but poor as well as rich are to have the benefit of the discovery.

Sir John St Leger

It don't appear that Helen is a real Protestant discoveror, because her conforming was approved of by her father as a proper means to bring this bill of discovery for the maintenance of the family, whereas all friendship is generally broke off where there is a real conformity and discovery, and the daughter is more to be suspected as a discoveror for the family than a creditor, who looks like a real discoveror by his buying in incumbrances. The Pauper Act[465] ordains that the lord chancellor shall direct etc., for the King is not to lose his fine for his writs, and we are answerable for the King's money, though we delegate this power over to counsel. As the court themselves formerly adjudged whether bills were good, though they now leave them to be signed by counsel. But if a pauper had first brought the bill, I see no reason why he should not be admitted; but I allow the cause in this case because the right was first vested in Chily.

ATTORNEY GENERAL v. NUGENT[466]

Friday, December the 3rd, [1731]

In Exchequer

Mr Prime Serjeant opened the information.

William Nugent late Lord Riveston[467] being seised in fee of the lands of Pallas in the county of Galway, in 1680 intermarried with Mariana the daughter of Nicholas, Lord Kingsland,[468] who was entitled to a portion of £2,000 at all events and to a further portion, if she married with [*95*] consent, and by articles previous or subsequent to the marriage Thomas, Lord Riveston in consideration of the said marriage and portion covenanted to settle the lands of Pallas and his future acquisitions on himself for life, remainder as to part to his wife for her jointure, remainder to the first and every other son of the marriage in tail male, and after made a settlement in pursuance of these articles. Thomas had issue several daughters, and three sons,

---

[465] 11 Hen. VII, c. 12 (Eng.), 1495 (action by paupers: suing *in forma pauperis*). See also G. J. Hand, ed., 'Rules and Orders to be Observed in the Proceedings of Causes in the High Court of Chancery in Ireland, 1659' (1974) *Irish Jurist* (n.s.) 110–165, at p. 143, 'Paupers', Rule LXVIII.

[466] Resumed on p. 298.

[467] Below, p. 81 n. 476.

[468] Nicholas Barnwall, Viscount Barnwall of Kingsland (1668–1725). He served in Lord Limerick's Dragoons, 1688, on behalf of King James II, and was consequently outlawed, but was within the Treaty of Limerick by which his outlawry was reversed: Cokayne, *Complete Peerage*, i. 428.

Richard Hyacinth[469] the eldest, and the defendants William, and Ignatius; Thomas being adjudged within the Articles of Limerick[470] did not forfeit, but Hyacinth when he was about seven years of age was attainted and outlawed for high treason,[471] and was carried out of the kingdom, and being tenant in tail, the remainder to his brothers is destroyed by the Act of Resumption,[472] which vests estates tail in the Crown in fee.

There were three parts of this settlement, one in the hands of Lord Netterville the trustee and grandfather of Marianna, which Thomas prevailed upon him to deliver up, another in the hands of Lord Kingsland, which Thomas as his executor got possession of, and the third was in his own hands, and in order to prevent the estate coming to the Crown by the attainder of Hyacinth, Thomas cancels and destroys the articles and settlement, and in 1700 makes a settlement of the lands of Pallas and other lands of Garny purchased with the portion of Marianna, on himself for life, remainder to Marianna for a jointure, remainder to William the defendant his second son in tail male, remainder to Ignatius his third son in tail male, etc. Thomas died above 14 years ago. Hyacinth obtained an Act of Parliament[473] in England to sue in the name of the Crown, and the scope of this information is to call William for an account of the rents and profits, and to have the possession [96] and the deeds and writings delivered up. Afterwards the counsel for the King only proved Hyacinth to be heir at law of Thomas, and there rested the case.

Mr Stannard for the defendants

They don't go into the case they have made by their information, but put us to the proof of our titles. All that is incumbent on us is to show, that Thomas in his lifetime conveyed away these lands, but we shall state our case in such a manner, as will oblige them to go into their evidence. Marianna the only daughter of Lord Kingsland was entitled at all events to £2,000 by the marriage articles in 1661 of her mother, the daughter of Lord Netterville, and intermarried with Thomas Nugent[474] the second son of the earl of Westmeath, afterwards chief justice of the King's Bench,[475] and created Lord Riveston[476] by King James the 2d after his abdication.[477]

[On] 16 November 1680 the portion was secured by a rentcharge of £400 a year on the estate of Lord Kingsland, and in consideration thereof Thomas only settled a

---

[469] Hyacinthus Richard Nugent (c. 1687–1738). In Cokayne, *Complete Peerage*, ix. 796–98, he appears as Hyacinth Richard Nugent, known as Baron Nugent of Riverston, or Lord Riverston. Above, p. cxxi.

[470] See 9 Will. III, c. 2 (Ir.), 1697 (confirmation of Articles of Limerick). Above, p. cxix n. 658.

[471] Under 7 Will. III, c. 4 (Ir.), 1695 (outlawry for foreign education). The statute not only made it an offence resulting in outlawry to send a child out of Ireland to be educated as a Catholic, but also made an offence for persons, i.e. children, 'being sent'. Above, p. cxvii.

[472] 11 Will. III, c. 2. (11 & 12 Will. III in Ruffhead) (Eng.) Trustee Act, Resumption Act (forfeited estates in Ireland vested in trustees), s. 1.

[473] 'An Act for Relief of Hyacinthus Richard Nugent', 1727, Private Act, 1 Geo. II, st. 2, c. 23, *HLRO*, 1 Geo. II, st. 2 no. 46. See Appendix C.

[474] (?–1715), Cokayne, *Complete Peerage*, ix. 796. Ball, *Judges in Ireland*, i. 300, 304–7, 309, 361–2.

[475] Appointed J.K.B. in autumn 1687: Ball, *Judges in Ireland*, i. 361. He was also given the title of chief justice of Ireland by King James II: Ball, *Judges in Ireland*, i. 361. Cokayne notes that the earl of Clarendon, lord lieutenant, on 20 April 1686, remarked on Thomas Nugent's appointment as puisne judge of the K.B., that being 'no lawyer will do no harm upon the account of his learning', Cokayne, *Complete Peerage*, ix. 796 n. c.

[476] So spelled in the MS. Ball, *Judges in Ireland*, i. 361 and Cokayne, *Complete Peerage*, ix. 796 have 'Riverston'. Above, p. cxiv.

[477] See also Ball, *Judges in Ireland* , i. 361.

jointure of £300 a year on Marianna, but no provision was made for the children of the marriage. In Michaelmas 1680 Lord Kingsland confessed judgment for £4,000 to secure the portion. These deeds could not be made with any design to cheat Hyacinth, or the Crown. Thomas had 13 daughters, eight born after 1700!

Thomas on the 25 of May 1700 made a settlement of all his lands on himself for life, remainder as to part of £300 a year to Marianna for life for her jointure, remainder to his son William for life, remainder to his first and every other son in tail male, with remainder to trustees to preserve the contingent remainders,[478] remainder to his son Ignatius in the same manner, etc.

Thomas died in 1715.[479] In 1710 the wife of Hyacinth obtained a [97] private Act of Parliament[480] to sue for the portion of Hyacinth, and in an answer to a bill filed by her for that purpose, Thomas in 1711 swears, that no settlement or provision was made for the children by the articles, but only a jointure for Marianna.

Patrick Brown, who married one of the daughters of Thomas, in 1720 filed also a bill for a discovery of marriage articles, and Marianna in answer to that bill swears, that her marriage was without consent, and that Thomas executed no articles after marriage in favour of children, but only made a provision for her. The defendant William Nugent intermarried with Bridget Daly, and in 1719 in consideration of her portion of £2500, covenants that he is tenant for life, remainder to his first and every other son in tail male; and that the lands should go accordingly, and his wife or her trustees had no notice of these pretended articles, or settlement. The defendant Ignatius Nugent in consideration of £5,000 portion settles his remainder, and his wife swears, she had no notice of these articles, and that this remainder was a motive for her marrying him.

Mr Calaghan

We desire to read the answer of Thomas against Hyacinth who has made no title but Ante 88. as heir to his father, and this is a private Act of Parliament to sue in the King's name.

---

[478] A technical device invented in the 17th century to avoid the destruction of contingent remainders. At common law seisin had to pass immediately from one freehold estate owner to the next in remainder. If land was settled on A for life, remainder to his first-born son in tail, remainder to B in fee simple, the entail to the son was contingent on his being born. A could destroy the remainder by wrongfully conveying in fee simple to X, thus renouncing his own life estate. A could also destroy the entail by buying B's remainder in fee simple, or by various other methods. A provision was therefore inserted in well-drafted settlements whereby, if A attempted to destroy his life estate, the legal estate passed for his lifetime to trustees to preserve contingent remainders. The device also protected the remainder against 'natural destruction', as where A's only children were posthumous, and so could not take immediately on A's death. The device was made unnecessary for this purpose by 8 Ann., c. 4 (Ir.), 1709; 10 Will. 3, c. 22 (Eng.), 1698. See Sir Robert Megarry and H. W. R. Wade, *The Law of Real Property* (4th ed., 1975), pp. 194–95; Andrew Lyall, *Land Law in Ireland* (2nd ed., 2000) pp. 381–82; *HEL*, vii. 112. L. Bonfield, *Marriage Settlements, 1601–1740: the Adoption of the Strict Settlement* (1983). Bonfield ascribes the rise of the family settlement in the seventeeth century to the invention of this device. The device was not without logical difficulty, in that it could be argued that the estate to the trustees was also contingent and could therefore also be destroyed by A. But its effectiveness was upheld in the courts.

[479] Cokayne, *Complete Peerage*, ix. 797 gives the date as 2 April 1715.

[480] She obtained an Irish Act: 'For relief of Susanna-Catherina Nugent', 10 Ann., c. 4 (Ir.) (private), listed in vol. 8 of the Irish *Statutes at Large*, and later a British Act: 'An Act to enable Susanna Catherina Nugent to sue for, recover and hold the Portion of fourteen hundred Pounds, provided for her out of her Father's Estate, notwithstanding her Coverture and the Outlawry of her Husband Hyacinthus Nugent Esquire', Private Act, 1716, 3 Geo. I, c. 10, *HLRO*, 3 Geo. I no. 16. See Appendix A.

Mr Daly

The answer of the father, and every act and deed of his, is evidence against his heir at law, and no estate vested in the Crown till the death of Thomas.

Lord Chief Baron

As the legislature have given Hyacinth a liberty to sue in the King's name, the answer won't bind him, unless it was put before the attainder. [98]

Mr Stannard

If your Lordship won't suffer us to give in evidence acts of the father, as a sale or the like, the descent must indeed fall on the son, for then we can't prove an alienation or sale.

Mr Prime Serjeant

This evidence is in behalf of William and Ignatius who claim under the settlement in 1710, by which Thomas passed by his eldest son Richard Hyacinth, and they would show from his own answer that Thomas had a power to make it.

Lord Chief Baron

You must take it as you state your own case. You have made your defence by a settlement in 1700, and would read the answer of Thomas in 1711 to support it. The Act of Parliament gives Hyacinth all the prerogatives of the Crown. The question then is, as an answer may be read against him who derives under the defendant, by parity of reason may it not be read against the Crown, though in strictness of law the King don't derive under any one? I think at present it can't be read, though the title of the Crown is only a possibility, because the King derives under none. The Attorney General has a right to examine the defendants on articles. He suggests this settlement was made to defeat the title of the Crown. This is the suggestion of the information, though he has put the case on another footing at the bar. This is not strictly legal evidence, because the Crown claims paramount the deed.

Then the settlement in May 1700 by lease and release[481] was read, which was recited to be in consideration of marriage, a portion, and of articles which Thomas entered into before marriage, whereby he covenanted to settle a rentcharge of £300 a year on his wife for life for her jointure, and to make [99] a competent provision for all the sons and daughters of the marriage of all the lands he then had and should thereafter acquire, and thereby the lands of Kilbride worth only about £40 a year are limited to Hyacinth the eldest son for life for his provision and maintenance, charged too with the debts of Thomas. Here appeared to be a rasure,[482] and it was

---

[481] A form of conveyance of the fee simple, common until the Real Property Act, 1845 (G.B., Ir.), in which a lease was first granted and then the freehold remainder released to the grantee, in order to avoid the inconveniences of the old common law feoffment with livery of seisin.

[482] I.e. an erasure.

insisted on for the Crown, that after the limitation of the jointure all was limited to William as it first stood limited to Hyacinth, which was after changed into those particular lands only, and the jointure was rased from £300 to £200, and then to £300 again, which Archer swore was done by Thomas to enable him to borrow money the better on the estate.

Mr Stannard

The question is, whether the deed of 1700 with these rasures made by Thomas is a good deed?

There are several distinctions as to rasures in the books.

A rasure in an immaterial part by one who takes by the deed vacates the deed, but if a stranger vacates the deed in a material part, the deed is void in law, but good in equity, for a stranger shan't prejudice me by his act. Another distinction is that he who makes the deed can't by rasing it defeat the interest of a third person, Cro. Ca. 398, 399,[483] Dyer 261,[484] Moo. 300[485] for then he might defeat his own act. Thomas the grantor made the rasure, but his act can't defeat the deed, and the rasure in the jointure which she has accepted, affected only Mariana.

I agree in this deed there is a recital of articles of intermarriage as a provision for the wife and children. But no court of equity could compel the father because of these articles to give his whole estate to Hyacinth, or if he was disobedient to give him the preference but the discretion was left in the father, and the provision he has made for him is not unreasonable, [*100*] the son being an attainted person, and the prerogatives of the Crown can't compel the father further than the son could. But here the articles being carried into execution, equity will not interfere, and subsequent marriages have been made on that consideration.

Objection: The children had notice they were to enjoy pursuant to the limitations in 1700.

Answer: But if the sense of them is dubious, the court won't strain it, but construe them favourably for them.

No proof has been made what estate Thomas was seised of at the time he executed the articles, and that only is bound by them. He made great acquisitions afterwards. The Crown can have no greater privilege than the forfeiting person but for the discovery of the title, but Thomas was an innocent person, and the court won't deprive him of his power to dispose of his estate among his children. If the deed is out of the case, Hyacinth is only heir at law to Thomas, which is such a contingent interest he may be evidence for his father. But as Thomas died in 1712[486] Hyacinth can be entitled only to a third part of the estate in gavelkind.[487] The defendant Ignatius is a Protestant, and there is an express saving for him in the Act, and the settlement of 1700 was before the Registry Act.[488]

[483] *Miller and Johns* v. *Manwaring* (1635) Cro. Car. 397, 79 E.R. 947.
[484] *A Case from Ireland* 3 Dy. 261b, 73 E.R. 580.
[485] *Degoze* v. *Rowe* (1591) Moo. K.B. 300, 72 E.R. 592.
[486] See above, n. 479.
[487] Above, p. cxxxv.
[488] Registration of Deeds Act, 1707, 6 Ann., c. 2 (Ir.).

Mr Attorney General

It don't appear in this case that either Thomas or the sons are Papists, so all that has been said as to their taking in gavelkind is immaterial.

Mr Bettesworth[489]

The rasure to Hyacinth is for his support and maintenance only, and not to his issue, but it would be absurd to suppose that the bulk of the estate was [*101*] settled on him for his maintenance. In the deed of 1680 the jointure of £300 a year only is recited, and that recital could not be supposed to be false to serve the turn of the attainder, which could not be thought of at the time.

Lord Chief Baron

Here is a strong presumption of articles, the King's title is either under the articles, or as heir, if the rasures make the deed void, and we must direct two issues, 1. Whether Thomas entered into articles on his intermarriage with Marianna? 2. What rasures there are in the deed of 1700, and by whom made?

Mr Calaghan

Here is no occasion for an issue. The rasures don't make a deed void either in law or equity. There is a difference as to rasures where the deed is an entire thing as a bond, and where it consists of different clauses; if the deed is an entire thing, any material alteration makes it void, but where the clauses are independent, an alteration on one don't affect the other, Cro. El. 545, *Matthewson's Case.*[490] 5 Co. 22.[491] 11 Co. *Pigot's Case.*[492] 1 Ventr. 185,[493] for then in effect they are several deeds. But 2 Lev. 35,[494] 2 Keb. 872, *Zouch* v. *Clay*[495] carry it further as to an entirety, and an alteration by consent of parties don't make a bond void. No alteration is proved that relates to William or Ignatius, the alteration is in a distinct independent clause that relates to Marianna. As to the recital of the articles previous to the marriage, that is a false recital, and the information itself says so, and that the marriage was without consent, and the articles subsequent to it. But it is said, that the information is good if any title appears for the Crown. If this was properly an information I grant it [*102*] would be so. The Act of Parliament is an act of restitution to put Hyacinth in the same state as if there had been no attainder, and to suppose more is to put him in a better condition than if he had never been attainted; and the deed of November 1680 makes it plain that there was no provision for the children, but the wife only. The jointure is recited as the consideration for securing the portion of Marianna, and if there had been a provision for the eldest son etc., that would have

[489] Above, p. clvii.
[490] *Matthewson* v. *Lydiate* (1597) Cro. Eliz. 546, 78 E.R. 792.
[491] *Mathewson's Case* (1597) 5 Co. Rep. 22b, 77 E.R. 84 (charterparty).
[492] *Pigot's Case* (1614) 11 Co. Rep. 26b, 77 E.R. 1177.
[493] *Zouch* v. *Clay* (1671) 1 Vent. 185, 86 E.R. 126 (space left in a bond).
[494] *Zouch* v. *Claye* (1671) 2 Lev. 35, 83 E.R. 441.
[495] *Zouch* v. *Clay* (1671) 2 Keb. 872, 84 E.R. 551.

been mentioned too. The Westmeath estate is out of the case, for a covenant to settle future acquisitions is not favoured in equity, as appears from the case of *Lowe* v. *Lowe*,[496] where the court carried into execution the articles as far as they related to the lands he was then siesed of, but not what he had acquired after. There is a saving for Protestants that claim under Thomas and William, as Ignatius doth, and registered deeds can only extend to those that ought to be registered.

Lord Westmeath ought to be before the court being remainderman after Ignatius, and the daughters have estates for the payment of their portions.

Mr Patrick French[497]

The Crown is not concerned in this case, for the prayer of the information is, that Hyacinth may be decreed to such right as he had before the attainder. It was an honest design in the deed of 1700 to provide for the children that could take; the deed is for the payment of debts, and the creditors, who don't appear to be satisfied, are not before the court.

Mr Darcy

Quoted 2 Lev. 113[498] as to the rasure.

Mr Daly

I must observe upon the evidence of Hyacinth, the witness swears, he heard and believes that Thomas at the time of his intermarriage was [*103*] seised of lands in the county of Galway. The rasure was not done by us, or in a part relative to us.

1. The only evidence for the Crown is the recital in our settlement, which is not such evidence the court ought to take notice of.

2. The rasure is not material to the point in consideration.

3. This is to be looked on as the suit of the party, and the information is evidence against him.

4. The recital of a deed or patent in another is not evidence of the deed or patent recited.

Lord Chief Baron

A recital is evidence against the recitor, and those that claim under him.

---

    [496]   No citation given.
    [497]   Patrick French, s. and heir of Robert, Monyval, Co. Galway. Middle Temple, 24 Jan. 1703/4. KI, Easter term, 1707. KI AP, p. 179.
    [498]   *Nelthorpe and Farrington* v. *Dorrington* (1674) 2 Lev. 113, 83 E.R. 475.

Mr Daly

Cragge v. *Norfolk*, 2 Lev. 108, 109,[499] and it might be of the worst consequence if a recital should be evidence; he who sets up a forged deed is punishable, but if he makes a false recital, he is not liable to punishment, and yet shall reap an advantage by it, and it is not evidence against the parties who claim under it. Vaugh: *Rowe* v. *Huntington*.[501] If one makes a lease to another reciting a former lease not in being, it shall commence immediately, and neither lessor [n]or lessee are bound or estopped by it. Co. Lit. 46b. 1 Vent. 83,[502] 84. 1 Sid. 460,[503] *Foot* v. *Berkly*, Vaugh. 82.[504] Mod. Cas. 44, *Ford* v. *Lord Grey*.[505] The recital of a lease in a release is evidence indeed, because they make but one conveyance, and the release is of no effect without it, and it is admitted against the lessor to make the lease of force, but where a deed is recited which is of no effect to corroborate the reciting deed, that is no evidence of it. A recital of the payment of money is no evidence.

Hob. 130. *St John* v. *Digges*.[500]

Lord Chief Baron

Yes, it is against the grantor, though the payment must be proved against the purchaser.

Mr Daly

This recital is no evidence because there is no [*104*] proof of such articles, and recitals are no legal evidence.

But if the recital was evidence, it can give no title to Hyacinth. The recital is of an article in general terms to make a competent provision for sons and daughters, these are too uncertain and general to be carried into execution, *West* v. *Lord Delawar*,[506] and it is straining an equity to create a forfeiture. Suppose instead of Hyacinth a young child had been attainted, would the court have carved out a reasonable provision for that child to have been forfeited?

William Nugent then has made a title under the deed of 1700 before the Popery Acts, and then the second question is, whether the rasure avoids the deed? But there is no instance where the rasure of the obligor has ever avoided a bond, though the rasure of a stranger may.

Lord Chief Baron

Formerly when the profert was produced, the court never sent a rased deed to a jury, but determined it themselves.

---

[499] *Cragge* v. *Norfolk* (1674) 2 Lev. 108 at 109, 83 E.R. 472; 2 Lev. 120, 83 E.R. 478.
[500] *St John* v. *Diggs* (1613) Hob. 130, 80 E.R. 279.
[501] *Rowe* v. *Huntington* (1670) Vaugh. 66, 124 E.R. 973.
[502] *Foot* v. *Berkley* (1670) 1 Vent. 83, 86 E.R. 581.
[503] *Foot* v. *Berkley* (1670) 1 Sid. 460, 82 E.R. 1216.
[504] *Sic*, for *Rowe* v. *Huntington* (1670) Vaugh. 66 at 82, 124 E.R. 973 at 980.
[505] *Ford* v. *Lord Grey* (1704) 6 Mod. 44, 87 E.R. 807.
[506] *West* v. *Lord Delaware* (1683) 1 Vern. 198, 23 E.R. 411; 2 Vent. 357, 86 E.R. 483.

Mr Daly

But a bond is a chose in action, and by the loss of the bond you lose your action, but where an estate passes by a deed, and that is cancelled, you only lose your evidence, but not your estate. A grantor can't destroy a voluntary settlement, 2 Vern. 476, *Lady Hudson's Case*,[507] but this doctrine would destroy that rule. 11 Co. *Piggot's Case*[508] is full in point: this is a deed for the use of several persons, and a destruction of one limitation, is not the destruction of another. William was innocent of what was done. It is collateral to his title, and does not destroy the deed as to him.

3. The estate by the Act is divested out of the Crown, and vested in the informer, and he has only a liberty to make use of the King's name, [*105*] as where one pays a debt to the Crown. He has the aid and process of the Crown to reimburse himself, but no prerogative of the Crown. I admit if in the case of strangers a title appears for the Crown that the court will give judgment.

If a remainder on an estate tail is in the Crown, no recovery can bar it, otherwise if it is divested and made over, for a subject shan't partake of the benefit of the Crown.[509] If then Thomas married without consent, and the articles are subsequent to the marriage, this is an evidence against Hyacinth.

But suppose this to be the suit of the King, the Crown makes an allegation, and the party applies himself to that, if the Crown might after give another matter in evidence, the party could not ward against it, which would be a prerogative destructive to the subject.

Lord Chief Baron

The Latin information only sets out a general title in the Crown, and the party was obliged to set out his title in particular, till the Act of Parliament gave him leave to plead the general issue, for the Crown is not at leisure to make out a particular case.

Mr Anthony Malone[510]

A grantor of a voluntary settlement can't make a second, but by their doctrine he might destroy the first by a rasure. If money is to be disposed of at the pleasure of the parent, he may increase or decrease the portions, and he has the same power in the case of lands, and in this case there is a sufficient reason for his doing so. But here is a settlement made pursuant to the articles; the party has shown his intention, which is a guide by which the court may decree an execution of the articles. [*106*]

---

[507] The case at that citation is *Clavering* v. *Clavering* (1704) 2 Vern. 473 at 476, 23 E.R. 904, which does not mention a Lady Hudson but concerns a voluntary settlement.

[508] *Pigot's Case* (1614) 11 Co. Rep. 26b, 77 E.R. 1177.

[509] I.e. 'benefit to the Crown' is the immunity from being barred by a recovery. If the remainder is divested from the Crown and conveyed to a private person, then it may be barred, for otherwise the private person would benefit from the Crown's immunity.

[510] KI AP, p. 325: Anthony Malone, son of Richard, of Dublin, educated Trinity College Dublin, admitted, Middle Temple, 30 March 1720; KI, admitted, Easter term 1726; P.S., patent, 9 May 1743, Smyth, *Law Officers of Ireland*, p. 189, (1700–76) *Hist. Ir. Parlt.* (no. 1336).

Mr Daly Junior[511]

Quoted as to the rasure, Moore 547.[512] Keilw 165.[513]

Mr Prime Serjeant contra.

We have made three points in this case:

1. That Hyacinth is heir if the descent is not broke, and whatever estate he had will come to the Crown.

2. The deed of 1700 is an evidence of the articles.

3. Of what weight the deed is.

It is strange to think that a recital in a deed under which the children claim is not [sic] evidence against them, though not against a purchaser. If this settlement was not produced, we have a title as heir, and shan't they be bound by the recitals in it when it is their title. Thomas was a younger branch of the Westmeath family, and if it appears that he was seised of the lands at the time of the settlement or at his death, it is sufficient. He marries a lady of quality and fortune, and enters into articles (which appear only by a recital in a deed) whereby he covenants to settle £300 a year on his wife for her jointure, and to make a competent provision etc., according to the estate he was then, or should be seised of etc. Where such articles are executed in consideration of marriage, and of a portion which deserves a better settlement than the husband can then make, the court will carry them into execution as to the children, though not where a creditor, or the purchaser of such future acquisitions is before the court. Hyacinth is a purchaser under these articles, and a bill filed by his prochein amy in his minority the court would have carried them into execution according to the usual course of marriage settlements. Would your Lordship distinguish him from other eldest sons, and give him only £40 a year [107] without any demerit but the attainder, at a time he could not deserve it, and which was occasioned only by his father being attainted? No, your Lordship would not divide the estate among the children, but observe the same course the rest of the kingdom do: give the bulk of the estate to the eldest son, and make a reasonable provision for the younger children.

Whatever right then Hyacinth had to carry articles into execution either in law or equity vested in the Crown and is now re-vested in him and Thomas is a trustee for the issue of the marriage. Thus it stands on the articles.

But supposing there were no articles, I shall next consider how far the rasures shall affect the deed.

The books make these distinctions as to rasures.

If a bond is rased in a material part either by the obligee or a stranger, that vitiates the whole bond. They who claim under a deed are obliged to take care of the safe custody of it, if it is not taken away by force or fraud. Rasure by the party in an immaterial part vitiates the whole for this reason.

If a deed contains several distinct covenants between A and B only, if one is rased, the whole is vitiated, because it is all one act and one deed between the two; but where distinct covenants are to be performed by different persons, the deed shall

---

511 Probably Denis Daly, listed in KI AP only as KI, Michaelmas term, 1710. KI AP, p. 118.

512 *Marckham* v. *Gomaston* (1598) Moo. K.B. 547, 72 E.R. 749.

513 *Milles* v. *Gilforde* (1511) Keilw. 165, 72 E.R. 339 at 340 (sub nom. *Millys* v. *Guldeford* 116 Seld. Soc. 625).

be vitiated as to one only, every covenant being to be considered as the deed of so many distinct persons, 2 Rol. Ab. 30,[514] and his act stands good, 5 Co. 23 *Matthewson's Case.*[515] But if several jointly covenant, a rasure vitiates the whole, or if the deed is altered in the date.

To apply these distinctions:

Archer swears that Thomas altered the jointure, and that there were other rasures. Here the presumption must be that these rasures were made after the execution of the deed, contrary to the common rule, because a rasure is a forgery; the jointure which is rased is a material part of the deed in respect of all the remainders, because their several estates are charged with it. These are the limitations of one estate, and are not [*108*] like separate but joint covenants by several persons and in one deed, and the rasure is a material part. This is a settled rule in equity, that he who makes a voluntary settlement, may destroy it, may burn or cancel it,[516] and here your Lordship can't set it up for the younger children against the heir, not more than if the father who made the settlement had thought fit to cancel or destroy it. This rasure then is made in a material part, in a deed which is one act, and by one who might vitiate and destroy it by any other act. The purchasers claim with notice of the recitals and of the rasures, which make the deed void ab initio, and consequently divests the estate Cro. Car. 397.[517] No estate passes since the Statute of Frauds and Perjuries without the lease and release,[518] so the rasure voids the deeds ab initio, which are necessary to pass the estate.

Lord Chief Baron

The Attorney General is not tied up to his allegations, but to inform the court that the defendant is an intruder, and the defendant before Ca. 1[519] could not plead the general issue, but was obliged to set out his title, and traverse generally.

Mr Attorney General

This is the suit of the King. In a cause between party and party if a right appears for the Crown, the court ex officio must determine for the King, as my Lord Hobart[520] says on a special verdict in a *quare impedit.*

The question is, whether the deed of 1700 is good or bad, or to what purpose? If it is totally bad, Hyacinth has a title as heir, 11 Co. *Piggot's Case*[521] the last resolution. Only the rasure in the jointure appears judicially before your Lordship, which was done by a stranger, by the direction of the grantor, when he was in possession of the deed, which was a concealed deed, not gone abroad,[522] or known.

---

[514] *Budden* v. *Wood* (1618) 2 Rolle 29 at 30, 81 E.R. 638.

[515] *Mathewson's Case* (1597) 5 Co. Rep. 22b, 77 E.R. 84.

[516] This is a crucial point in the case: if there were more than one party to the deed and consideration, then one party could not unilaterally alter the deed so as to escape his or her obligations, but a party may alter obligations which he or she entered into voluntarily.

[517] *Miller and Johns* v. *Manwaring* (1635) Cro. Car. 397, 79 E.R. 947.

[518] See above p. 83 n. 481.

[519] I.e. Charles I.

[520] *Sic.* Sir Henry Hobart (?–1625), C.J.C.P. in England, 1613. *ODNB*, A. W. B.Simpson, *Biographical Dictionary*, at p. 243. His reports were published in 1641, and the last, 1724 ed., is reprinted in 80 E.R.

[521] *Pigot's Case* (1614) 11 Co. Rep. 26b, 77 E.R. 1177.

[522] I.e. not made public.

There is great difference whether the rasure is in a charge precedent or subsequent to the estates of the defendants. The limitations to William and Ignatius are liable [*109*] to this charge, and it is very material to them whether they shall pay £200 or £300 a year, and by the lease and release[523] the whole estate passes to the trustees. And so the whole is vitiated by the rasure.

This deed binds William and Ignatius, because they have no other title, and they can't claim the benefit of one part, and not of the other.

William and Ignatius by their marriage settlement covenant, that their children shall enjoy according to this deed. Here then is constructive notice of the articles which are recited in it, and the deed is said to be made in pursuance and considera- *Ante* 51. tion of the articles.

But there is a strong presumption that they conceal the articles, for it appears that William is the executor of Thomas. This deed is not an execution of the articles, because though he had ever so many sons afterwards they could not take by it, which shows that this was a conveyance he did not design to make use of. How comes he to covenant that he was seised in fee, and that the estate was £600 a year, if he was not obliged to execute this settlement? Articles are to be carried into execution according to the intention of the parties. If one covenants to make a settlement on himself, and the issue of the marriage, the court will decree a settlement to be made to the father for life, remainder to trustees to preserve,[524] etc., remainder to the first and every other son etc., in the same manner if the covenant is to settle on himself and the heirs male of his body. 2 Vern. 420.[525]

The court undertook to say what was a competent discretionary provision, and gave the son a double portion.

In *Trevor* v. *Trevor*[526] Lord Macclesfield decreed a special execution of the articles, M͠S cas. in Canc. and the decree was affirmed in the House of Lords,[527] though by the words of the C.24. articles Sir John Trevor was tenant in tail. And if this deed is void in law, equity will not set it up in favour of the younger children against the [*110*] heir at law who is wholly unprovided for. He has only 138 acres settled on him subject to the debts of Thomas; and the mother's portion which was £2,000, is the standard provision for younger children.

Mr Solicitor General

First I shall consider whether the deed in 1700 is a good deed to defeat the title of Hyacinth as heir; 2. If it is a good deed, whether it is a good execution of the articles; 3. If not, whether the court can carry them into execution, and in what manner.

1. The deed is not good because of the rasures. If a material rasure is made by the party interested which goes through the deed it vitiates. The town and lands of Kilbride in the county of Galway: the last words are added only to cover the rasure, which must vary the whole deed if other lands were to pass to Hyacinth, so this is within the authority of the cases, and the whole deed is absolutely void, because this is not the deed of the parties originally, and this would make the deed void though

[523] See above p. 83 n. 481.
[524] I.e. trustees to preserve contingent remainders. A device to prevent the destruction of contingent remainders. Above, p. 82 n. 478.
[525] *Warburton* v. *Warburton* (1701) 2 Vern. 420, 23 E.R. 869.
[526] *Trevor* v. *Trevor* (1719) 1 Eq. Cas. Abr. 185, 21 E.R. 977.
[527] *Trevor* v. *Trevor* (1719) 5 Bro. P.C. 2nd ed. 122, 2 E.R. 574.

it were done by a stranger. Cro. El. 626, *Marham* v. *Gonaston*.[528] They ought to show this rasure was made before the execution of the deed, if it had been before the perfection. The parties would have taken notice of it, and we had not the deed in our custody.

2. The second point, which is the strength of the informant's case, is that this deed is not a good execution of the articles. The recital in a release is an evidence of the lease, because a recital is an evidence against the party but not for him. So this recital is as much evidence against William and Ignatius as against Thomas; but the deed is said to be in consideration and performance of the articles, and the [*111*] covenants that have been taken notice of by Mr Attorney General show it to be so. The defendants ought to produce these articles. They first denied them by their answer, the purport of them was to settle a rentcharge of £300 a year for the jointure of the wife, and a competent provision according to the estate which Thomas had or should acquire for the sons and daughters of the marriage. The settlement on Hyacinth is not a competent provision. The articles must be construed according to the intention of the parties at the time of their execution, and not from future circumstances. If money is devised to be divided at the discretion of the trustees, and they give it to one, equity will set the disposition aside. But the case is stronger on marriage articles, because the children are purchasers, *West* v. *Erisey*.[529] And it appears by the case of *Trevor* v. *Trevor*, that the father could bar Hyacinth of his right by reason of any misbehaviour, but that the articles must be executed according to the intention of the parties at the times they were entered into.

MS cas. in Canc. C.303.

3. The third question then is, how the court can carry these articles into execution, which must be by the common rule the court goes by, of limiting an estate to the father for life, remainder to his first and every other son in tail male etc., as if the husband sued for the wife's portion: this court would compel him to make a settlement in that manner, and to provide for the younger children suitable to their mother's portion. Thomas by this deed considers William as his eldest son, which is a measure for the court to go by in making a settlement on Hyacinth. This is a fraud on the Crown [and] ought not to receive a countenance.

Mr G. Bourk[530]

This is an act of restitution, which is more favoured than a grant by the Crown. 2 Mod. 2.[531] As to the rasures he quoted *Miller* v. *Mainwaring*[532] 2 Rol. Ab. 229, Cro. Ca. 1. [*112*]

---

[528] *Markham* v. *Gonaston* (1598) Cro. Eliz. 626, 78 E.R. 866.
[529] *West* v. *Erisey* (1727) 1 Com. 412, 92 E.R. 1135, 2 Eq. Cas. Abr. 40, 22 E.R. 33 (1727), 1 Bro. P.C. 2nd ed. 225, 1 E.R. 530.
[530] There is no barrister listed in KI AP of that name with that spelling, but there is one G. Burke in that period: Garret (or Gerard) Burke, 3rd. s. of Thomas, Tiaquin, Co. Galway; Middle Temple, 17 June 1699, KI, Hilary term, 1703, K.C., Michaelmas term, 1711, d. 23 April 1740; KI AP, p. 62.
[531] *Rex* v. *Bishop of Rochester* (1675) 2 Mod. 1 at 2, 86 E.R. 906.
[532] *Miller* v. *Maynewaring* (1635) Jones W. 354, 82 E.R. 186.

Tuesday, December the 7th [1731]

Mr Lindsey [*sic*]

We must make out our case from what the defendants have disclosed. And everything is to be presumed against them. Since they won't produce the deed of jointure, your Lordship will suppose it went further. And the presumption is strong of that side. Thomas could not recover the portion of Mariana without the aid of a court of equity. If he had filed a bill for that purpose against the father, equity would not have decreed for him without settling the money on the issue, but the father and son came to an agreement to provide for the wife only as they say. But it is probable for the issue too. The eldest son is attainted. If the settlement went no further, Thomas had a power to keep the estate in the family, and it was his interest, and of the wife, and sons, to prepare this deed if it went no further than to provide a jointure for Mariana, because that would show he had a power to make the settlement of 1700, and he kept the defeasance. So the presumption is, that this deed is either suppressed or concealed. If Thomas had only provided for his wife, he knew he had an absolute disposal of the rest of his estate, then he would have taken notice that this deed made no further provision, and that notice would have been good.

Objection. When the articles are carried into execution by a settlement, the court would interpose.

This indeed may be true where the portion of the wife is small, and a suitable provision is made for the issue. But the contrary appears to be true from the case of *Trevor* v. *Trevor*.

Objection. The recital is no proof of the articles. 1 Vent. 83,[533] 1 Sid. 460.[534] The case of *Rowe* v. *Huntington*[535] in Vaughan is only, that if the jury [*113*] find a deed in which another is recited, that is not a finding of the recited deed, but that case don't show, that such a recital is not good evidence of the deed to be laid before a jury.

This information is filed on the articles to carry them into execution. They set up a deed which discloses the articles. We insist upon having the original articles executed. The several distinctions on rasure appear in *Piggot's Case*.[536]

Mr Fortescue[537]

That articles have been carried into execution by the courts of equity, though settlements have been made, appears from 2 Vern. 658,[538] 670,[539] 703.[540]

---

[533] *Foot* v. *Berkley* (1670) 1 Vent. 83, 86 E.R. 581.
[534] *Foot* v. *Berkley* (1670) 1 Sid. 460, 82 E.R. 1216.
[535] *Rowe* v. *Huntington* (1670) Vaugh. 66, 124 E.R. 973.
[536] *Pigot's Case* (1614) 11 Co. Rep. 26b, 77 E.R. 1177.
[537] Probably Faithful Fortescue, 4th s. of William, Newragh, Co. Louth. Middle Temple, 18 Nov. 1717, KI, Easter term, 1723. KI AP, p. 174.
[538] *Corbett* v. *Maydwell* (1710) 2 Vern. 655, 23 E.R. 1027.
[539] *Baile* v. *Coleman* (1711) 2 Vern. 670, 23 E.R. 1036.
[540] *White* v. *Thornborough* (1715) 2 Vern. 702 at 703, 23 E.R. 1056.

Mr Hussy[541]

A deed recited in a deed which is found by a special verdict is not found by that verdict, but the verdict only finds such a recital. But surely the recital is in its own nature an evidence.

Lord Chief Baron

If Thomas had said in a letter, that articles were executed on his marriage, sure that would have been evidence.

Mr Hussy

1 Salk. 286,[542] the recital of a lease in a release is evidence against the releasor and all claiming under him. The suggestion of a bill is evidence, *Gayner* v. *Gayner* in Ante 58.[543] Chancery. The daughter sued for a portion under the will of her father, and by her bill set forth, that lands of £500 a year were settled on the marriage of her father and mother, and that he and her grandfather joined in a bond to make good the deficiency if any, this covenant of her own showing was to be first satisfied.

This evidence is not conclusive, but they should show the articles.

The intention of the articles was to make a provision for the children out of the power of the father, [*114*] and he who is the vendor is not to be the judge of what is a competent provision for them, but a court of equity.

As to the rasures the question is, whether they would destroy the deed at law, and not whether a court of equity will set it up. Here is no reason for equity to interpose.

Here is a fraud on the Crown to suppress evidence to disinherit an eldest son in favour of volunteers.

Thursday, December the 9th [1731]

Lord Chief Baron

In court: Sir John St Leger

Lord Chief Baron

Hyacinth Nugent is to have the same prerogative as if the information was for the benefit of the Crown, for it is granted to him generally by the Act.

Thomas was seised at the time of his death of the lands in the counties of Galway and Westmeath. In 1680 articles were entered into for making a certain jointure to the wife, and a competent provision for the children. These articles were previous to the marriage, and for a valuable consideration.

---

[541] Probably Ignatius Hussey, 3rd s. of Walter, Donore, Co. Kildare. Gray's Inn, 3 March 1704, Middle Temple, 25 Nov. 1719, called *ex gratia*, 27 Nov. 1719. KI, Michaelmas term, 1724, d. Jan. 1743. KI AP, p. 240.

[542] *Ford* v. *Lord Grey* (1704) 1 Salk. 285 at 286, 91 E.R. 253.

[543] The cross reference is to the point as to a bill being evidence, since it was drawn up by counsel from the available papers, though evidence 'of the slightest kind', as noted in *Ryan* v. *Cummin*, above, p. 49 [*58*], and *Snow* v. *Phillips* (1664) 1 Sid. 220 at 221, 82 E.R. 1069.

The question is, if this appears to the court? We think there is evidence sufficient that there were such articles. If they appear by the confession of the party, or of those claiming under him and they don't produce them, they are to be construed to the advantage of him that is to have a benefit by them, and strongest against those who ought to produce them. And they are to be presumed to have been to the use of the first and every other son in tail male, as is usual in such cases, and since it appears that there were articles in 1680, we are to consider them as burnt or destroyed [*115*] for one part of them at least must have been in the hands of Thomas.

If Richard then had not been attainted, and had come into a court of equity for an execution of these articles, the court would have decreed him an estate tail, subject to the jointure, and charged with a reasonable provision for his brothers and sisters.

But it is objected that recitals are no evidence. The case of *Rowe* v. *Huntington*[544] imports no more, than that where a deed is found in *hæc verba* in which a deed is recited, that is no evidence of the deed recited, for the court is not to infer but ought to direct them to find it. But a recital is evidence against the party himself, as a letter, or any other confession.

If then there were articles, the deed of 1700 is of no effect, that might have carried them into execution, but cannot control them. 'Tis a misexecution of them. The wife is to have but £300 a year *durante viduitate*,[545] and only £100 a year if she marry.

This deed being then out of the case, there is no need to enquire whether it is void or not. The question arises on *Piggot's Case*,[546] but I am of opinion that the deed is not void, but that it ought to be sent to a jury to see in what place it is rased. Formerly the court themselves judged of deeds, and if a deed was rased they held it to be void, because it was not the deed which was originally executed by the parties, and they construed them so strictly to prevent fraud, but it has been since determined otherwise in *Layfield's Case*[547] in 10 Co., that it shall be sent to a jury.

Be it therefore decreed, that the lands in the counties of Galway and Westmeath in the information mentioned be taken into the hands of the King, in trust, in pursuance of the Act, for Richard Hyacinth Nugent, and he is to enjoy them in tail male, remainder *eodem modo*[548] to William and Ignatius, remainder to the right heirs of Thomas, subject to the jointure to Mariana, and £40 a [*116*] year a piece to William and Ignatius for life and to £2,000 for the daughters who were unprovided for at the death of Thomas, and an account be taken of the rents and profits from the death of Thomas. The lands in the county of Westmeath are to go as the other lands by the covenant to settle future acquisitions, because no sale was ever made of them by Thomas for a valuable consideration in his lifetime, and an injunction is to issue to the sheriff to put the crown in possession. And the officer is to take an account, whether any and what part of the £2,000 has been paid since the death of Thomas, and the deed of 1700 is to be delivered out to William Nugent.

It was insisted on, that in the Act there was a saving for Ignatius, because William Nugent on his marriage covenanted to settle £80 a year on him. But the court were of another opinion, because no estate was actually made to him, and though purchasers are entitled to have covenants carried into execution by this court, they would not do it on this Act of Parliament.

---

[544] Above, p. 87 n. 501.
[545] L. during widowhood.
[546] *Pigot's Case* 11 Co. Rep. 26b, 77 E.R. 1177.
[547] *Leyfield's Case* (1611) 10 Co. Rep. 88a, 77 E.R. 1057.
[548] L. in the same manner.

Sir John St Leger

We ground our provisions for the younger sons on the estate of Kilbride, which it appears by the deed of 1700 the father thought sufficient for Hyacinth, and we decree the estate to Hyacinth, on the evidence of there being marriage articles which are suppressed.

Though by the Act of Resumption if the information had been for the benefit of the Crown an estate in fee must have been decreed to the King, yet the court said, they must take notice of this private Act of Parliament, and that his Majesty was not to hold the estate.

Mr Daly the same day moved for a rehearing on a petition. And it was argued for the defendants, that error may be brought on an information of intrusion.

Lord Chief Justice Holt was of opinion that error lay in civil cases against the Crown without leave of the Attorney General. [*117*]

On the other side it was said, That a rehearing is not a matter of right, that if the court should grant it, the injunction must go and they rehear out of possession, for the rehearing would not stay the King's process. On an information of intrusion the court must grant process till error is served on them, which is from another court.

A rehearing is in nature of error *coram vobis*. Mr Stannard said the issuing [of] the injunction was part of the decree they excepted to, because mortgages were concerned, and portions charged on the lands.

To which was answered, that there was a saving for them by the Act.

Post 384.   *Cur[ia] advisare vult.*

Monday, January the 24th.

The first day of Hilary Term 1731, 2 [1732].[549]

In Exchequer

You can't move to discharge an order made on hearing counsel on both sides without first paying the costs of the last motion.

Wednesday, February the 23rd. [1732]

In Exchequer

MOOR v. WORTHINGTON, & AL.,
THE EXECUTORS OF CHARLES CAMPBELL

Mrs Moor deposited £4,000 which belonged to her and her children under the Statute of Distributions,[550] in the hands of Mr Campbell, and he by a deed covenanted to put the money out at interest and declared the trust, and was to be allowed for his care and trouble. He puts the money to interest, but never declares the trust. After his death on a bill filed by the plaintiffs, an account was decreed, and the officer

---

[549] 24 January was a Monday in 1732 (Julian), Kratz, *Hist. Cal.* Note that the year changes here to 1732 and is given in the MS.

[550] Statute of Distributions (Ireland), 1695, (7 Will. III, c. 6).

having charged the executors with £71 for which Mr Campbell had sold the books of Mr Moor to Pepyat a bookseller,[551] and taken bond for them in his own name, and Pepyat after failed, the court thinking this a hard case, allowed him £75 for his care and trouble for nine years and a [*118*] half, which was near 9d in the pound, but no costs on either side.

MSŜ cas. in
Canc. A.198.
1 Vern. 316.[552]
(312)
Nels. Fol. Rep.
in Canc. 361.[553]

RUTLEDGE v. RUTLEDGE

Eodem die

In Exchequer

The mother settled all her real and personal estate in trust, for a provision to herself for life, and then for her sons and a daughter payable at marriage, the mother dies, the court refused to allow the daughter interest for her portion, because it moved from the mother, and it was not mentioned in the bill, or proved in the cause that she was otherwise unprovided for, though that was the case.

Thursday, February the 24. [1732]

In Exchequer

HUTCHINSON v. LAPP

The motion was for leave to examine witnesses after publication, the notice being so short that they were not able to examine their witnesses. What they would examine to was the very gist of the cause, whether the purchaser had notice. After great debate, and a consideration of the inconveniences of both sides, the court gave leave to examine to the matters in issue on showing the interrogatories to a baron. And several authorities were mentioned in support of the motion.

Shey v. *Burnford*.[554] On reading the depositions at the hearing it appeared that they had not proved all the circumstances requisite to complete a will, and the court ordered the cause to stand over, and they had leave to examine them.

Horan v. *Archdeckne*.[555] The bill was filed for a share in Gavelkind, and publication passed, then the plaintiff came of age, turned convert, and filed a bill for the whole estate, and he had leave to examine in the cross cause, on condition he did not examine to anything in issue in the [*119*] original cause.

Cummin v. *Ryan*.[556] Leave was given to examine in the cross cause, after publication was past in the original, they having examined no witnesses in the original cause.

---

[551] There were several booksellers by the name of Pepyat, the principal ones being Jeremiah Pepyat (fl. 1700–1740), and Sylvanus, his brother (d. 1739). Jeremiah got into debt and went to London. In January 1753 he and his wife were in the Fleet Prison for debt. See M. Pollard, *A Dictionary of Members of the Dublin Book Trade 1550–1800* (London, 2000), pp. 454–55.

[552] *Bonithon* v. *Hockmore* (1685) 1 Vern. 316, 23 E.R. 492.

[553] *How* v. *Godfrey* (1678) Cas. t. Finch 361, 23 E.R. 198 (trustee to have costs and charges but no allowance for care in managing the trust).

[554] No citation given.

[555] Below, p. 135 [*168*].

[556] Above, p. 49 [*58*].

Lord Chief Baron

Post 395, 140. *Nelson* v. *Welsh.*[557] On a reference publication past by consent, and the reference being broke off, they had leave to examine on showing the interrogatories to a baron.

Sir John St Leger

MSŜ ord in. Canc.
93, 95. A will or a deed may be examined to after publication, for there are fixed witnesses, whereas if they may examine to points at large after publication, when the parties see where the proof is defective, they may supply it with new witnesses.

HAWKINS v. PAGE

In Chancery

Sir William Sandys devised all his freehold lands, leases for years, chattels, and all his real and personal estate in Ireland, to trustees, to be sold by them or any three of them [a] quorum etc. and with the produce, the ready money and the debts called in, two of them [a] quorum etc, or any two of them were to purchase lands of inheritance[558] in England, to the use of John Sandys his son for life, remainder to trustees to preserve[559] etc, remainder to his first and every other son in tail male remainder to the second, and every other son of Sir William in tail male, remainder to Grace his daughter for life, remainder to her first and every other son in tail male, remainder to the defendant Page etc, and the profits till sale were to go to the same uses as the estate in England when it was purchased was to stand limited to, and made his son John Sandys sole executor, and John Shaw, John Page, John Sandys, William Sandys and Isaac Sandys his brothers executors *durante minoritate*[560] of John. Part of this estate was a term for years in a house in Castle Street held of the City of Dublin. The estate was [*120*] never sold, but came to Grace in remainder, who had a son William, and on his death she took out letters of administration to him, and by virtue thereof claimed this term which was limited to him in tail, and Mr Page the defendant one of the trustees claimed it by virtue of his remainder on William's dying without issue male. The plaintiff was a purchaser under Grace.

It was observed that this lease was taken in the name of Mr Gosse, in trust for Sir William Sandys and that Gosse being dead, the plaintiff had taken out letters of administration to him, and having thereby the legal estate of the term in him, he was not proper to sue in this court.

That it was the intention of the testator that this devise should be considered as real estate, that one may be tenant by the courtesie[561] of money devised to be invested in a purchase.

---

[557] No citation given.

[558] I.e. for an estate of inheritance, i.e. in fee simple or in fee tail, but in this context, since purchase is mentioned, in fee simple.

[559] Above, p. 82 n. 478.

[560] I.e. during the minority.

[561] Tenant by the curtesy, i.e. the life estate which a husband had at common law in his deceased wife's estate. The reference is to the equitable doctrine of conversion. The money is considered as converted to real estate from the point where there is a binding obligation to purchase real estate, and can therefore be held for the same estates as real property.

That if one articles to sell his estate, it shall be considered as personal estate, and the heir at law of the vendee may compel his executor to pay the purchase money.

That this court considers what ought to be done as done,[562] and the neglect of the trustees (supposing the sale to be personal to them) can't turn to the prejudice of the persons who are to take, nor can a trustee vary his trust. 2 Vern. *Audley* v. *Audley*.[563] If the committee of a lunatic vest his money in the purchase of lands, yet shall it be considered as personal estate,[564] because a trustee may execute, but can't vary his trust, so that other persons should take than those the testator intended. The limitation in the will can give the plaintiff only a title to it as real estate.

Lord Chancellor

The only question is, whether the court will take notice of this devise as real, or personal estate? I think it is real estate. And if a bill was brought for that purpose, I would carry the will into execution in favour of Alderman Page, the last in remainder. If the several estates devised [*121*] to be sold were to go according to their respective natures, they would not answer for the testator's intention, for they would go different ways.

I must dismiss the bill.

Friday, March the 3rd [1732]

In Chancery

THE CITY OF DUBLIN v. VERNON[565]

Mr Calaghan for the defendant

The title must be proved on these possessory bills, and everything in the affidavit is put in issue. Tenant[s] pur autre vie or for years must prove their title. *Mahony* v. *Lord Anglesea*.[566] My Lord was indicted for a forcible entry. The indictment was quashed for nonsense and restitution awarded to Lord Anglesea. And the court would not grant restitution to Mahony, because the term he held by was expired. So in *Eustace* v. *Brown*[567] 1706, the court would not grant restitution.

Possession alone is no evidence. But here the City have [*sic*] not been in possession within three years.[568] 'Tis proved indeed that Alderman Stoyte in his mayoralty

Mes App. G.13. SC.

---

[562] A maxim of equity.

[563] *Awdley* v. *Awdley* (1690) 2 Vern. 192, 23 E.R. 725.

[564] I.e. there is notional non-conversion in equity.

[565] See *Vernon* v. *City of Dublin* (1733) 4 Bro. P.C. 2nd ed. 398, 2 E.R. 270 ('It is usual in Ireland, for a lessee who has been three years in possession, and is disturbed, to file his bill in the Court of Chancery there, for an injunction to quiet him in possession, till evicted by due course of law; and this usage is founded upon the equity of the statutes made against forcible entries. But all bills of this kind must allege, and it must also be proved, that the sole and actual possession is in the plaintiff, and that no ownership or possession is in any other person.' Order of the Irish Chancery discharged.) Pleadings: King's Inns, Dublin, 'House of Lords Appeals', vol. 11, 1732–34.

[566] No citation given.

[567] No citation given.

[568] Under 10 Car. I, sess. 3, c. 13 (Ir.), 1634 (forcible entry).

about 15 years ago took several large fishes. If this had been within three years, 'tis
a possession of part of the profits only, which is not sufficient. No, the possession
that is required must be an actual, quiet and peaceable possession for three years,
and uninterrupted to the time of the interruption, as was adjudged in the House of
Lords; and if there is any disturbance within the three years by one who has a right
or not, 'tis an impediment to this bill. Here is no possession proved in Alderman
French. The liberty of laying down oysters is not brought down to the time in the
bill. The witnesses say, they were never disturbed but by Mr Vernon, but they don't
say when he disturbed them. But if they were in possession of this right, this is no
possession of the soil. This is the possession of one part of the profits only. The
possession of the land consists in anchorage and salvage, and many other profits of a
strand; grazing of cattle is not a possession of the land, [122] but a liberty only to eat
the grass, which is in the possession of another, and if you grant him the injunction,
it would be determining that the possession belongs to him alone, though it appears
in the cause that it belongs to another.

Lord Chancellor

If one in quiet possession for three years produce a lease, I would not inquire into
the right of him that made it.

Mr Calaghan

Here is no occasion for an issue, because if the proofs are true they have no title to
the possession. This is not like a bill on the merits, where the prayer of general relief
is of great service, but the question is, whether the defendant is in contempt of the
injunction to the party, and Your Lordship is tied up to grant the same injunction to
the sheriff. An equitable right in a court of equity is as good as a legal, and the court
won't quiet[569] a legal against an equitable right.

Mr Daly

This bill and the injunction is to be quieted in the possession of 199 acres in
Crablough. The injunction is for the soil, and the evidence for the plaintiffs varies
from their bill. It don't entitle them to the soil, but to a liberty of laying down oysters
in alieno solo.[570] But no injunction lies on these bills, but[571] where the defendant may
be indicted or sued in trespass.[572] But if one has a liberty of fishing or laying down
oysters, he can't bring trespass against him who enters on the soil, or indict him, as
was determined in King's Bench in the case of *Lord Hoath,*[573] who indicted several at
Ringsend for entering on his oyster bed, and it was adjudged that the indictment
was not good, because it was a separate grant from the Crown of a liberty only, but he

[569] I.e. secure.
[570] I.e. in the soil of another.
[571] I.e. except.
[572] I.e. equity could only grant an injunction where the plaintiff had a cause of action at common law for
trespass. Counsel goes on to argue that there is no action for trespass to the soil where the plaintiff has a lesser
right in the nature of a liberty.
[573] No citation given.

ought to have brought an action on the case.[574] And so ought Alderman French if he has this liberty only. This bill don't square with the lease, but it is said that the City are also plaintiffs, and they are owners of the soil. I say then a title ought to appear, a semblance at least. They must prove the affidavit, which is the foundation of their case. No injunction can go to the party without swearing a title still subsisting, and if they [123] don't prove this they have no right to the injunction to the sheriff, and the plaintiffs have made no proof of a title to the soil, but only to this liberty.

The statute of H. 6 in England[575] and of Ca. I in Ireland[576] is the foundation of these proceedings. There must be a triennial possession and a title undetermined, and he in reversion may enter by force though the lessee has been ever so long in possession, if his title is expired. Nay, the lessee on the contrary may be indicted for a forcible detainer, if his landlord enters quietly. The end of these bills is, that where one has a defective title, another by force should not turn him out, but he should have a fair trial to try his right.

Here is no occasion for an issue, because the plaintiffs have not proved their affidavit, for then the plaintiff ought not to be deprived of his right, though contrary evidence is offered by the defendant; but here is no contrariety of evidence, no proof of a quiet possession for three years before the filing [of] the bill. Mr French says, he is entitled since 1718. The proof [of] that [is that] he has only a possession in common with three others. If he had brought an action of trespass, it would be a good defence to say, that others had a right with him, who gave the defendant a liberty to enter.

Mr Stoyte Recorder for the plaintiffs

Nothing is required to be proved on these bills but what is on an indictment: three years uninterrupted possession, and a title at the time of the force, and of bringing the indictment; it is sworn that Mr French had a sole possession, and not in common with others of laying down oysters. And this soil yields no profit but the laying down [of] oysters. It is impossible to keep servants in all parts of it. And the taking of oysters from them is not taking possession. If it was admitted to be so, no quiet possession could ever be proved of these things. 2 Cro. *Bettesworth's Case.*[577] If the lessee is in possession of any part of the thing, no possession is gained by a stranger entering on any other part.

Objection: A title ought to be proved.

No such thing is required by the Act, but only an estate continuing, not such a title as must be shown on an ejectment. The plaintiff indeed must show a right to the possession, because otherwise he has no right [124] to a restitution. If we claim by a term for years, we must show that the term is still subsisting, because it might be pur auter vie,[578] or otherwise.

Objection: There can be no forcible entry on oyster beds, because they are a profit apprendre.[579]

---

[574] I.e. a separate form of action, an action on the special case.
[575] 8 Hen. VI, c. 9 (Eng.), 1429 (forcible entry).
[576] 10 Car. I, sess. 3, c. 13 (Ir.), 1634 (forcible entry).
[577] No case of that name in Croke in E.R.
[578] LF. for the life of another.
[579] I.e. profit à prendre. The right to enter the land of another and to remove something from it.

An indictment lies for a forcible entry on tithes, rent, and for a commoner, yet a common is as much a right apprendre as laying of oysters. The City of Dublin is said by the bill to be seised of the strand itself. French indeed has only a liberty to lay down oysters, and each desire to be quieted. Wrecks and salvage are not the rights of the soil, but the prerogative of the Crown. The title is not now in question, but whether the city has been in possession for three years past, and whether here is any contrariety of evidence?

Mr Attorney General

Here is a semblance of a title. The defendant admits the lease in 1718, and that £70 rent was paid and received by the city. This is *festinum remedium*,[580] the nicety of the title, or the right of inheritance is not to be looked into. A title indeed to the possession is required, but not to the inheritance. In *Eustace* v. *Brown's Case*,[581] Eustace was a tenant at will to Brown. He determines his will, and then Eustace was only a trustee for Brown. There the possession being determined, he could not be restored to it; here the city don't derive under Vernon, nay the court have given possession contrary to that right. This is not like the case of lands. It is impossible to have one always attending whether the tide is in or out. Nothing was done by force or violence, nor was any offered till the time of our complaint.

Mr Stannard

There reason of introducing these bills was, that the titles to estates were lost by the many rebellions in this kingdom, so that the rise of them, as well as the constant practice since shows that the title was not to [*125*] be proved but by the possession, and the title necessary to be sworn to, is not of an original title, but of the continuance of the possession; *Waddington* v. *Sherlock* in Jo. C.[582] Sherlock, though he claimed under Waddington, set up an ancient title, and by Loftus lord chancellor[583] and Aungier[584] the master of the rolls, all the depositions touching the title were ordered to be suppressed, and it is said that they were done so, by the opinion of the whole Bar, and on a complaint to the council in England they approved of it. Sherlock offered the Chancellor forty angels[585] to reverse this decree and the lord chancellor petitioned the House of Commons against him, who was a member for Waterford, complaining that he had aspersed him before the lords of the council. This is to be found in the journals of the House of Commons.[586]

Mes App. F.599.

---

[580] A swift remedy.

[581] No citation given.

[582] J. Ir. H. C. vol. 1, 1615, pp. 50–52, 57, 62, 74–75, at p. 50, 'Petition of Thomas, Archbishop of Dublin, and Lord Chancellor of this Realm.' 22 April 1615.

[583] The lord chancellor concerned in the account in the J. Ir. H. C. (see n. 582 and below, p. 102 n. 586), was Thomas Jones (*c.* 1550–1619), archbishop of Dublin, appointed L.C. in 1605 in succession to Adam Loftus (*c.* 1533–1605), archbishop of Armagh and Dublin: Ball, *Judges in Ireland*, i. 315–17, at 317. Below, p. 102 n. 586. It is unclear whether it was indeed Loftus, or Jones, who gave the decisions on the depositions.

[584] Sir Francis Aungier (1558–1632), Baron Aungier of Longford, 1621, Cokayne, *Complete Peerage*, viii. 118, 'Longford and Aungier of Longford'. M.R., 1609. Above, p. lxxx n. 218. He lived in Dublin in the former monastery of Whitefriars and died there, giving his name to Aungier Street: Ball, *Judges in Ireland*, i. 322.

[585] An old English gold coin, the angel-noble, so called because it depicted the archangel Michael standing upon, and spearing, a dragon. It was last coined under King Charles I. It was the coin always presented to a patient 'touched' for the King's Evil, i.e. scrofula: *OED*.

[586] J. Ir. H. C. vol. 1, 1615, pp. 50–52, 57, 62, 74–5. Jones L.C. in his petition states that in Michaelmas Term 1610 he gave a decree in the Court of Chancery in favour of Richard Purcell, plaintiff, against Paul

A continuing possession is required, because if the tenant has an ancient title, he shan't set it up, but shall be said to be in by the landlord.

It was necessary to make French a plaintiff, because he had a particular property in which to be quieted. The plaintiff in these bills is in nature of a defendant in ejectment, and rests on his possession. The bedding [of] oysters and cockles is only a trespass, which is an implied force as will entitle the plaintiffs to this bill, but the force we complain of is that Vernon gathered the oysters, and burnt them with a multitude of people.

But if it was a force, and he goes off again, 'tis at our pleasure whether we will complain or no, or stay till a second time, and the first force will be no bar, because it did not discontinue our possession.

Mr Lindsay

We have made out a title, for we have proved that the city are the reputed owners, have made leases, and that the tenants have enjoyed.

In the case of *Sir William Barker* v. *Lord Ikerin*[587] the question was, who were in possession of a piece of ground that lay between their estates. No deeds were produced to show the title, but there was proof of the lands being possessed of either side, so your Lordship dismissed [*126*] the bill, but upon enquiry of the Bar your Lordship found that the practice was upon contradictory evidence to direct an issue which your Lordship afterwards did in that case.

Lord Chancellor

A subsisting title from one who has a reputed right is sufficient. The injunction is to be quieted in the soil and profit apprendre,[588] but [if] the proof is only clear that the plaintiffs were in possession of the latter, then it is not proper to grant this injunction against Mr Vernon to be quieted in the soil. You claim an injunction for the soil, which is what Mr Vernon answers to. The injunction is already gone, and the question is, whether here is a breach of that injunction. When you come to have an injunction for the soil, you must show a possession in the soil too.

Attorney General

Their granting a liberty is an evidence of their right to the soil.

Sherlock, alderman of Waterford, defendant, in a case in Chancery for disturbance of the plaintiff's possession of about 50 acres of land adjoining the defendant's land. On 2 February 1615 Sherlock came to him in St Sepulchre's and offered him 40 angels to reverse the decree. As a result of Jones' complaint, Sherlock went with the serjeant at arms and two members of the House of Commons to the court of Chancery to apologise to the lord chancellor. He 'made submission on his knee', read a statement, reproduced at p. 74, and asked for pardon, which Jones granted 'with tears in eyes'. Sherlock was then discharged by the House.

[587] Below, p. 104 n. 594.
[588] Above, p. 101 n. 579.

Mr Daly

No, the land between high and low watermark is in the Crown, and must be shown out of him, and if so, then if French granted this over, that would be a presumption of his having a property in the soil.

Friday, March the 3rd [1732]

Lord Chancellor

There ought to be an issue from the nature of the evidence, which must be cleared up by a cross-examination. It is allowed that the City enjoyed by the neglect of the late Mrs Vernon. Perhaps it might be only the picking up [of] an oyster or so. The question is, whether the plaintiffs have enjoyed the whole circuit leased to them.

If I dismiss the bill I set them by the ears together. In this kingdom possessions are in a great measure the title.

In the case of *Lord Ikerin* v. *Barker*[589] it was complained that I dismissed the bill, so on the rehearing and consulting [*127*] the practisers[590] directed an issue.

A semblance of title is proof enough. Here is lease from the City, and a recital of a former lease.

These proceedings are as loose as on a petition, otherwise instead of being summary, there would be as much nicety required as in special pleading.

This is a different possession from the possession of lands, and consists in dragging for oysters. It don't appear from the evidence that the City enjoyed the whole Crablough. The anchorage is proved to be in Vernon, and the rest are royalties which may be *in alieno solo*.[591]

Issues were directed in two cases that went to the Lords, and the orders confirmed. *Ikerin* v. *Barker*,[592] *Hacket* v. *Smyth*.[593] Therefore let the preamble to the order be of this sort.

Mes App. B.29,
133.[594] Whereas it is the constant course on bills of this nature where there is variety of evidence to direct an issue to try the possession, as was done in the case of *Hacket* v. *Smyth*, and *Ikerin* v. *Barker*. Let therefore in this case an issue be directed to try, whether the plaintiffs, or any deriving under them, were in the actual quiet and peaceable possession for three years before the disturbance complained of, if any, and what part of Crablough? The issue to be tried by a jury of the county of Dublin.

In Chancery

It being a common practice to file a supplemental bill in order to save the 20s the plaintiff was to pay for amending his bill, and to continue an injunction, the Lord Chancellor Midleton[595] made an order that no supplemental bills should be filed without leave of the court before issue was joined, but that the plaintiff after issue was joined might file a supplemental bill of course. But *quære* if a supplemental bill may be filed without leave after publication is passed. [*128*]

---

[589] Below, n. 594.
[590] *Sic*, i.e. practitioners.
[591] Above, p. 100 n. 570.
[592] Below, n. 594.
[593] Below, n. 594.
[594] These seem to be references to court records in *Hacket* v. *Smyth* and *Ikerin* v. *Barker* respectively.
[595] Spelled 'Middleton' in MS. Above, p. clix and p. 22 n. 135.

SLOAN v. DONNEGAL

Eodem die

In Chancery

Mr Sloan[e] made his will and appointed Sir Hans Sloan[e][596] and Mr Anglesey his executors, and in case they died before his personal estate should be laid out in a purchase, he made Sir Robert Fowler and William Sloan the plaintiff executors. The first executors renounce, and administration is granted to William Sloan the plaintiff, who alone brought this bill.

And it was objected that Sir Robert Fowler ought to have been made a party, that if administration is granted to a wrong person it is void, not voidable, and that the court will take notice of it, as was adjudged in the case of *Otway* v. *Wey*[597] in Exchequer, where administration was granted while one executor was living, that equity was stricter than the law, that the executor *de son tort* can't be sued here without bringing the legal representative before the court.

Lord Chancellor

If the two executors renounce, administration must be granted, and the whole vests in the administrator. By their renunciation Mr Sloan died intestate, and the court could not grant administration to Sir Robert Fowler and the plaintiff as executors before the first executors died, because the testator had not made them so before, for only the testator, not the court, can make an executor.

LEADBETER v. LEADBETER[598]

February the 4th. [1732][599]

In Exchequer

The end of this bill was to have the title deeds delivered up with the possession discharged of the mortgage.

John Leadbeter who lived in England being seised [*129*] in fee of some rents in the city of Dublin, came over to this kingdom, and on his return left the title deeds of

---

[596] Sir Hans Sloane, Bt (b. 16 April 1660, Killileagh, or White's Castle, Co. Down; d. 11 January 1753, London), physician and naturalist whose collection of books, manuscripts, and curiosities formed the basis of the collection of the British Museum in London. He revived the publication of the 'Philosophical Transactions,' which had been suspended since 1687. In 1687 he went to the West Indies as physician to the governor of Jamaica, and made many natural history observations and formed a collection of specimens. In 1693 he published *A Voyage to the Islands of Madera, Barbadoes, Nieves, St Christopher's, and Jamaica, with the Natural History of the last.* In 1716 he was made a baronet, and in 1727 first physician to King George II. In 1722 he saved the Chelsea Physic Garden in London, which had been founded in 1673 by the Society of Apothecaries, by a donation. He became president of the Royal Society in 1727. *ODNB.*

[597] No citation given.

[598] Continued from p. 54.

[599] Note that it is earlier than the previous case.

his estate with Swift the banker and was drowned in a storm. About four months after William the son of his third brother came over from England, and demanded the deed as heir of John Leadbeter, and his father and uncle swore he was his heir, but Mr Swift, before he would deliver up the deeds, insisted on an affidavit from William, and a note for his indemnity. Some of the tenants attorned[600] to William, but Bowen a tenant would not, but contested his being heir, and on William's distraining him for rents, brought a replevin, and a bill. William made a mortgage to Mrs Wallis one of the defendants. Jonathan the plaintiff filed his bill as heir to John Leadbeter, and on an issue directed, was found to be his heir, and the cause now coming to be heard on the equity reserved, it was insisted on for the mortgagee that constructive notice ought not to prevail against a purchaser, 2 Vern. 160, *Phillips* v. *Redhill*,[601] 159, *Brampston* v. *Baker*.[602]

But it was argued for the plaintiff, that if notice was necessary it was proved in this case, for Bowen the tenant informed Johnson who was agent for Mrs Wallis that he had a suit depending against William on pretence of his being heir, and that he would not pay his rent to him, and she ought to have inquired of the tenants [as to] who was heir.

But supposing Mrs Wallis had no notice, she can't protect herself against an heir, and Mr Vernon was of this opinion in the case of *Sir Erasmus Smyth & ux.* v. *Sir Charles Adams*,[603] and it is plain Mr Swift had a suspicion of him by his insisting on the note, and affidavit.

Mr Stannard

Mes App. E.71.   Mentioned the case of *Mammon* v. *Coote & Godsil* in this court, which was affirmed on an appeal to the House of Lords.[604] Coote made a [*130*] lease for lives to Prothereau renewable forever, and having occasion to make a settlement of his estate, he applied to Prothereau to surrender his lease, which he did accordingly, and took a note from Coote to make him a new lease. Prothereau continued in possession but never demanded a new lease, and died leaving daughters who were minors. His widow and administratrix delivered possession to Coote, and he made a lease to Godsil. Coote insisted on the possession being delivered to him, and that Prothereau's never asking for a new lease was a waiver of it; Godsil owned he knew that Prothereau died in possession, but said he believed him to be a tenant at will, and denied he had any other notice. The bill was filed by Mammon who married one of the daughters to have a new lease made, and the court were of opinion that Godsil ought to have enquired by what title Prothereau held.

Here Mrs Wallis knew some of the tenants would not attorn.[605]

There need not be an express notice of bills, though there must of judgments.

---

[600] I.e. acknowledged William as their landlord.
[601] *Phillips* v. *Redhil* cited at (1679) 2 Vern. 160, 23 E.R. 70.
[602] *Brampton* v. *Barker* (1671) 1 Eq. Cas. Abr. 333, 21 E.R. 1083, cited at 2 Vern. 160, 23 E.R. 709.
[603] No citation given.
[604] *Coote* v. *Mammon* (1724) 5 Bro. P.C. 2nd ed. 355, 2 E.R. 727 (notice of the plaintiff's title to the agent or purchaser for another is notice to the party himself, because a presumptive notice to the party).
[605] I.e. acknowledge themselves to be tenants.

Mr Calaghan

It is not necessary that the mortgagee should have notice, because the pretended heir never was in possession of the whole.

Barrymore v. *Richardson*[606] in Chancery. Lawrence, Earl of Barrymore, being only tenant for his life, conveyed in fee to Mr Richardson, the grandfather of the present six clerk.[607] The bill was filed against Mr Richardson the son. It was allowed that notice was not sufficiently proved on Mr Richardson the purchaser, but all the judges who assisted the lord chancellor were of opinion, that no estate passed from Lawrence but for his own life.

And in the case of *Cotter* v. *Barrymore*[608] this [*131*] court were of the same opinion, where Sir James Cotter had made a purchase from Lawrence, Earl of Barrymore.

And if Mrs Wallis has no right to the estate, she has none to the deeds which are attendant to it.

Constructive notice is binding in equity, *Cusack* v. *Cusack*[609] in Chancery: Cusack on the marriage of his first wife covenants to settle lands on himself and the issue male of the marriage. In the articles on his second the first articles are recited, and he covenants to settle the said lands on himself and his children by Mrs Barnwell his second wife, and the lords were of opinion that this recital was sufficient notice of the first articles.   Ante 51.

In the case of *Kelly* v. *Ruth*[610] in Chancery there was no notice, but he might have informed himself from the tenants who were in actual possession.

Curia

Mrs Wallis must deliver up the deeds, and the possession. She had not only constructive, but presumptive, notice. She had the counterparts of the leases, and on inquiry from the tenants might have found, that William Leadbeter was never in possession of the whole. The heir of one who was said to be dead of the plague at Marseilles, made leases. The ancestor came over and broke them.

SIR THOMAS WEBSTER v. SIR E. JENSON

In Exchequer

Mr Solicitor General moved for an injunction to the party to put the plaintiff in possession on a possessory bill. The defendant is tenant to the plaintiff. In 1728 Mr Hill, who is a manager for the plaintiff, not having the counterpart of the lease, inquired of the defendant when his term expired, who assured him not in many years, so Mr Hill let him hold on, whereas it appears his title ended in 1728. But the court refused the injunction, the bill not being filed within three terms. [*132*] Mr Solicitor General made a difference, where the bill was against one who comes

---

[606] No citation given.
[607] I.e. one of the six clerks in Chancery.
[608] No citation given. See *Cotter* v. *Earl of Barrymore* (1733) 4 Bro. P.C. 2nd ed. 203, 2 E.R. 138.
[609] The House of Lords judgment is reported in *Cusack* v. *Cusack* (1714) 5 Bro. P.C. 2nd ed. 116, 2 E.R. 570.
[610] No citation given.

in by force, and where against a tenant holding over, and that in the last case they might file their bill at any time. That the reason of this manner of proceeding was not only to quiet possessions, but likewise that persons on every occasion might not be obliged to produce their title deeds, the rather in this kingdom, where so many deeds by the frequent troubles have been destroyed.

Curia

Though a tenant comes in by title, his holding over is a force, so there is no difference. Therefore you must proceed by ejectment, or original bill.

After on the 12 of February the motion was made by Mr Solicitor General in Chancery, and granted, because of the fraud in the tenant.

Monday, January the 24th [1732][611]

In Chancery

MARY HUISH AND FRANCIS HUISH v. ANN VERNON & AL.[612]

The defendants moved to set aside process to a sequestration that had issued against them, and a decree founded on the sequestration, that the bill should be taken *pro confesso*,[613] because the defendants had never been served with a subpœna, nor entered an appearance.

The plaintiff Mary Huish filed a bill to redeem, to which the defendants put in an answer, and pleaded the want of parties. The plaintiff allowed the plea, and moved to amend the bill by making Francis Huish a plaintiff. The plaintiff amended the defendants' copy of the bill, and paid the costs of the amendment to the defendants' six clerk, who gave commissioners names to the plaintiffs' six clerk to take the defendants' answer in England, [*133*] and gave him notice of a motion for time to answer.

It was allowed in this case that the amended bill was a new bill, a new plaintiff being added, and that the defendants ought to have been served with a subpœna and process *de novo*, but that the giving commissioners names by the defendants' clerk amounted to an appearance, and that the first answer was no bar to the bills being taken *pro confesso*.

The decree was set aside by consent, the defendants' clerk undertaking to plead answer or demur by the first of next term.

---

[611] Note that the date is earlier than the previous case, and is the same date as that above, p. 96, being first day of Hilary Term, 1732.

[612] Resumed on p. 138.

[613] If a bill was exhibited in equity to which the defendant appeared, but was later held in contempt for not entering a written answer, the matter in the bill was taken as if it had been admitted by the defendant.

In Chancery

MEYER v. SIR JOHN ST LEGER

The answer was *capt* in January, and the commission was dated last December. The defendant moved to amend the caption[614] on affidavit of the time the commission was taken out, but the chancellor thought it well enough as it was.

[ANON.]

In Chancery

A motion was made to dispauper unless the party would submit to a reference, and it was said to be the practice of the Court of Exchequer to dispauper unless the party would refer after the time for excepting to the answer was out.

But it was objected for the plaintiff, that he ought first to proceed to examine his witnesses for fear of death.

The lord chancellor made no order, but said he would be certified of the Exchequer practice.

HOLLAND v. THE CORPORATION OF LIMERICK

February the 12. [1732]

In Chancery

It was moved to fine the coroners for not returning a *distringas* against the corporation, and an order granted unless cause shown in four days. [*134*]

POMEROY v. STEADMAN

February the 16. [1732]

In Exchequer

If the bill is only for a discovery, the answer must be received without security to abide the decree, though the defendant has stood in contempt to a commission of rebellion returned, for an answer is all the relief prayed.

---

[614] Blount, *Law Dictionary*, 1670: 'When a Commission is executed, and the Commissioners names subscribed to a Certificate, declaring when and where the Commission was executed, that is called the Caption.'

MANLY & BAILY v. SHIMMIN & PURFIELD

February the 19th. [1732]

In Exchequer

Mr Baily previous to his marriage with Mrs Baily, conveyed £500 and some houses part of her portion to the plaintiff Manly, in trust for her separate use. She lent £50 to the defendant Purfield on a mortgage which was taken in the name of Manly, and after came to an agreement with Purfield to give him £60 for the equity of redempion, which he was to convey to Manly in trust for her, and gave him three half crown for earnest. Afterwards Purfield agrees with the defendant Shimmin for the purchase of these lands at two a clock and the conveyances being ready engrossed, the name of Manly was struck out, and Shimmin put in, and they were executed at eight a clock when Shimmin had notice of Baily's interest, and Mrs Baily and her trustee brought this bill to set aside this conveyance.

Mr Calaghan for the defendants

This agreement between Mrs Baily and Purfield ought not to be carried into execution, because it was not mutual, for she being a feme covert[615] it could not bind her, and there is no proof that this money was the arrear of the rents of the houses which were settled on her, or the interest of the £500. A feoffment[616] indeed to a feme covert [135] binds the feoffor, because the agreement is executed.

2. But she had a power to make such an agreement. She had also a power to waive it, which she has done. Purfield came to her and told her the deed was engrossed. She told him she was not ready. 'Why then', says he 'I must go to the country'. 'Do as you please', said she, so this parol agreement is waived by parol.

3. The Statute of Frauds etc. is a direct ban in this case. Trusts indeed that have been carried into execution by paying the consideration may have been adjudged out of the statute, because in equity the estate is no longer the owner's,[617] he having received a satisfaction for it; but here she paid only three half crowns earnest, and £3 after which is a trifling consideration.

Mr Daly

Here is only a communication of an agreement though Burnaby drew the deed. This was not a writing within the statute, because he was empowered only by Purfield to draw up a draft, whereas every agreement ought to be signed by the party, or by one authorised by him. Paying part of the consideration don't take it out of the statute, for that relates only to earnest on a sale of goods.

---

[615] LF. married woman.

[616] A means of conveyance of freehold at common law.

[617] Once there is an enforceable agreement, equity imposes a form of trust on the vendor, also called the purchaser's equity.

Mr Attorney General for the plaintiffs

First, Mrs Baily is to be considered as a feme sole, and could contract.

2. This agreement ought to be carried into execution.

3. The Statute of Frauds is out of the case.

4. Shimmin is a volunteer. Purfield owned[618] the agreement, and Shimmin is to be considered as his trustee.

By deed, previous to her marriage several houses and £500 was settled on Mrs Baily for her separate use, as to which she is to be considered as a feme sole, and they are not liable to the debts of the husband, [136] but she may dispose of them as she pleases. Purfield mortgages to Manly who was her trustee, for £50, and she agrees to pay him £50 for the equity of redemption. Shimmin makes the objection, who was not one of the contracting parties, and Purfield owns the agreement.

But suppose her a married woman, and employed for Mr Baily or Manly, their agreement would be binding, and Shimmin himself prevents the agreement from being executed.

This agreement is executed, the sum agreed for is received in part, the deed was drawn, and would have been perfected if Manly, the trustee, had been in the way, and she and her trustee were before in possession by preception[619] of the rents and profits, 1 Vern. 363, *Butcher* v. *Staly*,[620] putting in cattle was adjudged an execution of agreement.

But here is a fraud in Shimmin who sets up the statute, for he is the person who hinders Purfield to execute the deeds. If a son hinders his father from executing a will, by telling him he would see the legacies paid, and that they were his sisters, as well as that other's daughters, a court of equity will compel him to pay the legacies.[621]

Shimmin is a mere volunteer, for they have not proved the payment of any money.

Mr Stannard

I shall first consider this case as if Purfield only was before the court, and then as Shimmin is a defendant.

Purfield hearing Mrs Baily had money to put out, applied to her for £50, and for securing the repayment of the money made a mortgage to Manly her trustee. Purfield swears in his answer ['] I wanting more money applied to her and came to an agreement, but I don't remember for what, and I believe Manly and Baily are willing and ready to perform the agreement, so the trustee assents to this agreement, and therefore it is mutual[']. [137] But many agreements with minors and feme coverts[622] though not mutual are carried into execution, and the bargain shan't be avoided, because they knew they were not in their own power;[623] but here Purfield knew she had money.

---

[618] Eighteenth-century usage. Johnson's *Dictionary*: 1. To acknowledge; to avow for one's own.

[619] The right to receive.

[620] *Butcher* v. *Stapely* (1685) 1 Vern. 363, 23 E.R. 524 (a parol-agreement for a purchase and possession delivered, decreed to be performed against a subsequent purchaser with notice, who had a conveyance, and paid his money).

[621] Note that it would impose a constructive trust.

[622] *Sic.* femes covert.

[623] I.e. *sui iuris*, of full legal capacity.

As to the statute, it don't say that money given shall be binding, but only as to goods, yet wherever an agreement touching lands is executed in part, a court of equity will carry it into execution. The £3 note was not earnest, but an execution of the agreement, and part of the execution money, and equity carries such agreements into execution, because though the first treaty shan't bind, yet the further consideration shows a deliberate consent.

Lombard v. *Poltney*:[624] The agreement was to be in writing. The defendant refused to sign the writing. The court would not tie him up.

Calaghan v. *Dixon*[625] in this court. Dixon was a lessee under the Hollow Blades[626] with a condition to surrender upon notice. Hedges their agent gave him notice to surrender in May, and then sent to him to deliver the possession, which he received from the stewards. But the surrender not being in writing, Dixon brought an ejectment and recovered his lease. But Lord Chief Baron Gilbert granted a perpetual injunction, because it was executed by delivering the possession, and his Lordship said, that the statute[627] was made to prevent frauds and sudden bargains, and that Dixon should not set up the statute to support a fraud in himself. So that a parol agreement carried deliberately into execution shall bind.[628]

Shimmin is to be considered as Purfield, because he had notice of some agreement, and he ought at his peril to inquire what. He had a caution given him, and so the general notice is to affect him. He had notice at the time he paid his money, though not when he made the agreement. He should have kept his money. The agreement was at two a clock, and the deed was executed at eight, then he had notice, and Manly's name was erased [*138*] and his put in.

Mr Malone

Here are two bills, the original for an execution of the agreement, and a cross bill to redeem, and that Manly might assign the mortgage. Purfield gave directions to Burnaby to reduce the agreement into writing, which he did accordingly, and delivered it to him, and Purfield carried it to Manly to be executed, who happened to be from home. This agreement then ought to be carried into execution notwithstanding the Statute of Frauds, against Purfield on his own confession, and is not to be considered as a parol agreement, because it was ordered to be reduced into writing. 2 Vern. 200, *Cook* v. *Mascal.*[629]

The next day the lord chief baron delivered the opinion of the court.

Ord in. Canc. 167.   This is an agreement carried partly into execution, because not only earnest, but part of the consideration money was paid in pursuance of the bargain, and *Butcher* v. *Staly*[630] in 1 Vernon is a case in point. So in the case of an attornment,[631] and where the key is accepted, though the surrender is not in writing, it is good.

---

[624] No citation given.

[625] No citation given.

[626] Above, p. 1 n. 7.

[627] The Statute of Frauds (Ir.), 1695, 7 Will. III, c. 12 (Ir.).

[628] Gilbert here applies the doctrine of part performance. Although the statute required writing for a contract concerning land, equity would not allow a person to use this as a means itself of fraud, and held that part performance of the contract by the other party made the contract enforceable.

[629] *Cookes* v. *Mascall* (1690) 2 Vern. 200, 23 E.R. 730 (marriage articles in writing, not signed, decreed to be performed).

[630] *Butcher* v. *Stapely* (1685) 1 Vern. 363, 23 E.R. 524.

[631] I.e. acknowledgement that a person is a tenant.

Purfield knew Mrs Baily had money of her own, and treated with her on that account. This agreement is not out of the Statute, though it was reduced into writing by the direction of the parties, because it was not signed.

An answer in another cause can't be read in equity, or an exhibit proved *viva voce* without an order, because the only evidence in a court of equity are the depositions taken in the cause. But an answer may be read on a trial, because everything may be given in evidence to a jury. [*139*]

Monday, January the 24 [1732][632]

In Chancery

MOREHEAD v. LORD HOATH

A motion was made that it might be referred to a master to see who put Mr Geoffry Green's name to exceptions to an answer, and the motion was granted at peril of costs, though it was said to be the usual course never to make this motion without a certificate of the counsel, that he never signed the pleading.

Friday, May the 9th, [1732][633]

The first day of the Easter Term.

EDGWORTH v. DEMAR

In Chancery

The bill was brought to set aside a mortgage, and charged that his father who made it was only tenant for life, and that the mortgagor knew him to be so, having joined in a deed wherein the marriage articles were recited. Mr Coke formerly a notary public was one of the witnesses to the deed, and the plaintiff who was of a noted bad character went down to Finglass, and asked him if the name Coke to the deed was not in his handwriting, and he saying he believed it was, he hurried him to the Lion Tavern in Warbughs Street[634] [*sic*] to make affidavit of the execution of it before Dr Stephens, in order as he pretended to have it enrolled, which he never had done, and it was now moved for Mr Coke and the defendant, that this deed might be produced for his inspection, and that such orders had often been made by the court on a gross suspicion. And the Lord Chancellor made no order at this time to see if Mr Edgworth would consent to bring it before a master, but declared he would not

---

[632] 24 January was a Monday in 1732, Kratz, *Hist. Cal.*

[633] 9 May was a Tuesday in 1732 (Julian), Kratz, *Hist. Cal.* It was a Friday in 1729 and 1735, and a Sunday in 1731, but it seems likely the year is 1732, given the dates on either side. Note there is a gap here from the previous case between January and May, but earlier cases, above, are from February 1732.

[634] Werburgh Street, behind Dublin Castle. Named after St Werburgh's Church. See Gilbert, *A History of the City of Dublin*, i.43. Craig, *Dublin 1660–1860*, p. 178.

scruple to make such an order. The plaintiff having imposed on the master in taking the affidavit, without having any thoughts to enrol the deed, instead of proving it in the common way. [*140*]

In Chancery

Ante 118. Post 395.
MSS ord in. Canc.
93, 95.

A witness examined in chief may prove an exhibit after publication, and in the case of Colonel Sandford on a motion to suppress the depositions of a witness who had been examined on two commissions, the present lord chancellor ordered all the depositions to be suppressed, but to the execution of the deeds.

Friday, May the 26th. [1732][635]

In Chancery

SIR ROBERT ECHLIN v. MAURICE KEATING

The bill was filed against the father of the defendant in 1725, and the original bill of discovery against the defendant in 1730, and the defendant being in contempt to a serjeant at arms, put in a plea of a purchaser etc., and in July last moved to have it received, and the order was suspended, to see if the defendant would waive his privilege, and now when privilege is out, he moved again to have the plea received, but the motion was denied, because it was so long since rendered, and a plea is

Ante 58. a privilege to the party which the plaintiff can't force him to, though he may to answer.[636]

HOPKINS ET AL. v. STRETCH

In Chancery

A motion was made for the plaintiffs, that the deputation of the master of the rolls might be ordered to be read on the trial, on affidavit that the witnesses were men of business who lived in London, and could not be present at the trial.

The court denied the motion, because the plaintiffs had a remedy by rehearing their cause, and that this would be to alter the decree, which did not direct a trial, (in which case the lord chancellor thought he had a power over the terms of it) but only that the bill should be retained, that the plaintiff Hopkins might be at liberty to try his [plea] at law.

In Exchequer

The court don't give costs on discharging a notice, but won't let them move again without paying costs. [*141*]

---

[635] 26 May was indeed a Friday in 1732 (Julian), Kratz, *Hist. Cal.*.
[636] Below, p. 136.

MAIN ET AL. v. ROSE

In Exchequer

Wednesday, May the 17 [1732][637]

Mr Prime Serjeant objected to the reading the depositions of Zachariah Ward, a trustee in the settlement, because he was concerned in interest, being a co-plaintiff, and so liable to costs, if the bill should be dismissed; but as he was a party not concerned in interest, they might have struck him out before examination.

But the right way would have been to have made him a defendant, and then he might have disclaimed all interest upon oath, and the plaintiff is not entitled to costs against his own trustee, or if he was, there is a difference between his being plaintiff, and a defendant. A man may be made a defendant whether he will or not, but the commencing [of] a suit is his own act.[638]

The objection was allowed.

FARE v. CAESAR COUGHLEY ET AL.

In Exchequer

Saturday, May the 20th [1732][639]

Mr Stannard moved for a writ of estrepement to stay waste, and quiet the possession, that Dudley Coughley set out the bounds himself, and after 26 years quiet enjoyment by the plaintiff and those under who he claims, Caesar the son entered on the lands with 150 men, took away the wood and bark that had been cut and felled by the plaintiff, and was cutting down himself, and carrying away as fast as he could, and prayed that the writ might be directed to the sheriff, the force being so flagrant.

But Mr Malone said that was never granted but in case of an habitation.

The court granted the estrepement, and an injunction to the party.

The steward has been allowed to swear to a long enjoyment, where his principal was in England. [*142*]

Tuesday, May the 23rd [1732][640]

In Exchequer

MANWARING v. MCNAMARA

The bill was brought on the Popery Acts to have the benefit of a lease. The defendant put in three short answers, wherein he denied that the lease was in trust for the Papist,

---

[637] 17 May 1732 was indeed a Wednesday in 1732, Kratz, *Hist. Cal.* Note that the date is earlier than the previous case.

[638] I.e. a person can be compelled to be a defendant, but not a plaintiff.

[639] 20 May was a Saturday in 1732, Kratz, *Hist. Cal.*

[640] 23 May 1732 was a Tuesday in 1732, Kratz, *Hist. Cal.*

and the process being carried on to a sequestration, the bill was now decreed to be taken *pro confesso*.

The certificate of the three short answers was read, but the court would not allow the answers to be read.

MSS̃ cas. in Canc. A, 434, 574. D, 421. Hob. 115. *Glanvil v. Allen's Case.*[641]

Mr Calaghan objected that such a decree was erroneous, the material parts of the bill being denied by the answers, and that no judgment by default could be given on a bad plea; and that the defendant ought to answer *in vinculis.*[642]

LORD DARNLY v. CUSACK

In Exchequer

Lord Chief Baron

The question is, whether if an answer on another cause is read against a man, he can Ante 46. read it for him? In the case of *Lynch* v. *Kirwan*[643] a man's answer saved his ears,[644] and if you read a man's answer not in the cause, he may read it not only to explain that part, but to prove the contrary, for if you cross examine a witness, you establish his testimony though he is ever so interested.

But Sir John St Leger being of another opinion the answer was not suffered to be read for him, he said, that then a man might own some trifling matters, and swear to others in his own favour.

Another question was, whether parol proof, whether [*sic*] the depositions of Hopkins might be read to explain an agreement between John Bligh and Edward Cusack?

Mr Attorney General

MSS̃ cas. in Canc. A.242, 431. D.50. B.113, 145, 202.

2 Vern. 99.[648] (94)

252[649] (240).
648[650] (578).
675[651] (602).

Since the Statute of Frauds such proof is not allowed [*143*] either as to a deed or will of lands, but may as to a will of personal estate, as if there are two Edwards, to explain which shall have a legacy,[645] or that the executor shall have the residue in affirmance of the law,[646] but what relates to lands cannot be explained dehors,[647] and though this is but an agreement, 'tis to be considered in equity as executed, and must be proved by itself. The question is, whether they are to have the lands for 18 years, though the agreement says they are to have them only for 14, 'tis to give them a term of four years.

---

[641] *Glanvile and Allen's Case* (1616) Hob. 115, 80 E.R. 264.

[642] L. in bonds, fetters.

[643] No citation given.

[644] Perhaps refers to loss of ears or nailing of ears to the pillory for perjury. See pp. cii and clviii, above.

[645] If a gift was made to 'my nephew Edward' and there were two nephews called Edward, extrinsic evidence was admissible to show which the testator intended to benefit, since either one would answer the description in the will.

[646] I.e. at common law.

[647] LF. outside, i.e. evidence outside the will.

[648] *Towers* v. *Moore* (1689) 2 Vern. 98, 23 E.R. 673 (extrinsic evidence to explain a will), and see *Fane* v. *Fane* (1681) 1 Vern. 30 at 31, 23 E.R. 284 and case cited there in n. 2.

[649] *Countess of Gainsborough* v. *Earl of Gainsborough* (1691) 2 Vern. 252, 23 E.R. 764.

[650] *Lady Granvill* v. *Duchess of Beaufort* (1709) 2 Vern. 648, 23 E.R. 1023.

[651] *Ball* v. *Smith* (1711) 2 Vern. 675, 23 E.R. 1039.

Lord Chief Baron

In the case of *Archer* v. *Rochfort*[652] where the covenant was to make such a reasonable term as the plaintiff should desire, we thought 61 years a reasonable term, on proof that Rochfort generally made such leases, but there originally was no certainty in the words.

Mr Calaghan

This proof has been often allowed since the Statute of Frauds. In the case of *Foord* v. *Foord* in this court, where a doubt was on the will of Alderman Foord,[653] Stretch[654] who drew up the draft was read to his intention, and this was allowed on debate in the House of Lords.[655] They say the court would suffer proof to be read contrary to the plain words that he shall have but 14 years. We would read to prove that Bligh at that time apprehended he had only an interest for 14 years.

Mes App. A.9. E.535, 803.

Mr Daly

A will of lands ought to be in writing before the Statute of Frauds, yet the rule has always been, where the words were doubtful, to allow evidence not inconsistent with the will to explain them.[656]

Lord Chief Baron

In wills the court have [*sic*] gone a great way to explain the intention, and agreements also are founded [*144*] on the intention. These articles consist of two parts, a present demise, and a covenant for renewal if Mr Bligh take the said farm from Edward Corker, and this proof is to explain it to be a lease for the 18 years the time he had from Corker expressly agreement the words.

Hopkins can't be read.

HARVEY v. KENNEDY

In Exchequer

If a cause is set down to be heard by order *ad requisitionem def[enden]tis*, the order need not be served, but the defendants must serve a subpœna to hear judgment in the same manner as if they were plaintiffs, and the plaintiff may proceed to a hearing if he will, or the bill will be dismissed.

Here was no standing rule, but the court adjudged it not necessary.

---

[652] No citation given.

[653] John Foord, alderman of the city of Limerick: (1730) 3 Bro. P.C. at 127.

[654] It appears from *Foord* v. *Foord* (1730) 3 Bro. P.C. at 127 that his name was Bartholemew Stretch. No barrister or attorney of that name is listed in KI AP for the period. KI AP are incomplete: see KI AP, p. viii.

[655] *Foord* v. *Foord* (1730) 3 Bro. P.C. 2nd ed. 124, 1 E.R. 1219.

[656] This was the main rule as to the admission of extrinsic evidence in wills in the Republic of Ireland before section 90 of the Succession Act, 1965.

Friday, May the 12th. [1732][657]

CLERK v. SMYTH

In Exchequer

The cause was heard in exceptions to the officer's report, and all the exceptions being overruled, the court decreed the money to be paid though the cause was not set down on the report, and laid this down as a settled difference, that where the report leaves nothing to be done, the court will give judgment overruling the exceptions, but not where the order of reference is only interlocutory.

Saturday, May the 13 [1732][658]

In Exchequer

JOHNSON v. MARLAY

Ante 58. The chief baron mentioned the case of *Overand* v. *St John*, where the bill was dismissed in Chancery on his motion, it appearing by the plaintiffs own showing that he had been 109 years out of possession, but the court denied a motion to dismiss a bill for payment of a note for money won at play which was assigned over to the plaintiff, though there had been a decree on the [*145*] Civil Bill Act,[659] and an appeal which was dismissed for want of prosecution, because these facts did not appear by the Bill itself.

[Inserted note: Friday, November the 8. 1734. In Exchequer. Bill for relief against a decree on the Civil Bill Act dismissed with costs, on the motion of Mr Steward. *Gordon* v. *Matthew*.]

Sir John St Leger

If the defendant files a cross bill before issue is joined, he has a right to stop the plaintiff till he puts in an answer, that both causes may proceed *pari passu*;[660] but though by the general rule if he stays till after issue is joined, he can't stop the plaintiff but only oblige him to answer before he brings his cause to a hearing, yet if the plaintiff in the original cause is in contempt for not answering the cross bill, the court will not only stop the hearing of his cause, but publication also till he puts in

Ante 89. his answer, and then indeed when he has answered and cleared his contempts, he shall not be obliged to stop till they come up to him in the other cause.

---

[657] 12 May was a Friday in 1732, Kratz, *Hist. Cal.*
[658] 13 May was a Saturday in 1732, Kratz, *Hist. Cal.*
[659] 2 Geo. I, c. 11 (Ir.), 1715 (small debts), 1 Geo. II, c. 14 (Ir.), 1727 (Act to amend 2 Geo. I, c. 11). Above, p. cii.
[660] L. equally, without preference.

Monday, May the 15. [1732][661]

In Exchequer

CRANSTON v. EVANS

Mr Daly pro defendant

Tithe of mills are only payable by custom. They are not renovant,[662] but arise by the labour of man. 1 Rol. Rep. 405,[663] Lit. Rep. 314,[664] Cro. Ja. 523.[665]

Here are two mills under the same roof, and we build a new mill on the same race, this is not tithable. You may have estovers[666] though the chimneys are new built, and if the stream is changed by time, it is lawful to follow it, and the prescription is not lost, 1 Rol. Ab. 652.[667] So the plaintiffs have no tithe, because they have proved no prescription.

Mr Parkinson[668]

It appears by the Statute of *Articuli Cleri*[669] that old [*146*] mills are not tithable. This to be presumed an old mill, and no tithe was paid for 36 years, and they have made proof that 13s & 4d was paid for composition.

Mr Fortescue

The plaintiffs set them forth to be old mills. 4 Mod. 45.[670]

Mr Prime Serjeant for the plaintiffs

Here are two mills upon an ancient water under one roof, and the plaintiff as rector claims the tithes of these mills, or a composition if any such there be for the old mill, and tithes for the other.

The Second Institute[671] shows how the law stands. I agree since *Articuli Cleri*[672] no tithes in specie are to be paid for old mills, but the question is, what is an old mill

---

[661]   15 May was a Monday in 1732, Kratz, *Hist. Cal.*

[662]   Renewing, increasing by renewal.

[663]   *Jakes Case* (1616) 1 Rolle 405, 81 E.R. 568.

[664]   *Prohibition* (1629) Lit. 314, 124 E.R. 263.

[665]   *Danderidge* v. *Johnson* (1618) Cro. Jac. 523, 79 E.R. 448 (tithes not payable by common right for the profits arising from a fulling-mill, being personal).

[666]   Necessaries allowed by law. It is unclear what is meant in this context.

[667]   1 Roll. Abr. 652.

[668]   Probably Robert Parkinson, s. and heir of Edward, Ardee, Co. Louth, Doctor of Divinity. Educated, Trinity College Dublin, Middle Temple, June 1715; KI, Easter term, 1720. d. March 1761, KI AP, p. 394.

[669]   9 Edw. II, c. 1 (Eng.), 1315.

[670]   *Grimly* v. *Fawlkingham* (1691) 4 Mod. 45, 87 E.R. 253.

[671]   2 Co. Inst. ch. 5, p. 621.

[672]   9 Edw. II, c. 1 (Eng.), 1315.

beyond memory? Your Lordship will suppose it an old mill, unless a modus or tithes have been paid for it, for these are an evidence it was built within memory, but the proving it to be built beyond memory is no proof of it being an old mill, where there is proof in the cause of a tithe or modus have been paid. And Rol. Rep. 405[673] is no authority to the contrary. In 3 Bulst. 212[674] the same case is thus reported. There was a modus for mills, and the tithe of them was sued for. The occupier prayed a prohibition on suggestion of the modus, which was granted, and the next case in Bulstrode is a demonstration of it. A prohibition was prayed on suggestion of a modus for mills erected or to be erected, a new mill was built, and the court said, the modus can't go to the new mill, but allowed it as to the old.

If a mill lies waste, it yield [sic] no grist, no toll, yet when it brings in a profit, it shall pay, Cro. Ja. 429.[675] And all mills pay tithe without dispute. The question then is, what the parson is entitled to? [147] He charges himself to be entitled either to the tithes, or the composition money.

As to two old mills under one roof, though one is disused, the miller shall pay the whole. The act of the party shan't vary the modus. But here the miller thinks fit not to use one of his mills, but to build a new one on the same race as they swear, but our proofs are that the stream is different. But suppose it to be on the old stream, the tithe is payable for it. Where the mill race indeed is diverted by the act of the [sic] God, as by a storm, or the like, the miller may follow the stream, and the modus shall follow the new mill, and it shan't pay tithes, 1 Rol. Abr. 641, 652. But here is no proof why the miller disused the old one, or built a new mill, but suppose as they say, that he built it for his greater profit, he ought to pay tithes.

The question then remains, what shall be paid for the old mills? They say nothing, and we have made proof that 13s 4d, 6s 8d, and 40s has been paid, and your Lordship will consider that the parson comes into the parish a stranger, and not under the advantages of an heir.

Suppose then a composition is paid for two mills under one roof, and one is taken down, is the act of the party to lessen the demand of the minister, and vary, the modus.

Mr Lindsay

An old mill shan't pay tithe on the authority of *Articuli Cleri*, unless there is evidence that tithes or a modus have been paid for it, 1 Rol. Ab. 652. *De molendina nova erecta non jacet prohibitio*,[676] and 'tis a settled distinction whether the mill is old or new. If 'tis new and erected within the memory of man the court won't grant a prohibition. And your Lordship is to decree according to law not equity.

Maclanaghan sued for tithes of a new mill. A prohibition was granted in the Common Pleas, and the [148] rule was made by Mr Justice Macartney,[677] that they should declare in prohibition, and if it appeared to be a new mill that no prohibition

[673] *Jakes Case* 1 Roll. Rep. 405, 81 E.R. 568.

[674] *Jakes* v. *J.S.* (1616) 3 Bulst. 212, 81 E.R. 178.

[675] *Anonymous* (1617) Cro. Jac. 429, 79 E.R. 367 (new mill liable to tithe, though erected on land discharged of tithe).

[676] Prohibition does not lie for a recently erected mill.

[677] James Macartney (1651–1727), appointed 2nd J.K.B., 1701, superseded 1711 because of his political opinions, appointed successively 2nd J. and 3rd J. of the C.P. on the accession of George I in 1714. Ball, *Judges in Ireland*, ii. 65.

should go, and issue was joined, and found to be a new mill. Chamberlayn sued for tithes of a new mill in Chancery[678] in the time of Sir Constantine Phipps, and the House of Lords[679] decreed him the tithe, every tenth toll dish.

As to the old mills we have proved our predecessors received 13s & 4d. Now the question is, whether this shall be apportioned? And that it shall not appears from the authority of the 4 Mod. 45,[680] that has been quoted by the other side. Two stones being added to the mill, the parson sues for tithes. A prohibition was moved for and granted on the prescription, because it was still *unu[m] molendinum*,[681] so estovers belong to the house though more chimneys are erected; since then the prescription continues where there are two stones instead of one, it is equal justice it should; where one mill only works.

On Saturday July the 6th [1732][682]

being the last day of the following Hilary Term, the chief baron delivered the opinion of the court.

This bill is brought to have an account and payment of the tithe of one mill, or a prescriptive sum for it, and to have the tithe of the other set out and paid. Mills since *Articuli Cleri* are tithable, and as much a charge on the land as any prescriptive right to the landlord. They belong of common right to the rector or vicar, and under their titles by the Dissolution, etc. and no one is injured by paying what is inherent to his estate.

The new mill that is erected must pay tithe [*149*] by the authority in Roll[e']s if the stream is not altered by the hand of God, and the tithe is the tenth toll dish, and the defendant must account for it accordingly. If a mill continues on the same foundation, though new stones or wheels are added, 'tis still the old mill, Carth. 215,[683] 4 Mod. 45.[684]

The plaintiff having demanded only the prescription as to the ancient mills, is entitled to it.

---

[678] See *Newte* v. *Chamberlaine* (1706) 2 Eq. Cas. Abr. 732, 22 E.R. 617; see also *Peirson* v. *Miles* (1702) Colles 263, 1 E.R. 278 (ancient mill).

[679] *Chamberlaine* v. *Newte* (1706) 7 Bro. P.C. 2nd ed. 3, 3 E.R. 2.

[680] *Grimly* v. *Fawlkingham* (1691) 4 Mod. 45, 87 E.R. 253.

[681] L. one mill.

[682] 6 July was Thursday in 1732, Kratz, *Hist. Cal.*, but the note below date says it was the last day of the following term.

[683] *Gumble* v. *Falkingham* (1692) Carth. 215, 90 E.R. 729.

[684] *Grimly* v. *Fawlkingham* (1691) 4 Mod. 45, 87 E.R. 253.

Monday, May the 8th [1732]

In Exchequer

MARY HODSON
WIDOW AND ADMINISTRATRIX OF RICHARD HODSON DECEASED v. ROWLEY & UXR.[685]

Mr Prime Serjeant for the defendants

It is agreed that here was a subsisting interest in Thomas Dawson the elder (which was to determine in 1705) in 1692 when Clotworthy Upton took a new lease for 4 years to commence in 1705, in trust for the said Thomas Dawson as it was understood by the tenants and the country, and one gave a fine to Thomas the elder's wife, and two milch cows. Clotworthy Upton executes a letter of attorney to Arthur Upton to make leases, and he by virtue of thereof perfects the leases in question to Hodson and Henderson. The only proof of this letter is by Jackson, who only says, that he saw such a letter signed by Clotworthy Upton to make leases of the Manor of Drapers. He don't say, that he saw it executed, or was a witness to it. The legal proof of it is to produce it, and show it was executed. No copy of it is produced, to show whether the power warrants the leases, and there ought to be the strictest proof of it, since this is a power rarely granted to make leases indefinitely and [150] by a trustee too, without the privity or consent of the cestui que trust.

We swear, that in 1705 the lands were worth above £50 a year more than the rent reserved, and the question is, if here is sufficient evidence to establish these leases against the defendant, who is a purchaser by marriage?

If the letter of attorney is good and proved, this is only an equitable demise, for it is not made in the name of the principal, nor is his name and seal put to it.

There are many cases of conveyances and leases where equity won't interpose. The plaintiffs are purchasers not at the full improved rent. It is a fraud to take such a lease from a trustee himself without the privity of the cestui que trust, and equity won't establish it at least against a real purchaser. Length of time can be no objection to us. Thomas the father died before the commencement of the lease in reversion, and his son and daughter were infants, and the defendant was not at age till 1726. Joshua Dawson in 1709 executed a bond to Andrew Henderson and John Hodson in the penalty of £500, to confirm the lease to Andrew and John, an account of their attornment[686] to Joshua, and there is no proof that Mr Rowley the purchaser had any notice of this bond.

Objection: Mr Rowley, since his marriage, has confirmed these leases as appears by the receipts of Mr Cunningham his agent.

By the private Act of Parliament[687] several annuities were charged on this term. He was receiver for the annuitants, and gave the receipts on their account. In April

---

[685] Resumed on p. 125.
[686] I.e. acknowledgement of being a tenant.
[687] Below, p. 239. 'To enable Thomas Dawson of Castle Dawson, in Co. Londonderry, esq. to make sale of several lands for payment of debts, and for making provision out of other lands for Olivia Dawson his wife,

and August 1729 there are indeed two receipts given by Mr Rowley for rent, but they won't amount to a confirmation. Mr Rowley had before that time brought an ejectment, and the plaintiffs their bill. The intention in paying or receiving is to determine the Act. Now here one was suing at law to break the leases, and the other in equity for relief, and [*151*] to have them established. 1 Vern. 227, *Philips* v. *The Duke of Bucks.*[688]

Mr Stannard

We have the legal right because they have given us judgment at law, then let us see what equitable circumstances there are to divest us of it. A power given to a tenant for life to make leases won't warrant a lease in reversion, no more will a letter of attorney; and if I have only a reversion, I must wait till it comes in possession. If Clotworthy Upton had made these leases, equity would not interpose, but if he had only executed an article, this court would not establish and carry it into execution, because it would be a breach of trust in him to set the lands ten years beforehand, for he could not tell what value the lands would be of when the lease was to commence; the Popery Acts that say that leases are to be made at full two thirds of their real value, don't in words prohibit leases in reversion, but do in effect, because it is uncertain whether the rent reserved will be two thirds of the value of the land when the lease is to take effect in point of interest.

Since we don't know what are the words of it, we must suppose this to be a common letter of attorney to make leases.

Hudson and Henderson had in 1699 an interest under the old lease from Thomas Dawson, and this bond was only to confirm that interest.

Mr Calaghan

This lease is void in law because it is made in the attorney's name and signed by him; and a general receipt given to a man who has a void or voidable lease does not confirm it, as was adjudged by Lord Midleton[689] in the case of *Butler* v. *Worth*[690] and of *Lord Kingston* v. *Lord Shelburn.*[691] Tenant for life makes a lease which is void by his death. The remainderman receives the rent. This is no confirmation either in law or equity, because the tenant is in possession in nature of a tenant at will, the lease being void at law. [*152*]

Lord Chief Baron

But Lord Midleton[692] said it might amount to a new agreement.

and Arabella Dawson, late wife of Thomas Dawson the younger, his son, deceased, for their several jointures, and for Joshua Dawson and Arabella Dawson, infants, children of Thomas Dawson, deceased', 4 Ann., c. 7 (Ir.) (private). The long titles of Irish private Acts are listed in vol. 8 of the Irish *Statutes at Large.* There is a list of private statute rolls in *Irish Records Commission Reports, 8th Report, 1819,* Supplement pp. 380–83, but the titles of the statutes are only occasionally mentioned and the text is not reproduced. The original statutes held in the Public Record Office were destroyed in the fire of 1922. Individual printed statutes may survive in family papers.

[688] *Phillips* v. *Duke of Bucks* (1683) 1 Vern. 227, 23 E.R. 432.
[689] Spelled 'Middleton' in MS. Above, p. clix and p. 22 n. 135.
[690] No citation given. See *Worth* v. *Butler,* below, p. 245.
[691] No citation given.
[692] Spelled 'Middleton' in MS. Above, n. 689.

Mr Calaghan

It would not amount to a new agreement, because he was tenant at will, and it might amount to a payment of rent by him of such, and this receipt is only of so much rent for such townlands, but don't say under, or in pursuance of such a lease.

Post 227.   In the case of *Hodder* v. *Roberts*, the defendant had the settlement before him, by which his wife was entitled to £1,500. His counsel thought she had only a right to £500, which he receives, and gives a general release. The Lord Chief Baron Gilbert called this a release *in errorem*, and that it would not bind him, because he was misled by his counsel.

Mr Malone

Supposing the letter proved, it was a fraud in Clotworthy Upton to give a power to make leases without the concurrence of the cestui que trust. Here is a foundation to set aside these contracts, but the question now is, whether the court will establish them against a purchaser, which it would not do even against the party, unless the agreement was with a good conscience.

Brown v. *Rice*[693] in Chancery. There was an agreement for a sale of lands. The bill was brought for a specific execution of the agreement, and a cross bill to set it aside for fraud. The court stood neuter, and would not establish or set aside the agreement, because the purchase was obtained by surprise, and the other was to blame in some circumstances.

A void act is not capable of confirmation. Minors indeed after they come of age may make good things that are voidable.

In the case of *Taylor* v. *Logville*[694] in Chancery the case was dismissed, because the remainderman receives rent generally, that don't establish the lease. [*153*] Mr Jackson was examined for the plaintiffs to prove that there was such a letter of attorney. On his cross examination he was asked, whether he had a lease under this letter (he said he had) and whether he was interested (he said he was not) and it was objected that he was not a competent witness, because it did not appear that his lease was determined, and if he had assigned it over, he was still liable in covenant, though not in debt, and accountable for the mesne profits.

Contra: you may examine a witness on a voir dire[695] whether he is interested, and if he says he is not, you may examine him as to particulars. But you cannot prove the contrary by witnesses. It is to be presumed he has not the lease, and he might never have been in possession. He paid the reserved rent, and is not accountable for the real value, and Mr Rowley who has the counterparts of all the leases, might show the lease to be still in being, if it was so.

To this the defendants replied, that they could not examine to this fact, because they had cross examined him, which they might either do, or prove it by witnesses, or exhibit articles to his credit.

---

[693] No citation given.
[694] No citation given.
[695] I.F. oath to speak the truth when examined.

Lord Chief Baron

I think Jackson may be read. 'Tis the apprehension of the party that makes him a competent witness or not. He swears he is not interested, and though he may be obliquely accountable for the profits, if he thought he was not concerned, he was under no prejudice.   Post 154, 302.

May the 3rd [1732]

In Exchequer

WELDON v. LORD FINGAL, & È CONTRA

Weldon as agent charged himself with the receipts of all the rents from such a time, and in a schedule set forth so much to be in arrear for that time in the tenant's hands. One of these explains the other, and he shan't be charged with all the rents, for it amounts to no more, than that he received all not in arrear.

HIGGINS v. LEIGH

In Exchequer

The defendant was obliged at the hearing to produce the will of his brother James Leigh without an order because of [*154*] the words in his answer: 'Ready to be produced.'

HODSON v. ROWLEY [696]

Mr Attorney General for the plaintiffs

I humbly hope we shall have an injunction to stay the defendant's proceedings on the ejectment. Nineteen thousand acres in the hands of Protestants depend on this question.   Ante 149.

1. I shall consider the three leases, because there is a difference between the Grand one[697] in 1696, and the two others in 1698.

2. How things stood when the Grand one was made. Thomas Dawson the grandfather, who had a lease from the Drapers company to expire in 1705, made a lease in 1692 to Hodson and Henderson.

The said Thomas Dawson being a bad manager, Clotworthy Upton, whose sister he had married, without any application from him to whom he gave the benefit of it, takes a new lease of these lands, whereby he makes himself subject to the rent, and

[696] Continued from p. 122. Resumed on p. 235.
[697] I.e. the head lease.

a fine of £3,000, then he had it in his power to dispose of this lease as he pleased, because he was no original trustee, and it don't appear when he declared the trust.

Supposing him originally a trustee, yet as he had the legal estate in him, if we had no knowledge of his being so, the objection of the trustee is at an end. Now there is no proof that Henderson or Hudson knew of the trust when they took the lease.

But if they had notice, this differs from the common case, because he was no original trustee, but had an interest coupled with his power to see the rent and fine paid.

Thomas Dawson the grandfather having married his sister, the cestui que trust was his nephew. So it stands on the trust.

Next let us consider it as it stands on the lease. The letter of attorney don't appear, and it cannot be expected we should have it, because it extends to so many thousand acres.

But Arthur Upton a gentleman of character recites the letter and when it bore date in our lease, [155] which he could not be mistaken in, and the witnesses are Thomas Dawson the grandfather, William Cunningham, who had married another sister of Clotworthy Upton, and John Upton son of Arthur Upton and brother of Clotworthy. All these must be supposed to be in combination against their own relations in favour of a stranger. This is a family affair, and the witnesses were not called in by chance.

If there was no evidence but this recital, it would not perhaps bind the defendant, because he does not derive under Arthur Upton.

Mr Jackson says he was the clerk who engrossed the leases, and saw the letter of attorney. His calling it a supposed and pretended letter arises from the words of the cross interrogatory.

Objection: This letter might be to make leases before 1705, and not in reversion.

This must be a letter to make leases in reversion, because Clotworthy Upton had no interest till 1705, and therefore he could not give a power to let before.

The possession and acquiescence is in our favour, not against us.

Here I rest it as to the two other leases, they not being included in the bond.

But Thomas Dawson the son, if there was any defect in the power, has confirmed the third lease.

In 1699 Lord Masareen[608] was a mortgagee in possession, and the family in order to prevail on the tenants to attorn[699] to Joshua to whom the original and reversionary lease[s] were at that time assigned, agree if they will attorn to him, to confirm. (The words are) the lease or minutes etc. which must be understood of this lease, because Arthur Upton had nothing to do with the original lease, and you won't intend that he did what he had no power to do, when he had a power in the other case, and though these are only the words of a condition of a bond, are entitled to a specific

---

698   *Sic.* Clotworthy Skeffington, 3rd Viscount Massereene (*c.* 1660–1714). He supported with his father the Protestant cause in Ulster, being colonel of a regiment of Foot, and joint commmander-in-chief of Co. Antrim. He was attainted by James II's Parliament in 1689, and restored by William III. He succeeded his father in 1695. He died at Antrim, 14 March 1713/4, and was buried there. His unusual Christian name came from Sir John Clotworthy of Co. Antrim, from whom he had inherited his title. Sir John had supported Cromwell and as a reward received the greater part of the vast forfeited estates of the marquess of Antrim. However, he was later instrumental in procuring the Restoration, and received another reward, being created, on 21 November 1660, baron of Loughneagh and Viscount Massereene, both in Co. Antrim. The grant contained, unusually in an Irish peerage, a special remainder, under which, failing heirs male of his body, the title was to pass to Sir John Skeffington, Bt, of Fisherwick (his son-in-law), and the issue male of John by Mary, his wife, the only child of the grantee, with ultimate remainder to the heirs general of his own body. Cokayne, *Complete Peerage*, viii. 545.

699   I.e. acknowledge themselves to be tenants.

execution of it, [*156*] and Thomas Dawson the son was made a party to it, to show his consent, because Joshua Dawson was only his trustee, and they can't show that these words relate to any other lease, so Thomas Dawson the son agrees that the leases and minutes made by Arthur Upton shall be made good.

Objection: This is a reversionary lease, and the lands are not set[700] at their full value.

The witnesses speak only as to their belief, and give no reason for it, whereas there is no proof the court ought to be more exact in, because there is a great variety opinions on this head, and no proof is made of the value in 1696.

There are some clauses in the lease worthy of observation for the advantage of the lessor. If the rent is not paid in 21 days after it becomes due, he may make the lease void, and there are covenants on the lease to improve, which have been carried into execution, and the value arises from these buildings and improvements since the commencement of the lease.

So they would destroy the lease, because the value is raised by improvements, which the lessee had covenants to make.

But if the lands have rose in value naturally, there was the same chance they might have fallen, and the making them this reversionary lease was the encouragement to them to build, otherwise they would not have laid out the money. Some improvements were made in 1696, 1699, and 1708, when an orchard was planted.

I shall next consider Mr Rowley's defence.

First, that the leases were not registered. They were made before the Registry Act.[701]

2. That he is a purchaser, and had no notice. The latter part of his answer takes away this defence, for it appears he had express, and implied notice. He applied to Mr Arthur Dawson, who sent him a paper, wherein he informs him that the manor was in lease for 11 years. Ought he not then to have inquired what leases were made? He says, he was [*157*] told Mr Arthur Dawson had the counterparts. Why then wouldn't he see them? But he wrote to a friend to get them, and they not coming he was resolved to marry, so he would not stay for them, but married.

Objection: One lease was for 13 years.

He ought to have inquired after the leases, and the point is, whether he had notice or not, and not what was the length of the leases.

But if Rowley had no information from Mr Arthur Dawson, here is what will amount to a notice in equity: he knew the lady was only in possession of the rents, and he ought to have gone down on the estate and made inquiry among the tenants. *Delap* v. *Richardson*:[702] Richardson having a college lease[703] executed minutes to under-tenants with covenants of renewal, and then sells the lease to Archdeknc, Hamilton and Matthews, who renew from the college. On a bill brought by the under-tenants for a renewal, they plead themselves purchasers without notice of these covenants of renewal, and the plea was allowed with costs, but being replied to, Lord Midleton[704] said the want of notice was their own fault, because they might have seen and known, though they had no actual notice. So Mr Rowley might have gone to the tenants, and known how they held.

---

[700] See above, p. 10 n. 59.
[701] Registration of Deeds Act, 1707, 6 Ann., c. 2 (Ir.).
[702] No citation given. See *Delap* v. *Hamilton*, below, p. 248.
[703] I.e. lease from Trinity College Dublin.
[704] Spelled 'Middleton' in MS. Above, p. clix and p. 22 n. 135.

Mr Cunningham is appointed receiver of all the whole manor, and Rowley empowers him by letter of attorney to give all proper receipts. They say these receipts were given on account of the annuities, and rentcharges. By the Act[705] the whole estate was vested in Brice the surviving trustee, who assigned to Rowley, and he in his answer says, that Cunningham received all the rents, and after payment of the annuities, applied the remainder in discharge of the £3,000 fine. The tenants paid their rents to Cunningham, not to the annuitants. Where a lease is void, receiving the rent can't confirm it, because a confirmation can't operate on what is void, otherwise if it is only voidable, but a court of equity considers void and voidable in a different light, and makes no difference between them. Though this lease is void at law, it is good in equity. He who had the legal estate gave a power to make it, and Thomas Dawson the trustee confirmed it, and Rowley who had [*158*] notice claims it under Thomas Dawson, and has received the rents since 1725, which is an acquiescence under the lease. Since there was no contract between him and the plaintiff, of what pretence but only by way of confirmation did he receive this rent?

They say there is a difference between Rowley's coming to set aside these leases, and our coming to establish them. But if the demand is equitable, what signifies who is plaintiff or defendant, and we are not the aggressors, but come here to defend our possession of 36 years.

Mr Solicitor General

1. I shall consider how this case stands on the leases.

2. On the several acts of confirmation.

The defendants have mistaken the intent of our bill, which is not to carry the agreement into execution, but only to be protected against the ejectment. In the first case indeed the proof ought to be more particular than on a defence, in which it is sufficient to show that this agreement was really made and carried into execution by the parties.

There is no doubt that these leases were executed by Arthur Upton, who appears on the face of them to act by letter of attorney.

Objection: there is no sufficient evidence of such a letter.

The plaintiffs and those under whom they derive have been 24 years in possession, and they had no right to the letter, but it was to remain in the hands of Arthur Upton, who made several other leases; many estates being managed by agents who are armed with powers to make leases, their doctrine would overturn several interests.

Lord Chief Baron

But these letters of attorney are enrolled, and the enrolment, though evidence, is to be found in court.

---

[705] Above, p. 122 n. 687.

Mr Solicitor General

Objection: If the letter was proved, it is not to be warranted [*159*] but it was from a trustee to make leases in reversion, and the lease was made to one who had notice he was only a trustee.

Lord Chief Baron

Would a letter of attorney from a trustee to sell be good? Or would equity establish the purchaser?

Mr Solicitor General

It don't appear that Clotworthy Upton was a trustee when he executed the letter, and though by a deed in 1698 he declared the lease to be taken in trust, he don't say that he was originally a trustee, and if you suppose it to be an original trust by implication of law, it must be by a tenant right for Thomas the grandfather. The deed of 1698 is in their power, and they have not produced it.

But if this was originally a trust, it was not an absolute one, but attended with circumstances that gave him an interest in the lease to secure himself, and there is no proof that the lessees knew of this trust at the time of the lease. The transaction was with Arthur Upton as an agent, and the rent is made payable to Clotworthy Upton. Here was only a reversionary interest, so nothing could be set but what was derived out of it.

It was of great consequence at that time to have Protestant families on the land, to raise the large rent, and the fine.

The bond of 1699 appears to be a confirmation from the obligors, who are the trustees and cestui que trusts[706] and it could not be a confirmation of the leases in possession, because they were not controverted. Nobody has since attempted to disturb our possession, and though minors were concerned, yet their trustees would have taken advantage of so profitable a lease, if they had not apprehended this bond to be a confirmation of it. We are purchasers as well as Rowley, so equity will not favour him in case of negligence.

In the case of Lord Bernard the recital of a settlement was adjudged to be notice of what was in it. [*160*]

Mr Lindsey [*sic*]

First, I shall endeavour to establish the letter of attorney.

2. Consider the objections to the leases that are founded on the letter.

Rowley in his answer admits and believes that Arthur Upton pretended he had such a letter of attorney, and that he made the leases in pursuance of it. This letter of attorney then whether real or not was produced to these people. If it was not real, it was a forgery and fraud to impose on these farmers, which Mr Rowley can't suppose Mr Arthur Upton would have been guilty of, because he owns he believes him to have been a man of integrity.

---

706 *Sic* for cestuis que trust.

The date and purport of the letter recited in the three leases though they were made at different times is the same.

It appears by Rowley's answer that the trustees received the rents under these leases. Did not then Joshua Dawson who was the acting trustee know what lease was confirmed by the bond?

The declaration of trust was not till 1698, after the making of our lease, so the presumption is, we did not know of the trust at the time we took it. Clotworthy Upton was not guardian or trustee, or employed for his sister, or her children, but Thomas Dawson being negligent of his affairs, and Clotworthy Upton being in London, took this lease. This he was not compellable to, but did out of county, and he employs his father who lived in those parts to let leases, and there was no fraud or circumvention in the case, so that the tenants had notice of the trust. This is not to be compared to the common cases. Arthur Upton being the grandfather, and obliged to take care of his children.

Arthur Dawson informs Rowley the estate was let at such a rent. In the case of *Matthews* v. *Richardson*,[707] the articles were set out so obscurely by the bill, that it did not appear, whether they were [*161*] entitled to one renewal, or forever upon which they amended, and set them out clearer. In that case the Lord Chief Justices Levinz[708] and Whitshed assisted the lord chancellor and they all agreed that the purchaser ought to have enquired what interests the tenants had, because they knew the premises were in lease, and that otherwise no man could be sure of his lease.

1 Rol. 476,[709] the receipt of rent was adjudged a confirmation, in that case the bishop did not know it was a voidable lease, in this Rowley who knew this to be [a] defective lease, ought to have given his agent notice not to have received the rents.

Mr Arthur Dawson[710]

An incumbrance that is registered shall affect a purchaser in equity, because he ought to look over the register.

On Saturday the 6 day of July,[711]

Being the last day of the following Trinity term, the lord chief baron delivered the opinion of the court.

The case stands thus on the pleadings and the proof. The plaintiffs' bill is to stay the defendants proceedings at law on an ejectment, and to establish their title to certain leases.

[707] No citation given.

[708] *Sic*, for Sir Richard Levinge.

[709] *Colt* v. *Glover* (1612) 1 Roll. Rep. 451 at 476, 81 E.R. 600 at 617.

[710] KI AP, p. 125, mentions Arthur Dawson, s. and heir of Joshua, of Dawson Castle, Londonderry, Middle Temple, 27 September 1715, KI, Michaelmas term, 1723. The town is Castle-Dawson, or Castledawson, Co. Londonderry, mentioned in the private Act (above, p. 122). He was evidently the same Arthur Dawson mentioned above in this case and was appearing in person. He was the eldest son of Joshua Dawson, secretary in Dublin Castle and member for Wicklow. Arthur was born in 1698, matriculated in Trinity College Dublin as a fellow-commoner in 1712, and graduated B.A. in 1715. He succeeded as heir to his father in 1725. He married Jane, a sister of Charles O'Neill (d. 1679) of Shane's Castle, Co. Antrim. Arthur became K.C. in 1734, was appointed a baron of the court of Exchequer in 1741, and acted as a judge in the Annesley peerage case (see above, p. cxlviii n. 848) in 1743. He resigned his seat on the bench in 1768, and died in 1775, leaving no issue. Ball, *Judges in Ireland*, ii.206–07.

[711] 6 July was a Friday in 1732, Kratz, *Hist. Cal.*, but the text below says it was the last day of the following Trinity term, which would indicate from the previous dates that the year was 1732.

Thomas Dawson the grandfather of the defendant Mrs Rowley was possessed of a lease from the Drapers company in London which expired in 1705. In 1692 Clotworthy Upton brother to the wife of the said Thomas Dawson takes a lease of these lands in reversion for 41 years to commence in 1705, and the rent and fine were to be paid when the lease took effect in possession. In 1698 Clotworthy Upton declared the trust of this lease for Thomas Dawson the younger, the son of Thomas Dawson senior.

17 June 1696, nine years before the commencement of the lease, Arthur Upton the father of the said Clotworthy [*162*] upon reciting a letter of attorney from Clotworthy Upton the trustee, makes a lease of part to Henderson and Hudson from 1705, and afterwards two other leases of other parts for 31 years to John Hodgson. In December 1699 Joshua Dawson the brother of Thomas Dawson the elder and uncle to Thomas Dawson the younger enters into a bond to confirm all leases made by Arthur Upton, Clotworthy Upton, or Thomas Dawson, or any, or either of them.

Thomas Dawson the younger was killed at Gibraltar.[712] An Act of Parliament[713] [was] passed for vesting the real estate of Thomas Dawson senior discharged of any settlement on Thomas Dawson the younger, in trust for payment of debts, and in lieu thereof this term was lodged in trustees, charged with a provision for Thomas Dawson senior, his wife, and children and then in trust for the children of Thomas Dawson the younger.

On the marriage of Mr Rowley in 1725 Arthur Dawson conveys the legal estate of this term to him, and soon after Mrs Rowley came of age. The lessees enjoyed without interruption, and the rents were received by Joshua Dawson one of the trustees under the Act.

Improvements were made before and since the commencement of the lease.

If the letter of attorney had appeared and the lease had been made pursuant to it, the plaintiffs would have a good title at law.

Here is no sufficient proof of the letter, nor is it recited, but only that there was a letter.

Supposing there had been proof of this letter, and that this lease was made pursuant to it, and it not being good at law, I shall consider how far equity has, or can go.

Though courts of equity remedy defective powers, they never give powers where there are none, nor take away a right from a purchaser for a valuable consideration.

If [a] tenant in tail covenants to convey, and levy a fine, and dies under a sequestration for not obeying a decree to that purpose, his heir is not bound. [*163*] I admit no precedent[714] should confine a court from doing right, but a purchaser has a right at law which is not to be taken from him, because it is his property.

I won't say whether Mr Dawson's letter is notice, because Mrs Rowley is a purchaser under the Act of Parliament,[715] which is the most solemn conveyance. This term [vested] in her father was not subject to any charge for her grandfather, grandmother, or aunts, till it became charged by the Act, in which there is no notice taken of these leases, because they did not suppose a trustee would make a lease in reversion.

---

[712] His death may have been connected to the fact that Gibraltar was captured by the British in 1704.
[713] Above, p. 122 n. 687.
[714] Spelled 'president' in original.
[715] Above, p. 122 n. 687.

Objection: the lease is confirmed by subsequent acts, and though an interest which is void at law can't be confirmed by a subsequent act, yet such an act may in equity amount to a new agreement.

It was not the intention of the parties to the bond to confirm these leases. If a release in general is void, sure a confirmation in general is as void too. This bond was executed to secure the attornment of the tenant six years before the commencement of the lease, and rather looks like a fraud, than an intention to confirm.

The receipts were after the bill filed and ejectment brought, and are not in issue, nor can it be supposed that one who was attempting to break a lease, would at the same time do an act to confirm it.

Post 302.   The bill must be dismissed.

Trinity Term

Saturday, June the 9th [1732][716]

In Exchequer

BROMINGHAM v. LORD CARBERY

An order was made that the plaintiffs should submit to a reference, or be dispaupered nisi, and the plaintiffs now showed for cause that the bill concerned the inheritance, and the cause was allowed, and it was said this was not within the order of dispaupering, and was never made after a decree. [*164*]

BUCKNAL v. KENT

In Exchequer

John Kent made his will *inter alia* in these words:

> I give and devise to my brother Robert Kent and the heirs males [*sic*] of his body my whole real estate subject to my debts, and further subject to £500 to be paid to my wife immediately after my decease in lieu of her jointure, remainder to my nephew Samuel Matthews for life, remainder to John Matthews for life, remainder to the right heirs of Robert Kent in fee. Item, I give and devise £50 to the poor, and £500 to Ann Bucknal to be paid out of my estate, and my funerals. Item, I give and bequeath to my said wife any chaise, together with the horses, and all any crop of corn now growing, together with my plate and household goods, and I give and devise all the rest and residue of my personal estate to Daniel Gates and Charles Bucknal, and I do nominate and appoint the said Charles Bucknal and Daniel Osborn executors.

This cause being heard before the late Lord Chief Baron Dalton, and the question being, whether the personal estate should be applied in ease of the real? The court decreed an account to be taken, and the cause came back to be heard on the report, whereby it appeared, that the debts amounted to £280, and that the residue of the personal estate being but £250, was not sufficient to pay them.

---

[716] 9 June was a Friday in 1732, but from the context it seems the year was still 1732. Note that the date is earlier than the previous one.

Mr Marshal for the defendant[717]

To show that the personal estate ought to be applied [*165*] quoted 2 Vern. 469.[718] Here it is plain that the testator did not design the real estate should be sold, which makes this different from the common cases, 2 Vern. 718.[719] And after payment of the debts, and the jointure to which the estate is liable, only £44 a year would remain to his brother and heir.

Mr Malone

The real estate at the time of the devise was subject to dower and a mortgage of £2,000. The personal estate not being expressly devised, but the residue generally, ought to go in aid of the real estate.

'Tis a settled point that the devisee as well as heir is entitled to have the personal estate applied in ease of the real. 1 Ver. 36,[720] 2 Chan. Rep. 84.[721]

The executor has the personal estate subject to the executorship, though it is not expressly devised to him as executor. 2 Vern. 43,[722] 302,[723] 477.[724] If the personal estate is not applied, the intention of the testator as to the real estate will be defeated.

Mr Daly for the plaintiff

It is plain from the will that the testator designed the real estate should pay his debts, and the legacies which would otherwise affect the personal estate, and the reason was, because his personal estate was not sufficient, and he devises to Daniel Osborn and Charles Bucknal as devisees the residue, which they have as much right to, as the wife to her share, and he intended them a benefit by it. 1 Lev. 203,[725] 1 Chan. Cas. 296, 297.[726]

Mr Solicitor General

By the subsequent clauses which are relative to the first it is plain the real estate is to pay. The real estate is £266 a year clear, subject to a jointure of £74, the residue of the personal estate is but £250.

This is not a devise to them as executors, for only one [*166*] of the residuary devisees is made executor. Now if there are two executors, and one only has a particular legacy, neither are [*sic*] excluded from the residue. *Hale* v. *Brookall* 1711, MSŜ cas. in Canc. D.140.

---

[717] Probably Robert Marshall, s. and heir of John Marshal, Clonmel, Co. Tipperary, entered Middle Temple, 1 March 1717/18, called to Irish bar, Trinity term 1723 (KI AP, p. 327, Ball, *Judges in Ireland*, ii. 209); joint residuary legatee of Swift's Vanessa, 1723; 3rd serjeant, patent, 18 April 1738 (Smyth, *Law Officers*, p. 197); 2nd serjeant, 1741, recorder of Clonmel, M.P. for Clonmel, J.C.P., 1754 (Ball, *Judges in Ireland*, ii. 209).

[718] *Bishop* v. *Sharp* (1704) 2 Vern. 469, 23 E.R. 902.

[719] *Wainwright* v. *Bendlowes* (1716) 2 Vern. 718, 23 E.R. 1071.

[720] *Pockley* v. *Pockley* (1681) 1 Vern. 36, 23 E.R. 290.

[721] *Howard* v. *Hooker* (1672) 2 Ch. Rep. 81, 21 E.R. 622.

[722] *White* v. *White* (1688) 2 Vern. 43, 23 E.R. 638.

[723] *Cutler* v. *Coxeter* (1693) 2 Vern. 302, 23 E.R. 794.

[724] *Hawes* v. *Warner* (1704) 2 Vern. 477, 23 E.R. 906.

[725] *Feltham* v. *Executors of Harlston* (1667) 1 Lev. 203, 83 E.R. 369.

[726] *Lord Grey* v. *Lady Grey* (1677) 1 Ch. Cas. 296, 22 E.R. 809 (purchase by father in name of son unadvanced is an advancement).

Nels. 8vo Rep.
in Canc. 203.[727]
Post 210.

MSS̄ cas. in Canc. D
49.55.[728]

a devise to one in a separate clause, who is after named executor, is the same as a devise to a stranger, in which case there could be no doubt.

This was intended a beneficial bequest, and therefore it must not be defeated, as was adjudged in the case of *Wainwright* v. *Bendlo[w]es* the 3rd of the late King.

Mr Calaghan

In the same breath that he devises the real estate subject to debts etc., he devises the residue. The intention is the rule by which wills are to be expounded. The testator has an equal power over his real and personal estate, and the court can't direct them to be applied otherwise than he has done by his will. 1 Chan. Cas. 297,[729] 1 Lev. 203.[730] The devise of the personal estate to the executor is void, as a devise of lands is to the heir, which was the case of *Hale*; but here one of the devisees is a stranger, so both must take as legatees.

Mr Nash

The legatees are his brothers in law, and he left £500 to the daughter of one of them. The devisee of the lands is his brother and heir. 2 Vern. 675 *Ball* v. *Smyth*.[731] If Charles Bucknal had renounced the executorship, his legacy would notwithstanding have remained to him. 2 Vern. 121.[732]

This is like a specific legacy which turns the debts on the land.

Mr Attorney General

I allow the personal estate must go in aid of the real estate, unless it is expressly, or by necessary implication, excluded. *Hæres natus* and *factus* differ if the estate is made liable.

The whole personal estate would not pay the legacy of £500, which shows the debts are to be paid out of the real estate. [*167*] They don't pretend the horses, chaise etc., are to be liable, and in point of reason, all the rest and residue etc., is the same thing as if he had particularly named the remainder of his personal estate, and given it to them, except the plate, chaise etc., and it is given in the beginning of his will, before he had in contemplation whom he should make executors.

On Saturday July the 9th following[733]

The chief baron delivered the opinion of the court.

[727] Perhaps *Wood* v. *Caley* (1661) 1 Ch. Rep. 204, 21 E.R. 550.

[728] Cited as *Wainwright* v. *Bendlowe* (1716) 2 Vern. 707, by Marlay C.B. below at p. 135 [*167*] and Rogerson C.J. below, p. 163 [*210*], but the reference appears to be to *Wainwright* v. *Bendlowes* (1716) 2 Vern. 718, 23 E.R. 1071, as cited by Mr Marshal, see above, p. 133 n. 719. See also *Trott* v. *Vernon* (1715) 2 Vern. 708, 23 E.R. 1065.

[729] *Lord Grey* v. *Lady Grey* (1677) 1 Ch. Cas. 296, 22 E.R. 809.

[730] *Feltham* v. *Executors of Harlston* (1667) 1 Lev. 203, 83 E.R. 369.

[731] *Ball* v. *Smith* (1711) 2 Vern. 675, 23 E.R. 1039.

[732] *Mead* v. *Hide* (1690) 2 Vern. 120, 23 E.R. 687, and sub nom. *Gower* v. *Mead* (1689) Prec. Ch. 2, 24 E.R. 1.

[733] 9 July was a Sunday in 1732 (Julian), Kratz, *Hist. Cal.*, but from the context the year would still seem to be 1732.

This question depends on the will of John Kent. The scope of the bill was to charge the debts on the real estate, and that Charles Bucknal who was one of the devisees of the residue of the personal estate and one of the executors might be discharged from the debts etc. At the hearing it was referred to the officer to state the debts, and the value of the real and personal estate.

The personal estate is the natural fund to pay debts and legacies, because his real estate was not originally in the disposal of the testator, only by the custom of some boroughs, but since the Statute of Devises[734] and the taking away of wards and liveries,[735] the one is as much in his power as the other, and the words are to be considered according to his intention, which is the rule to go by in the construction of a devise either of the real or personal estate. Now the intention of John Kent was, that all the personal estate not given to his wife should go to Charles Bucknal and his brother, not as executors, and he had a power to leave it to them in this manner.

The rule in the case of *Wainwright* v. *Bendlowes*[736] in 2 Vern. 707 is not unreasonable, to construe the intention so as to make the legacy useful, and by another construction these legatees would have nothing, whereas he must be supposed to have intended them something, so the devise of the real estate must refund. 1 Vern. 45.[737] The real estate may be charged by the intention of the testator, though the words are not express. [*168*] Here the intention of the testator sufficiently appears to charge the real, and discharge the personal estate.

Tuesday, July the 4th [1732][738]

In Exchequer

HORAN v. ARCHDECKNE[739]

No receipt or other exhibit can be proved *viva voce* but by witnesses, and if they are not attested, they must be proved by commission, or in the office. For the rule to prove exhibits *viva voce* at the hearing extends only to prove the execution of a deed in the common way provided by the law, and supposes an attestation.   Ante 89.

The point in question was, whether the executors had paid beyond the assets, and might retain a mortgage.

And the defendant having failed to prove the payment of the money, it was insisted on since he could not prove the notes *viva voce* they not being witnessed, that he was entitled to a commission to examine to them, and the case of *Roquier* v. *Bolton*[740] in

---

[734] I.e. the Statute of Wills (Ireland), 1634 (10 Car. I, sess. 2, c. 2), and in England the Statute of Wills, 1540 (32 Hen. VIII, c. 1). Wills of real estate were not permitted at common law, the land passing under the rules of descent. In burgage tenure, wills of real property were allowed if sanctioned by the custom of the borough.

[735] Statute of Wills (Ireland), 1634, like the English Act, gave power to make wills of all land held in socage tenure and two-thirds of all land held by the military tenure of knight service. The Tenures Abolition Act, 1662 (Ir.) (14 & 15 Car. II, sess. 4, c. 19.) by converting all land in knight service to socage completed the freedom of testation.

[736] *Wainwright* v. *Bendlowes* (1716) 2 Vern. 718, 23 E.R. 1071; *Trott* v. *Vernon* (1715) 2 Vern. 708, 23 E.R. 1065.

[737] *Newman* v. *Johnson* (1682) 1 Vern. 45, 23 E.R. 298.

[738] 4 July 1732 (Julian) was a Tuesday, Kratz, *Hist. Cal.*.

[739] See above, p. 97. Resumed on p. 299.

[740] No citation given.

this court was mentioned, which was affirmed in the House of Lords.[741] And of *Wilson* v. *Mead*[742] in Chancery where the court give them leave to add an interrogatory to prove a banker's note, because they could not prove it *viva voce* for want of its having witnesses.[743]

Lord Chief Baron

The point here is to have the benefit of a mortgage, Jane one of the executors disclaiming all the benefit of it, and pleads she assigned it for the benefit of the creditors, and Nicholas has made no proof of this assignment, therefore we can give you no relief.

LORD PRIMATE v. MONTGOMERY[744]

In Exchequer

The court allowed a lease made in 1676 to be read, a witness having swore positively to the death [*169*] of two witnesses, and that he heard and believed the other was dead; and the chief baron mentioned the case of *Tasborough* v. *Mcnamara*.[745] Though it was objected, that they ought to have proved, that they had made some search and inquiry after the other witness.

Post 221.

SIR ROBERT ECHLIN, THOMAS TICKEL ESQR & CLOTILDA TICKEL ALIAS EUSTACE HIS WIFE, AND EUSTACE CHETWOOD ESQR PLAINTIFFS TASBOROUGH, & MCNAMARA DEFENDANTS

In Exchequer

The defendant Mcnamara after publication and a conditional decree obtained leave on a motion to exhibit articles to the credit of French a witness, and a motion was after made to set this order aside, and denied.

Post 366.

And the articles coming to be read, it was objected that they were wrong titled, Sir Robert Echlin[746] and Thomas Tickel Esqr plaintiffs.

But the lord chancellor said, without doubt they could amend their own orders, and that the only doubt lay as to the depositions, and that they had been amended in England.

Post 259, 281. Mes App. G.95.

---

[741] No citation given. The name 'Roquier' or 'Rouquier' does not occur in E.R. See pp. 206 and 310.
[742] No citation given.
[743] See also *Archdekin* [*sic*] v. *Horan*, above, p. civ.
[744] Resumed on p. 143.
[745] No citation given.
[746] See above, p. 114.

Mr Lindsay said, Lord Midleton[747] obliged the party to sign the articles, because if he did not prove them, the witness might have an action on the case.

Mr Calaghan said, no action would lie, because the court had a jurisdiction, but he allowed it would lie, if such articles had been exhibited in the Common Pleas.

The articles and examination were not only to the general reputation of the witness, but to his particular character, which the lord chancellor was offended at, and said, it was contrary to the established rules. A copy of the articles are given to the other side. French not only examined his witnesses, but cross examined those of Mcnamara. [*170*]

STAUNTON v. HATFIELD

In Exchequer

The defendant brought an *audita querela*[748] after execution executed, and Mr Calaghan moved that he might be bailed, and said he had the bail ready. Cro. Eliz. 634,[749]

Palm. 422.[750]

Mr Forbes contra, 1 Sid. 338.[751]

And Mr Daly mentioned a case in Common Pleas, where a judgment was by *cognovit*, and on a *scire facias*, the Statute of Usury[752] being pleaded was not allowed, because it ought to have been pleaded to the action. The court denied the motion, and said they must go into equity.

Monday July the 1st [1732][753]

In Chancery

On three summons and no attendance, 'tis a motion of course for leave to proceed before the master ex parte.

EYRE v. STAUNTON

In Chancery

An order was made that the plaintiff should leave the north-east passage on a salmon weir at Galway open for boats and an attachment being granted *nisi* for breach of the order, the plaintiff showed for cause, that though the order was made on hearing

---

[747] Spelled 'Middleton' in MS.

[748] A writ that lay for a defendant, against whom judgment had been recovered, to discharge the judgment by showing a good ground for discharging it which had arisen since the judgment had been given, such as a release.

[749] *Malyns v. Hawkins* (1596) Cro. Eliz. 634, 78 E.R. 874.

[750] Palm. 422, 81 E.R. 1152, AUDITA QUERELA.

[751] *Gee v. Fane* (1667) 1 Sid. 339, 82 E.R. 1144.

[752] 10 Car. I, sess. 2, c. 22 (Ir.), 1634 (against usury); 2 Ann., c. 16 (Ir.), 1703 (to reduce rate of interest on money to 8 per cent); 8 Geo. I, c. 13 (Ir.), 1721 (to reduce rate of interest on money to 7 per cent). 5 Geo. II, c. 7 (Ir.), 1731 (to reduce rate of interest on money to 6 per cent).

[753] 1 July was a Saturday in 1732, Kratz, *Hist. Cal.*. The previous date in the MS. is Tuesday, 4 July which is correct for 1732. From the context it seems the year was still 1732.

MSS̃ cas. in
Canc. A.300. counsel of both sides, yet it ought to have been drawn up, and he served with an
exemplification of it before he could be in contempt, and the cause was allowed,
because the plaintiff could not be in contempt, the order being never drawn up.

Tuesday, June the 27th [1732][754]

In Exchequer

HUISH v. VERNON[755]

Nels. 8vo Rep. in
Canc. 21.[756] The plaintiffs as devisees of an equity file a bill to redeem, the defendant pleads a
priority of suit for a foreclosure in England. The lands lay here, the parties [*171*]
lived in England. The plea was overruled.

ALLEN v. MANDEVIL

In Exchequer

Bail *de adjudicatis solvendis*. 27 April a motion was made for judgment, and a rule
made *nisi* etc.

1 May the defendant was surrendered in discharge of his bail.

10 May the rule for judgment was made absolute.

12 May the attorney for the plaintiff took out a *fieri facias*, the return of which is
out, by virtue whereof £25 only was levied, the debt was £200.

And Mr Calaghan moved, that the defendant might be discharged.

A *fieri facias* and a *capias*[757] can't subsist together. In debt and in assumpsit no
capias lay at common law where there was no trespass *vi et armis*,[758] but only a *fieri
facias*, and a *levari*, till the 25 Ed. 3,[759] and an account by West 2,[760] 3 Co. *Sir William
Herbert's Case*,[761] one is given in lieu of the other, and the party may make his election,
but can't have both. 2 Keb. 613[762] is in point, 1 Leon. 58[763] 1 Rol. Abr 904, letter X,
No. 8. Godbolt 296,[764] 5 Co. 87b[765] Moor 598.[766]

---

[754] 27 June was a Tuesday in 1732, Kratz, *Hist. Cal.*
[755] Continued from p. 108.
[756] *Emanuel Coll.* v. *Evans* (1625) 1 Ch. Rep. 18 at 21, 21 E.R. 494 at 495.
[757] A writ of execution ordering the sheriff to take the body of the debtor into custody so that he might
then appear in court to satisfy the judgment debt or be imprisoned for debt.
[758] L. with force and arms.
[759] I.e. 1350–51.
[760] Statute of Westminster II, c. 18.
[761] *Harbert's Case* (1581) 3 Co. Rep. 11b, 76 E.R. 647; *Sir William Herberts Case* (1581) Moo. K.B. 169, 72 E.R.
510.
[762] *Stokes* v. *Stokes* (1670) 2 Keb. 613, 84 E.R. 386 (goods and body cannot be liable at the same time, but
successively may be.)
[763] *Fullwood* v. *Fullwood* (1587) 1 Leo. 58, 74 E.R. 54.
[764] *Sir Edward Coke's Case* (1623) Godb. 289, 78 E.R. 169.
[765] *Blumfield's Case* (1596) 5 Co. Rep. 86b at 87b, 77 E.R. 185 at 187.
[766] *West* v. *Blackhead* (1592) Moo. K.B. 598, 72 E.R. 783.

If two are jointly and severally bound, and you sue both, you can't have a *capias* against one, and a *fieri facias* against the other, or vice versa. Hob. 69.[767] *Cane* v. *Ward*[768] in King's Bench. The officers of that court used to issue a *capias* and a *fieri facias* at the same time, and the sheriff returned the *capias*, and made no return on the other, and the defendant was discharged on the motion of Mr Daly, because both ought not to issue at the same time.

Objection: Here may be a difference in the case of his Majesty's debtor and farmer, for a *capias* is given to the King, which was the reason why it lay in trespass at common law, where there was a fine to the King.

The being [a] debtor don't gain the prerogatives of the crown, as appears by *Sir William Herbert's Case*.[769] The Act says [*172*] no *capias* lay for the subject, and don't except the King's debtors.

Mr Prime Serjeant for the plaintiff

I allow that the party can't have both a *fieri facias* and a *capias* at the same time yet the defendant is not to be discharged. If a *fieri facias* is taken out, and the goods are not sufficient to satisfy the debt, the plaintiff may have another *fieri facias*, or a *capias* at his election, therefore your Lordship will give us leave to lay hold of the party, for he is not yet in execution at our suit. The defendant is not in execution for the plaintiff by the surrender of the bail, and it could not be so in this case, because being before judgment, it could not be in execution of it. If the bail had surrendered him before the verdict, the case stood as if there had been no bail, and we might take out a *fieri facias* on the judgment, and if nothing was to be found, a *capias* afterwards. If the defendant is surrendered after judgment, he is not absolutely in execution, Hob. 210,[770] and 1 Leon. 58[771] is an authority against them, for the plaintiff has his election, and there must be a rule on him or his attorney to make his election, and if he dies, a *scire facias* against his executors.

So your Lordship will hold him till we have made our election, and not discharge him, the *fieri facias* well issued, and you won't thereupon discharge him, because only £25 is levied, and the debt is above £200, and we have an election either to take his body, or a new *fieri facias*.

Mr Attorney General

When the rule is made absolute, the judgment has relation only by fiction of law.

It was determined in the time of Lord Chief Baron [*173*] Gilbert, that on process of *quo minus* they might break open doors, but the court declared themselves of another opinion, because then it would have been done every day.

---

[767] *Rawden* v. *Strut* (1615) Hob. 69, 80 E.R. 218.
[768] No citation given.
[769] *Sir William Herberts Case* (1581) Moo. K.B. 169, 72 E.R. 510.
[770] *Welby* v. *Canning* (1617) Hob. 210, 80 E.R. 356 (*scire facias* bail).
[771] *Fullwood* v. *Fullwood* (1587) 1 Leo. 58, 74 E.R. 54.

Curia

The defendant was never in custody at the suit of the plaintiff, the surrender of the bail does not make him in execution for him, for that would destroy the plaintiff's election.

A *capias* and a *fieri facias* can't issue at the same time in a *quo minus*, for the Statute of Marlbridge[772] goes on a supposition, that there are no effects.

The motion is denied.

Friday, June the 30th [1732][773]

In Exchequer

CROMWELL PRICE v. SOPHY HAMILTON

The plaintiff moved for an injunction on equity confessed in the defendant's answer. The bill set forth that the plaintiff entered into a treaty of concubinage with the defendant as a woman of virtue, and that with that view, and under the influence of liquor, she prevailed on him to settle an annuity of £30 a year, which was to be increased to £40 after the death of his father, or she was to have £240 in money, and charged, that she was accustomed to draw young heirs in that manner.

The defendant by her answer denied, that she ever attempted to pass on him for a woman of virtue, that the plaintiff voluntarily and deliberately executed the deed of annuity after a night's deliberation, and that the consideration were agreeable favours, and if it was base or unlawful, that he was an equal sharer with her in the guilt.

And Mr Bettesworth for the defendant mentioned the case of *Sanderson* v. *Rose McCain, and Nichols,*[774] where my Lord Midleton[775] refused to interpose, there being no fraud in the case, because *turpis consideratio*[776] made it below the dignity of a court of equity, whereupon Sanderson reconciled himself to her, and [he] having in a fond hour prevailed on her to acknowledge satisfaction on [*174*] the judgment, the court of King's Bench would not set it aside, though she had before assigned the judgment to Nichols, and he also quoted the case of *Matthews*[777] in Vern.

Mes App. F.147.   Sir John St Leger being only in court refused the injunction till the hearing, because the deed was voluntary and the provision small, and the plaintiff was not imposed on by the defendant.

---

[772] 52 Hen. 3 (Eng.), 1267 (Statute of Marlborough).
[773] 30 June was a Friday in 1732, Kratz, *Hist. Cal.*
[774] No citation given.
[775] Spelled 'Middleton' in MS.
[776] L. base or immoral consideration.
[777] Possibly *Roberts* v. *Matthews* (1682) 1 Vern. 150, 23 E.R. 379.

Wednesday, June the 21st [1732][778]

In Exchequer

LORD PRIMATE v. BLACKWOOD

The 10 of July 1639 the then primate made a lease to Lord Clonaboy for 60 years, and the deed was enrolled for safe custody.

And it was objected to the reading of the enrolment, that it did not appear by whom it was enrolled, or at what time (it may be yesterday) or whether it was enrolled or no, that the enrolment ought not to be but on the affidavit of one of the parties who signed it, and that the officer ought not to enrol it upon the request of any person; that it don't appear whether this is the enrolment of the counterpart or original, and it is not certified by the officer to be enrolled.

That this being an old deed, though they need not prove the witnesses' hands, or the similitude of hands, yet they ought to show that the possession has gone along with it, and to give an account where it was found; and that the enrolment was of no use, the counterpart being produced.

Mr Malone

The prayer of the bill is to have the primate's right to the tithes established, and that the plaintiff Mr Hamilton may be decreed to the tithes of the year.

We have produced the counterpart, and the enrolment of the lease of the rectorial tithes of the parishes of etc. from the lord primate to the Lords Clonaboy [175] and Montgomery.

The enrolment was allowed to be read in the case of *Nugent* v. *Rochfort*,[779] because the parties had allowed the settlement in other causes, and claimed under it. And there is evidence of successive leases since by the following primates, and of the tenants paying the tithes to them.

Contra: No enrolment appears. They have produced a copy in paper of an enrolment for safe custody. The Rolls have no authority to enrol without proper directions from the master, and the affidavit of the execution endorsed.

It don't appear when, or how this copy was brought there, so your Lordship can't look upon it as a copy, or a regular enrolment.

This counterpart is no evidence, where the original is proved to have been executed and lost, and that possession has gone along with it, and the counterpart is found in proper hands, it is evidence, and where these fail, it is not.

They have produced a conveyance from the sheriff but not the *fieri facias*, whereas the writ is his authority. They have only made parol proof of the judgment and execution, and the return of the writ might as well be past before the sale as after.

---

[778] 21 June was a Wednesday in 1732, Kratz, *Hist. Cal.*
[779] No citation given.

Mr Stannard

The primate, being owner in right of his See of these rectories made a lease of them to ——[780] which was taken in execution by the sheriff, and sold to Mr Ross, in trust for the plaintiff Hamilton.

They must make out their title as on an ejectment, and recover by their own strength, but they can have all the defendant knows upon his oath to aid them. This being an impropriate[781] rectory could not always belong to him as primate, but must have belonged to the dissolved monasteries, and come from the crown. And it is recited so by the primate, and when once the estate is in the crown, it must come out of him [*176*] by matter of record, which they should have produced, and shown how they came by it, because they are out of possession. (If the defendant was out of possession, the proof would lie on him). They have shown no grant, but a licence to the lords to alien, but if they did not alien, where is their title? We have fixed it in the crown, so at law they must have been nonsuited, and their evidence is an admission of a title in the lords, but makes no title as to the lease, which is an estoppel to the parties only while it continues (this expired 33 years ago) and this lease is not mentioned as the foundation of their possession, but of the primate's right, but theirs is by a lease still subsisting in Hamilton, and they don't come here to be restored to their possession as against a tenant holding over, but to their right.

Mr Prime Serjeant

We have produced letters of licence to Lord Clonaboy to restore these impropriate[782] rectories to the See of Ardmagh. The grant indeed of Lord Clonaboy to the primate don't appear, but we have presumptive evidence of it, because ten days after the licence, viz on the 10 of July 1639, he takes a lease of these three rectories part of Blackabby. He had a licence to alien, from the then lord primate.

Objection: But they say there is no evidence of this lease. 1. Because this is no enrolment but a copy so we ought to prove the execution of the original.

But this is only for a term of years. The enrolment is evidence by the statute, and the tenant has been in possession.

2. It is not to be considered as enrolled for safe custody, because there is not the usual affidavit.

If they would produce the original lease the affidavit and endorsement would appear, but it can't be expected on our counterpart, for we claim in right of the See. [*177*] So the enrolment, and the counterpart, which being an old deed proves itself, is evidence against them, for they derive under Lord Clonaboy.

And though this is conclusive evidence only during the continuance of the lease, yet after the expiration of it 'tis good evidence with other circumstances to show a title in the primate.

'Tis not necessary for the sheriff to produce the judgment, that would retard the sale.

---

[780] Line in MS.
[781] A rectory placed in lay hands. *OED*.
[782] Above, n. 781.

Mr Calaghan

They have showed letters patent from the crown to Lord Clonaboy, and so have eased us of the trouble of taking the estate out of the crown. An enrolment for safe custody is allowed at common law, and such an old enrolment admitted as evidence 1 Salk. 389,[783] and in this court in the case of *Nugent* v. *Rochfort*.[784]

Deeds may be enrolled two ways, by acknowledgement of the party, or by affidavit of a witness to the execution.

A commission issued out of Chancery Hil[ary] vacation 1725 at Bray to enquire of the attainder of Sir William Kennedy a monk. The copy of the enrolment of the settlement was given in evidence, to show the estate was in him for life. The affidavit was endorsed on the settlement itself.

But in the case of an old enrolment the court will presume everything necessary to have been done. So if an old enrolment is given in evidence, and there has been a long enjoyment under it, the court will presume livery of seisin,[785] though it is not endorsed. And if the enrolment is evidence, it makes the counterpart so too, as a fine and recovery is a foundation to read the deed that leads the uses. It was adjudged by the Lord Chief Justice Rogerson[786] in the case of Mr Wilson the master of the packet-boat, that he who derives under a sheriff's sale need not produce the judgment, and the vendee may give parol proof of the execution, because the *fieri facias* is [*178*] the authority of the sheriff, and belongs to him, and he need not return it. 5 Co. *Semain's Case*.[787]

Thursday, June the 15 [1732][788]

In Exchequer

LORD PRIMATE v. MONTGOMERY[789]

Mr Prime Serjeant

The possessions of religious houses, being vested in the crown, and the crown being entitled to the forfeitures of the Oneals and others, a commission issued in King James's time to inquire what hereditaments belonging to the monasteries at the time of their dissolution in Down and Ardmagh were granted by the crown, and in what manner, with their names, and bounds, and to settle all disputes between the claimants. And the question is, whether we can give in evidence an inquisition taken by virtue of this commission to prove the limits of a parish about 100 years after. I

---

[783] *Taylor* v. *Jones* (1696) 1 Salk. 389, 91 E.R. 338.

[784] No citation given.

[785] I.e. transfer of seisin, or the legal possession of a freeholder, without which a conveyance at common law was ineffective.

[786] See *Hist. Ir. Parlt.* Rogerson (no. 1812). Ball, *Judges in Ireland,* ii. 199. John Rogerson, called to the bar of Middle Temple, 1698, to the Irish bar, 1701. S.G., 1714, on accession of George I. Recorder of Dublin in same year. A.G., 1720. C.J.K.B., 1727. Died 1741. Bu. St Werburgh's church, Dublin.

[787] *Semayne's Case* (1604) 5 Co. Rep. 91a, 77 E.R. 194.

[788] 15 June was a Thursday in 1732 (Julian), Kratz, *Hist. Cal.*.

[789] Continued from p. 136.

don't say the power to give the commissioners to determine disputes between the parties is legal, but to inquire etc., is a good commission, and traversable by one it affects. Inquisitions *post mortem* to inquire what land the King's tenant holds, that his heir may be in ward, and the profits go to the crown during his nonage, are allowed to be given in evidence. And if the King is entitled to the inquisition where he is only guardian, much more sure he has a right where the fee is in the crown *jure corone*. In a trial at the bar of the Common Pleas the bishop of Dublin's Black Book was allowed to be read to prove the bounds of St Catherine's and St James's. That was a book which only belonged to the diocese, which was taken out of his study, was no record, but only found among the books of his predecessors. It did not appear who made the entries, or by what [*179*] authority, yet it was read as an ancient book.

This commission is directed to the judges of the Common Pleas and the other judges, and is returned on record above 100 years ago.

Lord Chief Baron

That Black Book was refused as evidence at another trial.

Mr Attorney General

'Tis dangerous to say this is a bad inquisition because the commission is void, for most in this kingdom are in English, and are void without an Act of Parliament, and the Act of King William only confirms commissions against Papists.[790]

This commission is a good ground for an information, if any thing is withheld from the crown, or the tenure not observed.

There has been an acquiescence since the 21 Ja. I 1623.

Mr Lindsey [*sic*]

There was a perpetual war especially in the northern parts of this kingdom by the Oneals and others from the Dissolution of monasteries till this inquisition

I have seen such inquisitions taken in the time of King Charles I, and they were necessary, because Queen Elizabeth granted few lands or rectories belonging to the monasteries in fee, but only for terms of years, her successors therefore thought it proper at the expiration of these leases to make enquiries to enable them to grant. The present question is, as to two thirds of the parish of Donaghadee.

Mr Stannard contra

An inquisition *post mortem* may be read, because every one may traverse it.

The bishops the patentees need not traverse this inquisition, because their right is not bound. They might have cross-examined the witnesses, and produced their own, and any other depositions might as well be read. [*180*] And if they might read it because of the length of time, then a person would be in a worse condition for being the longer in possession.

This is evidence in a particular cause between private parties, but we were no parties, and this inquisition was taken 74 years after the dissolution.

---

[790] See 9 Will. III, c. 5 (Ir.), 1697, s. 5 (to hinder reversal of outlawries).

Sir John St Leger

The general direction is only preparatory to settle the right between those private persons, and the King's letter shows it was not for his benefit.

Lord Chief Baron

This might be read in evidence as to the reputation of the country of the possession on an ejectment, but not on a possessory bill to take away the possession of their lessor.

This is not a legal commission but void, and then how can the inquisition though of record in Chancery be read?

Courts have suffered inquisitions to be read, on a supposition of a commission, where it appeared that the commission was destroyed, and one commission has been read to explain another.

'Tis certain this kingdom was in troubles from the dissolution to Queen Elizabeth, and as it was governed by a military power, they issued many commissions, and Lord Strafford in his chamber in the Castle granted these commissions, and determined the rights of private persons.

In King James I's time these commissions were confirmed by Act of Parliament, and the letters patent by the 10 and 15 Ca. I.

Tuesday, June the 13 [1732][791]

In Chancery

SIR THOMAS SMYTH v. KING

It was moved to set aside the depositions of [*181*] Lady Lowth, because they were taken by the name of Lady Lowth, and not signed by her.

It was said for the defendant, that in the case of *Leadbeter* v. *Leadbeter*[792] in Exchequer it was adjudged that signing was not necessary, that on an indictment for perjury though they proved the signature, they might also prove it to be sworn by the party, and that it differed from an answer.

Ante 64.

But the lord chancellor not only read the rule of the court that required the signing, but showed that it might contribute greatly to convict the offender, for if it is proved that AB deposed, and there are several of that name, if they prove the signing by the traverser, that would fix it on him. But his Lordship took time to consider, whether he would set aside the depositions.

[791] 13 June was a Tuesday in 1731 (Julian), Kratz, *Hist. Cal.*
[792] See pp. 54, 105.

HOEY v. TAAF

In Chancery

The plaintiff obtained an order to amend his bill. The defendant after moved to dismiss the bill on a certificate from the Rolls, and an order was made accordingly, and the plaintiff now moved to set aside this order of dismission, because of his moving to amend, which was a proceeding.

But the lord chancellor was of another opinion, and the reason seemed to be, because he had not amended his bill before, for that is a motion of course, and the plaintiff don't serve the other side with notice, but the order is first served on the master of the rolls to take the old bill off the file, and when it is amended, put on the file again, then they give notice to the defendant.

Tuesday, June the 19th [1732][793]

In Exchequer

KELLY v. TAAF

Lady Fingal[794] signed her answer Frances Plunket but it was titled right the answer of Frances Plunket al[ia]s Taaf, and the plaintiff moved to go on with process [*182*] as if no answer was in, and the court were of opinion that the answer must be signed, and the defendant being in the country gave her a week's time to sign it, and staid process in the meantime.

---

[793] 19 June was a Monday in 1732, Kratz, *Hist. Cal.* It was a Tuesday in 1733, but from the context it seems the year was still 1732.

[794] Frances Plunkett, countess of Fingall. The earl of Fingall d. 1718 and Lady Fingall shortly afterwards married Stephen Taafe: Cokayne, *Complete Peerage*, v. 387.

Michaelmas Term

December the 17th [1732][795]

BEAUMONT ASTLE ESQR, PLAINTIFF
FRANCIS RICHARDSON ESQR, SIMON
RICHARDSON GENT, ET AL., DEFENDANTS[796]

In court: Lord Chancellor
                  Lord Chief Justice Rogerson
                  Lord Chief Baron Marlay

Mr Stannard for the defendants

Simon Richardson Esqr being seised in fee of several lands in the barony and county of Ardmagh, he and Catherine his wife in consideration of and previous to the marriage of Henry Richardson their eldest son with Jane Maxwell one of the daughters of Robert Maxwell, and in consideration of £1,000 portion, by deeds of lease and release[797] bearing date the 14 and 15 days of December 1685 did grant etc., unto Henry Maxwell and Samuel Warren and their heirs the said lands, in trust to the several uses in the said deed, and particularly, that after the said marriage should take effect, and after the decease of the said Simon Richardson and Catherine his wife, to Henry Lesly and Richard Close, in trust for the said Henry Richardson during his life, and after his decease to the intent to permit the said Jane in case she should survive him to receive the jointure provided for her by the [*183*] said deed, and after the decease of the said Henry to the use of his issue male by the said Jane, and in default of such issue, then as to all and singular the premises to Henry Echlin and the said Robert Maxwell their executors administrators and assigns for the term of 80 years, and then to the issue male of the said Henry by any other wife in tail male, and in default of such issue to Edward second son of the said Simon Richardson for life, and after his decease to the defendant Francis eldest son of the said Edward for his life and his issue male, with several remainders over, and the said term of 80 years is declared to be upon this special trust:

That in case the said Henry Richardson should have one or more daughter or daughters begotten on the body of the said Jane Maxwell who shall be living at the commencement of the said term of 80 years, the said Echlin and Maxwell and the survivor of them, and the executor and administrator of such survivor shall out of the issues and profits of the said lands raise and levy the several sums therein mentioned as portions for such daughter or daughters.

---

[795] 17 December was a Sunday in 1732, Kratz, *Hist. Cal.*, but from the context it seems the year was still 1732.
[796] Resumed on p. 324.
[797] See above p. 83 n. 481.

That in case there should be only one such daughter then to raise the sum of £2,000 for such daughter, with £40 per annum for her maintenance until she attained the age of 10 years, and thenceforth £80 per annum until she attained the age of 14 years, and thenceforth £120 per annum until such daughters' said portions should grow due, which said sums were to be paid half yearly as the same respectively should become due, until the marriage of such daughter or her age of 18 years which should first happen after the commencement of the said term of 80 years, when the said portion is by the said deed made payable. [184]

That in case the said portion for such daughter should not be paid at her marriage or her age of 18 years, or if she should be unmarried or attain the age of 18 years before the commencement of the said term, that then after the space of one year after the commencement of the said term, the said portion of £2,000 should bear interest of £8 per cent per annum until paid, which interest was also to be levied out of the rents and profits of the said lands by the said Echlin and Maxwell or the survivor, and the executor or administrator or the said survivor of them.

The said marriage soon after took effect, and the said Simon Richardson and Catherine his wife are since dead, by whose death the said Henry became seised of the said lands for life and the said Jane his wife died in the year 1690, leaving issue only one daughter named Jane, with whom in 1714 the plaintiff intermarried, who was then of age of 26 years. Henry Richardson died in March 1730 without issue male, whereby the remainder of the said lands subject to the said term of 80 years vested in the defendant Francis Richardson eldest son of the said Edward who is long since dead, and Jane also died in the lifetime of her father, and the plaintiff as her administrator 25 June 1730 brought this bill for an account of her maintenance from the death of her said mother, as also of the said sum of £2,000 and interest.

And the single question is, when interest is to be allowed for this portion?

The trustees had no right at law to enter till a failure of issue male, then the question in equity will be, whether it appears to have been the intention of the parties to the settlement, that if the daughters came to 18 or were married they should have their portions in the life of their father, if the mother died leaving no issue male.

In the case of *Greaves* v. *Maddison*[798] the wife died and left no issue male but two daughters and [185] the portions were raised in the life of the father because the contingency of dying without issue male happened by the death of the wife, and the portion was payable at 18 or marriage.

And in *Gerard* v. *Gerard*[799] 2 Vern. 458, because the intention was that they should have their portion at marriage.

But in these, and all the other book cases the contingency happened in the life of the father or jointuress, and the portions were absolutely payable. In *Staniforth* v. *Staniforth*[800] 2 Vern. 466 the contingency of dying without issue male happened, and no time was limited for the payment. I shall now consider how far our case squares with these, and differs from them.

In this case no part of the contingency on which the trust was to arise happened in the life of the father. The trust was for raising portions for such daughters as were living at the commencement of the term payable at 18 or marriage etc. The term

---

[798] *Greaves* v. *Mattison* (1682) Jones T. 201, 84 E.R. 1216 and see page 157 [199].
[799] *Gerrard* v. *Gerrard* (1703) 2 Vern. 458, 23 E.R. 894.
[800] *Staniforth* v. *Staniforth* (1703) 2 Vern. 460, 23 E.R. 895.

commenced in interest before the birth, and vested in the trustees when the deed was executed and therefore the words must relate to the commencement of the term in possession.

'Tis provided by the deed, that if the father paid any money in part of the portion it was to be deducted. Now this was unnecessary if they were entitled to it in his lifetime, and he was compellable to pay the whole; and the trustees are to account with these in remainder, which shows the father was not to be encumbered or troubled.

The portions are not payable at 18 or marriage but which should first happen after the commencement of the term, so the parties to the settlement have told us when it shall be raised, and have described what commencement they mean, whereas according to their description these phrases would be nugatory, 2 Vern. 760 *Butler* v. *Duncomb*.[801]

This portion then can't bear interest from her marriage in the lifetime of the father, because the contingency did not happen in his life. [*186*]

Mr Malone

Here are two questions:

1. Whether Jane being dead before the term commenced in possession, the plaintiff has any right to the portion?

2. If he has a title to the portion, whether it will bear interest till the death of the father?

As to the first, I agree that on the death of Jane the mother the term vested in the life of Henry in point of interest from the authority of many cases, but the contingencies annexed to the trust of the term did not happen.

The trust is for such daughters as shall be living at the commencement of the term, or if the wife is enseint,[802] as shall be born after. So the daughter which is born before and is alive at the commencement of the term, or is born after is to be provided for. The last clause goes farther. If no daughter is living at the commencement of the term, or if the portion is paid by Henry or the remainderman, the term is to cease. So this daughter not being living at the commencement of the term, is not within the meaning or intention of the settlement.

But if the plaintiff as her administrator has a title, let us consider the second point, and the intention of the parties must be the guide for the court to observe and govern themselves by. It appears from all the clauses that commencement must be meant in point of profit. It is an extraordinary construction that the father who by nature has the tuition and care of his children shall be obliged to raise portions or maintenance for them in his lifetime. He is bound by nature and is trusted by the law to provide for them. If the portions might be raised in his lifetime, the maintenances might, and here are different maintenances. By the first clause, portions are to be raised for such daughters as are alive at the commencement of the term, which was not till after the death of the father, and the failure of issue male. By the second the trust is to raise portions for such daughters, or those born after, this must have [*187*] relation to the commencement, or they would not distinguish between daughters born before or after. So it is plain they had in their minds a certain time for the commencement.

[801] *Butler* v. *Duncomb* (1718) 2 Vern. 760, 23 E.R. 1096.
[802] Or enceinte, LF. pregnant.

'Which said portion is payable to such daughter not born or married etc' so the words are plainer in every clause. 'That in case the said portion etc.', so that if the trust is to arise on failure of issue male there is otherwise no occasion for this restriction, and commencement must be meant of a certain time, or why is the portion to be paid within a year after? And the yearly maintenances are to be paid from the commencement. They are only to be paid if the daughters are under 18 or unmarried, but neither the portions nor maintenances are to be raised till after the death of the father. The trustees are not till then to come into possession, and they are to account with the remaindermen.

The case of *Corbet* v. *Maidwell*[803] and of *Butler* v. *Duncomb*[804] (which is an authority in point) show the court was willing to give a check to former authorities. So *Cotton* v. *Cotton*[805] at the Rolls.

Mr Coghlan for the plaintiff[806]

The case of *Staniforth* v. *Staniforth*[807] 2 Vern. 460 squares with ours, where the term arose as a charge in his lifetime, though not to put the tenant for life out of possession, the estate tail being out of the case. So *Gerard* v. *Gerard*[808] 2 Vern. 458, and the second resolution in the case of *Corbet* v. *Maidwell*[809] 2 Vern. 165 [*sic*].

Mr Daly

We are entitled to this portion and the maintenance provided in the lifetime of the father from the purport of the settlement. Jane survived her mother, whereby in construction of equity the father being dead without issue male of that marriage the portion arose.

The question is, what is the meaning of the word commencement? [*188*] This is an agreement on the part of the mother and her friends for a provision for her daughters in case the estate went to the collaterals. The plaintiff and defendant are both purchasers, and to be favoured.

The issue female were to be provided for at all events when they married or arrived at a proper age. At law the estate of tenant in tail after possibility[810] is changed into an estate for life. 'He must attorn', etc. Here everything contingent had happened, for it was no contingency whether the father would die or not, and how can the term be vested in point of interest on the death of the mother, and we not be entitled to the portion?

---

803   *Corbett* v. *Maydwell* (1710) 2 Vern. 640, 23 E.R. 1019; 2 Vern. 655, 23 E.R. 1027.

804   *Butler* v. *Duncomb* (1718) 2 Vern. 760, 23 E.R. 1096.

805   No citation given. Possibly *Cotton* v. *Cotton* (1690) 2 Vern. 290, 23 E.R. 787; or *Cotton* v. *Cotton* (1678) 2 Ch. Rep. 138, 21 E.R. 639.

806   Probably Francis Coghlan (or Coughlan), s. and heir of Cornelius, of King's Co. Middle Temple, 12 August 1707. Admitted King's Inns, Trinity term, 1712, d. 17 Jan. 1734 in London.

807   *Staniforth* v. *Staniforth* (1703) 2 Vern. 460, 23 E.R. 895.

808   *Gerrard* v. *Gerrard* (1703) 2 Vern. 458, 23 E.R. 894.

809   *Corbett* v. *Maydwell* (1710) 2 Vern. 655, 23 E.R. 1027.

810   Short for 'tenant in tail after possibility of issue extinct'. A grant 'to A and the heirs of his body by his wife B' creates a fee tail special. If B dies without leaving issue, A is a tenant in tail after possibility of issue extinct, and cannot bar the entail, and so in effect has a life estate.

We don't come to have it raised in the lifetime of the father, but after his death, and it appears we have a right to it from the case of *Gerard* v. *Gerard*,[811] and *Corbet* v. *Maidwell*.[812]

But the clause that the portion should be allowed if it was paid by the father makes it stronger, for it shows the parties had it in view that the portion might become payable in his lifetime, or how was what he should pay to be deducted out of the portion?

[']And in case said portion for such daughter should not be paid['] etc., that is if the daughters come to 18, or were married before the death of the father, though the portion was not actually paid, it was to carry interest.

The great question is as to the maintenance and interest. The portion was to arise on the contingency of no issue male, and it was the care of the marriage settlement that it should not be in the power of the father to hinder his daughter of a mainte-nance, or make an unreasonable bargain with her for her portion. Maintenance is a provision antecedent to the portion and no contingency is required to that but the not having issue male, so at all events maintenance is to accrue till marriage age or a certain age. [*189*]

Monday July the 2nd 1733.[813]

The lord chief baron having stated the case at large observed that there were two questions:

1. Whether the daughter who married and died in the lifetime of her father was entitled to the portion?

2. If she was, when it became payable, and would bear interest?

As to the first, he said that the intention of the parties to a deed where their real view could be collected was rather to be considered than the strict words, as far as there were agreeable to the rules of law.

That the difficulty arose from the multiplicity of the words of the trust of the term, and he observed in behalf of the profession, that long deeds were not introduced by lawyers, that persons of condition liked them for pomp and vanity, and that it was the interest of the engrosser to sooth[e] them in this opinion. He therefore thought a court of equity ought to enquire into the intention of the parties to this settlement, particularly of Mr Maxwell, (who gave what was a very large portion in 1685) which was to secure a provision for the issue male and female of the marriage independent of their father, indeed if the estate came into his family by his daughter having sons, the daughters were left to the discretion of their father, but they were to be provided for before the sons by a second venter.[814] Has then Mr Maxwell said anything in this settlement which shows he designed this daughter should not have her portion if her father survived her? This can't be collected from any words in the legal commencement of the term, for that is absolute, nor from any words in the trust of the term, indeed if commencement is to be understood as in *Butler* v. *Duncomb*[815] for the time when the term came into possession, she is entitled to no provision if she died in the life of her father, but [*190*] this term vested in point of interest when the

[811] *Gerrard* v. *Gerrard* (1703) 2 Vern. 458, 23 E.R. 894.
[812] *Corbett* v. *Maydwell* (1710) 2 Vern. 640, 23 E.R. 1019; 2 Vern. 655, 23 E.R. 1027.
[813] Note that the change of year is given in the MS. 2 July was a Monday in 1733. Note the gap of nearly seven months in the same case before the C.J. gives his opinion.
[814] L. womb.
[815] *Butler* v. *Duncomb* (1718) 2 Vern. 760, 23 E.R. 1096.

mother died without issue male, and it is this commencement of the term in point of interest that is here intended, and this is not a technical word that must be taken in a strict sense, and although 'tis used several times in the declaration of the trust of the term, it will answer in this sense, this portion therefore became payable on her marriage which was in the life of her father, and she is entitled from that time to interest.

This provision was designed to prefer the daughters in marriage, and the question is, if there are any authorities to overrule this construction, which constantly prevailed in the reigns of King Charles II and King William? The cases of *Corbet* v. *Maidwell*,[816] *Brome* v. *Berkeley*,[817] and *Butler* v. *Duncomb*[818] depended upon on particular circumstances which are not in this case, not is there any danger of destroying the estate by a sale or mortgage of the reversion, and Lord Cowper in the case of *Corbet* v. *Maidwell*[819] thought, that if the portion was to be raised in the life of the father, he must pay interest. Here the father is dead, the term vested in possession, and none of these inconveniences can happen, but it may be known what the sum and interest is, and for what to be had, for the court to decree on, but it cannot be known what people will advance money for on a mortgage of a reversion.

Lord Chief Justice Rogerson

We don't form our opinion on the foundation of any of the reported cases, where the bills were filed to have the portions raised in the life of the father or jointures, and the question was not, as in this, with the remainderman after the death of both of them. [*191*]

I shall first consider the precedents[820] that are reported.

In the case of *Corbet* v. *Maidwell*[821] the court refused to raise the portion, because the contingency had not happened, for who could know whether the father would provide for his daughter or not, and it varied in this from the case of *Staniforth* v. *Staniforth*,[822] and *Gerard* v. *Gerard*,[823] and if the bill had been brought against the remainderman, he could have shown, whether the daughter was provided for or not.

In *Butler* v. *Duncomb*[824] the mother was alive, and the term being vested in point of interest, and the portion not to be raised till the commencement, they understood that of the term's coming into possession, and would not charge the jointure. But if the bill had been brought against the remainderman, it would have been a charge, and the court must have raised it.

Brome v. *Berkeley*[825] was brought too in the life of the mother, and the portions being to be raised either out of the rents and profits, or etc., showed the term must first come into possession.

But here the father and mother being out of the case, let us see how it stands as to him in remainder? It is insisted on for the defendant, that though the term vested

---

816 *Corbett* v. *Maydwell* (1710) 2 Vern. 640, 23 E.R. 1019; 2 Vern. 655, 23 E.R. 1027.
817 *Brome* v. *Berkley* (1728) 6 Bro. P.C. 2nd ed. 108, 2 E.R. 965.
818 *Butler* v. *Duncomb* (1718) 2 Vern. 760, 23 E.R. 1096.
819 *Corbett* v. *Maydwell* (1710) 2 Vern. 640, 23 E.R. 1019; 2 Vern. 655, 23 E.R. 1027.
820 Spelled 'presidents' in MS.
821 *Corbett* v. *Maydwell* (1710) 2 Vern. 640, 23 E.R. 1019; 2 Vern. 655, 23 E.R. 1027.
822 *Staniforth* v. *Staniforth* (1703) 2 Vern. 460, 23 E.R. 895.
823 *Gerrard* v. *Gerrard* (1703) 2 Vern. 458, 23 E.R. 894.
824 *Butler* v. *Duncomb* (1718) 2 Vern. 760, 23 E.R. 1096.
825 *Brome* v. *Berkley* (1728) 6 Bro. P.C. 2nd ed. 108, 2 E.R. 965.

in the trustee on the death of the mother without issue male, yet by the trust of the term the portion cannot be raised because the contingency never happened, the daughter not being alive at the death of the father.

Though the second son is considered as a purchaser in equity, yet Mr Maxwell from whom the consideration and portion moved, only purchased for his daughter and grandchildren. If the word 'commencement' should be taken for actual possession, though the portion is made payable at 18 or marriage the daughter might want preferment if the father was not able or willing to provide for her, and though she was married and left children, by this construction they would not be entitled to the portion. So that commencement here must be understood when [192] the term commenced in point of interest, which was when the mother died without issue male, and the maintenance is to be raised in the same manner as the portion, so that if neither maintenance nor portion could be raised till the term came into possession, the daughter might starve in the meantime. Though I make a lease to begin *a fine et expiratione*[826] of another, it shall commence on the surrender of the former.

So I am of opinion that this portion with interest from the marriage of the daughter is to be raised out of this term.

Lord Chancellor

I shall take notice of what occurs to me in general.

If the case of *Greaves* v. *Mathison*[827] which was before the judges stood, everything that was contingent in this case happened by the death of the mother.

In the case of *Staniforth* v. *Staniforth*[828] the master of the rolls declared, that the contingency happened by the death of the father or mother and in the case of *Gerard* v. *Gerard*[829] the portion which depended on same contingency was decreed to be raised.

And this opinion lasted till the case of *Corbet* v. *Maidwell*.[830] There the court thought that as raising portions out of a reversion tended to the destruction of the estate, they would not do it without particular words that showed the intention of the parties to be so, and therefore distinguished that from other cases that had gone before.

Brome v. *Berkeley*[831] is the next case where the court was stopped from raising the portions by the words, [']the first payment to be made['] etc.

But the case of *Butler* v. *Duncomb*[832] has created the difficulty in this case, where it was expressly decreed, that the portion should not be raised till the death of the jointuress, nor bear interest, and that commencement [193] must be understood when the term came into possession.

But as that case stands single, and is not supported by authorities either before or since, I am not for carrying it so far, especially in this case where the wife was a purchaser, and this is all her family is to have for her £1,000, and that the remainderman is not to be considered in the same light appears from the case of *Tipping* v. *Piggot*[833]

---

[826] L. from the end and expiration.

[827] *Greaves* v. *Mattison* (1682) Jones T. 201, 84 E.R. 1216, apparently same case as *Greaves* v. *Mattison* '2 Jon. 201', cited at p. 157 [199].

[828] *Staniforth* v. *Staniforth* (1703) 2 Vern. 460, 23 E.R. 895.

[829] *Gerrard* v. *Gerrard* (1703) 2 Vern. 458, 23 E.R. 894.

[830] *Corbett* v. *Maydwell* (1710) 2 Vern. 640, 23 E.R. 1019; 2 Vern. 655, 23 E.R. 1027.

[831] *Brome* v. *Berkley* (1728) 6 Bro. P.C. 2nd ed. 108, 2 E.R. 965.

[832] *Butler* v. *Duncomb* (1718) 2 Vern. 760, 23 E.R. 1096.

[833] *Tipping* v. *Piggot* (1711) Gilb. 34, 25 E.R. 25.

adjudged by Lord Harcourt[834] in 1713, where his Lordship relieved the issue of the marriage against a breach of trust, but would not [relieve] him in remainder.

And I think we ought to consider how the law stood at the time this deed was executed, when these doubts had not been raised, but the commencement of the term was taken for the time when it vested in interest, and the reigning opinion was to guide lawyers in their drafts.

So I agree with my lords the judges that she is entitled to the portion, because she was a daughter living when the term commenced in point of interest, and her portion was payable at 18, but as she lived with her father till the time of her marriage, till she was 26 years of age, we will set the maintenance against the interest till that time, and the portion with interest from the time of her marriage is to be raised out of this term.

Post 412.

GEORGE STEPNEY ESQR PLAINTIFF

PHILIP RAWSON ESQR, MARTHA HIS WIFE,

AND THE REVEREND CHARLES STEPNEY DEFENDANTS

AND

PHILIP RAWSON ESQR, MARTHA RAWSON ALIAS
STEPNEY HIS WIFE,

AND STEPNEY RAWSON ELDEST SON

AND HEIR OF THE SAID PHILIP AND MARTHA, PLAINTIFFS

GEORGE STEPNEY ESQR, CHARLES STEPNEY CLERK, [*194*]
WILLIAM DANBERRY, THOMAS MAUNSELL, FRANCIS DUGGAN
AND THEODORA STEPNEY, ALIAS COOPER, DEFENDANTS[835]

Post 412.

Eodem die

In court: Lord Chancellor
                 Lord Chief Justice Rogerson
                 Lord Chief Baron Marlay

The Case

John Stepney the complaintiffs'[836] grandfather being seised in fee of several lands in the counties of Limerick and Cork, he and his eldest son Joseph Stepney by their deeds of lease and release[837] bearing date the 27 and 28 days of April 1682 in

834 Simon Harcourt (*c.* 1661–1727), 1st Viscount Harcourt, L.C.; L.K. 1710 to April 1713.
835 Cited on p. 324.
836 I.e. co-plaintiffs.
837 See above p. 83 n. 481.

consideration of a marriage to be had between the said Joseph Stepney and Martha
Cuffe daughter of Martha Cuffe widow, and in consideration of £2,200, and for other
considerations therein mentioned, did convey the said lands to Denny Muschamp,
Agmandisham Cuff,[838] James Plunket, and George Canning Esqrs and their heirs,
to the use of the said John Stepney till the said marriage took effect, and after the
said marriage, as to certain part of the said lands to the use of the said John and his
wife for their lives, and as to the residue of the said lands after the said marriage to
the said Joseph Stepney for life, and after his death to the use of the said Martha
for life, and after the death of the said John and Joseph and their wives then the
whole lands were limited to the use of the first and other sons of the said Joseph and
Martha in tail [*195*] male, and for want of such issue to the use of Hugh Harding,
Thomas Denny, Thomas Stepney, and Lancelot Stepney Esqrs, their executors, and
administrators, for the term of 99 years, and from the determination of that estate
to the use of the heirs males [*sic*] of the said Joseph, and for the want of such issue,
and a deposition of such remainder by a deed or will, to the use of the right heirs of
the said John Stepney for ever.

And by the said deed the trust of the said term was declared to be, that if the said
Joseph Stepney should die, and leave no issue male begotten of the said Martha then
alive, nor after born alive, or if having such issue male they should all die without
issue male before 21 years of age, and the said Joseph Stepney should in either case
leave one or more daughters begotten on the said Martha, that if but one daughter
the sum of £2,000, to be paid to such daughter, but if two daughters that then the said
sum of £2,000 should be equally divided between them, and should be raised by the
said trustees the survivors and survivor of them, or the executors or administrators
of the survivor either out of the rents issues and profits of the premises so to them
limited, or by leasing, mortgaging, charging, or sale of the premises, for all or any
part of the said term, or by all or any of the said ways or means, and to be paid
to and for such daughter or daughters respectively at their several ages of 18 years
or days of marriage which should first happen; Provided the persons to whom the
premises should next belong or appertain, have one whole year's time and notice
given him before such leasing mortgaging charging or sale thereof for payment of
the said portion. [*196*] And by the said settlement it was likewise agreed, that until
the said daughter or daughters attained their ages of 18 years or days of marriage,
that then she or they should until 7 years of age have £30 per annum, and from 7 to
12 years of age £40 per annum, and from thence to 18 years or day of marriage £70
per annum.

And the said term was to be void, whenever the said Joseph Stepney, or the person
to whom the premises should belong by the limitations therein mentioned should
pay the said portion, and the said sums before specified.

The said marriage took effect, and the said John Stepney and Frances his wife
died in the lifetime of the said Joseph Stepney, who had issue by Martha two sons,
Alban, who died in October 1714 without issue, aged about 28 years, and Robert,
who died about the year 1710 without issue about the age of 21, and one daughter
named Martha. Martha the wife died about 30 years ago, and Joseph Stepney, about
the year 1700 married a second wife, by whom he had issue the plaintiff, now his
only son.

In October 1714 the defendant Rawson married the said Martha the daughter.

---

[838] So spelled without the 'e'.

In the year 1720 the estate of the said Rawson being in mortgage to Richard late Lord Baron [Gowran] of Gowran,[839] who had filed a bill of foreclosure, the said Joseph Stepney, in order to raise the said sum for the said Philip Rawson, levied a fine of the said lands, and in or about the month of July 1721 borrowed from William Ludlow Esqr the sum of £2,500 at £7 per cent, and made a mortgage in fee of a considerable part of his said estate for securing the repayment thereof, and there being some disputes between the said Lord Gowran and Rawson concerning the sum that remained [197] due to him his Lordship refused to accept the said £2,000 whereupon the said Rawson on the 19 of August 1721 lent the said £2,000 to a banker at £5 per cent, and took his note for the same payable to the said Joseph Stepney.

In the year 1724 the said banker paid the said note to the said Joseph Stepney, who was prevailed on by the said Rawson not to pay it unto Ludlow, but to pay it to Rawson, which he did in the month of February 1724 by a cash note of Henry and Company by the hands of the complaintiff, and on the 17 day of the said February Rawson gave his note to the plaintiff for the said £2,000 note, and promised to be accountable for the same.

12 January 1716 the said Joseph Stepney made his will, wherein he recites that the said Martha was by the settlement entitled to £2,000 for her portion, and he thereby confirms it to her, and directed that it should be paid in twelve months next after his decease without interest for the said 12 months, and devised his real estate unto Thomas Stepney, John Cuff, Henry Obrien, and Edward Dean Esqrs and their heirs, to the use of William Denberry,[840] Thomas Maunsel,[841] and Francis Duggan and the survivor of them his executors and administrators for the term of 99 years from the day of his death, upon trust and after the determination of that estate to the use of the complaintiff for life, remainder to trustees to support contingent uses,[842] remainder to his first and every other son in tail male, and for want of such issue, to the said Martha for life, remainder to trustees to support contingent remainders, remainder to Stepney Lawson the eldest son of his said daughter for life, and after his decease to his first and every other son in tail male, and for want of such issue to the second and every other son of the said Martha in tail male, with several remainders over, [198] and declared the trust of the said term of 99 years to be, in case his wife Theodora should survive him, [that] the sum of £150 per annum should be paid her during her life, and that the trustees should out of the rents, issues and profits, or by sale, or mortgage, or otherwise raise or levy such sum or sums as should be sufficient for the payment of his just debts and legacies, and wills, that if George Stepney, or such other person as by virtue of his will should be entitled to his real estate, should pay the £150 per annum, and his said debts and legacies that then and not before the term of 99 years should cease, and devises that £150 to his nieces and some smaller legacies should be paid out of his personal estate if sufficient, or otherwise out of the rents of his real estate, and appointed the complaintiff his sole executor, and died the 22 of July 1725. Lancelot Stepney the surviving trustee of the term died in 1724, and the defendant Charles Stepney is his administrator.

---

[839] Richard FitzPatrick (c. 1662–1727), created Baron Gowran of Gowran in Co. Kilkenny in 1715, one of the peers created on the accession of George I. Cokayne, *Complete Peerage*, vi. 39.

[840] So spelled in MS.

[841] So spelled in MS.

[842] Above, p. 82 n. 478.

Mr Solicitor General for the defendants
in the original cause,
and the plaintiffs in the cross cause.

The contingency of the failure of issue male happened in the lifetime of Joseph Stepney, so the question is, from what time Martha's portion shall bear interest, whether from the death of Alban, or Joseph Stepney, and this depends partly though not altogether on another question, whether a court of equity would have raised the portion in the life of Joseph, for the objection that it would distress Joseph admits of a different consideration, but it might not carry interest in his life, and be a charge on the estate.

As to the practice of the courts of equity in raising [199] portions out of reversionary terms, I shall consider what introduced such practice, and the cases where such decrees have been made, and endeavour to show that this case squares with them, and then I shall consider those cases where the resolutions have been different, and the reasons of them.

Courts of equity always consider children as purchasers of these terms, and depart from the letter, and always construe portions and trust for them favourably, and so as best to answer the end of the parties, for these trusts are nothing but their agreement to make an effectual provision for such children, and as in mortgages they lengthen the time of payment, so in these cases they shorten it, if the term is once vested and the trust don't depend on a contingency; as if the trust is to A for life, then to B the jointuress for life, and then comes the term, in which there is no contingency as to the vesting, or declaration of trust, the court will sell or mortgage the term, so as best to answer the end of it, and this is the plainest case.

So where they could bring other cases to square with the reason of this, they have come to the same resolution.

The earliest case is *Greaves* v. *Mattison*[843] 2 Jon. 201, agreeable to which there are many subsequent resolutions, 2 Vern. 458,[844] 460,[845] and there are none to the contrary, but succeeding chancellors have always followed them, which shows them to be just, though they have declared they would have decreed otherwise, if it had been *res integra*.[846]

There are some cases indeed which at first seem contrary, but are very easily distinguished from it.

Corbet v. *Maidwell*[847] turned on this point, that the term was for raising portions for such daughters as were unmarried or unprovided for at the death of the father, which must be contingent during his life.

Butler v. *Duncomb*[848] turned on the manner the trust [200] of the term was declared, which was to take effect from the commencement of the term.

In the case of *Brome* v. *Berkeley*[849] the maintenance which is like the interest for the portion was not to commence till the term came in possession, and therefore the portion which was subsequent to the maintenance could not be raised before,

[843] *Greaves* v. *Mattison* (1682) Jones T. 201, 84 E.R. 1216. Apparently same case as *Greaves* v. *Maddison* cited above, p. 148 [*184*] and *Greaves* v. *Mathison* at p. 153 [*192*].
[844] *Gerrard* v. *Gerrard* (1703) 2 Vern. 458, 23 E.R. 894.
[845] *Butler* v. *Duncomb* (1718) 2 Vern. 760, 23 E.R. 1096.
[846] See above, p. 18 n. 100.
[847] *Corbett* v. *Maydwell* (1710) 2 Vern. 640, 23 E.R. 1019; 2 Vern. 655, 23 E.R. 1027.
[848] *Butler* v. *Duncomb* (1718) 2 Vern. 760, 23 E.R. 1096.
[849] *Brome* v. *Berkley* (1728) 6 Bro. P.C. 2nd ed. 108, 2 E.R. 965.

and it is said in the case of *Sandys* v. *Sandys*[850] quoted by Lord King in that case, that postponing the maintenance always postponed the portion.

The trust of this term don't differ from those cases where relief has been given, for the contingency happening by the death of Alban, and nothing contingent remaining, it became the ordinary case.

I suppose they will object the clause of notice, 'Provided the person', etc. But if this is joined with the subsequent clause, 'If Joseph or the person etc. should pay' etc. it appears of no weight, for then it means no more than that whoever is entitled to this estate when the portion is to be raised shall have timely notice of a sale or mortgage, that they may not be improvidently distressed, and was put in to restrain the power of the trustees.

But our case is stronger, because we come after the death of Joseph Stepney, and the portion in point of reason ought to carry interest when it vested.

The daughter is a purchaser, but the son is a volunteer under the will of his father.

Mr Stannard

I shan't go into the several cases, but endeavour to show that it appears by several clauses in the deed that this portion was to be paid in the life of the father.

'Tis a settled point, that if the contingency happens in the life of the father, and the portion is made payable at a certain age, which is past, that it [201] shall then be raised, unless something appears in the deed expressly to the contrary.

These portions are to be raised on a double contingency, if Joseph die without male issue, or if they die under 21.

Objection: Alban died about 28 in the life of his father, so this portion is not to be raised.

Answer: Dying before 21 must be understood after the death of the father.

The other parts of the deed relate to this double contingency. The next consideration of the parties was, if the contingency happened how these portions should be raised, either by the rents etc., or by leasing, etc., and this alternative way of raising is applicable to each contingency, and shows that if the contingency happened in the life of Joseph the portion was to be raised by mortgage or sale, if after his death, by the rents etc.

After the parties have thus provided for the contingencies and raising the portions, by another clause they declare how the term shall cease. 'If Joseph die without daughters, or if he, or the person to whom the premises' etc. If the portion was not to be raised in his life, why is it said, 'if Joseph pay'? So it is plain they thought it payable in his life.

Objection: The portions are not to be raised in his life from the clause 'Provided the person' etc.

Answer: This can't overturn the positive directions and clauses of the deed. But they are very consistent.

If the portion was raised in the life of Joseph, it must be by mortgage or sale, which would load the remainder, but be no prejudice to Joseph, who received the whole profits. So there was no need to take care of him, by giving him time to raise the portion, because he was not hurt. But when the trustees enter on the possession of the

---

[850] *Sandys* v. *Sandys* (1721) 1 P. Wms. 707, 24 E.R. 580, cited in *Brome* v. *Berkley* (1728) 6 Bro. P.C. 2nd ed. 108 at 112, 2 E.R. 965 at 967.

term which is precedent to the remainders, they were not to mangle the estate, if the remainderman was willing to pay the [202] portions, and it don't follow because the remainderman has a year given him, and Joseph not, that therefore portions are not to be raised in his life, because of the different reasons, that one would be injured, and the other not; and it was more advantageous to the daughters to receive the portions at once, though they waited a year, than out of the rents and profits. The portions are made payable at 18 or marriage, and maintenance is provided for and in the meantime, this shows that the parties intended them a sure provision, and that the money was then payable.

Mr Attorney General for the plaintiff

The question is, when the £2,000 shall carry interest?

I shall consider this case in two lights.

1. Whether on the construction of the deed the court would have decreed this reversionary term to be vested in the life of Joseph?

2. Whether it shall bear interest from the marriage of Martha, or the death of Joseph?

As to the first, if Rawson and his wife had filed a bill your Lordship would not have decreed a sale or mortgage in the life of Joseph. The legal estate don't arise till after the death of the father and mother.

I shall first consider this case as if it were *res nova*, and then with former resolutions, and show that it don't come under the old but later authorities.

If it were *res integra*[851] it would appear a very odd doctrine, because by the agreement of the parties the term is not to arise till after the death of the father and mother without issue male, so two things are necessary to the raising it, the death of the father and mother, and the want of issue male.

But equity in favour of daughters have shortened the time, as they have lengthened it [203] in behalf of mortgagors, which is rather a political than an equitable construction, and goes on a presumption which ought not to be made, that the father won't provide for his child, robs him of the duty to him, and is a temptation to the daughters to marry without his consent. But I must allow that courts of equity have in some cases decreed these reversionary terms to be sold, but these are different from ours, and they have of late years taken another turn, and never decreed the sale of a reversion, unless where the authorities are express, or the parties have plainly agreed it should be so.

Let us see then if the intention of the parties to the settlement appears to be, that the money should be raised before the death of the father and mother, and it is plain they did not from the words of the trust of the term. 'If Joseph Stepney shall die, and leave no issue male then alive' etc. 'Leave', and 'then alive' must relate, to the time of his death. So the provision for the daughters is only to take place at the death of the father. 'And if Joseph leave one or more daughter or daughters' etc. So the daughter who is entitled is one living at the death of the father, so that though she was married before, if she is not alive at his death, she is not entitled.

Next let us see how the maintenance and principal money are to be raised.

1. As to the principal, the trustees have a power to raise it either out of the rents, or by sale or mortgage etc. at their election, so it is clear this could not be raised in

---

[851] See above, p. 18 n. 100.

the life of Joseph, for they could not then raise it out of the rents, they not being entitled to the profits till his death. So they have no power to act till the father is dead.

The next clause of notice to the remainderman is very strong. It is a proviso or condition precedent, and the portion can't be raised till it be performed. [*204*]

The title of Joseph being precedent to the term, he can't be the person next entitled after the term. And this differs this case from all the resolutions that have been before, and is a condition [that] can't be dispensed with.

Objection: Joseph has a power to pay off the portion, and then the term is to cease, and the trustees are to account for the surplus profits.

Answer: It is left in the power of Joseph to pay the portion, but it don't from thence follow that he was obliged to it. The trustees are to account with him or them who are entitled to the possession. They are not to account with Mr Stepney, but with those in remainder. So it appears from these clauses that the principal is not to be raised in the life of the father.

[2.] But the clause of maintenance is stronger. The daughters are to have maintenances till 18, which sums are to be raised out of the rents, etc. and the residue of the profits are to go towards the portions. I shall consider this in two lights.

1. Profits have been construed to give a power to sell, where the money could not be raised in a proper time out of the annual rents and profits, and where it did not appear that annual profits were meant. But annual rents and profits must be meant here, to distinguish them from a sale or mortgage which are mentioned in the same breath. Then if the maintenance is to be paid out of rents, and the trustees are not entitled to these during the life of the father, it could not be raised while he lived, and in this case the maintenance must be previous to the portions, because the residue is to go towards the portions.

2. This arises also not only from the words of the deed, and the intention of the parties, but from [*205*] the nature of the thing, that the father will provide for them, and equity will not maintain them and there is no case in which the reversion has been decreed to be sold where the maintenance was directed to [be] raised out of the annual rents and profits.

I shall mention one or two cases to show that these portions are not payable till after the death of the father and mother.

Butler v. *Duncomb*,[852] in which case there are no words in favour of the defendant more than in this, but after the commencement, and the words here though not the same are as strong, because it is impossible to be done till after the death of the father and mother without issue male, and equity is not bound down by words, but the agreement of the parties.

In this the same intention appears though not in the same words as in the case of *Brome* v. *Berkeley*,[853] for here the maintenance being out of annual rents and profits could not arise till the term commenced in possession. There the trustees could not elect to raise the portion out of the rents, or by sale etc. in the life of the mother, which showed that the parties who gave them that election did not design the portions should be raised in her life. And this is our case.

In the case of *Sandys* v. *Sandys*[854] there was a term of 500 years in common form, and the trust was, that the trustees should by sale or mortgage, or by the overplus

---

[852] *Butler* v. *Duncomb* (1718) 2 Vern. 760, 23 E.R. 1096.
[853] *Brome* v. *Berkley* (1728) 6 Bro. P.C. 2nd ed. 108, 2 E.R. 965.
[854] *Sandys* v. *Sandys* (1721) 1 P. Wms. 707, 24 E.R. 580.

rents[855] above the maintenance raise[d], etc., and the bill was dismissed, because the principal was postponed to the maintenance, which condition arise[856] in the life of the mother, being to come out of the annual rents and profits.

Mr Malone

[*206*] This question depends upon the construction of the deed of settlement, and no case for raising portions out of a reversion squares with this, and the courts of equity have never decreed a maintenance and portion to be raised out of a reversion, where the intention appeared not to have them raised till after the death of the father.

The portion is to be raised out of the rents and profits, or by mortgage or sale. But the maintenance is only to come out of the rents and profits, so the deed distinguishes between the manner the portions and maintenance are to be raised, which are in their own nature annual. They are to have such a maintenance till 7, which from thence to 12 is to be increased to so much, and from that time to be further raised till 18, when the portions are payable, so the trustees have no election to raise the maintenances as they have the portions, but they must come out of the rents and profits. So they can't be raised in the life of the father, because he is entitled to all the profits. And this further appears from that part of the clause, which directs that the residue of the rents and profits after the payment of the maintenances shall be laid up towards the portions. If this was to be done in the life of the father he must starve, for it would deprive him of his whole subsistence, and therefore the maintenances must be intended to be raised after his death. The trustees have an election given them to raise the portions either out of the rents or by sale or mortgage, and it can't be supposed that the parties gave them this election in the life of the father, or that they might in his life raise them out of the rents, for then they might turn him out of possession. [*207*] 'Provided the person to whom the premises' etc., this proviso goes only in defeasance of the precedent part of the deed to restrain a sale or mortgage, but is no restraint on the trustees to raise them out of the rents and profits, which must be meant after the death of the father. The trustees receiving the rents was no mischief to the remainderman, but a sale or mortgage might, and therefore he has a power given him to prevent it by paying the portions. This proviso is to be considered in a different light for the benefit of the remainderman than of Joseph, whereas if the term might have been sold or mortgaged in his lifetime, it would have been as reasonable to have taken care of him, as of the remainderman.

As to the clause 'If Joseph or Martha die without daughters then living, or if the said Joseph, or any other in whom the premises shall vest shall well and truly pay to the trustees the said portions, together with all charges the term shall cease, and they shall account with and pay the surplusage of the rents if any shall remain in their hands to him or them that shall have the immediate possession of the premises by virtue of the limitations', this is a further manifestation of the intent of the parties, for Joseph has a liberty to pay, and as he had a remainder in tail general, it was reasonable to give him a power to discharge and pay these portions in favour of this remainder, and the latter part ought to be taken distinct, that Joseph or the remaindermen may pay, but the trustees are to account for the profits with him or them who are in possession by virtue of the remainders.

---

[855] I.e. balance of the rents.
[856] *Sic*, for arose.

After the daughters come to 18 or are married no interest can be raised in the life of Joseph, because that would break in upon the profits which belong to him as much maintenance. [*208*]

Mr Calaghan

The first question is, whether interest is payable from the death of Alban without issue? The second, whether interest can arise earlier than a year after the death of the testator?

The portion did not vest on the death Alban, but depended on two contingencies, the failure of issue male, and the daughters surviving the father. The words are, 'And shall leave one or more daughter or daughters' etc. so they have no right in the life of their father, but this is like the case of *Corbet* v. *Maidwell*.[857] There the trust was for the daughters who were not provided for at his death. This is for those who shall be then in being, and shall survive him, and is a contingency without which they are not entitled.

But if they had a right to these portions in the life of their father, they were not payable till after his death, but vested only in point of interest, and so could not bear interest till then. They are *debitum in presenti, solvend[um] in futuro.*[858]

If they were payable in the life of Joseph, why is notice made requisite only to those in remainder? But here are two circumstances that bring it within the case of *Brome* v. *Berkeley*,[859] and *Cotton* v. *Cotton*.[860]

1. That the trustees have it in their option to raise the portions either out of the rents and profits or by sale and mortgage, which shows, they are not to be raised in the life of the father, but when they had it in their power to do it by one way or the other. [*209*]

2. The maintenance is not to commence till the term comes into possession, and they have no election as to it, but it is to arise out of the rents and profits.

Two objections have been made:

1. That if Joseph pay, the term is to cease.

This is a common clause, and it don't follow because he might pay it, that therefore it should be raised whether he would or not.

2. The trustees are to account with him or them etc. for the surplus profits.

'Him or them' don't refer to Joseph, but to those in remainder, for the words are future.

As notice and a year's time is given to the remaindermen for payment, no interest is payable till a year after the death of the father.

Lord Chief Justice Rogerson

Having stated the case, spoke to this effect:

The term will arise in this case though Alban Stepney died not before 21, because it was to arise on a double contingency, if the said Joseph Stepney should die etc.,

---

[857] *Corbett* v. *Maydwell* (1710) 2 Vern. 640, 23 E.R. 1019; 2 Vern. 655, 23 E.R. 1027.

[858] L. owed in the present, payable in future.

[859] *Brome* v. *Berkley* (1728) 6 Bro. P.C. 2nd ed. 108, 2 E.R. 965.

[860] No citation given. Possibly *Cotton* v. *Cotton* (1690) 2 Vern. 290, 23 E.R. 787; or *Cotton* v. *Cotton* (1678) 2 Ch. Rep. 138, 21 E.R. 639.

and the other contingency of his dying without issue male of that marriage [which] happened.

There are three points [that] have been made in this cause. 1. At what time the portion of Martha is to be raised? 2. Whether the £2,000 for which Rawson gave his note shall be considered as the portion of his wife, or part of the assets of Joseph Stepney? 3. If the £2,000 is to be taken as part of his assets, whether it shall go to George Stepney as executor, or to exonerate the real estate?

1. As to the time when this portion is payable [*210*] it is agreed that the term vested in interest at the death of Alban Stepney.

The portions are to be paid at 18 or marriage and depend on a double contingency.

It is plain the trustees could not raise this portion in the life of the father from the election that is given them to raise it either out of the rents and profits or by leasing etc., and because the maintenance is to come out of the rents and profits, yet why should it not carry an interest now from the death of Alban, since from that time she was entitled to the portion, and the rather because she is to have no maintenance from 18 or marriage but is to have the benefit of her portion which is then payable. And it was reasonable to give the remainderman notice, that he might pay it off if he pleased.

2. It appears from the evidence that this note was taken as payment of the £2,000, and Mr Rawson in his cross bill says the portion was never paid, and the words of his note show this £2,000 could not be paid for the portion but was lent to Rawson, or why should he make himself accountable for it? And it appears by his letter that he paid interest for it to Mr Stepney.

3. If then this £2,000 is part of the assets of Joseph Stepney, the third question is, whether it shall go to George Stepney as executor, or in payment of the debts and legacies to ease the real estate? And I am of opinion it shall go in exoneration of the real estate. In the case of *Ford* v. *Lord Grey* 1 Chan. Cas. 96,[861] the executor was decreed to account for the personal estate. Lev. 298[862] don't come up to this case, and the power and right of the executors is altered, and declared to be otherwise since that resolution. Ante 164.

In *Wainwright* v. *Bendlowe* 2 Vern. 707,[863] the whole real estate was directed to be sold, so there was no reason to apply personal estate. 1 Vern. 37,[864] 2 Vern. 701,[865] where there is no [*211*] express devise to the executor the residue of the personal estate don't belong to him, but must go in a course of distribution, and Mrs Rawson being in remainder is entitled to have the estate exonerated. So I think the daughter is entitled to the portion and interest from the death of Alban, and that the £2,000 as part of the assets is to be accounted for, and to go in payment of debts and legacies.

Lord Chief Baron

I am of the same opinion in all the points.

---

[861] No case of that name at that citation, and case there does not appear relevant. See *Ford* v. *Lord Grey* (1704) 1 Salk. 285, 91 E.R. 253; 6 Mod. 44, 87 E.R. 807.
[862] Cases at 1 Lev. 298 and 2 Lev. 298 do not appear relevant.
[863] 2 Vern. 707: *Wainwright* v. *Bendlowes* (1716) 2 Vern. 718, 23 E.R. 1071.
[864] *Pockley* v. *Pockley* (1681) 1 Vern. 36, 23 E.R. 290.
[865] *Howell* v. *Price* (1715) 2 Vern. 701, 23 E.R. 1055.

Lord Chancellor

And so am I. The only difficulty is, whether the £2,000 fall to go to George Stepney as executor, but it is plain the testator had no personal estate in contemplation that should go to him, but thought there would be none left, because he orders £150 and other little legacies to be paid out of his personal estate, or if that was not sufficient, out of the rents of his real estate.

November the 24th [1732][866]

In Exchequer

FOORD QUI TAM[867] v. SULLIVAN AND ORPIN

Mr Stannard pro Rege[868]

After trial the defendants being found guilty, have moved in arrest of judgment.

This is an information for bringing East India goods from Nantes[869] to Waterford, whereby the ship etc. is forfeited, and I humbly pray judgment against the ship.

When a ship is seised, proclamation is made, and the goods etc. are forfeited if somebody don't come in and put in his claim, upon which a writ of appraisement issues, and the ship is discharged on security given for the advancement of trade, and he must plead not guilty. [*212*]

1. Objection: This information is faulty, because it is not required by the Act of Navigation that the goods should be shipped in England.

Answer: 'Tis laid on the 7 G. 1 ch. 21[870] made in England, whereby no East India goods are to be imported into Ireland etc., but such as are loaden and shipped in Great Britain,[871] and this was read on the trial in support of the information.

2. Objection: there is no averment in the information, that they were not brought from the place of their growth.

Answer: It says they were in the growth of France, but were brought from the East Indies.

3. Objection: The plea of *non cul[pabilis]* is senseless.

Answer: Not at all. It is the course of the courts, and by that they are parties to the record.

---

[866] The year seems to have returned to 1732, given that most of the dates following below are correct for 1732.

[867] See above, p. 66.

[868] L. for the king.

[869] Spelled Nants in the MS, the French city on the Loire estuary southwest of Paris.

[870] 7 Geo. I, st. 1, c. 21 (G.B.) 1720–21 (importing East India goods, etc.).

[871] Spelled 'Brittain' in MS.

Monday November the 27[872]

Mr Calaghan for the defendants

The Act don't warrant the information, which forbids East India goods to be imported but from the place of their production, or where they were usually shipped. These goods might have been shipped from England to France, and from thence here, which is not against the Act, and nothing must be intended, but the information must be plain and positive, and though the information says the goods were shipped at Nantes, yet they might have come from London: the offence must describe the statute strictly, though not at large, and the informer must bring his case within the very words of the statute, whether he sets it out or no. *Garny* v. *Green:*[873] The information was for treble damages for marking a writ, and it was held not good, though the variance was not in substance, but in words only. [*213*]

Hard. 487[874] was after the Act of Navigation, which prohibits East India goods, 1. Where the master and three fourths of the seamen are not English, 2. From places from whence they are not usually imported, and the design of it was to prohibit Dutch ships from bringing them in.

Here is no issue. The information says generally, that the goods were imported etc., but don't say by whom. The defendants say they are not guilty. They ought to have denied the importation from Nantes.

The practice of courts may model facts, but can't [model] a positive law, which says an issue must consist of an affirmative and negative. The goods might be imported by others, though the defendants are not guilty.

He only that comes in by proclamation takes defence, but it ought to be a proper one. The verdict finds the defendants guilty *modo et forma* as laid in the information, and no charge being against them in the information, the jury have found nothing.

Mr Solicitor General pro Rege

After the seizure proclamation is made to see if any one will come in and own the goods before the sale, and he that claims them takes upon him to justify that they were not seizable, he takes issue on the fact. The verdict is, *quod sunt cul[pabiles] de pre[missis] in infor[matione] pr[e]d[icta] ment[ionatis]*,[875] so the issue here is well joined, and proper, and the finding is according to it.

This information is well grounded either on the Navigation Act,[876] or the 7 G. 1.[877]

By section the 3 of the Navigation Act, all goods of Asia Africk and America are to be imported [*214*] in English bottoms, and the mariners are to be English.

By section 4, all foreign goods are to be imported from the place of their growth production or manufacture, or where they were usually shipped. This information

---

[872] 27 November was a Monday in 1732 (Julian), Kratz, *Hist. Cal.*
[873] No citation given.
[874] *Witheren* v. *Robinson* (1668) Hard. 487, 145 E.R. 561 (whether or not Malaga wines, of the growth of Spain in Europe, being imported not in English shipping, nor in vessels whereof two thirds of the mariners were English, are forfeitable by the said act, or not?).
[875] L. that they are guilty of the matters mentioned in the aforesaid information.
[876] 12 Car. II, c. 18 (Eng.), 1660; and see 7 Geo. I, st. 1, c. 21 (G.B.), 1721 (trade to the East Indies), s. 9.
[877] 7 Geo. I, st. 1, c. 21 (G.B.), 1720–21 (importing East India goods, etc.).

is on the fourth section, and says, that the goods were seised because they were imported from Nantes, and not from the place of their growth.

Foreign goods must include East India goods, from the words foreign goods so to be shipped in English bottoms, which is not requisite in the case of other goods.

If the information is not within the Act of Navigation, it is within the 7 G. 1, and there was no need to, given that they were not shipped in England, because if they were shipped at Nantes, they were not shipped in England, and if they were first shipped in England, and after at Nantes, they are prohibited by the Act, for the shipping from England ought to be immediate.

Friday, June the first. [1733][878]

Mr Prime Serjeant pro Rege

I am to show cause why judgment should not be arrested.

This is an information for East India goods of the growth, produce, and manufacture of East India that were shipped in the port of Nantes in France on board the Mary Magdalene, and from thence imported into Waterford, with an averment that Nantes is not any place of their growth, or produce, and charges this offence to be *contra for[mam] stat[uti]*,[879] and prays they may be condemned, and forfeited.

The first proclamation being made according to the course of the Exchequer for anyone to come in and [215] claim (for this information is not against any person, but the ship and goods). Sullivan and Orpin came in and claimed property, and [each] put in a separate plea that *In nullo e[s]t culpabilis prout* Foord *versus eos informavit*.[880] And trial was in the county of Waterford, and a verdict for the informer.

And there have been two objections made.

First, that no offence is charged in the information. 2. If charged, no issue is joined.

In order to answer the first of these objections, it is necessary to consider the Navigation Act, and the 7th of the late King, for on one, or both of these, the information is well laid.

By the Act of Navigation three things are done to oblige subjects to go for the East India goods themselves. 1. The ship must be English, or Irish built. 2. The master and two fourths of the sailors must be English, or Irish. 3. The goods must be brought from the place of their growth, or manufacture, or from the place where generally brought (because they might grow in the more inland parts).

These three qualifications are required by the Act of Navigation.

By the 7 Geo. 1[881] no goods of the produce etc., are to be imported into Ireland etc., but from Great Britain, though they have these qualifications.

The defendants would have information laid on the Navigation Act, and yet say it don't extend to it.

I shall consider, whether the Act of Navigation is repealed by the 7 Geo. 1.

---

[878] 1 June was a Thursday in 1732, a Friday in 1733, Kratz, *Hist. Cal.*
[879] L. contrary to the form of the statute.
[880] L. not guilty in the way that F has informed against them.
[881] 7 Geo. I, st. 1, c. 21 (G.B.), 1720–21 (importing East India goods, etc.)

As to the difference of the penalties, by the Act of Navigation only the ship and the goods are forfeited. By the 7 Geo. 1 the informer may resort either to the ship and goods, and condemn them, or sue for the value, to prevent the want of remedy, where the ship was got off.

This information is brought since the 7 Geo. 1 so the informer had his election to proceed against the ship and goods, or for the value, and he made the former his election, so he was under no necessity to mention the owner of the ship, which destroys the objection that no issue is joined. [*216*]

Next I shall consider how far the 7 Geo. 1 is a repeal of the Act of Navigation, and if we are within that.

There are two ways of repealing an Act of Parliament. 1. Either by an express clause in a subsequent Act. 2. Or by enacting in a subsequent Act anything inconsistent with the former. Here are no express words in the 7 Geo. 1. to repeal the Act of Navigation, and then it must be by enacting something inconsistent.

The 7 Geo. 1 is to be considered only as a further restraint on Ireland in relation to this trade, but not a repeal only in this particular. By the first Act those goods can't be carried into England or Ireland but under those qualifications, and Ireland by the other is under this restraint, that they can't buy them East India, but must take them from Great Britain.

Our charge is, that the defendants brought from Nantes to Ireland goods of the growth of India, and this we lay to be an offence against the statute. 'Tis an offence against the Act of Navigation, and against the 7 Geo. 1. And as to this point the 7 Geo. 1 is only a confirmation of the Act of Navigation, that says they shall be forfeited, if they are brought from France. The other says, they shall be brought only from Great Britain. They both affirm the same thing. One says, they shall not be brought from any other place than the East Indies, the other from Great Britain only.

Lord Chief Baron

If the Act of Navigation said, you should not bring them from Great Britain, and the 7 Geo. 1. that you should bring them only from Great Britain, would that not be an inconsistency? And don't they say the same thing? One says, you shall have them only from the East Indies, the other from Great Britain only.

Mr Prime Serjeant

But one says you shan't bring them from France, and the other says you shall bring them from Great Britain only, is not that a proclamation too against bringing them from France? [*217*] but we are within the 7 Geo. 1. If the Act of Navigation is in force as to not bringing goods from France, they allow our information is well laid. But if it is repealed *pro tanto*, these goods are found to be East India, and shipped at Nantes, and not in England, and so it is against 7 Geo. 1.

But it is objected, that it appears by our averment, that the information is laid on the Act of Navigation. If that is in force this is no good objection, nor if it is repealed, because all facts are found necessary to induce the penalty on the 7 Geo. 1. We charge them to be growth of India, and to be shipped at Nantes, which is a distinct kingdom from Great Britain. And all this is found by the verdict, which must necessarily be a breach of the Act, that says, they shall be brought out of Great Britain only, and since these two facts are found, the averment is superfluous.

If then the information is within one, or the other Act, the question is, whether any issue is joined. By the second Act an election, as I have before observed, being given, this information is brought *in rem*, in which case the practice is not to mention any person, for it may be impossible to know who is the owner, and the seizure don't alter the property, so that from the necessity of the thing though the information charged that they were the property of a person unknown, you would condemn the goods. So that as in some cases the information must necessarily be so, to make it in the same form it is practised in all, and you never issue process, but the proclamation is notice, and you proceed to condemn though no person comes in. The proclamations are in room of process, and the condemnation is like a judgment by default at law, and if they would save themselves, they must appear and claim, and all the precedents are in this manner, and the general issue is pleaded, and they must be so from the reason of the thing, the property that comes in being ever admitted as a defence.

But it is said, they plead they are not guilty as it is charged in the information, how as no charge is against them. Their saying they are not guilty don't amount to an affirmative and negative. [*218*] Where we proceed *in rem* we are not obliged to charge any particular person, and in many cases it is impossible. If then the information is well laid without naming any person, the party who claims makes himself a defendant, and denies the charge the crime that is laid in the information of importing those goods from a place not allowed by law, which is directly an affirmative of one side, and a negative of the other.

And what different is there, between saying the goods were not imported from France, and saying, we are not guilty of that importation?

The first precedent is after the Revolution on the Act Ca. 2.[882] 'Tis in Michaelmas term 4 W. 3 1692, for importing tobacco, and there is the same plea.

All penalties on the customs are to be recovered in this court, and how shall rum goods be recovered, if the party must be charged?

MS Cas. in canc D.330. The custom of the court, which is the law of the court, must be supported by judicial resolution, and will bind the court to give the like judgment, and they must presume that to be the law, or that the judges, or the parties, would not so long have acquiesced under it: in *Slanes Case*[883] in 4 Co. this rule is laid down, and this has warranted not only new writs not to be found in the register, but such as are contrary to reason and sense, and the case from the Year Book of a writ of error mentioned in that case is remarkable.

Mr Baron Wainwright

If nobody appears, the court must proceed, or there would be a failure of justice, but where they do appear, and take defence, I think a new information ought to be filed.

---

[882]   12 Car. II, c. 18 (Eng.), 1660 (Navigation Act).
[883]   This refers to *Slade's Case* (1602) 4 Co. Rep. 92b, 76 E.R. 1074, above, p. 57 n. 356.

Baron Wainwright

Justissimus Unus
Qui fuit in Tenebris & Servantissimus Equit.

Plate 6. John Wainwright, Baron Wainwright, baron of the Exchequer.

Monday, December the 4th [1732][884]

In Exchequer

NASH v. MORRIS

One having made a charge upon lands pursuant to a power, though the legal interest was at £7 per cent, and the estate of value, the court gave but £5 per cent interest, that being in their discretion, and not like lending money on securities etc. [*219*]

Tuesday, December the 5th [1732][885]

WALLER v. WHITE

In Exchequer

Partition by tenants in common, ejectment, and a bill for an account of profits, and an account decreed from service of the summons in ejectment.

Objection: the plaintiff never actually entered, and he is not entitled to an account of the profits till then, 2 Vern. 724.[886]

Answer: The defendants acted *mala fide*, and kept out the plaintiffs contrary to their agreement for a partition.

COLLIS v. ROACH

The plaintiff as a Protestant discoveror being decreed to the benefit of a lease, Mr Daly moved, that the trustee in whose name the lease was taken, might be indemnified against the lessor as to the rents and covenants by the plaintiff, for that in the plea side of this court, in the case of *Alcock* v. *Ashball*[887] in an action of debt it was adjudged the lease was not void as to the lessee after a discovery in Chancery. But *quære* if the action was not brought for rent in arrear after the decree in Chancery.

Sir John St Leger thought, he should have no favour, because he was an offender against the law.

Mr Daly said, he was now a trustee for the Protestant discoveror.

Curia advisar[e] vult.[888]

---

[884] 4 December was a Monday in 1732, Kratz, *Hist. Cal.*
[885] 5 December was a Tuesday in 1732, Kratz, *Hist. Cal.*
[886] *Hutton* v. *Simpson* (1716) 2 Vern. 722 at 724, 23 E.R. 107.
[887] No citation given.
[888] L. the court will be advised (before giving judgment).

[Inserted note:[889]

16 July 1734

In Chancery

MORRIS v. ESMOND

Plaintiff decreed to the benefit of an assignment of a lease for 3 lives, and to indemnify the original lessee, but that lease was taken after the first Act which makes it void, and before the second, which makes it subsist for the benefit of a Protestant discoveror, though the Chancellor didn't seem to found his decree on that distinction, but said it was reasonable in all cases to indemnify the lessee.]

Saturday, November the 11, and Thursday, the 16 [1732][890]

In Exchequer

MONK v. LOVAT

Some of the plaintiffs, and some of the defendants being dead, a bill of revivor was filed, and leave given on motion *nisi* etc., to serve the attorneys of the original defendants with subpœnas to revive.

And Mr Daly, and Mr Malone came to show cause against the order, and they allowed that the attorney of the plaintiff at law being abroad might be served, be-   MSŜ ord in. Canc.
cause otherwise the plaintiff might recover before they could serve him, but [after] the death of the defendant the cause is at an end till re[vived] and the authority of the attorney is determined, and [that] of the defendants [until] the children are come of age, and have a [chance] [*220*] to choose their own attorney, and amend their defence. Where the cause is still in being, and the defendant is above 40 miles, things of course, as a subpœna to rejoin, may on special motion be served on the attorney.

Cause allowed.

Friday, November the 10th [1732][891]

In Exchequer

CORKER v. LOWTHER

A bill was filed in 1727 to set aside a purchase made in 1708.

---

[889] The following note of the case of *Morris* v. *Esmond* was inserted later, as the writing in the MS. is small and spills into the margin, and the year is 1734.

[890] Both dates are correct for 1732, Kratz, *Hist. Cal.*

[891] 10 November was a Friday in 1732 (Julian), Kratz, *Hist. Cal.*

The defendant pleaded himself a purchaser for a valuable consideration without notice, and the plea was allowed, and enrolled, and the plaintiff now moved to amend his bill, but the motion was denied, because the enrolment was not to be opened, and the court had given their opinion on the merits.

Saturday, November the 11th [1732][892]

In Exchequer

SMYTH v. ROCHFORD

Ejectment for non-payment of rent. Bill for an injunction, and the plaintiff swore that all the material allegations of his bill were true.

This was adjudged not to be sufficient on the new Act.[893]

The Act don't require the affidavit to be annexed, but an order of court, as on the Popery Bills.

Thursday, November the 9th [1732][894]

In Exchequer

DELARUE v. LEWIS

Delarue claimed under a forfeiture of Kennedy to the Crown of lands in mortgage to Lewis, who in 1701 came to an agreement with the guardian of the plaintiff, to give up the lands at the expiration thereof, if he made him a lease for such a term of years. The lease was made to Ross in trust for Lewis, and being now determined, the plaintiff brought his bill to have the possession of the lands delivered up to him. [221] The question was, if Ross, the trustee, might be read to the proof of the lease.

Mr Calaghan

He is a good evidence, the lease is expired. He can have no bias, he can't be a gainer, but he may be a loser, because his being only a trustee don't discharge him of the covenants, and the deed is 30 years old. He proves that one witness is dead, and that he don't know whether the other is dead or alive.

Ante 168, 89.

Stanley v. *Stanley*[895] in Chancery: a party to a deed who is not concerned in interest may be examined. He sees his hand, and has the same opportunity to remember as a witness, and has no bias, and one who was present, though neither party, nor witness, may be examined to the execution.

---

[892] 11 November was a Saturday in 1732 (Julian), Kratz, *Hist. Cal.*

[893] 5 Geo. II, c. 4 (Ir.), 1731 (ejectment for non payment of rent), s. 1. The section gave a landlord the right to terminate the tenant's title if the tenant was at least one year's rent in arrear. See also the earlier Act 9 Ann., c. 8 (Ir.), 1710 (ejectment for non payment of rent) which gave the right after 6 months' rent in arrear.

[894] 9 November was a Thursday in 1732, Kratz, *Hist. Cal.*

[895] No citation given.

Powel, the surviving witness of Massy being examined said, he was old and could not remember whether he subscribed or not. Upon this he was examined in court and a trial directed, upon which he again swore he could not remember. Then Mrs Beard who was present when the deed was executed was produced as a witness, and 'twas objected, that there were three subscribing witnesses, and one of them alive, and therefore she could not be examined. But the Lord Chief Baron Gilbert allowed her evidence, and said, that setting the names was only to put the witness in mind of the execution, but don't authenticate it.

Mr Daly

Thirty years was allowed not to make an ancient deed in the case of *Lord Limerick* v. *Southwell*,[896] but they ought to swear, that they had made enquiry, and could get no account, and then they may prove the handwriting of one that is dead. Darcy, a trooper to Lord Ardglass,[897] was a witness to the deed of Southwell. There it was sworn that they had made enquiry after him, and that he was dead. [In] *Sir Arthur Shaen* v. *Lord Wharton*[898] the seven witnesses were proved to be dead, and their signing proved by similitude of hands.

Lord Chief Baron

In the case of *St John* v. *Overall*,[899] 30 years were [222] allowed to make an ancient deed. The books vary but the rule of reason, is the rule of evidence, where subscribing witnesses are suspected to be tampered with, it is not only proper, but necessary to examine others. Here the party may prove it, [be]cause not interested. If he may lose, it must be to the plaintiff, and he has declared him only a trustee for Lewis, and the lease being expired, the plaintiff can only sue him in equity, and he has discharged him.

Mr Baron Wainwright

The lease expired in 1719, so if rent is due, it is barred by the Statute of Limitations.[900] He is not interested, but is a good witness at law.

---

[896] See *Southwell* v. *Lord Limerick* (1729) 9 Mod. 133, 88 E.R. 360.

[897] Apparently a reference to Thomas Cromwell (1594–1653), cr. earl of Ardglass 1645. Supported the king in the Civil War and commanded a regiment of horse.

[898] No citation given.

[899] No citation given.

[900] 10 Car. I, sess. 2, c. 6 (Ir.), 1634 (limitation of actions), s. 14, arrears of rent, 6 years.

Friday, December the 8th [1732][901]

In Exchequer

HERDMAN v. MAXWELL

Mr Lindsey [*sic*] stated the case for the plaintiff.

Henry Maxwell father of the defendant John, being possessed of a lease held from the See of Ardmagh *inter alia* of the lands in question, in 1691 came to an agreement with John Herdman for a lease of part of the lands for 14 years at different rents till they should amount to £53 per annum, with a covenant to renew to Herdman as often as the Primate did to him; John Herdman entered, and made several improvements on the estate, and paid the rent to Henry till his death in 1710, and then John Maxwell the defendant became entitled, and received the rent till 1714, when John Herdman died, leaving a widow (the widow took out administration to John Herdman) and several children who were minors, and she paid the rent to the defendant John until 1718, but in 1719 the defendant John sent for her, and threatened to bring an ejectment, and told her the agreement with her husband was a void agreement, and that she should not hold under it, by which means she was prevailed on to surrender the old minute, and to come to a new agreement, to pay a fine of £50, to raise the rent to £83 per annum, besides receivers fees, and to subject herself to other [*223*] restrictions, as grinding at his mill, and there was no covenant for renewal on the part of the defendant.

The plaintiff is the eldest son of John Herdman and the end of his bill is to establish the agreement between his father John and Henry the father of the defendant, to set aside the agreement made with Margaret the administratrix, and for an account of the surplus rents over and above the old rent recovered by the minute.

Mr Whitney[902] stated the case for the defendant.

There is no proof that the £53 a year was ever paid, but rather that £48 a year only was paid, and by that proposal a lease was to be executed with the usual clauses in Mr Maxwell's leases, and a lease was accordingly drawn, and tendered to John Herdman with such usual covenants, which John refused to accept, but chose to abide by his minute, and after the death of Henry Maxwell John Herdman came to the defendant, and offered him £5 a year more than the £53, and proposed to take a new lease.

Mr Baron Wainwright

I am of opinion a lease ought to be made pursuant to the minute.

The first question is, whether this agreement was waived by John Herdman? Or secondly, afterwards extinguished by his administratrix? But the case is first to be cleared of two points not material.

1. Of the £50 fine, for the plaintiff is not entitled to that as part of the assets of his father.

---

[901]   8 December was a Friday in 1732, Kratz, *Hist. Cal.*

[902]   Boleyn, or Bullen, Whitney, 3rd s. of Thomas, Newpas, Co. Westmeath. Middle Temple, 24 June 1709. KI, Michaelmas, 1714, d. 18 April 1758. KI AP, p. 511.

2. Of the administration, which I think while unimpeached must stand, and we are not to take it as void.

The case then is, first whether John Herdman waived this agreement. But I shall first consider whether this was a mutual agreement though signed by Henry Maxwell only, and notwithstanding the words, 'may if he please have a lease', and as John entered on the lands, made improvements, and paid the rent, I think each might have compelled the other to execute the agreement.[903]

Supposing it then a good agreement, the question is, whether [224] it was rescinded or waived.

And upon this head the defendant has made three objections. First, that John Herdman refused to perfect a lease, 2. that he agreed to pay £5 a year more, 3. that the rent was paid otherwise than agreed to by the minute.

1. As to the refusal, it don't appear whether the covenants in the lease that was tendered where [sic] such as he was obliged to enter into. The only evidence is, that another tenant covenanted to grind, but he perhaps was not under the same circumstances.

2. As to the second, there is a proof of a reference, and that John Herdman said, 'I have offered him £5 a year more to give me a new lease', but it comes out on Maxwell's cross-examination, that he said, he offered it for peace' sake, and because he would have no words with his landlord.

3. The strongest objection is, that the rent was not duly paid according to the terms of the agreement. But it appears that till 1712 £48 a year was paid, and 'tis admitted by Maxwell that the whole rent was paid according to the agreement, and Pringle swears, that £24 was entered in the pocket book of Henry Maxwell for one half year, and the half of £53 towards the end of the book, so there is full proof of this.

The second question is, whether the administratrix of John Herdman by taking a new lease extinguished the old agreement.

It has been said here can't be such an extinguishment as if the legal estate had been in her, but I think it all one, if she had disposed of her interest for a valuable consideration, but the defendant got a profitable lease for nothing from her, and in breach of her trust which he was conusant[904] of, and shall this court see an administratrix dispose of her assets for nothing, and not bring them back? The defendant is not injured, but the plaintiff only.

This then is *nudum pactum*, an agreement without consideration, so I think the lease must be set aside, and a new lease made according to the agreement. [225]

Sir John St Leger

I am of the same opinion. In the case of *Coote* v. *Mammon*,[905] Coote agreed with Prothereau for a lease, and applied to him to execute a lease, which Prothereau refused because it was a hard bargain, not as in this case, because the lease tendered was not according to their agreement. Coote after prevails on Prothereau to surrender, to enable him to make a tenant to the *præcipe*, and after Coote makes a lease to Godsil.

---

903 I.e. through part performance in equity.
904 An early form of cognizant, i.e. having knowledge.
905 Above, p. 106 [*129*] and n. 604.

Coote insisted that Prothereau had waived the agreement. I being only in court decreed a lease against Godsil the purchaser, because he had notice of the interest of Prothereau, and that there was no waiver, because Coote might afterwards have compelled Prothereau to accept of a lease, and that the article could not be discharged by such words of passion, as that he would not execute it, because it was a bad bargain. And this decree was affirmed in the House of Lords.[906]

The widow here apprehended the agreement to be void by the defendant's threatening to bring an ejectment, and so applied to friends to get her a lease upon any terms, but this was not done willingly. She was afraid of his opinion as a lawyer, and accepted of the new lease for fear she should not get any. Maxwell had full notice of the right of the children, and was conusant of the law of intestates, and knew he purchased, nay got for nothing, the children's bread. As to John Herdman's agreeing to pay £5 more rent, he only said, he would give £5 more for peace sake, and that his landlord was very hard. So here is notice, no waiver, no purchase.

Lord Chief Baron

I am of the same opinion with my brothers. This is a cause of great consequence, for I have observed in causes not only in this court but in Chancery such covenants to renew in College and Church leases when [226] the lessor renews with the College or Church.

This is a good agreement, and has been carried into execution in the principal parts, by possession, and payment of rent,[907] and if made by parol, the agreement could not be set aside, or the Statute of Frauds[908] pleaded in bar.

The question is, whether the agreement was waived by John Herdman, or his administratrix, by acceptance of a new lease.

It was not waived by John, though he agreed to pay a greater rent, for that was only his proposal to waive it on terms which were not accepted, but others offered, but he insisted he was better as he was. So there was no waiver, but the old agreement subsisted, and he paid the rent agreed on till his death.

The question then is, whether taking this new lease is a surrender in equity of the old? The taking a new lease is a surrender of a former at law, but if a man makes an underlease, and then surrenders, that is not good even at law.

I shall consider in this case the party that made the surrender, and he to whom it was made. It was made by an administratrix, to him she paid the rent, and he knew under what title, and the agreement was referred to two gentlemen, so the defendant had full notice of her being administratrix.

The question then is, whether one who buys from an administratrix with notice of the trust is not subject to it, and whether the cestui que trust may not set the purchase aside to increase the assets.

A purchaser with notice is not to be allowed, *Whally* v. *Whally*[909] in 1 Vern. is a full resolution to this point.

---

[906] Above, p. 106 [*129*] and n. 604.
[907] I.e. by part performance in equity.
[908] Statute of Frauds, 1695, 7 Will. III, c. 12 (Ir.).
[909] *Walley* v. *Walley* (1687) 1 Vern. 484, 23 E.R. 609; *Whalley* v. *Whalley* (1687) 1 Eq. Cas. Abr. 332, 21 E.R. 1083.

Hendrick v. *Migee*[910] in Chancery: There was a lease of houses on the Blind Quay[911] held under Lord Moleworth. Migee and his wife sold the houses by the name of executors. The court was of opinion, the purchaser ought to have looked into the will, and set aside the sale, which was carrying the case further than in *Whally*, where the will was read.

But this is not the case of a purchaser, but of one [227] who comes in by surrender and gives nothing for what he gains and the case looks like a release in error. When Maxwell renewed he was entitled to a lease of £53 a year and she pays a fine of £50 and £83 a year rent. Suppose this then an agreement in error and that both sides were mistaken in the law, it is to be set aside in favour of the person who is prejudiced. *Hodder* v. *Roberts*[912] in this court: counsel were of opinion that a term for payment of £1,000 a piece for daughters' portions never arose. Upon this Hodder gave a release for his wife's portion and after filed a bill to have it raised and the settlement being Ante 152. read the release was set aside though there was no fraud in the case being a release in error.

Decree

That a lease be made for 18 years from 1731 at £53 a year rent, with such agreements, and covenants as were in the leases in 1691 from the See of Ardmagh, the lease, if disputed, to be settled by a baron, and an account to be taken of the £27 surplus rent from the time the administration was granted to the plaintiff, and costs reserved till after the report.

---

[910] No citation given.

[911] Spelled 'blind key' in the MS. Lower Exchange Street in Dublin was formerly known as the Blind Quay: Maurice Craig, *Dublin, 1660–1860. Bunbury* v. *Bolton* (1721) 1 Bro. P.C. 2nd ed. 434, 1 E.R. 671 concerns houses owned by Dudley Loftus in Blind Quay and mortgaged to the Bluecoat School. Dudley Loftus (1619–1695) was an orientalist and jurist. He was the third son of Sir Adam Loftus (b. 1590/91, d. in or after 1641), later lord justice and L.C. of Ireland. His grandfather, Sir Dudley Loftus, was the eldest son of Adam Loftus, the archbishop. A catalogue of 128 manuscripts belonging to Dudley Loftus was published in 1697. They included writings in Arabic, Armenian, English, French, Hebrew, Irish, Italian, Persian, Russian, Syriac and Welsh. Some of them are now in the British Library, the Bodleian library, Trinity College and Marsh's Library, Dublin, but several volumes of his manuscripts were destroyed as waste paper by the mother of Gorges Edmond Howard, who was a descendant, and her husband: above, p. clxii. He was a judge of admiralty from 1654, and in 1655 Cromwell appointed him master in Chancery. E. Boran, 'Loftus, Dudley (1618–1695)', *ODNB*, <http://www.oxforddnb.com/view/article/16936>, accessed 28 April 2008.

[912] No citation given.

Plate 7. The Bluecoat School, Dublin (now the Law Society of Ireland).

WHITLOW v. GORE

Wednesday, January the 31st [1733][913]

In Exchequer

Mr Stannard pro plaintiff

A provision was made by marriage articles for raising £400 a piece for daughters' portions, payable at 18 or the death of their father, with a maintenance of £40 a year till paid. And the single question is, whether this maintenance being for many years in arrear and unpaid to the daughters, shall bear interest.

And I think it will from reason and authority. This is not the case of interest upon interest, but for a certain sum for which debt would lie. They have no other provision, and how then could they support themselves but by taking up money at interest? And a sum that is certain and fixed by the parties, will bear interest though given in lieu of interest, and was ruled so in the case of a mortgage [228] 1 Vern. 191,[914] 2 Chan. Cas. 147.[915] If the parties designed only interest, they would have made the portions payable with interest, and so small a provision for younger children is to be taken favourably.

Mr Attorney General

There is a difference where the charge is personal, and where on lands. If it were *res integra*,[916] I should think it reasonable on a mortgage that interest should bear interest, since if it had been paid regularly, the mortgagee could have laid it out. Why then should the mortgagor keep him out of his money apparently to his disadvantage, and not make him amends? And the policy of the resolutions to the contrary were to induce people to throw their money into the public funds, where they were sure to have their interest constantly paid, and to prevent oppression. But here is no usury, no oppression to be feared, but the heir has had the benefit of their money, which we ought to have had the use of.

By deed, fine and recovery on the marriage of Sir Robert Gore, if there was one daughter of the marriage, she was to have £1,500, which the trustees were to receive by the annual payments of £150, if more than one, the eldest daughter was to have £1,000, and the trustees were to receive £100 per annum till it was paid, and the other daughters were to have £400 a piece, and £40 a year each till raised. And if there could be any doubt whether these sums of £40 a year were to be by way of maintenance or interest, or to go towards making up the principal sums themselves, this is cleared up by a subsequent transaction, for after the death of Sir Robert Gore, Sir Nathaniel his eldest son by a settlement on his marriage charges the estate with these principal sums, and with the yearly maintenances, or interest, and the daughters might have been 18 at the death of their father.

---

[913] Note the change of year. 31 January was a Wednesday in 1733, Kratz, *Hist. Cal.* The year changes to 1733 from now on.

[914] *Howard* v. *Harris* (1683) 1 Vern. 190 at 191, 23 E.R. 406 (no agreement in a mortgage can make it irredeemable; interest chargeable on interest reserved in deed).

[915] *Howard* v. *Harris* (1683) 2 Ch. Cas. 147, 22 E.R. 888.

[916] See above, p. 18 n. 100.

Mr Malone

This £40 a year was their daily bread, and if not paid [*229*] then they must starve, or live upon credit, which will carry interest. So it is different from interest on a mortgage or bond, and the daughters are not to be considered as moneylenders, and Sir Nathaniel by his own deed covenants to pay this money. In the case of *Roscommon* v. *Burgh*,[917] the present lord chancellor said, that where there was an express covenant in the mortgage deed to pay a certain sum, and the mortgagor was in the kingdom, and the interest demanded, and not paid, that the interest should bear interest.

Mr Daly

This is different from the case of a mortgagee or moneylender. The trust being to raise, the estate belonged to the trustees, and not to the heir, and Sir Nathaniel received the rents in his own wrong. If this was only an equitable charge, the estate would descend to the heir, and he might enter.

Mr Harward[918]

Mes App. D.303. Lex Præt. 59.[920] Ts cas. 167.

Chapman v. Chapman[921]

In the case of *Mahon* v. *Lord Blany*,[919] interest by the Court of Chancery was allowed for maintenance, and in that case 'twas said to have been decreed so by Lord Cowper in the case of *Ducain* a Frenchwoman, because the presumption was, that infants who were otherwise unprovided for must raise money on very disadvantageous terms, and that people would take advantage of their wants. If the mortgagee brings an ejectment, and the mortgagor sets up temporary bars, or otherwise hinders him from the possession, the court will give interest upon interest.

Lord Chief Baron

Nobody makes a defence. I observe in the deed of Sir Nathaniel, there is a clause of distress for non payment of the annuity.

Mr Geoghegan[922]

Then is the case stronger for us (for if we had distrained, he should have had damages) by the authority of the case of *Howard* v. *Harris* 1 Vern. 191.[923]

---

[917] No citation given.

[918] William Harward, admitted, KI, Michaelmas, 1718, d. 8 July 1770, KI AP, p. 217.

[919] See *Blaney* v. *Mohon* (1723) 2 Eq. Cas. Abr. 475, 22 E.R. 404, 2 Eq. Cas. Abr. 758, 22 E.R. 643; *Lord Blany* v. *Mahon* (1723) 22 Vin. Abr. 521, pl. 27, (1723) 4 Bro. P.C. 2nd ed. 76, 2 E.R. 52.

[920] See above, p. 35 n. 210.

[921] No citation given.

[922] Probably Francis Geoghegan, 3rd. s. of James, Killelin, Co. Westmeath. Middle Temple, 23 Sept. 1704, KI, Trinity term, 1713, d. 12 April 1767.

[923] *Howard* v. *Harris* (1683) 1 Vern. 190 at 191, 23 E.R. 406.

Monday, February the 19th, [1733][924]
The last day of the 8 days after Hilary Term

Mr Baron Wainwright

[230] In the deed dated the 13 of April 1678 there is a covenant or proviso, that if after the death of Sir Robert Gore those in remainder do not pay £40 a year to the trustees therein named, until they shall or might receive £400 a piece for the daughters, that then the trustees shall enter, and take that sum.

As it stands on this deed the charge is obscure, and it does not plainly appear how long the £40 is to be paid, but it is not controverted by the defendant, that the plaintiff Alice was entitled at her marriage to £400, and £40 a year till it could be raised, and this obscurity whether the £40 a year is for interest or maintenance for this £400, or whether that is to be made up of those annual payments, is cleared up by the marriage articles of Sir Nathaniel Gore, the son of Sir Robert, whereby the lands are charged with the payment of £400 a piece principal money for the daughters, and with £40 a year till paid.

The question then is on the first deed, whether this £40 a year is to be considered as the interest for the £400, which it amounts to at £10 per cent, and if so I think as it stands on that. This being so liberal an interest, the court would have allowed no interest on it.

And as it stands on the marriage articles of Sir Nathaniel, whether the court at the end of every year will give interest by way of damages. If a man had bound himself by covenant to pay interest for interest this court would not carry such a covenant into execution, and *Howard* v. *Harris*[925] is the only case where interest on interest was given by act of court, but there was a special covenant, that there should be no redemption, and the security being only £7 a year, it was equity not to let them redeem by making satisfaction for the rest, for which the security was not sufficient to answer.

There may be cases indeed, where if the annuity is demanded, and not paid, the court will give interest. [231] But this interest is so liberally given by Sir Nathaniel, there is no room for a court of equity to interpose.

Lord Chief Baron

I am of the same opinion.

If the question rested on the original articles, it would be a great doubt, whether more should have been received than £40 a year till the £400 was raised. But by the other deed £40 a year is secured till the £400 is paid, and 'tis plainly designed to be given as a recompense for the thing.

A court of equity will not give interest but in particular cases. Interest itself has been thought unlawful, but a court of equity looks on it as a just recompense for the use of the money, and it has therefore been reduced from time to time by the government as money has become more plentiful, and they have refused to decree interest upon interest, but have declared such bargains void, that the party might not lie by with design to eat out the pledge.

---

[924] 19 February was a Monday in 1733, Kratz, *Hist. Cal.*
[925] Above, p. 179 n. 915.

And it ought not to be allowed in this case from the intention of the parties to pay only £40 a year, which is £10 per cent, and a very large provision.

Wednesday, February the [2]1st.[1733][926]

A Rehearing

RIDGE v. HURLEY

In Exchequer

Mr Malone

The question in this case is, whether the decree of the trustees shall charge the estate for life of the jointuress?

By the attainder of Sir William Hurley they having the whole estate in them might charge the inheritance as they pleased. But his lady having claimed an estate for life, and it being decreed to her, they could not charge that estate, but all their proceedings were *coram non judice*. They were to allow of all claims out of these forfeited estates, and to [232] dispose of the residue for the use of the public. She claims under her old estate, and the trustees had no more power to charge that, than if she had claimed, and been decreed to the inheritance.

Claims were to be made that the trustees might sell only what the crown has a right to, and if their titles were ever so good, and they had made no claim, the claimants would have been barred forever by a sale of the trustees for a valuable consideration: but here is no conveyance from the trustees, but both claim under Sir Maurice Hurley, so the question is at large between the two claimants, who both claim by the same articles, one as a jointuress, and the other as an incumbrancer. Sir Maurice Hurly [*sic*] by articles on the marriage of his son William, whereby Sir William and Dame Catherine were joint tenants for life, remainder to Sir William in tail, had power to charge £300 for daughters portions, and by will in 1683 he executes this power, and charges the estate with £150 a piece for his two daughters. Burgh who had married Lettice, one of the daughters, claims this £150 with interest, and the trustees allow his claim for £250, and decreed Lady Hurly [*sic*] to account for the interest from 1694 to 1701. This power given to Sir Maurice is after the limitation of the jointure and the other estates, and such a power, whether given to a father or a stranger, the provisions made by virtue thereof can neither in law or equity affect the jointure, except where they are to be raised in a certain time.

Lord Chief Baron

A power to make leases will affect the jointure.

---

[926] 1 February was a Thursday in 1733, Kratz, *Hist. Cal.*, but from dates preceding and following, the year seems to be 1733. 21 February was a Wednesday in 1733.

Mr Malone

That power is not inconsistent with the limitation of the jointure. This would destroy it.

The trustees have no power to determine between claimants, but between claimants and themselves. Where they have decreed an estate to one, they cannot upon an afterclaim decree an incumbrancer to have a lien on that estate, and if they allow a greater estate, the proceedings are *coram non judice*, [*233*] and if after decreeing the estate to Lady Hurly they could incumber it, they might load it to the value and this subsequent claim was behind her back, and they have no such power given them, by the Act,[927] and this appears from the case of *Chamberlain* v. *White*.[928] Mr Chamberlain was a judge for a day or two in the reign of King James the second: and was afterwards attainted.[929] By settlement in 1672 Mr Chamberlain was tenant for life, remainder to his first and every other sons etc., with a provision of £200 a piece for daughters. By the forfeiture of Mr Chamberlain the estate vested in trustees. Christopher his eldest son puts in his claim, and the trustees decreed him an estate tail after the death of his father subject to the charges by the settlement. One of the daughters who had married Mr White claimed also £500 portion, and she was decreed to that sum. Mrs White brought her bill to have this £500 raised. Christopher insisted on the settlement, and that the trustees had no power to decree but according to that. Lord Midleton[930] was of opinion that the decree of the trustees was binding though they were mistaken in their judgment, because they had the inheritance in them. But this decree was reversed in the House of Lords,[931] and the acts of the trustees between claimants were adjudged void. He that claims a prior estate takes nothing from the trustees. He don't claim under them.

In the case of *Boyle* v. *Lord Dillon*[932] it was allowed by Lord Midleton,[933] that he who had a decree from the trustees did not claim under them, but a precedent title, and to keep his estate from being sold. Their decree will bind the reversion whether sold or undisposed of, because being vested in them, they had a power to charge it.

Lord Chief Baron

So then the claimant can have no charge on this reversion, but what they have decreed him to.

Mr Malone

The jointuress being first purchaser, the power can't break in upon her estate, but the reversion only.

---

[927] 11 Will. III, c. 2. 1698 (11 & 12 Will. III in Ruffhead) (Eng.).

[928] *Chamberlain* v. *White* (1720) 6 Bro. P.C. 2nd ed. 61, 2 E.R. 933. No citation given for first instance.

[929] In 2 E.R. 933 he is mentioned as Michael Chamberlain.

[930] Spelled 'Middleton' in MS.

[931] *Chamberlain* v. *White* (1720) 6 Bro. P.C. 2nd ed. 61, 2 E.R. 933. (By 11 Will. III, c. 2. 1698 (11 & 12 Will. III in Ruffhead) (Eng.) all the forfeitures in Ireland were vested in certain named trustees, who were authorized absolutely to determine all claims and rights to those lands.)

[932] No citation given.

[933] Spelled 'Middleton' in MS.

Mr Baron Wainwright

This proviso for so much takes away all the limitations, [*234*] being paramount in its nature. 'Tis a power given to the grandfather who made the settlement, and must his daughters wait till the jointure is determined? Can we make a better decree?

Mr Malone

It don't appear but that the daughters might have some other provision. This is not an actual charge, but a power, and the question is, whether 'tis a reasonable execution of it to charge the jointure? And we think it unreasonable, whether the charge is by a father, or grandfather, because the jointure is made in consideration of marriage, and her portion.

Lord Chief Baron

By the Resumption Act[934] 11 & 12 W. 3., the trustees are made a court of record, and their Acts are to be binding.

Mr Stannard

Here are two questions,
   1. Whether this provision for daughters can take place of the jointure.
   2. Whether the estate being vested in the crown by the forfeiture of Sir William, the claims have made any alteration in the case.
   1. This question depends on the articles, which were entered into previous to the marriage of Sir William, whereby Sir Maurice is to settle *prout*[935] in consideration of the portion (which Mr Blunt the father of Lady Hurley, and party to the articles, covenants to pay) and out of love and affection to the son, and to continue the estate in his name and blood, and to provide a jointure for Dame Catherine, and an estate is limited to Sir Maurice for life, with a power for him to incumber the estate with £300, for such of his children as should be unprovided for at the time of his death.
   The wife is the consideration of this settlement, and Sir Maurice has only a contingent power to provide and if a settlement had been made, Mr Blunt would not have consented to such a power as should prejudice the jointure.
   The settlement is by covenant to stand seised,[936] and £700 [*235*] part of her fortune is covenanted to be invested in a purchase of lands.
   2. By the vesting clause of the Trustee Act[937] page 2, all the right the forfeiting person had is vested, yet the right of those who do not claim is barred, and the Act obliged those to claim who had a right for the security of purchasers.
   A mortgagor put in his claim. The mortgagee made no claim, and the mortgagor insisted that his estate was discharged by the decree, and the question was, whether the mortgagee was not barred having made no claim, that if the trustees had sold

---

   [934] Above, n. 927 and n. 931.
   [935] L. accordingly.
   [936] I.e. a covenant to stand seised to uses.
   [937] 11 Will. III, c. 2. (11 & 12 Will. III in Ruffhead) (Eng.) Trustee Act (forfeited estates in Ireland vested in trustees).

the estate to a purchaser, nobody should take it from him, but that this estate that was claimed, lay as before.

In the case of *Grace* v. *The Hollow Blades*,[938] Grace was adjudged to be within the articles, made his claim, which was dismissed, and his estate sold to the Hollow Blades. He brought an ejectment, but the court of equity granted an injunction, and held the dismission conclusive, (though he need not have claimed, and the proceedings were *coram non judice*) because it was a fraud on the purchasers. Here appears no purchaser in this case.

Mr Attorney General pro Rege

The provision for the daughters is a charge on the estate, and to be paid in the life of Lady Hurly. Sir Maurice was seised in fee, and I shall first consider this, either as a legal or an equitable charge. If this is an equitable charge, the whole fee which descended to Sir William who was attained, subject to those charges, vests in the crown, and is conveyed to the trustees.

If the legal estate passed, (though I think a use won't arise, natural love and affection not being mentioned as part of the consideration) it was part of the agreement, and very reasonable, that Sir Maurice should have a power to provide for his children, and this is a reservation of so much of the old dominion over the estate he had never parted with, and is well executed at law. But they say the power is unreasonable in equity, [*236*] but if what she contracted for is complied with, she has no injury done to her, which was to have a jointure subject to these charges, or otherwise the words which are usual in family settlements would have been inserted, 'But not to impeach the jointure', or the like, and it was first in the view of the grandfather to provide for his own children, and otherwise this provision would not come to them at a proper age.

Lord Chief Baron

The question is, whether the £204 liquidated by the trustees shall bear interest against the jointuress? Against the reversion which is in the crown it certainly shall.

Mr Daly pro plaintiff

All the parties here are purchasers. The crown is a purchaser, as Sir William Hurley was by the articles. The power is to charge the estate Sir Maurice Hurley had when he entered into the articles, so the whole fee, and every estate derived out of it, is charged. Where the suit is only between the tenant for life and the remainderman, equity will only compel him to keep down the interest, but the tenant for life has no such equity against an incumbrancer, because he has a right to receive his principal and interest from him in possession, and is not to wait till the tenant for life dies.

As to the Trustee Act, the vesting clause vests the whole fee, (according to such estate as the forfeiting person had) and so does the claiming clause, for if any person has a use, or trust, they must claim, or are barred, so by this claiming clause uses or

---

[938] No citation given. Above, p. 1 n. 7.

trusts are vested, since the cestui que trusts[939] must claim. Otherwise suppose [the] tenant for life forfeits, if only the estate for life passed, those in remainder need not claim, but if they must put in their claim, then it is plain that the whole fee was vested, because it is to be divested by their claim.

And this is plain also from another clause. If any person has a right in the lands so vested he must claim, which shows the whole estate in the lands is vested. The decree of the trustees is to be conclusive to those who do not claim, etc., and to the King. Our incumbrance, being a charge on the estate, their decree is just, that the jointuress should keep down the interest. [237]

Mr Darcy

The husband and wife being joint tenants, the whole was forfeited by the attainder of the husband, for the King can't be jointly seised with a subject.

The case of *Chamberlain* v. *White*[940] differs from this. There only an estate for life was forfeited: here the reversion in fee.

Mr Francis Blake

The bill is to be paid the interest of £204 from 1694. By the 24th page of the Act, the lands, and not the estate of the forfeiting person being vested in the trustees, everyone must claim, or be barred, and 'tis like a non-claim on a fine: though the remainderman has a certain estate, he will be barred, if he don't claim.

Remainders on estates tail are excepted by the Act. The trustees allow the claim of Lady Hurley subject to other claims, so the Act that gives ordinaries a power to grant administrations, gives them a power by those words to revoke, to grant *sub modo*, etc.

Mr Baron Wainwright

Sir Maurice Hurly [*sic*] on the marriage of his son William, in consideration of £1,000 portion, etc., covenanted to stand seized to the use of himself for life, remainder to his son William and Catherine his wife for the lives, etc., with a power for Sir Maurice to charge the premises with £300 for the portions of his younger children. Sir Maurice afterwards executes this power, and charges the estate by his will with £150 a piece for his two daughters. Thomas Burgh intermarries with Lettice, one of the daughters of Sir Maurice, after whose death the estate came to Sir William Hurly, and by his attainder vested in the trustees etc. Sir William died in 1699. In 1701 Lady Hurley claimed before the trustees an estate for life, and in February following Thomas Burgh claimed in right of his wife Lettice the £150 and interest, which was lotted up by the trustees to £204, and they decreed that Lady Hurley should pay interest for the whole aggregate sum of £204 from 1694. [238]

I shall consider this case as it stands, 1. on the articles, 2. on the decree, and 3. whether the plaintiff has any right to bring this bill.

1. It was the view and intention of Sir Maurice to settle these lands on the marriage of his son, and to make a provision for himself and his younger children, and this

---

[939] I.e. cestuis que trust.
[940] *Chamberlain* v. *White* (1720) 6 Bro. P.C. 2nd ed. 61, 2 E.R. 933.

power though it stands subsequent to the limitations, is prior in reason, and ought to control them.

Whether an equitable or legal estate passed won't affect the defendant who is a purchaser.

This is not within the reason of *Mildmay's Case*,[941] because there the proviso was against the intention of the parties to provide equally, and could not be made good by averment, and would defeat the former uses. But these articles are said to be made for other good causes and considerations besides the £1,000, and this provision for his younger children, which is a good consideration, may be averred to be those other good causes and considerations; and if a legal estate had been raised, he might have made it a legal charge by mortgage etc., but as his will is only an equitable charge, it must be aided by equity.

These powers in courts of law were at first taken strictly, because they went in defeasance of the estate, but this has only relation to the execution of such powers, which makes no part of this case, and this artificial reasoning was never allowed in equity, where it came into competition with a provision for a wife or child. But this power in tenant for lifes [*sic*] was considered as part of the old dominion of the party who created the power, and I remember the late Lord Chief Baron Gilbert in the case of *Coventry* v. *Coventry*[942] expressed himself in these words, as I took them from his own mouth,[943] that after the statute of the 27 H. 8 etc.,[944] and this is applicable to the case before us. The power is general, and though subsequent to her estate is not to wait till the death of the jointuress, nay by the same reasoning it must wait till the death of the children of Sir William, if he had any. MSŜ cas. in Canc. D.255.

2. We shall reserve the consideration of the second point.

3. The third point is, whether the plaintiff who is [*239*] administrator *de bonis non* of Mr Burgh the husband, who survived Lettice, has a right to sue for this portion, though he is not administrator to Lettice.

And the question as to this is, whether the property of this portion vested in the husband by any act of his in his lifetime, or whether it remained a chose in action. A little matter will alter the property even of the chattels real[945] of the wife, as if the husband demises in his own name, or takes a covenant for further assurance, 1 Vern. 396.[946] So of choses in action he must reduce them into possession, or if he brings an action in his own name only, and has judgment, that shall go to his executors, and not to the wife, otherwise if he joins his wife with him in the action, for then he don't show his intention to alter the property.

---

[941] *Mildmay's Case* 1 Co. Rep. 175a, 76 E.R. 379.

[942] The case is reported in at least two reports: (1721) Gilb. 160, 25 E.R. 112, and 9 Mod. 12, 88 E.R. 284. Gilbert there appears in Chancery assisting Lord Macclesfield L.C. with Sir Joseph Jekyll M.R., and Price B. Wainwright's comment identifies Gilbert as delivering the judgment in the case, which does not appear from the report.

[943] Wainwright's comment seems to identify him as the reporter of the case.

[944] Statute of Uses (Eng.), 1536, 27 Hen. VIII, c. 10. The equivalent Irish statute is the Statute of Uses (Ir.), 1634. The quotation in Gilb. 160, 25 E.R. 112, at 166 is: 'after the statute 27 Hen. VIII for the transferring uses into possession, the courts of common law held, that powers of revocation of estates executed were to be taken strictly, and so if not pursued, they would not impeach or destroy an estate already executed by legal conveyances'. The corresponding passage in 9 Mod. 18, 88 E.R. 288 is: 'when powers were first created by the statute 27 Hen. VIII,, c. 10, they were strictly construed at law, and the reason was to avoid recalling and unsettling estates already settled'.

[945] E.g. leaseholds.

[946] *Oglander* v. *Baston* (1686) 1 Vern. 96, 23 E.R. 40.

Nightingale v. *Lockman*[947] is the strongest case in their favour, but here the husband has done more than in that case. He claims the portion in a court of record in his own name only, and his claim is allowed. So if this is not a charge on the estate for him, it is no charge at all. So money due to the wife awarded to the husband vests in him, and will go to his representatives, and not survive to the wife.

As to the second point, I shall leave the power of the trustees out of the case, for this being as to the quantum of the charge, the case may be eased of that, for as the plaintiff founds his bill for interest of the £204 from 1694 only, and 'tis in the discretion of the court what interest they will give, this account I believe will turn more to the favour of the defendant than if he had found his bill for the interest of £150 at 10 per cent from 1683.

Lord Chief Baron

Here are two points, 1. Whether the representative of the husband of Lettice be entitled to this bill, either on the articles, or 2. On the decree. And he clearly has a right on the articles. He who has the inheritance, may charge it as he pleases, and equity will make it good, if 'tis agreeable to the intention of the other parties.

This power refers to another conveyance, and was on other considerations, so equity will construe it according to the intention of the parties, which was to provide £300 for his daughters. This is so much reserved out of the grant [*240*] to the son, and this power the father has executed, and therefore it must take place at his death. The decree of the trustees is evidence against the husband, that all the interest was paid till 1694, but from thence he is entitled to 10 per cent for £150, but this decree is not conclusive to Lady Hurley, who is no party to it, so we can't decree it on the decree of the trustees.

Trinity Term. Monday, May the 28. [1733][948]

IVERS v. IVERS

In Exchequer

Mr Prime Serjeant stated the case for the plaintiff

John Ivers, who was seized of about £1,500 a year and the plaintiff of £700, entered into a treaty of marriage, and having four sons, and five daughters, because his hands were tied up by his marriage articles in 1692, he by settlement dated the 4th of August 1718 in consideration that his eldest son Henry did thereby discharge him from the covenants in the said marriage articles, and to settle the estate in his name and blood, limits £300 a year to Henry for his present maintenance and support, but subject to a mortgage of £2,000 to Mr Demar at £7 per cent, the remainder of the estate to himself for life, remainder to Henry for his life, remainder to his first

---

[947] *Nightingale* v. *Lockman* (1729) Fitzg. 148, 94 E.R. 694.
[948] 28 May was a Monday in 1733, Kratz, *Hist. Cal.*

and every other sons in tail male, remainder to Austen his second son for life, etc., remainder to John in fee, and a term of 600 years is created to raise £6,000 for the portions of the younger sons and daughters of John, with this proviso, that the said John, and his sons, etc. as they severally and respectively came into possession, might at any time or times by indenture executed under hand and seal in the presence of three or more credible witnesses limit any part of the said premises unto or for any woman or women they should marry for their lives for their jointure, so as the said premises did not exceed £200 per annum, and so as such jointure be not made dispunishable of waste, and on the same day John Ivers executed a bond to Mr Jephson[949] of the penalty of £2,000, payable on demand, conditioned that John after the marriage will on the request of the said Jephson settle lands of £200 a year [*241*] on the plaintiff Jane for her life for her jointure. The marriage was afterwards had on the same day, and before the death of John a draft of a settlement of particular lands was found among his papers, and John enjoyed the estate of the plaintiff 11 years.

And [the] prayer of this bill is either, that Henry may be compelled to execute the condition of the bond, which is in [the] nature of an agreement to settle £200 a year according to his power or that if this bond is not taken as an agreement to settle, or an execution of his power, it may be satisfied out of the personal assets of the father. John Ivers just before his death gave all his personal estate among his children, which shows he designed this bond should be satisfied out of his real estate.

Mr Attorney General

Stated the case of the defendant Henry Ivers.

John Ivers in 1692 intermarried with Helen Fitzgerald, with whom he had a portion of £1,000 and by articles previous thereto dated the 19th of April 1692, he settled £200 a year on his wife for her jointure, and covenants to settle his estate on himself and the heirs males [*sic*] of the marriage.

The defendant Henry was used very unkindly by his father, had no allowance, and was told by him he had the absolute power over the estate, and John desired Fitzgerald the uncle of Henry to conceal from him his mother's marriage articles, 'if you don't', [he] says he shall get no good of him. So though the plaintiff is a purchaser, she ought to have no remedy against the real estate on foot of the settlement in 1718, but out of the personal estate. Fitzgerald, being called into England, could not discover[950] this to Henry. So the father prevails on him to execute this settlement, and for £100 clear present maintenance. He gives him a power to charge the estate with a jointure of £200 a year, and £6,000 for his younger children, and £600 interest of the mortgage money was in arrear, and he locked up Henry, and made him engross the settlement, and said that nobody else should copy it, and that he would not for £500 [wish] it should come to the knowledge of his relations.

After stating the case, and reading the proofs, Mr Attorney [*242*] General spoke to this effect.

I hope your Lordship will dismiss this bill as to Henry Ivers, or at least that the personal estate shall be applied in the first place to satisfy the demands of the plaintiff.

---

949 Described as her counsel, below, p. 200.
950 I.e. disclose, make known. Johnson's *Dictionary*.

The father John by the will of the grandfather was only tenant in tail, and he never levied a fine or suffered a recovery, and at law as he was tenant in tail, so by his marriage articles in 1692 he was only tenant for life in equity, and if he made a settlement pursuant to those articles, he must have settled the lands in strict settlement.

Objection: But then 'tis objected, that if the court had carried these articles into strict settlement, they would have given John a power to make a jointure on a second wife.

Answer: When the court carries articles into execution, it considers the intention of the parties to them. The wife's father could only intend a provision for his daughter and her children, whereas such a power would be taking £200 a year from the eldest son, and there is no precedent[951] that the court gave such a power, where it was not contracted for, and the father by these articles has no power to provide for a second wife, or younger children.

I shall next beg leave to consider the preparatory steps the father took to the son to execute this settlement. He kept him without money to bring him to his measures. The articles were never laid before him, nor an opportunity given him to consult his friends, and the only notice he had was, that there were some articles or settlement on his mother's marriage, but he never saw them, and his father told him the estate was in his power.

The estate is only £800 a year, and his present maintenance by this settlement is only £240 a year, subject to a mortgage of £2,000 at 7 per cent, and for this he was to be made only tenant for life, and to pay £6,000 to the younger children, and the estate was incumbered £11,000, for £440 a year was gone forever, which it was not subject to by the articles of 1692, and £50 a year quit rent.

The question therefore is, whether on such a deed and power in it the court will give relief? [243] The bond was executed the same day with the articles, by which she sets up her rest on the penalty, and she must abide by it in this case, though it is not so in all cases.

Mr Baron Wainwright

The penalty is not forfeited at law, because Mr Jephson her trustee never made any request to John Ivers to settle a jointure.

Mr Attorney General

The trustee was of her nomination, not of ours. She is a witness to the deed, and they ought to show whether that was executed before or after the bond. Why should she not have the power executed immediately, but that she hoped to have more by the penalty.

Here the power is neither executed in law, or equity, nor is there any lien on the estate. Not at law, 'cause the draft never was executed. Nor is the bond, and the preparation to execute, and the promise to Mr Hasset[952] to execute it the Monday following, an execution in equity.

---

[951] Spelled 'Presidt' in MS.
[952] No person of the name of Hasset is listed in KI AP of the period as barrister, attorney or solicitor, but KI AP is incomplete: see KI AP, p. viii.

The bond would not be an execution if it had been perfected on another day, and can't on that day, because they might as easily have executed it by the deed, as by the bond. As to the draft of the deed, it was prepared in 1723, six years before the 2 December 1729, when John Ivers died, which was a sufficient time to execute it in, if he had a design to do so.

He sent for Mr Hasset not to execute the power in her favour, but of the young children, for the father had a power to distribute the £6,000 at his pleasure, and he sent down stairs for the settlement to that purpose, and when the deed was brought, this settlement was found in it. Then Mr Hasset with his consent and directions alters the date, and tells him of what service it would be to the family to execute it, which he promises to do on the Monday following, and as there is no pretence why he could not have executed it then as well as his will, it must be taken as a mere put off. This was on the Friday. On a fresh application on Saturday, he refuses it with warmth, said he had paid enough of her debts, and he had four days to have executed it in if had designed.

The question then is, whether we shall be obliged to execute it, [*244*] when the deed was fraudulent, and we [are] purchasers. So the father not having executed it, nor having a design, then as we are a purchaser as well as she, why should the court interpose, when they have not the law on their side?

Mr Bindon[953] quoted 1 Vern. 406,[954] 2 Ventr. 350.[955]

Mr Serjeant Purdon[956]

It appears from the case of *Nott* v. *Hill*[957] that a court of equity will look into purchases obtained even by foreigners from young heirs of reversions expectant on the life of their father, and will consider the measure of the purchase.

By the articles of 1694 John had only a power to charge the estate with £1,000 for younger children, but by the settlement of 1718 with £6,000, and Henry parted with his inheritance for about £100 a year for life for his present support.

Here is a non-execution of his power. The bond don't appear to be executed in view of his power, and he might have other lands. Jane was witness to the settlement. She might think it fraudulent, and would therefore rest on the penalty, and rely on his other estate. And in this case the father thought better upon what he had done. He reflected on his ill-usage to his son, and would not execute the draft.

---

[953] Henry Bindon, 5th son of David, Ennis, Co. Clare. Middle Temple, 10 Jan. 1715. KI, Easter term, 1724; KI AP, p. 36.

[954] *Earl of Kildare* v. *Eustace* (1686) 1 Vern. 405 at 406, 23 E.R. 546 (jurisdiction of English Chancery over land in Ireland where defendant resident in England); 1 Vern. 419, 23 E.R. 559 (the judgments on jurisdiction); 1 Vern. 423, 23 E.R. 561; 1 Vern. 428, 23 E.R. 565; 1 Vern. 437, 23 E.R. 571 and see also *Earl of Arglasse* v. *Muschamp* (1682) 1 Vern. 75, 23 E.R. 322 (court of equity in England would relieve against fraudulent conveyances gained of lands in Ireland, when defendant was in England); see also *Smith* v. *Wheeler* (1669) 1 Mod. 16, 86 E.R. 696; 1 Mod. 38, 86 E.R. 714; *Dowdale's Case* (1605) 6 Co. Rep. 46b, 77 E.R. 323 (land in Ireland to satisfy a bond debt in England).

[955] *Sayle and Freeland's Case* (1681) 2 Vent. 350, 86 E.R. 480 (redemption of mortgage).

[956] Recovered from his wound at the hands of Mr Lewis. See above, p. 25 n. 154.

[957] *Nott* v. *Hill* (1682) 1 Vern. 167, 23 E.R. 391; 2 Ch. Cas. 120, 22 E.R. 875 (bargain set aside for excessive value made in time of necessity).

Mr Recorder

Since they have shown fines by which it appears that John docked the entail[958] under his father's will, I shall consider the case on the articles of 1692, by which John in equity was only a tenant for life, and if a bill had been filed for a specific execution of them, the court would not have given him a power to make a jointure on a second wife. Some powers naturally run with the land, and are for the benefit of all the parties, as to make leases, and the like, and therefore a court might perhaps give the father that power in carrying such articles into execution, but then it would be at the best improved rent, but where the power is destructive of, and would load the interest of the parties, a court would not allow it.

In these articles only the first wife and her issue were in contemplation. Such a power in making of settlements [245] has been often refused, and he did not contract for a second marriage, but the parties to these articles contracted for the whole estate. *Brabazon* v. *Keating*,[959] in Chancery: the father of the defendant on his intermarriage one Obrien [*sic*] covenanted by articles to make a jointure, and to settle the estate on himself and the issue of their marriage. They had one son the defendant Richard. The wife dies, the father married again, and previous to his marriage grants a rentcharge of £200 a year to his second wife for life for her jointure. The father dies. The widow intermarries with the plaintiff. The son gets in a precedent mortgage, and by that means covered the estate from the rentcharge. She and her husband file a bill to have the mortgage assigned on payment of the money, and to have the arrears of the rent. The son insists, that by the second articles the father had a power only to settle £70 a year, and not £200, and after by a cross bill sets forth, that he had since found articles on the marriage of his mother, by which his father had no power to make a jointure on a second wife, and the court since her estate was only in equity, and the son had the law and a prior equity, would not interpose. It was then argued, that such a power to make a jointure on a second wife was a reasonable power, that she brought a portion of £1,000, and that the father declared he had such a power. But the court would not and, because it was not agreeable to the intention of the contracting parties to the first articles, and that it would be, instead of executing and old agreement, making a new one. So the bill was dismissed on a rehearing.

That this bond was not designed as a real lien on the estate is plain from these circumstances, that it was executed the same day with the settlement, and they might as easily have perfected articles, and John must have known his power, which was to be executed in the presence of three witnesses, and he could not have forgot the circumstances of it, and yet the bond was only attested by two, so this bond was not designed as a real lien, but she rested on his personal security; this is an absolute bond for £2,000 and is not to arise on a condition precedent, or to be defeated by a condition subsequent. So the condition becoming impossible by the act of God, it becomes absolute, and may be put [246] in suit. Jephson never made a demand on

---

[958] The effect of a fine was to bar the right of the issue in tail to inherit. This produced a base fee, i.e. a fee simple determinable when the issue in tail of the original entail died out. It further barred those entitled in remainder or reversion and their issue, if they failed to claim within 5 years (Baker, *OHLE*, p. 698); 1 Ric. III, c. 7 (Eng.), 1483 (5 years to claim, preserved fines at common law); 4 Hen. VII, c. 24 (Eng.), 1488 (5 years to claim) (statutes applicable to Ireland through Poynings' Law); 11 Hen. VII, c. 20 (Eng.), 1495 (doweress); 32 Hen. VIII, c. 36 (Eng.), 1540 (reversions in the crown not barred). 10 Car. I, sess. 2, c. 8 (Ir.), 1634, s. 3 applied 11 Hen. VII, c. 20 to Ireland, s. 5 applied 32 Hen. VIII, c. 36.

[959] No citation given.

John to settle during his life, and such a request is impossible after his death, and since he never made a demand in the life of the jointuress, that shows her election to abide by the penalty.

The general covenant in 1718, to discharge the father from all covenants in the deed of 1692 is to be looked upon as fraudulent, because he did not show him the deed, and the particular covenants therein. And though the fraud of the father don't devolve on the wife, yet you would oblige the father to indemnify the son, or give him this £2,000.

Mr Malone

I shall consider this case 1. as it stands on the articles of 1692, 2. on the power reserved to John by the deed of 1718, 3. whether this power be executed or whether it was their intention it should, 4. what effect this bond must now have, if 'tis not a complete or a defective execution of this power.

1. By the articles John was only tenant for life and I think when they were carried into execution, the court could not give him a power to incumber the estate.

Lord Chief Baron

In the case of *Lord Loftus* v. *Lord Drogheda*,[960] the court when they carried the articles into execution gave the father a liberty to transpose the uses, though it was not part of the agreement, and he gave them to the second son, who enjoyed accordingly.

Mr Malone

That case then is directly contrary to the case of *Trevor* v. *Trevor*,[961] which went upon this principle, that courts of equity don't make new agreements, but executes [*sic*] MSS cas. in Canc. those the parties have agreed on, and this is the very nature of a specific execution, C.24. and nothing is more common in this kingdom than not to make a provision for a second wife, or her issue, but leave them to the father's industry, except on failure of issue male and the court won't make them a better provision.

Kirwin v. *Kirwin*[962] in Chancery: the son turned Protestant and brought a bill against his father for a maintenance, and to carry his mother's marriage articles in to execution. [*247*] There the father insisted, that he had since married a second wife, and agreed to make her a jointure, and that he had no power by the articles to provide for younger children, and prayed that the court would in execution of the articles furnish him with reasonable powers. Lord Midleton[963] said it was a hard case, but that he could not alter the agreement. He could not lessen the interest of the parties, but he would make the Protestant maintenance as small as he could.

In the case of *Brabazon* v. *Keating*[964] the son discovered the articles after a decree against him, and then brought a cross bill, and the court said they would not have interposed, if the wife had had the legal estate.

---

[960] No citation given.
[961] *Trevor* v. *Trevor* (1719) 1 Eq. Cas. Abr. 185, 21 E.R. 977; affirmed by House of Lords (1719) 5 Bro. P.C. 2nd ed. 122, 2 E.R. 574.
[962] No citation given.
[963] Spelled 'Middleton' in MS.
[964] No citation given. See p. 192.

2. Henry antecedent to the deed of 1718 had the inheritance in him. The father after the articles sells part of the estate, and incumbers [the] other part, and then makes the son execute this settlement, whereby he gives him a power to settle £200 a year on a second wife, and £6,000 on younger children, and before this settlement he threw the son under the greatest difficulties for want of a maintenance, and concealed the articles from him, and yet makes him covenant to discharge him from all the covenants in those articles, which was a notorious badge of fraud and told him he had a power to act thus with him. This is giving the father the inheritance, for the power to make a jointure on a second wife must come out of that, and a bill between father and son here is sufficient to set these articles aside.

3. But here then is a third person in the case, which is like one purchasing without notice of the fraud, which I own varies the case, but yet she is not entitled to be benefit of this power, because here is no defective act done to carry it into execution, as was in *Lord Coventry's Case*.[965] If the condition of the bond had took notice of the power, and referred to it, that would have bound the land, but here is no covenant that refers to the power, and though she had notice of the power, she don't take a covenant to execute it, but a bond, which was perfected three hours before the marriage. Articles are the natural way to execute such a power, and might have been done in as short a time as the bond. This lady had a good estate, and might therefore think many better than land, and nothing has been done that looks like an express execution of it, and the condition is to settle [*248*] on request which has no reference to the power. Courts of equity indeed have executed powers for creditors, and made them assets, but this is an agreement *sub modo*, to execute it if requested, if not, to give her so much money.

Then the plaintiff can't have the benefit of this jointure, which may be made on the request of one who never made demand.

4. What decree then is the plaintiff entitled to? The condition of this bond is a plain agreement if she can't have one, to have the other. Mr John Ivers is not uneasy that he could not execute this draft, nor was he prevented from doing it by the absence of servants, or otherwise.

If the son had filed a bill to set aside the settlement, and the wife had brought her interpleading bill, the bond would be decreed to be satisfied out of his other estate that was in his power.

Mr Minchin[966]

Nels. 8vo Rep. in
Canc. 205.[968] 1 Chan. cas. 188[967] is an authority in point, that the plaintiff must resort to the personal assets, and rest on the penalty, and by the rule laid down in 1 Vern. 429, *Kildare* v. *Eustace*,[969] since they have proved assets, they may have a decree against them.

[That] our case differs from the other has been mentioned in which a constant intention continued to execute the deed, and several steps were taken towards it,

[965]   Above, p. 187 n. 942.
[966]   John Minchin, Clonohilton, Co. Tipperary, s. of Adam Minchin, surgeon; ed. Trinity College Dublin, Middle Temple, Hilary term, 1720, KI, Easter term, 1726.
[967]   *Bagg* v. *Foster* (1670) 1 Chan. Cas. 188, 22 E.R. 755 (conditional bond on marriage to settle property on wife).
[968]   *Holtham* v. *Ryland* (1692) Nels. 205, 21 E.R. 826.
[969]   *Earl of Kildare* v. *Eustace* (1686) 1 Vern. 428 at 429, 23 E.R. 565 (whether the estate in law was executed by the Act of Settlement).

and the perfection hindered by death, and the defendant was a volunteer, not a purchaser, and the power here is not part of the father's ancient dominion, because the inheritance was not before in him.

Mr Prime Serjeant for the plaintiff

I thought there were only two points in this case: 1. Whether the bond was an agreement in equity to make a jointure pursuant to his power. 2. Whether this was such an agreement, as a court of equity would carry into execution.

But another question has been introduced: whether John being tenant in tail by the will of his father, Henry is not entitled under it. No proof has been given that this estate was devised [249] by the father. No denominations are mentioned, but as fines have been levied, the issue are certainly barred[970] and John had a power to make this settlement, upon which so much has been said as of an act of oppression, and that though we were not involved in the act of the father, yet that makes it improper to pray a decree agreements the son, that I shall beg leave to look into the considerations of the settlement, and the manner of obtaining it.

I will suppose the value of the estate to be but £840 a year, and to be subjected to £4,000 debts, whereof Demar has a mortgage, and the rest are by judgment, and £6,000 for younger children's portions. Yet this is not an unconscionable bargain, and I will suppose them to be debts of John, though it don't appear by whom they were contracted. Now if these creditors had no notice of the articles of 1692, their debts would affect the estate in the hands of Henry. So that to have made this property part of his grievance, he should have showed his estate was not before liable to these debts, which he could only have done, by showing the creditors had notice of that settlement.

Of the £6,000 for the younger children, they were entitled to £1,000 by the articles of 1692, so that there was only an addition of £5,000, and since the son consented to it, though it had been without consideration, the court would not break the settlement upon this act, because such a provision ought to have been made at first, and it was more reasonable now, there being eight children, and £120 present maintenance will remain for the son, which would enable him to take that education his father's circumstances would not otherwise allow, and he enjoyed this eleven years. But what is this to the plaintiff, when whatever fraud was made use of, there is no proof that she was privy to it, or had notice of it?

Before I go into the power, I must also insist that the son had notice of the articles of 1692 for fourteen or fifteen days before Fitzgerald went to England, and why in all that time did he not see the said articles, which were in his hands, for there is no proof that the father hurried him.

If A purchases with notice of articles, he is bound, but if he sells to B without notice, he shall hold against the son that claims under them. [250] The bond is a violent presumption that the plaintiff, her trustee, and the father intended to execute the power, and that the plaintiff who was a witness to the settlement took care to inform herself of his power, and would she have future acquisitions in view, and not what he had in is power, considering his large family, and incumbrances.

The question then is, whether this bond is to be considered as an agreement. Formerly I allow courts of equity turned the obligee to law, but now they proceed on

---

[970] Above, p. 192 n. 958.

another foot, that the condition is an agreement to settle, and she has the choice of two remedies, and to fix her to one, to confine her to law, is to destroy that election, and this bond is to be construed in the strongest manner as well as against the son, as the father, it being part of that dominion which the son agreed his father should have over the estate in fee in the hands of the trustees.

How is this case different from *Coventry*, that I allow did recite the power, but if the condition of the bond is to be considered as a real agreement, there is no difference, for the lands are not mentioned in either case, and whether he refers to his power, or has it in his power, and covenants to do it, the court will consider it as done,[971] and if you don't refer it to this power, she can never have a specific execution, because he has no other lands.

This a provision before marriage, is to be taken liberally, and the wife is a creditor, and brought him £800 a year, and 'tis not to be considered like a provision for a younger child, and it looks as if she deferred the marriage till the settlement which gave him this power was executed, for she was married immediately after, and this act of the son led the lady into this marriage, relying on the power.

Mr Calaghan

1. I shall endeavour to prove, that John had a power to make a jointure on a second wife, 2. That there are circumstances in this equitable execution sufficient to induce the court to carry it into a [*251*] specific execution.

1. If the deed of 1718 was out of the case, John I think might have made this jointure, for if Henry had come into a court of equity for a specific execution of the articles of 1692, equity would not alter a hard agreement contrary to the words, unless the party would consent to what was reasonable.

The cases of *Kirwin*, and *Keating*, don't come up to this, for here by the very words John is tenant in tail, but defendant Ivers has expressly agreed to this power.

2. Whether, as John had this power, he has done anything that amounts to an equitable execution of it. Here are two equitable executions of it.

1. The bond. 'Tis a settled point in equity that a covenant to settle is an equitable execution, 2 Vern. 379.[972] Now a bond in equity is the same as covenant, and that the party shall stick to the penalty only was overruled by the House of Lords in the case of *Lady Prendergast* v. *Sir Toby Butler*,[973] where it was adjudged, that the condition to do, was an agreement, and that the penalty was not a waiver of it, but the better to enforce it, and that it was in the option of the party to pursue the penalty, or a specific execution.

Mes App. D.193. E.851.

2. Another equitable execution is the draft of the jointure deed, that was found among the papers of Mr Ivers, as appears from *Coventry's Case*,[974] and the declaration to Mr Hasset three or four days before his death that he would execute it on Monday,

---

[971] Under the maxim that 'equity considers as done that which ought to be done'. See *Trevor* v. *Trevor* (1719) 10 Mod. 436 at 437, 88 E.R. 798 ('That what the Court, if applied to, would have decreed, they would so far consider performed', per Parker L.C.), affirmed (1719) 5 Bro. P.C. 2nd ed. 122, 2 E.R. 574. Above, p. 91 [*109*] and n. 526.

[972] *Lady Clifford* v. *Earl of Burlington* (1700) 2 Vern. 379, 23 E.R. 841.

[973] For the litigation see *Butler* v. *Prendergrass* (1720) 2 Eq. Cas. Abr. 185, 482, 632, 22 E.R. 159, 409, 531. *Butler* v. *Prendergast* (1720) 4 Bro. P.C. 2nd ed. 175, 2 E.R. 119.

[974] Gilb. 160, 25 E.R. 112, 9 Mod. 12, 88 E.R. 284.

which was the day he died, and there appears on the face of the draft a reason why he did not execute it, that the lands there mentioned did not amount to £200 a year.

Where an agreement is executed, and the condition becomes impossible by the act of God, the estate is absolute, but where executory, the bond is void. The bond here is not forfeited, because there was no demand, but supposing it forfeited, she has her option.

Mr Wall[975]

It is plain the plaintiff did not rely on the penalty, from her procuring her friends to apply to John for a specific execution.

Ab. of equity cases 18 pl. 8, *Holtham* v. *Ryland*,[976] where the bond was saved, the equity carried the condition into execution, so here the obligation is saved by the death [252] of the obligor, before any request was made.

Mr Daly

The parties to the articles of 1692 by the deed of 1718 show what they thought a reasonable execution of them, which is the same thing as if they had been executed in that manner by a settlement previous to the marriage. 2. Chan. Cas. 28, *Hale* v. *Hale*[977] shows as to the execution of the power, that as the party had no other estate, he must be presumed to refer to that. If there was any fraud between the father and the son it is purged by handing it over to the wife.

Mr Spring[978]

In the case of *Brabazon* v. *Keating*[979] the articles were to settle on himself for life, remainder to trustees etc., remainder to his first and every other son in tail male. There the second wife had notice of these articles, whereby it appeared that the husband was only tenant for life, for they were recited in her deed of jointure.

26 June, [1733]

The last of the eight days.

Mr Baron Wainwright

In this cause Margaret Ivers is the plaintiff, Henry the eldest son of John Ivers deceased, his younger sons, and daughters, and others, are the defendants. The grandfather of the defendant Henry Ivers devised his real estate to John the father

---

[975] William Wall is listed in KI AP, with no date, but as probably 1725/6, s. of William, Dublin, Middle Temple, 1 Oct. 1729, d. 9 Oct. 1755.

[976] *Holtham* v. *Ryland* (1692) 1 Eq. Cas. Abr. 18, 21 E.R. 840.

[977] *Hele* v. *Hele* (1680) 2 Ch. Cas. 28, 22 E.R. 831.

[978] Thomas Spring, s. and heir of Thomas, Ballycrispin, Co. Kerry. Middle Temple, Hilary term, 1723. KI, Easter term, 1729, d. 6 Dec. 1761. KI AP, p. 459.

[979] No citation given. Above, p. 192.

in tail. By articles previous to his marriage dated in 1692 John in consideration of a portion of £1,000 agreed to settle his estate on himself and his heirs males, [*sic*] and to make a jointure of £100 a year for his wife, with a power to raise £1,000 for the portions of younger children, the marriage was had, and sometime after John and his wife levied fines, but no uses are declared of those fines. The wife died, and on the 4th day of August 1718 John intermarried with the plaintiff, and on the same day articles are entered into between John and [*253*] the defendant Henry, to which the defendant Fitzgerald his father in law who had the former articles in his keeping is witness, whereby Henry releases the covenants in the said articles to his father, and part of the lands subject to a mortgage are settled on Henry for a present provision, and the rest to John for life, remainder to trustees to preserve[980] etc., remainder to trustees for 600 years, then to Henry for life, remainder to trustees to preserve etc., remainder to his first and every other son in tail male, remainder to the second and every other son of John etc., remainder in fee to John, with a proviso, that John, and his sons, as they severally and respectively came into possession, might by indenture under hand and seal attested by three or more credible witnesses limit lands not exceeding £200 a year for a jointure to their wife, and the trust of the term is, declared to be for raising £6,000 for the young children of John. The plaintiff is a witness to this deed, and it is engrossed by Henry, and the same day John perfected a bond in trust for the plaintiff, with condition to settle lands of £200 a year on himself and his wife for their lives, and after his death to his wife for life for her jointure. The estate of the husband was about £800 a year, and his second wife had lands much of the same value, and £500 in money. After the marriage a jointure deed was prepared by the direction of the husband, but never executed, but by his will he executed the power in favour of his younger children, and made a donation of part of the personal estate to them in his lifetime, and he devised the rest to them.

And the plaintiff by her bill prays either a specific execution of these articles, or a satisfaction out of the assets to John.

Henry Ivers the defendant insists that his father by the marriage articles of 1692 was only a tenant for life in equity, that he was compelled to execute the articles of 1718 by hard means, that he was at that time ignorant of the articles of 1692, and that the wife ought to have her remedy out of the personal estate. And the younger children insist that the personal estate is not liable, but that the plaintiff is to be satisfied out of the power. [*254*]

The deed of 1718 is brought in by *duces tecum*, and is evidence against Henry, though not against his children the minors. It appears that Mr Hasset was present when John the father made his will, that he sent one of his sons for the settlement of 1718, that he might see how his power stood to provide for his younger children, that when it was brought, the draft of the jointure deed was in it, that Hasset said, it would prevent disputes if he executed this power, and that he promised to do it on the Monday following. Several lands are recited in that draft, but not of sufficient value.

Thomas Ivers swears, that he don't know whether the draft was prepared in pursuance of his power, or whether he designed to execute it, but that he designed to execute it in favour of his children, which he did accordingly by his will, and when Mr Francis Wilson came from the wife, and after Mr Hasset had been there, applied

---

[980]   I.e. trustees to preserve contingent remainders. Above, p. 82 n. 478.

to him to execute it. He refused with some warmth, and said, he would consider it till Monday.

The case of *Coventry* v. *Coventry*[981] though nearest to this, is materially different in some circumstances. In *Coventry* the power was part of the original fee, and not acquired by any fraud or hardship. It was intended to be executed, and several steps were taken towards it, and the earl was prevented by a concurrence of several accidents. Here was no concurrence of accidents to prevent the execution, but a different purpose in the party. There was a particular agreement to execute the power: here the condition of the bond is only to settle lands of such a value, and the security is by bond, for the payment of which the personal estate is the natural fund. Yet I think the plaintiff is entitled to a specific execution of the power, though there was no actual agreement for that purpose.

Whatever fraud or hardship appears on the son, the plaintiff not being accessory to it, cannot be affected by it, and she is a purchaser not only from the father, but from Henry the son, who joined in creating this [255] power, the day she was married, and that John executed the bond. So I am of opinion the bond was given in contemplation of the power, and shall in equity amount to an agreement, and must be presumed to be an agreement to settle lands according to the power, and there is no proof that John was in possession of other lands, and what is considerable in this case is, that the plaintiff can have no remedy on this bond but a specific execution of the condition, it not being forfeited, nor do real assets appear.

By the old resolutions indeed the parties to these bonds have been left to law to the remedy they had provided for themselves by the penalty, but the modern authorities run otherwise, and the court has considered them as contracts or agreements, and carried them into execution. As I remember in the case of *Holtham* v. *Rayland*[982] there the condition was to settle lands by a day certain. The other obligor died before the day, so the bond was not forfeited, and there the court decreed a specific execution. Here too the condition is to settle lands, and the bond is not forfeited. Nels. 8vo Rep. in Canc. 205. SC.

In the case of *Clifford* v. *Burlington*[983] the agreement had no reference to the power. He sent to his steward to be informed of what lands he could settle, and he accordingly settled those he returned him to the value of £700 a year, and took no further steps. There the portion was but £5,000, yet a specific execution was decreed against the heir in tail, and he was to make them up £1,000 a year, though there was only a general agreement to settle lands.

Sir John St Leger

I think this agrees with *Coventry's Case.*[984] The deed of 1718 was most fraudulently obtained to the total destruction of the defendant Henry. If then we can preserve the right of the heir, and provide for the plaintiff, I think that method most eligible; his father bred him up in poverty and obscurity, and from the beginning he intended to ruin him, for he sold £10,000 worth of the estate before he came of age, and it is for this reason Henry is made to release him from all the covenants [256] of the articles of 1692. John directs Fitzgerald not to let Henry have them, or know of them, because he was a stubborn fellow, and at other times he said he could make

---

[981]   (1721) Gilb. 160, 25 E.R. 112, and 9 Mod. 12, 88 E.R. 284.
[982]   *Holtham* v. *Ryland* (1692) Nels. 205, 21 E.R. 826; 1 Eq. Cas. Abr. 18, 21 E.R. 840.
[983]   *Lady Clifford* v. *Earl of Burlington* (1700) 2 Vern. 379, 23 E.R. 841.
[984]   *Coventry* v. *Coventry* (1721) Gilb. 160, 25 E.R. 112, and 9 Mod. 12, 88 E.R.284.

the settlement without him, so the articles were concealed, and the condition of the estate misrepresented to the son, then he makes him consent to pay his debts, and settle this jointure, though the father of his mother on her marriage did not think fit to give John this power, and he made him engross it, and confined him till he did it, because it was not fit to be known.

This fraud indeed won't affect the plaintiff, if she was ignorant of it, but she was a witness to the deed, and Mr Jephson her counsel[985] was present. Why did she not insist to have this power executed by deed? Now the case stands only on the bond to settle £200 a year, and why is not this power mentioned in the condition if it was in view of it, as in *Coventry's Case*? Nor can I construe it an execution of it.

In *Coventry's Case* the judges took the covenant to be an execution in equity. There were a variety of accidents to prevent the execution of the draft, in which there was a designation of the lands.

I think this gentleman did not design to execute this draft, since he let it lie by for four or five years, and did not take it up of himself. Mr Hasset was sent for to draw his will in favour of his children, and for that purpose he sent for the settlement to see his power, and when his son brought it, this draft being in it, Mr Hasset desired him in favour of his sister the plaintiff to execute it, and he promises to do it on Monday. Mr Stephens had directions from the wife to desire him to do it, but then having provided for his children, he changes his note, and tells him he will consider of it.

I don't think this bond is an execution of his power. Any friend might in her name as well as her trustee have applied for an execution. The condition is to settle £200 a year. He has the alternative, to settle, or forfeit. If Lord Coventry had made a [257] jointure of other lands than what the power reached to, that would have been a good execution of the covenant. The condition has no reference, nor recites, the power, nor the lands. The plaintiff was not ignorant of his power, and yet relied on this bond for the performance of her jointure. And here is no subsequent declaration that it was to relate to the power, nor any execution.

Since then she relied on the condition of the bond, which created no lien on these lands, and that there are personal assets, I think we ought to save the heir as much as we can, and apply the personal estate in the first place to exonerate his estate.

Lord Chief Baron

I think this bond is a charge on the lands, and there are two points to be considered.

1. Whether the power is created in such a manner as equity will carry it into execution, and I own there are strong appearances that the settlement in 1718 was not obtained with the greatest consideration, or paternal tenderness, but the plaintiff is a purchaser, and there is no evidence that she was a confederate, but she takes this settlement executed by the father and son as a good one, and consents to the marriage on the strength and relying on the power, so that the son contracts with her, that his father shall have a power to settle this jointure, so that however the son might be relieved against his father by a satisfaction out of his assets, he is to be considered in a different light as to the plaintiff, who if a purchaser of this power, is a purchaser without notice.

[985] Probably John Jephson, s. and heir of John, of Limerick. Middle Temple, 23 June 1697; KI, Easter term, 1702, KI AP, p. 248. A William Jephson was created serjeant in England in 1765: Baker, *The Order of Serjeants at Law*, pp. 215, 521. It is not known if he was related to John Jephson.

2. Whether the acts that have been done are such an execution of this power as equity will establish. In the case of *Lord Coventry*[986] the power is expressly mentioned, and he covenants to settle pursuant to it, or otherwise, but it is also taken notice of in the will of Lord Coventry, and that he had given her a further provision that that provided by the power.

Here the power was executed by the party defendant, and it don't appear as in *Coventry's Case*, that the personal assets are sufficient to satisfy the bond.

But I consider the case on this foot where one has a power to charge an estate in general with such a sum, [258] and he after contracts debts, equity will execute the power in favour of creditors in whosoever hands the estate comes. This contract then to settle is what in justice he ought to perform, and it don't appear that he can do it otherwise. Whatever it may have been formerly, it is not the present opinion that the party is bound up by[987] what they have held themselves to, and this was the opinion of the Lords in the case of *Sir Thomas Prendergast* v. *Sir Toby Butler*[988] on an appeal from a decree of the Court of Chancery in Ireland. Sir Toby had bound himself in the penalty of £5,000 to preserve the woods, and the demand on him was to double that value, and the Lords adjudged that the penalty should not limit her demands, and directed an issue to try what the estate was damaged by Sir Toby cutting the woods, contrary to the condition of his bond.

The bond is not forfeited at law, because no request was made to settle lands in the life of John, yet equity will relieve out of the assets of John, because this is to relieve against the strict rules of law. The plaintiff has desired her relief against the real estate, and it don't appear what the personal estate is worth, so we ought to give her the best remedy.

It would have taken up more time to execute this power than the bond, and this is an agreement which John ought in conscience to execute, and the power was given by the son, and I can't suppose the son not conusant of what was the design of the power when he executed it, and I take this to be the rule if he had left no other assets, though he had done no acts towards an execution of it, because he was obliged in justice to do it, and it was not such an act as he could in conscience do, or not do.

But here are steps taken towards an execution. The draft was prepared in 1723 by his orders. Some lands are set out to the value of £130 a year, and a blank left for other. Mr Hasset altered the date in his presence, and then he promises to perfect it on Monday, and after he did not tell Francis [259] Wilson that he would not perfect it, but that he would not at that time, which implies he would at another.

Therefore I think this power ought to be carried into execution, and the lands particularly mentioned in the draft are to be made up [to] £200, and settled on the plaintiff for life, and the arrears since the death of John Ivers are to stand a charge on the lands.

---

[986] *Coventry* v. *Coventry* (1721) Gilb. 160, 25 E.R. 112, 9 Mod. 12, 88 E.R. 284.

[987] I.e limited to.

[988] *Butler* v. *Prendergast* (1720) 4 Bro. P.C. 2nd ed. 175, 2 E.R. 119, from Irish Chancery; see also *Lady Prendergast* v. *Sir Toby Butler*, above, p. 196 n. 973 cited by Mr Calaghan and referred to in the marginal note there as 'Mes App. D.193, E.851.'

Saturday June the 9th [1733][989]

In Exchequer

DR ROBERTS v. DILLON POLLARD HAMPSON

An attachment was moved for against the defendant for putting in a short answer. The court ordered he should answer over, as on a baron's report of his answer being short, it plainly appearing to the court to be short, but by consent he was to put in a full answer in a month, or process was to go from the beginning.

Post 281.

May the 25th, 1733[990]

In Exchequer

COYNE v. GAYNER

The interrogatories and depositions were titled *Coyne* v. *Gayner et al.*, but the case was, there had been five defendants, and after answer the bill was dismissed against four of them, in order to examine them as witnesses, but some were examined before they were struck out, and some after, and a motion was made to amend the interrogatories and depositions, on the affidavit of the attorney, that there was no other cause, and yet he thought the bill was still subsisting against two of the defendants, and therefore titled the interrogatories, et al.

Ante 169.
Post 281.
Mes App. G.95.

Mr Recorder said there must be something to amend by, as the title of depositions may be amended by the commission, but here the examination was in the office, and that a record could not be altered in this manner.

Mr Baron Wainwright

Have you any authority, that if the title is altered by leave of the court, the witness is not indictable for perjury? [*260*] How can the title be altered [when] it is now good as to those defendants that were examined before they were struck out, and bad as to those that were examined after, and if it is altered, it will be bad as to those that were first examined, and good as to those who were examined after.

The court gave liberty to move it on the hearing.

---

[989] 9 June was a Saturday in 1733, Kratz, *Hist. Cal.*
[990] Note that the year is given in the MS.

NEWPORT v. MADDEN

In Exchequer

The defendant demurred because the bill contained no equity, and the demurrer was overruled for consistency, because the defendant had prayed a *dedimus*[991] without an injunction, and an order was made that the plaintiff should have an injunction in bringing the money into court.

June the 22nd [1733][992]

The 5th of the eight days after Trinity Term

In Exchequer

MARGARET BARLOW SPINSTER, AND ANN BURTON WIDOW, PLAINTIFFS

JOSEPH HARRIS, AND THEODORE BARLOW ESQR, DEFENDANTS

The question was, whether the answer of the defendant Harris should be read to the payment of the purchase money, not being contradicted by any proof?

The chief baron took this distinction: where only one witness proved the contrary, the negative of the defendant in his answer might be read; but that his answer could not be read to supply a defective proof of what it was incumbent on him to make out, for in the first case the *onus probandi*[993] lies on the plaintiff, in the other on the defendant.

But the answer was read, and the court said, they [*261*] would after consider what weight should be laid on it.

Mr Prime Serjeant for the defendant Harris

I shall argue on a supposition that we are real creditors, that the plaintiffs are not to be relieved on the decree of Martha, or Margaret in Chancery.

Martha was the widow of Lewis Barlow, and by articles previous to her marriage, she was to have a third of his personal estate. Lewis dies, having first made his will, and the defendant Theodore Barlow his son, and another [are] executors, and thereby made a provision for Martha and his daughters without any notice of the articles, and made Theodore Barlow residuary legatee.

Theodore immediately on the death of his father obtained a deed from Martha, whereby she waived the articles, and agreed to take £30 a year for her life.

---

[991] L. more fully *dedimus potestatem*, we have given the power, from the words of the writ. A writ empowering a person who is not a judge to do some act in place of a judge, such as those issued to authorize commissioners to take down the depositions of witnesses.

[992] 22 June was a Friday in 1733 (Julian), Kratz, *Hist. Cal.*

[993] L. burden of proof.

On the 29 April 1726 Martha filed a bill to set aside this deed, and to have a third part of the personal estate of Lewis Barlow under the articles. On the 26 of December following the defendant Harris lent Theodore on a mortgage of the leases £200, and on the 26 of January after £400.

And the question is, whether the executor had such a power over these leases as to make a purchaser a good title to them after Martha had filed her bill? And 'tis objected, that this bill is notice of these articles, though they were not mentioned in the will.

Answer: A purchaser would be safe, though he had notice of these articles.

Where an estate is generally devised for payment of debts, a purchaser is not bound to see the money applied. The articles don't convey a legal estate to her, so if they were mentioned, they would only show the husband had agreed the wife should have a third part of his personal estate, yet still the executor has a power to sell these leases: if Harris knew of a judgment against the testator, yet the sale would be good, [262] for the executor by law has a power to sell, and yet Martha has only a lien in equity, but the judgment creditor at law. 'Tis the duty of the executor to sell, and distribute the assets among the creditors according to the nature of the securities, and the purchase is good though the executor misapplies the assets; but a trustee has no power to sell but by the will, and therefore a purchaser ought to look into the will to see his power.

The question then is, how far Martha's bill is notice. There are authorities indeed that a purchaser must take notice of a bill, which demands a real estate, but there is a difference between a real estate and mere chattels, so supposing the bill [is] notice, the question is, whether that notice is material, which we think it is not from the power in the executor over the assets.

This decree was received by the plaintiff Margaret as executor of Martha.

But as to Margaret's bill on the foot of the articles [of] 22 March 1728, he had no notice for the articles as far as they provide the £400 for the children are not set out in the bill of Martha, so if we are a real creditor, there is no reason to give her portion the preference. If this legacy had been actually charged on these terms, the sale would be good, and the executor is to make the distribution, and the testator can't control his power, but he is to prevent a *devastavit*, and to sell and apply as he ought.

The plaintiff Ann's bill is on the same foot, and was filed a year after these mortgages.

Mr Solicitor General

This bill is brought to attach a sum of money raised by sale of the terms under a decree of this court, for the satisfaction of the mortgages of the defendant Harris. The plaintiff Margaret claims a third part of the personal estate of her father, as the representative of her mother Martha, and as legatee £300, and Ann claims by the said will £200.

Where the real estate is devised to executors to pay particular [263] debts the purchaser must take care to see the money applied, for the sale of the executor is an execution of that power which the purchaser must see well executed, but the personal estate is on a different foot.

These articles are no lien on any particular part of the personal estate, but she has her option, and it is not as strong as if she were to have a third part of these particular leases, and she must then have applied to the executor.

Now the executor has the same power over the estate as if there had been no articles, which only ascertain her quantum, but the executor as a trustee must sell perishing interests, such as leases, and turn them into money, which is more permanent, and therefore his sale is good, and the defendant need not inquire into who had the right.

This goes on a supposition he had notice, but [t]here is not enough in this case to destroy his purchase. The pretended notice is only by this bill, and it is not settled, how far such a bill is constructive notice to a purchaser, but depends on circumstances, and a search would be inconvenient to purchasers. The assignment to trustees to pay £400 a year to the children was not before the court, but they have lain by and suffered a sale to be in this court on a foreclosure.

Mr Recorder

Martha by her bill does not pray to be decreed to these terms, but to the third of the assets of Lewis Barlow, and the decree is according to her prayer, so neither the articles, or decree have created a particular lien on these terms, and if he had seen the decree, and then bought, he would not be bound, because the executor is a person trusted by the testator to sell.

The articles are no lien on any particular part of the personal estate, but the husband in his life might have sold these leases, or any other part of his personal estate.

If lands are devised generally to pay debts, the purchaser need not see to application, otherwise if the devise is for the payment of particular debts, for by that they are made a particular lien.

They have not the executors before the court, and they say [264] the testator left £5,000 assets, and yet they would fix their demands on these terms, whereas if the executor was before the court, and an account of assets were decreed, no charge would have been on these terms, if the rest were sufficient, and since they have made that unnecessary, shan't we have our money, who have the legal estate?

The payment of the purchase money is sufficiently proved against Barlow, by proving his receipt on the back of the deed, and we are not to look to his application of it. When the children file a bill for their legacies, it is a waiver of the articles, and they can't resort to them.

Mr Attorney General for the plaintiffs

The prayer of the bill is, that the money may remain in the officers' hands, till our three decrees in the Court of Chancery are determined.

1. I shall show, that we have a right to these terms; 2. That the defendant Harris has not a title either in law or equity; 3. That his title wears the badges of fraud; 4. That if he was a real purchaser, he had actual notice.

1. By the articles in 1693 these leases are made a security not only for the wife, but the children, and are actually conveyed to trustees, so Barlow the executor had not the legal estate.

2. She was to have a third part of the personal estate, though the remaining fund was deficient to make up the £400 for the children, and these leases were the consideration of the marriage, so the wife had an actual lien in equity on them, and by the will she £40 a year given her in lieu of dower, thirds,[994] or otherwise then Mr Harris ought to have inquired into what was meant by that part of the will, and what she insisted upon, for without the articles, she had no title to thirds.

The bill of Martha is notice, there are only two courts of equity in the kingdom, and he ought to have seen if she had attached her demands, and if he did not, he would not look, only for fear he should find. [*265*] You now can only consider this decree, which has said Martha shall be paid out of these terms, and the two other suits are not yet determined.

As to a trial, whether Harris paid the purchase money, in the case of *Roquier* v. Mes App. B.9.   *Bolton* in this court a trial was offered, but refused by the plaintiff, because being their defence they ought to have proved it, and it would be the greatest inlet to perjury.

Mr Serjeant Bettesworth

£40 a year is charged by the will on these terms for Martha, which is notice to Harris, and the executor could not sell to the prejudice of that annuity, and at that time a bill was filed by Martha for her election, for her thirds under the articles.

Harris swears, he never saw the will. Maybe so, but he might have seen a copy, or a probate of it, and having thus proved he had notice of the articles, he must have notice of them too as to the £400 for the children.

[On] 14 April 1731 Harris filed a bill for foreclosure in this court. [On] 19 May Theodore Barlow put in his answer without oath. Harris replied, and Barlow rejoined the same day, and in two months there was a final decree for a sale, so Barlow who received the money, owns it, and Harris swears he paid it, but Mr Somner knows nothing of it, but believes Boyd one of the witnesses who is dead, might.

Mr Hussy

He that designs to make a fraudulent sale will certainly give a receipt for the money. The witnesses say they see a receipt, and therefore believe the money was paid, why so does the court now. We expressly charge in our bill that no money was paid. He says in his answer there was, and we by our replication put it in issue.

But if he is a purchaser, he purchased in this town, where the bill of Martha was going on.

Mr Calaghan

A purchase from the executor with notice of the trust was [*266*] set aside in 1 Vern. 484, 5, 6,[995] yet in that case the executor had the legal estate. Here he has neither in law or equity any estate, and there, as in this case, the case was brought on without the executor, he being out of the kingdom, and the objection for want of parties overruled. 2 Vern. 616.[996]

---

[994]   The third of the personal property of a deceased husband allowed to his widow.
[995]   *Walley* v. *Walley* (1687) 1 Vern. 484, 23 E.R. 609.
[996]   *Crane* v. *Drake* (1708) 2 Vern. 616, 23 E.R. 1004.

A suit depending[997] is notice to all the world. Here the answer came in before the mortgage, 1 Vern. 318, 319,[998] and this is agreeable to the rules of equity in other cases, as of bankrupts, 2 Vern. 157,[999] and of decrees. So if an executor pays a debt by specialty without knowing of a decree, yet the decree shall bind him, 2 Vern. 37,[1000] and implicit notice is in many cases as cogent as actual notice. This notice to his scrivener shall bind the purchaser, though he had no notice, notwithstanding the hardship of the case. It would be of ill consequence to direct an issue, whether the purchase money was paid. It is put in issue and 'tis to be presumed he made the strongest proof he could. It would open a gap to perjury, and is the same as giving leave to examine after publication. As to the notice, he ought to have inquired into the articles as to the children, since they are mentioned in the bill of Martha, 2 Vern. 384.[1001]

These legacies are a charge on the assets in the hands of Barlow the executor, and as Harris purchased from him, he must have notice of the will, 2 Ventr. 349.[1002]

Mr Daly

A bill from the necessity of the thing is notice to everybody, or the defendant by conveying over might prevent the issue of the settlement, so Harris had full notice of the bill of Martha.

Mr Percival was trustee by the articles for the £400 for the children, then if Barlow had come to demand the legal estate from him, the court would not have granted it to him without his paying not only the £400, but their legacies also.

An issue is to be directed only where the proof is doubtful, and the court don't know to which side to give credit.

The quickness of Harris his[1003] proceedings in this court [267] where the security was not scanty, joined with this defective evidence of the payment of the purchase money, is a strong proof of fraud.

Mr Anthony Malone

Lis pendens is notice, if they proceed on to a decree, 1 Vern. 286 *Preston* v. *Tubbins.*[1004]

Though the residuum in this case is specifically devised to the executor, it is chargeable with the legacies, 2 Vern. 143.[1005] A devise of particular legacies is the same as a devise to pay particular debts, so the purchaser is obliged to see the money applied.

Ab. of Equity Cases. Tit. Purchase,[1006] a bill was brought for payment of a legacy. The defendant purchased from the executor the personal estate, charged with the

---

[997] I.e. a pending action, a *lis pendens.*

[998] *Anonymous* (1685) 1 Vern. 318, 23 E.R. 494 (subpœna and bill filed is a *lis pendens* against everyone).

[999] *Hitchcock* v. *Sedgwick* (1690) 2 Vern. 156, 23 E.R. 707

[1000] *Buccle* v. *Atleo* (1687) 2 Vern. 37, 23 E.R. 634.

[1001] *Ferrars* v. *Cherry* (1700) 2 Vern. 383, 23 E.R. 845 (settlement, sale to purchaser with notice).

[1002] *Thomas* v. *Kemeys* (1696) 2 Vern. 348, 23 E.R. 821 (settlement, trust of term to raise portions).

[1003] I.e. Harris's.

[1004] *Preston* v. *Tubbin* (1684) 1 Vern. 286, 23 E.R. 474.

[1005] *Elliot* v. *Hancock* (1690) 2 Vern. 143, 23 E.R. 699.

[1006] The reference appears to be to *Humble* v. *Bill* (1703) 1 Eq. Cas. Abr. 358, 21 E.R. 1101; 2 Vern. 444, 23 E.R. 884; rev. HL sub. nom *Savage* v. *Bill* (1703) 3 Bro. P. C. 2nd ed. 5, 1 E.R. 1140.

legacy. The bill was dismissed in the Court of Chancery, but this decree was reversed in the House of Lords, which is equal to this case if the estate was in the executor.

The court took a day or two to consider of it.

Mr Baron Wainright

This is a case of difficulty. We are unanimous on our opinion to attach the money, but what decree we shall make is the question.

I shall go over the different periods of time that are remarkable, and state the case truly.

Lewis Barlow in 1693 previous to his marriage with his wife Martha, in consideration of the marriage and her portion, entered into articles whereby the terms which are now sold were vested in trustees to secure £400 for the children of the marriage, and it was thereby agreed, that Martha should have her thirds, notwithstanding that conveyance to the trustees.

[On] 25 September 1723 Lewis Barlow made his will, wherein he takes no express notice of the articles but in this manner, he devised £40 a year to Martha in lieu of dower, thirds, etc., charged on these terms, and devised to his daughter Ann £200, and to Margaret £300, and wills that his executors pay his just debts and legacies, and the provision he had made for his wife, and [268] children, and made his eldest son Theodore Barlow, and Mr Smyth executors, and gave his said son all the residue etc., and all his interest etc. in the leases, and died the 12 January 1725.

The 17 of the same month Martha released to Theodore all the provision she was entitled to under the articles, in consideration of £50 for life per annum.

[On] 29 April 1726 Martha filed a bill to set aside this release, being unduly obtained from her, and to have her thirds according to the articles.

In June 1726 Barlow put in his answer.

[On] 6 December 1726 Barlow made the mortgage to Harris for £200, and the 20 January following the other for £400

[On] 27 June 1729 the release was set aside in the Court of Chancery, and Martha was decreed to the benefit of the articles. Martha died and left Margaret her executrix, who 31 march 1731 field a bill of revivor.

On the 14 of April following Harris filed his bill in this court.

The 19 of May he amended his bill, and obtained a final decree in about two months.

The other two bills for the legacies were exhibited after the mortgages.

First, I shall consider this case as if Harris was a real purchaser, 1. with regard to the articles, 2. with regard to the will, and I think him affected with notice both of the articles and will. What the consequence of such notice will be, I shall examine afterwards.

The articles are not only a legal conveyance for the benefit of the children, but of the wife too. The trustees in those articles are her trustees also, for she is to have her thirds notwithstanding that deed, and though the estate was not sufficient for the children, which shows them to be her trustees, and that the trust for the children is subsequent to the trust for her, and the husband could never have defeated this possession of the [269] trustees no more can his representative Theodore Barlow, or the person who claims under him.

But I will suppose she had only an equitable title to her thirds, and that the husband aliened only for the £400. Harris had not only constructive, but actual notice of the articles, and will, and therefore is bound though a purchaser.

The *lis pendens* is constructive notice, but here is actual notice too, for when he purchases under the will, which creates a charge of £40 a year upon these terms, in the mortgage, though no notice is taken that the will creates this charge of £40 a year in lieu of her thirds, yet since he recites the will, though he swears he never saw it, his blindness is notice, and this must have led him to the inquiry, what those thirds were, and he takes the mortgage absolutely,[1007] without taking notice of it, or that it was subject to the £40 a year.

But the decree, which I think right, though I won't examine into it, is an attachment, and here a purchaser, who under the decree of our court has brought in his money, would be bound by the decree in the Court of Chancery, being an attachment on these lands, and we should involve him in a law suit.

The next question, and I think the greatest difficulty is, whether Harris having notice of the will, could purchase from one who was one of the executors, and residuary legatee?

One executor may sell the whole term and this is stronger because he is devisee too, so no assent to the legacy is requisite. This therefore is a good equitable conveyance.

'Tis laid down for a rule in the case of *Omble* v. *Bill*[1008] which is good reason, though that case was reversed in the House of Lords,[1009] that wills could never take effect if such difficulties were laid upon those who purchased from executors, but in that case there was a particular charge which it was easy to see. Here the charge is only general and equally on the [*270*] real and personal estate. So by the reason of that case a purchaser might buy though he had notice of the will, if he is not controlled by subsequent circumstances.

But if Harris appears to be an accomplice with Theodore Barlow to strip the legatees of their legacies, if this court can believe they acted in concert, and if he made use of his legal right to that purpose, though he is a purchaser of the assets, they may be followed in his hands.

Theodore's design appears manifest to deprive them of the assets, by selling them, and going off and not being before the court, and it appears to me that Harris is his accomplice. He purchases under the will, and it is mentioned in the deeds. He swears he never saw it, though the quarrels in the family, and the bill in Chancery are a reasonable presumption he had notice of it, then when he did not so much as see the will, shan't I believe he concurred in that design, and from the difficulty Martha found to get a decree, Harris is party to the bill of revivor, and instead of contesting the matter in Chancery, he and Theodore come here, and obtain a decree for sale, and though the security was so sufficient all was done at once, and we are brought in to aid them in their contrivance, so if he was a purchaser, he ought to be postponed to the demands of both plaintiffs.

But supposing these badges of fraud out of the case, if he had notice of the articles whereby the estate is lodged in trustees to pay £400 to the children, and a further sum is charged on these terms in the hands of their trustees by the will, I question whether the court will give this legal estate to the purchaser without paying the whole.

[1007] I.e. without reciting the articles or will.
[1008] *Humble* v. *Bill* (1703) 2 Vern. 444, 23 E.R. 884, 1 Eq. Cas. Abr. 358, 21 E.R. 1101; 2 Vern. 444, 23 E.R. 884.
[1009] Sub nom. *Savage* v. *Bill* (1703) 3 Bro. P.C. 2nd ed. 5, 1 E.R. 1140.

As to the issue, I think it neither ought, [n]or can be directed. It ought not, because Harris says he never saw the will, and yet it is recited in his deeds, so that the best we can think of him is, that he swears a truth that amounts to a falsehood. 'Tis a truth to deceive, and though not perjury perhaps in King's Bench, 'tis *in foro conscientiæ*[1010] to be taken as a falsehood. It may be true if he saw only the probate, or copy of the will, [but] is it to be presumed he should purchase from an executor, and recite the will in the mortgage deed etc., yet never see it[?] Yet he has swore this, and that he paid the purchase money, and has examined witnesses to it who were present, who are so far from proving the money [271] paid, that I think they prove the contrary, for they don't know when, or how it was paid, but believe it was paid from the receipt.

Then we will give him no opportunity to supply this evidence, who by these circumstances has brought a suspicion on himself, and thereby ousted himself of that indulgence [which] might be given to other purchasers.

But if we had a mind, we could not grant it, because it would be fruitless for want of parties to be bound by it.

Therefore I think the money ought to remain in court, or be put out at interest, and let them make all who claim under the articles, and will, and Theodore Barlow parties, or proceed to a sequestration against him.

Sir John St Leger

This money in court is Barlow's. Harris had made no proof that the purchase was paid either in account, money, or bills. The scrivener says he believes it was paid from the receipt. He might as well believe it paid from the acknowledgement in the body of the deed. The signing the receipt is to be able to prove the payment, and if it was paid in bank notes, they might have recourse to their entries, and if by account, the scrivener was the person who probably would make it up. This was a hasty decree. Where there was a full security, would not Barlow have prayed time to pay off the money, if this had not been done to sanctify their proceedings, and to bring in a purchaser who had no notice, in order to secure them; and where Theodore was really concerned, he makes great delay and opposition.

Crassa, or *affectata ignorantia*[1011] is notice.

Lord Chief Baron

This is [in the] nature of an interpleading bill. One demand is ascertained by the decree of the Court of Chancery, which is as much a lien against a purchaser, as a judgment. The question then is, whether Harris is such a purchaser, as not to be affected with this decree. The plaintiffs have made out their demands, and he must prove himself a purchaser, and without notice, to defend himself against them. [272] He is a purchaser *pendente lite*, and could not have avoided that suit in Chancery, so he shan't by a suit here.

But I think he had actual notice, for the will is taken notice of by the deeds, and he that buys of an executor, must look into the will, which defeated the purchase in

---

[1010] L. in a court of conscience, i.e. in a court of equity.
[1011] L. gross or affected ignorance.

the case of *Hendrick* v. *Migee*[1012] in Chancery, and that would have showed him, that these terms were subject to £40 a year during the viduity[1013] of Martha, and to 3d a year after, and he should have applied to Martha to know her demands, so he has no right to take this money, and Theodore Barlow, who has a title to the residue, don't appear.

Here was a sequestration against Barlow for want of an appearance, and on affidavit of his being gone away with his family, and not to be found, an order was made to proceed with him.

Decree

It appearing therefore to us, that Harris is a purchaser with notice of the plaintiff's demands, this cause is to stand over with liberty to amend, and make proper parties, and the money to be retained in the mean time, and the parties may apply to have it put out at interest.

GREEN v. RYLAND,[1014]

FITZGERALD v. HIFFERNAM

GREEN v. FOLEY, AND OTHERS

Monday, February the 19th, 1732, 3 [1733][1015]

The fifth of the eight days after Hilary[1016] Term

This is a bill of discovery brought on the Popery Acts, and charges, that the defendant Fitzgerald a Papist purchased the equity of redemption of the lands in the bill mentioned from one Murphy, and took an assignment of the mortgages, that Gernon who was a real Protestant discoveror having filed a bill of discovery in Chancery, [and] Fitzgerald [having] employed [*273*] Hiffernam[1017] his attorney to buy off and compound with him, and the better to cover his purchase, set up the defendant Ryland, who filed a subsequent bill of discovery in trust for Fitzgerald, and questions Hiffernam as to the transaction between him and Gernon.

To this bill Hiffernam put in an answer, disclaimer and plea. By his answer he said, he believed the plaintiff was a Protestant and the defendant Fitzgerald a Papist, and denied combination. By his disclaimer, he disclaimed all right and title to the lands, and pleaded to the discovery, that he was an attorney, and that the knowledge of these matters came to him as attorney or agent for the defendant Fitzgerald, and

---

[1012] No citation given, but see above, p. 176 [*226*].

[1013] Widowhood.

[1014] Resumed on p. 356. See *Ryland* v. *Green* (1738) 5 Bro. P.C. 2nd ed. 403, 2 E.R. 759.

[1015] 1733 modern style. 19 February was a Monday in 1733. Note that the year is given in the MS. and that the date is earlier than the previous case.

[1016] Spelled 'Hillary' in MS.

[1017] *Sic.* There are two attorneys named Hiffernan in KI AP: James, listed as 4 June 1725, master of an apprentice; James, attorney of the Exchequer, *c.* 1734; KI AP, p. 227.

that it was contrary to his oath of an attorney (whereby he was to do no falsehood) and to the privilege of an attorney, to be obliged to answer.

And Mr Foley, an agent in Chancery to the other bill of the same nature put in the same plea.

And it was insisted on for the defendant:

That to oblige him to discover by the general words of the 8 Q. Ann. ch. 3 page 55[1018] the court not only made him break his oath, but made him liable to an action for doing so;

That in cases of treason, or felony, an attorney or barrister is not to disclose what they know as counsel;

That the general words of the Act no more extended to attorneys who had a privilege not to answer, than the general words in other Acts do to feme coverts,[1019] infants or those who are not *compos mentis*;[1020]

That if the legislature had designed to bar them, it would have named them particularly, as the 6 Ann. ch. 6 page 46,[1021] against popish solicitors does;

That the words of the Act extended only to those who were concerned originally in the trust, or purchase, etc., not those who came after to any subsequent knowledge of it;

That pleas and demurrers had been often allowed to these bills of discovery on the Popery Acts, *Evans* v. *Quin*:[1022] the defendant pleaded that at the time of the several purchases, charged to be made by him, he was a Protestant, and therefore not obliged to discover, and the plea was allowed by Lord Midleton.[1023]

Goodwin v. *Palmer*[1024] in Chancery: the bill was for a discovery against the defendant, who having married a Papist who had not conformed [*274*] within the time prescribed by the Act was incapable to purchase, being thereby a constructive Papist. The defendant demurred to the discovery, because the charge was a crime which would subject him to penalties, and the demurrer was allowed.

One who is proper to be examined as a witness only, and is not concerned in interest, as the defendant has sworn by the disclaimer he is not, ought not to answer, for his answer is no evidence against the other defendants, or for them, or [ought to] be made a defendant, for this gives the plaintiff an opportunity of seeing how far his evidence will go, and will as much tend to introduce perjury, as disclosing the evidence, or examining after publication, and of this opinion was the court in 2 Vernon under Title 'Award'.[1025]

Now if Hiffernam is not a proper defendant, if he had been examined as a witness, he might have pleaded or demurred to this purpose to the interrogator, for the Act goes no further than to oblige all persons to answer the bill and there is no provision in case of a witness, but he is not within the Act.

[1018] 8 Ann., c. 3 (Ir.), 1709 (popery, Protestant discoverors).

[1019] I.F. married women.

[1020] L. of sound mind, sane.

[1021] 6 Ann., c. 6 (Ir.), 1707 (to explain and amend an Act to prevent Papists being solicitors). See 10 Will. III, c. 13 (Ir.), 1698 (to prevent Papists being solicitors). Section 4 of the 6 Ann., c. 6 stated that no barrister, attorney or other practitioner was exempt from giving testimony relating to a question on that Act or on 10 Will. III, c. 13.

[1022] No citation given.

[1023] Spelled 'Middleton' in MS.

[1024] No citation given.

[1025] Vernon's Chancery Reports, 1681–1720, vol. 2, Index, 'Award'.

For the plaintiff it was insisted: That no plea or demurrer had been allowed to these bills, if the plaintiff brought himself within the Act, and made a proper case, or unless the defendant showed himself to be not within the Act, as in the two cases that were mentioned; That the words are general, and extend to all persons, whether attorneys or not; and in the case of *Digby* v. *Hanly*,[1026] Mr Ambrose Keon an attorney   Ante 11. demurred to an interrogatory in a cause for a discovery on the Popery Acts, and his demurrer was overruled.[1027]

Thursday, February the 22nd, 1732, 3 [1733]

The last of the eight days,

The court delivered the opinions.

Mr Baron Wainwright

There are several causes that wait the resolution of the court, and as the cause of *Green* v. *Hiffernam,* and *Green* v. *Foley* are upon dilatories, we shall first dispatch them out of the way.

The bill is to be decreed to lands as a Protestant discoveror against the defendant Fitzgerald, and that the plaintiff may [*275*] not be injured by priority of claim, he charges that a former bill was brought by collusion, and that the defendant Hiffernam was employed by Fitzgerald to compound with and buy of[f] Gripton the first Protestant discoveror. Mr Hiffernam by his answer disclaiming all interest in the lands, and pleads that he had no knowledge of the matters charged in the bill but as attorney or agent for Fitzgerald.

First, I shall consider if attorneys or agents in cases of this kind shall be obliged to answer and discover.

The points that have been made in this cause by the counsel for the defendant are, first, that the Act is relative only to the original sale, and don't extend to subsequent transactions; so by this construction which extends to all persons, any one not concerned originally, whether an attorney etc. or not, might refuse to answer.

The second point insisted on is, that one not concerned in interest ought not to be made a defendant, and if he is, he need not answer, because the plaintiff may examine him as a witness.

The third is, that if this plea should be overruled, the confidence between the attorney and his client would be destroyed, and he would be compelled to act contrary to his oath.

As to the first point, the Act I think extends to all subsequent transactions, as well as to the original. The statute was made to establish lands in the hands of Protestants, and is one of the pillars of the government, and reaches to all those who are privy to any circumstances that relate to such trust, or purchase etc.

As to the second, though it may be dangerous and not to be countenanced to permit the plaintiff to sift a man how far he can give evidence, where the discovery plainly tends to that purpose, yet the doctrine advanced under this head is pretty

---

[1026] See above, p. 11.
[1027] But note that the C.B. in *Digby*, above, p. 11, decided the point on a technical ground and left the substantive issue open.

uncertain, and liable to many exceptions, and 'tis a more settled point, that every defendant who is charged with fraud or confederacy is obliged to answer and discover.

As to the third point, which is the most material, and relates to attorneys etc., I allow that feme coverts, infants [276] and *non compos mentis*[1028] are not bound by the general words of an Act of Parliament, but it is not applicable to the present case, for what the defendant insists on as the privilege of the attorney, is really the privilege of the client, and since the client is barred by the statute from pleading or demurring, his attorney who is privileged only on his account, shall answer and discover as well as he, and the Act takes this natural right from the party himself, so it must be understood to do from the attorney, who is privileged only in regard to his client.

Mes App. A.39.

Radcliff v. *Fursman.*[1029] I mention this case only to show, that it was the opinion of the learned gentlemen who argued for the defendant that this privilege of the attorney was properly the privilege of his client, and is not so sacred as that they shall never be obliged to discover.

And since the covenants whereby the supra cargoes of East India and other ships have bound themselves to answer, and not to plead or demur to any bill [which] should be filed against them in equity, have been adjudged good and binding, and that they might renounce the right of not discovering anything to their prejudice, which is not a natural right, so this Act, to which every one is party, and privy, may take away this right from them as well as they may waive it by their own act.

Nels. 8vo Rep. in
Canc. 81.[1030]
1 Ventr. 197.[1031]
MSS law of
evidence 124, 125,
126, 127. March 83.
Styl. 449. Waldron v.
Ward.[1032] 1 Keb. 505
pl. 69.
Spark v. Sir Hugh
Middleton.[1033]

As to what is said that by answering, an attorney etc., would break his oath, whereby he swears to do no falsehood. He does none by obeying the law, by complying with the Act, but if by treating with a Protestant discoveror he endeavours to buy him off, he thereby attempts to evade the law, which is against his oath, and to do falsehood, and this is charged on him by the bill. And therefore the plea must be overruled.

Lord Chief Baron

I am of the same opinion with my brother.

I shall first consider, whether the privilege of an attorney is to be allowed in this case; 2. Whether that privilege is general, and to be allowed in all cases.

[1.] 'Tis a maxim, that all laws that are to be calculated more [277] immediately for the defence of the government, and the good of religion, are to have a beneficial construction. This Act appears to be so from the preamble to the Popery Acts, and was made to bind the evasion of the former Acts against popery, by enabling the Protestant to have a discovery upon oath.

And the general words of the Act include agents, attorneys, as well as others. Is not a sum of money given to a Protestant discoveror to drop his bill, relating to a Papist purchaser?

[1028] L. [those] of unsound mind.

[1029] *Radcliff* v. *Fursman* (1730) 2 Bro. P.C. 2nd ed. 514, 1 E.R. 1101.

[1030] *Cutts* v. *Pickering* (1671) Nels. 81, 21 E.R. 795; 3 Ch. Rep. 66, 21 E.R. 730.

[1031] *Cuts* v. *Pickering* (1671) 1 Vent. 197, 86 E.R. 133 (B., who had been solicitor for P., was produced as a witness concerning the erazure of a clause in a will, supposed to be done by P. It appeared that P. had disclosed this to B. before P. had retained him. Held, that he might be sworn. Otherwise if he had been retained as his solicitor before: the same as to attorney or counsel.)

[1032] *Waldron* v. *Ward* (1655) Style 449, 82 E.R. 853 (Rolle C.J.: '[counsel] is not bound to make answer for things which may disclose the secrets of his client's cause, and thereupon he was forborne to be examined').

[1033] *Sparke* v. *Middleton* (1663) 1 Keb. 505, 83 E.R. 1079 (counsel should only reveal such things as he either knew before he was of counsel, or that came to his knowledge since by other persons).

2. If these general words did not include barristers, attorneys etc., this plea is not good. Because he is charged with a transaction not as an attorney, for it is not their duty to take in titles, nor is included in their oath, by which they swear to do no falsehood. So they are not to injure the public, or a Protestant discoveror of the right he acquires by filing his bill of discovery. An attorney ought not to concern himself in evading the Act, nor to interfere with the purchase, where he was not concerned in the transaction, but employed in a suit relating to it.

The intention of the Act was, that no plea, or demurrer should be allowed either by an attorney, or anyone else, where the plaintiff by his bill brought himself within the Act.

'Tis no injury or contrary to the law of nature to discover an unlawful confidence, but on the contrary the party is obliged to discover it, for confidence is grounded on a presumption that the transaction is fair.

When a thing indifferent is prohibited by an Act of Parliament, it becomes unlawful, unless a penalty is annexed to the breach, and nobody can have a natural right to do a thing unlawful.

If an attorney etc. has the privilege they contend for, the Act has taken it away. The general words of an Act don't take away the right of infants, *non compos mentis*, and feme coverts, for they have a natural right not to be bound, wives, as being under the dominion and control of their husbands, infants, as not being arrived to a degree of understanding sufficient to conduct themselves, and idiots, as never having any. But this privilege is no natural right. [*278*] So I am of opinion that all persons are to put in a full answer upon oath, where the plaintiff has brought himself within the Act, and that the authorities [that] have been quoted no way prove the contrary, and therefore that this plea must be overruled.

Friday, May the 11th 1733

In Exchequer

The last of the four days after Easter Term.

ANN MILLS A MINOR, BY HER PROCHEIN AMY, PLAINTIFF
ALDERMAN JOSEPH NUTTAL, DEFENDANT[1034]

Mr Baron Wainwright

Heard this cause the day before alone, and now delivered his opinion.

Richard Mills senior devised £300 to the two daughters of Richard Mills junior, to be paid them a year after his death, and took notice that the plaintiff Ann one of the daughters was in New England, and made the defendant his executor, and residuary legatee. And the plaintiff brought her bill to be decreed to a moiety of this legacy, with interest from a year after the death of the testator, who died in 1719.

[1034] Resumed on p. 327.

Mr Nuttal, [on] 1 July 1720 wrote a letter, which was proved and read in the cause, to the now prochein amy, wherein he takes notice he had sent him a former letter, and that he wrote a second, for fear of the loss or miscarriage of the first, that he was ready to pay the legacy if he could give him a proper discharge, and desires him to advise with the lawyers of that place how it was to be done. This was in answer to one from New England which takes no notice of the receipt of his former letter. It don't appear that afterwards either the prochein amy, or Mr Nuttal took any steps towards the receipt or payment of this legacy. The bill charges the assets in the defendant's hands to amount to £3,000, and the defendant by his answer admits assets general [279] and insists that he made no advantage of this money, having always so much ready by him to answer her demands.

All cases in equity must be judged by their circumstances, and I shan't in this dwell on any that are minute and trivial, but consider it generally.

The testator devised £150 to an infant out of the realm to be paid within a year after his death, and takes notice that she was at the time of his making his will out of the kingdom, and the executor sends the now prochein amy advice that he was ready to pay this legacy etc.

This notice is of no consideration in the eye of the law, being to a person who was not guardian to the infant, or could give a discharge for the legacy, and though he is now prochein amy, that can have no relation backwards. If he had been guardian it might perhaps have varied the case, because he was a person capable to give a discharge, and if the infant was deprived of the interest by his means, she might have a remedy against him.

The next question is, whether laches[1035] shall prejudice the infant, and I think not, because I am of opinion they would not in this case [prejudice] one of full age for the notice being to a relation, and not to himself, would not have deprived him of the interest.

The executor can discharge himself from the payment of interest, either by paying the legacy to the infants own hands (for I have known it allowed to be a good payment, where the minor has appeared to be of discretion) or to his guardian, or in a court of equity, but none of these methods being taken by the defendant. He never applied properly for a discharge; but payment to the father of the infant is not good.

The question then is, whether in reason, or equity, he ought to pay interest.

The assets are charged in the bill to be very considerable, and are not denied to be so by the answer, and this was a proper charge to show how reasonable it was [that] the defendant should pay interest out of so large a fund, the general admission of assets is an allowance of a large sum, and if he had only enough to answer the principal sum, it was proper for him to have said so. [280]

But I shall consider this case as if he had only £150, and the residuum was to be looked upon as *bona propria*,[1036] whether after this offer he ought to pay interest.

A banker keeps a legacy in his hands without seeking for a proper discharge, and insists that it ought to yield no profit to the legatee, because he always kept money enough by him to answer the legacy. But if it yields profit to him, it ought to the legatee, and how can he suppose this money, which has no earmark, to lie dead in a different manner from the rest of his bank?

1035 MS. reads 'latches'.
1036 L. his own goods.

But suppose he had put it in a bag, so that it had an earmark, yet he ought to pay interest, because he took no proper method to discharge the assets of it. He gave notice to a stranger, to an improper person, and he made no declaration that he would not pay interest, if it was not received, or if he had, that would not avail him.

I shall mention two authorities, 2 Salk. 416, *Bell* v. *Dee*,[1037] from the authority of which case, as the time of payment is set in this, if the legatee was of age, interest [would?] run on the legacy without a demand.

Piggot v. *Foley*[1038] decreed at the Rolls in 1727, A devised that his executor after the death of B should pay to C £100, at such time, and in such a manner as should be most advantageous to C. B died about three years after the testator, and about 14 years after C filed his bill for this legacy with interest from the death of B. The executor admitted assets, and swore that the testator often declared his intention to be that C should have only £100, and that he had always as much money lying dead in his hands as would satisfy the legacy. The master of the rolls said, the testator showed by his will he designed to leave this legacy to C in the most beneficial manner, that it was more for his benefit to have interest than not, and that the executor, who was to pay it, was no proper judge what was so, that executors always endeavoured to excuse themselves from the payment of interest, by saying they had always money enough [*281*] in their hands, that the declaration of the testator was not to be minded, and therefore decreed interest.

So I am of opinion, that the defendant must pay interest after the rate of £5 per cent from the time of payment of the legacy directed by the will.

Lord Chief Baron

I think an executor ought to pay interest for legacies from a year after the death of Ante 45, 87. the testator, which is the time the law gives him to gather in and apply the assets, and it is for the interest of the public that money should not be locked up as in Spain,[1039] and though all interest was formerly held unlawful,[1040] that notion is now universally exploded, and therefore if the legatee is not to be come at, it is the business of an executor to apply to a court of equity, who will take care to put out the money for the advantage of the legatee, and to indemnify the executor, and this money in a banker's hands must yield a profit, as well as the rest of his cash. I didn't hear this cause, but I am of the same opinion with my brother.[1041]

[1037] *Smell* v. *Dee* (1707) 2 Salk. 415 at 416, 91 E.R. 360 at 361.
[1038] No citation given.
[1039] Unexplained reference. It is not clear whether this is a point of comparative law, as to the law of usury in Spain, or a comment on a lack of a banking culture in Spain, or perhaps both.
[1040] Under the usury laws.
[1041] Odd, then, that he delivers judgment.

CRAWLEY v. NUGENT

In Exchequer

May the 5th 1733

Ante 259.   Mr Recorder moved to amend the title of depositions according to the commission,
Mes App. G.95.   from Margaret to Catharine, and the defendant was styled so in the depositions
themselves. Order accordingly.

FITZGERALD v. FITZGERALD

Eodem die

In Exchequer

The defendant was desired by the bill before he answered to view [*282*] certain deeds
in the hands of the plaintiff's attorney. He put in his answer, and swore that he called
Ante 259.   at the attorney's house in order to view the deeds, and that he was not at home, this
Post 295.   appearing to be while the attorney was in court. The defendant on the motion of Mr
Prime Serjeant was obliged to answer over.

MOOR A BARRISTER v. BURTON,
ONE OF THE SIX CLERKS[1042]

Eodem die

In Exchequer

A motion was made on a possessory bill for an injunction to the party to be quieted
in the possession of a pew.

But the court denied the motion, because as he had been placed there by the
ordinary, he might apply to him on being disturbed.

The plaintiff in his affidavit set forth, that he had been in possession of the lands
upwards of 30 years, and that he was five years in the quiet possession of the pew, till
Mr Burton's family filled it up, and broke the lock, therefore this possession might
be under the ordinary, and how could the sheriff deliver possession of a pew[?]

[1042] Boyle Moore is listed in KI AP, p. 346, as a member in Michaelmas term, 1704. There is also Oliver
Moore, s. and heir of William, Salestown, Co. Meath. Middle Temple, 8 July 1702, KI Trinity term, 1711, KI AP,
p. 348.

Monday, April the 30th, 1733

In Exchequer

MORRIS v. HENERY

Mr Malone for the plaintiffs

This is a bill brought for an account against Sir Henry Cairnes the surviving partner, and the executor of the deceased partner. Process issued against Sir Henry Cairnes for not appearing to a sequestration, and the question is, whether the cause may be heard against the executors of the deceased partner only?

This is a joint and several contract, and at law where issue upon a joint and several bond, and one obligor is outlawed for want of appearance, I may proceed against the other, and judgment is given against both, because one confesses he can make no defence, by his not doing it, and we don't desire to proceed against Sir Henry Cairnes.

MSS̃ cas. in Canc. A.574.

Mr Calaghan

Mr Morris drew bills on Mitchel and Cairne, [*283*] and Mitchel made some payments, but above £590 remain unpaid. Sir Henry Cairnes lives in England, and there are two reasons why we are proper to proceed against the executors of Mitchel without him.

1. There was no reason to make him a party though he were in the kingdom, for partners in course of trade deal jointly and severally, and a promissory note of bankers may be sued jointly or severally, and is not like a joint obligation, and the contrary doctrine would tend to the destruction of trade, for by one going out of the way, they would render it impracticable to proceed against the other.

Factors and dealers by the law of merchants are jointly and severally bound.

2. When a fair creditor has done everything that lies in his power to bring both into court, surely he shall have the same measure and justice in equity as at law.

Mr Eustace[1043]

To prove the credit of partners to be joint and several quoted 1 Vern. 140,[1044] and said, that it did not appear in that case that the other factor was insolvent, out of the kingdom, or that he was served with process, all which appear in this case.

Lord Chief Baron

I think I can't go on without Sir Henry Cairnes. If four or five are partners in a bank, and one or more of them is sent out of the way, you may proceed against the rest at law after an outlawry, or in equity, upon suggesting this particular fraud.

[1043] Probably Rowland Eustace, 2nd s. of Laurence, Dublin; Middle Temple, 23 Oct. 1717, KI, Easter term, 1725, d. 12 July 1735; KI AP, p. 154.

[1044] *Barker* v. *Wyld* (1682) 1 Vern. 140, 23 E.R. 373.

Mr Attorney General for the defendants

'Tis a complaint that courts of equity have not this power, and the 5 Geo. 2^{1045} has provided a remedy. Only where you have carried on the process to a sequestration against a trustee for want of an appearance, for it was hard the party should lose his remedy when the bill could not be taken *pro confesso* for the want of the appearance of a person who was no ways concerned in interest. [*284*] If they had not been merchants, only Cairnes ought to have been before the court, but being merchants they are tenants in common, and the executor is not as proper a person to be sued as Cairnes the surviving partner, because he is not privy to the transactions. They are not without remedy. They might have set forth a contrivance in their bill, and proved it, and that they had done everything in their power to bring him before the court, but Cairnes has a good estate in this kingdom.

Mr Solicitor General

If there is any fraud in his not appearing, they should have framed their bill to that purpose, or filed a supplemental bill, and as Sir Harry Cairnes made several payments, 'tis possible he may have paid off and discharged the whole.

Mr Daly

The 5 Geo. 2^{1046} is an authority in point. An outlawry and sequestration are not alike. On an outlawry the party forfeits all his goods and chattels, and he can't appear, but is considered as a dead person. Supposing the security of two bankers in partnership to be joint or several, the plaintiff in this case has made his election to sue them jointly, and he can't afterwards on a sequestration say, 'I'll sue them separately.'

Mr Malone

No, we say Cairnes has failed, and is a bankrupt, and we pray a decree against the executors, who have made several payments.

Mr Calaghan

Where the defendant is a necessary party, yet on affidavit of his being out of the kingdom, the court may make an order to proceed without him, as in *Ward's Case* in Chancery on my motion, and in the case of *Webb* v. *Sharpless*,[1047] in 2 Vern.

[1045] 5 Geo. II, c. 8 (Ir.), 1731 (trustees who cannot be found, etc., treated as having been served with process). See also the earlier Act, 1 Geo. II, c. 17 (Ir.), 1727, s. 4, giving a remedy where trustees failed to make an appearance.

[1046] Above, n. 1045.

[1047] No case of that name in Vernon in E.R.

Lord Chief Baron

The question is, whether it was necessary to make [285] Cairnes a party in this cause, for if so, he is no more before the court than if he had been left out. The recital of the 5 Geo. the 2 shows the sense the Parliament had of the power of a court of equity, and it is a great presumption in them, to attempt to proceed further.

There are great inconveniences on either side, on one, the parties may be put to a double expense. Cairnes may have paid all, for he was solvent for two years after the death of Mitchel, and on the other, the creditors might be cheated and defrauded. If one partner might not be sued, as if six (as they may by Act of Parliament)[1048] should join in a bank, and one go out of the way on purpose, and though the plaintiff should charge this fraud in his bill, he might not be able to prove it.

Mr Baron Wainwright

Mr Cairnes was solvent in April 1722. The bill was brought against both, so the decree might have been against both, and carried into execution against either. The plaintiffs have done everything in their power. One of the partners is insolvent, and there must be a stop to justice; 'tis said some fraud or contrivance ought to be suggested in the bill. This would put the plaintiff to unnecessary expense, for then he could have no decree without proving the fraud: I think this is of great consequence to trade, to delay payment while one keeps out of the way. The making all the partners parties, is rather for the sake of the defendants, than the plaintiffs, that if one pay all, he may be exonerated.

THE EXECUTORS OF MORRIS

v.

SIR HARRY CAIRNES, HENERY, AND OTHERS, THE EXECUTORS OF MITCHEL

June the 26, the last of the eight days after Trinity Term, 1733

Mr Baron Wainwright

I think the plaintiffs may proceed in this cause without [286] bringing Sir Harry Cairnes before the court.

The case is this. Abraham Morris, a banker in Cork, had dealings with Mitchel and Cairnes partners in a bank in London. Mitchel in 1719 died, leaving Mr Henery and others his executors. In 1721 Morris made drafts on Sir Harry Cairnes and the executors, to which objections were made, but some of the money paid. Morris dies,

---

[1048] This appears to be a reference to the British Act 6 Ann., c. 50 (G.B.), 1707 (taxation, Bank of England) s. 10 of which provided that no banks other than the Bank of England could consist of more than six partners. The similar provision in Ireland, in relation to the Bank of Ireland, was not enacted until 21 & 22 Geo. III, c. 16 (Ir.), 1781–82, s. 14. See also J. Breslin, *Banking Law in the Republic of Ireland* (Dublin, 1998).

and makes the plaintiffs his executors, who file this bill against Sir Harry Cairnes, and the executors of Mitchel, for the balance. Sir Harry being in England stood out to a sequestration for want of an appearance, and in 1722 became a bankrupt.

I must observe first, that I don't think the acceptance of the former drafts, and payment of part, binds the executors of Mitchel to pay the rest. Nor do any subsequent dealings of Morris and Cairnes discharge the executors of Mitchel.

Nels. 8vo Rep. in
Canc. 139.[1049] In all partnerships the joint and separate effects are liable to the creditors; on commissions of bankrupts taken out against partners, the joint estate is first to be resorted to, and the separate estate only in case of deficiency, and I think both the partners or their representatives on a demand against them ought to be made parties, and brought before the court, that if one pays the whole, he may have contribution from the other, and because one of them might prove the debt paid.

But this equality which equity is always desirous to observe where it reasonably may, is not to tie up their hands where they can't do justice to the parties without breaking it, and therefore if one of the parties is not amenable[1050] by the process of the court, I think they may proceed against the other; so if you bring an action against two joint obligors, and proceed against one to an outlawry for want of an appearance, you may go on, and recover against the other.

I don't rely on the case in 1 Vern. 140,[1051] that has been [287] quoted, but as it stands limited and qualified by the *quære*, not by itself, and the reason of it is to prevent a failure of justice, or an unreasonable delay, and the court will rather leave the partner to his remedy against the other, than put such hardships on an innocent creditor, who relied on the joint and separate security. I think 2 Vern. 369[1052] an authority in point. There no objection is made but to the irregularity of the sequestration, and implies, that if the sequestration had been regular, they might have proceeded.

So I am of opinion both from the reason of the thing, and this authority, that they may go on without Sir Harry Cairnes, since there is no pretence that the other partner did not leave assets.

Lord Chief Baron

The effects of each of the partners are liable to the debts of the partnership, and as it is necessary to make both parties, 'cause one may have paid, and each is entitled to contribution from the other. So they must show in order to have liberty to proceed against one only, that they have done everything in their power to make the other a party, and I rely on that case in 2 Vern. That has been quoted by my brother, and the other in the same book mentioned from the Bar.

No bill can be taken *pro confesso* in this court for want of an appearance, because equity never decrees *in absentia*. Where a man is outlawed he is considered in law as dead, but a court of equity must have the party before them, and when he is once there by his appearance, and won't answer, 'tis the same thing as if he was brought up *in vinculis*,[1053] and actually refused to answer.

[1049] *Holcomb* v. *Rivis* (1670) Nels. 139, 21 E.R. 810; *Holstcomb* v. *Rivers* (1669) 1 Ch. Cas. 127, 22 E.R. 726.
[1050] Spelled 'amesnable' in the orginal.
[1051] *Barker* v. *Wyld* (1682) 1 Vern. 140, 23 E.R. 373.
[1052] *Parker* v. *Blackbourne* (1699) 2 Vern. 369, 23 E.R. 833
[1053] L. lit. in chains, in custody.

In this case no order was had to proceed against Henry Cairnes as if he had appeared, or if it had been moved for, it must have appeared by affidavit, that he had nothing in this kingdom by which he could be sequestered, for the return of the sequesters of *nulla bona*[1054] is not sufficient. Everyone knows that to be of course, and done in order to procure [288] a decree, and he is a necessary party, because there were several transactions between him and the executors of Morris after the partnership.

So as he is a necessary party, and as much as has not been done as might be to bring him before the court, I think this cause ought to stand over, till further steps are taken to bring him in.

Sir John St Leger

I did not hear this cause,[1055] so can say nothing to the merits, but shall only speak to my experience of our rules, and I never knew a bill taken *pro confesso* but after appearance, and that is for the contempt done to the court. 'Tis like a departure at law in despite of the court. This I take to be the practice of the court, and I think we can't alter it.

Tuesday, January the 26, 1732, 3 [1733][1056]

BLENERHASSET v. BABINGTON

Mr Calaghan pro defendant

The question is, whether notice is necessary. We say it is not material, because the Act[1057] makes the note void to all intents and purposes: Acts are to be construed by the rules and maxims of law, one of which is *quod ab initio non valet, [in] tractu temporis non convalescebit*,[1059] and they would make the act of the drawee by endors[ing] it, make that good which is void in itself. Freem. 232.[1058]

2 Mod. 279,[1060] Yelv. 47,[1061] there the securities were for money really lent, here Mr Hasset's security, which is the note, was originally void.

In 1 Salk. 134,[1062] in case of an acceptance it was determined against the party, and the endorsement is the same thing. Both are only for further security.

[1054] L. no goods.

[1055] Above, p. 217 n. 1041.

[1056] 26 January was a Tuesday in 1733, Kratz, *Hist. Cal.*

[1057] 11 Ann., c. 5 (Ir.), 1712 (for the better preventing of excessive and deceitful gaming). See also the English statute 16 Car. II, c. 7 (Eng.) 1664 (gaming).

[1058] May be a reference to *Corderoy's Case* 1 Free. 312, 22 E.R. 1233 (note assignable in equity).

[1059] That which is invalid from the beginning is not improved by the passage of time: *Vernon's Case* (1572) 4 Co. Rep. 1a at 2b, 76 E.R. 845 at 852.

[1060] *Anonymous* (1677) 2 Mod. 279, 86 E.R. 1071 (a bond given to a third person in discharge of a gaming debt, not void by the statute 16 Ch. 2, c. 7 s. 3, if the obligee had no notice that the money was won at play).

[1061] *Ellis* v. *Warnes* (1604) Yelv. 47, 80 E.R. 34.

[1062] Possibly *Hill* v. *Lewis* (1709) 1 Salk. 132, 91 E.R. 124, or *Harry* v. *Perrit* (1710) 1 Salk. 133, 91 E.R. 126.

In the case of *Costegan*,[1063] the security at law was adjudged by Chief Baron Gilbert to be void by the Registry Act,[1064] though the party had notice, though it may be otherwise in equity.[1065]

Mr Wall for the plaintiff

Notice is material, and as such is made part [*289*] of the plea. By the 8 Ann.[1066] promissory notes are made endorsable, and if notice of their being for money won at play was not necessary, innocence would be punished, and trade discouraged, and if the endorsee must enquire into the consideration, that would elude the Act, and put a stop to trade.

In 2 Mod.[1067] the consideration why the loser joined with the winner in the bond was, because he was indebted at play (which is the same case as this) and the obligee being a stranger to the transaction was not bound, and the same construction has been made on the Statute of Usury,[1068] Hill. 9 Ann. 3 February 1709,[1069] *Turner* v. *Albert*, the court of equity said, if the note had been assigned in course of trade, they would have established it, but not being so, directed an issue as to the consideration.

MSŝ cas. in Canc.
B.166.

Mr Baron Wainwright

Negotiable notes were left out of the Act, because of the late statute.

The case of a mortgage is different. 'Tis not a vested security, but is divested, and placed in the next heir, etc.

Tuesday, February the 6th [1733][1070]

Mr Hasset pro plaintiff[1071]

The action is brought by the endorsee of a promissory note, which was assigned to the plaintiff by one Baron. The defendant pleads the note was given for money won at play, and the plaintiff had notice. The plaintiff replies, he had no notice. The defendant demurs, and the question is, whether notice is material. The defendant says it is not, because the statute [of] Anne makes all notes for money won at play void. The plaintiff could take issue on this part of the plea, which charges him with notice, and though he was a fair creditor, the issue would be found against him. This shows it is not for gaming. The judges of England always gave their opinion on the

---

[1063] No citation given.

[1064] Registration of Deeds Act, 1707 (6 Ann., c. 2).

[1065] The point is still relevant in Ireland: see *Re Fuller* [1982] IR 161 (actual notice of an unregistered deed).

[1066] 8 Ann., c. 11 (Ir.), 1709 (promissory notes endorsable).

[1067] *Anonymous* (1677) 2 Mod. 279, 86 E.R. 1071 (bond in payment of gaming debt given to third party, not void against third party).

[1068] 10 Car. I, sess. 2, c. 22 (Ir.), 1634 (against usury); 2 Ann., c. 16 (Ir.), 1703 (to reduce rate of interest on money to 8 per cent); 8 Geo. I, c. 13 (Ir.), 1721 (to reduce rate of interest on money to 7 per cent).

[1069] I.e. Hilary Term. The date appears to refer to the case.

[1070] 6 February was a Tuesday in 1733, Kratz, *Hist. Cal.* Note that the date is earlier than the previous case.

[1071] No person of that name is listed in KI AP for the period as a barrister. KI AP are incomplete: see KI AP, p. viii.

2[n]d clause in the English Act in favour of the endorsee, or assignee, if they had no notice. [*290*] But it is said, there is a difference between the English and the Irish Act. The difference extends no further than where lands are concerned, and to prevent the construction that had been made on the English Act that they [*sic*] vested mortgages [were] always adjudged void as to [the] assignee, and issue is taken upon the notice, and insisted upon in all the books.

Objection: 'Tis objected, that in 2 Mod. the original security was not for money won at play, but here the note was.

Answer: The endorsement to the plaintiff by virtue of the statute is in [the] nature of a new security, and the plaintiff don't sue on the note, but endorsement, 1 Salk. 126.[1072] A new property is vested by the endorsement.

Mr Attorney General's reply

Mortgages are made void by both Acts as to the gamester, but by the Irish Act the remainderman is to have the benefit by the 2[n]d clause, and that is the reason of it. We have admitted by our demurrer, that they had no notice, and they by their replication, that the money was won at play.

By the Irish Act[1073] all notes etc. for play are made void, 'notwithstanding any law' etc., which words are not in the English Act.

All the cases mentioned for the plaintiff are not promissory notes, but bills of exchange.

Before the statute notes were not assignable, but were only evidence of the defendant, but by the Act they are put on a foot with inland bills of exchange.

This note is void as to Baron, and the words of the statute to prevent an assignment of such promissory notes notwithstanding any law etc., are not to be rejected, when a meaning can be put on them.

5 Mod. 170.[1074] Carthew 356, *Hussy* v. *Jacob*,[1075] differs from Salkeld. There is no notice taken in 5 Mod., that it would be otherwise in case of an assignment. Lex Præt. 100, 2, 4.[1076]

The note when it was drawn by Babington was void, and he has done nothing since to make it good, as is an acceptance.

Their construction would quite elude the gaming Act, whereas the note will be good against the endorser, because [*291*] that is a new contract, so the whole security to trade is not gone by our construction, and notes are generally taken on the credit of the endorser, not drawer.

[1072] *Clark* v. *Pigot* (1698) 1 Salk. 126, 91 E.R. 118.
[1073] 11 Ann., c. 5 (Ir.), 1712.
[1074] *Hussey* v. *Jacob* (1695) 5 Mod. 170, 87 E.R. 588.
[1075] *Hussey* v. *Jacob* (1695) Carth. 356, 90 E.R. 808.
[1076] See above, p. 35 n. 210.

Monday, May the 7th [1733][1077]

The last day of Easter Term.

This day the court delivered their opinion

Mr Baron Wainwright

The plaintiff declares on a promissory note for the payment of £128 to Baron, or order, which Baron endorsed to the plaintiff, whereof the defendant had notice, and so became chargeable by virtue of the statute.

The defendant pleads he is not chargeable, because he and the said Randal Baron played dice, at which the defendant lost £128, for which he gave this note as a security, and so by virtue of the statute the note and promise are void, and that the plaintiff had notice thereof.

The plaintiff replies, and thereby denies that he had notice at the time of the endorsement or before that this note was given for money won at play.

The defendant demurs, and the plaintiff joins in demurrer, so the only question is, whether this demurrer is good, which depends upon this, whether notice in this case is material or not.

Three statutes are to be considered in this case.

The 8 Ann. ch. 11[1078] whereby promissory notes are made assignable and an action is given against the drawer or endorser of them.

The 11 Ann. ch. 5[1079] For the better [to] prevent excessive and deceitful gaming which is subsequent to an English statute of the same kind.

And the 16 Ca. 2[1080] against gaming which concludes like the 11 Q. Ann: 'any statute law or usage to the contrary thereof in any wise notwithstanding.'

All the authorities have been quoted arise on the 16 Ca. 2 and were determined antecedent to the two former statutes and there are no resolutions in point since the making [of] the 11 Ann. and only an opinion in the case of *Hussy* v. *Jacob*.[1081] [292]

1. I shall consider the general rule for the construction of statutes; 2. The construction that has been put on the 16 Ca. 2, and how it is applicable to this case; 3. Or, whether these statutes are so penned, that the resolutions upon that Act, can't be applied to the 11 Anne.

But however we determine this point, the mischief designed to be prevented by one or other of the statutes will be evaded. If we adjudge the demurrer good, the good of the public and trade which was considered by making notes negotiable, will be evaded, and if we shall judge it not good, the good and welfare of private families, which the statute designed to promote, will be evaded.

The first rule to construe statutes by is laid down in 1 Inst. 381b, that a statute is to be construed in suppression of the mischief, and advancement of the remedy designed by the statute.

[1077] 7 May was a Monday in 1733, Kratz, *Hist. Cal.*
[1078] 8 Ann., c. 11 (Ir.) (promissory notes endorsable).
[1079] 11 Ann., c. 5 (Ir.), 1712 (for the better preventing of excessive and deceitful gaming).
[1080] 16 Car. II, c. 7 (Eng.), 1664 (gaming).
[1081] *Hussey* v. *Jacob* (1695) 5 Mod. 170, 87 E.R. 588; Carth. 356, 90 E.R. 808.

Another rule is also in 1 Inst. 11, that a statute is not to be so interpreted, as to injure an innocent person.

To make all notes, bills etc. for money won at play void, would tend to suppress the mischief, and advance the remedy designed by the 11 Anne; but then what would become of innocent persons who have paid money for these notes, and taken an endorsement of them on the credit [of] 8 Anne?

The second rule is a breach of natural justice, and ought always to be observed, the first is only to be observed *sub modo*, and qualified, and it is said in Yelv. 47,[1082] that the Statute of Usury is to be taken strongly for the suppression of usury, as to the parties to the corruption, but not so as to punish the innocent.

It was said from the Bar, that the 11 Anne is a repeal of the 8th, by the words, 'any statute, law, usage to the contrary thereof in any wise notwithstanding', and the words 'notes, bills', being expressly mentioned in the Act.

But Lord Coke[1083] in 11 Rep. 63[1084] says, that former Acts are not to be supposed to be abrogated by a strained construction of subsequent. [*293*] We are therefore to interpret these statutes consistent with natural justice, so as not to hurt the innocent, and if the statute can be satisfied with making these notes, etc., void in one instance, we are not to extend them to another.

2. Next I shall consider how the judges have construed the Act 16 Ca. 2.[1085]

And this was, as they had formerly done the Statute of Usury, Yelv. 47, *Ellison* v. *Warnes*.[1086] Moo. 32.[1087] Cro. Ja. 32.[1088] so as not to let the general words of the Act hurt an innocent person.

Mich. 29 Ca. 2. One won £100 at play and the winner owing £100, the loser gave a bond of £100 to the creditor, the bond being put in suit. The Statute of Gaming was pleaded. Notice was denied in the replication, which was demurred to, which case agrees with ours both in substance and form, and the judges agreed the money was to be paid, the creditor not being privy, though the contract was void as to the original parties to it. 2 Mod. 259.[1089] So Carth. 356[1090] is the same distinction between a privy and a stranger, though in that case the party would have relied on the custom of merchants, though he was privy.

3. What alteration their 9 Anne[1091] in England on the 11 Anne in this kingdom have made in the cases, so as to lessen the weight of the authorities on the 16 Ca. 2.[1092] And they have made no alteration, but as to the sum lost, the time, and the personal ignominy on the winner, but they seem to confirm all those authorities, for the makers of the Act knew of such a distinction, and therefore both the English and Irish statute obviate it as to mortgages, but don't carry it to bills, notes, though they are expressly recited, so the expression of one, is the exclusion of the other,[1093] and this they did for the convenience of trade.

[1082] *Ellis* v. *Warnes* (1604) Yelv. 47, 80 E.R. 34.

[1083] *Sic.* Sir Edward Coke.

[1084] *Foster's Case* 11 Co. Rep. 56b at 63a, 77 E.R. 1222 at 1231.

[1085] 16 Car. II, c. 7 (Eng.), 1664 (gaming).

[1086] *Ellis* v. *Warnes* (1604) Yelv. 47, 80 E.R. 34.

[1087] *Anonymous* (1651) Moo. K. B. 32, 72 E.R. 421.

[1088] *Ellis* v. *Warnes* (1604) Cro. Jac. 33, 79 E.R. 26.

[1089] *Sic*, for *Anonymous* (1677) 2 Mod. 279, 86 E.R. 1071.

[1090] *Hussey* v. *Jacob* (1695) Carth. 356, 90 E.R. 808.

[1091] 9 Ann., c. 19 (G.B.), 1710 (gaming).

[1092] 16 Car. II, c. 7 (Eng.), 1664 (gaming).

[1093] Cf. Latin maxim *expressio unius exclusio alterius*.

But if there was no authority to guide us, this case is not within the words 11 Anne, 'The bill', etc., and contract is void between the drawer and drawee, and the statute which makes notes negotiable, creates a new contract between the drawer and the endorsee. Their [*sic*] was not before, so though the mischief of gaming is to be suppressed, yet an innocent person is not to be injured, nor is the 11 Anne an [*294*] abrogation of the 8th Anne, and it must have the same construction as 16 Ca. 2.

So I am of opinion the demurrer must be overruled.

Sir John St Leger did not hear the case argued, but declared himself of the same opinion.[1094]

Lord Chief Baron

The only question is, whether the endorsee of a note won at play be at liberty notwithstanding the 11 Anne to sue the drawer, and this depends on the words, that 'from and after the 1 day of November 1711 all notes' etc. by the express words as to reimbursing or repaying money it must be knowingly lent or advanced for such gaming or betting, though mortgages in this clause are made absolutely void, yet in the next they are to be for the use of the person to whom the lands would have come after the death of the person encumbering.

So I shall consider, 1. whether by the natural import of these words, if it were *res integra*, we could declare the note to be void against the endorsee, or, 2. If we can do it since the resolutions on the 16 Ca. 2.

1. Supposing there were no authorities to guide us, the statute don't say against whom they are to be void. As to reimbursement care is expressly taken whether the lender had notice or not, then since the statute don't say against whom they are to be void, we must see how this statute operates on the 8 Anne, and if the better opinion is, that an action did not lie on the endorsement before the statute, then this Act gives a new right to the endorsee, which he had not before, and therefore if this right is not expressly taken from him, it shall not be included in the general words of the 11 Anne, and these securities are not absolutely void, for mortgages are after declared to be some purposes subsisting. So the 11 Anne would not from the natural import of the words take away the right given to the endorsee by the 8th, and much less from the intention of it can we suppose that these general words were made to destroy a statute calculated to promote credit, and for the benefit of trade, and the public advantage [*295*] of the kingdom.

Mes App. I.287.
Baldwin v. *Van Charrante.*[1095]

[2.] But this is not *res integra*, for the 16 Ca. 2 in the *non obstante* clause is the same, and since that there have been several authorities, as *Hussy* v. *Jacob*,[1096] that these notes are not void against the endorsee without notice, and that is the opinion in that case of the court as well as of the reporter. So we must make the same construction in a like clause in favour of the assignee, and overrule the demurrer.

[1094] Above, p. 217 n. 1041 and p. 223 n. 1055.
[1095] *Van Charante* v. *Baldwin*, KI, (1736) 'House of Lords Appeals', iii. 374 (Scottish Appeal) (payment of bankrupt's bills of exchange).
[1096] *Hussey* v. *Jacob* (1695) 5 Mod. 170, 87 E.R. 588; Carth. 356, 90 E.R. 808.

WHILLY v. HUSSY

In Exchequer

The bill requires the defendant to view papers the plaintiff left in the hands of his attorney. Before he answered, the defendant answers without viewing them, though the attorney went to the inn where he lodged, and gave him notice, and the court made an order on him to show cause why he should not take out a *dedimus* at his own expense to take his further answer.

And Mr Recorder mentioned the case of *Hicks* v. *Sir William Barker*[1097] in this court. The defendant was desired to view papers in the hands of the commissioners, if he answered in the country, or of the attorney, if he answered in town, and Sir William being in the country, the plaintiff sends down the papers. Then Sir William comes up, and answers in town. Upon this he is ordered to answer over, and we send for the papers to town. Then he takes out a *dedimus*, he answered in town, and Sir William being in the country, the plaintiff sends down the papers. Then Sir William comes up, and answers in town. Upon this he is ordered to answer over, and we send for the papers to town. Then he takes out a *dedimus* and swears his answer in the country before we can send the papers down again. Upon disclosing this matter to the court, he is ordered to answer over, and the plaintiff sends down the papers to one of his dwelling houses in the county of Limerick, and the defendant takes out a *dedimus*, and answers at another of his houses, upon which the court obliged him to take out a third *dedimus* at his own expense.

Ante 281.

Thursday, June the 21 [1733][1098]

The third of the eight days after Trinity Term.

KING v. LORD ORRERY

Lord Chief Baron

Lord Orrery brought an ejectment against the now plaintiff [*296*] as of last Hilary Term, which was served before the essoign[1099] day of Easter Term. The defendant did not appear till the 11 of May, the last day, when judgment would otherwise have gone against the casual ejector.[1100] Then he takes defence, issue is joined, and the same day he files this bill. Lord Orrey answers, exceptions are taken to his answer, and the baron this day reports his answer short, and in a material point too, but not wilfully. He is asked, whether Mr Oughnaghan, who was employed by the later Lord Orrery his father, had not a power from him to make leases for 99 years, and he

---

[1097] No citation given.

[1098] 21 June was a Thursday in 1733, Kratz, *Hist. Cal.*

[1099] LF. from OF. *essoine, essoign* from verb *essoigner*, an allegation of an excuse for nonappearance in court on the appointed day, or the accepted excuse itself.

[1100] See above, p. lxxvi.

answers, he had a power to make leases for 99 years determinable on three lives. This report was signed only this morning, and the question is, whether we shall grant an injunction on this report of a short answer.

The practice stood a long time in this as in the Court of Chancery, not to grant an injunction till the confirmation of the report, but that rule has been altered here, and injunctions granted on the report in special cases, because of the difficulty to bring on exceptions to the report, but this is not a written rule. The words are, 'or, on not perfectly answering'. The report is only ministerial till it is confirmed. Common practice and rules in writing can't be varied in particular cases, but for the future only, but since the defendant offers to put in a full answer in two days, and to attend the baron on Monday, and procure a report, or let the injunction go, therefore since the plaintiff delayed to take the defence till the last, let the injunction go, unless the defendant puts in an answer, and attends the baron for a report on Monday.

Mr Baron Wainwright

I think we ought not to grant this injunction, because the defendant will have no time to dissolve it, if he should put in a full answer.

NB: The practice in Chancery is to continue an injunction on the master's report, but not to grant it.

Quære if more credit ought not to be paid to a baron's than a master's report? [*297*] Said, that a witness to a deed, or will, may give evidence of the insanity of the party who executes the deed, or makes the will, for he may be uncertain how far the the circumstances of the man will render him unable to execute a deed, or make a will, and if he refuses to testify, he does him a manifest wrong.

Friday, December the 14, 1732, 3 [1733]

In Exchequer

LORD RANELAGH v. FITZGERALD

The bill was brought to compel the tenants to execute a counterpart. The agent made affidavit, that he had searched for it, and could not find it. The defendant demurred to the relief and discovery, and the affidavit was allowed improper as to the relief, because he had not swore his employer was in England.

NOWLAND v. BAGGET

A case quoted. The plaintiff took a lease at a small rent from the defendant's father who on his intermarriage makes a settlement of the lands in lease, with a power to himself to make leases etc. Nowland surrenders his old lease, and takes a new lease for lives from the defendant's father at an advanced rent, not warranted by his power. The father dies, the son brings an ejectment, and the tenant brings a bill to have the surrendered lease set up again in equity, which was decreed by Lord Midleton,[1101] with an account of the surplus rent.[1102] See Hutton 104, 105.[1103]

BAKER v. MURPHY

In Exchequer

The case of *Gibson* v. *Curry*[1104] was quoted, where a note was given for 50s payable at marriage, or the death of the father. He that passed the note marries, upon which the note is put in suit, and the defendant brought a bill for relief, which was dismissed by Lord Chief Baron Dalton as below the dignity of the court. But the court were now of opinion, that nothing was below the dignity of this court, nor be the sum what it will, if the party was forced into court, or if there was [*298*] any fraud in the case, would they dismiss the bill.

12 February 1732, 3 [1733]

In Exchequer

LESSEE OF MALONE v. HOLMES [AND] RIDGES

Mr Baron Wainwright

The question is, whether this declaration in ejectment for certain lands in a moiety, be so uncertain the sheriff cannot safely give possession.

It appears by the authorities to be a fundamental rule in pleading, that the words are to be taken according to their legal sense. This question then will depend on the meaning of the word *medietas*, of which we shall trace the several significations, and see how it came into the law. Tully[1105] says, he scarce dare make use of it. The Greek $\mu\epsilon\sigma\sigma\sigma\tau\eta\varsigma$ signifies a medium between two extremes. The Barbarians used several old Latin words in a legal sense different from their former, and gave a new stamp to them, as may be seen in 'villain', and in Maddox's [*sic*] *History of the Exchequer*,[1106] and *medietas* is one of them. Co. Lit. Sect. 298 says a moiety is an undivided estate, and Sect. 299 the land still remains undivided, and in reason when a division is actually made, it ceases to be a moiety, and is an entierty.[1107]

[1101] Spelled 'Middleton' in MS.

[1102] I.e. the father granted a lease to Nowland which was within the father's power to grant. Nowland later surrendered it to the father in return for a lease for lives, which, unknown to Nowland, was not within the father's power to grant. If the son insisted on his legal right to eject Nowland, then Nowland had an equity to have the surrendered lease restored and an account for the difference in rent.

[1103] *Watt* v. *Maydewell* (1628) Hut. 104 at 105, 123 E.R. 1132.

[1104] No citation given.

[1105] English byname of Marcus Tullius Cicero (106 BC–43 BC), Roman statesman, lawyer, scholar, and writer.

[1106] Thomas Madox, Richard Fitzneale, and Gervasius, *The History and Antiquities of the Exchequer of the Kings of England from the Norman Conquest to the End of the Reign of K. Edward II* (London, 1711). Copy in King's Inns Library, Dublin.

[1107] *OED*: obsolete, for entirety.

Objection: But a saying of Doderidge[1108] in Latch 224[1109] is objected, that before partition a parcener[1110] has *dimidium,* and after *medietas.*

Answer: This is only a saying of Doderidge, and is apparently a mistake from Co. Lit. 197a, *de mediet[ate] unius libræ piperis,*[1111] not *dimid[ium]* which is further confirmed by Calvinus *Lexicon iuridicum,* that *dimidiu[m] e[st] pars dimidiati.*[1112] Lord Parker says in 6 Mod. 231,[1113] *dimidia pars*[1114] is a certain moiety, *medietas*[1115] an uncertain one, but that it ought to be taken and understood *secundum subjectam materia[m].*[1116]

Objection: Though this don't appear to be an ejectment brought on [*299*] a legal possession given by the sheriff on an elegit,[1117] yet it must be understood so after a verdict.

[Answer:] But such an intendment would not help. The sheriff only returns that he has given a *medietas* generally, and till there is an actual partition the tenant by elegit and the defendant are tenants in common, and if we should not arrest judgment, we should do a manifest injury, by letting the sheriff give him possession, when another is in possession with him.

Lord Chief Baron

I am of the opinion, *medietas* has always the same sense my brother has taken notice of, and it is, as if an ejectment was brought for a thing for which it does not lie.

SLATERY v. THE CASUAL EJECTOR

Eodem die

Slatery a creditor by judgment of Dr Ryley sued out an elegit, and having obtained a legal possession from the sheriff, brought an ejectment, and served the tenants on the lands, and a stranger made oath, he knew nobody else who was concerned in interest. Mr Recorder moved to set aside the judgment against the casual ejector,

---

[1108] Sir John Dodderidge (or Doddridge), J.K.B. (Eng.), 1612. David Ibbetson, 'Dodderidge, Sir John (1555–1628)', *ODNB*, <http://www.oxforddnb.com/view/article/7745>, accessed 14 May 2008.

[1109] *Beverly's Case* (1627) Lat. 224, 82 E.R. 357: 'Doderidge dit q[ue] devant partition, l'un parcener ad dimidium manerii, apres medietatem; quia dimidium est d'un chose devant division, come inter tenants in common & joynt-tenants.'

[1110] See above, p. 27 n. 166.

[1111] Co. Litt. 197a: 'Now for the rent, as namely twenty shillings, or a pound of pepper may be severed; the one tenant in common may have an assise for the moiety of 20 shillings, and the moitie of a pound of pepper, *de medietate libræ piperis,* but he cannot have an assise of ten shillings, or *de dimidio libræ piperis*'; i.e. a tenant in common who was entitled to half the rent of 20 shillings could not plead a claim of 10 shillings, but had to claim a half interest in 20 shillings. The distinction was more subtle in relation to the pepper: he could not claim half a pound of pepper, but had to claim a half of one pound of pepper, i.e. not a whole interest in a half pound, but a half interest in a whole pound.

[1112] L. a half is the part of what is divided into two.

[1113] *Knight* v. *Burton* (1704) 6 Mod. 231, 87 E.R. 982.

[1114] L. a half part.

[1115] L. half.

[1116] L. according to the subject matter.

[1117] L. he has chosen. A writ of execution, so-called because the creditor chose to use it, by which a creditor was put in possession of half (later, the whole) of the goods and lands of a debtor, until his claim was satisfied. See above, p. cvii.

because Mr Ryley was not summoned, nor Mr Towers who was a purchaser under him, his purchase registered, and he in actual possession, and that this was done in the case of the *City of Cork* v. *Anon.*[1118]

Mr Calaghan

If we stop judgment, you shall appear, and take the defence.

Lord Chief Baron

No service would be good, if we should say this was not, but having late notice, you should move to put off the trial, not having time to prepare. I think the parties after took the old course to move for a trial at bar, which was granted.

February the 22[n]d 1732, 3 [1733]

LORD ORRERY v. BADHAM

The question in this case is, whether the party is in [*300*] contempt.

A proclamation was returned [on] the 10th, and not sealed till the 12th, and the commission of rebellion was sealed [on] the 13th.

And it was said that here could be no contempt, which is a disobedience to process under seal, but that the proclamation was not sealed till after it was returned, and if the return is out before you seal the former process, it is irregular, and no proceedings can be grounded on it till it is sealed, and the rule is said to be, that you may seal at any time after the return is out, but it must be sealed before further process can be grounded on it.

And Mr Attorney General said, this was a point of law, that the practice of the court could not dispense with, and that there could be no contempt where the writ was not under seal, which was a notification of the order.

On the other side Mr Calaghan said, that the practice of a court was the law of the court, and that if it was necessary to serve these processes, the sealing them after their return would be irregular, but the process is not actually served. By the usage of the court this proclamation is never served, and therefore 'tis not irregular to seal it after its return, and the practisers[1119] agree where further process is entered before the former is sealed, it is irregular, but not if the former is sealed though after the return. The sheriff makes no proclamation: it is all a fiction. At common law the process of outlawry is all sealed at once on the same day.

The officer being asked by the court as to this point said, that the process ought to have been sealed before the return, and that he did not know that the several processes were sealed at once, unless where there was an order of process *tunc pro nunc.*[1120]

[1118] No citation given.

[1119] I.e. practitioners.

[1120] L. now for then. A retrospective order used to make good an omission by the court. Ferguson, *Treatise* i. 308.

Mr Attorney General

To what purpose is it sealed on the 12th[?] It must [*301*] be sealed before the sheriff can have power to proclaim it. This would be to give life to a dead body.

Lord Chief Baron

The reason is certainly against the thing. By practice of the court, which is the law of the court, many of these processes are not served, but it is all fiction, but the party can't be in contempt without disobeying the process notified.

Mr Baron Wainwright

The proclamation is irregular being sealed after the return, and this is the practice too. So it must be set aside, and since the reason of the thing is that the process should be sealed before it issues, but they are indulged to seal them before the return, why should we indulge them further[?]

Hilary Term. February the 21, 1732, 3 [1733]

Before the Commissioners of Appeals[1121]

Dr Trotter
Mr Robert French
Mr Tenison

FOSTER v. MURRY

On a Petition to Rehear

Mr Prime Serjeant

On the 31 October the proceedings were returned according to the injunction. On the 7th November your honours made an order for the cause to be heard on the 17th, by consent of the appellant, who had ten days time given him, which he thought sufficient, but there was no hearing till the 24th, when the counsel and agent for the appellant appeared, who had two causes. The proceedings were read, counsel heard, and judgment given on the merits in one of them. Upon this the appellant would not attend, but wilfully neglected the prosecution on the other, and never desired to put off the cause, or have the time for hearing enlarged. So the cause was heard, the decree affirmed, and the ship that was condemned, sold, and Foster the petitioner did not apply for a rehearing till the 27th. You will therefore

---

[1121] Robert French (1690–1772), appointed commissioner of revenue appeals, 1732, J.C.P., 1745. Ball, *Judges in Ireland*, ii. 208; Thomas Tenison (1707–1779), commissioner of revenue appeals 1732–38, 1741–59, P.S., 1759, J.C.P., 1761. Ball, *Judges in Ireland*, ii. 212–13.

Gentlemen consider to what purpose you should allow a rehearing. If you reverse, you must do what the commissioners below ought to have done, [*302*] you must give judgment that the ship be restored, but the ship is not in the power of the informer or crown, so the rehearing would be nugatory, because you can't give that judgment, you can't take the ship out of the hands of the purchaser, who bought under the faith of the decree. The Commissioners of Reducements may mitigate the fine before it is paid into the Exchequer, but not after, for when the fine is levied, they have no power over it. They can't bring it back again, no more can you the ship in this case, nor can you make a compensation.

Mr[1122] Trotter

The appellant desired to put off the cause, but produced no affidavit. I shan't enter into that question, whether we can grant a rehearing, but the appellant's withdrawing is a sufficient reason we should not grant it in this case. If we have such a power, there are many inconveniences that would follow from rehearings to induce us not to grant them but for cogent reasons.

HODSON v. ROWLEY[1123]

A Rehearing, and twice argued.[1124]

January the 29th 1732, 3 [1733]

Thursday, February the 15, and April the 28th.

By one of a side.

Mr Attorney General stated the case for the plaintiffs.

Arthur Upton had two sons, Clotworthy and the defendant John, and two daughters, Ante 149, 154. Olivia and Ann, married to William Cunningham. The said Clotworthy Upton being in London, came to an agreement with the Drapers company for a reversionary lease, to commence at the expiration of the former, paying a fine of £3,000, and the rent of £200 a year, and Clotworthy Upton sometime after executes a declaration, that he took this lease in trust for the children of Thomas Dawson the younger, after payment of the fine. But it did not appear at the time of the transactions I shall mention, that he was a trustee. [*303*] In 1696 a Protestant colony was settled on these lands, and to establish and encourage them a lease for nine years was not sufficient, so the family thought proper, as an encouragement to them to build, to grant them a term of 33 years out of this reversionary lease, and accordingly Clotworthy Upton by letter of attorney empowers his father Arthur Upton to make leases of this reversion.

The said Arthur Upton [on the] 17 June 1696 makes a lease to John Hudson and Andrew Henderson, to commence at the 1 November 1705, at £100 a year for 33 years, and they covenant to build, and improve.

[1122] *Sic.* Referred to in the heading as 'Dr Trotter'.
[1123] Continued from p. 125.
[1124] See above, pp. 122, 125, 130.

[On] 24 May 1698 Arthur Upton makes two leases to John Hudson, to commence [on] 1 November 1705, one for nine, the other for 14 years, and they enjoyed these lands, and built and improved on them to the value of £600.

In 1710 these leases were conveyed to Richard Hudson previous to his marriage with Mary Henderson. Richard dies, and the plaintiff Mary by taking out administration to him became entitled to these leases.

The defendant Rowley brings an ejectment under this title.

Thomas Dawson junior left a son Joshua, and a daughter the defendant Arabella, to whom the benefit of these leases belonged by survivorship, and with her Rowley intermarried in 1725, and having thereby the legal estate in him, brought this ejectment, to which we could make no defence at law, because the original letter of attorney from Clotworthy to Arthur Upton was not in our power, (several other leases being made by the same authority) and because the leases were made in the name of Arthur Upton, and not of his principal, though the rent was reserved and made payable to Clotworthy Upton. Mr Rowley insists, that he is a purchaser without notice. But Arthur Dawson before his marriage informed him of the state of the lands, of the leases, rents reserved, etc., and so he was a purchaser of no more, and Rowley would not wait [304] for the counterparts but married in the meantime. This lease is made by Arthur Upton, the great grandfather of the defendant, and attested by her two great uncles.

Evidence

The leases recite them to be made by Arthur Upton, by virtue of a power, or letter of attorney from Clotworthy Upton, bearing date 1 February 1695.

[On] 29 December 1699 Joshua Dawson, and Thomas Dawson junior, enter into a bond of £500 to John Hudson and Andrew Henderson, conditioned, that Joshua Dawson shall confirm the lease or minutes made to Hodson and Henderson, etc., (being the same denominations as in the grand lease) by Arthur Upton, Clotworthy Upton, and Thomas Dawson senior, or any of them, and that Joshua should indemnify them and their tenants from any costs or damages they should be put to by the Lord Mazareen, for their attornment to Joshua Dawson. The old and new lease was conveyed over to John Dawson.

The plaintiff offered to read Mr Jackson to the proof of the letter of attorney.

To which Mr Prime Serjeant objected, because it appeared by his cross-examination, that he had a lease from Arthur Upton by virtue of this letter of attorney, so that he swore to support his own lease. He don't indeed swear that this interest is still subsisting in him, but as the term don't appear, it is to be presumed still subsisting, since he has nor shown it to be determined.

His cross-deposition is in these words, that he had a lease jointly with A from the said Arthur Upton by virtue of said letter of attorney, that he was not to gain or lose by the success of the cause, and that he knew the defendant Rowley was endeavouring to break these leases. But he don't answer, whether he is tenant of the lands, or has now a lease.

Mr Recorder

Our acquiescence is not to hinder us as it ought on an answer to a bill, because we could not tell his [305] answer to our interrogatories, or except to it. That he don't gain or lose is nothing but his [re]collection. If he has assigned his lease over, he could not be a witness, because he is bound after assignment.

Mr Malone

He is asked, whether he is not apprehensive Rowley will break his lease. He makes no answer to this question, but involves it in the general answer, 'I don't get or lose' etc. This may be true, and yet he may be interested, for his lease is not in question in this cause, and 'tis to be presumed not determined, since he don't answer the other questions.

Mr Steward[1125]

Part of the cross interrogatory is, has not Rowley threatened to break their lease, or brought an ejectment. He says, he hears Rowley is endeavouring to break. This is no answer.

Lord Chief Baron

If a witness was produced *via voce* at law, if he prevaricated, would we let him go on, or give his evidence to a jury?

Mr Calaghan

The answer is short and evasive, so the presumption is, that the lease is still subsisting.

Mr Attorney General

Every witness is a competent witness till the contrary appears. Depositions are different from an answer, which is drawn by the advice and assistance of counsel. And therefore the defendant ought to suffer, if he don't put in a full answer.

The commissioners either read this part of the interrogatory to him, or they did not. If they did not, the plaintiff ought not to suffer for that. If they did, he either made some answer to it, or none. If he made an answer, they should have returned it. If he made no answer, they should have returned so, and took notice of his contempt, and the court would have obliged him to answer; and the defendant is not to suffer by the neglect of the commissioners. [*306*]

If any doubt arise on the words of a deposition, the court will inform themselves by trial, even where the party is in fault, and the witness not examined before publication. He has said nothing to take off his evidence, and then the presumption is, that he has sworn true, which he has not done if his lease is subsisting, for then he must either gain or lose by the success of the cause.

[1125] Charles Steward, or Stewart, listed in KI AP, p. 464, *c*. 1734.

Mr Solicitor General

This objection arises not from the original, but cross-examination. He has said all that is proper to the general question, that he don't gain or lose. An admission that he had a lease, is not an admission that he has one now, but the court will presume he has not now.

Mr Lindsey [*sic*]

If he has not sworn as explicitly as he might, less weight is to be given to his evidence, but he ought to be read. If a witness prevaricates, this lessens the force of his testimony, but still he is examined.

Mr Baron Wainwright

I am of opinion he cannot be read. The question he is asked is, 'Have or had you, or any in trust for you, any lease,' etc, by virtue of this pretended letter of attorney[?]

He answers, that he had a lease, and drops, whether he has one now or not.

He is asked again, whether any relation of his has, or had, a lease etc. As to this he answers fully, and makes the distinction as the question does, that they neither have, nor had.

He is asked again, whether any ejectment is brought against him to evict him, and he answers, that an ejectment is brought to break the leases made by virtue of the power, which is a strong implication that it was brought to break his, then we are to suppose the lease either subsisting in him, or assigned over by him.

So he must be interested, though he neither wins, or loses. [*307*] This is an affected, not an inadvertent answer. He answers like a man of skill, and seems wilfully to have avoided the question, and could not be convicted of perjury on this answer.

Sir John St Leger

If the answer is short and evasive, the party might have a remedy before the hearing, and it ought to be referred to a baron. The commissioners should have certified any misbehaviour, and we are not to judge of it now. If he has not answered fully to one part, why should not he be read to the rest? Their evidence is by cross-examination. I don't like his answer, but we can direct a trial.

Lord Chief Baron

I am of opinion he cannot be read, but we can help the want of his evidence by an issue, if we find the question necessary, whether such a letter of attorney was executed or not. This is a matter of consequence. Depositions are not to be set aside on rehearing, but if the credit of a witness appears suspected by his answer, he must clear it before he can be read. It is a maxim, that a person whose credit is suspected, cannot be read.

If he has a lease under this letter of attorney, or is affected by it, he cannot be read, nor is a competent witness.

If he assigned it, and is not exonerated from the covenants, he is still affected.

The question then is, whether he appears to be cleared. He says he had a lease, then it is to be suspected that he still has, if he don't show he has not, which he does not do.

Perjury must be *scienter*,[1126] and corrupt! But he says, he don't win or lose by the success of the cause. He might not know, that the success of one cause would influence the other.

And he says ejectments are brought against all the leases. His evidence then is justly to be suspected, and he can't clear himself by implication.

Interrogatories are often read at the hearing to explain depositions. [*308*]

Friday, February the 16th. [1733][1127]

Mr Prime Serjeant for the defendants.

Clotworthy Upton in 1692 obtained a lease from the Drapers' company for 46 years, to commence in 1705, when the former lease expired.

[On the] 8th of December 1698 he by deed declares this lease to be in trust for Thomas Dawson the younger; and as [for] the plaintiff, if she has any title derives it under Clotworthy Upton. What is recited in this deed is evidence against her, and he recites, that by an instrument dated the 30 August 1692, he declared his name to be made use of in trust for the heirs begotten and to be begotten on the body of Olivia his sister by Thomas Dawson the elder.

Having thus declared himself to be only a trustee, he on the 1 February 1695 perfected the letter of attorney to Arthur Upton his father under which the plaintiffs claim, three years after this first declaration of trust.

Arthur Upton on the 17 June 1696 made one of the leases in question to Henderson and Hodson for 33 years, and the two other leases on the 24 May 1698 for 31 years at £9 13s per annum rent.

And by articles of intermarriage these three leases were vested in Richard the husband. And the plaintiff is entitled to them as his administratrix. Thomas Dawson the elder assigned the old lease to Joshua Dawson, and on the 29 December 1699 the bond was given by Joshua and Thomas Dawson the younger, which is no confirmation of these leases, but can extend only to those derived out of the first lease.

Joshua Dawson came into possession by the fraudulent attornment of these tenants.

Thomas Dawson the younger was killed at [*309*] Gibraltar in 1703, having first devised these terms to Joshua his son, and the defendant Arabella his daughter, who is also administratrix to her brother.

On the intermarriage of Thomas the younger with Arabella Carr in the year 1700, Thomas Dawson the elder previous thereto, settles his real estate on Thomas the younger and Arabella in strict settlement, after an estate to himself and his wife Olivia for their lives.

The friends and relations of the family procure an Act of Parliament,[1128] in which this settlement is recited, and the estate divested of the old uses is vested in trustees, to

---

1126 L. knowingly.
1127 16 February was a Friday in 1733, Kratz, *Hist. Cal.*
1128 4 Ann., c. 7 (Ir.) (private). Above, p. 122 n. 687.

be sold for the payment of the debts of Thomas the elder, and this term in lieu thereof is vested in trustees, subject to a jointure for Olivia and Arabella, as maintenance for Thomas Dawson the elder, and portions for his daughters, Rose and Rachel, to the use of Joshua Dawson the son in tail male, remainder to the defendant Arabella. Joshua Dawson who died in 1709 was not above two years old when the Act passed, and the defendant Arabella was born after the death of her father, and came of age in 1725.

I allow the lessees made some improvements in hopes to enjoy this reversionary term. But we have proved the value of the lands to be double of what they were set for by Arthur Upton in 1698. The bill charges, that the plaintiff was informed that Clotworthy Upton was a trustee and it was the general reputation of the manor from the beginning that he was so.

It is so that Mr Cunningham the agent for Mr Rowley received four years' rent for this manor, and that Mr Rowley had notice of these leases, and confirmed them by giving two receipts for the rent, but his ejectment was brought the Easter before, and on the 20th of June precedent the bill was filed for a perpetual injunction to stay his proceedings at law, which is the same thing as if the plaintiff had prayed a specific execution of these leases. [*310*]

A court of equity has always made a difference between setting aside contracts, and carrying them into execution, and though it won't set aside a hard bargain, it won't countenance, or establish it.

Here are three questions:

1. Whether here is any evidence of this letter of attorney.

2. Supposing such a letter was produced, and proved, whether the power given by it, or the acts under it, or these leases, are such contracts of which your Lordship would supply the defects, or carry them into execution.

3. Supposing them reasonable, and to be carried into execution, yet whether the court would do so in this case, against Mr Rowley, who is a purchaser without notice.

1. Here is no evidence of such a letter of attorney, but the declaration of Arthur Upton and the possession. The declaration arises only from the recital of the lease, that he demised by virtue of a letter of attorney etc. This is no evidence to affect a third person not being upon oath, of if he had been examined as a witness in this cause, and had sworn to such power, he would not be a good witness either in law or equity. And if the recital is no evidence, the enjoyment cannot. This term commenced after passing the Act of Parliament.[1129] Joshua and Arabella were both minors, and she contests the lease as soon as she came of age, and was married.

There have been cases where thirty years' quiet possession having gone along with the deed [the court] has read it without proof, though the time of enjoyment is not settled, but they went on this reason, that it could not be presumed a man would stand by and see another enjoy his estate, if he knew he had a title, but they who should contest this matter, where [*sic*] minors when the term commenced, and the neglect of their trustees or [*311*] guardians shan't turn to the prejudice of the minors. But this presumption is the weaker, though it ought to be the stronger, because the power is unreasonable, and against the interest of the family.

It is said that these reversionary leases were made to preserve a Protestant colony on the lands. But the religion of the lessees don't appear in the cause, and only that Henderson was a clerk.

[1129] Above, p. 122 n. 687.

But the plaintiff says, she can't produce this letter of attorney, because several other leases were made by virtue of it.

But though every lessee could not have this letter annexed to his lease, it might have been enrolled on the oath of Clotworthy Upton before a master. This was a precaution they might have observed. And then the power would have appeared, but they haven't taken the common security of annexing a copy to the lease, nor taken a covenant from Arthur Upton to produce this letter, if needful. Then the nature of the power would have appeared, and whether the trustee took notice of the trust, and the nature of it; so here is no presumptive proof of this letter of attorney. And though the gentlemen were men of distinction, and probity, they might exceed their power, or not pursue it.

[2.] The rule of equity is this, that an agreement which a court of equity will carry into execution ought not only to be obtained without fraud or circumvention, but reasonable in itself, otherwise the court will leave the parties to their damages at law.

And of this nature is the present contract. Supposing it made by Clotworthy Upton, whom I will consider in two lights, 1. as a bare trustee, and 2, as a trustee joined with an interest, being a purchaser, because he stood engaged for the rent of £200 a year, and the fine of £3,000, £1,000 whereof was to be paid in 1705, £1,000 in 1715, when the lease commenced, and the other £1,000 in 1725. [*312*]

1. As a bare trustee, he execute[d] a lease in 1698 to one who had notice of the trust, to commence in 1705, without the concurrence of the cestui que trust. If this was only a contract, the court would not carry it into execution against the cestui que trust. If as a bare trustee, he had no power in equity over the estate, so no power to demise to one who had notice, and the rather in this case, 1. Because Thomas Dawson the younger lived in the neighbourhood of these lands, so that nothing could establish such a lease but its appearing to be for the benefit of the cestui que trust. How could this in the creation of it be for his benefit, though it might prove so[?] But this contract is to be considered as if it had been called in question immediately after the execution, and 2ndly, no necessity is shown for making it, and to allow such a power to a trustee without or against the consent of the cestui que trust, is to give him dominion over the estate.

[3.] Next I shall consider how Clotworthy Upton appears as a purchaser. He has told us that a few weeks after taking the lease he declared the trust. The lease in equity is a pledge for the fines, so he is [in the] nature of a mortgagee for these sums, and seven years before any of them became due, he makes a lease for 33 years without the consent of the mortgagor. A mortgagee can at most bind the lands only during the subsistence of his interest, and if the mortgagor redeems, his leases fall to the ground, and here all the money was paid before the bill was filed. The legal estate don't pass by this demise, because the name and seal of Clotworthy Upton is not put to it.

If Clotworthy had given a power to Arthur to make leases in the name of Arthur or Clotworthy, these leases would be void at law, because the legal estate would still remain in [*313*] Clotworthy, and there was only a power in Arthur Upton to take it out of him, so nothing flows from Arthur, but it must be by an act in the name of Clotworthy Upton, and if they had filed their bill against Clotworthy Upton and Thomas Dawson the younger, and Clotworthy in his answer should say he was willing to execute a lease, and Thomas Dawson should insist he could not bind his property, the court would not supply the defect.

These leases are not to be encouraged. As we don't know what the power was, I shall suppose it to be to make leases generally, yet such a power must have a reasonable construction, and suitable to the nature of the estate, for this being a naked power, must be construed strictly, nay though it was a power coupled with an interest, as if [a] tenant for life has a power to make leases, this must be understood of leases in possession, 6 Co. 33a, and it was adjudged by the House of Lords[1130] in the case of Mr Worthington, that a Papist cannot take a lease in reversion, though both his leases don't exceed 31 years. The trustee could not tell what value these lands would be of nine years after, when the term was to commence.

Mes: App. D.77.[1131]

The question then is, what has been done by Clotworthy Upton or Thomas Dawson the younger to confirm this lease?

First, the bond is insisted on, the condition of which is, if the allowed bound Joshua Dawson[1132] shall confirm the lease or minutes made to Hodgson or Henderson, or either of them, of the lands of Moykelan etc, (the lands in the first lease mentioned) and shall save harmless the said Hodgson and Henderson from Lord Mazareen, an account of their attornment to the said Joshua Dawson. Lord Mazareen was an incumbrancer in possession of the old term, and Joshua, who was the assignee of it, tampers with the tenants to get possession from him. So this bond, on which they would raise an [*314*] equity for the plaintiff, is grounded on a fraudulent attornment, and can only go to the first lease, to such leases as they were in possession of under Thomas Dawson the elder, and if it was intended as a confirmation of the reversionary leases, why is only one of them taken notice of?

But how could this bond if a confirmation affect the son of Thomas Dawson the younger, who is a purchaser under the Act without notice? Or if the son had notice, Mr Rowley or his wife had no notice of this bond, or confirmation and on this supposition this bond would show the leases not to be good, for they would purchase a confirmation of them by this fraudful act.

The next thing to be considered is the operation of the Act of Parliament.[1133] Thomas the younger was then dead, and Joshua his son about two years old, and by this Act he is divested of the real estate whereof he was a purchaser, which is to be sold for payment of the debts of his grandfather, and he is to have this lease subject to the charges in the Act in lieu thereof. The legislature then designed that nothing should be a lien on this term not particularly mentioned, and as the legislature were trustees for the minors, they would not have subjected it to these charges only, if they thought that these leases too were good.

'Tis said, that Joshua Dawson one of the trustees by this Act had notice of these leases, but that won't affect the eldest son by constructive notice, the Act having set[1134] this term as a compensation for the real estate.

Joshua the son then was a purchaser without notice, and Mr Rowley having married Arabella his administratrix, if he stood only in his place, he must enjoy it with the same security, for a purchaser may sell to one that has notice, otherwise he would not have dominion over his estate to dispose of it,[1135] and as Mr Rowley is an

---

[1130] *Cusack* v. *Bulkley* (1717) 5 Bro. P.C. 369 at 371, 2 E.R. 737 at 738.

[1131] Note that, unusually, 'Mes:' has a colon in the MS, the normal indication of an abbreviation.

[1132] I.e. Joshua Dawson, who is admitted to be bound. Original word is spelled 'alowed'.

[1133] Above, p. 122 n. 687.

[1134] See p. 10 n. 59.

[1135] I.e. a purchaser without notice takes free of equitable interests and furthermore may sell to a purchaser *with* notice who will also take free. If it were otherwise, the purchaser without notice could not obtain the value

honest purchaser, the court will be very tender how they affect him with constructive notice.

Mr Recorder

I shall rest the first point on what has been offered by Mr Prime Serjeant, and it is not necessary to rely on it, because enough appears on the two other points to dismiss the bill. [*315*]

There is no charge in the bill of any power but to set[1136] leases. So it is to be presumed that the letter of attorney to Arthur Upton was in common form, and not to set leases in his own name. Therefore it can't be pretended that these leases are good in law, he not having a special power.

2. If they are good, I shall consider whether they ought to be carried into execution.

Your Lordship would not carry an article under the hand of Clotworthy Upton himself into execution. The estate is to be considered as resting in the cestui que trust and the trust is to be looked on only as a power, and the cestui que trust in tail by fine and recovery may bar his issue, and those in remainder. Could Clotworthy Upton then having only a general power make leases in reversion? No, because he had no power over this estate to the detriment of it, and a trustee of a reversionary term has no power to make leases till the term comes *in esse*,[1137] because that would tend to the ruin of the estate.

The bond does not confirm the leases made out of the reversion, but out of the running term, or supposing it did, they can't be carried into execution against us, for we are purchasers under the Act, not under Thomas the younger, and have this term in lieu of our remainder in the real estate, which he could not bar, or encumber. Henderson's lease was until 1705, and the bond is to warrant against Lord Masareen, who was a mortgagee only of the term in Thomas the elder, and was given on their attornment. 'I won't', says Henderson, 'attorn only on the bond of Thomas the elder, unless Thomas the younger who has a future interest in these lands joins with him', so it can't bind Thomas the younger to make good future leases, and if it had been made to confirmation, it would have extended to all, and in one only.

We claim not under Thomas our father, and supposing this [to be] his confirmation, it extends only to a single lease, and Mr Rowley and his wife had no notice of this bond, so they must recover damages against the representatives of Thomas the younger.

The Act has not taken any notice of these leases, because the law makers could not presume a trustee in reversion had made leases, so there is no saving for them.

Mr Rowley who is a purchaser of this term, has the legal estate conveyed to him by the surviving trustee. [*316*] As to notice, Mr Rowley could not be presumed to enquire after leases which it was unreasonable to make, so he had no notice of leases in reversion made by a trustee, for a fraud was not to be presumed, and they did not appear by the Act under which he claims, so he was in no default not to enquire into these leases. A judgment shall not bind the estate of a purchaser by constructive notice; but if he had notice, he comes in by way of remainder, therefore the leases

---

of his or her property on sale. This is a point of equity later held in *Re Stewart's Estate* (1893) 31 LR Ir. 405 per Monroe J. at 415 in Ireland and in *Wilkes* v. *Spooner* [1911] 2 K.B. 473 in England.

[1136] See p. 10 n. 59.

[1137] L. into existence.

made before the term commenced can't bind, but are void as to him, so he has the legal estate, and has equity too on his side.

Mr Malone

No words can empower an attorney to convey an estate in the lands, because the estate is in his employer, so the legal estate remained in Clotworthy Upton after making the leases, but no ownership.

This letter of attorney is to set all the manor, without restriction as to the number of years, or the rent, and is never to receive the sanction of a court of equity, because there can't appear any necessity for such a power, that any part of the manor was out of lease.

Next let us consider how this letter of attorney is carried into execution. A power to make leases especially when given to a trustee must be understood of leases in possession, nay if the owner of the lands gave such a power, it could not be understood of unusual leases. A covenant to renew in a lease made by virtue of a letter of attorney has been adjudged to be void. These leases would not be good if made by the trustee, because of the uncertainty of the value of the lands when the lease commences. He don't know but he may do an injury to the cestui que trust.

And the number of years these leases are granted for is material. One is for 33 years, and the other for 21, out of a reversionary term of 46, and they ought not to be established, because the cestui que trust was in the kingdom, and his approbation might have been had, and as he was a minor, the trustee is to be considered as his guardian, and is guilty of a breach of trust if he makes a leases [*sic*] longer than his minority.

But the lessees were tenants of this manor, and had notice of the trust, for it was generally known and reputed that Clotworthy Upton was only a trustee. So here was a fraud in them, as well as in the trustee.

As to the bond, if the leases that were in being will satisfy [*317*] the words of the condition, will you look after future leases that are not taken notice of in it, have they showed that these leases were at the time and the contemplation of Thomas Dawson junior, or that he intended to confirm them? And the attornment is to Joshua Dawson, and the rent is payable to him. Now these reversionary leases were not made by him, nor was the rent reserved to him.

The real estate could not have been sold without the consent of Thomas Dawson junior. All parties agree to the sale of it, and this lease is to come in lieu of the estate tail in the lands taken from Joshua Dawson, the son of Thomas the younger.

A receipt from an agent without an express authority is no confirmation of a lease, nor from the party, unless it were in contemplation, for a confirmation in equity must arise from the agreement and intention of the parties. If a man indeed acquiesces, and gives receipts not in error, this though it can't confirm a void lease, is understood in equity as, and will amount to a new agreement.

Mr Calaghan

No legal estate could pass by the letter of attorney, though Arthur Upton had been empowered to make leases in his own name, for he could not give what he had not. And 'tis the essence of a letter of attorney to act in the name of his employer, and is a true difference between a letter of attorney and a power, and that at law is not good, if they act in their own name. If the testator directs that his executors shall sell his lands, they have a bare power, and they can't convey in this case of a will, and to avoid this, the law has found out an executory devise.

Let us then consider if any equitable right could pass, and here the same rule will hold. He could not pass the legal estate, because it was [vested] in Clotworthy. The equitable estate also was not [vested] in him but [in] Thomas the younger. How then could the attorney of Clotworthy Upton convey, what even Clotworthy himself had not? And no right could pass in equity, because the making such leases was an injurious act, and inconsistent with the trust reposed in him who made the power, and by his own declaration he publishes himself to be a trustee, and by that no power is given him [318] to make leases, and unless by the deed a power is given the trustee to make leases, his lease won't bind the cestui que trust, and this declaration though subsequent in point of time, must have relation to the time of taking the lease.

Then what circumstances are there in this case to raise an equity for the plaintiff[?]

She would be relieved on the head of possession, the bond, notia, and receipt of the rents, the possession is of no weight, because it begun during minority, and the bond is a fraud from the general words of it. 'Tis not said by whom, or to whom, to them, or one of them the lease was made. The date, commencement, duration, or by what power made, is not set out. If they designed to have brought these leases under the view of Thomas Dawson the younger, they would have been more particular. The attornment must relate to a lease then in being, and could not to a reversionary lease, and though they might have more in their view, Thomas Dawson the younger had not.

But the condition of this bond is only that Joshua Dawson the incumbrancer should confirm, and not destroy them, whereas if they had designed to confirm these leases, the condition would have been, that neither Joshua, nor Thomas Dawson the younger should destroy them, and the incumbrance being paid off, the condition is gone.

But suppose Thomas Dawson the younger was bound to confirm these leases, Mr Rowley and his lady claim under the Act of Parliament,[1138] which has a saving for all persons, but those that claim under Thomas Dawson the younger. As to notice, the express has destroyed the constructive notice, where a man buys lands whereof others are in possession, he must inquire into the title they hold by. But here he has notice given him of a lease not in being, on which he rests, and makes no further inquiry, but is hindered by it.

But whether he had notice or not is no ways material, because the plaintiff has neither law or equity on her side. *Barrymore* v. *Richardson*[1139] adjudged in 1705. Lawrence Earl of Barrymore who was only tenant for life conveyed in fee. The question was, whether the purchaser had notice, as to which evidence was imperfect, but the court was of opinion, there was no need to prove notice, because he could not pass the legal estate, and in equity [319] he could convey no more than he had in him.

As to the acts of the agent, in the case of *Worth* v. *Butler*[1140] a lease was made by [a] tenant for life, and Lord Midleton[1141] held, that the receipt of the rent by the

---

[1138] Above, p. 122 n. 687.
[1139] No citation given.
[1140] No citation given. See *Butler* v. *Worth*, above at p. 123.
[1141] Spelled 'Middleton' in MS.

remainderman, was no confirmation of the lease, but was receiving rent from him as tenant at will, and quoted the case of *Lord Shelburn* v. *Lord Kingston*.[1142]

Mr Magawley[1143]

The attornment was to Joshua Dawson who was to have a benefit by it, and he was for that reason to confirm the lease. But he had no benefit by the reversionary lease.

These leases were made at an undervalue. Some of the lands which had been set for £20 a year, are set by this for [£]14.

There must indeed be proof of fraud, where this court will set aside an agreement, but they will refuse relief, where there is any suspicion of fraud, though not fully proved, 2 Vern. 632.[1144] Here is a suspicion of fraud that the lessees had notice, from the general reputation, that this reversionary lease was taken in trust for Thomas Dawson the younger.

In the case of *Delap* v. *Richardson*,[1145] notice of the lease was construed to be constructive notice of a covenant in it to renew.

Mr Attorney General for the plaintiff

I shall consider these leases, 1. As if Clotworthy Upton was but a bare trustee, 2. As he is concerned in interest, 3. In respect of the plaintiff, as to whom he had a legal estate in him, and was the owner, 4. I shall show that this is not impeached by the Act, or 5. By the settlement of Mr Rowley.

1. If there had been no declaration of trust, Clotworthy Upton must have been if at all a trustee for Thomas Dawson senior, to whom the subsisting lease belonged, and not for Thomas his son, who had no interest in the lands. Clotworthy Upton was under no obligation to take this new lease. It was his voluntary act, and he was not employed by the Dawsons, and was greatly concerned in point of interest, for he thereby subjected his person to the payment of £200 a year rent, and to a fine of £3,000, and if he is to [*320*] be considered as a trustee, it is only after the satisfaction of this money, and therefore he is not on the foot of a common trustee, who is answerable only for misbehaviour, but is a purchaser in equity.

But if he is to be considered as a common trustee, and the plaintiff had notice he was so, he has acted with great honesty, and the defendants are highly obliged to him.

Their assertion, that no trustee ought to set a reversionary lease, has no foundation in reason or authority. The war[1146] being just ended, it was a happiness to landlords to secure Protestant tenants, and by the covenants in their leases they are not to assign or alien to Papists, and no one would build or improve on so short an interest as between 1696 or 1698 and 1705 but upon this further encouragement given them, these tenants covenant to build a farm house on every denomination of land in the lease mentioned, which are eleven, and the size of the houses is mentioned, and they were to be delivered in good repair at the end of the lease.

[1142]   No citation given. See *Lord Kingston* v. *Lord Shelburn*, above at p. 123.

[1143]   There is no person of that name in KI AP, but it may refer to Alexander McAuley, s. and heir of Alexander, Drumnegesson, nr. Coleraine. Middle Temple, 24 Aug. 1722. KI, Hilary term, 1729; KI AP, p. 300.

[1144]   *Green* v. *Wood* (1708) 2 Vern. 632, 23 E.R. 1013.

[1145]   No citation given. See above, p. 127 and below, p. 248 n. 1148.

[1146]   This seems to refer to the War of Spanish Succession (1701–14).

As to the value, they have given no proof of it in 1696 when the lease was made, and the value they have proved in 1705 is a strong evidence for us. The rent reserved is £148 10s[?] 00d, and they have proved the lands to be worth in 1705 £157 10s 00d, and before that we had laid out £3[?] 45 12s 5d in improvements, for which we get about £9 a year, so this is not only an honest transaction, but for the advantage of the family.

This is such a lease as a court of equity should establish. The lease recites the letter of attorney, and our long enjoyment and payment of rent is a proof of it, and the defendant in his answer takes notice of tenants in possession by virtue of this letter, and all the leases though of different dates recite the same letter, and as Mr Rowley in his answer owns Arthur Upton to be a man of honour and integrity, it can't be supposed that he would under his hand and seal have certified a falsehood, and the tenants enjoyed under it, and laid out their money in improvements.

But it is said, the power don't appear, and is to be construed strictly. But the thing speaks itself, because the interest of Thomas the elder continued till 1705, and Clotworthy Upton had only an interest in reversion. Then when he gives a power, it must be intended to make leases in reversion, and Jackson swears the power was to make leases for 31 years. [321] What has been said on the Act is of no weight at all. These Acts in equity are considered but as more solemn private conveyances, and the intention of them is not to hurt strangers who had no notice, and were not parties to them, but to enable persons to make a settlement, or the like, who otherwise had no power. If the landlord applies to Parliament to enable him to pay his debts, and there is no saving for the tenants, who were not then under the contemplation of the makers of the Act, are they to be injured by it? At that rate every tenant might be ruined, and the lord chancellor was of opinion, that a private Act would not destroy the right of the lessees, in a late cause in that court between Mr Rowley and some of the tenants.

Thomas, Olivia, and Arabella Dawson in behalf of themselves and their children apply for this Act, and no others are bound by it, and in the saving clause the right of every one is saved who before had any, except their, and their creditors, right, and of those who derived under them, or any of them.

But supposing the lessees bound, it appears by the bond, and his receipt of the rents, that Joshua Dawson had notice of this lease, and he being a trustee by the Act for the minors, his notice is notice to them, and the notice of one trustee will affect all.

We are purchasers without notice that this lease was not in Clotworthy Upton for his own use. No express notice has been proved, and none can be presumed from the lease, but the contrary from the covenants they have entered into. No trust is declared till 1698, after the making the leases, indeed in that declaration 'tis recited that a trust was declared in 1692, but that recital is no evidence against us, because any act of the lessor after his making a lease can't find the lessee.

If [a] tenant for life makes a lease longer than his own life it is void,[1147] and any act of the remainderman can't confirm it, because [the] tenant for life can't make such a lease; but Arthur Upton had a power to make leases for 31 years, and though he has not well executed that power, it shall bind, because he had a power to make [them]. Then if Clotworthy Upton gives a letter to another to make leases, who don't

---

[1147] A tenant for life at common law might make leasehold grants, but they were *voidable* at the instance of those entitled in remainder when their interests fell into possession: Co. Litt. 251b.

execute that power as it ought, would in equity oblige Clotworthy Upton to make [*322*] such leases good, after the tenants had laid out their money in improvements.

Mr Rowley is not a purchaser without notice, for he had not only implied, but express notice.

A purchaser ought not only to enquire who has the inheritance, but who is in possession of the lands, and his neglect of what he might know, shall not prejudice the right of another, *Delap* v. *Hamilton*:[1148] Mr Richardson purchased a lease, with a covenant to renew as often as his lessor did from the College.[1149] Matthews purchased from the lessor without notice of this renewal, and yet he was bound to renew, because as he knew the land was in lease, he ought to have enquired into the leases, and asked the lessees, and if they had refused to show their leases, it might have been another thing, but of two innocent men he that is negligent ought to suffer.

But here is express notice, because Arthur Dawson told him of the leases: so that he is only a purchaser of the rents reserved by them, for he tells him the whole manor was in lease, and what rent was reserved, and though he did not see the counterparts of the leases, it was his fault to marry before they were sent him.

By the declaration of trust in 1698 no lease is to be made without the consent of Clotworthy Upton, and Arthur Dawson, and they had both consented to these leases, by the letter of attorney, and the bond. It was the interest of Clotworthy Upton to be secured against the fine and rent, and Joshua Dawson was a creditor. It was therefore reasonable that no leases should be made without the consent, and dominion is given to them by the subsequent clause, 'Subject to such money as Clotworthy Upton, and Joshua Dawson shall charge on the estate.' Thomas Dawson the younger being a voluntary cestui que trust, Clotworthy Upton reserved a power over it, and might charge it as he pleased. If I take an estate in another man's name, he has nothing to do with the estate, but if he takes it, he may declare the trust as he pleases, and such a declaration is not inconsistent with the trust.

'Tis said, the bond relates only to the first lease. The condition is, to indemnify the lessees, and to confirm, and [*323*] ratify the lease or minutes made by Thomas Dawson the elder, Clotworthy Upton, Arthur Upton, or either of them. Clotworthy Upton, or Arthur Upton had nothing to do but with this reversionary lease. They were not concerned in the old lease. Here then is a sufficient description, and as they were in possession under Thomas Dawson senior, so it was necessary to make him a party, to secure the possession till 1705 under him, as from thence, under the others.

This is not general, either as to the lands, or the persons, but both are particularly mentioned, so *dolosus*[1150] *versat[u]r in generalibus*[1151] won't hold, and it was necessary to mention both Clotworthy Upton, and Arthur Upton, because the lease was in the name of Arthur, but the rent was reserved to Clotworthy, and no other lease has been shown, to which the words can be applied.

If Mr Rowley had no notice of these leases, the acceptance of the rent by Cunningham is a confirmation of them, (though his own acceptance after bringing the ejectment I own won't bind).

[1148] No citation given. See *Delap* v. *Richardson*, above, pp. 127, 246. The cases now cited for the principle are *Hamilton* v. *Lyster* (1844) 7 Ir.Eq.R. 560, and *Hunt* v. *Luck* [1902] 1 Ch. 428.

[1149] I.e. Trinity College Dublin.

[1150] *Sic*, for *dolus*.

[1151] L. fraud dwells in generalities. *Doddington's Case* (1593) 2 Co. Rep. 32b at 34a, 76 E.R. 484 at 488.

As to which there have been made two objections, [1.] that this was a receipt by an agent, which won't bind his employer, 2. that it was for his benefit to have the annuities paid off.

Mr Rowley in his answer admits he made him agent to receive all his rents, and not only the annuitants but the fine too were paid with them. So it is the same thing as if paid out of his own pocket, and ours is not a void but a voidable lease in a court of equity.

A lease is void when it is made by one who had no power, but if the person has a power, though the lease don't strictly pursue it, 'tis not void, but defective, and good for so much as it pursues the power.

A lease for three lives to commence *in futuro*, though made by the tenant in fee, is void at law, yet shall it be made good in equity.

This lease being made in the name of the attorney is only void at law for the informality, and the employer had a good power to make the lease, though his attorney executed it in an improper manner.

Possession has gone with us twenty-nine years.

Saturday, February the [2]4th. [1733][1152]

Mr Solicitor General

This an equitable agreement, under which the lessees have long enjoyed, performed their covenants, and paid their rent, which has been accepted. [*324*]

It is said we have given no evidence of a letter of attorney. But that is either to be taken for granted, or put in a method of trial, and is evident from the recital of the leases, our enjoyment, and the answer of Mr Rowley, that several leases were made by virtue of a pretended letter, and from the bond which confirms the leases made by Arthur Upton.

Here are two questions. 1. Whether these leases are such an equitable agreement as shall be aided in a court of equity. 2. Whether any aid is to be granted against Mr Rowley.

If Clotworthy Upton had a power to make leases, though there are some defects in these leases, we are entitled to have them made good. He had the legal estate, and though he was only a trustee, it was no fraud in him to make these reversionary leases, and if he was a bare trustee, they have made no proof that the plaintiff knew it. And this will appear no fraud, from a consideration of the nature of his trust, and when it began. He had not a naked trust, but one coupled with an interest. He that is a bare trustee must in all his acts have a regard to the cestui que trust. But where he has an interest, he may also in reason and justice take care to protect himself.

Clotworthy Upton was not originally a trustee. If he was, it must either be by operation of law, or his own express declaration.

The trust for Thomas Dawson the younger could not arise by operation of law. He never employed him, or paid the consideration money, and if any trust arose by law it must be for Thomas Dawson senior, who was in possession, and had a tenant right.

The first declaration of trust is in 1698, that indeed takes notice that in August 1692 Clotworthy Upton had declared the trust for the children of Thomas Dawson

---

[1152] Since this continues the same case, it would seem to be 24 February and the year 1733. 24 February was a Saturday in 1733 (Julian), Kratz, *Hist. Cal.*

senior. But that is no evidence against the plaintiff, who had no notice, whatever it may be against Clotworthy himself, and this declaration shows, Clotworthy thought it had dominion over the estate, and therefore declared the trust Upton terms, and this varies, and is a departure [*325*] from the first trust, whereby he reserved a power to charge this estate with the consent of Joshua Dawson with any sum of money, at any time, and for any purpose.

A lease made in reversion by a trustee is only a presumptive evidence of fraud, but not if it appears not to be at an undervalue, but for benefit of the estate as in this case, and was proper, because he was concerned in interest, and bound by his covenants to the payment of the rent and fine, and if he had staid till the estate was out of lease, the tenants would have made their own terms, and the estate been neglected and spoiled by the tenants, who were to quit it, if these reversionary leases had not been made.

The fairness of the transaction appears from the characters of the persons who transacted, which is admitted by the defendant, and what end could they have in making them, they received no fine.

As to the Act of Parliament,[1153] notice to the trustees is notice to the manor, and Arthur Dawson had notice, was an incumbrancer, had an assignment from the cestui que trust of this lease, is made by the Act one of the trustees, and was the only one who acted under it.

Mr Arthur Dawson

'Tis a strong proof of a letter of attorney, that twelve leases were taken from Arthur Upton, who had otherwise no power to make them.

Why may not a trustee as well make a lease in reversion for 31 years, as take a surrender of a lease for ten years to come, and grant a lease in possession for 41?

The case in Rol. Ab. 436 proves, that the receipt of Mr Rowley amounts to a confirmation. A bishop makes a lease voidable by his successor, and dies. The bailiff tells the successor what rents were due, who orders him to receive them, which he does, and among other from the tenant. This was held to be a confirmation of the lease.

Hale says in 1 Ventr. —,[1154] that there is no occasion for a saving of the rights of any person in a private act of Parliament. 8 Co. *Barrington's Case.*[1155]

Lord Chief Baron

Acceptance of rent on a void lease is not a confirmation in equity, for the tenant has paid quid pro quo, and is to pay [*326*] for every year's enjoyment.

This cause was after comprised.[1156]

[1153]   Above, p. 122 n. 687.

[1154]   *Lucy* v. *Levington* (1671) 1 Vent. 175 at 177, 86 E.R. 119 at 120. Hale: 'Suppose an Act says, Whereas there is a controversy concerning land between A. and B. 'tis enacted, that A. shall enjoy it. This does not bind others, tho' there be no saving, because it was only intended to end the difference between them two.' Twisden: 'There is an old book which says, that if an attainder be reversed by Parliament, the person shall have trespass against him, which took the profits of his land in the interim.' This seems to refer to private Acts.

[1155]   *Barrington's Case* (1610) 8 Co. Rep. 136b, 77 E.R. 681 (22 Edw. IV, c. 7 (Eng.), 1482 (forest) and 35 Hen. VIII, c. 17 (Eng.), 1543 (woods), held to be general acts).

[1156]   *Sic*, probably for compromised.

By a late order of the Court of Exchequer, if an attachment issues for non-performance of a decree, and a *non inventus*[1157] is returned, the process is shortened to a serjeant at arms.

Mes App. D.361.
Ante 81.
MSS̃ Ord in. Canc.
49, 117, 133, 135.

Easter Term

Friday, April the 13, 1733

LESSEE OF OGARA v. FLEMING

On a trial at the bar of the Court of Exchequer in ejectment.

Mr Prime Serjeant for the defendant

Sir John Fleming being tenant in tail, by deeds of lease and release[1158] subsequent to the marriage of his son conveys the lands in question to Lord Gormanstown[1159] in fee to the intent to make him tenant to the præcipe, and covenants to levy a fine before the end of the next Easter Term, to the use of his son and his wife, and the survivor of them for life. But no fine was levied, or recovery suffered till the Trinity term following. Sir John died, and his son's widow was afterwards waived[1160] for high treason, and married to Mr Ogara who lived in France, and by a private Act of Parliament[1161] she is enabled to sue for her jointure, as the King might.

Mrs Ogara is barred by the Statute of Limitations 8 Geo. 1,[1162] not having been in possession for 20 years before, but it is 44 years since Sir John Fleming died, and she was then in the kingdom. Besides she has no power to demise, for the legal estate remains in Lord Gormanstown, and no use arises, the fine not being levied at the time covenanted.

[1157] L. he is not found.

[1158] See above p. 83 n. 481.

[1159] Cokayne, *Complete Peerage*, vi. 18, 'Gormanston'. If Sir John Fleming died in 1689, i.e. 44 years before (see next paragraph), the Lord Gormanston referred to was probably Jenico Preston, 7th Viscount Gormanston (before 1647–1691).

[1160] I.e. outlawed.

[1161] 'An Act to enable Mary O'Gara Widow, to sue for her jointure lands', 13 Geo. I, c. 31 (G.B.), 1726 (private), *HLRO*, 13 Geo. I, no. 66. See Appendix B. See also 'For relief of the protestant creditors and lessees of Sir John Fleming knt. deceased, and of Mich. Fleming, esq. only son of the said Sir John; and for effectually executing certain articles of agreement entered into between said Michael, and Mary O'Gara, widow', 9 Geo. II, c. 4 (Ir.) (private), listed in vol. 8 of Irish *Statutes at Large*.

[1162] This is not a reference to the principal Act dealing with limitation of actions, 10 Car. I, sess. 2, c. 6 (Ir.), 1634, but to the specific statute 8 Geo. I, c. 4 (Ir.), 1721, s. 4. The section provides that persons not already barred, and claiming an estate or interest or an incumbrance on lands, of which they were not in possession for 20 years before 12 September 1721, were to have 5 years from that date within which to bring an action. Section 7 of the Act preserved the right of the king to sue notwithstanding anything in the Act. The 1721 Act was aimed at dealing with problems of establishing titles in the confused state of land ownership in the aftermath of the accession of William and Mary.

Mr Stannard

The estate was not to be to the use of Mrs Ogara till such a fine was levied, so either Lord Gormanstown continued seized, or the estate resulted back to the use of the grantor. [*327*]

In case of a fine, if the time begins in the life of the ancestor, it shall run on even against infants, and the Statute of Limitations is to be construed in the same manner.

To go out of the kingdom was her own fault, which the statute did not design to provide for, but the ignorance of those who were out of the kingdom.

Mr Daly

Cartr. 5.[1163] Though the fine of another term is good between the parties in equity, yet having tied themselves to a particular term and time, by the fine of Trinity term the uses are not taken out of Lord Gormanstown, no more than if the fine had been levied to another person, for a variance of time, is as material as of the term.

Mr Calaghan

If Sir John Fleming before the execution of these deeds had levied a fine and suffered a recovery, this fine would be only [a] matter of form, yet must have been levied, and the time is material from the nature of this case, for Sir John Fleming being tenant in tail, might die before it was levied, and then the uses for this lady would not arise.

Mr Attorney General contra

These deeds being by way of lease and release are to be construed in such a manner both in law and equity as to carry the intention of the parties into execution and were designed for the benefit of the Flemings, not of Lord Gormanstown, and no time is limited for suffering a common recovery, so if the uses are well declared, no matter whether there was a fine or not, for Lord Gormanstown being tenant to the præcipe, the estate is taken out of him, and if uses well raised; and if the parties had not expressed this to be their intention, their Lordships would presume the fine to be levied, with intention to make Lord Gormanstown a good tenant to the præcipe.

Lord Chief Baron

'Tis objected that the estate in law remains in Lord Gormanstown, but that can't be, because the common recovery was against him, which is to the uses of the settlement, and if the fine can't inure, yet the recovery shall, though if the recovery had been confined to time as well as the fine, no doubt the legal estate would still remain in Lord Gormanstown.

Then the defendants insisted, that the plaintiff claimed under a voluntary settlement after marriage, whereas they were purchasers and mortgagees. [*328*] The

---

[1163] *Davies* v. *Kempe* (1664) Cartr. 2 at 5, 124 E.R. 789 at 791.

plaintiff insisted, that she was a purchaser of this jointure, her portion being paid at the time of the settlement, and to prove this, would have read the answer of Sir John Fleming to an information filed against him by the Attorney General for this jointure, wherein he confesses the receipt of the portion, but the defendants objected, that this answer could not be read against them.

But Mr Attorney, and Solicitor General for the plaintiff insisted, that the answer was good evidence, being put in before the purchase, that the allowed distinction was between acts done by the mortgagor or vendor before, and after the purchase, and mortgage, that the first would bind the mortgagee of vendee, but not the latter, that acts done before were evidence, because they can't be supposed with a view, and if they were fraudulent, the other side must show them to be so. An answer is upon oath, and so different from any loose conversation, and though not conclusive, 'tis such evidence as ought to be received, and they said, he can't alter his title and that he that buys, can't have a better [title] than he that sells.

Objection: This don't appear in the settlement.

Answer: If he had acknowledged the receipt in the deed, and all the witnesses were dead, that would be good evidence, and 'tis the same thing if he owns it by any other act before the mortgage or sale. Suppose Sir John Fleming had given a receipt for the money, would not that have been evidence?

Mr Calaghan

This distinction is not founded on reason, justice, or authority. Fleming in 1699 mortgaged to Porter, but in an answer two years before he says something to destroy that mortgage. If this evidence should be allowed, no purchaser could be safe. A purchaser may come to a knowledge of incumbrances, but now they would have him search for bills and answers, to see if the seller has owned anything prejudicial to him, and this would be impossible, for there is no alphabet for answers, so though I know who is the defendant, I can't tell who may be plaintiff, and this was determined not to be evidence in a trial at bar in Salk. *Ford* v. *Grey*,[1164] and that case makes no distinction whether the answer is precedent or subsequent, and the decree can't be evidence, because we are not party to it.

Mr Malone

If Porter had been one of the defendants to that information [*329*] the answer of the other defendant Fleming could not be read in evidence against him, but here they would have his answer evidence against one who was no party. If a seller had a mind to deceive, he might cause a bill to be filed against him, and put in such an answer. But supposing this answer was evidence of the payment of the portion, and that we knew of it. It don't appear in that answer how the fact is to be applied, that it related to the settlement and limitations, that she was thereby to have a jointure etc.

[1164] *Ford* v. *Lord Grey* (1704) 1 Salk. 285 at 286, 91 E.R. 253.

Mr Daly

If this doctrine should be established, the Statute of Fraudulent Conveyances[1165] would be of no use, for then a receipt for the money, or an acknowledgement of the consideration would be evidence, though no money was really paid. How are these private evidences to be made out? A purchaser in equity need not take notice of records, but he must have actual notice of a judgment, or it will not bind him.

The lord chief baron having left the court, Mr Baron Wainwright said, it would be dangerous to admit this kind of evidence. The Act of Parliament was made for the sake of purchasers. Settlements made after marriage are prima facie fraudulent, and there ought to be the strongest proof of their being otherwise, as if the receipt was on the back of the deed, and all latent settlements are fraudulent. You would have me take the admission of the party for evidence that the settlement is not voluntary, and I am not satisfied that according to the rule of evidence I can read the answer of a defendant against one not party to the suit. The distinction that has been made is true as to all acts executed. But I don't think this proper evidence to be laid before a jury.

The plaintiff appeared, and the jury brought in a verdict for the defendant, and the baron saved this point to the plaintiff.

Saturday, April the 14th. [1733][1166]

STEWARD v. EVERS

A bill was brought against a tenant holding over, and an injunction granted to the party *nisi*, and Mr Recorder came to show cause why the order should not be made absolute. The bill was brought by the devisees of General Steward who resided in England, and by the affidavit their title is set out as executors of General Steward, whereas they have none as such, and 'tis only by way of recital, nor do they show, that General Steward was in his lifetime seized of these lands, and his heir ought to be before the court. *Townshend* v. *Barry*:[1167] the lands were devised [*330*] to daughters, and their guardian brought a bill to be quieted against the heir who was in possession, and the court denied the injunction until the right was tried at law, because the law throws the reversion on the heir.

On the other side it was said, that where the parties lived out of the kingdom it was sufficient to swear to the belief of a title, to obtain an injunction either against a tenant holding over, or against force, that it was not necessary to set forth that the General was seized, but only that the lease was executed, which was sufficient to have the possession restored, that this is only an injunction to the party, which is in nature of a summons to him to make his defence, and a probable cause is a sufficient ground for it. The court will decree possession to a devisee, or assignee, though the heir is not before them, if the title is not in question, and here not the mere right, but who ought to have the possession is in question, and the plaintiff may hold the possession till evicted by the heir.

[1165] 10 Car. I, sess. 2, c. 3 (Ir.), 1634 (fraudulent conveyances).
[1166] 14 April was a Saturday in 1733, Kratz, *Hist. Cal.*
[1167] No citation given.

Lord Chief Baron

These bills ought to be favoured, and if there is sufficient sworn for the court to believe that such a lease was made and expired, the court will quiet; here neither the seisin of Steward, or a counterpart is sworn, and you are not without remedy, but may be helped by another affidavit. So the cause must be allowed.

December the 3rd, 1733

DIGBY AND ANN HIS WIFE v. AUGUSTINE CLERK AND OTHERS[1168]

Mr Prime Serjeant for the defendants

James Clerk made his will, and thereof his two elder sons Luke and Augustine Clerk executors, and left a residue of his personal estate undisposed of. Luke made his will and thereby devised £600 to the plaintiff Ann his daughter, and this bill is brought for a payment of the said legacy, against the executors of the said Luke, and against Augustine Clerk, that the moiety of the residue of the personal estate of the said James Clerk might be considered as part of the assets of Luke, to which he was entitled as one of the executors of James. James Clerk by his will made a provision for all his children and grandchildren, and by a codicil divided all his plate equally among his children. [*331*]

Luke married in the life of his father, and James on his intermarriage lodged a sum of money with trustees, to be invested in a purchase of lands to be settled on Luke, etc. Luke died about six months after his father, and Augustine alone after his death proved the will of James.

The question is, whether a moiety of the residue of the personal estate of James Clerk undisposed of by his will shall be looked on as the personal estate of Luke? Or, whether the whole shall survive to Augustine?[1169]

First, I shall consider the cases generally, 2. As the father was a trading man, and whether anything was done by the executors in trade to alter the law.[1170]

There can be no doubt that by law the whole will survive. Then I shall consider what reason there is for a court of equity to alter the law, and what they have done in these cases.

There are many resolutions in equity agreeable to the law, whereby it has been adjudged, that if the residuum is devised to executors, or strangers, it shall survive in equity, as well as at law.

[1168] See *Digby* v. *Hall* (1735) 4 Bro. P. C. 1st ed. 524; 4 Bro. P.C. 2nd ed. 577, 2 E.R. 393, below, p. 266 n. 1227.

[1169] I.e. if Luke and Augustine held as joint tenants at Luke's death, the whole would pass to Augustine on the principle of *ius accrescendi* or survivorship, that a surviving joint tenant is entitled to the whole. If, on the other hand, the property had been held as a tenancy in common, or if it had been a joint tenancy but had been severed in equity before Luke's death, in this case by the fact that they had dealt with the assets as merchants, they would have been tenants in common at Luke's death and a half share would have been held by Luke and passed to his executors and been available to satisfy the legacy of his daughter, Ann.

[1170] I.e. alter the position at law.

That it survives at law in the case of bare legatees, appears from 1 Lev. 164,[1171] 2 Lev. 209,[1172] 2 Jon. 130.[1173]

And in equity the case is the same of executors, as well as legatees, *Creagh* v. *Willis*, Trin. 1729, at the Rolls.[1174] 2 Chan. Cas. 65, *Draper's Case*,[1175] and this is said to be a settled rule in equity in 1 Vern. 482, *Lady Shower* v. *Billingsly*.[1176] But your Lordship has a doubt upon the resolutions that have been, that the executors being considered only as trustees of the residuum undisposed of for the next of kin, ought to be considered as trustees for one another.

But here is no creditor or child unprovided for, and if you consider them as trustees of the residuum, the next of kin ought to be before the court.

The second question then is, whether James being a merchant, and dying in trade, and his executors likewise merchants, they have done anything to alter this from the common cases. If the residuum had consisted in leases, the whole was survive, unless there was a special agreement to the contrary. 2 Vern. 385, *Boyce* v. *Giles*.[1177]

And however odious joint tenancy may be in equity, there must be something done to prevent it, 2 Vern. 63, *Musgrave* v. *Dashwood*.[1178] An agreement to sell won't prevent survivorship.[1179] Survivorship don't hold indeed among merchants, to prevent the accidents of life, as well as of trade.

This was not a fund originally created by these executors to carry on a trade. [*332*] If all the residuum had been in this kingdom, and they had actually turned the ship which was part of it into money, and sold it as soon as they could, that would be only an act of necessity, and not an agreement to sever the residue. This would be only a necessary act to discharge the trust as executors, and the money arising by the sale would survive, because they did nothing which showed an intention in them to alter the law. But part of the assets being in foreign parts, if they had only brought these home, that too being only an act of necessity, would not alter the case. They must either do that, or sell them abroad. Suppose this ship at the time of his death had been well freighted at Cork, might not the executors have ordered it to be brought coast ways to Dublin: this would not be an act of trade, but necessity.

And if they let the ship to freight, and ordered the products to be invested in brandy, and sell it here, this is no proof of a partnership, or agreement to alter the law. But they are supposed to act out of duty, and as executors.

'Tis objected they have traded as partners.

But Augustine swears, they never agreed to trade as partners, but as executors.

[1171] *Guillan* v. *Gill* (1665) 1 Lev. 164, 83 E.R. 350.
[1172] *Bastard* v. *Stukely* (1677) 2 Lev. 209, 83 E.R. 522 (no survivorship by the ecclesiastical law).
[1173] *Bastard* v. *Stukeley* (1677) Jones T. 130, 84 E.R. 1181.
[1174] Below, p. 264 n. 1214.
[1175] *Draper's Case* (1681) 2 Ch. Cas. 64, 22 E.R. 848 (joint-tenants or tenants in common).
[1176] *Lady Shore* v. *Billingsley* (1687) 1 Vern. 482, 23 E.R. 607.
[1177] *Moyse* v. *Giles* (1700) 2 Vern. 385, 23 E.R. 846.
[1178] *Musgrave* v. *Dashwood* (1688) 2 Vern. 63, 23 E.R. 650.
[1179] An agreement by one joint tenant to sell to a third party would not produce a severance of a joint tenancy at law, and so would not prevent the survivor taking by survivorship, since it did not, and does not, transfer an interest in the property, but it would cause a severance in equity today, even though the contract itself could not be enforced by specific performance, *Burgess* v. *Rawnsley* [1975] 1 Ch. 429, and indeed even a 'course of dealing' would do so: Page-Wood V.-C. in *Williams* v. *Hensman* (1861) 1 J. & H. 546 at 557, 70 E.R. 862 at 867. The position in equity may not have been so clear in the 1730s, or the prime serjeant is referring to a contract by all the joint tenants to sell to a third party, which would not necessarily cause a severance of the proceeds *inter se*: *Byrne* v. *Byrne*, unreported, High Court, R.I., McWilliam J., 18 January 1980; *Re Hayes' Estate* [1920] 1 I.R. 207.

Now when instead of selling the ship, they thought it would be more for the benefit of the assets, to let it to freight, and turn the money into brandy, and sell it here, the question is, whether this shall make them joint traders.

If this should be looked on as a fund belonging to themselves, and which would not survive, this residuum would have different constructions, for the debts standing out would survive to Augustine, and the ship not, but we must consider in what right they had the ship, and all the profits arising from thence, must follow it.

Mr Malone

The question is, whether the surviving executor is entitled to the residuum not disposed of, or whether the executors of Luke can call him to account.

It don't appear but that Luke left other assets sufficient to satisfy the plaintiff.

No question but at law the surviving executor shall have the whole, and though the executor was always a trustee to pay the debts and funerals, 'tis but of late only that he has been construed in some cases as a trustee of the surplus, in which before he had a property, because he was to sue and be sued, yet the resolutions as to this have varied according to the circumstances of the case. If the executor is a stranger, and has a particular legacy, or other marks of a trust, that show the [*333*] intention of the testator the next shall take the residuum, but where the executors are in equal degree with the other relations, and the testator has made a provision for them all, they have been adjudged to hold the surplus as in *Elliot* v. *Beauchamp*[1180] in Chancery: there the testator left legacies to all his children, made a provision for his wife, whom he appointed sole executrix, and had portioned some of his children in his lifetime, and the surplus was £1,000, yet it was decreed to the executrix. Here the executors are the two eldest sons of the testator, and he has provided for all his children and grandchildren, so there is no room to say this surplus is a trust.

Where a personal estate was devised to two, I own it has been decreed that it should not survive, as *Cox* v. *Quantock*, 1 Chan. Cas. 238,[1181] but in the case in Levinz this point came directly in question, and it was resolved otherwise in the case of *Shore* v. *Billingsley*.[1182]

But the case of executors who take by act of law is stronger, where there is an actual devise: there is some colour to think the testator designed each of the devisees an equal benefit, and this is the notion of the civil law. But this intention don't appear to be so in the case of executors, though they are his sons, for this is only giving them such an office with all its burthens and advantages, and this appears from *Drapers' Case*,[1183] and *Hunt* v. *Berkley*,[1184] in Abr. of Equity Cas. 242; and the testator by his will has made distinct provisions for Augustine and Luke Clerk. He has given them distinct estates and legacies. He was indeed a merchant, but this will make no alteration in the construction of his will, and his executors were merchants too, but nothing is devised to them to be employed in trade. The will was not proved in the life of Luke. The assets were in the possession of both, and they acted as executors in

MSŠ cas. in Canc. A.74, SC.

1180 No citation given.
1181 *Cox* v. *Quantock* (1674) 1 Ch. Cas. 238, 22 E.R. 779.
1182 *Lady Shore* v. *Billingsley* (1687) 1 Vern. 482, 23 E.R. 607.
1183 *Draper's Case* (1681) 2 Ch. Cas. 64, 22 E.R. 848.
1184 *Hunt* v. *Berkley* (1730) 1 Eq. Cas. Abr. 243, 21 E.R. 1020 (A. left a will, making B., C. and D. residuary legatees and executors. B. died before A. Did the surviving executors, C. and D., take the whole or was one third part to be distributed among next of kin? Held, M.R., surviving executors took the whole).

the disposal of them *in auter droit*,[1185] and did not consider them as their own. A ship part of the assets by consent of both is set to freight, and the produce is laid out in brandies, and those sold here. This is so far from being an evidence of a partnership, that it excludes all notions of it. If the ship had been sold, and the money put out at interest, would not the interest have been assets, and the executors accountable for it, and nothing more has been done in this case. Instead of putting the money to interest, they have put the ship to freight.

Partners are considered as acting in stock of their own [*334*] not in assets, which would be of disadvantage to creditors and legatees.

Suppose immediately after the death of James Clerk Luke should have come into equity for a moiety of the surplus. Would the court have decreed it to him? No, it would have changed the nature of the assets to have decreed him a property distinct from the other executor, so the profits arising from the cargo can't be considered as private, but as to done to increase the assets.

Mr Calaghan

These executors are to be considered in two lights, 1. As executors, 2. As merchants from the evidence of their trading.

If they are considered as executors, there can be no doubt but the whole will survive to Augustine. This is certain in the case of joint legatees, *Farewell* v. *Coker*,[1186] and the case of joint executors where there is no express devise of the residuum comes within the same reason, for one only takes by the act of the party, the other of the law, and 'tis a rational intent to suppose the effects are to go in a course of administration, and otherwise all survivorship would be destroyed in equity. The evidence of their joint trading is very uncertain, but I will suppose they did. 'Tis the mercantile law which rescinds survivorship, which depends upon usage and custom. That can't relate to executors while they are entitled as such, but if they trade with the effects, the return of them will be assets. If the executor lends the assets on a mortgage, the interest is still assets.

MSS̃ cas. in Canc.
C.344.
Mes App. E.701.

Lord Chief Baron

I would have you gentlemen who are to speak for the plaintiffs to consider survivorship between executors, and whether the residue in all cases shall survive to them, or whether the decrees that have been for a distribution shan't have an influence on this question, and as the courts have decreed the executors to be trustees of the surplus, whether they shan't construe how far this trust shall extend.

2. Whether merchants by dealing in one thing shall be considered in general as merchants, but the question is, whether executors agreeing to deposit a fund in trade, won't [*335*] make them joint traders.

[1185] LF. in right of another.
[1186] *Farewell* v. *Coker* (1728) 2 P. Wms. 460, 24 E.R. 814; *Coker* v. *Farewell* (1729) 1 Swan. 403, 36 E.R. 436 (doctrine of election); 2 Eq. Cas. Abr. 737, 22 E.R. 625; 2 P. Wms. 563, 24 E.R. 863.

Wednesday, December the 5th. [1733][1187]

Mr Daly pro Quer

The points in this case are, what interest the two executors have in this residue, whether they have it in their own right, or liable to a distribution, and whether the whole will survive.

By the first part of his will it appears that the testator designed to dispose of all of his effects: 'I think fit to dispose of all my fortune in manner following.' He orders his debts to be paid out of his lutestrings,[1188] alamodes,[1189] and household goods in Coke's Street, and the surplus of the money arising from the sale of them to go as the rest of his fortune. Then he devises some real estates, leases and mortgages to his son Luke, and some to his son Augustine, and directs that the portions and legacies he thereby devises to his younger children should not be taken out of the devises to Luke and Augustine, and that the same should not be liable to them, but that they, as well as the legacies he devised afterwards, should come out of the rest of his fortune, thus he carried out to his younger children what provision he desired for them, and he did not intend by making his sons executors, to give them an office of trouble only, but benefit.

Your Lordship will consider the nearness of the relation between these executors and the testator. He designed to provide for them by this residue. 2 Vern. 375, *Ball* v. *Smyth*,[1190] this distinction is made between relations and strangers, and particular legacies being left to the relations, his intention appears that they should have no more.

Then the question that remains is, whether the surviving executor shall take the whole surplus.

Survivorship in Chancery is looked upon as odious and unequitable. If a mortgage is made to two jointly and they pay equal parts of the money, equity will not let it survive, 1 Chan. Rep. 57.[1191]

2. 'Tis to be considered how far survivorship hold among traders, and how far these executors appear to be such.

The custom of merchants extends to all kinds of trades, so if two farmers jointly stock a farm, it shan't survive. 1 Vern. 217.[1192]

In the case of children, where the father intends them a [*336*] benefit and provision, the court will go as far as they can to prevent survivorship to answer his intention, which is the foundation of the decree in *Sanderson* v. *Brown*, 2 Vern. 46.[1193] I admit that the common rule at law is, that the surviving executor shall have the whole, but equity may decree the contrary from the circumstances of the will, as where the residue is designed as a provision, 1 Chan. Cas. 238, *Cox* v. *Quantock*,[1194]

[1187] 5 December was a Wednesday in 1733, Kratz, *Hist. Cal.*

[1188] Lutestring: a kind of glossy silk fabric; a dress or a ribbon of this material. An alteration of *lustring*: *OED*. English statutes of the period have *lustring*, e.g. 4 Geo. II, c. 15. Johnson's *Dictionary*: 'LUSTRING. n.s. [from *lustre*.] A shining silk; commonly pronounced *lutestring*.'

[1189] Alamodes, from Fr. *à la mode*, lit. 'fashionable items': a thin, light, glossy black silk. *OED*.

[1190] *Ball* v. *Smith* (1711) 2 Vern. 675, 23 E.R. 1039.

[1191] *Petty* v. *Styward* (1631) 1 Ch. Rep. 57, 21 E.R. 506 (survivorship does not apply to joint mortgagees).

[1192] *Jeffreys* v. *Small* (1683) 1 Vern. 217, 23 E.R. 424.

[1193] *Saunders* v. *Brown* (1688) 2 Vern. 46, 23 E.R. 640.

[1194] *Cox* v. *Quantock* (1674) 1 Ch. Cas. 238, 22 E.R. 779.

and in 2 Chan. Cas. 64, 65, *Drapers Case*.[1195] The lord chancellor was dissatisfied, but said, 'I will decree it to the survivor, because the judges will have it so.'

But here are circumstances that arise from the will and the proofs to vary that rule in this case.

Alderman Clerk the testator was a merchant, and his effects lay in trade, for the provisions for his younger children were devised out of his effects in France, and his lutestrings and household goods were to answer his debts. The executors too were merchants, and it appears they were employed in trade under him. The freighting the ship, bringing home the goods, and the selling them makes them joint traders, and gives them an interest in what they brought home. If they had sold the ship, it would have another consideration, but they freighted it, had a return in brandy, and sold that, and Shale consigned wine to them, which they sold as factors only, so they traded with the goods of the testator. This was a joint trade, and not their duty as executors, and they were joint factors for others.

Since then it appears that the testator designed his sons a benefit by making them his executors, as he and his sons were traders, he intended this surplus as such, and to advance them in their trade, and that they accordingly traded with the assets, and dealt jointly, your Lordship will consider them as tenants in common of this residue, and that the whole shall not survive to the defendant Augustine.

Mr Recorder

The single point is, whether here is enough on the circumstances of the case for your Lordship to decree a share of the surplus to Luke, who died first.

It has been insisted, that at law survivorship takes place between executors.

I admit it to be so, but the reason of that, and of survivorship [*337*] at law is not to guide and govern this case.

Executors take the assets in *auter droit* as the testators, and are looked on as trustees, and the trust will survive, so though one executor is an infant, they may all sue by attorney, Cro. Fl. 376, 7.,[1196] nay if joint executors divide the assets, the partition is void at law, and the whole shall survive to the other, and he may bring his action Bro. Tit. Exr. Pl. 7., so even an actual division won't bind at law. But an action lies for the survivor for the benefit of creditors.

But in equity where there are no debts, your Lordship will consider it otherwise. Here is no creditor, and the common law is altered as to the residuum, by the Statute of Frauds. The executor now holds all the residue after payment of debts and legacies in his own right, for if a man give legacies to all his relations, and his executors, and they are relations too, the court won't decree a distribution, but looks on any surplus as designed them for their own benefit, and won't consider it according to the rules of the common law, but the civil, as in the case of *Cox* v. *Quantock*,[1197] and the bar was dissatisfied there, because the law of survivorship was overturned by implication.

Here is enough in this case to destroy the survivorship. The executors were traders, and dealt with this surplus. Augustine indeed swears, that they traded only as joint executors, but the deduction is this, that if joint executors put the residuum in trade,

[1195] *Draper's Case* (1681) 2 Ch. Cas. 64, 22 E.R. 848.

[1196] *Baldwin* v. *Wiseman* (1595) Cro. Eliz. 377, 78 E.R. 624; *Elizabeth, Countess of Rutland* v. *Isabel, Countess of Rutland* (1594) Cro. Eliz. 377, 78 E.R. 624.

[1197] *Cox* v. *Quantock* (1674) 1 Ch. Cas. 238, 22 E.R. 779.

it shall exempt the stock from survivorship, and is the same thing, as if they had put such a sum of money in trade, and when it is once in trade, it must be subject to the rules of trade, whether they get the money by will, or otherwise.

The instances of their trading are, that they let the ship Mary Ann to freight. This was no act of necessity. If they did not design to trade they would have sold it. If the ship had been lost, this would have been a *devastavit*. This then is making that fund their own, and their own assets liable, and they turn the freight into goods, and bring them home again. This ship though it was the testator's, by this risk becomes their own. Augustine swears it was done to improve the assets. But as thereby they might have wasted, as well as improved them, that risk makes them their own, and 'tis plain as the father and the sons were traders, and that he left them assets abroad, and they trade in them, that they pursued his intention, and if the executors came to a [*338*] division of the residuum, that is good in equity, though not in law, and equity would stop their action, nay equity is so far from following the strict rules of common law, that one executor may compel the other to a division in Chancery. And their putting this fund into trade is the same thing as an actual partition, because the law divides it for them.

Mr Geoghegan

There is no survivorship among executors by the civil law, and this rule is to be observed in equity, and at law, being a matter testamentary, 1 Lev. 164,[1198] and for this reason the Statute of Distributions[1199] is explained according to the civil law, as that the half bloods shall inherit. The intention in a will is to be our guide, 1 Co. 100. If an estate is devised to a daughter, a posthumous son shall take it from her. So here it could not be the intention of the testator that the residue should survive, for he could not [have] intended that Augustine should have all if he survived, who was his second son, and at that time unmarried, but Luke was his eldest son, married, and had children.

Sir John St Leger

Would not these dealings have made the executors buyers and sellers within the Statute of Bankrupts?[1200]

[1198] *Guillan* v. *Gill* (1665) 1 Lev. 164, 83 E.R. 350.
[1199] Statute of Distributions (Ireland), 1695, 7 Will. III, c. 6, and see 22 & 23 Car. II, c. 10 (Eng.), 1670, 1 Jac. II, c. 17 (Eng.), 1685.
[1200] 34 & 35 Hen. VIII, c. 4 (Eng.), 1542. See also 13 Eliz. I, c. 7 (Eng.), 1571 (acts of bankruptcy); 21 Jac. I, c. 19 (Eng.), 1623 (adjudged bankrupt, who shall be). The first statute dealing with bankruptcy in Ireland was 11 & 12 Geo. III, c. 8 (Ir.), 1772.

Saturday, February the 23rd. [1734][1201]

The last of the eight days after Hilary Term.

Mr Baron Wainwright

As the equity of every case arises and depends on the circumstances of it, it is necessary to state the circumstances of this case.

James Clerk, Alderman, made his will dated the 27 of September 1712, and thereby made a provision for all his children. He devised to each of his sons Luke and Augustine a moiety of a yard wherein his warehouse stood, subjected his personal estate to the payment of several legacies, appointed the said Luke and Augustine his executors, and two others overseers of his will.

By a codicil he confirms the bequests in his will, and gives his plate equally to his children, and soon after dies, leaving a considerable personal estate, consisting of money, merchandise, and other goods, whereby a large surplus undisposed of by his will came to his [*339*] said executors, who made no division thereof in the lifetime of Luke.

[On] 4 June 1713 Luke Clerk makes his will, and thereby devises several specific legacies to his son, and to the plaintiff Ann £600, and died four days after, and about eight months after the death of the father.

The will of James was never proved in the life of Luke, but after his death Augustine proved the same as surviving executor.

This bill is to have a satisfaction for the £600 legacy out of a moiety of the surplus of the assets of James the grandfather, which belonged to her father Luke as one of his executors, the said Luke not leaving other assets sufficient to pay and satisfy the legacy.

Augustine clerk by his answer admits, that the assets of Luke were very inconsiderable.

The bill is founded upon this principle of law, that survivorship ought not to take place among joint traders.

The defendant Augustine by his answer insists, that his father was a merchant, and a great part of his assets consisted of lutestrings, wine, and other merchandise, and that he and Luke only disposed of the goods and effects as occasion required as executors, that they received no ships in, or freighted, or traded, but as joint executors to bring home the assets which lay abroad. He admits that he and his brother Luke in the life of their father as joint factors had a parcel of hermitage[1202] and pipe staves consigned to them by one Sheal, that they never traded jointly, but that by commission they returned the produce of these goods in merchandise to Sheal. He admits that they were possessed of the Mary Ann. He denies that it was freighted with the effects of Luke, but that they set it out to freight to Francis Lynch to better the assets, and that the freight by their joint order was laid out in brandy, that the ship returned home, and landed at Dublin after the death of Luke, and he admits the grandfather left sufficient assets.

[1201] 23 February was a Saturday in 1734, Kratz, *Hist. Cal.* The report continues the previous hearing of the case, which is dated December 1733.

[1202] A French wine produced from vineyards on a hill near Valence: so called from a ruin on the summit supposed to have been a hermit's cell. *OED.*

It appears from the proofs that Luke and Augustine were bred merchants, and that Au[gu]stin[e] was out of his apprenticeship but a short time before the death of his father.

I shall consider how survivorship stands between executors at law, and how in equity.

At law if two purchase either lands, or chattels, [*340*] by the same title and conveyance, and one dies before any partition, the whole survives to the other.

Another principle of law is this, that this survivorship can't be severed by the will of the companion.

But a joint tenancy arises by implication in no case but of executors, which is evident from hence, as well as from many other reasons [which] might be offered, that where children take a third by custom, they can't join in a *rationabili parte*, or detinue for the goods, but take them in common, and are not joint tenants by operation of law, and yet the custom casts their part on them, as much as the law does the surplus on the executors, Bro. Joinder in Action, Pl. 93.

Nor did the law thus operate originally as to executors, for all the executors were but one in the eye of the law, and all the effects vested in them as one person.

For many ages personal estates were very inconsiderable, and guided by no certain rules. Executors were formerly accountable before the ordinary,[1203] who allowed them what they expended *pro salute animæ*,[1204] as masses, which they looked on as preferable to debts, or providing for the wife and children, so then they could not be considered as trustees for one another, or the next of kin, but for this charity.

But then the common law interposed, and obliged the executors to be just in the first place, and then they retained the surplus, on pretence, and for fear that debts might appear, and after many changes and struggles the same practice prevailed as to administrators.

Swinburn,[1205] which is a book of great authority, says, that the executor after payment of debts and legacies ought to distribute the residue in pious uses, and has no title to it himself, but only to what the ordinary shall think fit to give him, etc., 2 Book 235, a. Hence survivorship in course of time arose among executors, but survivorship by the feudal law was always uncontroverted, whereas by the testamentary law the surviving executor was only a trustee for charitable uses, 1 Lev. 164.[1206] The surviving executor takes all by our law, but not by the testamentary.

This survivorship then among executors is very different from that established by the feudal law, for no act done by one executor can alter it, nay though they have made an actual partition, they must join in action. [*341*]

I shall next consider the resolutions in equity as to this right of survivorship.

As administrators by degrees acquired the right of executors, so after a positive law was made for distribution,[1207] and administrators were made trustees for the next of kin, and personal estates were greatly increased in value, courts of equity decreed executors also trustees for the next of kin of a surplus undisposed of by the will, and conformed to the ancient common law by which executors were accountable, and

---

[1203] One who has, of his own right and not by special deputation, immediate jurisdiction in ecclesiastical cases, as the archbishop in a province, or the bishop or bishop's deputy in a diocese. *OED*.

[1204] L. for the health of the soul.

[1205] Henry Swinburne (*c.* 1551–1624), *A Treatise of Testaments and Last Wills* (1st ed. 1590, 5th ed., 1728).

[1206] *Guillan v. Gill* (1665) 1 Lev. 164, 83 E.R. 350.

[1207] Statute of Distributions (Ireland), 1695, 7 Will. III, c. 6, above, p. 261 n. 1199.

the time may come when the executors shall be adjudged trustees for one another, as well as for the next of kin.

Is not the step as natural and easy to consider two brothers who are executors trustees for each other, as for the next of kin? And is one case a greater invasion on the common law than the other?

Suppose a father dies worth £10,000, and leaves his two sons executors, and each of them have children, and one dies without any division of the surplus. Why should one be rich, and the other poor, and necessitous. But this is not the present case.

However it has been a question in equity, whether the surviving executor shall have the whole. In the case of *Cox* v. *Quantock*, as it is reported in 1 Chan. Cas. 238,[1208] the [moiety][1209] of the surplus was decreed to [the] representative of the executor, but the decree is said to be to the dissatisfaction of court. But as that case is stated in Finches [*sic*] Reports 176,[1210] it comes very near this case, for Margaret one of the executors died before probate, and the residuum was not devised to the executors, therefore Lord Finch[1211] *sic* first decreed the moiety, for those excellent reasons that are set out in that report, though he was afterwards pleased to dismiss the bill. This was in 1676. Afterwards in 1684 in *Drapers Case*, 2 Chan. Cas. 65,[1212] he said the surviving executor must have all, since the judges would have it so, and the case of *Shower* v. *Billingsley*[1213] 1 Vern. 482 was in 1687, in which the case of *Cox* v. *Quantock* is recited. And there the devise was decreed to be joint, and to survive. 28 June 1679 *Cray* v. *Willis* at the Rolls:[1214] there the devise was to A and B their executors and administrators.

I shall make this observation on all these cases, that they differ from the case before us in this, that there was an actual devise of the surplus to the executors, and the [*342*] survivorship did not arise barely by implication of law. Here is the original foundation for saying they are accountable, whereas by these wills they took jointly. But seeing the courts of equity since the time of Lord Nottingham have made executors accountable, and trustees for the next of kin, I think they ought to be accountable to each other in this case of brothers, and one by survivorship ought not to carry away the whole, but it would be hard for us perhaps to make such a precedent, and in this case there is no occasion for it.

So I shall next consider whether survivorship ought to take place in this case, 1. either in regard to the intention of the testator, or 2. as to subsequent acts.

As to the first, the father was a merchant, and bred his sons Luke and Augustine merchants, and the latter was just out of his time, and he seems to have nominated them executors to encourage them to go on with the business, having devised to them the yard wherein his merchandises stood, and he knew they must trade with the assets, and they had been joint factors in his life. He devises the yard to them as tenants in common, but makes them joint executors, because he knew as they were merchants, they would trade with the surplus, and therefore it would not survive.

[1208] *Cox* v. *Quantock* (1674) 1 Ch. Cas. 238, 22 E.R. 779.

[1209] The word is unclear in the MS. 'Moiety' is suggested by the report of the case.

[1210] *Cox* v. *Quantock* (1674) Rep. Temp. Fin. 176, 23 E.R. 9.

[1211] *Sic*. Sir Heneage Finch (1621–1682) afterwards 1st earl of Nottingham, L.C., known as 'the father of modern equity'. D. E. C. Yale, 'Finch, Heneage, first earl of Nottingham (1621–1682)', *ODNB*, <http://www.oxforddnb.com/view/article/9433>, accessed 9 June 2008.

[1212] *Draper's Case* (1681) 2 Ch. Cas. 64 at 65, 22 E.R. 848 at 849.

[1213] *Lady Shore* v. *Billingsley* (1687) 1 Vern. 482, 23 E.R. 607.

[1214] *Cray* v. *Willis* (1679) Rolls Court, no citation given. See *Cray* v. *Willis* (1729) 1 Eq. Cas. Abr. 243, 21 E.R. 1020; 2 Eq. Cas. Abr. 537, 22 E.R. 453; 2 P. Wms. 529, 24 E.R. 847 although much later is on the same point.

A word 'equally' in a will has destroyed survivorship, and the case of *Morris* v. *Gyles* 1 Vern. 385[1215] shows equity will not interfere to prevent survivorship.

But here the law will decree it a joint tenancy or in common from the intention of the testator, which appears from his making them joint executors, and the necessity there was they should trade with the surplus.

But if his intention is not sufficient, the 2nd point is, whether the acts of the parties haven't made a severance of this even at common law.

The act of either party that alters the privity or tenure severs a joint tenancy, nay less solemn acts *in pais*,[1216] than which alter either, will sever a joint tenure, Bro. Ab. Tit. Joyntenants pl. 37, where survivorship was destroyed by a separate reparation. To apply this to the present case, is not the letting the Ann and Mary [*343*] to freight, as much a severance as the reparation in that case[?] Is not this as strong a proof of their joint trading, as the other of their severance, so the salvo[1217] that they traded only as joint executors will not avail, because 'tis the salvo of the party, and he shan't construe what the law is, since his trading by the custom of merchants will prevent survivorship, Lit. Sect. 282.[1218]

This law is *pro bono publico*,[1219] and the sons of a merchant, who are bred up merchants, and had been joint factors in his life, trading with the joint surplus to improve the assets, and get in those which were abroad, are within the reason of this law, and the distinction that they traded as executors will be of no service, because their trading in any sort brings them within the law.

The only question that remains then is, whether the trading in one instance shall sever the whole assets, or only that part with which they traded. But I shall give no opinion, because the answer makes no distinction, but says, if the plaintiff is entitled, I admit assets. I think her entitled, and that in the case of traders, every advantage ought to be taken in equity. That the law was originally against the survivorship of the assets to executors *jure proprio*, and that to decree them trustees for each other would no more control the law, than the decrees that have been made adjudging them trustees for the next of kin. So I am of opinion that the plaintiff must have a decree for her legacy with interest against Augustine Clerk.

Lord Chief Baron

I am of the same opinion with my brothers for these reasons.

Here are two points of great importance, one, a point of law, the other a construction of fact.

The first is, whether one executor shall account with the other. On the first settlements personal estates were of very small value, and governed by no fixed rules till the establishment of the Christian religion among us, when the ordinary determined according to the common law, and took care of the estates of the deceased, whether they died intestate, or with a will, for he looked on himself as the person who should take care of his soul, which he did by first paying his debts, and disposing of the surplus *pro salute animæ*[1220] in charity, for I so far differ from my brother, that they

---

[1215] *Sic* for *Moyse* v. *Giles* (1700) 2 Vern. 385, 23 E.R. 846.
[1216] LF. lit. 'in the country,' i.e. outside the court.
[1217] In the sense of a saving clause, or reservation. *OED*.
[1218] Co. Litt. s. 282.
[1219] L. for the public good.
[1220] L. for the health of the soul.

always preferred his debts to charities, as appears because an action always [*344*] lay for a creditor.

The administrator was only the committee of the ordinary, not his attorney, for if there were several administrators, the whole survived, he collected, and distributed the assets, and disposed of the surplus at the discretion of the ordinary, as well as the executor. How then came the executor to have the surplus? In the time of H. 8 when the power of the spiritual court was confined, the executor began to think, being exempted from the arbitrary power of the ordinary, that he had the same right as the *hæres* among the Romans. But after the making of the Statute of Distributions,[1221] the courts of equity thought, as an executor was originally a trustee only, and sued and recovered *in jure alieno*,[1222] that he ought to be accountable to the next of kin for any surplus undisposed of by the will, as if the testator had *pro tanto* died without a will, as then he is accountable to the next of kin, why not to his companion, where they take only as executors as if a man names three executors, and two of them are his sons, and gives the stranger a legacy. I believe he would be accountable. *Foster* v. *Munt*[1223] was the first case of this kind. There is one rule to distinguish all these cases by, the intention of the testator, for where the executor has no legacy, 'tis plain the residue was intended him for a benefit, especially if a wife, or relation. After the reversal of *Granville's Case*[1224] all these several cases were reviewed by Lord Harcourt,[1225] and he goes on the intention, and therefore a distribution in one case, because the will was made before the decree in *Foster* v. *Munt*, but I can't say in this case that the co-executor is a trustee for the other, because the bill is not framed so.

But it is the second point which turns me, that it is plain these two brothers were joint traders, and equity will break through survivorship where a family interest comes in question. The separate reparation in Rolls[1226] made a division of the mills, and if joint tenants run a ditch between their lands this is a severance, and there is no survivorship in trade, because it is necessary to be carried on in partnership, and the ruin of a family might be risked by it.

The answer plainly proves them to be joint traders. They traded, it says, as executors. If any loss had happened to the assets, must they have made them good? They invested them in trade, and traded with them jointly according [*345*] to the intention of the testator, though to be sure they might have severed them notwithstanding. So the plaintiff must have a decree for her legacy of £600. But without costs.

But this decree was reversed in the House of Lords on Wednesday the 18th day of February 1735.[1227]

[1221] Statute of Distributions (Ireland), 1695, 7 Will. III, c. 6, above, p. 261 n. 1199.

[1222] L. in the right of another.

[1223] *Foster* v. *Munt* (1687) 1 Vern. 473, 23 E.R. 598 (A. B. by will gives legacies to his children and grand-children, and £10 a-piece to his executors for their care, and makes no disposition of the surplus. Decreed the executors to be trustees for the children, as to the surplus); 2 Eq. Cas. Abr. 443, 22 E.R. 378.

[1224] *Lady Beaufort* v. *Lady Granville* (1710) 3 Bro. P.C. 2nd ed. 37, 1 E.R. 1161 (B made his wife executor, and devised to her the use of his table-plate for life, and after to C, his grandson; but made no disposition of the surplus of his personal estate. Parol evidence was admitted, that the testator intended his wife should have the surplus to her own use; it being only to rebut the construction of a Court of Equity, which would create a resulting trust, and make the executor a trustee for the next of kin).

[1225] Simon Harcourt (*c.* 1661–1727), 1st Viscount Harcourt, L.C.; L.K. 1710 to April 1713.

[1226] Above, p. 264 n. 1214.

[1227] Above, p. 255 n. 1168. *Digby* v. *Hall* (1735) 4 Bro. P. C. 1st ed. 524; 4 Bro. P.C. 2nd ed. 577, 2 E.R. 393. Augustine died intestate and his administrator, Hall, revived the appeal to the House of Lords. Arguments of counsel, but no speeches, are reported in the House of Lords.

Saturday, April the 14, 1733[1228]

In Exchequer

HIS MAJESTY v. SIR WILLIAM COURTNEY

An information of intrusion was filed against Sir William who lived in England, and on an order made, that service of a subpœna to appear on his agent Mr Smyth, should be good service to him, and a motion was now made to set aside this order, and that no precedent could be found of such service being allowed, either of a common law subpœna, or in equity. This was attempted, and refused in Chancery, where a tenant having filed a bill against the trustees and cestui que trusts[1229] of Mr Nutley, moved that service of the trustees might be good service of the cestui que trusts, who lived in England.

Mr Smyth the agent swore, that he believed Sir William was then at his house in Westminster.

Curia

The King here has no prerogative. The agent may not inform his employer, and you may serve his house in England.

Said by Mr Daly, that a demurrer and answer stand singly, and are not to be considered together and as one defence like a plea and answer, and that though all the facts charged in the bill were not denied, that would not vitiate the demurrer, but the plaintiff might except to the answer.

Friday, April the 20 [1733][1230]

LESSEE OF WEST v. SIR HARRY TUTE

This was a trial at bar on an ejectment for non payment of rent on the 8 Geo. 1.[1231]

Sir Joseph Tute executed the counterpart, and Sir Harry who took the defence was a stranger, because not executor of Sir Joseph Tute, nor did he claim as heir.

Question: What [was] the meaning of the words in the Act, 'three year's possession.'

Agreed that the counterpart of the lease would be good evidence against Sir Joseph Tute, or his executors. [346]

The case was this, Mr Haughton having filed a bill against Sir Joseph Tute for a recovery of the lands in question. The parties came to an agreement, whereby Sir Joseph in consideration of £1,000 levied a fine, and conveyed to Haughton in fee

---

[1228] Note that the year is in the MS. and reverts to 1733.
[1229] *Sic*, for cestuis que trust.
[1230] 20 April was a Friday in 1733, Kratz, *Hist. Cal.*
[1231] 8 Geo. I, c. 2 (Ir.), 1721 (preventing frauds by tenants).

(under whom the lessor of the plaintiff claimed) and he redemised to Sir Joseph for 99 years, rendering rent of £500 per annum.

The defendant offered to enter into his title, and to produce a marriage settlement, whereby Sir Joseph was only tenant for life, and consequently had no power to make this sale to Haughton.

The question arose on the defendants being a stranger, and it was said, that no title could be given in evidence, but what went in affirmance of the lease, as if the heir brings an ejectment for the rent. The devisee of the reversion may show his title, because that goes in affirmance of the lease, and that if the defendant should be let in to show a title, that would rob the lessor of the very benefit assigned him by the Act, for if the lease don't bind him, then we must show another title, and be put to make out an original one, contrary to the very end and intention of the Act.

Mr Prime Serjeant for the defendants

We may make out a title against yours, and are not hindered either by the letter, or meaning, of this Act. The intention of all these Acts was to make the recovery of rents easier, and to remove difficulties and delays. And if these Acts had not been made, we might have entered into our title at common law. The question is then, whether they have deprived us of this benefit, and I say not. And that they were made only to overthrow the niceties of re-entry.

This is an explanatory Act of the 9 Ann,[1232] and others, and all explanatory laws are not to be extended by equity, but must be confined to the very words.

Either Sir Harry has a remedy, or not. If not, Sir Joseph might defeat his son who is a purchaser, and load him with the full value of the estate, and the legislature could not intend to give him a greater estate, than he had dominion over. [*347*] But they say we have a remedy by ejectment, that is, that the defendant who is in possession shan't defend himself by that title, but by which he may recover as one out of possession.

[']Or shall show sufficient title['], etc. These words must mean a title upon hearing both sides. What [was the] occasion for these words upon their construction[?] The plaintiff must show a better title than that offered by the defendant.

Lord Chief Baron

These Acts might design to put the stranger on the same foot with the lessee, and had a view to the Acts against force, where three years possession made a title.

Mr Malone

Sir Harry Tute had a right of entry for a forfeiture on Sir Joseph's levying the fine, and another on his death, and he has been in possession since the death of his father, but not under the lease, nor has paid rent. The question then is, whether the Act hinders him to show this right, this title, and defend himself thereby.

[1232] 9 Ann., c. 8 (Ir.), 1710 (landlord and tenant).

Lord Chief Baron

Yes, where the notice is given, that the ejectment is brought for non-payment of rent.

Mr Malone

The title of these Acts is to prevent the frauds of tenants etc. Sir Joseph the tenant never assigned, or attorned to us. What fraud has Sir Harry committed[?] He is no tenant, but the lease determined with the death of Sir Joseph. Where an ejectment is brought under this Act, the lease must be in being, and possession going with it, or handed over to another in possession thereby, and the lessor must have a reversion, and a right of entry in him. But this case has none of these qualities. The lease don't continue, and the defendant is not in possession either by assignment, or attornment.

I would put this case which is not so strong. Suppose Sir Joseph a disseisor, and the disseisee had entered within five years, could Haughton or West bring an ejectment for non-payment of rent, Sir Harry's entry being lawful, is the same thing as if he had recovered by ejectment[?]

Mr Calaghan

This case is not within the mischief of this Act, that the tenant by taking defence in the name of a stranger hindered the plaintiff from giving the counterpart in evidence, and put the lessor to his original title, as in the case of *Byrn* v. *Billingsley*,[1233] and this was the cause of making the Act, which says, that he that [348] has been three years in quiet possession, and shall give a counterpart in evidence, shall be in the same plight as if he had shown an original title, but before this Act if he had shown a bad title he could not recover.

Mr Daly

I shall consider the meaning of the first, and subsequent Acts whereby ejectments are given for no-payment of rent.

By the first, half a year's rent must be due, no sufficient distress, and a re-entry. The next thought fit to tie it up to a year, but gave the ejectment though there was a distress. A mischief was, that tenants by taking defence in the name of a stranger who had no title, hindered the lessor from giving in evidence the counterpart, or arrear of rent, by which means the Act was eluded, and to prevent this, the Act in question was made. But this case is not within that mischief. Here the person in possession is the remainderman, and in by a title paramount, and is not set up by the tenant, or by his fraud, who don't concur in the defence, nor been in possession since the death of Sir Joseph.

The conveyance of the tenant for life was lawful, though by fine for a valuable consideration and passed no more than an estate for his own life, for the fine, the lease, and release, make but one conveyance. If then the remainder continued in him, the possession of the tenant for life was his possession, for the estate for life

---

[1233] No citation given.

and in remainder make but one estate, and if his remainder was turned to a right, he has entered.

The executors might have showed the right to be in a third person, that the reversion was conveyed over to another.

Mr Attorney General for the plaintiff

They cannot show a title both from the letter and intention of the Act.

The defendants have argued from a case not before your Lordship, that we had made out title on the words, 'Other sufficient title['], etc.

This law has laid down what proof is necessary, and if that is made the plaintiff shall recover. He must make due proof of the perfection of the counterpart, that he has been in possession three years, or if he can't make out these, he must show any sufficient title to the premises etc.

'Tis objected, that if West assigned over the reversion [349] the defendants might have showed it.

True, but not as a title in the defendants, but to show that the plaintiff had no title, because of the words. 'Rent due to landlord, or lessor' etc., for this shows that no rent is due to the lessor, and it shall not be recovered, but by the proper person, so that this is a good objection, not from the strength of the defendant's title, but from the weakness of the plaintiff's.

If the counterpart was lost, the proof of it, and the loss of it, would be a good title. *Lord Orrery* v. *Onaghan*.[1234] Bill filed on loss of counterpart. Onaghan sets out the counterpart, but not the clause of re-entry. This point was saved, and this court said, they had showed sufficient title, the counterpart, and payment of the rent, if they could not comply with other parts of the Act.

Under this Act they can't say what estate they have. If the landlord receives his rent, that is all the possession he can have. The possession may be altered, and an assignment made without his notice, and therefore the counterpart is sufficient evidence.

If Sir Joseph Tute was alive, no stranger could have set up a separate[1235] title, and can his death injure us[?] The fine has wrought a discontinuance, and we claim under it, and there is no proof of re-entry by Sir Harry. The mischief this Act was to remedy was, that the plaintiff might not show the title of his lessor, but if they are at liberty to show their title, we must show a prior, and this law supposes, that they who take the defence, came in under this title.

Mr Solicitor General

If the executors of Sir Joseph Tute had handed over the possession to the defendant, or him that had the right, we might recover against them. They are not to suffer another to enter, but preserve our possession to us.

Ante 12.

[1234] Above, p. 13.
[1235] Spelled 'seperate' in original.

Mr Recorder

By the notice the stranger is put in the place of the lessee, and the words, [']or other sufficient title,['] etc., were put in for the sake of the plaintiff, not of the defendant. In the case of *Edwards* v. *Crosby*[1236] 19 years' rent was in arrear. He showed as other sufficient title, lease, entry, and enjoyment. The intent of the legislature was that the plaintiff should not go into the original title, for then he must first have showed seisin, and not have begun with the lease. [*350*] Their title would defeat our lease, but they can set up no title but to show that they have a right to the rent. If Haughton had made a prior conveyance, his right might have been shown, for thereby it would have appeared, that he had a right to the rent.

Mr Baron Wainwright

This is plain from the words of the Act, that if the owner of the land, whether in fee or for years, made a lease, the counterpart should be a good title against the lessee, or his assignee. This prevented the mischief that every one but his own lessee put the landlord under the difficulty of proving his seisin, or title. But on this or other good title, he shall recover according to his title, if the defendant is lessee, or claims under him, by producing the counterpart, but not at all events, if the lease be determined, or the defendant has a prior title, and this title is not destructive of the whole right of the plaintiff, but goes in affirmance of it, for a lease of 99 years is a less estate than for life, and affirms his title during the life of Sir Joseph, and may not the defendant show how this lease is determined in fact, or laid, and so no rent is due[?]

If the fine is a discontinuance, there would be a right of entry in the defendant, which is admitted.

Lord Chief Baron

This is not quite a new case, and many inconveniences may follow from either construction of the Act. One may set up pretended titles in lessors, and tenants on the other hand may put their landlords to show their title against the Act. I think the Acts go no further yet than to take away re-entry, to give the ejectment without distress if rescued, though no proof of sufficient distress, if a year's rent is in arrear.

The construction of the words of the Act, of three years' possession, is not that the lessor must have received rent within three years, or for three years, but to make it appear that the possession was not altered for three years, but continued in their tenants. Now here the possession was altered by the entry of the defendant for the forfeiture, and he may show his title, as well as make it out in case he was plaintiff. So I am of opinion the defendant may join his title.

It appeared that one denomination was in the settlement, [*351*] so whether he could recover for that was the question, or whether the rent must not be apportioned, since part was evicted. In the case of *Usher* v. *Crosby*,[1237] the plaintiff by entry into part, which was her own act, after the ejectment suspended the whole rent, and consequently defeated her whole rent. But in this case the plaintiff can't recover, for how will it appear, that a whole year's rent is due.

Verdict for the defendant, and this point saved.

[1236] No citation given.
[1237] No citation given.

Thursday, April the 26. [1733][1238]

In Exchequer

WHEELER v. HAINES

This bill was brought for a moiety of certain leases, jewels, plate, and other goods, given to the plaintiff by the will of Mrs Haynes,[1239] which her husband the defendant had cancelled, or would not produce.

Mrs Haynes being entitled to several leasehold interests, plate and goods as executrix and devisee of her former husband, Marcus Usher. By articles previous to her marriage with the defendant dated the 14 of October 1699, to which he was a party, conveyed these leases, etc. in trust to pay her the produce for her separate[1240] use during life, with a power to dispose of them by deed or will, which power she executed by will in favour of the plaintiff.

Mr Haines made this defence, that Jane being entitled to these leases as executrix to her first husband subject to his debts and legacies, after several disputes between her and her son Usher, the said son, the defendant, and she [on] 4 December 1707 entered into articles, whereby she was to have £100 a year for life, the son was to pay some of the debts, and to have some of the leases delivered up to him immediately, and the £100 a year after the death of his mother, and the husband was to pay other debts, which he thereby covenanted to do, and to enter into bonds for performance, and then the rest of the assets were to remain to the husband and wife, their heirs, executors, and administrators, and that he accordingly paid £1,800 debts of the testator, whereby he became a purchaser of these assets, and the wife had no power to make this will.

Mr Attorney General for the defendant

Here are two points, 1. What the plaintiff is entitled to [352] under the articles of 1699, 2. If the deed of 1707, and the payment of the money is not a discharge of these articles.

1. She was entitled to the leases mentioned in the articles only as executrix of Marcus Usher her husband, and subject to his debts, but she takes upon her to settle them as her own, and the husband being party, is bound indeed by the assignment.

But the plaintiff has made no title against us under these articles, 1. because the contents of the will are not proved, 2. nor that it came to our hands, and therefore it shall be supposed to be cancelled by Jane and this is confirmed by the oath of the defendant, that he believes it was.

1. One witness only says the will was in favour of the plaintiff, and the defendant Thomasin, which is not a sufficient foundation for a decree. Others swear that her brothers and sisters had a share left them, and they are not before the court.

2. It is not traced into the hands of the defendant. I allow a will, if stifled by the person who is prejudiced by it, may be proved *viva voce*.[1241] The housekeeper only

---

[1238] 26 April was a Thursday in 1733, Kratz, *Hist. Cal.*
[1239] So spelled in MS.
[1240] Spelled 'seperate' in MS.
[1241] L. lit. by or with the living voice, i.e. by oral evidence.

swears that she ordered her will to be made and lodged it with her, with a desire not to show it, that sometime after her husband prevailed on her to show it him, and promised on his honour to give it back again, and that about three hours after he delivered her a paper she believes was the will, which she locked up again in her escritoire, which she delivered after the death of the wife with the key to the defendant, and he swears he returned the will, which is not inconsistent with this deposition, and that he believes his wife cancelled it, and fraud is not to be presumed, and this transaction was 22 years ago.

[2.] As to the second point, if she had made a will she had no such power. This is only an equitable power, which we have rebutted by the equity of the agreement in 1707. There had been several controversies at law on the will of Marcus Usher, and a verdict in the Common Pleas against Henry Usher the son, in favour of the will, at the expense of Mrs Haynes, after Henry filed a bill, and then the parties came to an agreement. She was to have £100 a year in lieu of her jointure, and Henry was to have one lease, and the other, with the rest of the personal estate [353] was to remain to the husband and wife their executors and administrators, and the husband covenants to pay such debts, and makes himself liable to them which he was not before, and so becomes a purchaser of these assets; and it appears by the release of Henry Usher that he has paid them, which is good evidence, because the covenant to pay was made to him, and the wife had a chance to have the whole again by survivorship. So Mr Haynes is a purchaser, and the plaintiff only a voluntary devisee, and though the articles are not mentioned in the deed of 1707, that is not material, if the parties were conusant of their right.

Mr Solicitor General

1. I shall consider whether there is any evidence that Jane executed her power by will, and to decree against the defendant, 2. If there is any proof that this will was secreted, or destroyed by the defendant, 3. If the deed of 1707 is not a waiver of the articles in 1699.

1. I shall consider what evidence there is of this will. 'Tis proved she gave Aspin[1242] directions to draw her will, but the purport of it don't appear, only a general evidence that she designed to do for the plaintiff.

2. A fraud is not to be presumed, but must be expressly proved. The defendant by the return of the will discharged himself, and it is not proved that it ever came again into his hands, for the housekeeper don't swear it was in the escritoire when she delivered it to him. So here is no sufficient proof of the purport of the will, nor is the laceration, or suppression of it fixed on the defendant.

3. By the deed of 1707 the wife executed her power, and this will was void. This agreement varies her interest. The deed is under hand and seal, and is a disposition in favour of her husband. If she had executed her power to the use of her and her husband, the execution would be good, and here the husband paid the consideration. Or if the debts are not paid, he is still liable by his covenant.

[1242]   There is no attorney or solicitor of that name listed in KI AP. KI AP are incomplete: see KI AP, p. viii.

Mr Recorder

I shall insist upon one point only beyond what has been offered, that the defendant by the deed of 1707 was a purchaser of these assets, and that Jane thereby executed her power. Notwithstanding the deed of separate trust, [*354*] the assets were still liable to the debts and legacies of Marcus Usher and if they had been wasted by the wife, the husband would have been liable to a *devastavit*, and can it be supposed that Mr Haynes would by this deed have made himself still answerable for these debts, if they were still to continue in the wife for her separate use, and yet you must put this construction on the deed, if you don't suppose it a revocation, and therefore the covenant is, that they shall hold and retain to their use, and of their executors, administrators, and assigns. So the assets are not to be held for her separate use, and Jane, to make her husband safe, revokes the former articles, and our equitable title is good against yours by way of rebutter.

Mr Hussy

The will was left in Aspin's hands, because it was reasonable to put it out of the power of the husband, and she sent for it, and 'twas brought her home.

Mr Prime Serjeant for the plaintiff

As no creditor of Marcus Usher is before the court, I would consider this case as if Jane was a party, and the dispute between her and the defendant after the execution of the deed of 1707. She was a purchaser in equity of these leases, the right of which would have accrued to her husband by the intermarriage, and she married him upon these terms, and if she is a purchaser, so is the plaintiff the devisee who stands in her place.

2. The second question then is, whether she has executed the power reserved to her by this deed. Aspin swears she give him instructions to draw her will, which he did accordingly, and that she signed and published it, and that it was in favour of the plaintiff, that she delivered it to him, and after got it from him, and gave it to Drinkall the housekeeper, who give it to the husband a few days before her death, that he had it in his custody for three hours, that he returned her some paper she don't know what, which she locked up in the escritoire, and after the death of the wife delivered the keys to the husband. And he swears that after the deed of 1707 he went at her desire to John Fitzpatrick to prepare her will, which he did, and he delivered it to her, and that [*355*] it was in his favour, but she never executed it, then he admits that she was prevailed on to make the will under which we claim to his prejudice. So since once made, and proved to have come to his hands, it lies on him to set it forth, or *in odium spoliatoris*[1243] it must be taken to be as we have shown it.

3. So we are entitled under the will if the deed of 1707 has made no alteration, which it has not. They would imply the husband to be an absolute purchaser from the words 'to the use of them, their executors', etc., whereas nothing was then in contemplation but to settle the differences between the mother and her son, and in equity no one is construed to part with more than he designed, and nothing passes at law, because the legal estate is in the trustee.

[1243] L. through hatred of the robber, thief.

Mr Baron Wainwright

It appears by the marriage articles that the wife had a separate estate in the real and personal chattels during coverture, with a power to dispose of them by deed, will, or writing.

It is said, supposing she made a will, yet by a deed prior to that, these leases were to remain to her, and her husband, their executors, administrators, etc., and that this was a revocation in equity, though not of the legal estate which stood out in Rochfort, or an execution of the power. The wife had no consideration for this deed. The husband could not alter the property, and she had no chance by survivorship, and shall we by implication of law say she has parted with her separate estate, when 'tis plain that this was never the intention of the parties, not even of the husband[?] He says that Fitzpatrick by his orders prepared the draft of a will in his favour. Now how could this will have operated, if her power had been executed by the deed of 1707, and he was very solicitous to see the other will? So equity won't consider this deed as an execution of her power, or revocation.

As to the will, it was last in his hands, and Drinkall says, he returned it, or some other paper, and that she kept it locked up, and delivered the keys to him. So the will is proved, and the execution of it, and that it was last in his hands. He don't swear in his answer he did not cancel it, but that he delivered it to the housekeeper, and that he believes the wife cancelled it. So this is a strong case of spoliation, and everything is to be considered in the strongest light against him. [*356*]

Lord Chief Baron

Here are several concurrent testimonies that this will was destroyed by the husband, though only one positively swears it, and though he is not asked by the bill, whether he cancelled it, he ought for his own honour and reputation to have denied he did. It is proved she desired him not to go to law with his grandchildren, but let them have their legacy quietly, and that the husband desired to have these leases for three or four years after her death, to enable him to pay his debts, though he has denied it by his answer.

As to the question, whether the deed of 1707 has taken away her power, 'tis not good at law, because the legal estate was in the trustees, and could not pass to the husband. So the question is, whether the words, 'To their use', etc. are an equitable conveyance to the husband.

It is a maxim in equity, that the parties shall be construed to have parted with nothing but what they designed, and it was plainly her intention not to part with it, so if her husband took anything, it could be only as his trustee.

Friday, December the 7th [1733][1244]

BOYD v. MONTGOMERY

Mr Daly

Hugh Earl of Mount Alexander in 1716 made his will *inter alia* in these words:

> I do, failing issue of my own body, leave, devise, and bequeath all my lands, tithes, and fee farm rents issuing out of the same, and all my tenements and hereditaments whatsoever, except what is otherwise disposed of by this my will, to my brother Henry for life, remainder to his son Thomas for life, remainder to the first, and every other son of his body in tail, and for want of such issue, to my cousin James Montgomery, remainder to his son William for life, remainder to his 1st, 2nd, 3rd, 4th, & 5th sons in tail, remainder to his brother my cousin Edmondson Montgomery for life, remainder to his 1st and every other son in tail male, remainder to my own right heirs. I do devise my faithful servant Jane Meredith and her heirs all my lands of inheritance [*357*] in the parish of Kilmore, she the said Jane and her heirs paying yearly to my heirs £2 sterling, and no more. I do also devise and bequeath to the said Jane and her heirs the lease of land and tithe I hold from the Bishop of Down. I do also devise and bequeath unto the said Jane and her heirs my house and demesnes of Mount Alexander, and the lease of the 80 acres adjoining to it, which I hold from Mr Ross, and also the chief rent payable to me out of the Cherrysally, with the horse course reserved to me. I do likewise devise and bequeath to the said Jane and her heirs the townland of Ballyhayes, etc., paying to my heirs out of each townland 40s and no more. I do also devise and bequeath to the said Jane and her heirs the lease of my house in Dublin. I do also devise and bequeath to the said Jane all my stock, goods, and chattels, of what nature, or kind soever, and all rents, and arrears of rent that shall be due to me at the time of my decease, over and above what payeth the interest of my debts then due, and my funeral expenses, which I do order and direct do not exceed £100. I do constitute and appoint the abovenamed Jane Meredith my sole executrix.

Then he devises other parts of his real estate to others, and then proceeds:

> I do hereby charge and subject all my real estate to the payment of my debts and legacies, and order and will, and my will is, that if any of my creditors sue my executrix, and recover against her any debt, and the same be paid out of my personal estate, that my said executrix be reimbursed the same out of my real estate, with interest for the same till paid, and all costs she shall be put to on account of such suit; and whereas I am indebted to the above-named Jane by bond dated the 13 November 1709 in the sum of £1,398 9s 10d, I do hereby will and direct, and my will is, that the said Jane be paid the same out of my real estate, and interest for the same until she is paid both principal and interest, and I do hereby make my said real estate liable to the payment of the same, together with what other sums may appear to be due to the said Jane upon the balance of accounts, notwithstanding of the before bequeathed to her, and [*358*] of her being executrix.

The creditors file a bill for sale of this estate, and William Montgomery and his son who are [entitled] in remainder under the will file a cross bill for an account of what debts are really due, that the interest due at the death of the testator might be paid out of his personal assets, and kept down by the tenant for life.

[1244] 7 December was a Friday in 1733, Kratz, *Hist. Cal.*

[1.] The first point we insist on is, that by this will all the interest of the money due Jane by the bond at the time of the death of Earl Henry ought to be paid and discharged out of the personal estate.

The interest of all the debts of the testator is first charged on his personal estate, then the interest of this bond that is charged upon his real estate till paid, must be understood of what interest grew due after his death, when it became a charge on the real estate, and the personal was exonerated.

[2.] The second point is, that all the estate devised to Jane and others, are as well subject to the debts and interest due to Jane, as the bulk of real estate which was devised to Earl Henry.

In the beginning of his will he subjects all his real estate to the payment of his debts and legacies, when he was as well seised of the real estate devised to Jane as of the others, so that whatever real estate seised of at the time of his death was to be charged, and he don't exempt her part by any words of the will. Whereas the dispute being between her and the heir of the family, the devise to her ought not to be discharged, unless the words are plain and explicit.

'That if any of my creditors sue' etc. These words were inserted, because it was in the option of the creditors whether they would fix their demand on the real or personal estate, and he designed to give her the personal estate entire.

3. Henry Earl of Mount Alexander compounded the debt due to Jane, and purchased that, and her interest under the will for £4,000, and he and Hugh the present earl his eldest son joined in a mortgage to Charles Campbell for securing the same, upon which Jane renounced the executorship, and Henry took out administration to Earl Hugh. So Earl Henry being administrator, he is to [359] be considered as a trustee, and whatever composition he made, we in remainder are entitled to the benefit of it.

Or fourthly, as he was in possession of the estate under the first limitation for life, he was trustee not only for himself, but those in remainder, not only to keep down the interest, but for the principal sums.

Mr Coghlan[1245]

[1.] The first point we insist on is, that by this will the personal estate is to keep down the interest of all the debts till paid.

He devises to Jane all the personal estate, except what should be sufficient for his funerals, and to keep down the interest of his debts, so that he gives to her on trust to bury him, and keep down the interest, and the words 'Then due', are to be applied only to the debts, not to the interest. She was to keep down the interest, but to be refunded if any creditor obliged her to pay the principal.

[2.] The next question is, whether the purchase from Jane by Earl Henry shall be solely for his benefit. If I am right in the first point, that the personal estate is the fund for payment of interest, then it is still liable in his hands.

If a trustee buys with a fund that other have an interest in, the benefit of the purchase will accrue to them.

3. Jane conveyed her interest to Charles Campbell, in trust for Henry Earl of Mount Alexander, and she covenants, that neither she, nor Earl Hugh had done

---

[1245] Francis Coughlan, or Coghlan, s. and heir of Cornelius, of King's County; Middle Temple, 12 Aug. 1707, KI, Trinity term, 1712, d. 17 Jan. 1734 in London. KI AP, p. 104.

anything to prejudice the right etc., the said recited will whereby his real estate was made subject to his debts and legacies only excepted. So she was of opinion that his whole estate was liable, and if it should be decreed to be liable, and Campbell paid off any of the debts, he was to have interest for all such sums.

Mr Parkinson

I shall only speak to the point, whether the real estate devised to Jane shall contribute to the payment of the debts. The testator subjects all his real estate, so if the question is asked, what is charged, the answer must be every part, and to apply it only to part of the estate devised, is to contradict the will, and the word 'all' is here expressive. [*360*] 6 Mod. 110.[1246] It shows his intention, and is not to be rejected, but must have a meaning put on it, Fitzgib. 23,[1247] and all devises are to be considered equally, unless there are words in the will to show a distinction, 2 Vern. *Short* v. *Long*.[1248]

Mr Prime Serjeant contra

I shall endeavour to answer the four points [that] have been made by Mr Daly.

1. Whether the interest of the bond due to Jane is to be taken out of the personal estate, or is to stand a charge on the real. The will has directed what burthen the personal estate shall bear, and your Lordship can impose no heavier.

But I shall first beg leave to take notice of the deed of 1718.

Henry disputed the validity of the will with Jane. At last they came to an agreement, that Jane should renounce the executorship, and Henry take administration, that the funerals should be discharged out of the rents, and arrears, and the interest of the debts, if it was not sufficient, out of the other parts of the personal estate, and she was to assign all her interest under the will to Campbell for security of the purchase money, redeemable by Earl Henry, which she did accordingly by this deed in 1718.

[1.] As to my first point, 'tis plain from the will that he designed Jane an absolute estate. He devises to her all his lands in Kilmore paying so much to his heirs, and the whole personal estate was to be hers, paying his funerals, and the interest of the debts then due, and to prevent her being overcharged, he limits the sum which his funerals were not to exceed. So the question is, whether this personal estate shall pay any interest of the debts due to her.

I agree that the personal estate is the proper fund to pay debts, unless there are words to exonerate it as to those who claim by the will, but the creditors indeed must have the option, and though one clause subjects his personal estate to the interest of his debts then due, yet she is not to pay herself the interest of her own debt, but this [*361*] would be going against the words of the will. 'And whereas I am indebted' etc. This part of the will shows he had the former part in contemplation, and is as much as to say, 'though I have devised all my personal estate subject to the interest of all my debts etc., yet notwithstanding this bond debt, and all interest due thereon, shall stand a charge on my real estate.'

[1246]   *Countess of Bridgewater* v. *Duke of Bolton* (1704) 6 Mod. 106 at 110, 87 E.R. 866.
[1247]   *Shaw* v. *Weigh* (1728) Fitzg. 7 at 23, 94 E.R. 628 at 636 (where a word is capable of a proper signification, and may stand, it must not be rejected, but must have such a construction as will make it take its effect).
[1248]   *Short* v. *Long* (1717) 2 Vern. 756, 23 E.R. 1094.

[2.] The second question then is, what real estate shall bear the burthen. The words indeed seem to extend as much as to one estate devised as to another, being subsequent to all the devises of the lands. Yet the real estate intended to be subjected by the will can only be that which is devised to Earl Henry, which plainly appears from these words, 'and my will is that if any of my creditors sue', etc., and he made this provision, because he knew the bond creditors had still a power to come on his personal estate. A reimbursement was designed as a benefit for her. Now what benefit could it be to her, unless it be confined to the lands devised to Earl Henry, unless she is reimbursed by some other person[?] 'Tis not proper to say she shall be reimbursed by herself, but must be by a stranger, by another hand. This is to give her no ease, for 'tis indifferent to her, whether she pay it out of one fund or the other.

[3. & 4.] The third and fourth points are, whether Henry is to be considered as a trustee for those in remainder, either as tenant for life, or as administrator. The personal estate after payment of the interest belonged wholly to Jane, and she might have given it away. Henry purchases both the real and personal estate that was devised to her. What right then has one who is in remainder of another estate to the benefit of this[?] He is a perfect stranger, and as to the real estate nothing can follow but this, that if the real estate devised to her was subject pro rata to her bond debt, this purchase can't alter the nature of the lien, but it must be still subject to a contribution. But this estate has no relation to that of which Henry was tenant for life, and the consequence of their doctrine is only, that a proportion of what was paid for the bond can be charged on the remainderman, but they can't go so far, for Earl Henry at the time of the agreement with Jane had not taken out letters [*362*] of administration to Earl Henry, but administered after, so he was a mere stranger, and if he pays off a debt, the remainderman must pay him two thirds. If Jane had given it him, should the remainderman have the benefit of her bounty, contrary to her intention?

Mr Attorney General

[1.] The first question is, whether the interest due on the bond of Jane Meredith shall be charged on the real estate, or whether the interest due at his death shall be charged on the personal estate, and what incurred after on his real, and the question is, whether he has either expressly exonerated the personal estate from it, or show any intention to do so.

Mrs Meredith is a devisee, executor, and a creditor and she don't claim the personal estate as executor, but as devisee. He not only devises to her all his personal estate, but that she might the better have the full benefit of it, if the creditors came upon it, she was to be reimbursed. But it is said, that this must be understood only of debts recovered against her, but that she could not sue herself. But there was no occasion to indemnify her against her own retainer, but against others suing her. But his intention plainly appears from the *non obstante* clause, 'Notwithstanding the before bequeaths' etc. 'Bequeaths' relate to both the real and personal estate devised to her. Suppose she had assigned over this bond, and the assignee had sued her in equity as executor, then she must have paid this out of the personal estate, and would have been within the very words of the will.

[2.] As to the second point: if this was a controversy between the creditors and devisees the court would make the most liberal construction for their benefit, but here the dispute is between the devisees only, and the fund is sufficient. If this bond had been assigned, she must, as I have already observed, reimbursed herself out of real estate, 'Notwithstanding' etc., that is, 'Notwithstanding I have before given her a real estate which would have been otherwise subject' [*363*] and he subjects her devise to the payment of so much rent only, and no more, so he has charged it expressly, and shown the burthen it should bear.

3 & 4. Henry is not to be considered as a trustee, either as administrator, or devisee. The dispute between Henry and Jane was, whether the will was real. How is the remainderman concerned in that[?] If the will was set aside, he would take nothing, and this composition was made with him not as devisee, but heir, not to insist on that right, and the remainderman has the benefit of this confirmation of the will, and would he have the benefit of the composition too, though he was a stranger to the controversy.

But if Henry was not heir, the remainderman would have no pretension. One devisee buys the interest of another. What right has the remainderman to this[?] It would be something indeed if he had a remainder in the estate purchased.

Mr Malone

It appears to be the interest of the testator that no part of the interest of the bond ought to come out of the personal estate. By the clause whereby he devises her the personal estate, all the interest of his debts is to be paid out of that. But the subsequent clause, 'And whereas I am indebted', etc., explains the former, and shows that the interest of her bond was not to be comprehended under the general word, 'interest', because then there would have been no occasion for this further clause, and the last sentence of it demonstrated that this interest was not to be charged on his personal estate. This explains his intention to be to guard against any such thought, or mistake, that the interest of that also as well as of his other debts was to be taken out of his personal estate.

As to the second point, he describes the devise to Henry by the name of all his lands etc., except what is otherwise disposed of etc., which imports no more than he says, 'I do hereby charge and subject all my real estate' etc., which imports no more than in the first devise to Henry, and the exception is to be carried on to this clause, and only all he had devised to his brother Henry is charged with the payment of his [*364*] debts and legacies, which appears from the subsequent clauses, 'If any of my creditors sue my executrix', etc., which shows Jane was to bear no part of the debts. She is not to be reimbursed any proportional part of what she shall pay, but the whole, and all costs, and she is not to be reimbursed out of her own estate. She is likewise to be reimbursed with interest. Shall she pay herself interest? This shows it was to be a continuing charge on the other lands.

3 & 4. Here is no pretence to say that the purchase made by Henry is in trust for the remaindermen.

First, here is an evidence indeed of an agreement with Jane, but not of any composition, but only of a beneficial bargain to the heir at law.

They can have no trust on the real estate, because the lands were absolutely devised to Jane in fee. Nor they neither had [*sic*], not could have any estate in those lands, because they were neither devisees, or heirs.

As to the money, what pretence have the remaindermen to the debts of Jane, but whether they are wholly a charge, or in part. They must bear their proportion, then will her voluntary disposition of it alter the conditions of it in the hands of Earl

Henry. By the deed of 1718 he gives Charles Campbell security for the payment of it, and his eldest son Hugh, the present earl, joins in the mortgage, and he gives him £100 a year as a consideration, and this estate devised to Henry is carried away from Hugh, and devised to the next son Thomas.

Monday, December the 10th [1733][1249]

Mr Baron Wainwright

The points in question arise on the will of the Earl of Mount Alexander, 1. Whether the whole interest of all the debts shall be paid by Jane Meredith. By the clause, 'I do also devise and bequeath to the said Jane and stock' etc., she is to pay the interest of all the debts then due, and by the clause, 'If any of my creditors sue' etc., she is not to be reimbursed any interest due at his death, because by the former clause she was to pay all then due, but for every principal sum she paid out of the personal estate, she was to be reimbursed with interest out of the real estate. So she was to have no allowance for the interest out of the real estate, but only for the principal money she advanced. [*365*]

The question then is, whether the last clause, 'And whereas I am indebted' etc., the testator has not distinctly considered her debt with the interest of it from his other debts, and made it a particular charge, so that this clause must be considered distinct from the rest, and as a will by itself, without any relation to them. She is to pay the interest only of those debts which she ought to discharge as executrix, the debts of other people, and the words don't extend to her own debt, which she might pay herself by way of retainer. If the will is to be considered in this light her debt is a separate charge on the real estate, and is not one of those whose principal if she paid, she was to be reimbursed.

The question then is, whether she being a devisee of part of the real estate under this will, which subjects all his real estate to the payment of his debts and legacies, whether the estate devised to her shan't bear its proportion, and as all other estates are as much specific devises as hers, so I think hers ought to bear a proportion of all, and her own debt too.

The words '£4 and no more', extend only to the chief rent that is payable to his heirs.

There is no reason to make the estate either real or personal purchased from Jane a trust for those in remainder.

Lord Chief Baron

This bill was brought by the creditors against the devisees, and those claiming under Jane Meredith as devisee, and when the cause was first heard, it was referred to the officer, to take an account of the debts of the testator, and the interest due at, and since his death, and how much had been paid, and to state separately the value of the estates devised, and the officer has made his report, to which no exceptions have been taken.

And these points have been made on the will:

[1249] 10 December was a Monday in 1733, Kratz, *Hist. Cal.*

1. Whether the interest of the money due to Jane at the death of the testator shall be paid out of his personal estate. It is plain it shall not. The whole personal estate is exempted from the payment of the debts, and the principal and interest of her debt is to remain a charge on the real estate.

2. The debts are left a charge on the whole real estate, and it appears to be his intention to exempt the personal estate from all incumbrances, and he has made his real estate liable, and given Jane his executrix a remedy [366] in case she was forced to pay any creditor out of his personal estate. He has made no exception as to the real estate. The will goes no further than to exempt the personal estate from the debts, and to transfer them on the real estate. So the whole real estate devised is liable pro rata to hers and all the other debts.

3. As to the remaindermen having the benefit of the composition, as Henry was administrator, I don't find any evidence of a composition. She has indeed given up her right to the heir. She might have a value for the family whereof she was a servant. She has parted with the whole that was devised to her and given him the benefit of it, and he took out administration after the agreement. Not are they entitled to it as he was a tenant for life. These were different estates, and he has purchased a fee, in which the remainderman had no right.

Be it therefore decreed, that the whole real estate be subject to the principal and interest due to Jane, and to all the other debts due by the testator pro rata, and in proportion to the value reported by the officer.

By the practice of the Court of Exchequer, if the plaintiff obtained a decree, or the defendant a dismission, the party prevailing has costs of course, unless 'tis expressly proved otherwise by the decree, and in a decree to account costs are reserved.

Michaelmas Term, 1733

Saturday, November the 10.[1250]

FRANKS v. ISAAC

Mr Fortescue moved, (after publication was past, and the cause set down to be heard) for leave to exhibit articles to the credit of a witness, on affidavit of her being interested in the cause, and partial to his client, having swore she would pursue her to hell for revenge, if she thought she would come back again, that this was sufficient to discredit a witness, and that the examination being by commission, they had no notice that this woman was to be examined, or they would have exhibited cross interrogatories to her, [367] that they could not apply till after publication because they did not know before who were witnesses, that partiality and interest were sufficient to discredit a witness, and that this was a motion of course in Chancery, and prayed a commission to examine to the proof of the articles.

The chief baron said, it was frequent in the spiritual court to examine to the credit of a witness, because their trials were by witnesses, but that it was sparingly granted by courts of equity, because if they had any reason to suspect their credit, they could send the matter to a trial, and seemed unwilling, and at first denied the motion.

<hr />

[1250] 10 November was a Saturday in 1733, Kratz, *Hist. Cal.*

And Mr Baron Wainwright said, they ought to have shown by their affidavit that her proof was material, and went to the gist of the cause.

At length on importunity the court granted the motion on terms, that the hearing of the cause should be put off, that they should appear gratis, and suffer no Ante 169. conditional decree.

December the 1st. [1733][1251]

In Chancery

BYRN v. RATHBORNE

A lease of the lands of Kilmore in the county of Dublin were decreed to be in trust for the plaintiff, and an account directed of the mesne profits. On exception taken to the master's report *inter alia* of the value of the land, though the profits were contradictory, yet the defendant having been guilty of a breach of trust, and above 80 years of age, the Chancellor would not direct a trial, unless the defendant gave security to pay the balance, which by the report was above £700, but struck a medium himself of £1 3s an acre, for so many years, and 30s an acre after, when the defendant set[1252] a lease of them at that price.

The master had charged the value according to the plaintiff's evidence, at 25s, 26s, 27s, 28s, 29s, 30s an acre, raising every year a shilling, the defendant's proofs were from 15s, to 18s an acre.

June the 30th [1733][1253]

In Chancery

DONERAIL v. DONERAIL[1254]

[*368*]

Lord Chancellor

This bill is brought by Lady Donerail for a specific execution of articles made after marriage, whereby a term of 99 years is raised in trust to pay the plaintiff £300 a year pin money.

The defendant insists, he don't know if he ever married her, or executed the deed, and if he did, 'twas when he was in liquor, by the means and persuasions of the plaintiff.

[1251] Date follows from previous case which was Michaelmas term 1733.
[1252] See above, p. 10 n. 59.
[1253] See below, n. 1254.
[1254] See House of Lords decision in *Doneraile* v. *Doneraile* (1734) 1 Coop. t. Cott. 534, 47 E.R. 987. The report states that the hearing before the Irish court of Chancery was in June 1733: 1 Coop. t. Cott. at 535, 47 E.R. at 988.

But I think if this deed was fairly obtained, as it was after marriage, and the plaintiff brought no fortune, it ought not on the circumstances of the case to be carried into execution.

Though the courtship and marriage were in one day, yet the proofs of his acknowledging her to be his wife are too strong to be denied.

The deed is not an agreement to allow her £300 a year for alimony, but for pin money, and goes on a supposition of their living and cohabiting together. Only four or five were present at the execution of it. The same were by at the marriage, and they swear he was sober when he executed it, and that it was fairly obtained, that he found fault even with the spelling of some words, and that he filled up the blank with £300.

But the transactions that were before, and after this deed create a suspicion. It appears that he was continually fuddled[1255] for some days before and after the execution, and that he was asked some time before to execute it, and he refused.

And there are other circumstances to make me believe it was not a fair deed. There is full evidence of an ill-treatment of his lordship, and a misbehaviour of the lady, such as I don't care to take notice of, even her trustee in these articles, so that the consideration of the deed, which was her good behaviour, is not good, for there is proof of her misbehaviour, and ill-treatment preparatory to the deed.

It is uncertain by what appears on this cause what my lord's estate is, but I have as much [369] reason to believe that I shan't leave him £300 a year, if I take this from him, as that I shall.

Next I shall consider what happened after the execution of the deed.

She immediately withdrew from him, and he advertised that nobody should supply her with necessaries,[1256] and that he was not married to her, so that I would not relieve him against this deed, if he came here as plaintiff.

No relation of my lord was present at the marriage, or execution of the deed, or any lawyer of note.

But I will suppose this deed fairly obtained.[1257] Equity has never decreed alimony in the first instance, but in the case of *Bar* v. *Bar*,[1258] 1 Chan. Cas. 250, at which time the power of the spiritual court was vested by commission in the Chancery, but only out of the wife's own fortune, 1 Vern. 671,[1259] 493.[1260] But the spiritual court can't give alimony till they first decree a separation, which is the foundation. Equity indeed will carry articles, or an agreement for a separate maintenance into execution, because the spiritual court can't assist such contracts, and in that case the husband is to be indemnified against the debts of the wife, as in the case of *Angier* v. *Angier*.[1261] But here the plaintiff would have me decree her alimony, on a deed which was made for a provision for her during cohabitation, and the separation puts an end to the consideration of it.

MSS̃ cas. in Canc.
D.93.

[1255] I.e. intoxicated.

[1256] A husband was liable at common law on contracts entered into by his wife during marriage for necessaries. The husband was here indicating that he would no longer accept such liability.

[1257] I.e. the lord chancellor in the following passages sets out the position, even assuming that the deed was fairly obtained, which he does not accept.

[1258] Case at that reference is *Whorewood* v. *Whorewood* (1675) 1 Ch. Cas. 250, 22 E.R. 785, and concerns alimony.

[1259] 1 Vern. ends at 490 in E.R. See *Nicholls* v. *Danvers* (1711) 2 Vern. 671, 23 E.R. 1037.

[1260] 1 Vern. ends at 490 in E.R. See *Oxenden* v. *Oxenden* (1705) 2 Vern. 493, 23 E.R. 916 (marriage articles).

[1261] *Angier* v. *Angier* (1718) Prec. Ch. 496, 24 E.R. 222; Gilb. 152, 25 E.R. 107; 2 Eq. Cas. Abr. 150, 22 E.R. 129 (alimony).

Here is no evidence of a portion, so it is absolutely a voluntary conveyance in consideration of her good behaviour and cohabitation, and they would have me carry it into execution on another consideration.

He ought not to have published such an advertisement, and she ought to have gone into the spiritual court for a separation and alimony.

This I speak on a supposition the deed was fairly obtained. In this case the plaintiff is not without remedy, but may try her fate at law on the covenant, which was the remedy she provided for herself, and I shan't set the deed aside.[1262]

In *Mildmay* v. *Mildmay*,[1263] the court removed the fraud [*370*] of the husband in buying up leases after an agreement for alimony.

Considering therefore who were present at this marriage, and the execution of the deed, that none of his relations were consulted, that the blank for the allowance was left open, that he was for some time fuddled both before and after the day he executed it, and that he wrote her several kind letters after the separation, that the courtship and marriage were in one day, that no suit was brought in three years, that this was intended as a provision during and in consideration of their cohabitation, considering the facts charged on this lady, and with her trustee too, that I am not satisfied the estate will bear it, that I can't consider this deed as fairly obtained. 'Tis too hard for me to assist the lady, or put the estate in the hands of such a trustee.

Monday, February the 17, 1733, 4 [1734][1264]

POWER v. POWER

Mr Attorney General for the defendants

If her husband transact the jointure, and not the wife, or her friends, and part is evicted, she shall have a compensation by the 10 Ca. 1 ch. 1,[1265] but here it appears by the verdict she had notice by her counsel, so she took it for better for worse, and must stand by it. And if she knew it was only a mortgage, and took it as an inheritance, this was a fraud in her, for if she had no notice, she had law and equity for her.

The lease given her by the will of her husband must be looked on as a satisfaction, for there was a controversy as to Kennedy's demands in his life. She says indeed in her answer, that the lease was given her on terms, that she would permit the executors to take index[1266] of her jointure lands, but she has made no proof of it, and this the executor had a right to do.

The husband warrants only against himself, and those deriving under him, but the mortgage is a title paramount, 1 Chan. Cas. 15.[1267]

[1262] I.e. she had a remedy at law.

[1263] *Mildmay* v. *Mildmay* (1682) 1 Vern. 53, 23 E.R. 305; 2 Ch. Cas. 102, 22 E.R. 866.

[1264] 1734 modern style.

[1265] 10 Car. I, sess. 2, c. 1 (Ir.), 1634 (Statute of Uses). Under section 5 a wife who was given a jointure forfeited her right to dower, but section 6 provided that if a wife were evicted from her jointure, she could again claim dower.

[1266] Word somewhat unclear in MS. Looks like 'indec'. *OED*: 'Index 5 c. A reference list. *Obs.*'

[1267] *Coldcot* v. *Hill* (1689) 1 Ch. Cas. 15, 22 E.R. 671.

Mr Calaghan

If the wife is entitled to any relief on this eviction, [*371*] it must either be on the covenant in the feoffment, on the fraud of the husband, or on the Act.

First, the covenant is no foundation, because it is only against persons deriving under him the said Peter Power, who was only mortgagee, but Kennedy the mortgagor had no title under him.

2. And Peter notwithstanding this special covenant could not be guilty of a fraud in settling this mortgage as an absolute estate, because she had notice of this title.

3. And she is not entitled by the Act, for by it she is to recover out of the other lands whereof she was dowable, but she was not dowable of the other lands, for this settlement being before marriage barred her of dower out of any of them. A jointure was not a bar to dower at law, but his act makes it one, and designed to leave the wife as well as if she had been endowed, but the lands she now enjoys are above half the value of the estate, so she is not within the words, or meaning of the Act, for she never could have dower out of these lands, and she is not in possession of lands of more value.

But if this eviction would entitle her to a satisfaction, she takes under the will cattle, etc., £136, and a lease worth £39 6s a year, which is a sufficient compensation, and 'tis probable the husband intended it one, and made her this additional provision and amends, because he supposed the lands would be evicted, for Kennedy filed his bill in the life of Power, and he owns it in his answer to be but a mortgage. But
Mes App. A.61.   equity will apply it, or not, 2 Vern. 347.[1268] So in *Levinge* v. *Levinge*,[1269] Sir Richard Levinge was entitled to a legacy under the will of his grandfather. The father laid out several sums for him. These were adjudged a compensation for that legacy, though they were advanced by a father, who is obliged to provide for his son.

Mr Prime Serjeant

The defendant Anthony is not executor of Peter, or claims anything by descent from him, or enjoys any estate [*372*] of which she was dowable.

As to the Act, the estate out of which she claims compensation is settled on Thomas the father of the defendant, by that deed on which she grounds her equity, and was a party to, and she takes this for her jointure, though she had no notice that 60 acres were a mortgage, then the question is, whether on an eviction she is entitled to a compensation, and I think on the common rules of equity she is not, because she took it knowing it to be a mortgage, and relied on it, as is plain from the warranty, otherwise the covenant would have been a general warranty to make it good. The statute will not help her, for she was never endowable of these lands, for the settlement whereby her husband was only tenant for life being before marriage, prevents her title, and she being a party to the settlement, consents to the remainder limited to Thomas the brother of Peter, though she would now defeat it.

So she has no foundation for relief, if Peter's will was out of the case.

She says the legacies were not given her as a satisfaction for the deficiency, but the question is, if equity will consider them so. Peter knowing from the confession in his

---

[1268]   *Smith* v. *Burroughs* (1696) 2 Vern. 346, 23 E.R. 820.
[1269]   No citation given.

answer that there was likely to be an eviction, makes this further provision for her, and the lease is still subsisting. 2 Vern. 484,[1270] 558.[1271]

A jointure of a term of years has been adjudged on the equity of the statute to be bar of dower. As this lease then if it had been originally settled would have been a bar to her dower, it may be construed as a satisfaction for it.

Mr Malone for the plaintiff

We ought to have a satisfaction for the lands evicted. And without the aid of the Act the plaintiff is entitled to an original equity.

The plaintiff is a purchaser, and the defendant Anthony claims as nephew and heir of Peter, and under a voluntary settlement, of which he was not within the consideration.

This jointure was antecedent to marriage, and made in consideration of it, and her portion, and part of it is evicted. Why then we are in the common case of any other purchaser [373] who has an original right to be reprized.[1272]

She has also a title from the fraud of Peter, who settled lands in jointure he had no power to do.

But this mortgage comes under the special covenant, for Kennedy derives under Peter the right to redeem, who agreed, and covenanted with him to the purpose.

But though this is a clear point, we need not rest on the covenant, but on the absolute limitation to her for life, which was a fraud, because he knew he had no power to make it.

But 'tis said we are *particeps criminis*,[1273] having notice of the mortgage.

But this objection is of no weight, because there is no evidence that she or those that were concerned in the treaty for her had actual notice, but here is constructive notice of counsel, who was employed by both parties, and not her counsel only, which might make room for the mortgagor to redeem, and the counsel swears he did not advise the woman or her friends of this mortgage. So no fraud can be imputed to her, because she had no actual notice.

As to the Act, they say we have no remedy but on lands whereof she was dowable. The meaning of the Act must be, that she shall have a recompense, not only out of the lands whereof she is dowable, but out of which she would have had a right of dower, if there had been no settlement, otherwise when the jointure is made before marriage, she could have no recompense. Now if there had been no settlement, she would have been endowed out of the reversion in the hands of the heir.

This is not an eviction to recover dower at law, for being only a decree to redeem, it could not be given in evidence. 'Tis said we have had a satisfaction, but the lease may be determined now, though it was in being when the depositions were taken.

But this can't go in compensation, not being devised so. But it is to be considered as a gift, the husband having no children, and his lands being to go to his brother, and equity can't apply this lease as a satisfaction for [374] a freehold. A personal estate may indeed in equity be settled in jointure in bar of dower, but then it must be expressly said to be in recompense and bar, or otherwise it will not, because 'tis

---

[1270] *Mackdowell* v. *Halfpenny* (1704) 2 Vern. 484, 23 E.R. 911.
[1271] *Wilcocks* v. *Wilcocks* (1706) 2 Vern. 558, 23 E.R. 961.
[1272] I.e. compensated.
[1273] L. participants in the crime.

of another nature. It was given her many years before the eviction, the mortgage was old, and might never have been redeemed, so no personalty can go in satisfaction of a freehold without express words.

As to want of parties, it appears the executor of Peter has no assets. If then we have an original equity to be reprized, and we can't have a compensation from him, we must have it out of the real estate, because every limitation of the deed is a covenant from him and his heirs for an enjoyment of those limitations.

But they say, he comes in[1274] under a remainder. But if the heir comes in under a voluntary devise, or remainder, he is to be considered as heir.

So we have an original equity on the fraud, and on the Act, because she was entitled to dower out of these lands, received no satisfaction by the will, and was guilty of no fraud.

Mr Solicitor General

Neither the plaintiff Elizabeth, or any concerned for her, had notice. Lynch the drawer of the deed had notice from a common servant, and he swears he gave no credit to it, and did not tell her, or her friends. This may be sufficient notice perhaps in case of a purchaser, but not of a volunteer. Then on an eviction she is entitled to a recompense not only by the statute, but an original equity.

As the Act was made to protect jointures under settlements, it is hard to say those very settlements should destroy their remedy.

But without the statute she has a general equity as a purchaser of this jointure. All the lands are concluded in the agreement for the jointure, that it will yield such a sum, and the lands bound by the agreement are to make it good, and she is to have a remedy not only against a stranger, but the very issue of the marriage, *Carpenter* v. *Carpenter*, 1 Vern. 440.[1275] So we have a right to be satisfied out of the real estate, and the lands settled are bound to make it good.

The legacies can't be a satisfaction, for 'tis a rule in equity, that nothing can be taken as a satisfaction which is not adequate, but here the lease is not of equal permanency with her jointure, *Savil* v. *Savil*,[1276] but she might outlive the term [*375*] nor will equity decree that a satisfaction, which don't appear to be intended one.

Mr Darcy

Fraud, or covin in the statute, must mean an eviction recovered by fraud with the jointuress, but this suit was adversary.

Mr Daly

We have an original equity, and on the Act without bringing the executors before the court. Peter Power by the settlement is not tenant for life, but in tail, for the

---

[1274] I.e. claims title.

[1275] *Carpenter* v. *Carpenter* (1686) 1 Vern. 440, 23 E.R. 572; *Wasborne* v. *Downes* (1686) 1 Vern. 440, 23 E.R. 572.

[1276] No citation given. *Savel's Case* (1614) 11 Co. Rep. 55a, 77 E.R. 1221.

limitation is to him for life, remainder to the heirs males of their two bodies[1277] etc, so she is endowable of this estate, but if it were otherwise, and he only tenant for life, by their construction a jointure made before marriage could have no recompense, but she is to have a recompense out of that estate, out of which she would have had dower if there had been no settlement. So in equity we are within the letter of the Act, because this eviction is by decree of the court.

The notice is no hindrance, since he settled it absolutely, but if she had actual notice, by the Act she is to have a recompense out of the rest of the estate, then she might take it in this view, 'I don't care if it is a mortgage, for I shall have a recompense out of his other lands.'

And this by the Act is a lien on the endowable lands, and if we could sue at law, we should recover damages off them, so there is no occasion for the executor, and we should not only recover dower but damages from the time of the eviction against her, and won't equity do as much for us?

As to the legacy, there must appear some intention of satisfaction. Though a bill was filed against the husband, he proceeded only to answer, does it appear when he made his will?

This is not an eviction in the life of Peter Power, but when the second remainder came in possession. How can the executors account upon such an eviction? The equity of redemption of one denomination is assets to make satisfaction, though we are not endowable out of it. All the lands descend but the jointure lands.

Mr Francis Blake

The devise of an estate in fee is not a satisfaction at law, unless expressly mentioned to be in recompense of dower, 4 Co. *Vernon's Case*,[1278] and 'tis the same in equity, 2 Vern. 365,[1279] for devises are considered favourably in equity, as well as at law, and by the intention.

Curia

The defendant must account for £18 a year, the value of the lands evicted, from the death of the husband, for the plaintiff accounted for the profits to the mortgagor.

The notice would affect her, if it had been proved, that she [*376*] agreed to take these lands such as they were in lieu of dower.

Their original equity would be proper, if they had parties, but here 'tis founded on the Act.

As she has paid for the eviction from the death of her husband, she ought to have an account from that time.

[1277] Counsel here refers to the effect of the Rule in *Shelley's Case* (1581) 1 Co. Rep. 88b, 76 E.R. 199, 3 Dy. 373b, 73 E.R. 838. The effect of the rule on the limitation as given by Daly is that the life estate to Power would merge with the fee tail given jointly to Power and his wife. The effect of a joint fee tail given to husband and wife, or to persons capable of marrying, is that once the marriage takes place they hold an estate in special tail, descendable only to the issue of the marriage (see Williams, *Principles of the Law of Real Property*, (23rd ed., 1920) p. 143, Lyall, *Land Law in Ireland,* (2nd ed., 2000), p. 231 et seq.) Since in this instance, because of *Shelley's Case,* the life estate would merge with it, they would hold an estate in special tail in possession.

[1278] *Vernon's Case* (1572) 4 Co. Rep. 1a, 76 E.R. 845 (dower).

[1279] *Lawrence* v. *Lawrence* (1699) 2 Vern. 365, 23 E.R. 829 (dower, when barred).

The meaning of the statute is, that dower shall be barred by such means, but if any part is evicted, as to so much it shall be no bar of dower. Then the consequence is, that she shall recover dower as at common law, and damages by the Statute of Merton,[1282] and this being an eviction in equity, we ought to give the remedy she would have had at law.

Mr Baron Wainwright thought, she ought to recover from the time of the eviction only, and the £191 damages from the representatives of the husband, who were to make it good in the first place.

The parties were to consider, whether they would account, or pay the £191 damages, and the £18 a year from the eviction.

HIS MAJESTY v. GARRET BOURKE

Mr Caulfield for the defendant[1283]

This comes before the court on a demurrer of the Attorney General to the traverse of an inquisition upon an outlawry. Mr Bourk[1284] as an inducement to his traverse sets forth, that Wm Burk[1285] being indebted by bond to Andrew Blake, he obtained judgment, and extended the lands of six denominations, and assigned his interest in three of them to the defendant, and avers the three denominations to be part of the lands found by the inquisition, and that the debts are not paid.

The questions are, whether we have a good title, and have set it forth well.

We have a good title for three reasons. 1. The crown has no prerogative that can be applied to this case. 2. The duration of the estate don't depend on the extended value. 3. It don't appear that the debts could have been satisfied by the extended value.

1. The King is to be satisfied before other debts, but here his title is to the forfeiture, and not to a debt, and the interest a third person had before the outlawry is not to be defeated, nay after the outlawry, and before seizure [377] an extent, or alienation will defeat the forfeiture. This is an outlawry in a civil action on mesne process.[1286] Raym. 17, 1 Lev. 33 *Windsor* v. *Saywell.*[1287] This estate by elegit is an estate that vests by operation of law, which is stronger than where it is created by the party, and vested

---

[1280] *Gervoyes Case* (1592) Moo. K.B. 717, 72 E.R. 860 (baron and feme).

[1281] *Wrotesleys Case* (1540) Moo. K.B. 721, 72 E.R. 863.

[1282] 20 Hen. III, c. 1, 1235 (damages on writ of dower), extended to Ireland by writ, 1236, confirmed 13 Edw. II, c. 2 (Ir.): Berry, *Statutes, Ireland,* at pp. 27–30, p. 281, Donaldson, 'The Application in Ireland of English and British Legislation', p. 381.

[1283] Probably St George Caulfeild (spelled 'Caulfield' in MS.), fourth son of Caulfeild J. and Lettice, da. of Sir Arthur Gore. Entered Middle Temple, 1716, called to Irish bar, 1723, M.P. for Tulsk, 1727, counsel to revenue board, 1734, S.G., 1739, A.G., 1741, C.J.K.B., 1751, d. 1778 (Ball, *Judges in Ireland,* ii. 208; KI AP, p. 81.)

[1284] So spelled in MS.

[1285] So spelled in MS.

[1286] Process of the court which began after an action was commenced and continued only until judgment was given. The complementary term 'original process' referred to the issue of an original writ beginning an action, but after the practice was adopted of beginning an action by judicial writ, 'mesne' process was no longer used in its literal sense. Final process was the process of the court concerned with the execution, i.e. enforcement, of judgments.

[1287] *Windsor* v. *Saywell* (1661) 1 Lev. 33, 83 E.R. 283; *Windser* v. *Saywell* (1661) Raym. Sir T. 17, 83 E.R. 10; *Windsor* v. *Seywell* (1661) 1 Keb. 74, 83 E.R. 820 (outlawry, alienation before seisure).

even before the outlawry. So no prerogative can be applied to this case, but it must be considered as if it stood between party and party.

2. The estate of the tenant by elegit may continue longer or shorter than it will if computed by the extended value. Casual profits will determine it sooner. So where the creditors can't enjoy the profits, it may continue longer, as if the widow of the debtor recover dower, the tenant shall hold over, or if the debtor ousts the tenant, or if the profits are lost without his wilful default, as by inundation, or the like, 2 Saund. 71 *Underhill* v. *Anon.*[1288] So the law takes notice that in several cases the extended [value] ought not to be the measure, and we have averred all the debts to be still due, and that general averment is sufficient, without entering into all the particular reasons why 'tis not satisfied, Hard. 75 *Attorney General* v. *Buckridge,*[1289] and the distinctions in that case are observable, and a more particular averment is not necessary. This is a collateral circumstance to defeat his estate, and therefore they must plead it.

3. The six quarters are extended at £140 per annum. What are the value of the parts assigned don't appear to the court, and though we say Andrew Blake was seised, it don't appear he was in actual possession, and the sheriff don't, nor ought to give actual possession on an elegit, least he should turn out a tenant who has a title, 4 Co. 8,[1290] *Bevil's Case.* So if he was seised in law 'tis sufficient to justify this form of pleading, so that Andrew Blake might never have any benefit of this extent, or been in actual seisin.

Tuesday, February the 6th 1732, 3 [1733][1291]

Mr Roach for the defendant[1292]

By 33 H. 8 ch. 39,[1293] the King is to be preferred if there is no judgment, which shows he is not, if there is one. Hardr. 23,[1294] Shower Parlt. Cas. 72,[1295] Raym. 17.[1296]

The extended value does not bind: Hard. 79.[1297]

Mr Attorney General

The traverse is bad in form, and substance. He [*378*] that would traverse the King's title must set out a good title in himself, and here is no traverse of Mr Bourk, if he hadn't set out a good title in law or equity. He traverses three denominations which are not in our inquisition, but in his plea. He avers them to be part of Kilcornan found in our inquisition, and if he had made a good title he might have traversed them. But he has made no title, for by the inquisition under which he claims they

---

[1288]   *Underhill* v. *Devereux* (1669) 2 Wms. Saund. 68 at 71, 85 E.R. 698 at 713.
[1289]   *Attorney-General* v. *Buckeridge* (1652) Hard. 75, 145 E.R. 388.
[1290]   *Bevil's Case* (1575) 4 Co. Rep. 8a, 76 E.R. 862.
[1291]   1733 modern style. Note that the year has reverted to 1733.
[1292]   There is no barrister of that name listed in KI AP, but it may be misspelled, and KI AP are incomplete: see KI AP, p. viii. There is a James Roche, listed only as a barrister, *c.* 1734; KI AP, p. 425.
[1293]   33 Hen. VIII, c. 39 (Eng.), 1541 (English crown debts).
[1294]   *Attorney-General* v. *Andrew* (1655) Hard. 23, 145 E.R. 360.
[1295]   *Rex* v. *Baden* (1694) Show. P.C. 72, 1 E.R. 50 (outlawry).
[1296]   *Windser* v. *Saywell* (1661) Raym. Sir T. 17, 83 E.R. 10.
[1297]   *Attorney-General* v. *Buckeridge* (1652) Hard. 75 at 79, 145 E.R. 388 at 390.

go by another name, and he has not averred them to be the same. But as to one that is the same, he has shown no title, and it is part of the King's prerogative, that the King's title, which is by record, should not be disturbed without showing a title. The judgments were obtained by Andrew Blake, and not assignable at law, and he traverses in his own name, and makes title to other judgments on which no elegits issued, and there was no possession in the other. There were four judgments, elegits taken out on two of them, and not on the other two, and the other not in possession, so they are not assignable, and Bourk pleads them all, and insists on the benefit of them all.

But suppose he had pleaded the same denominations, and elegit. He has not shown a sufficient title.

The money on the first judgment extended was £142, and on the other £40, and the extended value of the moiety is £141 19s 0d. Both elegits are extended the same day, 19 August 1726. And both are judgments of the same term, and therefore he has the whole lands given him by the elegit, then he must be paid off in 1728, and yet he says the last Trinity term the whole money was remaining unpaid, though he says Blake was in possession in 1726, and he in 1728. And this is conclusive on him, for at law he is to take them at the extended value, and the party must show on record the fact to be otherwise. And casual loss or profit is not to be presumed, but must be averred, in 4 Co. 67b, Hardr. 75[1298] The difference appears between a statute merchant[1299] and an elegit. It appears by the record Bourk must have received more than six times his money, and he can't aver against the record, nay against what he has shown himself, but such averment is a nullity.

Wednesday, November the 28, 1733.[1300]

Mr Baron Wainwright

[*379*] The plea of the defendant is bad in four particulars.

1. Because he don't say, that those under whom he claims were in possession by virtue of the elegit, but only sets out a title at law in them.

2. Supposing them in possession, no legal conveyance to himself is set out. He only says, they conveyed their right and interest.

3. If they were in possession, it appears the judgments were satisfied, and if they are not satisfied, the defendant ought particularly to have shown it, and the reasons why they were not.

4. If these points were with the defendant, it don't appear that the lands in the inquisition and elegit are the same, only one denomination, Knoctigaranbane, is the same.

It appears in his own plea, that the judgments only, which are choses in action, were assigned to him.

[1298] *Attorney-General* v. *Buckeridge* (1652) Hard. 75, 145 E.R. 388.

[1299] An ancient form of bond, introduced by the Statute of Merchants, 1285, 13 Edw. I, st. 3, (applicable to Ireland through Poynings' Law: see above, p. cli) allowing land to be charged with debts incurred in trade, which would otherwise have been contrary to feudal principles.

[1300] 28 November was a Wednesday in 1733, Kratz, *Hist. Cal.*

Lord Chief Baron

The traverse is not to be supported, and the demurrer must be allowed. He has not maintained by his plea, that Wm Burk was not seised at the time of the inquisition, for no actual possession was given on the elegit, and if an ejectment had been brought, a legal defence might have been made to it.

Tuesday, November the 20, 1733.[1301]

DAWSON v. SPIERS

Mr Calaghan

Moved, that the defendant being an executor might not be obliged to give security, though process of contempt to a commission of rebellion had issued against him, and mentioned the case of *Blake* v. *Kirwin*,[1302] 9 December 1723, *L[. . .]ot* v. *White*,[1303] 23 June 1721, both in this court, where it had been so ruled.

Mr Attorney General

There are many late precedents to the contrary.

Curia

Produce precedents next motion day, and stop in the meantime.

Saturday, December the 7th. [1733][1304]

The case of *Head* v. *Lake* 26 June 1733[1305] in this court was read, where the court ordered on the motion of Mr Tench,[1306] that the defendant should make affidavit to ascertain the value of the assets, and that upon paying the costs of the process of contempt, the defendant be at liberty to give security to the value of the assets to abide the decree. Made by consent. [*380*]

Mr Calaghan

The executor is not at all events to pay, whether he has assets or not, and that they would have him give bail under that difficulty, though he may not be liable to pay anything. On a common law subpœna if the process runs to a commission of rebellion, the executor don't give security.

[1301] 20 November was a Tuesday in 1733, Kratz, *Hist. Cal.*
[1302] Above, pp. 23 [*27*], 73 [*87*].
[1303] The middle of the plaintiff's name is obscured by an ink blot in the MS.
[1304] 7 December was a Friday in 1733, a Saturday in 1734, Kratz *Hist. Cal.*, but the previous date in the MS. is stated to be November 1733 and the case continues.
[1305] No citation given.
[1306] Robert Tench, KI, Michaelmas, 1713; KI AP, p. 476.

Mr Eustace

On other cases where the party won't answer, the presumption is that the demand of the plaintiff is just, and that therefore shall be the measure of the bail, but what measure can the court go by to compel the executor to give security, for though the demand should be presumed just, he is not to pay it unless he has assets, and it don't appear, whether he has any, or what effects, because they won't receive the answer till he give security.

Mr Attorney General

They have lain by three terms, and in the answer they admit assets. We only ask security for them, and this can't be grounded on the prerogative process, for then it would be so in the Exchequer of England.

Sir John St Leger

Either the executor is guilty of a *devastavit*, or not. If he is, he ought to give security, and must answer it *de bonis propriis*. If he is not, it will do him no hurt, for the security is only to abide the decree which can be but to answer as far as he has assets. The executor is equally a contemner[1307] of the court with one sued in his own right. This may encourage them to stand out, and in the meantime they may waste the assets.

Mr Baron Wainwright

This prerogative is not in Chancery, but is founded on the writ on the common law side, where the giving security don't extend to executors. How then can we alter it[?] We should hurt the subject to extend it, and we have no measure to go by. The defendant in other cases knows, whether the demand of the plaintiff is right, but the executor may not know whether it is or no, and considering the many suits he is liable to, it is hard he should give security. And the defendant has produced two precedents for him, and the other against him was scarce allowed. We ought not to go farther.

Lord Chief Baron

This is a prerogative process. 'Tis only the suggestion of [*381*] His Majesty's debtor and farmer that gives us a jurisdiction.

We will see how far the prerogative process, which was calculated for the advantage of the King and his debts, could influence this equity process, in which the court takes the best method they can. Sequestrations were not at first carried as far as they are at present. The court may now take the party on an attachment, and admit him to purge himself as they please. Chancery don't require security. This court does where the process has run to a commission of rebellion. We may proceed for contumacy as we please, but 'tis hard in a particular case to bind the party, for till he has purged

1307 I.e. one who commits a contempt of court.

himself he can't put in his answer. How then shall we measure the security? We must believe precedents,[1308] and the party has a right according to the course of the court to have his answer received. So the executor need not give security, for if by the rule of the court he is entitled on purging his contempt to have the answer received, we can't alter it in a particular instance.

A notice to set aside process for irregularities will not stop process either in the Court of Exchequer, or Chancery.

'Twas settled in the Chancery on consultation with the Court of Exchequer by the present lord chancellor, that a pauper and a dives[1309] should not be joined as plaintiffs, for one may be made a defendant. This rule was made on complaint of the officers, that the copies of pleadings and orders were always taken out in the name of the pauper.

In Chancery, if either side take out a commission to examine witnesses, the other has a commission of course, but in the Exchequer, to prevent delay, neither the plaintiff nor defendant can have a separate commission, without an affidavit of the reasons why they could not examine on the joint commission.

Monday, November the 12 [1733][1310]

SKIRRET v. PIERCE

Moor gave a certificate of what passed at a conversation, and being examined as a witness, swore this certificate was true. The court would not allow the certificate to be read, but said, they should have examined him to the facts certified.

And Mr Baron Wainwright said, he did not know how he could be indicted for perjury, if any part of the certificate was true. [*382*]

Wednesday, June the 6th [1733][1311]

LEWIS v. DELARUE

Delarue filed a bill of redemption. The defendant in his answer insisted he had no right to redeem, and claimed the benefit of articles, an account, and redemption was decreed, and a bill was filed by Lewis for a discovery and relief as to improvements in aid of the account, and that the proceedings might stay in the meantime, to which the defendant demurred, and Mr Daly for the plaintiff mentioned the case of *French* v. *Kirwin*[1312] in Chancery. The bill was to redeem. The defendant insisted on a release of the equity, but it being obtained by fraud the plaintiff had a decree to redeem, yet

---

[1308] Spelled 'presidts' in MS.

[1309] L. *dives*, rich, a rich man. Thought to have entered English from the Latin Bible, Luke 16.1. See Henry Parker, *Here endith a compendiouse treetise dyalogue of Diues [and] paup[er], that is to say, the riche [and] the pore fructuously tretyng vpon the x. co[m]manmentes*, (London, 1493).

[1310] 12 November was a Monday in 1733, Kratz, *Hist. Cal.*

[1311] 6 June was a Wednesday in 1733, Kratz, *Hist. Cal.*

[1312] No citation given.

in that case the defendant was allowed his improvements, a house he had built, and an issue was directed.

And Mr Solicitor General quoted the case of *Reeves* v. *Reeves*[1313] in Chancery; he was decreed to such money as he stood engaged for his brother on securities, after he filed a bill in aid of the account for an allowance of what he had advanced for his use. NB. There was no demurrer.

Lord Chief Baron

A bill may be filed to set aside a decree in the whole, or in part, but if a bill prays such general relief which if true would set aside or vary the decree, and in aid of the account, he prays things that are inconsistent, for there must be a decree of the court upon such a bill too.

Sir John St Leger

This is to pray a new allowance, a new account.

Mr Baron Wainwright

A bill in aid of an account is for a discovery only, and must affirm the decree, and the account as directed, but if one comes to the knowledge of a thing after a decree, 'tis proper to bring a bill: this bill is to subvert the account of which you pray in aid, and if it prevailed, we must direct a new account: from the circumstances of the case we would not decree a general account from the time the defendant came into possession, but only from the filing [of] the bill, but till that time set the profits against the interest, this bill is to have the account taken from the beginning. [*383*]

Thursday, June the 7th. [1733][1314]

In Exchequer

CAMPBELL HAMILTON ET UX. v. JANE HAMILTON, ADMINISTRATOR TO HER HUSBAND

Sir Hans Hamilton being obliged to go into Holland, deposited some deeds, family pictures, and other things of value with Mr Hamilton, and this bill is brought by the plaintiff his daughter as his heir and executor against the administrators of Hamilton to have them delivered up.

The defendant insisted on being first paid £100, which the husband had lent, advanced or remitted to Sir Hans, and the proof not being clear, an issue was directed, but the court were all of opinion, that this being a demand on the assets and no other appearing, the defendant had a right to retain them, though they

MSŠ cas. in Canc.
D.13.

[1313] No citation given.
[1314] 7 June was a Thursday in 1733, Kratz, *Hist. Cal.*

were not originally designed as a pledge, but were deposited in trust, for when Mr Hamilton after lent him the money, the original trust as to so much was altered, as if goods are consigned to a merchant, if he has any demand on the consignor, he may retain them till satisfied.

The case of *Lord Mountcashell* v. *Delamere*[1315] in this court was mentioned. The bill was filed for the title deeds. The defendant insisted on being first paid a bill of costs, but the court obliged him to deliver up the deeds, because the debt did not bind the heir, and was no lien on the estate, but the executor, and from the great inconvenience [that] might follow, to keep an heir out of his deeds, when he wants them to go to law.

Tuesday, June the 12 [1733][1316]

In Exchequer

WIDNAM v. TUBBS

An order for an attachment being made absolute, Mr Recorder came to show cause on their own affidavit, and took this distinction, that the person in contempt can't discharge himself by other affidavits, but must answer personal interrogatories, but he may except to the affidavit in which it is grounded, and show it to be insufficient. The affidavit charges him with arson and murder, and he ought not to be put to answer to criminate himself, [*384*] that personal interrogatories being in favour of the person sworn in contempt, if he should demur to them, that would be taken as an admission of the crime, and mentioned the case of *Blake*, who came to the Lord Chief Baron Gilbert's,[1317] and told his Lordship, he had lately made a decree in his favour, that such a cause of a friend of his stood in the paper, and if he would bring it in the eight days[1318] he had a hundred guineas at his Lordship's service. The lord chief baron afterwards seeing him in court, had him on the table,[1319] where he swore one Martin persuaded him to make the offer, upon which Martin was attached, and demurring to the personal interrogatories, Sir John St Leger took the charge to be true, and fined him £100.

The court in this case said, they ought not to compel him to what the judges of assize would fine a justice of [the] peace if he obliged the party to answer, but they thought though the court would commit him for the contempt as true by his demurrer, that that would not be evidence against him at law, and so would not allow the cause.

[1315] No citation given.
[1316] 12 June was a Tuesday in 1733, Kratz, *Hist. Cal.*
[1317] I.e. to his house, presumably.
[1318] The eight days after the end of the regular term when the Exchequer continued to sit.
[1319] Perhaps standing on the Cheque. Below, p. 334 n. 1475.

Tuesday, June the 26. [1733][1320]

The first of the eight days after Trinity term.

KING v. THOMPSON AND LORD ORRERY

The bill was to be relieved against an ejectment brought by Thompson lessee of Lord Orrery.[1321] Thompson obtains a *dedimus* without an injunction. The commission not being taken out in the usual time, the plaintiff seals an attachment against him, and obtains an injunction on it as a motion of course. The court set aside this injunction on the motion of Lord Orrery, because he being only a nominal person, his answer could be of no service to the plaintiff, not could he be in contempt, but the defendant was to pay the costs of the attachment.

Saturday, November the 25, 1732.[1322]

In Exchequer

ATTORNEY GENERAL v. NUGENT[1323]

Ante 46. Counsel for Ignatius Nugent moved for a rehearing. No precedents could be found for, or against, a rehearing. The Attorney General would not cons[en]t.
Curia advisare vult.[1324]
Denied. [*385*]

MSŠ ord in. Canc. 67, 63. It was laid down as a rule in the common law side of the Court of Exchequer, that a rule to pay money ought to be served personally, and that there must be affidavit of such service, and a power to the person to receive the costs, before the other could be in contempt.

[1320] 26 June was a Tuesday in 1733, Kratz, *Hist. Cal.*
[1321] Above, p. 229.
[1322] 25 November was a Saturday in 1732, Kratz, *Hist. Cal.* Note that the year reverts to 1732.
[1323] Continued from p. 80.
[1324] L. the court will be advised (before giving judgment).

Tuesday, November the 14, 1732.[1325]

In Exchequer

HORAN v. ARCHDEKNE[1326]

A rehearing was granted the 8th of July, but the £5 was not lodged till the 18th (whereas by the course of the Exchequer the petition is to be preferred before the enrolment of the decree, and the money lodged in four days after) which was plainly done to delay the enrolment, and now it was moved on a new petition to rehear, and they insisted that the money not being paid within the four days, they might have enrolled the decree, which they had neglected, and by that given them a new title.

But the case of *Donellan* v. *Eyre*[1327] in Easter term 1731 was quoted. There the money was tendered in six days to the attorney who refused it, and a second rehearing was denied, because the terms of the order were not complied with, and if there is no tender, or payment of the money in four days, the petition is discharged of course. But 'twas said in that case, there had been a conditional decree, that made absolute, the petition to rehear granted, and that Eyre having brought a cross bill for delay, the money not being lodged, the petition was discharged, and no second petition was lodged.

Post 432.

Mes App. G.119.

The rehearing denied.

Wednesday, November the 22nd [1732][1328]

In Exchequer

BAKER, A MINOR, BY HER PROCHEIN AMY v. LEIGH

The bill was to set aside a purchase as obtained from the father of the plaintiff during his minority, and charged notice in the defendant of his being a minor.

The defendant pleaded himself a purchaser for a valuable consideration and denied the nonage, and notice. The plaintiff allowed the plea, and filed a general replication, and a special one as to the nonage, and at the hearing made no satisfactory proof of the nonage, none of the notice. [*386*]

John Baker the plaintiff's father in 1704 sold the lands in question to James Leigh, who was married to his mother, and lived ten years after, and never impeached the purchase, but three years after the sale James and he executed general releases. James Leigh sold these lands to Higgins, and he to the defendant, the brother of James. 'Twas insisted for the plaintiff, that James was only 19 years and a half old when he sold.

The defendant proved that he had before, and at the time of the sale, levied fines, executed bonds, confessed judgments, and solicited an Act of Parliament in England in behalf of himself, his mother, and sisters.

[1325] 14 November was a Tuesday in 1732, Kratz, *Hist. Cal.*
[1326] Continued from p. 135.
[1327] No citation given.
[1328] 22 November was a Wednesday in 1732, Kratz, *Hist. Cal.*

The court thought here was too long an acquiescence to give any relief, even if the bill had been brought against James Leigh, that a fine levied by an infant can only be reversed during nonage, and supposing him a minor, we must presume at least that the purchase money was paid, or that John Baker would have sued either for that, or his estate; as the law gives infants great privileges, as that bonds given by them even for necessaries are not good, so are purchasers favourites of this court, and matters are to be construed with equity and justice even against minors, and if John Leigh the defendant had notice that John Baker was an infant at the time he sold to James Leigh, yet his release, and long acquiescence after, amount in reason and equity to a confirmation after he came of age.

Tuesday, and Wednesday, November the 27 and 28, 1733[1329]

Michaelmas Term

In Exchequer

LESSEE OF HILL v. LORD HILLSBOROUGH

Mr Parkinson

This ejectment was brought in the last Trinity term, as of Easter, and on the last day of the term there was the common rule for judgment, unless a plea in four days. The fourth day was the 18th of June. The 19th in the morning before the judgment was entered, we [387] tender a plea of *non cul[pabilis]*, and the costs, which the officer refused to accept, because the plaintiff's attorney had been just before with him, and marked the declaration for judgment, though the assizes were not till the first of August. Then we moved the barons in the chamber, who told us they could do nothing in it, the common law side of the court being shut,[1330] upon which we apply to the attorney, show him the plea, and offer to take any notice of trial, which he refusing, we brought a writ of error; we have an affidavit of all these matters and the judgment is not yet entered. I therefore humbly hope your Lordship will set the judgment aside, and order our plea to be received.

The court have set aside a regular judgment, where the plaintiff has not lost his trial, Salk. 402,[1331] 518,[1332] and in 516[1333] 'tis laid down as a rule, that it may be done till possession is delivered.

We applied to your Lordships, did everything in our power, and affected no delay.

[1329] The dates are correct for 1733, Kratz, *Hist. Cal.* Note that the year changes to 1733.

[1330] A peculiarity of procedure. They were the same judges in law and equity, but the common law courts did not sit outside term, whereas a court of equity could do so.

[1331] *Sisted* v. *Lee* (1704) 1 Salk. 403, 91 E.R. 349.

[1332] *Wood* v. *Cleveland* (1700) 2 Salk. 518, 91 E.R. 441.

[1333] *Anonymous* (1697) 2 Salk. 516, 91 E.R. 440.

Lord Chief Baron

This is not in our power, for you have removed the cause by writ of error returnable the first of this Easter term. Show us some precedents in our own court where this has been done. The rule in England are [*sic*] not the law of our court.

Mr Recorder

Judges in their chambers have a power over ejectments, and we'll waive our privilege. Though the judgment in ejectment is not conclusive, it ought to be set aside, because they had been at no loss when we tendered our plea. The last case quoted from Salkeld is in ejectment. Here no judgment was entered, but only the declaration marked, and the officer might have received it, and your Lordship can't put us in the same plight. We must lose the possession, and be plaintiff instead of defendant in a new ejectment, and the judges in these cases always consider whether the right has been tried.

Mr Daly

These motions to set aside judgments and put in pleas are in the discretion of the court. These are feigned proceedings, which are confined indeed to rules, but your Lordship will rather relax them, than strip us of the possession, and if the plaintiff had accepted the plea on the 19th, he would have lost no advantage he had by its coming in the 18th.

Mr Arthur Dawson

The Executors of Bargery v. *Pierce*,[1334] action on a bond. [*388*] The declaration was marked for judgment for want of a plea, and your Lordship allowed the defendant to take defence, on paying costs, and tendering an issuable plea.

We have complied with the reason of the rule, that the plaintiff might be sure of his trial at the next assizes.

The record remains in court to some purposes after a writ of error is brought, as to amend, etc., and we consent to withdraw it.

Mr Attorney General for the plaintiff

I shall consider these two points, 1. Whether your Lordship could set aside this judgment, when the record is before you, 2. Whether you are not barred by the writ of error.

As to the first, 'tis allowed that the judgment was regularly signed for want of a plea according to the rules of the court, but they would have your Lordship dispense with them. The rules of the court are the law of the court, of which the subject has a right to have the benefit, unless he has been guilty of some fraud.

Two of the cases from Salkeld are not in ejectment, and the court would stretch a rule as far as they could, where otherwise the party would be barred forever, but

---

[1334] No citation given.

here the defendant only loses the possession, but his right if he has any, remain still with him.

The other case in Salkeld is indeed in ejectment, but it is only the saying of Lord Chief Justice Holt, but the practice of every court is the law of that court, and 'tis nothing to their purpose, if 'tis not the law, and practice of this court.

But such a practice is contrary to law, because the judgment is the act of the whole court, and one judge can't set aside, or control it.

But if they had a mind to do everything in their power, if they expected a favour, they should have consented to waive their privilege.

As to the second point, suppose your Lordships would interpose, I presume it is not in your power after the writ of error is returned, for the proceedings are now in the Exchequer Chamber, and though you can amend the record after error brought, that is by virtue of the Act of Parliament, and you could not do it at common law. But when once the writ of error is allowed, your jurisdiction ceases, and you are only ministers. You are commanded to send it *crast[ino] Anima[rum]*,[1335] and if the plaintiff in error had done his duty, it would have been [*389*] actually in the Exchequer Chamber, and if it is sent up hereafter, yet it will be considered returned in *crasī animā*, and the writ of error is a *supersedeas* from the *teste* to all the proceedings, though the Act says it shan't supersede execution unless bail is given by such a time, and the court can't award execution after, and therefore the court can't set aside the judgment, Salk. 402[1336] the reference was adjudged regular, because of the writ of error which affirmed the judgment, and they can't withdraw that writ of error here, but in the Exchequer Chamber.

Mr Calaghan

You are desired to set aside a regular judgment of another term, which is now enrolled. The case of *Bargery* v. *Pierce*[1337] was in debt on a bond, and the court was then sitting when application was made.

And the party can't withdraw his writ of error, because if by the allowance 'tis a writ of another court, the act of the party shan't rob that other court of the record which belongs to them even by his act without a *remittit[u]r*.[1338]

Mr Daly

We consent to withdraw our writ of error though the return is out, but they say it is not in our power. This is a writ of right to have justice done, and there is no difference between it and any other original writ to the Common Bench, which is a commission to the court to proceed. He can enter a *retraxit*, and this record is here now. 'Tis directed to the treasurer and the barons, which is sent back with the writ, and certificate. The return of the writ is out but no return is yet made, or signed. The record remains here till it is legally sent to the Exchequer Chamber, or if it was sent

---

[1335] L. the morrow of All Souls. The first return day of the Michaelmas term. Return days for the Michaelmas term were set by 6 Geo. I, c. 1 (Ir.), 1719. The equivalent English statute was 16 Car. I, c. 6 (Eng.), 1640.

[1336] *Sisted* v. *Lee* (1704) 1 Salk. 403, 91 E.R. 349.

[1337] No citation given.

[1338] L. it is remitted. The sending back of the record to the court from whence it came. The entry of this fact was called the *remittitur*. Jacob, *Law Dictionary*.

there, it is not legally there till the return is made, and the party may waive the writ
he has purchased without leave of the Crown. In the case of *Aston*[1339] in Common
Bench the writ of error was brought by the casual ejector. The real person after taking
defence would not confess lease, entry and ouster etc. The court would not allow him
to bring a writ of error, because though by his taking defence the casual ejector was
out of the case, yet he was brought in again by the non-confession of the tenant, and
judgment was given against him. He moved in the Common Bench and had liberty
to withdraw his writ of error after the allowance of it, and so it must be plainly before
them. *Lord Antrim* v. *The Hollow Blades*[1340] in Chief Baron Gilbert's time: there was a
bill of exceptions, and 'twas moved that execution might be taken out of the record,
was not removed, which [*390*] shows the record still remains in court. *Lessee of Ram*
v. *The Casual Ejector*[1341] in this court, there was no defence, and judgment was given
against the casual ejector, execution taken out, and a writ of error brought, and the
sheriff would not execute the *habere*, because he was served with the writ of error.
There the judgment was set aside, and a defence allowed, though execution had
been awarded, on affidavit of Mr Purdon who managed for Mr Clayton the owner
of the estate, that he was at that time wounded, which is a precedent[1342] in point,
where the court because of the fatality would not tie themselves up to their rules.

But it was said, that there the writ of error was not allowed but it was taken out in
vacation time.

Mr Flack said, it was usual for them in the office to receive pleas after the four
days, if the declaration was not marked, but not after, and that he did not know of
any precedents,[1343] but believed there might be some in favour of the defendant.

Mr Recorder

Though the writ of error is not allowed, the bringing it stops their hands. *Newel* v.
Massy:[1344] Massy being told that Newel had brought a writ of error, runs out of court
and got an *habere*, and the Lord Chief Baron Gilbert restored Newel to the possession,
Massy having notice the writ was brought, though it was not allowed, so that bringing
the writ binds the court, and the party.

Mr Fortesque

In the case of *Aston*, the court only asked if the record were actually removed. If not,
they said they might withdraw their writ of error.

If judgment of another term could not be set aside in ejectment, no judgment in
that action could be set aside, because 'tis always moved for the last day of the term.

Mr Flack observed, that formerly they moved for judgment in ejectment at any
time, but to prevent surprise the rule was made, that it should be moved for the last
day of the term, and after they had four days to plead, and he said that the barons
of this court never made rules out of court relating to ejectments.

1339   No citation given.
1340   No citation given. For the Hollow Blades, see above, p. 1 n. 7.
1341   Above, p. 25 [*30*].
1342   Spelled 'President' in MS.
1343   Spelled 'precedts' in MS.
1344   No citation given.

Mr Baron Wainwright

Observed, that then they could not apply sooner, nor defend their [*391*] possession but by bringing a writ of error, that on judgment in a *scire facias* the court gives them time to plead putting in an issuable plea.

Lord Chief Baron

We may alter the practice for the future from any inconvenience we see in it, but can't do it in a particular case.

Monday, February the 11th [1734][1345]

Lord Chief Baron

The writ of error is the only thing now in this case, for the *Lessee of Ram* v. *The Casual* Ante 30. *Ejector, and others,*[1346] are precedents in point. The defendant must pay all the costs, discharge his writ of error, and go to trial the next assizes, or at bar.

Friday, January the 25, 1733, 4 [1734][1347]

Hilary Term

In Exchequer

WELDON v. HAMMOND

The defendant an executor of above 18 years of age had possessed himself of the assets of the testator to a very considerable amount or value, and answered by guardian, who swore himself a stranger to all the charges of the bill. An order was made *nisi* etc. on the motion of Mr Tench, that the defendant should answer on oath, and no cause being shown, the order was now made absolute.

You may read the pleadings of the court without proving them true copies, for the court will credit them, being signed by the officer.

Friday, February the 1st [1734][1348]

WELLINGTON v. LODER

Mr Baron Wainwright

The declaration is on the 6 Ann. ch. 7,[1349] the words of which are, 'If the party or parties at whose suit... etc., and the declaration is, that the defendant 'præ[1350]

[1345] 11 February was a Monday in 1734, Kratz, *Hist. Cal.* The hearing continues from November 1733.
[1346] Above, p. 25.
[1347] 1734 modern style. 25 January was a Friday in 1734, Kratz, *Hist. Cal.*
[1348] 1 February was a Friday in 1734, Kratz, *Hist. Cal.* The MS. continues from January 1734, above.
[1349] 6 Ann., c. 7 (Ir.), 1707 (sheriffs' fees; treble damages for wrongly marking writs).
[1350] Meaning unclear.

oneravit eum ad 60 libras ultra feodum et occasione præmissorum sustinuit dampna ad valenciam[1351] 181 librarum unde virtute statuti actio accrevit[1352],[1353] and the jury find the damages he declares for.

The question is, whether this declaration is right on this penal statute, that gives treble damages, or if the obligation is good in arrest of judgment after a verdict. [*392*] He declares not as on treble damages, but as if he was to have treble the forfeiture. In one case the sum is certain, but damages are uncertain till ascertained by the jury. So it is wrong in point of form, and on [a] penal statute the party may lay his damages as high as he pleases, and the jury are to find what they think the real damages, and the increment is the work of the court, not of the jury, Co. Entr. 44, 45. Lib. Placit. 77, 83. Rast. Entr. 44b. Noy 62.[1354]

And judgment must be agreeable to the pleadings, and being on the penal statute we must give treble the sum declared for which the jury have given, which is plain injustice, and giving the plaintiff nine times the damages.

'Tis said, that other damages might have been sustained by the imprisonment, but 'tis plain they are totted up to a sum certain.

In *Sandys Case* 3 Lev. 351[1355] the damages in the special verdict were express *in duplo*, which was a certainty the jury gave double damages, but here the damages are not said *in triplo*, so that we might have given judgment on the statute and pleadings. That case is also reported in Salk. 31,[1356] 4 Mod. 176,[1357] but best in Carth. 294.[1358]

So this declaration can't be supported after a verdict, because it does not run as for something uncertain, but for a certain sum and then tots it up threefold.

Lord Chief Baron

The judgment must be arrested, because damages are given that it appears by the declaration the plaintiff has no title to, for the sums totted up don't come to so much, like the case in 2 Salk. 663,[1359] Hob. 189.[1360] So he can't have those damages which 'tis plain he has no right to. The judgment therefore can't subsist, because the verdict gives him more than he has a right to.

[1351]   MS. reads 'valac'.

[1352]   MS. reads 'acrevit'.

[1353]   L. charged him with £60 above the fee, and by reason of the foregoing [the plaintiff] has sustained damages to the extent of £181, wherefor by virtue of the statute an action has accrued [to him].

[1354]   *Patridge* v. *Emson* (1597) Noy 62, 74 E.R. 1030 (action started in admiralty for thing done on land: penalty).

[1355]   *Sands Qui Tam* v. *Child, Franklin and Leach* (1693) 3 Lev. 351, 83 E.R. 725.

[1356]   *Child* v. *Sands* (1693) 1 Salk. 31, 91 E.R. 33.

[1357]   *Sands* v. *Child* (1692) 4 Mod. 176, 87 E.R. 332.

[1358]   *Child* v. *Sands* (1693) Carth. 294, 90 E.R. 774.

[1359]   *Prince* v. *Molt* (1697) 2 Salk. 663, 91 E.R. 565.

[1360]   *Harbin* v. *Green* (1616) Hob. 189, 80 E.R. 336.

DUFFY v. BATH

February the 9th, and February the 11th. [1734][1361]

Mr Bradstreet

A bond was entered into conditioned to account with White and Bath for the profits of the woods of Mellifont,[1362] with warrant of attorney to confess judgment etc., and White is accountable to Bath for a moiety, for which he assigned this bond to Bath, and after acknowledges satisfaction. Bath takes out a *capias* on the judgment marked for [£]200 [*393*] and the defendant in that action brings his action for treble damages for marking the writ, nothing being due on the bond, and the question is, whether the defendant shall be held to bail.

No special bail is required on [a] penal statute, unless 'tis expressly provided, as the 11 Anne against tenants holding over, says expressly, that they shall be held to bail. Otherwise they would not. In the case of *Hatfield* v. *Sutton* in this court on the Statute of Usury,[1363] no bail was required, but a common appearance only, so on the statute of maintenance in the Common Bench, Yelv. 52.[1364]

Ante 33.

2 Danv. Tit. Bail,[1365] in all penal statutes the defendant need not put in bail, as on the statute [of] Eliz. of Fraudulent Devises.[1366] Indeed in *scandalum magnatum* bail is required, because there is a fine to the King, and the peers have many privileges, as the words are to be taken in the strongest sense against the speaker, and they may lay the venue where they please.

Mr Steward

This is not a popular action, but is only given to the party damaged, and an action on the case would lie for wrong marking a writ before the statute, and the Act did not design to put a party in a worse case. This is overmarking an execution, Yelv. 53.[1367]

In the case of *Graydon* v. *Bumpford*[1368] on this very Act the party was held to bail for the treble damages in King's Bench. So in *Newland* v. *Wellington*[1369] in this court where the damages were £100.

Ante 48.

Sir John St Leger

The severity of the penalty is the reason the party is not held to bail, for when once the action is vested, a popular action is as fixed and certain as any other.

[1361] Ms. continues from 1 February 1734.
[1362] Spelled 'Mellefont' in MS.
[1363] 10 Car. I, sess. 2, c. 22 (Ir.), 1634; see also 13 Eliz. I, c. 8 (Eng.), 1571.
[1364] *Hargrave* v. *Rogers* (1605) Yelv. 52, 80 E.R. 37 (bail).
[1365] D'Anvers, *Abridgement of Common Law* (2nd ed., 2 vols., 1705–37, 1725–37). Bail is in volume 1 in this edition.
[1366] 13 Eliz., c. 5 (Eng.), 1571 (fraudulent conveyances).
[1367] *St George's Case* (1604) Yelv. 53, 80 E.R. 38 (penal statutes).
[1368] No citation given.
[1369] See *Wellington* v. *Nowland*, above, p. 41 [*48*].

Lord Chief Baron

Here are precedents in point that bail is required on this statute, but 'tis discretionary in us whether we shall require bail. Their affidavits don't show a probable cause. It must be done wilfully, knowingly and maliciously. He don't show he gave him notice that nothing was due before he marked the writ. It don't appear he knew all was satisfied to his co-obligee, so the common appearance must stand. [*394*]

Saturday, November the 24th, 1733[1370]

HACKET v. HACKET

A *capias quo minus* issued against the defendant *ret. tres Trin.*[1371] The plaintiff's attorney delivered the writ to the sub-sheriff, and desired him to draw up a warrant, and sign it in the name of the sheriff to what bailiffs he pleased, which he did accordingly, and therein recited the writ returnable *cras[tino] Trin[itatis]*,[1372] which was the day before the caption, and the defendant being arrested, it was moved to set it aside. And Mr Daly said, that a blank warrant to be filled up with the bailiff's name was bad.

On the other side, it was said, that the writ was in the sheriff's hands before the arrest, that though a deputy can't make a deputy,[1373] he may appoint one to do a single act in the name of the sheriff, that this was a real debt by bond and warrant, and the caption was avowed by the sheriff.

Lord Chief Baron

One taken on a Sunday for a pretended breach of the peace, and kept till Monday in order to lay an action on him, was discharged in Common Bench. Here was no arrest, there being no warrant, the writ being misrecited. It was not a warrant on that writ, and this is in a court of law. We can't enquire into the reality of the debt, or hardness of the case. The caption must be discharged.

ADMINISTRATOR OF POWER v. SARSFIELD

This cause being set down to be reheard, a motion was made for a commission to prove a codicil, on affidavit of a witness to the execution of it.

And it was argued, that wills are every day proved after a hearing, which are in nature of exhibits, which may be proved on a rehearing.

[1370] 24 November was a Saturday in 1733, Kratz, *Hist. Cal.* Note that the year reverts to 1733.

[1371] L. returnable the third day of Trinity term. *tres Trin.* would normally mean the third week of Trinity term, but from the context here is appears to mean the third [return] day. 32 Hen. VIII, c. 21 (Eng.), 1540 revised the return days for Trinity term. The preamble relates that the term was shortened to reduce the incidence of plague. The Irish equivalent statute was 11 Eliz. I, sess. 3, c. 2 (Ir.), 1569.

[1372] L. on the morrow of the Trinity.

[1373] Cf. the maxim *delegatus non potest delegare*, a delegate cannot delegate, 2 Inst. 597.

Shea v. *Smyth*[1374] on a possessory bill, where the title depended on a will, on a reference to a baron the proof of the will being defective, a commission was granted to prove it, because there was no danger of practice. That the cause is open on a rehearing, and that till the decree is enrolled, there is no need of an affidavit that it came to their knowledge since the decree, and you may have the answer of the party in aid of a rehearing. [*395*]

The Attorney General on the other side insisted, that a rehearing was of grace, and ought not to be delayed by these means. This codicil is not in issue. We might have shown it revoked.

2. They don't swear they had no knowledge of it before, or why they did not prove it, nor they don't insert it in their general petition to rehear, and though wills and deeds may be proved after publication, 'tis dangerous to allow it after it is known how the judgment of the court is.

Lord Chief Baron

Granted a commission on payment of costs, and thought it reasonable, since the witness was 72 years of age, and he swears the codicil was executed, and it has been proved in the spiritual court, and his Lordship said, he should not have granted it, but that the party perhaps might have been deceived in thinking he could prove it as an exhibit, as wills were formerly.

BARLOW v. HARRIS

Monday, December the 10. [1733][1375]

Mr Prime Serjeant moved, that the defendant Harris might have leave to examine to the payment of the mortgage money, on affidavits which he offered to read.

Mr Solicitor General

It is proper the court should have a power to grant an examination after publication, and which they have accordingly exerted in several instances, where there was no danger of perjury; we only desire to prove the payment of this money in bankers' notes from written evidence from the books of the banker, which are not in the power of either of the parties.

Mr Recorder

This being a point in issue, and examined to in the original cause, by the course of the court we could not file a cross bill, and what we would prove, can't be fraud by us on purpose, being written testimony before the institution of the cause.

[1374] No citation given.
[1375] 10 December was a Monday in 1733, Kratz, *Hist. Cal.*

The Executors of Sir Patrick Dun v. *Mitchel and the College of Physicians.*[1376] The chancellor after publication suffered the [*396*] Archbishop of Dublin to be examined to a fact in his own knowledge, because of his probity and character. In *Hodder* v. *Sarsfield,*[1377] the bill was for a legacy under the will of Sarsfield. 'Twas insisted at the hearing that the plaintiff was only a trustee, and before the cause was reheard, leave was given to prove a codicil.

Smyth v. *Ryan.*[1378] A will was proved after the hearing though it was the gist of the cause, the probate being produced, though it could not be read.

Mr Bradstreet

The plaintiffs make two demands, as purchasers under the marriage articles of the father, and as volunteers under his will. If the defendant had notice of the articles he must be bound by them, yet if he is a real purchaser, though he had notice of the will, he must prevail and be preferred to the legacies, which amount to about two thirds of the assets; so 'tis very material for us to prove the payment of the purchase money.

Mr Smyth[1379]

Hard. 180,[1380] *Sir John Langham* v. *Anon.* An issue being directed, a bill was brought to produce books on the trial, and a demurrer to it was overruled, because this was not to have supplemental proof in the same cause, but at the trial, which I hope is an authority for us. The discovery of these vouchers was accidental. [In] 1 Chan. Cas. 229, *The Mayor of London* v. *The Earl of Dorset,*[1381] a witness was examined after publication on several special circumstances

Henvil v. *Holland*[1382] 2 Vern. 437. After a verdict on *plene administravit,*[1383] a new trial was granted, a material witness being out of the way, and a new voucher discovered.

Mr Bettesworth for the plaintiffs

The defendant all along knew this was the chief thing in the cause which he was to prove, in order to charge the assets, and he swears, as they now open the affidavits, that he would have made other proof at the hearing, but that Mr Somner the notary public told him, he could swear to the payment of the money, if the *litera scripta* was previous to the examination, and in his own knowledge. 'Twas his [*397*] fault he did not examine to it before the hearing.

[1376] No citation given.

[1377] No citation given.

[1378] No citation given.

[1379] Probably Charles Smyth, 3rd s. of Thomas, bishop of Limerick. Middle Temple, 19 March 1717/18, called 12 Feb. 1724/5. KI, Michaelmas, 1725; KI AP, p. 455.

[1380] *Sir John Langham* v. *Sir Edward Lawrence* (1661) Hard 180, 145 E.R. 440.

[1381] *Mayor of London* v. *Earl of Dorset* (1674) 1 Ch. Cas. 228, 22 E.R. 774.

[1382] Cases at that reference are *Tovey* v. *Young* (1702) 2 Vern. 437, 23 E.R. 880 and *Earl of Huntington* v. *Countess of Huntington* (1702) 2 Vern. 437, 23 E.R. 881. There are no cases in Vernon in E.R. which mention both 'plene' and 'voucher'.

[1383] L. fully administered.

Mr Calaghan

There are three reasons why your Lordship should not grant this examination. 1. Because it would be a plain introduction to perjury. 2. Because it is to a point not material. 3. If the merits of the motion were with them, this is not a proper time.

1. Where the party makes a defective proof on the hearing, to give him a new examination is plainly introductive of perjury.

Mes App. B.9.

In *Rouquier* v. *Bolton*[1384] in this court, an issue was offered to make up this defect, but the House of Lords would not allow it.

Ante 118, 140.
MSS ord in. Canc.
93, 95.

In the case of *Sir Patrick Dun*, though the publication was past, the party, agent, and clerk swore, they had not, nor would see or know the depositions till after the examination.

In *Hodder* v. *Sarsfield*,[1385] there was no examination before the hearing, and the codicil was but in nature of an exhibit: but entries in bankers' books are not exhibits, nor can come under the meaning of them, but are in nature of parol proof, for he that enter them must swear the money was paid, and they are only a refreshment of his memory.

2. This is not material. We produced authorities in point, that the legacies are a charge on the estate, and *caveat emptor*.[1386]

3. This is an improper time, because it is necessary that the parties your Lordship thought wanting, should be before you on this question, as at the hearing.

Mr Daly

This application is improper, because this court was of opinion, that if he had proved the payment of the money, that would not have varied your determination. This must arise from a recollection of the cause, which is not a proper motion.

A purchaser of the assets can't defeat the legacies. If he had been a creditor, or purchaser under the testator, he could.

We by our bill charged the defendant with a fraud, and that the pretended mortgage money was never paid, and as our evidence set out the hastiness of the pro ceedings to foreclose. He joins in issue of these points, and examines witnesses to them, and they don't prove the payment of the money. He never applied for a new examination between the publication [*398*] and the hearing of the cause, nor from that till this time, and there is no precedent that such a motion was ever granted. There are many indeed where wills have been allowed to be proved, but this is not written evidence. The memorandums of it in a book are not written evidence.

Mr Anthony Malone

The court never gives leave to examine after publication but to exhibits, or new matter not in the knowledge of the parties at the time of the former examination.

[1384] Above, p. 135 [*168*] where the case is cited as *Roquier* v. *Bolton*, affirmed in the House of Lords, but no citation given. The name 'Roquier' or 'Rouquier' does not occur in E.R.

[1385] No citation given.

[1386] L. let the buyer beware.

Lord Chief Baron

This is a motion the last day of our sitting, though they had the whole term to have made it in. 'Tis in the power of the court to grant an examination after publication, but they always do it very sparingly, from the great inconvenience [that] may follow.

Where a fact is properly in issue, and proof defective, we can grant a trial. This proof of the fact was in the knowledge of the defendant, and in issue in the cause, and the bankers' books are not sufficient proof of the payment of the money, unless it be proved to be paid to Barlow, or order. Our decree is only to secure the money.

We can't grant the motion.

Mr Baron Wainwright

This is not a motion to examine after publication, but to supply evidence after the court have given their opinion, and they see where the cause presses, when 'tis heard again. If we see occasion we can direct an issue, whether the money was paid, so the defendant is not prejudiced by the denial of the motion.

In Exchequer

On a bill of discovery on the Popery Acts, if they don't annex an affidavit, you may move that they stop *quosq[ue]*.[1387]

In Exchequer

After a verdict the certificate must be confirmed, and the order served four days before the cause can be set down to be heard. [*399*]

READ v. HAMILTON

The bill was referred for impertinence. The baron reported it pertinent. The defendant took a general exception to the report, which was disallowed for that reason, because he should have shown wherein it was impertinent, but the exception would have been good, if the baron had not made a general report, but had reported the particular parts.

HANDREKIN v. POWER

In Exchequer

Order on motion to prove a pedigree after publication.

[1387] L. until.

Saturday, February the 9th [1734][1388]

In Exchequer

MILLER v. DINELLY

Order on motion of Mr Recorder, that service of the defendant's last place of abode be good service of a decree and injunction, on affidavit that the plaintiff had made inquiry for the defendant at her usual place of abode in the country and in Dublin, which was particularly named, and that they heard and believed she was gone to England to avoid service.

Ante 81.
MSS̃ ord in. Canc.
117.

Thursday, February the 22nd[1389]

In Exchequer

BURKE v. HACKET, ET È CONTRA.

Bill to stay proceedings on an ejectment, cross bill to set aside the lease made by the husband not warranted by the settlement, on the motion of Mr Bradstreet for the defendant the widow. The court said, it was not usual to grant money where the party impeached the lease, because they might be the representative of the lessor from whom they might recover over, but here being very poor, they granted her £100, as they had before £150, for if she broke the lease, they must answer for the value of the land, if it stood, for the rent reserved, and they have the benefit of the injunction by staying.

[1388] 9 February was a Saturday in 1734, Kratz, *Hist. Cal.* MS. continues from December 1733. The year remains 1734 from here until the end of the MS.

[1389] 22 February was a Friday in 1734, a Thursday in 1733, Kratz, *Hist. Cal.*, but the MS. continues from previous date which appears to be February 1734, and the next date given below is Easter term 1734.

Easter Term, 1734

Friday, May the 11th[1390]

In Exchequer

Upon a trial at bar in ejectment

UNDERHILL LESSEE OF GALWAY v. ARTHUR ECHLIN

[*400*] The question was on the 1 Geo. 2 ch. 5,[1391] whether the affirmation of Pemberton a Quaker should be admitted, on his producing a certificate, without affidavit of the signing it.

Mr Recorder

That the certificate need not be proved by oath has been allowed above 40 times on the circuit. In the case of *Mayna[rd]* v. *Power*[1392] at Clonmel, a Quaker was brought as an evidence to prove a man living who went to Pennsylvania.[1393] He produced a certificate, and 'twas adjudged it need not be proved by affidavit.

'Tis received and annexed to answers, and affirmation by way of affidavits in equity, and why not on trials, and as 'tis usual, so 'tis reasonable to admit it without proving the certificate, because by producing it, he has made it evidence against himself, and he can't say that the six were not Quakers etc, and 'tis not to be evidence against any other person. The affirmation by this Act is to come in room of an oath. He is as much bound by it, as by an oath, and if he affirms falsely, he is indictable for perjury, and the certificate is lodged in court, and will be evidence against him that he was a Quaker.

Mr Attorney General

If it was required that the certificate should be sworn to, the Act would be eluded, and rendered impracticable, and therefore I presume the Act did not require such an oath. The certificate must not only be by six Quakers, but of the same congregation. The oath then must be not only that the certificate was signed by six Quakers, but that also they were of that congregation, and who could prove them to be all of one congregation but Quakers, who will not take an oath. Here not the party, but the

---

[1390] 11 May was a Saturday in 1734, Kratz, *Hist. Cal.*, but the year is given in the line above as 1734.

[1391] 1 Geo. II, c. 5 (Ir.), 1727 (Quakers). Note that under 6 Geo. I, c. 6 (Ir.), 1723, the earlier temporary Act, section 5 provided for Quakers to make affirmation, and under section 6 a person claiming to be a Quaker was to produce a certificate to that effect by six members of a Quaker congregation. These provisions were re-enacted later in the general provision as to testimony by Quakers in 1 Geo. II, c. 5. Below, p. 316 n. 1397.

[1392] No citation given.

[1393] Spelled 'Pensilvania' in MS. By an indenture dated 12 December 1698 William Penn, Governor and Proprietor of the province of Pennsylvania demised 10,000 acres in that province to Joseph Pyke of Cork: O. C. Goodbody, *Guide to Irish Quaker Records 1654–1860* (Dublin, IMC, 1967), at p. 159, no. 213. In 1690 a number of Quakers travelled to Pennsylvania on the ship *Trial of Pennsylvania*: ibid., p. 120 D.

witness himself must produce the certificate, if required, which was inserted in the Act, that it might be evidence against him.

Mr Daly contra

Certificates at common law are not evidence unless they are under seal. The certificate is to satisfy the court that he is a Quaker, and is not filed in the office.

Mr Hussy

How can we indict him for perjury, when perhaps [*401*] he is not a Quaker? 'Tis not only required by the Act they should be Quakers, but also credible ones, and of the same congregation, and the certificate don't say what sort of people they are. So 'tis plain the Act designed this should be made out by oath, and required something more than the bare certificate.

The certificate of the clerk of the peace of proclamations is not evidence without oath of his signing it.

Mr Steward

They must be six Quakers all of one congregation, and when the certificate is signed, they may have those present who are not Quakers.

An office copy though signed by a public officer of a court must be proved a true copy.

Mr Carleton[1394]

In the Tholsel Court[1395] before Mr Stoyte the late Recorder the affirmation of an insolvent debtor a Quaker was refused, because the certificate was not sworn to, and he took an oath.

[1394] Probably Alexander Carleton, 2nd s. of George, Tullymargie, Co. Fermanagh. Middle Temple, Easter 1724. KI, admitted Trinity term, 1729. KI AP, p. 75.

[1395] *OED*: ME. tolseld, tollsell, f. OE. toll. OE. seld seat, or sl, hall: cf. OE. tollsetl, 'tolbooth, custom-house'. The ancient name in some English and Irish towns for the guildhall, tolbooth, or borough court-house; also for the local court of justice (more fully, tolsel or tolzey court there held). The original form, long retained in Ireland, has been reduced in some English towns to tolsey (sometimes only the traditional name of the building), or tolzey. 1486: Galway Arch. in 10th Rep. Hist. MSS. Comm. App. v. 385 'His matter or suite be pledid and tried in the Tollsell or Courte-housse befor the Mayor.' 1584: Ibid. 435 'To appeare in the Towllsill or court howse.' 1621: Ibid. 469 'The Towsell or Courthowse of Galwey.' 1632: Ibid. 480 'The Mayor and Comonaltie of Galwey assembled in their Towelshill.' 1680: Ibid. 505 'The concerne of the Corporation formerly acted by Tholsell was vested in the Council by charter.' 1701: Ibid. 515 'Nor doe they enjoy any houses except the Tholsell and gaole thereunder.' 1701: Lond. Gaz. No. 3721/3 Dublin. 'The Lord Mayor, with the Aldermen, and Commons of the City, assembled at the Tholsell at Four a Clock.' 1769: Wesley, Jrnl. 15 June, 'I preached in the Tholsel [Kilkenny].' The Dublin Tolsel court is referred to in 10 Geo. I, c. 10 (Ir.), 1723 s. 1, providing that salesmen in the Smithfield sheep and cattle market had to enter a bond with the mayor deposited in the Tolsel court to carry on business without fraud.

Plate 8. The Tholsel Court, Skinners Row, Dublin, 1798.

Mr Flack[1396]

The certificate is not filed on trials, but only when 'tis annexed to the affirmation by way of affidavits.

N.B. The certificate is not sworn to in the Chancery side of the Exchequer, but in the Court of Chancery there is an oath of their signing it.

Mr Baron Wainwright

When a certificate is produced, the law never presumes a man's hand to be forged, and it may be against the conscience of a Quaker to make others swear.

The certificate of the minister and churchwardens is received, though no oath is made that they are the minister and churchwardens, or that they signed it, but 'tis took on the public faith. They often sign the certificate privately without anyone being present. I don't say that the cases are the same, but that that Act requires a certificate, and say who shall make it, and that these certificates have been received and filed without oath. So this Act says that six shall certify, and the courts have hitherto received them without oath. How must then handwritings be proved? Must the witness be carried about to see them signed? Since the Act did not require an oath, 'tis to be presumed to be a [402] fair certificate, and that the Act went upon this foundation. So it grounded on reason and practice. Why may not we go so far as to examine the Quaker himself whether the six signed it?

Sir John St Leger

The certificate of the minister and churchwardens is a superabundant caution by that Act, for two also must swear they were present when the party received. I have allowed answers with a certificate, because they are annexed, and will certainly be evidence against the defendant, but these certificates on trials are not lodged in the office, and if it don't appear that he is a Quaker, taking the affirmation don't lay him under a religious obligation. If the certificate was filed, then it would be as on the equity side, but still the religious obligation would be taken away.

Lord Chief Baron[1397]

The practice has always been to receive these certificates without oath, and there is no instance to the contrary. An oath is required that the certificate was signed by the clerk of the council *in favore[m] vitæ*.[1398] I think we may allow his affirmation without proof of the certificate, though it is contrary to that rule of law, that all papers but records must be proved, and the Act says it was necessary to carry on trade to give the

[1396] There is no barrister of that name listed in KI AP. KI AP are incomplete: see KI AP, at p. viii. It is more likely he was an attorney, since he was addressing the court as to practice. See above, pp. 303, 303, below, p. 318. There are three attorneys listed in KI AP of the period, with the surname Flack, all called James: James, listed in Feb. 1718 as master of an apprentice, James, snr., attorney of the Exchequer, *c.* 1734, d. Oct. 1741, and James, jnr. attorney of the Exchequer, *c.* 1734; KI AP, p. 169.

[1397] It was Marlay who, as A.G. in 1727, had introduced the bill which became 1 Geo. II, c. 5 (Ir.): *Hist. Ir. Parlt.* (no. 1344) Marlay.

[1398] L. lit. in favour of life.

Quakers this liberty, and if their testimony was taken away the sole witness in a cause might pretend to be a Quaker; by this Act Quakers are allowed to affirm instead of swear except in criminal cases, but with this proviso, that they are not to be deemed Quakers, unless they produce a certificate etc. if required. So 'tis left in the discretion of the court to require a certificate, and it would be a hardship if it was always to be proved. If a Quaker comes from England he may easily procure a certificate, but with great difficulty prove it. So though the law don't allow certificates to be evidence, yet the statute don't require those who qualify to prove the certificate was signed by the minister and churchwardens. [403] Let us consider the inconveniences. An oath is good from the apprehension the party has of perjury. Now Quakers have the same belief of their word, because every word is spoke in the presence of God. But I think this ought to be the opinion of everyman, that what he affirms solemnly in court to the prejudice of another, deserves vengeance, and the penalties are the same as in case of perjury, and he may be examined on his affirmation if he is a Quaker, and has been so for five years and upwards. So no difficulty can arise upon an indictment. Therefore I think we may receive the certificate, and let it be filed on record by the proper officer.

Accordingly the court examined Pemberton whether he had been a Quaker for above five years, whether he saw the six sign the certificate, and whether they were of his congregation.

The court took it ill they were forced to give their opinion when it was not necessary, but the evidence was sufficient without examining Pemberton; but Mr Prime Serjeant said, they thought it very proper to have the sense of the court, since this point happened every day on the circuit.

PRENDERGAST,
ONE OF THE ATTORNEYS v. GODFREY GREEN[1399]

May the 18th[1400]

Lord Chief Baron

The serjeant at arms is to show cause, why the execution on his Kerry bond should not be set aside.

The serjeant at arms has no right to his day fees of 6s 8d (for which he demands £60) till he returns his writ, which he has not yet done, but has only signed it since he came into court, so that the plaintiff could have no benefit of the execution, by compelling him by fine or attachment to bring in the body; but he has a right to his caption fee of £50, though the process was irregular, for he must obey the writ brought to him under seal, so that I think he had no right to take out execution on his bond and judgment, but that the same must be set aside, and he must give a warrant to acknowledge satisfaction on the judgment. The serjeant shall never have his day fees, unless he return his writ in due time.[404]

Post 404.

[1399] Thomas Prendergast is listed in KI AP in the period, as attorney of the Exchequer, c. 1734, KI AP, p. 410.
[1400] Presumably still Easter term 1734.

Mr Baron Wainwright observed, that the original of the serjeant at arms was, that where the party had stood long in contempt, the court sent their own officer to bring him in immediately, but as they proceed now, justice instead of being furthered, is greatly delayed by them, to the expense and vexation of the suitor. If the defendant is rich, the serjeant will not return his writ till the plaintiff force him by several fines, and an attachment, and when he has returned a *cepi*,[1401] if the defendant is able to indemnify him, he will not bring in the body, till he is compelled by the same methods.

The court perhaps may connive at these bonds, which are really a great ease to the party in a long vacation, but since day fees are allowed them for the safe custody and maintenance of the defendant, and that on these bonds they suffer him to go at large, the court will take advantage of any misexecution of the officer, as here he has not returned his writ, to set aside an execution for these fees, when they come to as moderate a sum as £60! And he would make use of these bonds to oppress the party.

Where process by consent of the party is to issue *tunc pro nunc*,[1402] they take out all the process to a sequestration together, and take care to give them proper return. But no process can be taken out without a rule (which Mr Flack said was entered of course) and a return of a former process to warrant it. But Mr Attorney General said, it was plain the attorney must move for the rule, and see it entered, because he is allowed half a crown for his fee, though the officer has 1s 6d for entering it.

Friday, May the 17th.[1403]

HIGGINS v. BUTLER

The serjeant at arms came to show cause, why he took out execution on his bond and judgment.

Ante 403. An attachment to the serjeant at arms was read, *teste* 28 June Trin. 6 Geo. 2 1732, *ret. crast[ino] Anima[rum]*[1404] which is read by the attorney for the plaintiff. In September Butler was taken, [*105*] and executed a bail bond in the penalty of £1,500 with a warrant in the body of it to confess judgment, and the serjeant returned a *cepi corpus*,[1405] and took out execution on the bond for £136, his day fees, and £15 his expenses in travelling to the county of Clare, and his 12 days stay there. A rule dated Friday the 5 of June 1713 as to the *supersedeas* a serjeant at arms was read.

On the humble petition of Richard Povey the serjeant at arms, and the pursuivant,[1406] that they were often at great expense in searching for those against whom attachments issued, and could not take them, and that the party after issued a *supersedeas* without paying them their fees. It was therefore ordered, that when an attachment issued to the serjeant, or pursuivant, no discharge from the attorney should hinder execution, unless their fees were first paid, and that no *supersedeas* should issue till they were first paid, and that they may renew the attachments till their fees were paid. Mr Flack being asked as to the practice on the statute took

---

[1401] L. I have taken, or seized.

[1402] L. lit. then for now.

[1403] 17 May was a Friday in 1734, Kratz, *Hist. Cal.*

[1404] L. the morrow of All Souls, the first return day of the Michaelmas term. Above, p. 302 n. 1335.

[1405] L. I have taken the body.

[1406] Fr. A royal or state messenger with power to execute warrants: *OED.* Spelled 'poursuivant' in MS.

this difference, that when he took out an execution for the non-appearance of the defendant, the serjeant never marked his execution, but told the sheriff the sum, but where the execution was for his fees only, he marked the writ.

Mr Prime Serjeant

This is a question of consequence to all the officers, and suitors of the court.

The first attachment to the serjeant was *teste* the 5 February *ret. quind[ena] Pasch[æ]*.[1407] On this no return was made. The second was taken out in Trinity term without order.

But if this process is erroneous, that is no reason why the officer should be deprived of his fees.

In Trinity term the officer has the attachment put into his hands *ret. crast[ino] Anima[rum]*.[1408] He according to the duty of his office grants a warrant to take the defendant, and gives his bailiff, as is the usual practice, a bond to be filled up if the party was taken. The defendant being taken executes the bond. We enter judgment, and take out execution for £136.

There are several objections to this execution. First, that here are two attachments, and that there being no return of *n[on] e[st] inventus*[1409] on the first, the second could not issue without that return, and an order. [*406*] But though the attachment is erroneous, where the officer sees the seal, that is his command to execute it, and he is only ministerial, and 'tis no excuse for him to say the order is erroneous, but while it subsists, he must execute it.

When the party is apprehended, the serjeant has no gaol to lay him in, and the gaolers do, and may refuse him, so that taking this bond for his appearance is not only of necessity for the officer, but of great ease to the defendant, and if he don't think fit to execute it, he may go with the officer. This was the original design of these bonds, and this is usual practice, and the bond of itself is not irregular. If the officer must arrest, 'tis not unreasonable he should take bond for his security, or at least till the return of the writ, nor is it against law, there being no Act of Parliament to the contrary.

The attachment is to attach the person, and make a return. The condition of the bond is, to appear on the return, or when demanded by the officer, and for payment of his fees, costs, and charges.

This is an extraordinary objection in the motion of the defendant. Why didn't he perform the condition of the bond? He might have appeared in court, and your Lordship would have obliged the serjeant to deliver up his bond, and stay his fees, and on the return *cepi*, the officer is liable to pay the plaintiff's demand.

The next question is, whether the execution ought to be marked.

The 6th Anne[1410] requires the execution to be marked by the officer who grants it, and the party who takes it out is to return a certificate or docket of what is due. This Act extends only to private contracts, and not to the officer, because where a bond is given to secure him his fees they are ascertained, and he is under an oath to execute his office faithfully, which is not to oppress the subject, but other plaintiffs are not under this obligation.

[1407] L. in the quindene of Easter.

[1408] L. the morrow of All Souls, the first return day of the Michaelmas term. Above, p. 302 n. 1335.

[1409] L. he is not found.

[1410] 6 Ann., c. 7 (Ir.), 1707 (sheriffs; treble damages for wrongly marking writs).

Objection: This bond is a private contract.

No, because the bond refers to what is certain, the payment of the usual fee, and were it otherwise, being taken in [407] duress it would be void.

Objection: But it extends to costs and charges, which are uncertain.

This has been the constant usage for 37 years since the making [of] this Act. And the officer has told your Lordship in what cases they are marked, but where the suit is still subsisting and the execution goes for the whole sum, because he won't appear to the process of the court.

But the court of Common Bench made a rule 20 June 1711, which I mention to your Lordship only as an authority or precedent, and gave their opinion, that their tipstaff was not within the Act.

Mr Solicitor General

It has been a constant practice in all the courts where attachments have issued to take these bonds for appearance, etc, and the courts have never censured them, because of their necessity, for the sheriffs are not obliged to take persons into custody who are attach[ed] on contempts of your courts. And as very many be taken up, and there is no public gaol for them, it was not the design of the court they should be close confined till they gave particular orders, for which there are frequent motions.

But 'tis said, when these bonds lie for a great while, 'tis an oppression to sue for the whole sum. By the condition of the bond he is only to be paid his due fees, & the swelling the sum is not the act of the officer but of the party. He knew he ought to appear and discharge his contempts, and he might have put an end to them.

The officer doesn't know the consequence of his not appearing, but the party does. And Reeves the agent for the plaintiff swears he told the defendant if he did not make satisfaction he would be put to great expense.

The taking out of the *fi. fa.* is said to be contrary to the 6 Anne, not being marked, and there being no certificate. Though this case is not expressly excepted out of the Act, it must be so from the intention of it, and the necessity of the thing.

The design of the Act was, that the party should not be laid in execution for a greater sum than was due, but the fees are certain, and the time from whence they commence appears on the bond. [408] If the bond be put in suit for the party not appearing, the whole penalty must be recovered, and no writ of enquiry is necessary where the fees are certain. And the officer is a stranger to the misbehaviour of the sheriff, if any, in executing the writ.

The serjeant's travelling fees are 9d a day going down.

Mr Serjeant Bettesworth

The first attachment is an *album breve*,[1411] and without any return, and therefore the party may renew it within such a time.

The suit indeed is but for £5, but the officer is not supposed to know that, but is to take a sufficient bond. If the fees are exorbitant, it must be in the fee, and not in the quantum, for the swelling them was the fault of the party, and he don't complain he was overcharged.

[1411] L. a blank writ.

Sir John St Leger

The same process may be renewed though the first was never returned, as if it is lost, etc., but if you would ground a new process on it, the former must be returned.

Mr Recorder

The order for the process subsists for a year and a day, and if the writ is not returned, it may be renewed by the party or serjeant without motion, or order. 'Tis the same process, only a long time is given to execute it, which is for the benefit of the defendant, so the second writ of attachment to the serjeant issued regularly. The taking [of] these bonds is an advantage to the party, for otherwise if he is attached in the beginning of the long vacation, he must lie in close custody all the summer.

The question is, if the officer should have stirred before the plaintiff pressed him, and I think he ought, otherwise the parties by compromising might deprive him of his fees, and he may go on till a *supersedeas*, and the rule [that] has been read is to that purpose. [*409*]

The next question is, if he should have marked the execution, if he has not marked it. The statute don't make the execution void, but gives the party treble damages in an action, for the plaintiff might at law take out an execution for the whole penalty. And you won't set the execution aside in this summary way by affidavits. You can't judge of the credibility of the witnesses without a jury. But the practice shows the courts thought these bonds not within the intention of the Act.

But 'tis said, we should have issued a writ of inquiry on the 9 W. 3.

There is no occasion, because the fees are certain, and the Act extends only to damages.

Mr Jos. Robins[1412]

The condition of the bond to appear at the return of the writ or when required is not unequitable. He might appear at the return, and be confined, or if he valued his liberty every day above 6s 8d, he ought to pay it, and the officer don't hasten him till a rule is put on him by the plaintiff.

Mr Attorney General contra

This is a question of great concernment to the fees of the officer, and the liberty of the subject.

I allow the officer can't say the writ is irregular, but must obey the seal.

The plaintiff brought his action for an apothecary's bill of £5, and prayed a subpœna. Upon this proceedings were carried on till a lease worth £1,000 was sold, (which execution and sale your Lordship has set aside) and the serjeant at arms got £100.

He has not cleared up this point: how he came to execute this writ.

[1412] There is a Joseph Robbins in KI AP, 2nd s. of Joseph, Ballyduffe, Co. Kilkenny. Middle Temple, 21 Feb. 1716/7. KI, Hilary term, 1721, d. March, 1761; and also a Joseph Robbins listed only as *c.* 1734.

The attachment issued in the name of Kennedy,[1413] an attorney of this court, but he knew nothing of it, but gave leave to Reeves, an attorney of the Common Bench,[1414] to use his name. Reeves says, he ordered the writ to issue. If he had a mind to have it executed, wouldn't he have delivered it to the officer, and told him where [*410*] the defendant lived. So he gets a writ from his bailiff without any request from the attorney or party to execute it. This bond was executed in an open field in September 1732. Does the plaintiff demand any return of this writ? Does he make any application for a fine on the serjeant for not returning his writ? Yet he sends down an execution for £138, which I take to be irregular for these three reasons.

1. Because the bond was not forfeited.

2. Because there was no writ of inquiry of damages.

3. Because it was not marked.

1. The bond was not forfeited, 1. because the obligor had an election, and the serjeant never made any demand on him to appear, 2. he was to indemnify him, what pretence for that, 3. he was to pay him his fees, and such costs and charges as were usual, or accustomed to be paid. Will you suffer the officer to take but execution, without telling the party what he is to pay? But he is to take accustomed fees. Why none are due, for he is not entitled to the caption fee, if he is not employed by the plaintiff, or his attorney, but where he raises up business for himself. These are not accustomed fees.

2. If the bond was forfeited, this execution is irregular by the 9 W. 3 ch. 35,[1415] for want of a writ of inquiry of damages. Before this statute the plaintiff on a bond could assign only one breach, but was to recover the penalty. This was hard on the plaintiff, that he could not show all the reasons he had to complain, and on the defendant, who ought to pay no more than the plaintiff had really suffered. But this Act gives the plaintiff a liberty to assign as many breaches as he pleases, but he is not to judge of his damages, but they must be left to a jury. The rule of the Common Bench only says, the Sixth of Queen Anne[1416] don't extend to their tipstaff.

3. As to the 6 Anne, that was made for two purposes, both in favour of the defendant, 1. that the sheriff should raise [*411*] no more poundage than for the real debt, 2. nor the plaintiff oppress the defendant without laying open to treble damages. The action for the treble damages is given for over-marking the writ, but the statute is express, that the execution shall be marked, then you would set aside the execution if it was taken out by a common person, and more so in the case of the officer.

The certificate of what is due is given to the officer, and then he marks the writ. So the whole £500 was to be raised by the sheriff, though £138 only was due.

Next I shall consider the practice of this court, and the rule of the Common Bench, and neither will justify the officer. The officer has made a distinction: when the bond is executed for the non-appearance of the party, and when for his fees. But reason seems to go the contrary way, for if he don't appear to be more damaged in the first than the other case, it seems more contrary to the intention of the Act, he should levy the whole penalty.

[1413] Possibly Charles Kennedy, listed in KI AP, p. 263 as attorney of Exchequer, no date.

[1414] There is no attorney of the Common Pleas of the name of Reeves listed in KI AP for the period. KI AP are incomplete: see KI AP, p. viii.

[1415] 9 Will. III, c. 10 (Ir.), 1697 (frivolous actions, etc), 9 Will. III, c. 35 (Ir.) in Statutes at Large, 1692–1711, (Grierson ed., 1733), i. 124.

[1416] 6 Ann., c. 7 (Ir.), 1707 (sheriffs fees; treble damages for over-marking writs).

But if this is a practice that has passed *sub silentio*, and is not founded on judicial determinations, 'tis of no weight, but your Lordship will judge on the Act. And if the practice were so, he ought to have marked it, because it is for his fees.

If the officer is commanded, and does his duty, he is to have his fees, but no contrivance to take out the writ without the direction of the plaintiff or his agent will justify this bond. He was in no danger of being fined, because he was not employed, and £46 has been levied.

Mr Wall

1. This bond is void by the 23 Hen. 6.[1417]

2. If 'twas good, 'tis not forfeited, the disjunctive being for the benefit of the defendant.

3. If 'twas forfeited, the execution is bad, because the terms of the two Acts are not complied with.

1. Under the word sheriff in the Act are described all persons concerned in the execution of process. This bond is not for fees only, but all costs and charges.

3. This execution is against the two Acts. How are his travelling charges ascertained? The Act avoids the execution if it is not marked, as well [*412*] as gives an action of treble damages for over-marking.

Saturday, May the 25th. [1734][1418]

Mr Baron Wainwright

I won't determine whether this bond is good, or whether the execution ought to be marked, but here is a manifest oppression sufficient to make them set aside their own writ.

Lord Chief Baron

The statute is penal, so we won't determine these questions on a motion.

The serjeant at arms, hearing the sense of the court, came to an agreement with the party.

By order of the Court of Chancery, a notice of motion by a pauper must be signed by counsel.

By order of the Court of Chancery previous to the late Act of Parliament,[1419] no injunction shall be moved for, after the appearance of the defendant, to stay proceedings at law for rent, without a special notice.

[1417] 23 Hen. VI, c. 9 (Eng.), 1444 (sheriffs' bonds).

[1418] 25 May was a Saturday in 1734, Kratz, *Hist. Cal.*

[1419] Statute not identified. Perhaps 5 Geo. II, c. 4 (Ir.) (ejectment for non payment of rent).

POPE v. POPE

July the 20th, 1734

If a pauper sues for a maintenance on the Popery Acts, he shall not be obliged to refer, or be disempaupered, for the appointing [of] a maintenance is personal to the Chancellor.

Friday May the 24th, 1734.[1420]

NESBIT v. NESBIT

1 Vern. 103.[1421]
(89).
MSS̃ cas. in Canc.
A.310, 450.

Mr Daly moved to set aside an order obtained by the defendant before he had answered, for the plaintiff to make his election, whether he would proceed at law, or in equity.

Mr Baron Wainwright set aside the order.

Tuesday, June the 18th, 1734[1422]

Lord Chancellor

In court: Lord Chief Justice Rogerson
                     Lord Chief Baron Marlay

STEPNEY v. RAWSON,[1423]
ASTEL v. RICHARDSON[1424]

Ante 182, 194.   [413] These causes were reheard by the Chancellor, assisted by the same judges who had formerly given opinions.

Lord Chief Baron

In *Stepney* v. *Rawson*, from a view and consideration of later authorities, I think the decree ought to be so far reversed, that no interest shall arise till a year after the death of the father.

[1420] 24 May was a Friday in 1734, Kratz, *Hist. Cal.*
[1421] *Tillotson* v. *Ganson* (1682) 1 Vern. 103, 23 E.R. 344 (plaintiff not bound to make election, till defendant has answered.)
[1422] 18 June was a Tuesday in 1734, Kratz, *Hist. Cal.*
[1423] Continued from p. 154.
[1424] Continued from p. 147.

In *Astel* v. *Richardson* there are two questions:

1. Whether the plaintiff in right of his wife is entitled to the portion, because she was not a daughter alive at the commencement etc., but died in the lifetime of her father.

2. If he is entitled, when the interest for her portion shall arise.

1. Equity construes settlements so as they may best answer the end and intention of the contracting parties, and therefore I think the word here must be understood, commencement in point of interest.

2. The interest is not to be paid till the death of the father.

Lord Chief Justice

I think that later authorities both in the Court of Chancery and House of Lords of England go against raising the portion in the life of the father or mother.

I think the case of *Stepney* v. *Rowson* bears a resemblance to *Brome* v. *Berkely*.[1425] The maintenances are provided for in much the same manner, so I have changed my opinion, and think we must come to the same resolution, and that interest is not due till a year after the death of the father.

As to *Astel* v. *Richardson*, I think it would be hard on the circumstances of the case to deprive the plaintiff of this portion, and to make such a construction, when the words are not express, that a daughter who was not alive when the term commenced in possession, though she married with the consent of her friends, and had children, should have no portion. And it can't be supposed that the lady's friends who contracted for this settlement could have such an intention, but must mean when the term commenced in point of interest, by the mother's dying without issue male, though I think the interest ought not to arise but from the death of father. [*414*]

Lord Chancellor

These cases turn upon a point [that] has been very variously construed.

The question began originally in the courts of law, in the case of *Greaves* v. *Mattison*,[1426] and the courts of equity followed the law till they found the inconveniences of such resolutions for raising portions in the life of the father, and have ever since avoided it, where the words were not express for that purpose, for in the case of *Brome* v. *Berkley*,[1427] and *Butler* v. *Duncomb*,[1428] according to the rule and reasoning in former cases the portions ought to have been raised in the life of the particular tenant, and they seem to have searched and looked into the deeds that they might lay hold of any words to get out of the authorities of the old cases, but whether these were their reasons or not, I'm sure they have gone back from the elder precedents.[1429]

Butler v. *Duncomb*[1430] turned on the word commencement; *Brome* v. *Berkley*,[1431] that the maintenances preceded the portions, and they were not to be raised till the first

---

[1425] (1728) 6 Bro. P.C. 2nd ed. 108, 2 E.R. 965. Above, p. 152.
[1426] *Greaves* v. *Mattison* (1682) Jones T. 201, 84 E.R. 1216, and see pp. 148, 153, 157.
[1427] *Brome* v. *Berkley* (1728) 6 Bro. P.C. 2nd ed. 108, 2 E.R. 965.
[1428] *Butler* v. *Duncomb* (1718) 2 Vern. 760, 23 E.R. 1096.
[1429] Spelled 'presidts' in MS.
[1430] *Butler* v. *Duncomb* (1718) 2 Vern. 760, 23 E.R. 1096.
[1431] *Brome* v. *Berkley* (1728) 6 Bro. P.C. 2nd ed. 108, 2 E.R. 965.

feast after the term took effect in possession; *Corbet* v. *Maidwell*[1432] that the portion was for a daughter unprovided for at the death of her father.

So their opinion is, that the portions are not to be raised in the life of the particular tenant, where the intention don't appear expressly from the words, whereby the portions or the maintenances are to be raised, therefore as in *Brome* v. *Berkley*, I'm of opinion in *Stepney* v. *Rawson*, that no interests arise till a year after the death of the father.

As to the first point in *Astel* v. *Richardson*, I will stick by the old rule for raising portions, that they vested when the term commenced in interest, when by the contingencies being over, it came *in esse*, though not in possession, and another construction would being doing an injustice to the mother, who was a purchaser, and brought a good fortune, and this is all her children are to have. This would alter the old cases in a point which is not necessary, and where the construction is of no detriment to the estate, and is not within the mischief of raising them by sale or mortgage in the life of the father, when it might undo a family to allow the interest for a portion which the father had spent and lived upon, and I think some [*415*] inconveniences and contradictions would arise from the words of the deed, by allowing interest in the life of the father. So I think the portion vested, when the term commenced in interest, but that it ought not to be raised till the term commenced in possession, so that no interest is due for it till the death of the father. But I will allow the legal interest for it at the time of the death of the father, when it became due.

Monday, June the 17th, Trinity Term, 1734[1433]

In Exchequer

MARNEY v. FRISSEL

The plaintiff, an old man of eighty, employed the defendant to write his letters, and he brought him a bond in the penalty of £240 for payment of £120, with warrant of attorney to confess judgment, and after he had signed it as a letter, he carried it to two in the house, who on seeing the plaintiff's name to it, signed it as witnesses. The defendant took out execution on the judgment, which he caused to be entered, and seized by virtue thereof three gabbards,[1434] which were the only support of the plaintiff.

The defendant in his answer denied all these charges, and swore that he stated an account with the plaintiff of what was due to him for wages, and that the bond was given for the balance, admitted he was employed by the plaintiff to write his letters. Yet the court relieved the plaintiff from the air of fraud that ran through the case, on the affidavit of the plaintiff, and one of the witnesses, which they suffered to be read, the other being out of the kingdom, and on his giving security for the sum and costs, the court ordered him the gabbarts[1435] out of execution, the working them

---

[1432] *Corbett* v. *Maydwell* (1710) 2 Vern. 655, 23 E.R. 1027.

[1433] 17 June was a Monday in 1734, Kratz, *Hist. Cal.*

[1434] Also spelled 'gabbart', a barge or lighter, for conveying cargo from sailing ships to shore. Above, pp. cxxv, 66 [*76*].

[1435] So spelled in MS.

being his only subsistence, and being very poor, they would not oblige him to bring the money into court.

This was on the motion of Mr Daly for an injunction to stay the sale.

Monday, July the 16th 1734.[1436]

MILLS v. NUTTAL [1437]

In Exchequer

A legacy was decreed to be paid by the defendant Nuttal. He and Maguire who were partners in the banking trade, before a sequestration for his non-performance of the decree [416] the day before they stopped payment, vested the real and personal estates in trustees for the payment of their creditors. And one of the trustees deposited a chest in which their ready money was lodged in the bank of Henry and Company as a deposit, and he now came to show cause why a sequestration for non-performance of the decree against Mr Nuttal should not attach on it.

And the court allowed the cause, that the decree no more than a judgment at law attached on the goods till the execution was served, that here was no fraud, but if this had been an assignment only by Mr Nuttal of his private estate it would not have been fraudulent, for the effects by this assignment are out of his power, and no longer his, and the assignment being by both of their partnership effects makes the case much the stronger, so the plaintiff must come in as a creditor.

Friday, July the 13, 1734[1438]

COSTELLO v. COSTELLO[1439]

In Exchequer

The motion was for an injunction on equity confessed in the answer, that the defendants had brought two ejectments, which were tried by *nisi prius*, and a verdict in each ejectment for the now plaintiffs, of which there had been no complaint, and that the defendants had brought a third ejectment to which this injunction was prayed, that a real action is a bar to another of the same kind,

MSŠ Ord in. Canc. 129.

MSŠ cas. in Canc. C. 162

[Inserted note:[1440] *Leighton* v. *Leighton*. In Canc. Mich. 7 Geo. 1.[1441] Where two verdicts on trials at bar in favour of the plaintiff's title, a perpetual injunction was decreed according to the case of *Lord Bath* v. *Sherwin*,[1442] which practice was introduced, that the right might be quieted in

---

[1436]   16 July was a Tuesday in 1734, Kratz, *Hist. Cal.*
[1437]   Continued from p. 215.
[1438]   13 July was a Saturday in 1734, Kratz, *Hist. Cal.*
[1439]   Resumed on p. 342.
[1440]   The note is inserted in the margin at this point in the MS.
[1441]   *Leighton* v. *Leighton* (1720) 1 P. Wms. 671, 24 E.R. 563, (1720) 4 Bro. P.C. 2nd ed. 378, 2 E.R. 256.
[1442]   *Lord Bath* v. *Sherwin* (1709) Prec. Ch. 261, 24 E.R. 126; *Earl of Bath* v. *Sherwin* (1709) 4 Bro. P.C. 2nd ed. 373, 2 E.R. 253 (after five trials at bar, and five verdicts all the same, the court of Chancery will grant a perpetual injunction to restrain all further proceedings at law on the same title by the parties, or anyone claiming under them).

ejectments where at law the party is always at liberty to bring a new one, as it was in real actions, where the verdict was final, and this was affirmed in the House of Lords,[1443] March 1720. N.B. there had been several county verdicts to the contrary, but the trials at bar were last. MSS Cas. in BR, D.157, SC.]

and the party can only resort to a higher action, as from a writ of entry *sur disseisin*, to a writ of right, and that these two verdicts ought to be thought equal to verdicts in disseisin and a writ of right which would have been final, since ejectments are substituted in the room of real actions.

'Twas said for the defendants, that trials in disseisin and writs of right were very different from and more solemn than trials by *nisi prius* or even at bar.

The court ordered the defendants to stop till hearing, and the plaintiffs speed their cause, and at the hearing they would [*417*] judge whether the injunction should be continued, or the bill dismissed.

Monday, June the 17th, 1734[1444]

Trinity Term

LORD GAGE, MR CRAWFORD AND OTHERS

v.

THE ATTORNEY GENERAL
AND HAYINGTON

This cause was spoke to before two [*sic*] several times.

Mr Recorder for the plaintiffs

This bill is to be decreed to the sum of £810 levied by the defendant Hayington, when he was high sheriff of the county of Wicklow, the rent reserved on a custodiam, and totted[1445] for him before the private Act of Parliament passed for the relief of Dame Elizabeth Dudley[1446] etc., by which we apprehend this money to be vested in Lord Gage, and William Piers Esqr.

Private Bills B.425.

The doubt is on the vesting clause, whereby all and every the manors etc., and all rent accrued to the Crown etc., not paid into His Majesty's Exchequer in Ireland etc., be sued for and recovered in the name of His Majesty etc. The question then is, whether totting is a payment into His Majesty's Exchequer, for if it is, His Majesty and not the plaintiffs, is entitled to this sum.

[1443]   *Leighton* v. *Leighton* (1720) 4 Bro. P.C. 2nd ed. 378, 2 E.R. 256.
[1444]   17 June was a Monday in 1734, Kratz, *Hist. Cal.*
[1445]   L. *tot*, so much, so many; according to Blount, short for *tot pecuniæ Regi debenitur*, so many sums of money are due to the king. See above, p. lxiv.
[1446]   The reference in the marginal note is evidently to private bills kept in Ireland, and probably kept in the Public Record Office in the Four Courts, in which case they were destroyed in the fire of 1922. However, there is an existing English private Act: 'An Act for Relief of Dame Elizabeth Dudley, relating to an Estate in the Kingdom of Ireland, forfeited to the Crown during the Life of William Kennedy her great Uncle', 1729, Private Act, 3 Geo. II, c. 21, *HLRO*, 3 Geo. II, no. 58. See Appendix D.

'Tis plain from the recitals of the Act that by the Exchequer in this clause must be meant the receipt of the Exchequer.

The Act recites the settlement of Sir Richard Kennedy, that William Kennedy the second son was outlawed for treason, whereby the estate limited to him by the said settlement became forfeited to the Crown, then recites the Trustee Act,[1447] and an Act made 1 Anne,[1448] whereby the money arising by the forfeited estates and interests therein mentioned was to be paid into the receipt of the Exchequer in Ireland, and there to be kept apart from other Her Majesty's treasure and revenue. Here the Act tells us [418] what Exchequer they mean: the receipt of the Exchequer. Then the inquisition, and custodiam are recited, and the rent reserved thereon. The petition of Sir William Dudley and Dame Elizabeth his wife, and then comes the said vesting clause.

I think the doubt is created by the word Exchequer, which has several meanings, and in which of them is to be understood here, must be gathered from the context. It may signify the whole court, sometimes the Exchequer Chamber, sometimes the court of pleas before the barons, which has no power over money when it is paid into the receipt of the Exchequer. Formerly a summons issued to the party for payment of money returnable at Easter and Michaelmas, and in the old books these times of payment are often called the Exchequer, as the Exchequer of Easter, of Michaelmas. These several meanings may be seen in the fourth chapter of Maddox's *History of the Exchequer*,[1449] and the word is applicable to any of them according to the subsequent matter. Here by the word is intended the receipt, which of late years has obtained the name of the Inferior Exchequer, answer is fixed upon by the Act, because then the money becomes part of His Majesty's revenue, and the barons have no power over it, but it must be taken out by the King himself, though *in transitu* the barons have a power over it. By the recited Act 1 Anne the money arising by the sale etc. is to be paid into the receipt of the Exchequer, and the rent not paid into the Exchequer being vested by this Act, because these clauses are relative to one another.

So whether totting is a payment or not, 'tis not a payment into the receipt of the Exchequer, but is *in transitu*.

Originally as the King issued writs to the sheriffs, and others who had the charge of his casual or certain revenue. The barons when they came to pay this money, had no power to make them any allowances without a writ under the Great or Privy Seal, till 5 R. 2.[1450] The sheriff is charged with the several fines issued in Green Wax,[1451] and accounts before the barons. All this is in [419] *transitu*, and he tots, that is charges himself with the receipt of them, or o.ni.'s,[1452] which is an actual charge, unless the next sheriff levies it, and he prays in aid of the King, and 'tis respited.

[1447] 11 Will. III, c. 2. (11 & 12 Will. III in Ruffhead) (Eng.), 1698–99, Trustee Act, Resumption Act (forfeited estates in Ireland vested in trustees). The Private Act 3 Geo. II, c. 21 refers to it by the Ruffhead citation, 11 & 12 Will. III, 'An Act for granting an Aid to His Majesty by Sale of the forfeited and other estates and interests in Ireland.'

[1448] 1 Ann., st. 2, c. 18 (Eng.) (c. 21 in Ruffhead) 1702 (crown estates, forfeited estates in Ireland, receipt by Irish Exchequer), s. 7.

[1449] Thomas Madox, *The History and Antiquities of the Exchequer of the Kings of England* (2nd ed. 1711, reprinted, 1969).

[1450] I.e. 1381/2.

[1451] Above, p. lx.

[1452] An abbreviation of the Latin words *oneratur, nisi habeat sufficientem exonerationem*, he is charged (or legally responsible) unless he have a sufficient discharge. Above, p. lxiv.

By the practice of the court the sheriff has four days to bring in his tots, and he may after totting crave allowances, or the court may respite the time for his payment: Sommer's argument in the *Banker's Case*,[1453] and the precedents[1454] there cited out of Ryley.[1455] So the tot is not money paid into His Majesty's Exchequer, because then the money being out of your power you could not respite the payment, or make the sheriff any allowance out of it, but it must come out by the Great, or Privy Seal.

Money even in the chamberlain's hands is not money paid into the Exchequer, but this court has a power over it, 2 Inst. 572, 573. So there is a difference between money paid into the Exchequer, when 'tis confessed to be within the sheriff's hands, nay though it was out of the sheriff's hands, and he had laid it down here in the officer's hands, by the 2 Inst. you would still have a power over it. Your Lordships are not the receipt, but to issue process, and enforce payment, but you can't receive, or give a discharge for the money as an actual payment.

So that the Exchequer without reference to the recited Act must mean the final receipt, and this is stronger than if it was in the hands of the chamberlains, so though the sheriff had laid down this money in bags as formerly, the tot would not be a payment into the Exchequer. You may issue process against the sheriff to bring in this money, which shows 'tis not yet in the receipt. So the tot is not a payment into the Exchequer, by which must be meant the receipt of the Exchequer, which can give a discharge for it, and the makers of the Act knew that till then it was not the King's money.

Mr Daly

Went over the several recitals of the Act, and observed with Mr Recorder the variety of senses in which the word Exchequer is taken, and that Lord Coke[1456] in 4 Inst. 119 says, that in the Exchequer there are seven courts, and [*420*] mentions the officers of each of them.

The general charge is contained in the Great Roll of the remembrancer. There is an annual, and an exannual roll,[1457] which arose on the Statute of Rutland.[1458] Nothing is put in the annual roll but 'tis probable the sheriff may levy, but the whole revenue is in the exannual. The sheriff is to account on the first, and the other is to be read, that he may give an account if there is a probability of levying any of the sums that are in it. The inconvenience before was, that the sheriff used to worry the subjects alike either for good or desperate debts. So he was to keep these two rolls, and to tot for those on the annual roll which were good debts. So no inference can be drawn from the totting, that the money was levied, but only that it is a good debt.

As to the sheriffs taking security, 'tis determined in the case of *Sir Daniel Norton*, Lane 74,[1459] that the party is not discharged thereby.

[1453] *The King* v. *Hornby (the Banker's Case)* (1695) 5 Mod. 29, 87 E.R. 500, per Lord Somers. Howard, *Treatise of the Exchequer*, p. 8. Above, p. lxii.

[1454] Spelled 'presidts' in MS.

[1455] Ryl. Plac. Parl.

[1456] *Sic.* Sir Edward Coke.

[1457] A roll kept at the Exchequer to which debts to the Crown presumed to be irrecoverable were transferred, instead of being carried forward in the 'Annual Roll' from year to year. *OED.*

[1458] 12 Edw. I (10 Edw. I, c. 11 in Ruffhead) (Eng.), 1281, Statute of Rutland (provisions as to the Exchequer), *Statutes of The Realm, Chronological Table of the Statutes, covering the period from 1235 to the end of 1971* (London, 1972). See also Jacob & Tomlin, *Law Dictionary*, 'Exchequer'.

[1459] *Sir Daniel Norton's Case* Lane 74, 145 E.R. 310.

Totting was first introduced by 42 Ed. 3 ch. 9.[1460] Before the statute the process of the Pipe used to issue against the party if the sheriff would not account, to prevent which this Act obliges the sheriff after he has received the money to tot for it, or pay treble damages, and by the 3 Ed. 1 ch. 19,[1461] no summons is to go to the party after the sheriff has owned the account, and on this depends the cases in Keilw. 172b,[1462] 185a[1463] that the o.ni.[1464] makes the sheriff debtor to the King, and the party to the sheriff, and after a tot and o.ni. the sheriff may be discharged. Suppose a recognisance for appearance is estreated[1465] and goes in Green Wax to the sheriff, which he levies and tots for, the recognisor on the reducement shows he appeared to the indictment, and was acquitted, won't your Lordship reduce the recognisance? So totting is not a payment, but the sheriff is only a debtor to the Crown for it, whereas if it amounted to an actual payment into the Exchequer, he could not be a debtor for it.

By tot or o.ni. the sheriff is made a debtor, 4 Inst. 116, Hardr. 424[1466] and if he refuses to pay, process must issue against him, and if process may issue upon his tots, that shows totting is no payment into the Exchequer.

This Act then must mean money paid into the Exchequer according to law, and such a payment as will discharge [421] the debtor, which only into the receipt can do. There was no occasion to recite 1 Anne, but to show where the rent was to be paid into, and the words must mean such money as the barons had no power over.

This money then, being in an accountant's hands, for which process must issue if he don't pay it, shows it can't be considered as an actual payment.

Sir John St Leger

The sheriff becomes the King's debtor from the o.ni., Keilw. 187,[1467] and the Crown can't resort to the party, but he is discharged. Now the o.ni. is only an act of the court, where the sheriff won't tot, or give an excuse and we give him a constat[1468] to levy the fines and amerciaments, whereas the tot is his own act, and an account.

Mr Jones procures a custodiam reserving a fourth part of the rent to himself. He receives the whole rents. The tenants petition that the money may be respited in the sheriff's hands, because he was to account for three fourths, and that their lands might not be sued in hopes to get the money from Jones. The tenants are discharged *quoad* the King, and he can only come on the sheriff. This Act grants no debt due to the King. Here the King has no suit against the tenants, or strangers, but only a *capias*, or other execution against the sheriff.

Mr Crawford, to whom Jones had assigned this money, having desired leave of the court, spoke to this effect:

[1460] 42 Edw. III, c. 9 (Eng.), 1368 (crown debts, sheriffs, totting).

[1461] 3 Edw. I, c. 19 (Eng.), 1275 (crown debts).

[1462] Keilw. 172, 72 E.R. 347 (text).

[1463] Keilw. 185, 72 E.R. 362 (text).

[1464] Above, p. 329 n. 1452.

[1465] An estreat was the true extract, copy or note of some original writing or record, of fines, amercements, etc., entered on the rolls of a court to be levied by the bailiff or other officer.

[1466] *Attorney-General* v. *Beston* (1666) Hard. 424, 145 E.R. 529.

[1467] Keilw. 187, 72 E.R. 364 (text).

[1468] L. *constat*, it is certain, it is established. A certificate stating what appears (*constat*) upon record concerning a matter, given by the clerk of the pipe and auditors of the Exchequer at the request of a person who intends to plead or move in that court for the discharge of any matter. Also an exemplification of the enrolment of letters-patent under the Great Seal.

The question is, whether this is money paid. The recitals of the Act are to be observed. These rents are to be actually paid into the receipt of the Exchequer etc., whilst the estate was in the hands of the Crown. Either the tenants or the custodee must pay it into the Exchequer. And it is not meant of a constructive payment by a tot, but of an actual payment into the Exchequer, because it is to be kept there separate and apart from other money.

A tot is only a general account.

At the time of making this Act £540 was actually levied by the former sheriff, and paid in, and these words were put [422] in to except and distinguish this money, which was not to be restored to the family.

The custodiam is recited. 'All rents accrued to the Crown.' etc.: these words must refer to those rents. The recitals must explain what payments are meant, and the Act must be construed beneficially for the honour of the Crown. And if there could be any doubts, the words, 'All right, title', etc. will remove it.

As to the direction to sue in His Majesty's name, what remedy have we, how could we compel the sheriff to answer the tot, but in His Majesty's name, and the right of the Crown ceased, and Lord Gage and William Piers Esqr could not otherwise recover, but the sheriff would say, 'I have totted'.

Provided that the several tenants and lessees etc. shall not be made further answerable etc., these words show the Act could not mean old rents, but those reserved on the custodiam, which would otherwise be without meaning.

Mr Attorney General

It could not be the intention of the Act to give those arrears which the sheriff by his duty ought to have paid. In November the sheriff was opposed, and in six days after he ought to have paid the money. The Act was made six months after, and supposed these were paid in, and only designed to give those arrears the sheriff had not accounted for.

Mr Hussy for the plaintiff

Money totted for is not money paid, *Articuli Super Chartas* ch. 19,[1469] 2 Inst. 572, and Lord Sommers in his argument in the *Banker's Case*[1470] says, that it is a settled maxim, that money paid into the Treasury can never be taken out, but while 'tis *in transitu*, though 'tis paid into the hands of a receiver, or collector, it may be restored, and that money paid into the chamberlain's is not money paid into the Exchequer, because they retain it in their hands, that if the subject has any right, they may do them justice.

Lord Chief Baron

'Tis the indulgence of the court to give the sheriff six days [423] to pay his tots, to go through the offices, and get the chamberlain's receipts for his account.

[1469] The title of the statute 28 Edw. I, c. 19 (Eng.), 1300 (*Articuli Super Cartas*) confirming Magna Carta, but without the saving clauses in 25 Edw. I (*Confirmatio Chartarum*).

[1470] Above, p. 330 n. 1453.

The sheriffs formerly brought their tots into court in bags, and tendered it in court, which Mr Harrison[1471] remembers.

Mr Baron Wainwright

Tot is, *totu[m] illud habeo.*[1472]

Sir John St Leger

Tot is a payment. The sheriff was committed if he did not produce it. Tot is so much money is in that bag, and is a discharge to the debtor, and the King can't after resort to the tenant or farmer, but to the sheriff, who is the receiver of the demesnes of the Crown.

Six days is given to the sheriff, not by the indulgence of the court, but to get the vice-treasurer's receipt, and because they have not time to reckon it in court.

The meaning of this Act is, that they shall be at liberty to use the name of the Crown for the arrears. This must mean a remedy against the tenants, but here they are discharged by this Act, by which the money not levied, is to be levied by the authority of the Crown.

Mr Harrison[1473]

The sheriffs formerly brought the tots in bags sealed, and they remained with the Clerk of the Pipe, who kept a chest in court to deposit them. And he had a fee for his certificate to the chamberlains. And if the sheriff don't bring in his tots, we lays three fines on him, four days between each of them, and then an attachment.

Monday, July the 16.[1474]

The last day of the eight days after Trinity Term 1734

Lord Chief Baron

I think by the words of the Act page 6, 'All rent accrued to the Crown' etc., the plaintiffs are entitled to this sum, and the words, 'To be sued for in the name of His Majesty' etc., don't confine the words, that nothing shall be recovered but what may be sued for in the name of the King, but only gives them this liberty for so [*424*] much of the rent as in arrear and to be sued for, and the ground of my opinion is this, that totting is no discharge to the sheriff of his debt, till it has gone through the proper hands, but he is still liable to process, and money totted for is not actually paid in, but *in transitu,* and the sheriff is entitled to proper allowances.

[1471] Probably Joseph Harrison, an attorney, listed in KI AP as master of an apprentice, 11 Feb. 1719. KI AP, p. 215. Above, p. lxiv.

[1472] L. all that thing I have.

[1473] Above, n. 1471 and above, p. lxiv.

[1474] 16 July was a Tuesday in 1734, Kratz, *Hist. Cal.,* but the year is given in the line below. Note that it is the same date as that above, p. 327.

Sir John St Leger

I am sorry I differ in opinion from my brother. I won't go into a consideration of the several courts of the Exchequer, or the different acceptances of the word Exchequer, because I don't believe the makers of the Act had them in their view, but only designed to give the King's name to sue for the arrears that were in the hands of the tenants. I don't think this Act is to have a liberal construction. This is public money distinct from the money of the Crown, and is to be kept apart from his other treasure and revenue, and if any favour is to be shown in the construction of it, 'tis in favour of the public creditors.

To give this money to the plaintiffs, we must supply what is not in the Act, and to the words, 'not paid into His Majesty's Exchequer of Ireland', we must add, 'into the receipt of his Exchequer.' In the recitals of the Act 1 Anne page 3 the words, 'Into the receipt of the Exchequer' are made use of, and it has been from thence inferred, that by the Exchequer in this clause must be meant the receipt of the Exchequer too, but I think the contrary is to be inferred, that they did not mean the receipt, or they would have made use of the word, and it was necessary to mention it in the reciting clause, where it was ultimately to come, and be kept apart from other Her Majesty's treasure and revenue. The Act says, 'you shall have all rent' etc. This can't be called rent, you can't sue the tenant for it in the King's name, for he is discharged by the tot, and the sheriff is the King's debtor.

Shall these words then give Lord Gage and William Piers Esqr a right by this bill to sue His Majesty's [425] Attorney General? The words are only, that they may sue and recover in the King's name. The money was properly that day on the table when it was totted for, and by the practice in the reign of Queen Elizabeth if the sheriff did not produce the money he totted for, he was to be attached in court immediately, though this practice is now relaxed while the money is *in transitu*, out of indulgence to the sheriff, and in old Magna Charta there is a picture of the Exchequer, where the several officers are seated round the Cheque,[1475] looking at the tots in the sheriff's bags.

This money ought to have been paid in four years ago, and I won't add the word receipt by construction to take this money from the creditors of the public, and when I think it plain the legislature meant at large, rent not paid into the Exchequer.

Mr Baron Wainwright

I have been very much divided upon this Act, but have settled it as well as I can, and am of the same opinion with my lord chief baron for these reasons. I consider it as an Act of restitution, and therefore to have a liberal construction, and these words in 2 Inst. 572 ch. 19 weigh with me, De Rechief etc, where my Lord Coke[1476] in his comment says, that by issues are intended rents and things leviable by the escheator, which may be restored though the escheator has accounted for them, and not paid, but the money being once in the King's coffers shall not be restored, and that these being beneficial laws for restitution, extend to things not mentioned, as livery, etc.

The 5th page of this Act recites, that Sir Richard Kennedy, and Sir William Dudley, and Dame Elizabeth his wife had been always well affected to the Protestant interest,

---

1475 The chequered table used in the Exchequer for counting money. Above, p. lxiv.
1476 *Sic.* Sir Edward Coke.

and designed to restore them, and the words in page 6 are very extensive, whereby not only all rent etc., but all and every right, etc., is vested etc., and though we have no power over money when paid into the receipt from the authority of the *Banker's Case*,[1477] yet I think this money is only *in transitu*, and that money in the accountants' hands is not paid into the Exchequer, but only accounted for. One thing indeed weighed with me to be of a contrary [*426*] opinion if the Act would let me, that there seems not to have been a full discovery of this matter to the King or Parliament, but they industriously took care to respite and delay this payment, but I think this can't hinder the operation and effect of the Act which must bind us. And there is some artifice too in wording the Act. 'Tis inferred from the Act that is recited, that by the Exchequer in the vesting clause must be meant the receipt of the Exchequer, but I should think the words if they stood singly turned the argument the contrary way, and that by Exchequer must be meant something other than receipt, but the reason I go on is this, that this is an Act of restitution, and like the case of a traverse or *monstrans de droit*[1478] against the King where the party being restored to the mesne profits, is restored not only to the arrears, but to the tots if not actually paid into the receipt, and this Act being drawn by men of skill and knowledge in the profession, I take to be formed on those judgments, and designed to restore what was not *domino regi respons̃*, and this Act being a restitution of a forfeiture, deserves a liberal construction, and meant to restore what was in the power of this court to restore.

Sir John St Leger

On a *monstrans de droit* judgment is given because the King had no right, and therefore the party is to be fully restored, but the King here had a just right to these arrears.

Wednesday, May the 15th, 1734[1479]

In Exchequer

LADY DILLON v. HUSSY ET UXR. ET AL.

Mr Recorder for the defendants

Though this bill is said to be only for discovery. 'Tis for relief also, for the conclusion is, that the confederates may stand to and abide etc., this being a bill for discovery only against the confederates.

The plaintiff is one of the daughters of Lady Tyrconnel [*427*] and has shown by her bill she has no right to distribution. She charges that Lady Tyrconnel in 1704 made her will, and appointed the Duchess of Marlborough executor, and thereby

---

[1477] *The King* v. *Hornby (the Banker's Case)* (1695) 5 Mod.29, 87 E.R. 500, per Lord Somers. Howard, *Treatise of the Exchequer*, p. 8.

[1478] LF. demonstration, showing, of right. Proceedings originally in Chancery or the Exchequer to determine, on facts already established, whether the subject or the Crown had title to property real or personal.

[1479] 15 May was a Wednesday in 1734, Kratz, *Hist. Cal.*

devised her real estate to trustees to sell, and to pay one third of the money arising by the sale to her daughters, and the other two thirds to George Parsons her grandson, that it is pretended she made another will in 1726, and Lord Berkeley executor thereof, which was lodged with William Guidot Esqr in London, that Lord Berkeley exhibited this will in the Prerogative court of Canterbury, and proved it after her death, though Mr Guidot promised it should not be opened till all parties concerned were present, that Lady Tyrconnel died on the 6 March 1730, and some time before her death was pressed to make her will, but refused, but that the defendants Collins and Somner took hints on a piece of paper which she was prevailed on by importunity to give them, but had no intent to execute, that a lawyer was sent for, and she refused to make a will, that Mr Hussy produced these scraps as her will, that a cause was thereupon instituted in the Prerogative court of this kingdom, that witnesses were examined, and cross-examined, that sentence was given in favour of the will, and that she[1480] had appealed from this sentence, as well as from that in favour of Lord Berkeley to the Delegates in England, and then she lays her equity thus, that she was her daughter, and that the wills ought not to be established, but that she had a right to administer, and a distributive share, that she had appealed from those sentences, that the sentence in this kingdom ought not to have been given, because the witnesses varied in their cross-examination from their first depositions, that there were many rasures in these scraps propounded as a will, that her appeals are now depending before the Delegates in England, and that she could only have relief in equity from the answers of Hussy and his wife, and of Collins and Somner.

This on the face of it is a bill for relief, from the words to stand to, etc., which are as full as to pray relief, and the other words won't take it away, for if the cause [428] came to a hearing, these general words would entitle the court to make what decree they thought fit on the merits, and the plaintiff's saying she prays only a discovery, won't alter the nature of the bill, and on bills for a bare discovery, the plaintiff prays a subpœna to answer only, and when the defendant has discovered, he has a right to dismiss the bill.

The defendant may demur to the relief and discovery, where the bill is not proper for a discovery only, though there are many instances where a bill for discovery is proper, though not for relief.

On a demurrer to the relief in the case of *Sir Walter Burroughs*,[1481] this court thought the words 'such further and other relief' etc., made it a bill for relief.

If this is a bill for relief our demurrers are good, for the bill is improper, for this court can't relieve against two sentences in the spiritual court, or overhaul them. They have gone this far indeed, that if any fraud has been practised in obtaining a will, and anyone under the probate comes here for relief, the court will refuse it, will not touch the probate, and the plaintiff admits jurisdiction of the spiritual courts by her appeal.

But if this is a bill for a discovery only, 'tis not proper, and this is the distinction, equity will be auxiliary to a court in which the cause is originally, if you can't there have a discovery, as to a court of law, where you can't have the oath of the party. But here is no necessity for a discovery, but the bill is vexatious, for the plaintiff may have an answer to all she seeks by it before the Delegates, so 'tis not only making this court

---

[1480] I.e. the plaintiff.
[1481] No citation given.

auxiliary, but to do what is wholly unnecessary, for she may libel[1482] anew before the Delegates, examine new witnesses, and have the personal answers of the parties. And though the King's justice is distributed among the several courts, and the original courts have given sentence, and the plaintiff has appealed, and may have a discovery before the Delegates, yet she would draw it *ad aliud examen.*[1483]

Lutterel v. *Lutterel:*[1484] the plaintiff libelled in the spiritual [*429*] court for a separate maintenance, and they proceeded against the husband to a writ *de excommunicato capiendo.* Then she filed a bill for aid *in personam,* and that his real and personal estate might be sequestered, because the spiritual court could only proceed against his person for contumacy. The cause was heard by Lord Midleton,[1485] and reheard by Lord Chancellor West, who dismissed the bill, because the matter was originally conusable in the spiritual court, and the court would not assist a defect in the law, that they could not make their sentence more effectual. In that case there seemed to be some necessity for the bill, because if he would continue *contumax*[1486] the suit would be fruitless, but the plaintiff can be no sufferer by allowing our demurrers, for she may produce new witnesses before the Delegates.

What signifies a discovery of that part of the bill which charges the will to be razed and defaced? The plaintiff says it appears on the will, and what can we say more. She don't say whether these witnesses were examined below or not, if they were examined below, you won't encourage a re-examination of them, and do what that court would not do after sentence and publication, and what you would not suffer to aid your own jurisdiction, to overturn a decree upon a re-examination. Who knows what tampering there may be after publication. Then it is worth while to bribe, when they see what is sworn, and what is the gist of the cause.

If these were new witnesses, she has no right to a discovery, because they were either parties below, or witnesses, and they may libel against them on the appeal, or might in the first instance, and where this court helps, they will see whether the party did all he might in the inferior court, and won't aid him, where he was indolent, negligent, or slips his advantage.

Lord Chief Baron

This is a bill for discovery only. If it had prayed relief, I think it might be supported. The bill of *Lutterel* was to carry the sentence of the spiritual court [*430*] into execution against the effects of the husband, he having gone out of the kingdom, and Lord Midleton[1487] carried the sentence into execution as to what was past, but lessened the alimony as to the time to come, but Lord Chancellor West dismissed the bill.   Mes App. B.119.

Mr Solicitor General for the plaintiff

This cause comes before the court on two separate demurrers, one of James Hussy, and Catharine his wife, the other of William Somner, and James Collins. It appears

---

[1482] In the sense used in ecclesiastical courts, meaning the pleading setting out the nature of the plaintiff's case.
[1483] L. to another jurisdiction.
[1484] See the marginal note below, giving the reference as 'Mes App. B.119.'
[1485] Spelled 'Middleton' in MS.
[1486] L. in contempt of court.
[1487] Spelled 'Middleton' in MS.

by the bill, that the plaintiff is one of the daughters of Lady Tyrconnel, who in 1704 made a will in England, and thereby directed her estate to be sold, and part of the money to go to her daughters, and that the plaintiff had no notice of this will till after the death of her mother, and her applying to the spiritual court for administration. She says that 'tis pretended another will was made in 1726, and Lord Berkeley executor, and that she made a codicil in favour of the defendants, but she charges this to be only a draft, and preparatory to a will, and that she often declared her will in 1704 should stand. This will was lodged in Mr Guidot's hands, and he promised not to open it till all that were concerned attended, yet he opened it in our absence, that the defendant Hussy says she made a will *in extremis* more in his favour, and the plaintiff mentions the artifices and importunities to prevail on her to make a will, the proof of it in the prerogative court of this kingdom and her appeal, and she has a right to come her for a discovery as a daughter either as being entitled to the administration, or under the will of 1704, in order to establish which she prays a discovery of all transactions since 1704, and this not only to assist her before the Delegates, but that she may turn it into a bill of relief, if she sees proper.

The first demurrer is for special causes that reach to both, that this discovery is a matter the plaintiffs may have before the Delegates, and that the Court of Exchequer is not to be ancillary to it. [431] But your Lordship won't take into the consideration what use is to be made of this discovery, or whether this court will be ancillary, but whether it is not proper to oblige them to discover this fraud in a devise, as well as in other cases, which is to the prejudice of Lady Dillon, relates to all the transactions, and the concealment of the will in 1704, which is a matter not relative to the appeal, and a discovery of it can only be had here. Indeed in separate suits such an examination might be in the spiritual court, but one discovery will do here, and as Mr Hussy and his lady are to reap the benefit, 'tis proper to have the discovery from them.

Sentence was given in the case of *Lutterel*, and they would have made the Court of Chancery ancillary to the execution, but if the husband had made over his effects in trust to defraud her of the benefit of the sentence, this court would have obliged him to discover, but this discovery is not relative to a suit in equity.

As to the demurrer of Somner and Collins, they insist that it don't appear by the bill, that they were examined below, and that therefore their answers could not be made use of before the Delegates. If they were not examined before the reason on that head as to them falls to the ground, but they being charged as parties to the fraud, they ought to answer.

Curia

The prayer of this bill is to have a discovery, that the plaintiff may use the answers of the defendants on the appeal. The demurrers must be allowed. This bill would make us in nature of commissioners to examine witnesses for the spiritual court, and a discovery would be needless, and of no use, for the plaintiff may examine the defendants to these matters as well on the appeal, and I don't know whether their answers to this bill could be read against them before the Delgates. [432]

CLERK v. CHARTRES

Saturday, June the 22nd, 1734[1488]

The bill was for payment of a legacy, and a conditional decree for an account. The officer reported £754 due to the plaintiff, and the decree on the report was made absolute, and the defendant now moved for a rehearing. And the petition was signed by two counsel, who certified they had examined the decree. And the case of *Vaughan* v. *Plunket*[1489] in Chancery was mentioned, where a plea was reheard after a decretal order nisi, and that made absolute, though no counsel attended, on affidavit of a compromise, which was a stronger case than this, because though the plea was overruled, they might insist on the benefit of it in their answer, and 'twas said, that rehearings ought to be granted readier in this kingdom than in England, because of the expense of an appeal.

Lord Chief Baron

There is no standing order in this court that may not be set aside in a particular case, but the defendant has made no particular case, has produced no affidavit, there is no standing order against rehearing a decree made absolute, but 'tis against the general reason of rehearings, which are granted in the faith of the counsel who attended on the hearing, that the court would not have made such a decree if everything had been fully laid before them at the time of the hearing, and since it is settled that rehearings are *ex gratia*, I think this ought not to be granted for fear of a precedent. The right of the defendant's sister to this legacy accrued in 1723. The defendant was served with the conditional decree. Why should this indulgence be granted him to put back the plaintiff? He may file a bill of review, for the cause you pretended for a rehearing is, that the daughter is decreed to interest at 7 per cent for her legacy from the death of her father [*433*] and you object you say only to the quantum, not to the time from which the interest is allowed.

Sir John St Leger

The brother is made executor, and has obliged his sister to spend her fortune in law. I was told by Lord Cowper, that no appeal would lie for interest, or costs, of which the court are supposed good judges. This conditional decree was made on the voluntary neglect of the party, and there is no affidavit to the contrary, and a conditional decree is not drawn up by the direction of the judges, but at the peril of the party and therefore can't be supposed as exact, as if the cause had been heard, and thoroughly spoke to, and so is more liable to be overturned on a rehearing.

Mr Solicitor General said, if an appeal would not lie for interest, or costs, he thought there was the more reason to grant a rehearing, because otherwise the defendant would be without remedy; that the conditional decree by the practice of this court is served on the attorney, and not on the party, (though 'tis served on the party in Chancery) and four days after service 'tis set down to be made absolute.

[1488] 22 June was a Saturday in 1734, Kratz, *Hist. Cal.*
[1489] No citation given.

Mr Baron Wainwright

Mes App. G.119.

Ante 385. This is an affectation of delay to gain the long vacation. The rehearing was denied.

WATSON v. COOK AND HENDRICK

Hendrick drew bills in favour of Watson on Mackay and Craighead in London. The bills were protested, and Hendrick failing, and going out of the way, Watson attached money in the hands of Cook due to Hendrick on a balance of account he had delivered to him, and then filed this bill for a discovery.

Cook demurred, because this was to discover in aid of an action in an inferior court, and because he was not accountable to Watson.

Mr Baron Wainwright being alone in court overruled [434] the demurrer, and said that where a debtor was out of the kingdom he thought it very reasonable to attach the money, that it might not be paid over to him, and that since the late Act[1490] the account with the plaintiff and Cook would bind Hendrick, if he let process go against him to a sequestration, and that though he had not waived his foreign attachment,[1491] the defendant might oblige him to make his election.

But Mr Prime Serjeant insisted, that when they had answered, the plaintiff might make his election to proceed at law, and give their answer in evidence in aid of the foreign attachment.

So the plaintiff having waived it, the court overruled the demurrer, but without costs, and obliged the plaintiff to consent to waive the foreign attachment.

CORR v. CORR

In Exchequer

The court will give the plaintiff leave to file a supplement bill on the Popery Acts, to avoid the doubt, whether an amending bill is to be considered as a new bill.

[1490] Below, n. 1491.

[1491] Watson could attach money in the hands of Cook owed to Hendrick under garnishee procedure, which applied in 'liberties', i.e. certain ancient cities. For foreign attachment see Jacob and Tomlins, *Law Dictionary*, 'Attachment foreign', 'an attachment of the goods of foreigners, found in some liberty, to satisfy their creditors within such liberty'. Brown, *Law Dictionary*, 'Attachment, foreign', states that foreign attachment applied in London, Exeter and 'some other ancient cities'. It seems to have been developed from the custom of merchants. The 'late Act' is not identified. Jacob cites Comyns, *Digest*, 'Attachment foreign', as citing '22 Edw. IV. 30'. See also *Magrath* v. *Hardy* (1838) 4 Bing. N.C. 785, 132 E.R. 990.

Tuesday, June the 18, 1734[1492]

LESSEE OF BULL v. LORD DARNLEY

Mr Attorney General for the defendant moved in arrest of judgment.

The first demise is on a lease made by Nathaniel Bull, dated 1 January 1732, of 'duo acras terre arabilis, decem acras pasture [et] decem acras prati communiter vocatas quinque parvas insulas jacentes et existentes inter [. . .][1493] et unam acram prati'.[1494]

And the second is on a lease made by Owen. And the *postea* is, 'dicunt super sacramentum [suum] quod defendentes sunt culpabiles de transgressione quoad duas insulas communiter vocatas per nomen de Mult et insulam de Anodyna existentes duo[1495] insularum in narratione infrascripta mentionatarum, et non sunt culpabiles etc. quoad alias tres insulas et unam acram prati prout etc.'[1496]

1. This declaration is uncertain, and no *habere* could issue.

2. If 'twas certain, the verdict is uncertain, and the sheriff can't tell of what the defendants are acquitted, of what found guilty.

3. Here is a discontinuance in the verdict, part not being [*435*] disposed of by the jury, 3 Lev. 55,[1497] 3 Cro. 133.[1498] Here are two demises, each of which is to be disposed of. If the demise relates to Owen, nothing is said to Bull; if to Bull, nothing to Owen. Is it the islands demised by Bull or Owen? 'Unam acram prati' can't go to both, and 'tis not said to which.

But if there is no discontinuance, the plaintiff can't have execution. By five islands, must be understood one denomination, or really five islands. If five islands there is not a sufficient description in what parish or barony they lie. They have said indeed that they lie between such lands, but those may be in different counties, and no ville is mentioned.

The verdict says they are guilty as to two islands, but it don't appear whether there is one acre of meadow, pasture, or arable in them. They should have mentioned what kind of land they contained, whether arable, etc. and how much of each kind. They may contain none of the land in the declaration, and ten times as much as declared for, Cro. Jam. 113,[1499] Noy 67.[1500]

This ejectment is not for five islands, but for such lands in them.

The plaintiff must allow that judgment must be so certain, that the sheriffs may give possession.

[1492] 18 June was a Tuesday in 1734, Kratz, *Hist. Cal.*

[1493] Blank in MS.

[1494] L. two acres of arable land, ten acres of pasture and ten acres of meadow commonly called five small islands lying and being between [. . .], and one acre of meadow.

[1495] MS reads 'du'.

[1496] L. [the jurors] say upon their oath that the defendants are guilty of the trespass with respect to two islands commonly called by the name of Mult' and the Island of Anodyne, being two of the islands mentioned in the within-written declaration, and not guilty etc. with respect to the other three islands and one acre of pasture, as etc.

[1497] *Graves* v. *Morley* (1682) 3 Lev. 55, 83 E.R. 574 (verdict: discontinuance).

[1498] *Finymore* v. *Sanky* (1588) Cro. Eliz. 133, 78 E.R. 390.

[1499] *Woolmer* v. *Caston* (1606) Cro. Jac. 113, 79 E.R. 98 (partial verdict).

[1500] *Beum* v. *Felton* (1598) Noy 67, 74 E.R. 1035 (partial verdict).

Cro. Eliz. 465[1501] is quite different from this, because there was only one species of land. Here are several kinds.

Cro. Ja. 435,[1502] in that [case] the closes are said to contain only three acres, and all arable. That went against the authority of *Savil's Case*[1503] in 11 Co., which is now allowed to be law, and the court was divided, 1 Brownl. 137.[1504]

Objection: Here is a view.

Answer: That don't appear on the record. So your Lordship can take no notice of it, nor will that entitle the plaintiff to ask more than he has a right to.

Mr Stannard

Quoted Yelv. 114,[1505] 166[1506] Ow. 18,[1507] 133.[1508] 1 Brown. 146.[1509]

Here is no vill in the declaration. Hob. 89.[1510] Comberb. 198.[1511] 1 Salk. 254.[1512]

But see the Statute for Want of Hundreds,[1513] by which the amendment is not fatal. [*436*]

COSTELLO v. COSTELLO[1514]

Friday, 5 July, 1734[1515]

The bill was filed the 26 of June. On the 8th of November the defendant appeared, and had time to answer till the 23, or process. On the 23 of January following on appearing *gratis* he obtained further time till Easter. On the 29 the plaintiff obtained an order to amend his bill. On the 3d of March the answer was sworn, two months before the time was out, but was not filed, upon which the plaintiff took out process to a commission of rebellion, and refused to accept the answer, and [on the] plea of the defendant of another bill depending and at issue for the same matter, the defendant obtained an order to refer the process for irregularity. The officer reported the process to be regular notwithstanding the order for the amendment, and that that order was no suspension of the process.

[1501] Case at the reference Cro. Eliz. 465 does not appear relevant.

[1502] *Wykes* v. *Sparrow* (1617) Cro. Jac. 435, 79 E.R. 372.

[1503] *Savel's Case* (1614) 11 Co. Rep. 55a, 77 E.R. 1221.

[1504] *Ward* v. *Willingsby* (1607) 1 Brownl. 137, 123 E.R. 714.

[1505] *Winkworth* v. *Man* (1607) Yelv. 114, 80 E.R. 77 (ejectment: precision in pleading).

[1506] *Troughton* v. *Googe* (1609) Yelv. 166, 80 E.R. 111 (ejectment: close mentioned by name).

[1507] *Palmers Case* Ow. 18, 74 E.R. 868 (ejectment: certainty).

[1508] *Day* v. *Fynn* (1601) Ow. 133, 74 E.R. 954 (ejectment: certainty).

[1509] *Davis* v. *Pardy* (1610) 1 Brownl. 146, 123 E.R. 720.

[1510] *Rich* v. *Shere* (1608) Hob. 89, 80 E.R. 238 (ejectment: failure to mention location, town, etc.).

[1511] *Knight* v. *Symms* (1692) Comb. 198, 90 E.R. 426 (ejectment: quantity of each type of land to be specified).

[1512] *Knight* v. *Syms* (1692) 1 Salk. 254, 91 E.R. 223.

[1513] 2 Edw. III, c. 12 (Eng.), 1328, Statute of Lincoln (hundreds and wapentakes annexed to counties), and see *Atkyns* v. *Holford Clare* (1671) 1 Ventr. 399, 86 E.R. 254; *Cole* v. *Ireland* (1608) 2 Show. K.B. 98, 89 E.R. 819; *Rex* v. *Kingsmill* (1606) 3 Mod. 199, 87 E.R. 128; *Simpson* v. *Hundred of Ashwardhern* (1772) 2 Black. W. 842 at 844, 96 E.R. 496 at 497.

[1514] Continued from p. 327.

[1515] 5 July was a Friday in 1734, Kratz, *Hist. Cal.*

The defendant now moved to set aside the report. On the affidavit of his attorney, that the plaintiff's attorney had informed him he would amend, and that he was in court when he moved for the order, that the amendment might require a further answer, and therefore he delayed to file the answer, but that he had it swore, and kept by him, for fear the plaintiff should waive his order for the amendment, and that he thought the plaintiff's order was a suspension of their order, and that on a motion to amend everyone supposed the plaintiff will amend.

It was argued for the plaintiff, that this order was only a liberty to amend, that the report was regular, and that the order was no dispensation with the order to answer or process, which the defendant had submitted to, that the order was only an authority to the officer to suffer the plaintiff to amend, and though the record was actually amended, the defendant need not take notice of it, till his copy was amended, and if a further answer was requisite, he has costs for the amendment.

Curia

The defendant has given a rational account why he did not [437] file his answer, and his attorney swears he thought the order for amendment was a suspension of the order for time to answer. So we think the officer's report right, but that the defendant is in no fault, and that the plea and answer ought to stand, and the process be set aside.

BLACKHALL v. BLACKHALL

Saturday, July the 13, 1734[1516]

Mr Recorder for the defendant

Thomond Blackhall being seized of lands in County Kildare, and possessed of a personal estate to the amount of £10,000, made his will in 1715, and Sarah his wife executor thereof, and devised his real estate to her for life, remainder to George and his heirs, and gave part of his personal estate to the said George Blackhall his son, and the other part to the rest of his children. Sarah proved the will, and died in 1716, leaving George the defendant and other executors and George guardian to George the son, who continued a minor to 1729, and intermarried with the plaintiff before he came of age, and died in 1733, and devised one moiety of his personal estate to his wife Ann, and the other to his daughter Elizabeth, who bring this bill against the defendant George for an account and discovery of the assets of Thomond Blackhall, and George Blackhall.

The defendant Blackhall denies combination, and as to the relief and discovery of assets he pleads the 6 Anne ch. 16[1517] to prevent marriages against the will of guardians etc., that he was appointed guardian to George during his minority, which

---

[1516] 13 July was a Saturday in 1734, Kratz, *Hist. Cal.*

[1517] 6 Ann., c. 16 (Ir.), 1707 (to prevent taking away and marrying children against the will of parent or guardians).

continued to 1729, and that in 1726 the plaintiff Anne seduced him to marry her without his[1518] consent, whereby she is incapable to take by will.

She may take issue on this plea, and if she can prove that the marriage was not had by her insinuations, the Act will not bar her. One would think indeed that marrying a minor was a sufficient proof of seducing him, but the authorities have gone otherwise, and [438] issue may be taken on it, and the seduction must be proved, as in *Kent* v. *Kent*,[1519] where the jury found, that the wife did not seduce the husband.

To save the benefit of the plea to the hearing would lead us into an unnecessary account, and we have answered to all but what she sues for in her own right.

Mr Smyth

The wife being made executrix, though a moiety of the personal estate is devised to her, yet it will be assets in her hands.

This Act indeed is a strong personal disability, but so is outlawry, yet it can't be pleaded to a suit as executor. But she is entitled to a discovery and relief, whether she is concerned in interest or not.

This being a penal statute, every circumstance to be observed ought to be pleaded strictly, and it should appear that George the defendant was guardian to George the husband, but he was appointed guardian by Sarah the mother, whereas the Act only gives the father a power to name a guardian to his child, so his consent was not requisite.

The defendant don't aver, that George the husband was entitled to £50 a year, or £500 personal estate, but he only says, we allege so in our bill, but that won't make his plea good, but he should have said so.

Curia

Let the plea stand for an answer, with liberty to except, and the benefit be reserved to the hearing.

TUCKER AND DUDGEN v. DELISLE

Friday, June the 28th, 1734[1520]

In Exchequer

Mr Caulfield for the defendant

This is an oath brought by the sheriffs of the city of Dublin for their fees, wherein they declare, that they executed a *capias* marked £154, by reason whereof [439] and

---

[1518] I.e. George the guardian.
[1519] No citation given.
[1520] 28 June was a Friday in 1734, Kratz, *Hist. Cal.*

vigore stat[uti] *[nu]p[e]r edit[i]*[1521] the defendant became indebted to them in £6, which he promised to pay.

The defendant demurred specially to this declaration, and assigned three causes:

1. That the Act is not set forth, on which the plaintiffs sue for their fees.

2. That they don't say the *capias* was delivered to them by the defendant, or that he desired them to execute it.

I need not mention the third cause, for I shan't insist on it.

1. At law the sheriff is not entitled to fees for executing writs, but is obliged thereto by the duty of his office. But he pretended a right to fees, and the statute 6 Anne[1522] in this kingdom, which is the same with the 29 Eliz.[1523] in England, was made to regulate them, 1 Roll. Rep. 404.[1524] 'twas adjudged an action would lie for the sheriff on this Act otherwise he would be without a remedy, Cro. Ja. 103,[1525] and in Latch 54,[1526] that executing a writ was no consideration, because 'twas his duty.

And the clause of the Act whereby they are entitled ought to be particularly set forth, because it is not a general Act, which the court are *ex officio* to take notice of.

Acts that relate to sheriffs and bishops, but not to all officers, or the clergy, are particular, as the 23 H. 6 ch. 23,[1527] which relates to sheriffs' bonds, 4 Co. 74, that that is more extensive than this Act, and has been adjudged to reach to the marshal of the King's Bench.

The 23 H. 6 is a particular law, Hob. 13.[1528] And the 29 Eliz.[1529] is adjudged to be a public law in Moor 468[1530] (669), but on a writ of error, Moor 699[1531] (972) the judgment was reversed, because the statute was not set out in the declaration. Brown. Redv. 463, 4[1532] is a precedent for us as to both points.

The second cause rests on the reason of the thing, that the execution should be at the instance of the party, and not officiously, and the question of Mr Justice Jones in Latch 17[1533] is to this purpose: 'If I deliver the writ to the sheriff, but forbid him to arrest, and yet he does, the party may have his action against the sheriff, but *quære* whether the [*440*] sheriff in that case can have an action for his fees?' And this question he leaves undetermined.

Tuesday, July the 2d[1534]

Mr Darcy for the plaintiffs

This is an action on the case by the sheriffs of the county of Dublin for their fees, wherein the plaintiffs declare that the defendant in Michaelmas Term 5 of the

---

[1521] L. by force of the statute recently published.

[1522] 6 Ann., c. 7 (Ir.), 1707 (sheriffs' fees; treble damages for wrongly marking writs).

[1523] 29 Eliz., c. 4 (Eng.), 1586 (sheriffs' fees).

[1524] *Viscounts de London* v. *Michell* (1616) 1 Roll. Rep. 404, 81 E.R. 567.

[1525] *Bridge* v. *Cage* (1605) Cro. Jac. 103, 79 E.R. 89 (promise to pay money to sheriff in consideration for doing something for which the law does not permit them to be paid, is void).

[1526] *Batho* v. *Salter* (1662) Lat. 54, 82 E.R. 271.

[1527] Probably an error for 23 Hen. VI, c. 9 (Eng.), 1444 (sheriff's bonds), given the repetition of '23'.

[1528] *Norton* v. *Simmes* (1623) Hob. 12 at 13, 80 E.R. 163 at 164.

[1529] 29 Eliz., c. 4 (Eng.), 1586 (sheriff's fees).

[1530] *Suliard* v. *Stamp* (1597) Moo. K.B. 468, 72 E.R. 701.

[1531] *Stamton* v. *Suliard* (1597) Moo. K.B. 699, 72 E.R. 849.

[1532] Brownl. Redv. 463.

[1533] *Walden* v. *Vessey* (1626) Lat. 17, 82 E.R. 252 (29 Eliz., c. 4).

[1534] 2 July was a Tuesday in 1734, Kratz, *Hist. Cal.*

King[1535] having recovered in King's Bench against David Paine £400 and costs, he *prosecutus fuisset*[1536] a *capias ad satisfaciendum* against the said Pain,[1537] directed to the plaintiffs, marked £154 8s 6d, which the defendant certified at the foot of the judgment to be due to him. By which *preceptu[m] fuit*[1538] to the plaintiffs to take Pain, *virtute* of which they being then sheriffs arrested Pain, and have him in custody, by which the defendant, at whose suit the execution was, became indebted to them in 6s 7d, being 12d in the pound according to the statute.

To this declaration the defendant demurs:

1. Because it don't appear that the execution was delivered to the sheriffs to be executed, whereas 'tis the delivery of the writ entitled them to their fees.

2. That it don't appear, in what place or county the court of Chief Pleas was held.

3. That it don't appear, by what statute the plaintiffs are entitled.

1. It appears sufficiently to be delivered to the sheriffs, and was in their hands when they executed it. Here is sufficient certainty to satisfy the defendant of a cause of action, 1 Inst. 303, that such an execution was taken out, that Pain was arrested by virtue of it, and it must be presumed to be delivered, 1 Sand. 298[1539] and if it was not, it ought to have been shown on the other side, and they should have pleaded it, and the court will intend it, notwithstanding the demurrer, 2 Lev. 19,[1540] 2 Lutw. 1289,[1541] like the case in 1 Ventr. 34,[1542] 1 Sand. 29.[1543] And if the sheriff took it out, or the defendant did not desire him to execute it, he should plead it. If a writ issues he may execute it before delivery, 3 Lev. 93,[1544] and 'tis the execution entitles him to his fees, and *prosecutus fuisset* by the plaintiff is sufficient, and the precedents are both ways, as is observed in 1 Sand. 298.[1545]

2. As to the second point, the county being in the margin, the court shall be supposed to lie there, 1 Sid. 345.[1546]

3. The preamble to 6 Anne ch. 7 looks as if the sheriffs before that Act were entitled to their fees. The 29 Eliz. ch. 4 in England is much of the same kind, which in Moor 468[1547] is allowed to be a general law,[1548] and the judgment was affirmed in the Exchequer Chamber. Debt will lie for the sheriffs' fees, Moor 853[1549] (1166), 1 Roll. Rep. 404.[1550]

It appears by *Holland's Case,*[1551] that this is a general law, for it relates to sheriffs, and all concerned in the execution of writs. That is a general law that includes all the

---

[1535] I.e. Michaelmas term 1731.

[1536] L. had sued.

[1537] So spelled in MS.

[1538] L. it was ordered.

[1539] *Greene v. Jones* (1670) 1 Wms. Saund. 298, 85 E.R. 407.

[1540] *Jones v. Greene* (1672) 2 Lev. 19, 83 E.R. 433.

[1541] *Pepper v. Gay* (1693) 2 Lut. 1288 at 1289, 125 E.R. 713.

[1542] *Perry's Case* (1669) 1 Vent. 35, 86 E.R. 25.

[1543] *Birks v. Trippet* (1666) 1 Wms. Saund. 28, 85 E.R. 32.

[1544] *Osborne v. Brookhouse* (1683) 3 Lev. 93, 83 E.R. 594.

[1545] *Greene v. Jones* (1670) 1 Wms. Saund. 298, 85 E.R. 407.

[1546] *Parker v. Sadd* (1667) 1 Sid. 345, 82 E.R. 1147.

[1547] *Perrots Case* (1594) Moo. K.B. 368, 72 E.R. 634.

[1548] I.e. one which court will apply without its being pleaded.

[1549] *Probey v. Michell* (1616) Moo. K.B. 853, 72 E.R. 950 (29 Eliz., c. 4).

[1550] *Viscounts de London v. Michell* (1616) 1 Roll. Rep. 404, 81 E.R. 567.

[1551] *Holland's Case* (1597) 4 Co. Rep. 75a, 76 E.R. 1047 (general and special laws).

species, as all spiritual persons, though not all the subjects. The 23 H. 6 ch. 10[1552] is reckoned a general law, 1 Sid. 23,[1553] 4,[1554] 1 Lev. 86,[1555] 2 Lev. 103, 104.[1556]

Mr Caulfield's Reply

The declaration is defective:

1. the plaintiffs not having declared on any particular Act,

2. nor averred the delivery by the defendant, or his request to the plaintiffs to execute the writ.

1. This is a particular Act. I allow if the 23 H. 6 is a general law, this is so too. I think *Holland's Case* is an authority for me, and not for the plaintiffs, on the distinction that is there laid down between general and particular laws, and that statute is there reckoned among the particular laws, and 'tis judicially determined so in 2 Sand. 154,[1557] Hob. 13,[1558] and Moo. 468,[1559] 699,[1560] is an authority for me too, for the judges changed their opinion, and designed to reverse the judgment, though the matter was compounded. In 1 Lev. 86[1561] there is no judgment of the court, nor in 2 Lev. 103,[1562] but the cause was adjourned, and 'tis only Hales's opinion. 1 Roll. Abr. 26 pl. 41, is a strong authority that the delivery must be averred, and ought not to be presumed, and how can we deny by our plea, what is not asserted in the declaration? In Latch 17,[1563] in an action of false imprisonment, if the sheriff has a writ, he may justify, though it was not delivered to him, because the writ is an authority, but the party may have an action for the damage done him, and shall the sheriff have a right to fees for doing that which is a wrong to the party?

Curia advisare vult.[1564] [442]

[1552] 23 Hen. VI, c. 10 (Eng.), 1444 (wages of knights of parliament).

[1553] *Allan and Robinson's Case* 1 Sid. 22 at 23, 82 E.R. 946.

[1554] 1 Sid. 4 at 5, 82 E.R. 936 (text).

[1555] *Bentley* v. *Hore* (1662) 1 Lev. 86, 83 E.R. 310 (23 H. 6, sheriff obliged to let the party to bail by sufficient mainpernors).

[1556] *Oky* v. *Sell* (1674) 2 Lev. 103, 83 E.R. 470 (court takes account of general statutes without their being pleaded).

[1557] *Benson* v. *Welby* (1669) 2 Wms. Saund. 154, 85 E.R. 891 (23 H. 6, c. 9, on sheriffs' bonds, is a particular statute, of which the court will not take notice unless it is pleaded).

[1558] *Norton* v. *Simmes* (1623) Hob. 12 at 13, 80 E.R. 163 at 164.

[1559] *Suliard* v. *Stamp* (1597) Moo. K.B. 468, 72 E.R. 701.

[1560] *Stamton* v. *Suliard* (1597) Moo. K.B. 699, 72 E.R. 849.

[1561] *Bentley* v. *Hore* (1662) 1 Lev. 86, 83 E.R. 310.

[1562] *Oky* v. *Sell* (1674) 2 Lev. 103, 83 E.R. 470 (debt on sheriff's bond).

[1563] *Walden* v. *Vessey* (1626) Lat. 17, 82 E.R. 252 (29 Eliz. I, c. 4).

[1564] L. the court will be advised (before giving judgment).

Wednesday, June the 26, 1734.[1565]

THE DEAN AND CHAPTER OF WATERFORD

v.

CONGREVE

Mr Prime Serjeant for the Plaintiffs

The Dean and Chapter were originally Dean and Canons and are perpetual incumbents of the rectory of the Holy Trinity, which is one of the seven parishes in Waterford, and is part within and part without the walls, and adjoins to the Parish of St John. In Trinity Parish lay the ancient quay on Millers Marsh, which was originally without the walls and was the ancient and only landing place for all goods imported into Waterford. Millers Marsh anciently belonged to the Priory of Grey Friars,[1566] now to the Hospital of the Holy Ghost, and was set[1567] by them in 1726 to the defendant Congreve, who built a new quay on Congreve's Marsh, which occasioned a controversy as to payment of tithe fish. Congreve claiming an exemption from tithes in Millers Marsh as belonging to the hospital, whereupon the plaintiffs filed their bill for the payment of the tithe of fish, and have alleged therein three customs:

1. That by a custom in the said city and seven parishes, and every part thereof, at all times heretofore had and approved, the whole, or entire tithe or tenth fish, and particularly herrings, whether taken in the open sea, and outside of the harbour's mouth, or within the said harbour's mouth of the said city, by any boat or vessel belonging to any person dwelling within the said city, or parishes and landed or put on shore in any place within the said city, or parishes, has been duly set out, and paid to the plaintiffs and their predecessors to their own use, without any disturbance, or substraction until etc.

2. The second is for half tithe for fish imported in foreign boats.

3. For half tithe of fish taken by any inhabitant, though landed out of the city.

The first is the foundation of our bill, and enough for us to prove. [*443*] This is a personal tithe payable by custom of which usage and quiet enjoyment is evidence and before the memory of man till 1729 we enjoyed this custom without disturbance, the defendant allows the tithe ought to be paid when the fish is landed on the old quay, but I made, says he, Congreve's Marsh a new quay, and they have no right to the tithe of fish landed there; But his building a new quay won't take away our former right to the tithe of all fish landed, etc. and he can have no exemption, for the hospital always paid.

Mr Solicitor General

They say they have a right to tithe of fish landed in Congreve's Marsh, which is in the parish of St John, but Mr. Fell the rector of that parish claims a right to it, and therefore he ought to be before the court.

[1565] 26 June was a Wednesday in 1734, Kratz, *Hist. Cal.*

[1566] See A. Gwynn and N. R. Hadcock, *Medieval Religious Houses: Ireland* (1988).

[1567] See above, p. 10 n. 59.

Mr Prime Serjeant

We only pray a decree for tithe of fish landed in Miller's Marsh, which is the only tithe is substracted.

Mr Solicitor General for the Defendant

The tithe of fish is due by custom, and being a personal tithe must be presumed to be granted for the service of the person officiating; two of these modusses[1568] are given us; but as the prayer of the bill is to establish them, the court must determine them all.

The substance of a custom ought to be as precisely alleged in equity, as at law, because it is the plaintiff's title, and he cannot recover unless he proves it as he has set it forth for otherwise no defence could be made to it, and customs are innovations on common right. And if a custom is unreasonable, the court won't give relief.

Here are two questions:

1. Whether the plaintiffs have made any proof of the customs, as they have laid them.

2. If they have proved them, whether our grant don't show the title to them belongs to the master and brothers of the Holy Ghost Hospital.

I shall speak to the second point first, because if that is with us it will make an end of the case.

The Letters Patent are a grant to the hospital of all the tithes within the precincts of the late dissolved monastery. Millers Marsh is proved to belong to the hospital and to be part of the precincts of the Monastery, and your Lordship will presume this personal tithe to be payable to them for their officiating. But as to the main point, your Lordship will dismiss their bill, because [444] they have made no proof of the custom as they have set it forth.

They have made proof of their having the tithe of fish landed on the quay, but not in any other part, and in St John's parish there was no place to land them in till 14 years past, and there has been no regular payment, but the usage often interrupted.

But supposing the modus to be well proved, if it is unreasonable your Lordship will not decree it.

It is for the whole city to pay tithe though not within the seven parishes, and we have proved to other parishes to be within the liberties, though not the walls of the city.

This custom is for the tithe without deducting the expenses, which is a void custom. 2 Rol. Rep. 419,[1569] 1 Rol. Ab. 656.

Mes App. F.361.
2 Inst. 621.

Lord Chief Baron

It is not necessary to allege the custom as precisely in a bill, as at law, but if it is set forth in such a manner as to lay the whole before the court, we will give relief, though the plaintiff mistake his title.

[1568] L. Modus, usual abbreviation of *modus decimandi*, the manner of paying tithes. A discharge from paying tithes in the normal manner of paying in kind, allowing them to be paid in a particular manner by custom or prescription, sometimes effected by compensation in money. Jacob, *Law Dictionary*.

[1569] *Jones* v. *Lord Sheffield and Ratcliffe* (1624) 2 Roll. Rep. 416 at 419, 81 E.R. 888 at 890.

Mr Recorder

This is a personal tithe that arises from labour, and is not due of common right.

One tithe cannot be pleaded in discharge of another where both are due *de communi jure*, but labour may be thrown in and pleaded, because tithe arising by labour and industry is not the natural tithe. Hob. 250, *Hyde* v. *Ellis*.[1570]

The substance of all customs, which creates the duty, must be strictly set out, though not formally, on this principle, because you charge a particular fact, and the party comes to defend that, and if it varies it is a different custom. The demand and evidence must be the same in equity as at law, though they are not tied down in equity to the same manner of setting it out, and you can direct no other custom to be tried, but what they claim. Clayt. Rep. sect. 135, *Sir Alexander Robinson's Case*,[1571] a custom varying in an acre gone, this was at law.

The plaintiffs don't officiate in the seven parishes, but are rectors of one only, and they don't say they ever were rectors of the other, so this custom cannot have a reasonable commencement, because the inhabitants of the other six parishes cannot have the benefit of them, so your Lordship must dismiss the bill, though the modus was well proved, because [*445*] there must be *quid pro quo*, a spiritual assistance for their labour, so their own ministers have a better title to these tithes.

A layman may prescribe, but not in *Decimando*,[1572] because the custom might be valuable at that time.

They allow Alcock to be rector of a parish within the liberties of the city, to which they have no right to tithes, yet by this custom he must pay.

The Council of Lateran[1573] erected parishes, and settled the right to tithes, and this custom must arise since the division of parishes, for the English laws did not prevail here till H. 2. So you cannot presume these seven to have been once one parish, and the right to have arose from thence.

People who lived in different parishes might by landing their fish in a particular parish give a foundation for a custom to pay tithe there, they might be sick, and have the advantage of the minister while they stayed there, but why should they pay if they landed fish in a different parish, where they could not have their assistance?

The Dean and Chapter are the rectors of this parish, but the Dean is vicar, and these are vicarial tithes which can belong to him only. So the plaintiffs have no right to sue for them as a corporate body, but the Dean only, therefore if they had proved these modusses, they could not have a decree to establish them, because they are not rectorial tithes but personal that belong to the vicar.

A modus ought to be constant and uninterrupted, but they have not proved that the same modus was always paid, but sometimes a tenth, sometimes a fifteenth, or twentieth. A boat would give a small matter rather than stand a suit, and it is in proof that the plaintiffs often offered to take anything from them.

We have produced a grant from H. 8 to the master and brothers of the Hospital of the Holy Ghost of all tithes of all persons living within the precinct of the monastery

---

[1570] *Hide* v. *Ellis* (1618) Hob. 250, 80 E.R. 397: 'for tythe naturally is but the tenth of the revenue of my ground, not of my labour and industry'.

[1571] *Sir Arthur Robinson's Case* (1639) Clayton's Reports, York Assizes (Dublin, 1741), s. 135, p. 81 [not in E.R.].

[1572] In that manner of tithing. L. decima: tenth or tithe.

[1573] The fourth Lateran Council, the 12th ecumenical council, 1215.

and considering the distance of time it is impossible to prove the King was seized of these tithes.

The King's forests were exempted from tithes being excepted out of the grant of tithes to the clergy by Ethelred the First Saxon King,[1574] so that in England they first came from the Crown, and this is called *commune jus*, [*446*] and is in force here since the reign of H. 2, who as a conqueror settled the common law in this kingdom, and the tithe of fish could not be granted by him because it is not due of common right, but by custom, and we can have no other right than the people of England. Yet if there were such tithe due at the time of the grant, it passed by it. If it arose since, they have given no proof of payment of tithe fish in Congreve's Marsh in the parish of St John.

Mr Malone

This bill ought to be dismissed, which is brought by the plaintiffs as rectors of a single parish in Waterford, for all the tithe of fish in the seven.

They have endeavoured to give no proof but of an entire tithe or tenth, which is a void and unreasonable custom, and against natural law and justice.

All customs have several properties peculiar to them:

1. Every custom must have a reasonable commencement.

2. Must be certain, not of one kind today, of another tomorrow.

3. Must be time out of mind, and without interruption and cannot be by grant or Act of Parliament, but is *jus non scriptum*,[1575] and founded on an agreement. Davis 32.[1576]

As their whole title is founded on custom, if there is no such custom, or if it has not these qualities, they have no title to relief.

The tithe of fish can be warranted only by custom and is not payable of common right, especially if they are taken at sea, 1. because fish are *feræ naturæ*,[1577] 2. because they are taken *extra parochiam*[1578] and so cannot be a tithe to any incumbent.

A custom for any dweller within the seven parishes to pay tithe for fish imported into the parish of Trinity may perhaps be justified, but here are six more parishes, some of which have distinct incumbents, of which the plaintiffs have not alleged themselves rectors, and they claim the tithe of fish landed in any of the others, which is unreasonable, because they have not the cure of souls [*447*] in the others, whereas *propter officium datur beneficium*.[1579] This is a personal tithe and where it is due even *de jure* the expenses and charges of labour and machinery are to be allowed, but here the whole entire tithe is claimed, which is unreasonable.

This custom is not proved as it is laid in the bill, to be immemorial, and without interruption. Some swear to 12, 14, 30 and one to 98 years enjoyment. The canonists think a prescription of 20 years by a spiritual person good, but a custom which is good at law, or which equity will establish, must be immemorial, and better evidence ought to be expected from so populous a place, and this differs from others. Where

---

[1574] Aethelred I (d. April 871), King of Wessex and of Kent (865/866–871).
[1575] I.e. unwritten law.
[1576] *Case of Tanistry* (1608) Dav. 32, 80 E.R. 516 at 519.
[1577] L. of a wild nature.
[1578] L. outside the parish.
[1579] L. the benefit is given because of the duty. See *Shaw* v. *Woods* (1855) 5 Ir.C.L.R. 156.

though the party mistakes his case, the court will relieve him if an equity appears for him, but here they have founded themselves on a particular special custom and it is as if they had claimed the lands of Blackacre by a particular deed, and at the hearing produce another. Hardr. 130,[1580] which shows the necessity of setting only the title by which they claim, that the defendants may controvert it.

The tithe is to be paid by the occupier, but to be established against the inheritor, and he is not before the court.

As to the exemption, Millers Marsh is part of the monastery, and all tithes within that surround are granted to the hospital, this then would be a good grant if it appeared by inquisition, or other evidence, that the King was seized of these tithes, or if the monastery was proved to be seized of them, it is recited by the grant, that they came to the Crown by the Dissolution. So at this distance of time the presumption is the monastery was seized of them.

Mr N. Nash[1581]

Personal tithes are to be paid deducting expenses. 2 Danv. Tit. Dismes 583.[1582] This bill claims tithes in other parishes, and they don't charge all the parishes to be in one diocese, so they cannot pretend that they were originally one parish and might as well claim the tithe in any diocese in England.

Lord Chief Baron

Those who obtained these grants from the Crown had them by a particular which they gave in to the Attorney General [448] and though they took care not to misinform him for fear their patent should be repealed; yet often things were inserted in patents the King was never in possession of.

Mr Prime Serjeant for the Plaintiffs

All that has been said may be reduced to these three points:
1. Whether these modusses are reasonable as charged in the bill.
2. Whether they are proved.
3. Supposing them reasonable, and well proved, whether the grant is not a bar.

1. All agree that tithe of fish may be payable by custom, though they are *feræ naturæ*, and not taken in any parish, and may be due and payable in another parish than where the fisherman lives, 2 Inst 641. Lord Coke[1583] admits that before the Council of Lateran, or some other decree, tithes were payable *ad libitum* to any spiritual person, that the revenues were brought into one stock, and afterwards distributed, that A and B as rectors could not resort to any particular persons but to the common stock, but he disputes tithes being made parochial by the Council of Lateran, but by a decretal epistle of Pope Innocent III[1584] to the Archbishop of Canterbury, which we

---

[1580] *Button* v. *Honey* (1658) Hard. 130, 145 E.R. 415.
[1581] Probably Nicholas Nash, 3rd s. of James, Killahill, Co. Limerick. Middle Temple, Oct. 1714. KI, Hilary term, 1719, d. April 1746, KI AP, p. 360.
[1582] D'Anvers, *Abridgement of Common Law* (2nd ed., 2 vols., 1705–37, 1725–37), 'Dismes' (LF.), tithes.
[1583] *Sic.* Sir Edward Coke.
[1584] Pope from 1198 to 1216.

received as reasonable in England, though not binding on us, but it is not material whether tithes were originally parochial or not, for this is certain, that the minister of one parish may have tithes in another, because all the possessions might originally have been disposed of by consent of parson, patron and ordinary, and the usage and payment of the tithes is a presumptive evidence of such a grant. *Complete Incumbent* 405.[1585]

The second modus is for the payment of half tithe of fish brought into any of the seven parishes by foreign boats, and it is reasonable a foreigner should pay this upon his coming into any of the parishes, because whilst he is commorant[1586] there, he is under the cure of that parish.

The second question is, whether we have given evidence of such customs, the defendant by his answer says, I believe the [*449*] quay, which was formerly the only landing place for fish, is in Trinity parish, and that there was no other landing place till of late, and that the tithe, and half tithe of fish landed on that place, has been paid. This is a full proof, because he says there was no other landing place for fish or other goods.

And though the canon law is no authority, a decretal epistle of the said Pope Innocent III to the plaintiffs in the year 1200, confirming these tithes to the Dean and Canons of Waterford is a strong proof, and may be given in evidence as an ancient history, Balusius 461 (Paris edition, 1682).[1587]

The defendant insists on these being unreasonable customs, and yet claims them by the grant from the H. 8, and if that grant was an exemption, it could only go to the tithes of their own possessions, as the

Grey Friars were exempted, but what is that to personal tithes, which are payable out of labour, and not out of lands.

It is objected, that the hospital, and the minister of the parish of St John ought to be parties.

If the tithe was due of common right the presumption would be it belonged to the minister, and then he ought to be a party, but as this is founded on custom, it might be payable to the minister of another parish, and we have been long in possession, and they have never claimed them.

Though the Dean is vicar, he may not be entitled to these tithes, for a vicarage is no certain endowment, and the defendant says, the vicar is entitled to all the tithe, except of fish.

The court won't trust the determination of these points to a jury without absolute necessity.

The third custom is, that all inhabitants shall pay half tithe of fish landed anywhere, both parishes, where he lives, and where he lands his fish have care of the fisherman. But as the defendant is not concerned in this modus, the bill may be dismissed as to it without prejudice. [*450*]

[1585]   William Watson, *The Clergy-man's Law: or the Complete Incumbent* (1st ed., London, 1701).

[1586]   *OED*: dwelling, resident. *Obs.*

[1587]   The reference is to Étienne Baluze (1630–1718), also known in the Latin form as Stephanus Baluzius, *Epistolarum Innocentii III* (Letters of Pope Innocent III) (Paris, 1682), vol. 2, p. 461 (Marsh's Library, Dublin). Singleton is citing the decretal epistle referred to in the text, granting tithes to the Dean and canons of Waterford. The letter is reproduced in Appendix E. And see above, p. cl.

Mr Attorney General

Tithe of fish may be due by custom, and was sooner established here than in England, Cro. Car. 264,[1588] 339;[1589] 1 Rol. Rep. 419.[1590] The court was inclined to grant a prohibition till Mr. Justice Jones told them which modusses had been paid in Ireland and Wales.

These customs are reasonable, and well proved. The fisherman is entitled to the care of the minister while he is resident with his fish, and this may be a reasonable custom, though not if the tithe were due *de jure*, because custom may make it payable in one parish, and not in that where he lives.

A trial is never directed against the defendants admission by his answer.

Mr Calaghan

Fish is titheable by custom. 1 Lev. 179,[1591] there the custom was for half tithe, like our second modus.

Evidence of a usage of 40 years is a good proof of a modus, 2 Inst. 649, but we have made better proof. As to the reasonableness of these modusses, if you consider the plaintiffs as the council of the bishop, the whole city has the benefit of their advice, and is influenced by it, and they have cure of all the souls, or you consider them only as a religious house, there is the same foundation for these customs as for the other charities, which were bestowed on them, and the whole city might at first have been one parish, and after on its growing populous divided into several, but what unreasonableness is there in a custom, for the rector of one parish to have tithe in another. This is laid down in the *Bishop of Winchester's Case*, 2 Co. 43,[1592] and in 11 Co., *Priddle and Napper's Case*,[1593] and this might arise before the Council of Lateran, when there were no parishes, or after by Bull, but the case is stronger, because these are tithes due by custom only, for before the disabling statute,[1594] the parson, patron and ordinary might have disposed of them, as of their private estate. [*451*]

As to the exemption, see 2 Co. 44, 47;[1595] 11 Co. 13.[1596] There is no pretence that this custom extended to the ministers of the other parishes, and this tithe did not originally belong to them *de jure*, or if it did, these customs would be a proof they had parted with them, and they might as well object that a man who was in possession 100 years ago, and had parted with his right, ought to be made a party.

Mr Daly

We have made full proof of the payment of these modusses for above 60 years, and they are not prejudicial to the rectors of the other parishes, because they have no right to them *communi jure*.

[1588] *Watts* v. *Baker* (1632) Cro. Car. 264, 79 E.R. 830.
[1589] *Dawes* v. *Huddleston* (1634) Cro. Car. 339, 79 E.R. 897.
[1590] *Goslin* v. *Harden* (1616) 1 Roll. Rep. 419, 81 E.R. 578.
[1591] *Sheppard* v. *Penrose* (1666) 1 Lev. 179, 83 E.R. 357.
[1592] *Bishop of Winchester's Case* (1596) 2 Co. Rep. 43, 76 E.R. 509.
[1593] *Priddle & Napper's Case* 11 Co. Rep. 8b, 77 E.R. 1155.
[1594] Statute not identified.
[1595] *Bishop of Winchester's Case* (1596) 2 Co. Rep. 44 at 47, 76 E.R. 509 at 510; *Archbishop of Canterbury's Case* 2 Co. Rep. 46a at 47, 76 E.R. 519 at 521.
[1596] *Priddle & Napper's Case* 11 Co. Rep. 8b at 13, 77 E.R. 1155 at 1162.

The rector of one parish may prescribe to have tithes in another parish, Bro. Tit. Jurisdiction, pl. 28; Bro. Tit. Prescription, pl. 86, and there might have been originally an exchange between the rectors, and some bishops in this kingdom have tithes running through several parishes of their dioceses, which must be by original grant to them.

The Dean and Chapter have the cure of souls through the whole diocese as well as the bishop, and if the case were so, the defendants might easily have proved that the rector of the other parishes received these tithes.

Mr Marshal

This is a reasonable modus. The inhabitants may resort to the cathedral to hear divine service. *Chapman* v. *Mounson*, Ab. of equity cases 367.[1597]

MSS cas. in Canc. a. 393, 412.

Mr Nash

Tithe fish is payable by custom. Palm. 527,[1598] Het 13, 14.[1599] The reasonableness of custom cannot be inquired into, 6 Co. 61, 62;[1600] 4 Co. 31b, 32a,[1601] though a prescription which is laid in the person must, and there is no coming at a custom, for if you trace it to its source, it is lost.

Tithe may be demanded in the parish of another, 4 Co. 34, *Bezouns Case*,[1602] in the margin of Dy. 83a, *The Dean and Chapter of Bristol* v. [*Clerke*].[1603] The King's grant cannot operate to a double intent, so that this grant can extend only to tithes due *de jure*, and not by custom.

Monday July the 16.[1734]

The court gave the opinion, that the Dean and Chapter [*452*] had shown themselves to be entitled, and had a right to the two first modusses, but that they could establish them only against the parties [*sic*] defendants.

[1597] Title: 'Of a Modus' 1 Eq. Cas. Abr. 367, 21 E.R. 1107. *Chapman* v. *Monson* (1729) 2 Eq. Cas. Abr. 735, 22 E.R. 623.

[1598] *Anon.* (1652) Palm. 527, 81 E.R. 1204.

[1599] Title: 'Tithes' Het. 13–14, 124 E.R. 303.

[1600] *Gateward's Case* 6 Co. Rep. 59b at 61a, 77 E.R. 344 at 346.

[1601] *Foiston* v. *Crachroode* (1587) 4 Co. Rep. 31b at 32a, 76 E.R. 962 at 964.

[1602] *Bezoun's Case* 4 Co. Rep. 34b, 76 E.R. 970.

[1603] *Dean and Chapter of Bristol* v. *Clerke* (1553) 1 Dy. 83a, 73 E.R. 181.

GREEN v. RYLAND[1604]

July the 8th 1734

Mr Recorder for the Defendants

Benjamin Green filed a bill on the Popery Acts for a real estate purchased by Edward Fitzgerald, a Papist, formerly the estate of Michael Murphy. Green made his will bearing date the 13 of August 1733, and thereby devised to James Roach Green one of the plaintiffs the benefit of this discovery, and made the plaintiffs his executors, and died the September following, whereupon the plaintiffs filed this bill of revivor, to which we have demurred for two causes:

1. Because such an interest was not vested in Green as could be revived.

2. Supposing such an interest was vested, yet James Roach Green being devisee only, and not the representative of Benjamin Green, could not bring this bill of revivor, but an original bill in nature of a bill of revivor.

1. This is a bill for an inheritance, so if it vests, it must be in the heir, if it is not devised away. This information is in nature of a popular action and is not vested in anybody. By the first Act,[1605] the estate is void, by the second,[1606] it subsists for the benefit of a Protestant discoveror. No interest is given to anyone, but generally to the first discoveror. The heir, or executor of an informer can't revive, Noy 100,[1607] and I cannot see a difference between this and a popular action. In one the penalty is given to the subject to encourage him to inform, in the other, the estate, for the better execution of the Act. [*453*] And the case of *Bar[r]y* v. *Goold*[1608] is the only case I know where this demurrer was overruled by the Lord Chief Baron Gilbert.

2. But if this was such an interest vested in the ancestor that the heir might revive, yet the devisee can't.

The devisee can't by the Act have a better interest than if the estate had come to the ancestor by descent, or purchase, in which cases neither a devisee, or remainderman can revive, because they come not in under a representation as an heir, or executor, *Whally* v. *Wingfield*,[1609] and though James Roach Green in the bill says he is the son and heir of Benjamin Green, yet by claiming under the will he waives his title by descent, and has made his election as devisee, and this is no hardship, because the devisee may bring an original bill in nature of a bill of revivor.

Objection: the case of a plaintiff is different from that of a defendant.

No, because none but a representative can revive a suit, or have it revived against him, and though 'tis on the Popery Acts, the proceedings must be in the same

Mes App. D.318.

[1604]   Continued from p. 211. See *Ryland* v. *Green* (1738) 5 Bro. P.C. 2nd ed. 403, 2 E.R. 759 (British House of Lords. Order of Irish court of Exchequer reversed: where a person sues as a Protestant discoverer under the Popery Acts, he becomes entitled to the rents and profits of the estate from the time of filing his bill; and if he dies pending the suit having made a will those rents and profits will belong to his devisee. But such devisee cannot regularly exhibit a bill of revivor; but must exhibit an original bill, as a protestant discoverer in his own right.) And see Howard, *Equity Side*, i. 262, where the case is mentioned.

[1605]   2 Ann., c. 6 (Ir.), 1703 (to prevent the further growth of popery).

[1606]   8 Ann., c. 3 (Ir.), 1709 (Popery: Protestant discoverers).

[1607]   *Agars Case* Noy 100, 74 E.R. 1066.

[1608]   Below, p. 359 n. 1621.

[1609]   *Wingfield* v. *Whalley* (1722) 5 Vin. Abr. 534 pl 38, 2 Eq. Cas. Abr. 19, 22 E.R. 16; (1722) 1 Bro. P.C. 2nd ed. 200, 1 E.R. 513, reversing the Irish Chancery (dormant contract: no specific performance. Foliot Wingfield, afterwards Viscount Powerscourt, m. Elizabeth, daughter of the earl of Orrery).

manner. No demurrer will lie to a bill on the Popery Acts where the plaintiff comes properly into court, but it will where he don't, and Green's executors can have no right, or if they have, they ought to be made defendants, for they can have no decree for the inheritance.

Mr Daly

A devisee can't revive, but the representative only: the executor, if a personal estate in demand, the heir, if a real, and this is no inconvenience, because he may easily file an original bill, and what is it to the public that by this means another discoveror may step in, if he is a real Protestant discoveror? If this is such an interest as may be devised, 'tis plain by the bill that Benjamin Green has devised it, and the other plaintiffs are executors, and they pray a revivor.

This is a particular action which vests no right in anyone till suit. The Act says, that any Protestant who shall sue, after verdict, judgment, or decree shall be entitled. If such a cause might be revived, the next of kin to the discoveror, or his [454] heir might be a Papist, and would have a right to revive contrary to the Act, and you won't vary the Act so as to say if the representatives are Protestants the right shall descend, but not if they are Papists.

The informer has only an initial right till verdict or judgment, and here were no further proceedings than to an answer.

Mr Wm. Nash[1610]

Where an Act of Parliament gives the suit to any person there he is a common informer, 1 And. 116, *Nivet* v. *The Butchers*,[1611] and if an informer dies, the suit is at an end, 1 Salk. 30, *Kirkham* v. *Whally*.[1612] If a common informer has proceeded to a judgment or decree, the heir or administrator may suggest the death of the ancestor, and take out execution, Hardr. 161.[1613]

Where the statute gives a penalty for what was not an offence before the making the Act, no other means can be pursued, nor no other person have a remedy, Cro. Ja. 643.[1614] Now the informer by the act after a recovery or decree is to hold etc.

A descendable freehold is not within the Gavelkind Act,[1615] but will go from a Protestant to a Papist. In such a case should the heir revive, though a Papist?

A devisee can't revive. 2 Vern. 548,[1616] 676.[1617]

[1610] William Nash, s. and heir of James, Kilatel, Co. Limerick. Middle Temple, July, 1720, called June 1724. KI, Michaelmas term, 1724, d. Aug. 1744.

[1611] *Knevet* v. *London Butchers* (1583) 1 And. 116, 123 E.R. 383.

[1612] *Kirkham* v. *Wheeley* (1695) 1 Salk. 30, 91 E.R. 31 (action *qui tam* will not lie against attorney of the Common Pleas in any other court).

[1613] *Morbye* v. *Urlin* (1659) Hard. 161, 145 E.R. 432.

[1614] *Castle's Case* (1622) Cro. Jac. 644, 79 E.R. 555.

[1615] 2 Ann., c. 6 (Ir.) s. 10 ('gavelkind' imposed on Catholics).

[1616] *Clare* v. *Wordell* (1706) 2 Vern. 548, 23 E.R. 955.

[1617] *Ball* v. *Smith* (1711) 2 Vern. 675 at 676, 23 E.R. 1039.

Mr Rowan for the plaintiffs[1618]

Two objections are made, 1. That this bill can't be revived, 2. If it can, that the plaintiffs have no right to revive it.

1. As to the first, 'tis said that popular actions can't be revived, and that, this is of the same nature, but this suit is of a very different nature. Popular actions are not perhaps to be revived, because there is no need to give such encouragement to sue for penalties. 'Tis enough to give the informer the benefit of it if he brings his action to and [*sic*] end, if not, to any one else. But this Act being necessary to the good and [*455*] welfare of the kingdom is to be encouraged in the highest manner, and though penal laws are to be construed strictly, this is to have a liberal construction, and 'twill be a greater encouragement to institute a suit, when the discoverer knows though the defendant tires him out, the benefit of it will go to his representative; and otherwise the Act might be defeated. The defendant sets up all delays, and another discoverer, then if he can put of[f] the first cause till the plaintiff dies, he carries his point. But allowing these bills to be revived will obviate those inconveniences, and all demurrers are forbid by the Act, but where the plaintiff don't entitle himself; and *Barry* v. *Gould* is an authority, that bills on the Popery Acts may be revived.

2. As to the second point, the plaintiff Green sets forth that he is heir at law to Benjamin Green, and the original bill prayed an account of the mesne profits, so the executors as well as the heir ought to bring this bill of revivor, because one has a right to an account of the profits, the other to the lands, and the bill says, that Benjamin Green made his will, and the plaintiff Green devisee thereof, whereby, and in manner aforesaid, &, the first of which words relate to the will, the rest to the other title of the plaintiff Green as heir, and if I set out a good title, and after[wards] a bad one, the first is sufficient, the other superfluous.

Mr Malone

This is a demurrer to the whole bill, not to that part of it (if there is any such) which prays to have the proceedings revived as devisee. The executors are proper parties, because an account of the profits is to be taken from the time of filing the bill, by the settled course both of the Court of Chancery and Exchequer, nay in the case of *Blake* v. *Blake*,[1619] the House of Lords decreed an account from the time the defendant came into possession of the several discoverable interests. [*456*] 'Tis settled that a bill of discovery may be revived. A pecuniary sum was not looked upon as an adequate recompense for this offence. But the Act gives a remedy to recover the thing itself, and from the time of the filing of the bill, the court considers the Papist as a trustee for the plaintiff. If the informer releases the penalty, there's an end of all prosecution, but if a Protestant discoveror should release to a Papist, that would not secure the estate to him from the intention of the Act, that a Papist should not hold lands, but a new discoveror would have the same right, so this Act is very different from those, whereby forfeitures and penalties are given, and is made for this particular purpose, to take estates out of the hands of Papists. The interest in these lands became vested in the plaintiff on the filing of his bill, and if the suit was to be determined by his death, it would be a great discouragement to him from the uncertainty of life to

Mes App. E.51.

1618   William Rowan is listed in KI AP as a barrister, *c.* 1734; KI AP, p. 430.
1619   *Blake* v. *Blake* (1721) 7 Bro. P.C. 2nd ed. 241, 3 E.R. 157; (1724) 5 Bro. P.C. 2nd ed. 384–391, 2 E.R. 747.

pursue it. So from the nature of it, and the inconveniences which would otherwise follow, your Lordship would decree this to be such an interest as would devolve upon the representative of the plaintiff, though there was no precedent.

But 'tis said, the heir or executor of a Protestant discoveror may be a Papist. But the Act provides for this. Where a Protestant dies seized of lands, they shan't descend to Papist but his next Protestant heir, and where the bill is for a personal estate, if the party that revives is not a Protestant and has the same qualifications with his ancestor, he has no right to a decree, and the interest vested by this Act in the Protestant discoveror must have the same fate with all other interests that are vested in Protestants.

The next day a precedent[1620] was produced in this court, Monday, 11 December 1721, Richard Barry [457] administrator of Abraham Allen brought a bill of revivor on the Popery Acts, v. Ignatius Goold, and Garret Goold,[1621] who put in a demurrer, that the bill could not be revived. 'Twas insisted on for the defendants, that no right vested till the decree, being a personal thing, and a chose in action till that time, and his counsel demurred on terms, that the plaintiff might be a Papist, and so could not revive.

'Twas said for the plaintiff, that the discoveror was entitled to an account of the profits from the time of filing the bill, and that the right accrued from that very day.

Curia

Let the plaintiff file another bill, and he shall have the priority. But I apprehend a Papist shall not have the benefit of reviving, for though a right does not vest, yet when the court decrees, there is a retrospect as to the account. But if the representatives are Protestants, they shall have priority, and be admitted to revive, and that grounded on the equity of the Act, which intends the benefit to the first discoveror. But this demurrer on terms, that the administrator does not show he is a Protestant, must be allowed without costs, and the plaintiff is at liberty to amend his bill of revivor paying 20s costs; and after the bill being amended, and the same demurrer put in, and coming to be argued 22 February 1723, it was overruled with costs, *Richard Allen and Richard Barry executors of Abraham Allen v. Ignatius Goold.*[1622]

Lord Chief Baron

This has been settled before on a full debate that a bill on the Popery Acts may be revived, because an interest vests in the plaintiff from the time of filing the bill, and the heir in this case comes properly to revive. [458]

In *Barry* v. *Goold* the demurrer was allowed, because the plaintiff had not charged in his bill that he was a Protestant, though he swore in his examination on the table.

[1620] Spelled 'presit' in MS.

[1621] *Barry, administrator of Allen* v. *Goold and Goold,* 11 December 1721, Irish court of Exchequer. Above, p. 356 n. 1608 and below, n. 1622.

[1622] No citation given. Above, p. 356 n. 1608 and above, n. 1621.

Sir John St Leger

A popish heir or executor can't carry on the suit, because the Act says only a Protestant shall sue. The executors here ought to be co-plaintiffs, because the profits from the time of filing the bill belong to them.

In *Barry* v. *Goold,* the plaintiff thought it would have been sufficient to have swore he was a Protestant, and when according to the old way he came to be examined on the table.

Mr Baron Wainwright

I submit to the authority, and reason of the thing, that the first Protestant discoveror may not lose his priority, and another be set up.

This is not like a popular action. Not only an interest, but the estate too is vested in the discoveror, or how could he maintain an ejectment?

There is no objection on the second head, but that the plaintiff Green is devisee, but since all are plaintiffs who have a right to revive, we are not to regard such niceties.

So I think the demurrer must be overruled, and that this is an interest vested from the nature of the Act, and the proceedings at law on it.

The demurrer was overruled.

[*459*]

A Table
of the Principal Matters
Contained in the Foregoing Cases

[Note: for Enrolment see Inrollment]

Abatement

See Execution, 1. Bill of revivor, under Bills

Account

See Foreign Attachment 2. Under Attachment, Joint tenants, etc.

1. A bill being brought in aid of an Act, the court ordered the report to stay, till the defendant had put in a full answer. 64

2. On a decree to account, the defendant may examine the plaintiff on personal interrogatories, of course in Chancery, and on the officer's certificate in Exchequer. 88

3. An agent in his answer charges himself with the receipt of all the rents from such a time, and in a schedule set forth so much to be in arrear for that time. He shan't be charged with all the rents, for this amounts to no more than that he received all not in arrear. 153

4. A demurrer to a bill in aid of an account allowed, it praying things inconsistent, that would vary the former decree and subvert the account. 382

Action

See *scire facias* under writ.

Assumpsit

[no entry]

Indebitatus Assumpsit

Whether the evidence in an indebitatus assumpsit can vary from the declaration. 85

Administrator

Administration See Bill of Discovery, 1. Evidence, 6. Purchase, 1.

Whether a court of equity will take notice that administration is granted to a wrong person. 128

Affidavit

See Possessory bills under Bill. Certificate. Injunction, 3, 8. Papist, 5. Attachment, 4. Under Process, Quaker.

To a bill for an injunction [*460*] against an ejectment for non-payment of rent, the statute don't require the affidavit to be annexed, but an order of the court of Chancery. 220

2. The affidavit of the agent of the loss of a deed is not good, without swearing his employer abroad. 297

Agent

See attorney.

Agistment

See Tithe, 2.

Agreement. Articles

See Parol proof, 2.

1. A meadow left out of Articles was decreed to be inserted. 66

2. An agreement adjudged not to be waived. 222

When to be performed in specie

See Marriage articles. Jointure, 2, under Baron etc. Bond. 2.

1. A Papist may file a bill for a specific execution of a discoverable interest. 25,79

2. A executed a minute to B to make him a lease for 3 lives, B filed a bill for an execution of the minute, and had a decree, and after A conveys the estate to C, and B brought a bill to have the decree made good against C the assignee. 65

3. Court carried into execution marriage articles as far as they related to the lands the husband was seised of at the execution of the articles, but not as to what he had acquired after. 102

4. In what cases equity will stand neuter, and neither set aside, or carry an agreement into execution. 152

5. A bill for specific execution of articles made after marriage for paying the plaintiff £300 a year pin money dismissed, on he circumstances of the case. 367

Parol Agreement

Statute of Frauds and Perjuries. See Trusts. 2.

1. A bill was dismissed, the trust not being in writing, though fully proved, and the Statute not insisted on in the answer. 26

Attorney, Agent

Solicitor, Counsel

See Account, 3. Affidavit, 2. Answer, 1. Confirmations, 1. Deeds, 2. Fraud. Pauper, 6. Service, 1, 2, 3, 4. Tender.

1. A witness pleaded to interrogatories, that he came to the knowledge of the facts contained in them as agent to A. This plea was overruled, because he did not swear, he came to the knowledge of the facts only as agent. 11

2. *quære* whether an attorney is obliged by the Popery Acts to answer interrogatories. 11

3. Bill to have part of his clerk's fee returned, his master dying before his time was out. Decree and directions. 86

4. On motion 'twas referred to a Master to see who put counsel's name to exceptions. 139

5. A plea to a bill for a discovery on the Popery Acts, that he was an attorney, and that the knowledge of the matters came to him as an attorney, was overruled. 272

Average
and Contribution

See devise of lands etc. 2. Under Will.

Audita Querela

See under Writ.

Award

See Certificate. Pauper, 2, 3, 4.

1. Whether the court of Chancery is within the 9. W. 3. 52

2. Arming arbitrators with a power to examine witnesses, is not an order on them to examine, but only gives them a power. 53

3. Award made an order of [*464*] the court of Chancery confirmed, and the several objections, or causes showed why it should not be confirmed, overruled. 51

Bail

See *fieri facias*, under Writ.

1. On an habeas corpus cum causa, the court denied a motion for the plaintiff to show cause of bail, because has had showed cause below. 31

2. In an action on the Statute of Usury, the court would not hold the party to bail. 33

3. In an action for treble damages on 8 Anne for overmarking a writ, the defendant must give bail. 48, 392.

4. A note of £10,000 was produced as cause of bail for value received, but the plaintiff allowed it to be given for favours. The court ordered the defendant to give £1,000 bail. 86

Baron and Feme

See Evidence, 23. Will.

Estates and Interests of the Wife

The claim of the husband to his wife's portion is allowed by the trustees for sale of the forfeited estates. She dies, then the husband dies. This portion is vested in the husband and shall go to his administrator. 231

Alimony

and Separate Maintenance

See Agreement when to be performed in specie 5.

A bill to carry a sentence of the spiritual court for alimony into execution by a sequestration, dismissed 428

Jointure

See Who must be Parties, 3, under Bill. Bond, 2. Satisfaction.

A on the marriage of his son covenants to stand seized to the use of his son and his intended wife for life, remainder to the son in tail, etc. with a power to A to charge £300 for the portions of his daughters. A executes this power. The portions are an incumbrance on the jointure, as well as the other estates 231

2. By marriage articles A covenants to settle lands on himself and the issue of the marriage. *quære* if a court of [*465*] equity when they carry these articles into execution, will give the father a power to make a jointure on a second wife, ought to transpose the uses. 240

3. A jointuress is entitled to a satisfaction on an eviction by the Act, and by an original equity, if the executor is before the court. 370

Dower

See Jointure, 3, under Baron, etc.

Bill

See Amendment, 3. Evidence, 4, 9, 10.

Dismission of a Bill

See Bill of Review, 5. Plea, 3.

1. The court dismissed a bill on a motion without a demurrer, it appearing on the bill, that the defendant, and those under whom he claimed, had been 109 years in possession. 58

2. But denied a motion to dismiss a bill for payment of a note for money won at play assigned to the plaintiff, though there had been a decree on the Civil Bill Act, and an appeal dismissed for want of prosecution, because the facts did not appear by the bill. 144

3. Bill to be relieved against the Civil Bill Act dismissed with costs on motion. 145

4. An order to amend is not such a prosecution as will hinder the defendant from dismissing the bill. 181

Who must be Parties

1. A devised £100 to his son if he returned in 2 years, if not, to the plaintiff, the 2 years being expired, the plaintiff brought his bill for the legacy, the court gave him leave to bring the cause to a hearing without the son.   81

2. A cause brought on without the executor, he being out of the kingdom.   260

3. The executor need not be a party where dower issued for on the Statute on an eviction of part of the jointure.   370

4. Bill for an account against A the surviving partner, and the executors of the other. A sequestration is taken out against A for not appearing, who becomes bankrupt. *quære* if the cause may be heard against the executors only.   282

Bill pro Confesso

Bill taken pro confesso on a sequestration after 3 short answers.   142 [*466*]

Bill of Revivor

See service, 2.

A decree not enrolled being revived by scire facias, and not by bill, the court would not discharge it on motion, but left the party to his bill of review, the defendant having acquiesced for two years, and proceeded before the officers.   80

2. A devisee, or remainderman can't revive, but must bring a bill in nature of a bill of revivor.   452

3. A bill of revivor may be brought on the Popery Acts.   452

Possessory Bill

1. The court dismissed a possessory bill, though a plain force at midnight was fully proved, the plaintiff's title being fraudulent.   80

2. Issue directed on a possessory bill, the evidence being contradictory.   121

3. Granted after 3 terms against a tenant holding over by fraud.   131

4. When the court will direct the injunction to the sheriff.   141

5. The affidavit of the steward has been allowed on these bills, where his principal was abroad.   141

6. An injunction was denied on a possessory bill by a devisee against a tenant holding over, neither the seisin of the devisor, or a counterpart being sworn.   329

7. A possessory bill don't lie to be quieted in the possession of a pew.   282

Bill of Review

What introduced bills of review.   15, 16

2. One can't have a second bill of review.   16

3. What must be done to bring a bill of review properly before the court.   16, 17

4. Errors at law, and in fact may be assigned in the same bill of review.   14

5. A demurrer to a bill of review allowed as to the errors at law, and the bill dismissed as to the errors in fact, not coming properly before the court.   14
[*467*]

Supplemental Bill

In Chancery you can't file a supplemental bill before issue is joined without leave of the court, but you may after issue is joined.   127

2. The court will give leave to file a supplemental bill on the Popery Acts to prevent the doubt whether an amended bill is a new bill.   434

Bill of Discovery

See Attorney 5, 6. Papist, 5. Commission of Rebellion, 2, under Process.

1. Bill against an administrator to discover assets, and be decreed to money due by assumpsit, the defendant by her answer confessed assets, but denied the assumpsit, and demurred to the relief, and the demurrer was overruled, the defendant being brought into equity to discover assets.   12

2. The plaintiff has no right to the discovery of a forfeiture, unless he waives the benefit of it.   91

3. In the end of the bill the words were that the confederates might stand aside etc., this being a bill for discovery only against the confederates this is only a bill of discovery.   426

4. A demurrer to a bill of discovery in aid of an appeal before the Delegates was allowed, as being wholly needless, because the plaintiff might have the same examination and discovery before the Delegates. 426

Cross Bill

If the cross bill is filed before issue in the original, the defendant has a right to stay proceedings, but if it is not filed till after issue, he is only entitled to an answer before the hearing of the original cause.   89

2. But if the defendant in the cross cause is in contempt for not answering, the court will not only stop the hearing of his cause, but publication also, till he puts in an answer, though when he has answered, he shall not be obliged to stop till they come up to him in the other cause.   145

Bill of Exceptions

Allowed in a trial at bar.   10 [*468*]

Bond

See injunction, 8. Judgment. Serjeant at arms, 4, 5, 6 under Process.

The party has his election to pursue the penalty of the bond, or a specific execution of the condition of it.   251

2. A by deed of settlement executed by him and his eldest son reserves a power to himself etc., to limit any part of the premises in jointure not exceeding £200 per annum, and on the same day executes a bond, conditioned, that after the marriage he will on request of the obligee settle lands of £200 a year for the jointure of his intended wife. The marriage is had the same day, and after a draft of a jointure was prepared, but never executed. The husband dies, the eldest son was obliged to execute the condition of the bond, which was in nature of an agreement, and the court would not decree it out of the personal estate, though the settlement was not fairly obtained from the son, because the wife was not privy to it, nor the bond forfeited.   240

Bail Bond

See Sheriffs, 3.

Capias

See under Writ.

Caption

See Arrest.

An answer was capt in January, the commission was dated in December. This caption is good enough, and need not be amended.   133

Certificate

See Evidence, 6, 12, 13 24. Papist, 1. Quaker. Trial, 5.

Commissioners may certify, but referees must make affidavit, unless of what they do by virtue of a commission.   37

Claim

See Statute, 2.

Codicil

See under Will.

Commission

Commissioners

See Certificate. Evidence, 21. Examination, 1, 2. Rehearing 2.
     Ordered by the Court of Exchequer, that commissioners to [469] examine witnesses should return the diminicals of the commission.   64

Dedimus

Confirmation

See Injunction, 4, 5. Trial, 5.

1. Whether the receipt of rent by the agent or principal is a confirmation of a lease.   149, 317, 325

2. If the remainderman receives rent, whether this is a confirmation of a void lease made by the tenant for life.   151, 152, 319, 325.

Composition

Devisee for life makes an agreement with the executor and devisee in fee of other lands, for all she took under the will. The remaindermen shan't have the benefit of this composition, or agreement, [n]or is there any trust for them.   356

Construction of Words

See Lease, 1, 2.

1. The word 'months' in the 4 G[eo.] 1, which gives an ejectment for non-payment of rent, must be understood not of lunar, but of calendar months.   73

2. The meaning of the word 'medietas'.   298

3. Of the word 'Exchequer'.   417

Contempt

See under Process.

Contract

Whether a contract with the M[aste]r of the ship, is a contract with the owner.   85

Coparceners

See Estrepement, under Writ.

Copy

See Evidence, 11, 17.

The court will allow copies of their own pleadings signed by their officer to be read, without being proved true copies.   391

Corporation

See Fines.

Costs

See Deeds, 2. Ejectment, 6, 7. Motions. Plea, 2. [470]

1. The Court of Exchequer don't give costs on discharging a notice of motion, but won't let the party move again without paying costs.   140

2. By the practice of the Court of Exchequer the party prevailing has always costs of course, unless 'tis otherwise provided by the decree.   366

Covenant

See Assignment.

If one covenants to build a bridge and uphold it for 20 years, on an action on this covenant, 'tis no plea to say, the bridge was thrown down by a sudden tempest.
70

Counsel

See Attorney.

Counterpart

See Evidence, 3, 17, 18.

Court

The custom of the court will bind, and must be presumed to be law, or that the judges, and the parties would not have so long acquiesced under it.   218

Court of Exchequer
See Writ of Error, 1. Under Writ.

No sum is below the dignity of that court, and may be sued for, either if the plaintiff is forced into court or there is any fraud in the case.   297

Inferior Court
See Bail, 1.

Court of Delegates
See Bill of Discovery, under Bill.

Death

See Sheriff, 2.

Debtor and Creditor

See Personal Estate. Power. Sequestration 4, under Process.

Decree

See Costs, 2. Account, 2, 4. Bill of Revivor, 1, under Bill. Infant, 1. Attachment, 1. under Process. Register. Rehearing, 3, 4. Report. Service, 1, 6. Statute, 17.

When a decree shall bind the heir.   25

2. In Chancery a conditional decree is served on the party, in the Exchequer on the attorney.   433

Dedimus

See Commission.
[471]

Deeds

See Answer, 3, 6. Depositions, 4. Duces tecum. Exhibits. Revocation.

A notary public being hurried before a M[aste]r to prove the execution of a deed, in order as the party pretended to have it enrolled, but without any such design, moved the deed might be produced for his inspection, and the Lord Chancellor made no order, to see if the party would consent to produce it before a M[aste]r.   139

2. Deeds shall be delivered up to the heir without paying the attorney his bill of costs.   383

3. A counsel has a right to have the purport of a deed opened before 'tis proved, but not to see it.   89

4. A deed may be proved by one person at the execution, though it has witnesses.   89, 220.

5. May be proved as an exhibit, though no subscribing witness.   89

6. You may prove the hands of the witnesses to an old deed without proving them dead.   89, 220.

7. What makes an old deed.   220.

Deeds Rased and Cancelled
When a rasure will make the whole deed void when only in part.   99

Loss of a Deed
See Affidavit, 2.

Voluntary Deed
See Injunction, 2.

Whether he who makes a voluntary settlement can alter, or destroy it.   108

Defendant

See Depositions, 1.

A defendant who is never served with process, may be examined as a witness without leave of the court.   30

Demurrer

See Bill of Discovery, 1, 4, under Bill. Account, 4. Dismission etc., 1, and Bill of Review, 5, under Bill. Evidence, 7. Attachment, 5, under Process. Commission of Rebellion, 1, under Process.

You may demur to a plea in abatement after imparlance.   86

2. A demurrer that the bill contained no equity was overruled, the defendant having prayed a dedimus without an injunction.   260
[472]

3. A demurrer and answer stand singly, and though the answer is short, that will not vitiate the demurrer.
345

Depositions

See Amendment, 1. Perjury.

1. Depositions were adjudged to be well titled, though two of the defendants were left out, they having never been served with process. 30

2. So depositions could not be read, which were titled A v. B, & al, when B was only served with process, and appeared. 36

3. By order of the Court of Chancery depositions must be signed. But there is no such order in the Court of Exchequer. 64, 180

4. Depositions of a witness examined on two commissions were ordered to be suppressed, but as to the examination of deeds. 140

5. Interrogatories and depositions may be amended by the commission, *Quære* if they can, when the examination is in the office? 259

Devise

See under Will.

Devastavit

See under Executor.

Dies Non

See Subpœna, under Process.

Discovery

See under Bill.

Distringas

See under Process.

Duces tecum

In what cases the plaintiff has a right to a duces tecum. 37, 90.

2. The court on motion would not order the defendant to bring in deeds according to the submission in his answer but ordered the plaintiff to move for a duces tecum. 37

East India Goods

See Information.

An information on the 7 G 1 ch. 21, whereby no East India goods are to be imported directly into Ireland. 211

2. How the Act of Navigation has regulated the East India trade. 211 [*473*]

Ejectment

See Construction of Words, 1, 2. Evidence, 3. Injunction, 3, 6, 7, 9. Joint tenants, etc., 1. Lease, 4. Trial, 1. Estrepement, 1 under Writ of Error 5 under Writ.

1. By the 4 G 1 no clause of re-entry is necessary to support an ejectment for non-payment of rent. 12

2. Though the demised lands lie in several counties, an ejectment may be brought for the lands in either county. 13

3. On a recovery in ejectment for non-payment of rent, how the rent is to be ascertained. 23

4. Court set aside judgment in ejectment against the casual ejector, and gave the defendant leave to put in a plea, though a writ of error was brought, on their consent to withdraw it. 30, 386

5. If the defendant in ejectment died within the year and a day, *Quære* whether by the common law a scire facias lay for the damages, though not for the realty? 49

6. The court ordered the tenant to take the defence or security be given to pay the costs on affidavit that he who had taken the defence was a person unknown. 61

7. He who takes defence shall not give security, on affidavit of his poverty, and living abroad, if he is not possession. 75

8. Moved in arrest of judgment, that the declaration in ejectment was uncertain. 75, 298.

9. On an ejectment for non-payment of rent on the 8 G 1, in what cases the defendant may go into his title. 345

10. If it appears by the defence that part is evicted, the plaintiff can't recover, for how will it appear a years' rent is due? 351

11. If the plaintiff in ejectment enters into part he can't recover, for he thereby suspends the whole rent. 351

12. Whether the declaration, or verdict uncertain. 434

Election

See Fieri Facias under Writ.

The plaintiff is not obliged to make his election whether he will proceed here or at law, till the defendant has put in an answer. 412
[*474*]

Elegit

See under Writ.

Entry

See Ejectment, 1, 11. Joint Tenants, 1.

Error

See under Writ, 4.

Estrepement

See under Writ.

Eviction

See Jointure, 3 under Baron etc. Satisfaction.

Evidence

See Indebitatus Assumpsit under Action. Deeds, 1, 3, 4, 5, 6. Marriage Articles under Agreement. Copy.

1. An inquisition was allowed as evidence of a lease found without commencement, but that 498 years of the term continued, the return whereof was endorsed, but the endorsement not signed by any officer. 10

2. A memorial of a deed was refused as evidence, that the lessor of the plaintiff had sold to A before the commencement of the plaintiffs lease. 11

3. On an ejectment for non-payment of rent a counterpart of a lease made in 1673 found among the family papers was allowed to be read, without proving the execution or attestation of it, or that the witnesses were dead, payment of the rent to him that was last seized being proved, or if seisin can be proved within 20 years. 22

4. Bill admitted to be read as evidence against the heir of the plaintiff, from a presumption that it was filed with consent, the plaintiff being admitted pauper, and having the benefit of it by injunction, though the registers' notes were produced, for an order to dismiss the bill, being filed without the knowledge or privity of the plaintiff. 26

5. The evidence of one who was plaintiff, guardian, and trustee allowed to be read. 44, 141

6. The certificate of the judge under seal that letters of administration were granted, or the book, is good evidence. 44

7. If you demur to evidence, *Quære* if the jury ought to give a verdict? 45

8. If any part of an answer is given in evidence, the defendant may read the rest at law, but not in equity. 46, 142

9. A bill by prochein amy was read as evidence against the infant, he having after he came of age, reaped the fruit of the decree. 58

10. A bill is the slightest evidence. 58, 113
   [*475*]

11. Whether the copy of a parish register in England shall be read to prove the death of a person. 59

12. The certificate of the registrar of Paris of the death of a person allowed to be read. 60

13. The acts of foreign admiralties may be certified. 23

14. Against whom an answer is evidence. 88, 97

15. A letter of the vendor not allowed to be read against the purchaser, it not being proved when it was wrote. 89

16. The court allowed a lease in 1676 to be read, one having swore positively to the death of two of the witnesses, and that he heard, and believed the other was dead. 168

17. Whether the counterpart of a lease in 1639, and a copy of the enrolment for safe custody is good evidence. 174

18. When a counterpart is good evidence. 175

19. When an enrolment is good evidence. 174

20. The bishop of Dublin's Black book allowed to be read, to prove the bounds of parishes. 178

21. Whether an inquisition taken by virtue of an illegal commission above 100 years ago, may be read to prove the limits of a parish. 178

22. The answer of the defendant read to the payment of the purchase money not being contradicted by proof, though he had failed in proving it. 260

23. The answer of the grantor not admitted to be read against a purchaser, to prove that a jointure made after marriage was not voluntary, but in consideration of a portion then paid. 326

24. A certificate proved by the person who gave it is not good evidence, but he ought to be examined to the facts contained in the certificate. 381

Exchequer

See Construction of Words, 3. Court of Exchequer under Court.

Examination

Account, 2. Defendant. Exhibit, 3. Publication.

In Chancery if either side take out a commission, the other has a commission of course, but in the Exchequer neither can have a separate commission, without an affidavit of the reasons why they could not [*476*] examine their witnesses on the other commission. 381

2. A commission granted to prove a codicil on a rehearing, upon affidavit of its execution by one of the witnesses and the probate in the spiritual court. 394

3. The court denied leave to examine to the proof of the payment of the mortgage money after the cause had been heard. 395

Cross Examination

Cross examining a witness in equity after he appears to be interested, will not make him a good witness, though it will before a jury. 27

Exception

See Woods.

Exceptions

See Answer, 5, 6.

No time is fixed for taking exceptions to a baron's report, but you quicken the other side by moving to confirm it. 38

2. If a baron reports a bill pertinent, a general exception to the report is bad, but it ought to show wherein the bill is impertinent. 399

Execution

See Sheriff, 2. Fieri facias under Writ. See Audita Querela under Writ.

There can be no abatement after an execution taken out. 32

2. The execution takes place between the parties from the teste of the writ, though not till the delivery as to strangers by the Statute of Frauds. 33

Executors

See Who must be parties, 2, 3, 4, under Bill. Infant, 4. Joint tenants, etc., 2, 3. Interest, 3. Notice, 4. Parol proof, 1. Commission of Rebellion, 3, under Process. Purchase, 1. Return, 1.

1. Motion denied, that the executors might plead one plea. 31

2. A surplus undisposed of adjudged to the next of kin, and not to the executor. 41

3. The general rule is, that the executor shall pay interest for the assets from a year after the death of the testator, but this admits of great variation. [278]

Devastavit

See Return, 1. [477]

Exhibits

See Depositions, 4. Deeds, 5. Publication, 3.

An exhibit can't be proved viva voce without an order. 138

2. The rule to prove exhibits viva voce extends only to prove the execution of a deed in the common way provided by the law, and supposes an attestation. 168

3. The court refused a commission to prove a note, which could not be proved as an exhibit, not being witnessed. 168

Fees

See Serjeant at Arms, 1, 2 under Process.

Fieri Facias

See under Writ.

Fine

Tenant in tail conveys to B in fee to the intent to make him a tenant to the praecipe, and covenants to levy a fine before the end of next Easter term to such uses, but no fine was levied, or recovery suffered till the Trinity term following, though the fine can't inure, the recovery, which is limited to no time shall to the uses of the settlement. 326

Fines

See Sheriff, 3.

An order to fine the coroners *nisi* for not returning a distringas against a corporation. 133

Fish

See Tithes.

Forfeiture

See Bill of Discovery, 2.

Fraud, Collusion, Covin, Imposition.

See Possessory Bill, 1, 3 under Bill. Court of Exchequer under Court. Injunction, 8. Sequestration, 4 under Process.

A purchase set aside, being gained by the misrepresentation of the defendant, who was agent, friend, and brother in law to the vendor. 34

Gaming

See Promissory Notes.

Guardian

See Evidence, 5. Infant, 4. Marriage. [478]

Hearing

See Subpœna, 1, 3, 4 under Process. Report. Trial, 5.

The order for the cause to be set down to be heard *ad requisitionem* defendant need not be served, but the plaintiff must be served with a subpœna to hear judgment. 144

Heir and Ancestor

See Deeds, 2. Decree, 1. Evidence, 4, 5. Lease, 5. Notice, 3. Papist, 1.

Idiot, Lunatic

A witness to a deed, or will, may give evidence of the insanity of the party executing them.   297

Imparlance

See Demurrer, 1.

Infant

See Evidence 5, 9. Interest, 3. Marriage.

An infant filed a bill to set aside a decree, the defendants pleaded the decree enrolled, and the plea was allowed, because the cause had been reheard, and a trial at bar directed, whereby the fact the infant suggested must have been fully under the consideration of the court.   36

2. The plea of an infant was overruled. After he came of age he had liberty to amend, and put in a new plea.
                    36

3. A bill to set aside a purchase obtained from the father of the plaintiff during his minority was dismissed, on the long acquiescence of the father, and other circumstances.   385

4. An infant executor above 18 was ordered to answer, the guardian having swore himself a stranger to the charges of the bill.   391

Information

See East India Goods, 1.

Whether the issue *non culpabilis* on an information for importing East India Goods into Ireland from Nantes is senseless.   211

Injunction

1. To stay waste granted without affidavit there being a special verdict.   74

2. The court would not grant an injunction on equity in the defendant's answer, that the consideration was favours received, because the deed was voluntary, and the provision small [479] and the plaintiff was not imposed on be the defendant.   173

3. On a bill for an injunction to stay an ejectment for non-payment of rent, an affidavit that all the material allegations are true is not good.   220

4. By the practice in Chancery, the court will continue an injunction on the master's report, but not grant it till the report is confirmed.   296

5. But the Exchequer in special cases will grant an injunction on the report of a short answer.   295

6. Bill to be relieved against an ejectment, the lessee obtaining a dedimus without an injunction, the commission not being taken out in the usual time, the plaintiff seals an attachment, and obtaining an injunction on it, this was set aside on the motion of the lessor, the lessee being only a nominal person.   384

7. By an order of the Court of Chancery previous to the Act, no injunction without notice is to be moved for to stop proceedings for rent, after the defendant has appeared.   412

8. Granted to stay a sheriff's sale, though the defendant had denied the chief charges of the bill, from an air of fraud that ran through it, and an affidavit of the plaintiff and one of the witnesses to the bond.   415

9. To stop proceedings on an ejectment till the hearing, the plaintiff having two verdicts in his favour in two former ejectments.   416

Inquisition

See Evidence, 1, 21. Elegit under Writ.

Inrollment

See Amendment, 3. Evidence, 17. Rehearing, 3.

Interrogatories

See Attachment, 5, 6, under Process.

Joint tenants, and Tenants in Common

Tenants in common came to a partition, and the one having kept out the other, he brought an ejectment, and a bill for an account of the profits, and though he never entered, an account was decreed from the service of the summons in ejectment.   219

2. *quære* whether the residue undisposed of shall go in moieties, or to the surviving executor.   330

3. If the executors trade with any part of the assets, this will prevent the survivorship of the residue.   330

4. A small matter will make a severance of a joint tenancy, either at law or in equity.   330

Jointure

See under Baron, etc. [480]

Issue

See Information. Possessory Bill, 2 under Bill. Lease, 3.

The court refused an issue whether the purchase money was paid, the defendant having failed in the proof, and his pretended purchase being suspicious.   260

Judgment

See Hearing. Ejectment, 4. Sequestration, 4 under Process. Return, 1. Scire facias under Writ.

In an action on a bond though the declaration was marked for judgment for want of a plea, the court allowed the defendant on paying costs to put in an issuable plea. 387

Interest

See Executors, 3. Mortgage. Portions, 1, 2.

One having charged lands pursuant to a power, the court gave but £5 per cent interest, though the legal was at £7 per cent. 218

2. The court refused interest for the interest of a portion, it being at £10 per cent. 227

3. A legacy was devised to an infant out of the realm to be paid within a year after the testator's death. The executor a banker insists, that he always kept money enough by him to answer the legacy, yet the court decreed him to pay interest for the legacy from a year after the death of the testator. 278

Kin

See Executor, 2.

Lease

See Agreement, when to be performed etc., 2, under Agreement. Confirmation. Evidence, 1, 2, 3, 16, 17, 18. Assignment. Money. Papist, 3, 4. Renewal. Trust, 1. Witness, 4. Woods.

1. *quære* whether by the words in a lease of lives, that the lessee should pay all taxes, country charges, and impositions whatsoever imposed on the premises, the lessee is obliged to pay the quit rent. 9

2. *quære* whether parliamentary taxes after the demise are chargeable on the lessee? 10

3. A bill being brought against a tenant holding over to account for the full value of the land, the court refused to grant an issue, till the officer had reported he could not ascertain it. 44

4. Bill to stay proceedings on an ejectment, and to establish a lease made by virtue of a letter of attorney from a trustee. 149, 154, 302

5. A surrenders his lease to B, who makes him a new lease not warranted by his power at a greater rent. The heir of B after his death brings an [*481*] ejectment to break the lease, the court of equity decreed the surrendered lease to be set up again, and an account of the surplus rent. 297

Legacy

See Who must be parties, 1, under Bill. Interest, 3. Satisfaction.

A devised £200 to his son then supposed in the east Indies, if he returned in two years, if not, to the plaintiff. The court would not decree the money, without the plaintiff's giving security to refund in case the son returned. 81

Letter

See Evidence, 15.

Letter of Attorney

See Lease, 4. Witness, 2.

Letters Patent

Where the first description is wrong, the letters patent are void, and a *non obstante* clause won't help. 61

Lunatic

See under Idiot.

Maintenance

See Interest, 3.

Cestui que use at common law might maintain the suit at his own costs. 88

Manor

See Common Recovery.

Marriage

6 An. ch. 16 to prevent marriages against the will of guardians, etc., pleaded to a bill brought by the widow, as executrix, and devisee of her husband. 437

2. If this Act is pleaded the seduction must be proved. 437

Marriage Articles

See under Agreement.

M[aste]r in Chancery

After 3 summons you may move to proceed ex parte before the M[aste]r. 170

Memorial

See Evidence, 2.

Merchant

See Joint Tenants etc., 3.

Mills

See Tithe, 2.

Misnomer

Edward Chevers was outlawed [*482*] of treason by the name of Christopher Chevers of Killany, commonly called Lord Mount Leinster, *quære* whether this misnomer shall make the outlawry void notwithstanding the 9 W. 3.   1

Modus

See Tithe.

Money

See Service, 4. Sheriff, 4.

Money was decreed to the plaintiff being poor, who sought to break a lease, for if she prevailed, they were to account for the value, if not, for the rent reserved.
                                                                399

Mortgage

See Plea, 5.

The assignee of a mortgage shall not have interest for interest.   5

2. In what cases the court will allow interest upon interest on a mortgage.   229

Motions

See Costs, 1. Notice, 5. Pauper, 6.

You can't move to discharge an order made on hearing counsel of both sides, without paying the costs of the last motion.   117

Non obstante

See Letters Patent under Letter.

Promissory Notes

The indorsee of an note won at play without notice may by the 8 Anne sue the drawer notwithstanding the 11 Anne.   288

Notice

See Parol agreement, 2 under Agreement. Promissory note. Costs, 1. Pauper, 6. Purchase. Sheriff, 2. Writ of Error, 5, under Writ.

1. A recital of articles in a deed is sufficient notice to those who claim under it of those articles, though they are misrecited.   51, 94

2. What notice shall bind a purchaser.   128, 154

3. Whether a purchase without notice is good against an heir.   128

4. Whether one may purchase the personal estate from the executor, with notice of the will.   260

5. Notice of motion to set aside process for irregularity, will not stop process.   581

Order

See Motions. Attachment, 2 under Process. [*483*]

Outlawry

See Misnomer. Elegit under Writ.

Papist

See Attorney etc., 2, 5. Bill of Revivor 3, under Bill. Pauper, 1, 4. Agreement when to be performed etc., under Agreement. Supplemental Bill, 2. Under Bill.

By the 6 Anne the heir of a Papist may file his certificate before his age of 21, and may conform at any time from the death of the testator to the age of 22 years. 6

2. A Papist makes his will before the disabling Act 2 Anne, but dies after. The will is void.   6

3. If a Protestant is decreed to the benefit of the trust of a lease on the Popery Acts, *quære* whether he shall indemnify the lessee against the rents and covenants?
                                                                219

4. *quære* whether the lease is void as to the lessee, after a discovery, and decree in equity.   219

5. In Exchequer if you don't annex an affidavit to a bill of discovery on the Popery Acts, the defendant may move that the plaintiff stop *quosq[ue]*.   398

6. A constructive papist by marriage can't file a bill of discovery .   92

Parol Proof

See Trusts, 2. Fieri facias, 4 under Writ.

Parol proof admitted to show the testator intended the executor the surplus.   42

2. Parol proof refused to be read to explain an agreement contrary to the words.   142

Partners

See Who must be Parties, 4, under Bill. Sequestration 4 under Process.

Partners are bound jointly and severally.   282

Partition

See Joint Tenants etc., 1.

Patent

See Letters Patent under Letter.

Pauper

1. A plaintiff on the Popery Acts may be admitted a pauper, but refused where the plaintiff conformed purely to bring a bill against her father, & to worry a Protestant discoveror. 92

2. When the party shall be dispaupered unless he submit to a reference. 133

3. Not if the bill concerns an inheritance. 163

4. Or he sues for a maintenance on the Popery Acts. 412

[*484*]

5. A pauper shan't be joined as a plaintiff with a Dives. 381

6. By an order of the court of Chancery notice of motion by a pauper must be signed by counsel. 412

Payment

[no entry]

Perjury

If the title of depositions is amended by the court, *quære* if the witness is indictable for perjury. 259

Personal Estate

The whole personal estate exempted by will, and the debts charged on the real estate. 356

2. The personal estate adjudged not to be applied in ease of the real estate. 164

3. Decreed to be applied. 193

Pew

See Possessory bill, 7 under Bill.

Plaintiff

See Evidence, 5. Witness.

Plea

See Demurrer, 1. Amendment, 3. Judgment. Marriage. Infant, 1, 2. Executors, 1. Attorney etc., 1, 5. Covenant. Ejectment, 4. Commission of Rebellion, 1 under Process. Publication, 1. Scire facias under Writ. Elegit under Writ.

1. On a scire facias to revive a judgment, because it contradicts the sheriff's return, which is matter of record. 70

2. Upon a *respondeas* ouster no plea can be admitted till the costs are paid. 72

3. A plea being allowed, the plaintiff moved to dismiss his bill, and files the same in Chancery. The defendant moved that his bill might be retained, that he might plead the decretal order to the bill in Chancery, but the motion was denied, because he might plead the dismission. 90

4. The defendant being in contempt to a serjeant at arms, and having delayed the plaintiff by privilege, the court refused to receive a plea of a purchaser etc. 140

5. A files a bill to redeem, the defendant pleads, she had brought a prior bill of foreclosure in England. This plea was overruled. 170

Pledge

See Retainer. [*485*]

Portions

See Interest, 2. Estates etc. Jointure, 1 under Baron.

The court refused to allow a daughter interest for a portion, because it moved from the mother, and it did not appear she was otherwise unprovided for. 118

2. On a bill brought against the remainderman, the court would not allow interest for a portion till after the death of the father. 182, 194, 412

3. The trust was for such daughter as should be living at the commencement of the term, yet the court decreed the portion to vest in a daughter who married, and died in the life of her father. 182, 412

Power

See Bond, 2. Jointure, 1, 2, under Baron etc. Revocation. Will.

A power to charge lands with a sum of money is assets in favour of creditors, if there prove a deficiency. 87

Process

Subpœna

See Amendment, 2. Defendant. Attachment, 1, 3. Hearing. Return, 2. Service, 2, 3, 4.

1. A subpœna to hear judgment in the Exchequer returnable on a *dies non* good. 64

2. Of the manner of taking out process on a subpœna. 403

3. The petitioner must serve the defendant's attorney with a subpœna to hear judgment, though he consents to appear gratis. 35

4. Such a subpœna returnable the 1st day of term in Chancery is bad. 64

Attachment, Contempt

See Sequestration 1, 2, under Process.

By an order of the Court of Exchequer, if an attachment issues for non-performance of a decree, and a *non est inventus* is returned, the process is shortened to a serjeant at arms.   326

2. You can't be in contempt for disobedience of an order till 'tis drawn up and served though 'tis made on hearing counsel of both sides.   170

3. Every process must be sealed before the return, or the party is not in contempt, and the several processes are not sealed at once, unless where there is an order of process *tunc pro nunc*.   299

4. A person in contempt can't discharge himself by affidavit, but he may show the affidavit on which the contempt was grounded insufficient.   383

5. If one in contempt demurs to interrogatories, the charge shall be taken for true.   383

6. Whether one in contempt shall answer personal interrogatories that would criminate him.   383
[*486*]

Distringas

See Fines.

Commission of Rebellion

No plea, or demurrer can be put in after a commission of rebellion returned, without leave of the court.   58

2. After a commission of rebellion returned, the answer must be received without security, if the bill is for discovery only.   134

3. *Quære* an executor on the equity side of the Exchequer, who has stood out process to a commission of rebellion, shall give security?   379

Sequestration

See Bill *pro confesso* under Bill.

The court refused to revive process of attachment after a sequestration.   38

2. Or to grant a sequestration where one was taken on an attachment, and lay in gaol for not performing the decree.   38

3. On the defendant's absconding, the decree being served on his attorney, a sequestration was granted without any intermediate process for non-performance.   81

4. After a decree the defendant and his partner who were bankers, vest their real and personal estate in trustees for the payment of debts; adjudged that a sequestration that issued after for non-performance of the decree could not attach on the effects, that this assignment was not fraudulent, and that a decree, no more than a judgment, attached on goods till execution served.   415

Serjeant at Arms

The serjeant shall never have his day fees, unless he return his writ in due time.   403

2. He is entitled to the caption fee, though the process is irregular.   403, 404

3. The original of the serjeant at arms.   404

4. Of the bonds they take for the appearance of the defendant.   403, 404

5. Whether the execution on these bonds ought to be marked by the 6 Anne.   404

6. Or whether there ought to be a writ of enquiry of damages by the 9 Wm. 3 ch. 35.   404

Promise

See Promissory Notes under Notes.

Publication

[*487*] One having pleaded to an interrogatory, and the plea overruled, he was ordered to be examined to the interrogatory, though publication has past in the meantime and after he was examined, the plaintiff was obliged to move the rules for publication *de novo*. 12

2. Leave given to examine witnesses after publication.   118, 395

3. A witness examined in chief may prove an exhibit after publication.   140

4. Leave given to prove a pedigree after publication.   399

Purchase, Purchaser

See Agreement, Parol 2, under Agreement. Evidence 15, 22, 23. Fraud. Infant, 3. Issue. Notice, 1, 2, 3,4. Plea, 4.

He who purchases from an administrator, or executor, is subject to the trust, and has notice.   222

2. A purchaser bound having not only constructive, but actual notice of a will, and articles.   260

Quaker

Adjudged on a trial at bar in ejectment on the 1 G. 1 ch. 5, that a Quaker might be a witness, on his producing a certificate, without affidavit of the signing it, on examining the Quaker, whether he had been a Quaker for above 5 years, whether he saw the 6 signing the certificate, and whether they were of his congregation.   400

Quo minus

See under Writ.

Rasure

See deeds rased etc, under Deeds.

Real Estate

See Personal Estate. Devise of Lands etc., 1 under Will.

Recital

See Notice, 1.

Record

See Plea, 1.

Common Recovery

By a common recovery of a manor, the reversion of part on a lease for life will pass. 22

Register

See Evidence, 11, 12.

quære whether a deed not registered shall be void against a creditor by decree. 26

Regularity

See Serjeant at Arms, 2, under Process. Notice, 5. [*488*]

Rehearing

See Examination, 2.

The court denied a rehearing of an English information. 116, 384

2. The Commissioners of Appeals denied a rehearing, the appellant having wilfully neglected the prosecution of his cause, without desiring to have it put off. 301

3. A rehearing being granted, and the money not lodged in due time, though the decree was not enrolled, the court refused a new rehearing. 385

4. A rehearing after a conditional decree made absolute denied. 432

Rejoinder

See Service, 3.

Release

A release *in errorem* will not bind. 152, 227.

Relief

See Bill of Discovery, 1, 3 under Bill.

Remainder

See Composition. Confirmation, 2.

Renewal

A lease for 31 years, with a covenant that the lessor should at the end of the term make a new lease for 31 years, with the same clauses, covenants, and reservations as in the former, *quære* if in the new lease there should be a covenant of renewal. 14

Rent

See Injunction, 3, 7. Confirmation. Account, 3. Tender.

Repeal

See Statute, 16.

Report

See Injunction, 4, 5. Exceptions.

Exceptions to a report being overruled, the court made a decree though the cause was not set down to be heard on the report, it not being interlocutory, but leaving nothing to be done. 144

Retainer

The court would not oblige an administrator to deliver deeds and other things of value to the heir and executor of the person who deposited them, without paying the money the intestate after lent him, and said she had a right to retain them, though they were not originally designed as a pledge, but deposited in trust, for when the intestate after lent the money, the [*489*] original trust as to so much was altered. 383

Return

See Serjeant at Arms, 1, under Process. Attachment, 3, under Process. subpœna, 1, 4, under Process. Fines. Sheriff, 3. Fieri facias, 4, under Writ.

Judgment being against an executor by default, the coroner returned *nulla bona*, the court would not oblige him to amend his return, and return a devastavit, he not designing to abuse the court, but left the plaintiff to his action. 49, 69, 71

2. The same process may be renewed without a return, but you can't ground a subsequent process on it till 'tis returned. 404

Reversion

See Common Recovery.

Revivor

See Bill of Revivor under Bill. Service, 2.

Revocation

A subsequent deed adjudged not to be a revocation of a former or an execution of a power in it. 351

Satisfaction

[See Sale.]

Sale

See Sheriff, 1, 2. Devise of lands etc. under Will.

A legacy to the wife adjudged not to be taken as a compensation or satisfaction for part of her jointure which was evicted. 370

Scandal

The defendant can't refer a bill for scandal after answer but as an *amicus*, and shall have no costs, but a stranger may. 79

Scire facias

See under Writ.

Seal

See Attachment, 3 under Process.

Security

See Trial.

Sequestration

See under Process.

Serjeant at Arms

See under Process.

Service

See Decree, 2. Attachment, 2 under Process. subpœna, 3 under Process. Hearing. Trial, 5.

1. An affidavit of the defendant's absconding, serving the attorney with the decree, was allowed good service. 81

[*490*] 2. A subpœna to revive can't be served on the attorney of the original defendant. 219

3. In the Exchequer a subpœna to rejoin may on motion be served on the attorney, if the defendant lives above 40 miles. 220

4. The attorney of the plaintiff at law may be served with a subpœna. 219

5. A rule to pay money by the course of the Pleas side of the Exchequer must be served personally. 385

6. Ordered on affidavit etc. that service of the defendant's last place of abode be good service of a decree and injunction. 399

Sheriff

See Fieri facias, 4, under Writ.

Adjudged that on a fieri facias the sheriff can't employ an auctioneer to sell the goods, or sell them on trust with the consent of the parties. 313

2. The sheriff is not bound to take notice of the death either of the plaintiff or defendant, but must execute his writ by sale, and though he is out of his office, he must go on with the sale. 33

3. The sheriff can't oblige the plaintiff to accept an assignment of the bail bond, but if the plaintiff refuses, the court will stop the fines against the sheriff for not making his return. 42

4. Money totted for by the sheriff was adjudged not to be money paid into the Exchequer, within the words of a private Act of parliament. 417

5. The old and present manner of totting. 417

Ship

See Contract.

Solicitor

See under Attorney.

Spoliation

See Spoliation.

Statutes

9 W 3 of outlawries. See Misnomer.

2. By the 6 Anne the Statute of Periods persons in possession need not claim. 1.

3. 2 & 6 Ann. to prevent the further growth of popery. See Papist

4. 4 & 8 G. 1 Ejectment for non-payment of rent. See Ejectment, 1, 3, 9. Construction of words, 1. Tender.

5. 6 Ann. the Register Act. See Register

6. Statute of Frauds. See Parol agreement, under Agreement. Execution, 2. Trusts, 2.

7. Statute of Usury. See Bail, 2.

[*491*] 8. 6 Ann. ch. 7 Treble damages for over-marking a writ. 48

9. 9 W. 3 of awards. See Award

10. 7 & 8 W. 3 extends to goods not enumerated. 76

11. Goods were entered as come from St Lucia, the duty paid, and the warrant given for bringing them

ashore, and some were in the gabbart, and some were in the ship, when they were seized by a warrant from the commissioners by virtue of this statute, being goods directly imported from Barbados, landed and put in the King's stores. This was adjudged not to be a landing within the Act to make the goods forfeited. 76

12. Civil Bill Acts. See Dismission of bill, 2 under Bill.

13. Articuli Cleri. [145]

14. The nature of a private Act of Parliament. 49, 154, 302

15. 7 G. 1 ch. 21 Against importing East India goods into Ireland. See East India Goods, 1, 2.

16. Navigation Act, *quære* if repealed by the former Act. 215

17. Trustee Act, how far the decrees of the trustees are conclusive. 231

18. 8 Ann. which makes notes negotiable. Promissory Notes.

19. 11 Anne To prevent gaming. See Promissory Notes.

20. 16 Ca. 2 in England against gaming. See Promissory Notes.

21. 10 Ca. 1 ch. 1 Of jointure. See Jointure, 3, under Baron & Feme.

22. 1 Geo. 2 ch. 5 Of the affirmation of Quakers. See Quaker.

23. 9 W. 3 ch. 35. Writ of enquiry of damages. See Serjeant at Arms, 6, under Process.

24. 6 An. ch. 16. To prevent marriages against the will of guardians. See Marriage.

Subpœna

See under Process.

Surrender

See Lease, 5. Fieri facias, 1, under Writ.

Suspension

See Amendment, 1.

Taxes

See Lease, 1, 2.

Tenant

Possessory Bill, 3, 6, under Bill. Evidence, 1, 3, 16, 17, 18.

Tender

A tender of the rent and costs according to the 4 G. 1 ch. 5 to the agent is a tender to the lessor. 73

Tot

See Sheriff, 4, 5.

Traverse

See Elegit under Writ.
[*492*]

Treason

See Misnomer.

Trial

The courts will grant a new trial in many cases after a trial at bar, but not after a trial at bar in ejectment. 28

2. A new trial prayed because the jury took out with them a letter, and a draft of a deed, but denied by the Court of Chancery. 82

3. Where a court of equity directs a trial, it has power over the terms of it, but not where it only retains the bill, that the parties may be at liberty to proceed to trial. 140

4. The defendant having been guilty of a breach of trust, & above 80 years of age, the court struck a medium from the proofs, and set a value on the lands, and would not grant a trial, unless the defendant gave security for the balance due by the Master's report. 367

5. After a verdict on an issue out of the Exchequer, the certificate must be confirmed, and the order served 4 days before the cause can be set down to be heard. 398

Trust, Trustee

See Agreement Parol, under Agreement. Composition. Retainer. Lease, 4. Witness, 1, 4.

1. A new lease adjudged to be taken in trust for the former lessee. 39

2. Trusts arising by operation of law may arise and be destroyed by parol since the Statute of Frauds. 40, 88.

How to be charged,
and what allowances to have.

A trustee was allowed £75 for his care and trouble being charged with £71 for which he had sold books part of the trust estate, and taken a bond from the bookseller in his own name, who failed. 117

Breach of Trust

See Trial, 4.

Tithe, Modus

1. Decree for the tithe of the agistment of barren cattle.   44

2. For the tithe of mills.   145

3. Custom in the city of Waterford and 7 parishes, that the whole, or entire tithe [493] or tenth fish, and particularly herrings, whether taken in the open sea, and outside of the harbour's mouth, or within the said harbour's mouth of the said city, by any boat, or vessel belonging to any person dwelling within the said city, or parishes, and landed in any place within the said city, or parishes, be paid to the Dean and Chapter of Waterford and their predecessors, as rectors of the parish of the Holy Trinity in the said city, adjudged to be a good modus.   442

Venue

In what cases the court will change the venue.   32

Verdict

See Evidence, 7.

Warrant

See Arrest.

Waiver

See Agreement, 2.

Will

See Papist, 2.

A will made by a feme covert by virtue of a power, was decreed against the husband on the foot of spoliation, he having cancelled it, or would not produce it.   351

Codicil

See Examination, 2.

Devises of lands to be sold etc., for payment of debts, and legacies, etc.

See Personal Estate.

A devises all his lands, leases for years, and all his real and personal estate to be sold, and the money to be laid out in a purchase, to be settled etc., the trustees never sell, yet the whole devise is to be considered as real estate, for the benefit of those who are to take by the purchase.   119

2. Where a man subjects all his real and personal estate to the payment of his debts and legacies, the several devises shall stand charged in proportion.   356

Waste

See Injunction, 1. Estrepement, 2, under Writ.

Witness

See Defendant. Cross-examination, under Examination. Perjury. Deeds 4, 5, 6. Idiot. Attorney, 1.

1. A plaintiff not allowed to be a good witness, though a bare trustee, being liable to pay costs.   141

2. A not allowed to be read to the proof of a letter of attorney, he having on his cross-examination denied he was to gain or lose by the success of the cause, but owned he had a lease made by virtue of the said letter, but did not say, [494] whether he was tenant of the lands or had then a lease.   153, 304

3. Leave given to exhibit articles to the credit of a witness after publication, and the cause set down to be heard, and in another cause after a conditional decree.   169, 366

4. A lessee in trust allowed a good witness to prove an old lease which was expired, though he only swore, that one witness was dead, and that he did not know, whether the other was dead, or alive.   220

Woods

A lease, except the woods, passes the soil.   66

Writ

See Execution. Serjeant etc., under Process.

Declaration on the 6 Anne for over-marking a writ, which totted, and tripled the damages as a sum certain, and totted them too high, ill.   391

Writ of Enquiry

See Serjeant at Arms, 6, under Process.

Capias

See Fieri facias, 2, 3, under Writ.

Scire facias

See Plea, 1. Bill of Revivor, under Bill. Ejectment, 5.

What might have been pleaded to the action can't be pleaded to a scire facias on the judgment.   170

Fieri facias

See Sheriff, 1.
         After surrender by the bail, the plaintiff may take out a fieri facias, for by the surrender, the party is not in execution without the election of the plaintiff. 171

2. A capias and a fieri facias can't issue at the same time.   171

3. If on a fi. fa. the goods are not sufficient, the plaintiff may have another fi. fa., or a capias at his election.   172

4. The vendee may give parol proof of a fi. fa., because that belongs to the sheriff, and he need not return it.   174

Estrepement

Granted to one who claimed only a sixth as co-parcener, on a writ of error in ejectment. 32

2. An estrepement to stay waste. 141

Elegit

The plea of an elegit on traversing an inquisition on an outlawry overruled. 376
  [495]

Quo Minus

Whether on a quo minus you can break open doors. 173

Writ of Error

See estrepement, 1, under Writ.

1. Whether error in fact lies in the Court of Exchequer, by a writ of error *coram vobis*. 43, 46, 49, 61, 68.

2. A writ of error may be quashed after an allowance, or withdrawn, if not actually removed. 43, 387

3. A writ of error quashed, the treasurer and barons being commanded to etc., because the treasurer is no judge of law matters. 43

4. *Quære*, whether the writ must be directed to the treasurer and barons, who have the custody of the records, for barons to review, or to the barons. 46, 149

5. An *habere* was set aside though the writ of error was not allowed, the plaintiff having notice of it. 390

Audita Querela

Won't lie after execution executed. 170

[Note: At this point the MS. ends with a Table of the Names of Cases, i.e. cases reported in the volume. This has not been transcribed, and reference should be made to the list of Cases Reported at p. xxi.]

APPENDICES

APPENDIX A

An Act to enable Susanna Catherina Nugent, to sue for, recover and hold the Portion provided for her out of her Father's Estate, notwithstanding her Coverture and the Outlawry of her Husband Hyacinthus Nugent Esquire, 1716

Private Act, 3 Geo. I, c. 10 (G.B.)
HLRO, Original Act, 3 Geo. I no. 16 (G.B.)

Whereas Susanna Catherina Nugent eldest daughter of Sir Tristram Berisford deceased when she was but fourteen years of age was by her guardian the late Dame Nichola Sophia Berisford her mother and Arrabella Susanna Viscountess Dungannon her aunt married to Hyacinthus Richard Nugent esquire son and heir apparent of Thomas Nugent esquire which said Hyacinthus Richard was then a Protestant *And Whereas* the said Hyacinthus Richard Nugent is since the said marriage turned papist and has forsaken his said wife and lives in foreign parts in the service of the French King and left her destitute of a support *And Whereas* the said Hyacinthus Richard was when he was an infant of thirteen years old outlawed for high treason in Ireland *And Whereas* the said Susanna Catherina Nugent by virtue of the last will or marriage settlement of her said father or otherwise claims or is intitled to a portion or provision of one thousand four hundred pounds charged on the estate of her said father but by reason of her coverture and of the attainder of her said husband she is by law disabled to recover or hold the same for remedy whereof your most dutiful subject the said Susanna Catherina Nugent most humbly beseeches your most excellent Majesty That it may be enacted *And* be it *Enacted* by the King's most excellent Majesty by and with the advice and consent of the Lords Spiritual and Temporal and Commons in Parliament assembled and by the authority of the same That all the estate right title interest trust property claim and demand which the said Hyacinthus Richard Nugent and Susanna Catherina his wife or either of them have has or ever had or might have had in case the said Hyacinthus Richard Nugent had never been outlawed or shall or may hereafter have of in or to the said sum of one thousand four hundred pounds and the interest thereof and of in or to all and every other legacy and legacies gifts grants devises sum and sums of money whatsoever granted devised provided or secured unto or for or in trust for the said Susanna Catherina Nugent by the last will and testament or any deed or deeds settlement or settlements of the said Sir Tristram Berisford her father or of in or to which they the said Hyacinthus Richard Nugent and Susanna Catherina Nugent or either of them are is or shall or may be entitled by virtue of such last will and testament settlement or settlements shall be and is and are hereby vested in the Right Reverend father in God William Lord Arch Bishop of Dublin and the Honourable Lieutenant General Richard Gorges Esquire and the survivor of them and the executors and administrators of such survivor

383

and that it shall and may be lawful to and for the said William Lord Arch Bishop of Dublin and Lieutenant General Richard Gorges and the survivor of them and the executors and administrators of such survivor to commence and prosecute any action or actions suit or suits in any of His Majesties courts of law or equity in Great Britain or Ireland for the recovery of the same or any part thereof and to receive and give proper discharges for the same in trust nevertheless that all and every sum and sums of money so recovered or received by the said William Lord Arch Bishop of Dublin and Lieutenant General Richard Gorges or the survivor of them or the executors and administrators of such survivor shall be paid laid out and disposed of to and for the sole separate and proper use benefit and behoof of the said Susanna Catherina Nugent her executors administrators and assigns and shall be paid laid out disposed of and applied in such manner and to such interests and purposes as the said Susanna Catherina Nugent by any writing or writings under her hand and seal or by her last will and testament which she is hereby enabled to make shall direct or appoint and that the said Hyacinthus Richard Nugent shall in no ways intermeddle therewith or with any part thereof any law statute usage or custom to the contrary notwithstanding *Provided* always And be it further *Enacted* That if Sir Marius Berisford Baronet only son and heir of the said Sir Tristram Berisford shall and do within three months after he has notice of the passing of this Act pay or well and sufficiently secure to the said William Lord Arch Bishop of Dublin and Lieutenant General Richard Gorges and the survivor of them and the executors and administrators of such survivor the just and full sum of fifteen hundred pounds sterling current money of Ireland with interest for the same as now allowed by law in the said kingdom from the day of passing this Act to be applied to the trusts intents and purposes above-mentioned that the same shall be and is hereby declared to be in full payment discharge and satisfaction of the said principal sum or portion of one thousand four hundred pounds granted devised or settled on or to the said Susanna Catherina Nugent by the said last will and marriage settlement of the said Sir Tristram Berisford or either of them and of all interest that is or may be due thereupon But in case the said Sir Marius Berisford shall neglect or refuse to pay the said fifteen hundred pounds and interest as aforesaid that then and in such case the said sum of one thousand four hundred pounds and all interest now due and which hereafter shall grow due for the same shall be and is hereby vested in the said William Lord Arch Bishop of Dublin and Lieutenant General Richard Gorges and the survivor of them and the executors and administrators of such survivor upon the trusts and to the intents and purposes above-mentioned anything herein contained to the contrary notwithstanding.

APPENDIX B

An Act to Enable Mary O'Gara, Widow to Sue for her Jointure-Lands, 1726

Private Act, 13 Geo. I, c. 31 (G.B.)
HLRO, Original Act, 13 Geo. I no. 66 (G.B.)

Note: The text of the Act is printed, as is the bill.

Whereas by one indenture tripartite, of bargain and sale for a year, bearing date the fourteenth day of February in the year of our Lord God, One thousand six hundred and eighty-seven, and an indenture tripartite, of release, bearing date the fifteenth day of the same month, made, or expressed to be made, between Sir John Fleming of Stoholmock in the County of Meath, knight, and Richard Fleming, son and heir apparent of the said Sir John Fleming of the first part; the Right Honourable Jenico Lord Viscount Gormanston, the Right Honourable Christopher Lord Baron of Slane, and Sir Patrick Barnewall of Crickstown, baronet, of the second part; Sir Richard Bellings of the City of London, knight, and Sir John Barnewall, knight, recorder of the city of Dublin, of the third part, in consideration of a marriage before had, and solemnized, between the said Richard Fleming and the Honourable Mary Fleming his wife, one of the daughters of the Right Honourable Randal late Lord Baron of Slane; and also in consideration of the sum of one thousand five hundred pounds, secured to be paid by the said Randal Lord Baron of Slane, out of his estate, as a portion for his said daughter, pursuant to a certain agreement made and concluded on, between the said Sir John Fleming on the one part, and the said Sir John Barnewall, uncle of the said Mary Fleming, on the other part the lands, tenements, and hereditaments of Rahood, and Butler's-town, situate in the county of Meath in the Kingdom of Ireland and also the manor, town, and tathes[1623] of land of Derry, Knockboy, alias Gouldrey, with a court-leet, and court-baron, and all fairs and markets thereon; Tullynure, and the mill thereof; Mullaghmore, Killdowagh, Shallews, Culmultkilly, Culmult-Bane Cornally, alias Croyle, and Covenreagh, Corbeg, Drumrootagh, Cornally, and Crumlin, situate in the county of Monaghan in the said Kingdom of Ireland, [2] with their appurtenances; are therein expressed to be conveyed, limited or settled to the use of, or in trust for, the said Richard Fleming and Mary his wife, during their lives, and during the life of the longer liver of them, without impeachment of waste, during the life of the said Richard Fleming only, as a jointure for the said Mary Fleming, and in lieu and full satisfaction of all dowers and thirds that should be due to the said Mary Fleming, out of the Lands, Tenements, and Hereditaments of the said Richard Fleming.

[1623] Fields in which cattle or sheep were kept in order to manure it. OED.

And Whereas the said Richard Fleming soon afterwards departed this life, and the said Mary Fleming did, in some short time afterwards, marry Oliver O'Gara Esquire, who is since likewise deceased, and claims to be intituled unto the said several lands, as her jointure by virtue of the said recited indentures of lease and release.

And Whereas the said Mary O'Gara, widow, stands outlawed or waved in the Kingdom of Ireland, for, or on account of foreign, or other treason, by her committed, or supposed to have been committed, against their late Majesties King William and Queen Mary, or one of them, by reason whereof she is disabled to sue for, recover, or have any estate, right, title, or interest, which she was intituled unto at the time of the said outlawry, or at any time before; whereby she is reduced to extreme misery and want, and therefore hath most humbly petitioned His most Excellent Majesty, that she may be enabled, notwithstanding the laid outlawry, to sue for and recover her said jointure lands and mesne profits thereof; which His Majesty hath been graciously pleased to allow of;

May it therefore please Your most Excellent MAJESTY;

That, at the humble request of the said Mary O'Gara, it may be *Enacted; And be it Enacted* by the King's most Excellent Majesty, by and with the Advice and Consent of the Lords Spiritual and Temporal, and Commons, in this present Parliament assembled and by the Authority of the same, that it shall and may be lawful to and for her the said Mary O'Gara, her executors, administrators or assigns, to have, use and take all such remedies, ways, means, actions and suits, both at law and in equity, for recovering, obtaining, and enjoying, to her the said Mary O'Gara, her executors, administrators and assigns, all lands, tenements and hereditaments conveyed or limited by way of jointure to her, or to her use, at or after her marriage with her first husband Richard Fleming, together with the rents and mesne profits thereof, in as ample and beneficial a manner, as she might, or could have used or taken, at any time before the aforesaid outlawry or attainder, or as the King's Majesty might have used or taken immediately before the making hereof; any outlawry or outlawries, attainder or attainders of the said Mary O'Gara, for high-treason, or misprision of treason, by [3] what name, surname, or addition soever; or any law or statute heretofore made in this Kingdom, or in the said Kingdom of Ireland, to the contrary in any wise notwithstanding.

Provided always that nothing in this Act contained shall extend, or be construed to extend, to avoid, make null, impeach, defeat, or charge any estate or interest that hath been sold or disposed of by the trustees named and appointed in and by an Act of parliament made in the eleventh year of the reign of His late Majesty King William the Third, intituled, *An Act for Granting an Aid to His Majesty, by Sale of the Forfeited and other Estates and Interests in Ireland; and by a Land-Tax in England, for the Several Purposes therein mentioned.*[1624]

Saving nevertheless, to the King's Most Excellent Majesty, his heirs and successors, all such estates right, title, interest, claim and demand, of, in, to, or out of the premises, as belonged to the Crown on, or before the first day of November, which was in the year of our Lord God one thousand six hundred and eighty-eight; and saving to all and every other person or persons, bodies, politick and corporate, their heirs and successors, all such estate, right, title, interest, claim and demand whatsoever, either in law or in equity, as they, or any of them have at the time of the making of this Act, of, in, to, or out of any of the said premises, other than the estates, rights, titles,

---

[1624]   11 Will. III, c. 2. (11 & 12 Will. III in Ruffhead) (Eng.)

interests and demands which the said Mary O'Gara is hereby enabled to sue for, recover, or enjoy, as fully and, beneficially, as if this Act had never been made.

Provided also, that nothing in this Act contained, shall extend or be construed to extend, to avoid, make null, impeach, defeat, or charge any estate or estates, lease or leases, mortgage or mortgages made by Sir John Fleming, of Stoholmock in the county of Meath in the Kingdom of Ireland, knight, deceased, and Michael Fleming, Son and Heir of the said Sir John, or by either of them, unto any Protestant or Protestants (of any part of the lands, tenements and hereditaments, situate, or being in the said county of Monaghan, which the said Mary O'Gara claims to have been conveyed or limited by way of jointure to her, or to her use, for her life) but that all and every such Protestant and Protestants, their heirs, executors, administrators, and assigns respectively, shall have, hold, possess, and enjoy all and every such estate and estates, lease and leases, mortgage and mortgages, for and during, and according to the several and respective estates, terms, and interests, and under the several rents, covenants, conditions, provisoes and agreements in them or any of them severally and respectively mentioned and contained, freed and discharged of, from, and against all, claims of His Majesty, his heirs and successors, in respect of any forfeiture vested in His Majesty, his heirs and successors, by means or on account of the attainder or outlawry of the said Mary O'Gara, and the claims of the said Mary O'Gara, and all and every person and persons [4] whomsoever, claiming or to claim, any right, title, estate, or interest under the said Mary O'Gara, or under His Majesty, his heirs and successors, in respect, and by means, or on account of such forfeiture, attainder or outlawry as aforesaid any thing herein before contained to the contrary notwithstanding.

Provided nevertheless, that it shall and may be lawful to and for the said Mary O'Gara, her executors, administrators and assigns, to take, have, and use all such remedies, ways and means, both at law and in equity, for recovering the rents reserved by the said lease or leases which shall hereafter become due, as the said Mary O'Gara might have taken, or would have been intituled unto, in case she had made such lease or leases, and had been actually seized of the lands so leased at the time of making thereof; and also to have and received full satisfaction from the said Michael Fleming, or out of, all, or any of his other lands, tenements, and hereditaments, for such losses and damages as shall or may happen to, or be sustained by her for her executors administrators or assigns, by means or occasion of the said mortgages, and leases, or any of them.

APPENDIX C

An Act For Relief of Hyacinthus Richard Nugent, 1727

Private Act, 1 Geo. II, c. 23. (G.B.)
HLRO, Original Act, 1 Geo. II no. 46 (G.B.)

Whereas Thomas Nugent Esquire commonly called Lord Riverston second son of Richard Earl of Westmeath of the kingdom of Ireland was included in the Articles of Limerick and by and under the said Articles all along held and enjoyed his estate so that no part thereof was forfeited or granted by the Crown to any Protestant whatsoever And *Whereas* the said Thomas Nugent was at the time of his death seized of and in all that and those the capital and mansion house of Pallas and the lands thereunto belonging and adjoining making in the whole three cartrons[1625] and two thirds containing three hundred and twenty acres Lissenard half a quarter one hundred thirty seven acres Killiorban half a quarter one hundred fifty seven acres in Balleline half a quarter one hundred fifty two acres Gortnesillagh half a quarter ninety eight acres Cappachur quarter thirty six acres Oltertyan one cartron eighty five acres in Gurrane and Ballinsulla two thirds of a quarter two hundred fifty two acres all profitable land Irish plantation measure situate lying and being in the half barony of Leitrim and county of Gallway Sunaghbegg one quarter two hundred forty five acres of like profitable land of like measure lying and being in the barony of Longford and county of Galway aforesaid Killbride one quarter one hundred thirty eight acres in Coolebane twenty acres of like profitable land and like measure lying and being in the half barony of Leitrim and county of Gallway aforesaid Bolosteragh one quarter one hundred seventy seven acres Knockanevine and Coolenegart two hundred and six acres of like profitable land and measure lying and being in the barony of Longford and county of Gallway the town and lands of Feybract Bailevallin Gortnegallass alias Gortnegallagh and Lecarrow two quarters containing two hundred thirty seven acres in Kill one cartron thirty two acres in Gortfine one cartron twenty acres Tourfallagh alias Tanufullagh fifty five acres two half cartrons of the three half of Cahir alias Caigher fifty seven acres in Concrashy alias Cloncoshan over and above the cartron belonging to the Earl of Clanrickard forty eight acres of like profitable land and like measure Knockanevine one cartron of Garrane one hundred twenty five acres of like profitable of Irish plantation measure lying and being in the barony of Longford and county of Gallway

---

[1625] The *OED* has the word as an Irish variant of quartern and the quotation: 1683 J. Keogh, 'Account [of] Roscommon' in O'Donovan, *Tribes Hy-Fiachraich* (1844) at p. 454 'The lands here are generally set and let by the name of quarters, cartrons, and gnieves, a quarter being the fourth part of a townland and a cartron the fourth part of a quarter.' But under quarter, 7c. it has 'An Irish land-measure (translation [of the] Irish *ceathramhadh*, sometimes anglicized as carrow)' and the quotation, 1883, Seebohm, *English Village Communities*, vii. 223, 'Annexed is an example of an ancient bally divided into quarters. Two of the quarters, now townlands, still bear the names of 'Cartrons' and 'Carrow', or 'Quarter'.

aforesaid Gandy alias Garrhy containing five hundred thirty nine acres four roods and thirty nine perches in the town and lands of Killenegallagh thirty eight acres one rood thirty four perches the town and lands of Skyne and Monyduff containing two hundred fifty five acres two roods the town and lands of Kill and Straduffe containing one hundred forty five acres making in all nine hundred seventy one acres one rood and thirty three perches all profitable land Irish plantation measure all lying and being in the barony of Mayrashell and county of Westmeath and all and singular the castles messuages houses edifices building barns stables dove houses yards orchards gardens closes enclosures loghs rivers mills waters watercourses fairs turbarys heaths mines known and unknown commons pastures and also all waifs strays privileges franchises immunities liberties jurisdictions profits emoluments commodities hereditaments and appurtenances whatsoever by what name or names soever the same be called or known to premises or any part thereof belonging or in any wise appertaining *And Whereas* Hyacinthus Richard Nugent commonly called Lord Riverston and heir of the said Thomas Nugent to whom the said capital messuage towns lands hereditaments and premises would otherwise have descended or come stands outlawed in Ireland for or on account of treason by him supposed to have been committed against their late Majesties King William and Queen Mary or one of them and is thereby made incapable to sue for recover hold or enjoy the same although as well at the time when the said treason is alleged to have been committed as at the time of pronouncing the said outlawry he the said Hyacinthus Richard Nugent was an infant of so tender years as made it impossible for him to be guilty of such treason or to use any endeavours to prevent his outlawry and the ill consequences thereof by which said outlawry and in the incapacity under which he is fallen thereby he is reduced to great necessity and by the particular hardships of his case is a fit object of his Majesty's princely compassion and the said capital messuage towns lands hereditaments and premises are held and enjoyed by his younger brother William Nugent who is a papist and therefore the said Hyacinthus Richard Nugent hath most humbly petitioned His Most Excellent Majesty that he may be enabled notwithstanding his said outlawry to sue for recover take hold and enjoy the said capital messuage towns lands tenements hereditaments and privileges with their appurtenances and the mesne profits thereof which His Majesty hath been graciously pleased to allow of *May* it therefore please Your Most Excellent Majesty that at the humble request of the said Hyacinthus Richard Nugent your Majesty's most dutiful subject it may be enacted *And* be it *enacted* by the King's most Excellent Majesty by and with the advice and consent of the Lords Spiritual and Temporal and Commons in this present Parliament assembled and by the authority of the same that it shall and may be lawful to and for the said Hyacinthus Richard Nugent his heirs executors administrators and assigns respectively to have use and take all such remedies ways means actions and suits both at law and in equity for recovering and obtaining to him and them the said capital messuage towns lands tenements hereditaments and premises hereinbefore particularly mentioned with their and every of their appurtenances together with the rents and mesne profits thereof subject to the several estates leases and mortgages hereinafter saved and provided for in as ample and beneficial manner as the said Hyacinthus Richard Nugent might or could have used or taken if he had not been outlawed or as the King's Majesty might have used or taken immediately before the making hereof the same to be used or taken either in the name of His Majesty his heirs and successors or otherwise howsoever and also that it shall and may be lawful to and for the said Hyacinthus

Richard Nugent his heirs and assigns to take hold and enjoy all and singular the said capital messuage towns lands tenements hereditaments and premises and every part and parcel thereof with their and every of their appurtenances the said hereinbefore mentioned outlawry or any other outlawry or outlawries attainder or attainder of him the said Hyacinthus Richard Nugent for high treason misprision of treason or any other account whatsoever by what name surname or addition soever or any act or Act of Parliament passed in England Great Britain or Ireland confirming the same to the contrary in any wise notwithstanding *Provided* always that nothing in this Act contained shall extend or be construed to extend to avoid make null impeach defeat or charge any estate or interest which hath been sold or disposed of by the trustees named and appointed in and by any Act of Parliament made in the eleventh year of his late Majesty King William the Third entitled *An Act for Granting an Aid to his Majesty by Sale of the Forfeited and Other Estates and Interest in Ireland and by a Land Tax in England for the several purposes therein mentioned,*[1626] *Saving* nevertheless to the King's Most Excellent Majesty his heirs and successors all such estate right title interest claim and demand of in to or out of the said premises as belonged to the Crown on or before the first day of November which was in the year of our Lord one thousand six hundred eighty eight and saving to all and every other person and persons body politic and corporate their heirs executors administrators and successors all such estate right title interest claim and demand whatsoever either in law or equity as they or any of them have at the time of making this Act of in to or out of the said premises other than the estates rights titles interests and demands which the said Hyacinthus Richard Nugent his heirs executors administrators and assigns are hereby enabled to sue for recover hold and enjoy as fully and beneficially as if this Act had never been made *Provided* also that nothing in this Act contained shall extend or be construed to extend to avoid make null impeach defeat or charge any estate or estates lease or leases mortgage or mortgages of the said premises or any part thereof made or executed bona fide and for valuable consideration by the said Thomas Nugent and William Nugent or either of them to any Protestant or Protestants so as such lease or leases estate or estates mortgage or mortgages except two several deeds of mortgage made to Francis Palmer late of Farrow in the county of Mayo in the kingdom of Ireland Esquire deceased were duly registered any time before the twenty fifth day of March one thousand seven hundred and twenty six pursuant to an Act of Parliament in the kingdom of Ireland entitled *An Act for the Public Registering of all Deeds and Conveyances and Wills which concern any honours manors lands tenements and hereditaments within this kingdom* but that all and every such Protestant and Protestants their heirs executors administrators and assigns respectively shall have hold possess and enjoy all and every such estate and estates lease and leases mortgage and mortgages for and during and according to the several estates terms and interests and under the several rents covenants conditions provisions and agreements in their conveyances leases and mortgages severally and respectively mentioned and contained freed and discharged of from and against all claims of His Majesty his heirs and successors in respect of any forfeiture vested in His Majesty his heirs answer successors by means or on account of the attainder or outlawry of the said Hyacinthus Richard Nugent and the claims of the said Hyacinthus Richard Nugent and all and every person and persons whomsoever claiming or to claim any right title estate or interest under him the said Hyacinthus

---

[1626] 11 Will. III, c. 2 (Eng.), 1698–99 (Trustee Act).

Richard Nugent or under his Majesty his heirs or successors in respect of or by means or on account of such forfeiture attainder or outlawry as aforesaid anything hereinbefore contained to the contrary notwithstanding *Provided* nevertheless that it shall and may be lawful to and for the said Hyacinthus Richard Nugent his heirs executors administrators and assigns to take have and use all such remedies ways and means both at law and in equity for recovering the rents reserved by the said lease or leases which shall hereafter become due as he the said Hyacinthus Richard Nugent might have taken and none other or would have been entitled unto in case he had made such lease or leases and had been actually seized of the said lands tenements or hereditaments so leased at the time of making thereof.

APPENDIX D

An Act for Relief of Dame Elizabeth Dudley, relating to an Estate in the Kingdom of Ireland, forfeited to the Crown during the Life of William Kennedy her great Uncle, 1729

Private Act, 3 Geo. II, c. 21 (G.B.)
HLRO, Original Act, 3 Geo. II no. 58 (G.B.)

Whereas Sir Richard Kennedy of Mount Kennedy in the county of Wicklow[1627] and kingdom of Ireland Baronet by indentures of lease and release bearing date the seventeenth and eighteenth days of February one thousand six hundred and seventy nine in consideration of the marriage portion before had and received with Dame Anne his wife and for the settling and assuring to her the jointure therein mentioned and for settling and assuring all his manors lordships towns lands tenements and premises therein mentioned in his name and blood did convey to Michael Lord Arch Bishop of Armagh John Lord Arch Bishop of Dublin Sir Maurice Eustace Knight Henry Hene Sir William Domville Sir John Temple Edward Jones Walter Walsh and George Kennedy and their heirs and assigns for ever *All* that the manor of Mount Kennedy and divers towns lands tenements and hereditaments in the said county of Wicklow and also all those the towns and lands of Kishoge and Balladonde in the county of Dublin lands and tenements and in the county of the City of Dublin To the use of him the said Sir Richard Kennedy for his life without impeachment of waste remainder as to part of the premises to the use of Dame Anne then wife of the said Sir Richard Kennedy for her life remainder as to all the said premises from and after the respective deceases of the said Sir Richard Kennedy and Dame Anne to the use of Robert Kennedy son and heir apparent of the said Sir Richard Kennedy for his life without impeachment of waste with remainder to the use of the trustee therein named and his heirs during the life of the said Robert Kennedy in trust to preserve the contingent remainders with remainder to the first and second and every other son of the said Robert Kennedy in tail male successively with remainder to the use of William Kennedy second son of the said Sir Richard Kennedy for his life without impeachment of waste with remainder to the use of the said trustee and his heirs during the life of the said William Kennedy to preserve the contingent remainders with remainder to the first second and every other son of the said William in tail male with remainder to the use of the said heirs male of the body of the said Sir Richard Kennedy with like remainders to Thomas Kennedy and his sons as by the said indenture of release duly inrolled in the Rolls Office in Ireland relation being thereto had may appear *And Whereas* the said Thomas Kennedy died without issue male in the lifetime of the said Sir Richard Kennedy and

---

[1627] The 'manor of Mount Kennedy in Co. Wicklow' was granted on 28 September 1664 by King Charles II to Robert Kennedy: *Cal. St. Papers Ir. 1663-65*, p. 438.

the said Sir Richard Kennedy afterwards videlicet[1628] on or about the twenty ninth day of February one thousand six hundred and eighty four departed this life having issue male only his said two sons Robert then Sir Robert Kennedy and William Kennedy which said Robert entered upon the said manors lands and premises and soon afterwards videlicet on or about the tenth day of June one thousand six hundred and eighty eight departed this life having issue two sons Richard Kennedy and Howard Kennedy both infants under the age of twenty one years *And Whereas* afterwards videlicet on the sixth day of April one thousand six hundred and ninety one the said William Kennedy was outlawed for treason for being engaged in the Irish Rebellion of one thousand six hundred and eighty eight whereby the estate and interest of and in the said the said manors lands and premises limited to him by the said first recited settlement in case of failure of the issue male of his deceased brother Sir Robert Kennedy became forfeited to the crown *And Whereas* the said Howard Kennedy afterwards (in the lifetime of his said brother Sir Richard Kennedy) died without issue and the guardians of the said Sir Richard Kennedy died during his infancy and he the said Sir Richard Kennedy after his attaining the age of twenty one years did enter upon all and every the said manors lands and premises and quietly enjoy the same until the tenth day of April one thousand seven hundred and ten when he departed this life having issue only Elizabeth his daughter and heir who hath since intermarried with William Dudley Esquire now Sir William Dudley Baronet *And Whereas* in and by a certain Act of parliament made in the eleventh and twelfth years of the reign of his late Majesty King William the Third intituled *An Act for granting an aid to his Majesty by Sale of the Forfeited and other Estates and Interests in Ireland and by a Land Tax in England for the several purposes therein mentioned*[1629] all the estates rights and interests of persons convicted or attainted of the said Rebellion were vested in trustees therein named to be sold and disposed of for the benefit of the public with a power thereby given to the said trustees to make an allowance not exceeding a fourth part of such real estate and five shillings in the pound of all personal estates and interests so forfeited as aforesaid to the discoverer or discoverers of such forfeiture in the manner therein mentioned *And Whereas* by another Act of parliament made in the first year of the reign of her late Majesty Queen Anne entituled *An Act for Advancing the Sale of the Forfeited Estates in Ireland and for other purposes therein mentioned*[1630] all and every the estates rights and interests by the said former Act vested in the said trustees and which were not or should not be sold before the twenty fourth day of June one thousand seven hundred and three were vested and settled in her Majesty her heirs and successors for the several and respective uses and purposes aforesaid subject to such orders and appointments as should thereafter be given by the parliament of England in that behalf and that the money arising by such forfeited estates and interests (the necessary charges of levying collecting suing and recovering and other incident charges relating to the said forfeitures excepted) should be paid into the Receipt of the Exchequer in Ireland and there kept apart from other her Majesties treasure and revenue to be disposed as hereafter directed by the parliament of England *And Whereas* after the decease of the said Sir Richard Kennedy the grandson Elizabeth Jones widow of the said Edward Jones afterwards Lord Bishop of Saint Asaph and

---

[1628] L. that is to say, often abbreviated to viz.

[1629] 11 Will. III, c. 2. (11 & 12 Will. III in Ruffhead) (Eng.) 1698-99, Statute of Trustees.

[1630] 1 Ann. St. 2, c. 18 (Eng.) (c. 21 in Ruffhead) 1702 (advancing sale of forfeited estates in Ireland).

one of the daughters of the first named Sir Richard Kennedy first discovered the said forfeiture and outlawry of her said brother William Kennedy to her late Majesty Queen Anne who by warrant under the Sign Manual bearing date the nineteenth day of July one thousand seven hundred and fourteen did in consideration of such discovery direct a commission to be issued for finding and seizing the said forfeited estate and upon return of such commission to pass a lease or custodiam thereof under the seal of the court of Exchequer in Ireland to the said Elizabeth Jones her executors administrators or assigns for the term of ninety nine years if the said William Kennedy should so long live reserving to her said Majesty her heirs and successors three fourth parts of the clear yearly value of the said estate and did also thereby direct that in case the said estate should be found and seized into her said Majesties hands then out of the arrears of the said estate which ought to have been answered to her said Majesty since the death of the said Sir Richard Kennedy one full fourth part should be allowed or paid over to the said Elizabeth Jones her executors administrators and assigns as of her said Majesties free gift and royal bounty *And Whereas* the said Elizabeth Jones dying without farther prosecuting the discovery of the said forfeiture Robert Jones esquire her son having obtained by warrant date the nineteenth day of August in the twelfth year of the reign of his late Majesty King George the First a revival of the said warrant and grant to his said mother did effectually prosecute the same and on or about the second day of January one thousand seven hundred and twenty six obtain a lease or custodiam of so much of the said forfeited estate as lies in the county of Wicklow of the yearly value of seven hundred and twenty pounds to hold to the said Robert Jones his executors and administrators and assigns for the term of ninety nine years if the said William Kennedy so long live thereby reserving to his said Majesty his heirs and successors three fourths of the said seven hundred and twenty pounds per annum according to the proportions reserved for the use of the public by the said recited Acts and the direction of the recited warrants as in and by the said custodiam or lease under the seal of the court of Exchequer in Ireland may appear *And Whereas* by means of the said attainder and by force of the said recited Acts not only the right and interest of the said William Kennedy was so as aforesaid vested in the Crown for the use of the public but it is also apprehended that the reversion and inheritance of the said manors lands and premises expectant on the estate of the said William Kennedy without issue male not being claimed by the said Sir Richard Kennedy the infant his guardians or trustees in such manner as by the said recited Act of the eleventh and twelfth of William the Third is directed is or may be involved in the forfeiture of the said William Kennedy and together with the said life estate also vested in the Crown and forasmuch as the said Sir William Dudley and Elizabeth his wife have been always well affected to the Protestant interest and from the circumstances of their case the said Sir William Dudley and Dame Elizabeth his wife are objects of compassion and may deserve the relief of Parliament *And Whereas* upon the humble petition of the said Sir William Dudley and Dame Elizabeth his wife his Majesty has been graciously pleased to signify his consent that a bill be brought into Parliament for the relief Therefore may it please Your Majesty that it may be enacted *And* be it *Enacted* by the King's most Excellent Majesty by and with the advice and consent of the Lords Spiritual and Temporal and Commons in this present Parliament assembled and by the authority of the same that from and immediately after the first day of June one thousand seven hundred and thirty all and every the said manors messuages lands tenements and hereditaments settled and conveyed by the said

Sir Richard Kennedy by the aforesaid recited settlement and all rent accrued to the Crown from the premises or in respect thereof since the death of the said Sir Richard Kennedy the grandson not paid into His Majesties Exchequer in Ireland to be sued for and recovered in the name of His Majesty his heirs and successors as need shall be or require and all and every right title and interest whatsoever of and in the same forfeited by the said William Kennedy as aforesaid or vested in the Crown as aforesaid shall be and the same is and are hereby vested and settled in the Right Honourable the Lord Viscount Gage of the kingdom of Ireland and William Peirs esquire and their heirs subject to the said custodiam or lease which together with the fourth part of the said arrears of rent in the said warrants mentioned to be granted is and are hereby made effectual and confirmed to the said Robert Jones his executors and administrators and assigns on trust nevertheless that they the said Lord Viscount Gage and William Peirs or the survivor of them or the heirs of such survivor shall and may settle and convey the same to such uses intents and purposes as the said Dame Elizabeth Dudley in and by certain Articles of Agreement enrolled or intended to be enrolled in the High Court of Chancery bearing date the eighteenth day of April one thousand seven hundred and thirty and made and mentioned to be made between the said Sir William Dudley by the name of Sir William Dudley of Clapton in the county of Northampton baronet and the said Dame Elizabeth by the name of Dame Elizabeth his wife the only daughter and heir of Sir Richard Kennedy of Mount Kennedy in the county of Wicklow and kingdom of Ireland baronet deceased of the one part and Robert Jones of the parish of Saint Margarets Westminster in the county of Middlesex esquire of the other part hath directed and appointed or therein agreed to direct and appoint which said Articles of Agreement and the several uses conditions clauses covenants and agreements therein contained shall be as valid and effectual in the law to all intents and purposes as if the said Dame Elizabeth Dudley at the time of making and executing the said the same had been sole and unmarried and notwithstanding her coverture and as if she had levied fines and suffered recoveries and to and for no other use intent or purpose whatsoever the said outlawry or forfeiture or any matter of thing whatsoever in the said recited Acts of Parliament or either of them contained to the contrary in any wise notwithstanding *Provided* always *And* be it *Enacted* and declared by the authority aforesaid That all and singular the manors and premises intended to be hereby vested as aforesaid shall be subject to such Crown rents Quit rents and Chiefries issuing thereout respectively as the same were respectively liable to and charged with on the thirteenth day of February one thousand six hundred and eighty eight *And* be it also *Enacted* that nothing herein contained shall be construed or taken to charge incumber defeat or prejudice the said custodiam or lease of the estate right or interest of the said Robert Jones his executors administrators or assigns hereinbefore confirmed and that during the continuance of the said custodiam or lease the rent thereon reserved to his Majesty his heirs and successors shall be from time to time paid to and had taken and received by such person or persons as by force or virtue of this present Act is are or may be intituled to the reversion and inheritance of the said manor and premises subject to the several charges and incumbrances herein mentioned *Provided* always *And* be it *Enacted* and declared by the authority aforesaid that nothing herein contained shall be construed or taken to defeat or prejudice any other debt charge or incumbrance which may any ways charge or affect the said manors lands and premises or any part thereof but that the same shall be and remain in the same plight and condition to all intents and purposes as if this present Act had not been made any thing therein contained to the contrary thereof in any wise notwithstanding *Provided* also *And* be it *Enacted* and declared by the authority aforesaid That all and singular the said manors lands and premises hereby intended to be vested as aforesaid shall be and the same are hereby charged with the yearly rent charge of three hundred and fifty pounds to Katherine Howard widow and relict of Frederick Henry Howard esquire commonly called the Lord Frederick Howard during her life according to the true intent and meaning of the last will of Sir Richard Kennedy the grandson her first husband bearing date the twenty second day of July in the year of our Lord one thousand seven hundred and seven and with all arrears of such rent charge now remaining due and unpaid to be levied or reserved in such manner as in the said will is directed notwithstanding such outlawry forfeiture and non claim as aforesaid in satisfaction of her dower and of all other the claims she hath or is entitled unto out of the said manors and premises or other the estate of the said Sir Richard Kennedy the grandson deceased *Provided* also *And* be it *Enacted* by the authority aforesaid that the right and claim of John Toole gentleman and Martha his wife to a debt or debts or incumbrances of one thousand seven hundred pounds principal money and of Peter Godby esquire to a debt or incumbrance of four hundred ninety six pounds four shillings and eleven pence principal money and all other debts and incumbrances originally charged and secured on the said manors lands and premises by the said Sir Richard Kennedy the grandfather or the said Sir Robert Kennedy his son or the said or the said Sir Richard Kennedy the grandson with the interest respectively due or to grow due thereon and the right and title of William Godby clerk to the lands of Kishoge in the said county of Dublin purchased by his late father John Godby deceased of Sir Richard Kennedy the grandfather and the several legacies given bequeathed and charged on the said manors lands and premises by the said will of the said Sir Richard Kennedy and likewise the several estates rights and interests of John Sale esquire Richard Arthur John Arthur John Ford Miles Barnwall John Walsh and Edward Metcalfe gentleman severally granted to or otherwise vested in them by or under leases or grants made by the said Sir Richard Kennedy the grandfather or the said Sir Robert Kennedy or the said Sir Richard Kennedy the grandson or the said Sir William Dudley or Dame Elizabeth his wife shall not be any ways defeated or prejudiced hereby but shall be and remain as good valid and effectual in the law to all intents and purposes as if the said William Kennedy had not been attainted or outlawed as aforesaid and as if the said recited Acts of the eleventh and twelfth years of the reign of his late Majesty King William the third and the first year of the reign of her late Majesty Queen Anne or any other Act or Acts for vesting the said forfeited estate or this present Act or any of them had not been made *Provided* also that the several tenants and lessees of all and every part of the said manors lands and premises who have from time to time paid the rents respectively due from them to the person or persons in possession shall not be made farther answerable for the same by any thing herein contained *And* saving to all every person and persons bodies politick and corporate other than as aforesaid and other than his said Majesty his heirs and successors all such right title and interest as they or any of them had of or in the premises or before the making of this Act and as if this Act had not been made.

APPENDIX E

LETTER OF POPE INNOCENT III

Grant of Tithes of Fish

Étienne Baluze (Stephanus Baluzius) *Epistolarum Innocentii III.*
(Letters of Pope Innocent III) (Paris, 1682). vol. 2, at p. 461;
Registrum Vaticanum 8 f. XXVIr = Reg. Innoc. III, XIII 95 (c. 92);
Pontificia Hibernica (M. Sheehy, ed., 1962), vol. 1, no. 70, pp. 144–5.

DECANO ET CANONICIS WATERFORDEN.

Sacrosancta Romana Ecclesia humiles & devotos filios ex assuetæ pietatis officio propensius diligere consuevit, & ne pravorum hominum molestiis agitentur, eos, tamquam pia mater, suæ protectionis munimine confovere. Eapropter, delicti in Domino fi[l]ij, devotionem quam erga beatum Petrum & nos ipsos habere dinoscimini attendentes, personas vestras & universa bona quæ in præsentiarum rationabiliter possideris, aut in futurum justis modis dante Domino poteritis adipisci, sub beati Petri & nostra protectione suscipimus. Specialiter autem locum in quo Eccclesia vestra sita est cum pertinentiis suis, Ecclesiam de Kilros, Ecclesiam de Kilmelassi, Ecclesiam de Cluoneda, Ecclesiam de Tibrada, Ecclesiam de Kilimelach, Ecclesiam de Kilmaclug. cum omnibus pertinentiis suis, decimas piscium in Waterford, beneficia terrarum Ricc. Scadan. & Terri, villam de Corbali, villam de Balikassin, villam de Tachethen, terram de Kaldebech, terram Roberti le Franceis juxta Kilmemilog. cum omnibus pertinentiis suis, & omnia bona communitati & sustentationi vestrae nihilominus assignata; sicut ea juste ac pacifice possidetis, vobis & per vos Ecclesiæ vestræ auctoritate apostolica confirmamus & præsentis scripti patrocinio communimus. Nulli ergo &c. hanc paginam nostrae protectionis & confirmationis infringere vel ei &c. usque incursurum. Datum Laterani vi. Kal. Iulij, pontificatus nostri anno tertiodecimo.

[Translation by Dr Michael Staunton]

To the dean and canons of Waterford

The holy Roman Church is accustomed to hold especially dear her humble and devoted sons on account of the duty of customary piety, and lest they be disturbed by the annoyances of wicked men, to favour them with the shelter of her protection, as a pious mother. On which account, beloved sons in the Lord, attending to the devotion which you are known to have towards St Peter and toward us, we take under our protection and that of St Peter your persons and all goods which you reasonably possess at present, or in future by just means and by God's gift you are able to add: especially the place in which your church is established and its appurtenances, the church of Kilrush, the church of Kilmolash, the church of Clonea (?), the church of Tubrid, the church of Kilmolash, the church of Kilmacleague with all its appurtenances, a tenth of the fish in Waterford, benefices of the lands of Richard Scadan. et Terri, the vill of Corbally, the vill of Ballycashin (?), the vill of Templetney (?), the land of Cahirbreac (?), the land of Robert le Frances near Kilmogemogue with all its appurtenances, and likewise all goods assigned to your community and sustenance as you hold justly and peacefully. These we confirm to you and through you to your church by apostolic authority and we strengthen by the protection of the present letter. Let no one then infringe upon this letter of protection and confirmation ... etc. Given at the Lateran 26 June, the thirteenth year of our pontificate. [1210 A.D.]

BIBLIOGRAPHY

AND

INDEXES

BIBLIOGRAPHY

RULES OF COURT

Darley, William F., *General Orders of the Court of Chancery in Ireland; Also General Orders of the Lord Chancellor in Matters of Bankruptcy and Lunacy*. Dublin, Hodges and Smith, 1843.

Hand, G. J. and V. W. Treadwell, eds., 'His Majesty's Directions for the Irish Courts, 1622.' 26 *Analecta Hibernica* 177–212.

Hand, G. J. ed., 'Rules and Orders to be Observed in the Proceedings of Causes in the High Court of Chancery in Ireland, 1659.' (1974) Ir. Jur. (n.s.) 110–165.

Ireland, Parliament, 'Rules and Orders to be Observed in the Upper House of Parliament upon Writs of Error and Appeals.' 1 Ridg. P. C. pp. xix–xxi.

Moore, Ross Stewart and Lowry Thomas Kennedy, *A Collection of the General Rules and Orders of the Courts of Queen's Bench, Common Pleas and Exchequer of Pleas in Ireland; . . . With Practical and Explanatory Notes, and an Appendix of Statutes*. Dublin, 1842.

'New Rules of the Chancery [side] of the Court of the Exchequer'. *c.* 1730. King's Inns, Dublin, MS No. 50.

'Rules and Orders of the Court of Common Pleas in Ireland - Trinity Term, 22 Charles II [1670]'. Columbia University. Singleton MS. No. 25.

'Rules in the Chancery Side of His Majesty's Court of Exchequer in Ireland.' Gilbert C.B.[?]. Early 18th century. Harvard Law School Library, MS 505.

'Rules of the Court of Exchequer in Ireland, with notes and observations.' *c.* 1734. King's Inns, Dublin, MS No. 90.

United Kingdom, Parliament, *Standing Orders of the House of Lords relative to Writs of Error and Appeals*. London, 1843.

PRINTED PRIMARY SOURCES

Berry, H. F. ed., *Early Statutes, Ireland, John to Henry VI*. The Irish Record Office Series of Early Statutes, vol. 1. Dublin, 1907.

British Parliamentary Papers series. Shannon, Irish Academic Press.

Foster, Joseph, *The Register of Admissions to Gray's Inn, 1521–1889*. London, 1889.

Gilbert, Lady ed., *Calendar of the Ancient Records of Dublin*. Dublin, Dublin Corporation.

Goodbody, Olive C., *Guide to Irish Quaker Records 1654–1860*. Dublin, Irish Manuscripts Commission, 1967.

Ireland, House of Lords, *Rules and Orders to be observed in the Upper House of Paliament of Ireland*. Dublin, 1790.

Keane, Edward, P. Beryl Phair and Thomas U. Sadleir eds., *King's Inns Admissions Papers 1607–1867.* Dublin, Irish Manuscripts Commission, 1982.

Lascelles, Rowley, ed., *Liber munerum publicorum Hiberniae, ab an. 1152 usque ad. 1827; or, The establishments of Ireland from the nineteenth of King Stephen to the seventh of George IV. Being the report of Rowley Lascelles . . . Extracted from the records and other authorities, by special command, pursuant to an address, an. 1810, of the Commons of the United Kingdom. Ordered to be printed 1824.* London?, ca. 1830–1852.

O'Byrne, E., ed., *The Convert Rolls: the Calendar of the Convert Rolls, 1703–1838.* Dublin, Irish Manuscripts Commission, 1981; 2nd ed., with Fr Wallace Clare's annotated list of converts, 1703–78, ed. Anne Chamney, 2005.

The Statutes at Large of Ireland. [Public General Acts. 1310–1800]. 21 vols. Dublin, George Grierson, 1786–1804.

The Statutes at Large of Ireland. [Public General Acts. 1692–1711]. 2 vols. Dublin, George Grierson, 1734. Note: Vol. 1 contains the statutes of King William III and Queen Mary II and is dated 1733. The chapter numbers of the statutes of 9 Will. III follow on from those of 7 Will. III. Vol. 2 contains the statutes of Queen Anne and is dated 1734.

Sturgess, H.A.C., *Register of Admissions to the Honourable Society of the Middle Temple, from the fifteenth century to the year 1944.* London, Butterworth, 1949.

PLEADINGS, HOUSE OF LORDS

House of Lords Record Office, London, Main Papers (printed and unprinted). 1499–. Appeal Cases (printed) 1702–.

King's Inns, Dublin, 'House of Lords Appeals.' (Irish and British).

Lincoln's Inn, 'House of Lords Printed Cases, Judgments and Appeal Documents.' 1664 onwards.

National Library of Ireland, 'Appeals: Printed statements of cases of appellants, respondents, etc., in cases to be heard before the House of Lords.' 1710–1800.

Trinity College Dublin, 'Appeals to the House of Lords brought by various persons mostly residents of Ireland.' 202 r. 31–35, 1710–1739; I. cc. 21–23, 1729–1739; 202 r. 36, Index of appellants, typescript 1956.

CD ROM FORMAT AND SOFTWARE

Cokayne, G. E., *The Complete Peerage.* 2nd edition revised & enlarged by V. Gibbs and others. CD Rom. ABC Publications.

Johnson, Samuel, *A Dictionary of the English Language.* 1st & 4th editions. CD ROM. Anne McDermott ed. Johnson's Dictionary Project, University of Birmingham. Cambridge, University of Cambridge, 1996.

Kratz, Bernd, *Historical Calendar of Western Europe A.D. 550 to 1970 (1 to 2700).* Freeware. Lexington, USA, Department of Germanic Languages and Literatures, University of Kentucky, 1989.

Oxford English Dictionary. 2nd ed. CD ROM version 3. Oxford, Oxford University Press, 2002.

Seipp, David J., *An Index and Paraphrase of Printed Year Book Reports, 1268–1535*. Boston University Law School, Internet online. <http://www.bu.edu/law/seipp/>, accessed 17 Jul 2008.

COLLECTED WORKS, COMPILATIONS, LETTERS, ETC.

Baker, John Hamilton, *English Legal Manuscripts in the United States of America: a Descriptive List*. London, Selden Society, 1985–1990.

Baluze, Étienne; Innocent III, Pope, *Epistolarum Innocentii III. Romani Pontificis libri undecim; Gesta ejusdem Innocentii, et prima collectio Decretalium composita ÖÌ Rainerio Diacono et monacho Pomposiano; Stephanus Baluzius in unum collegit, magnam partem nunc primÖ„m edidit, reliqua emendavit*. Parisiis; Apud Franciscum Muguet Typographum Regis et illustrissimi Archiepiscopi Parisiensis; 1682. (*Letters of Pope Innocent III*. Paris, 1682).

Berkeley, George, bishop of Cloyne, *The Works of George Berkeley Bishop of Cloyne*. A. A. Luce and T. E. Jessop eds., Edinburgh, Nelson, 1956.

Boulter, Hugh, *Letters written by His Excellency Hugh Boulter, D.D., Lord Primate of All Ireland, &c. to several ministers of state in England, and some others*. Dublin , Printed for George Faulkner and James Williams, 1770.

Granville, Mary (Mrs Delany), *The Autobiography and Correspondence of Mary Granville, Mrs Delany*. Lady Llanover, ed. London, Bentley, 1861.

Hyde, Henry, earl of Clarendon, *The Correspondence of Henry Hyde, Earl of Clarendon, and his brother Laurence Hyde, Earl of Rochester*. S. W. Singer, ed. London, H. Colburn, 1828.

Swift, Jonathan, *The Correspondence of Jonathan Swift*. Harold Williams, ed. Oxford, Clarendon, 1965.

Swift, Jonathan, *The Prose Works of Jonathan Swift*. Davis, ed. Oxford, Blackwell, 1966.

Swift, Jonathan, *Poems of Jonathan Swift D.D.* W. E. Browning, ed. London, 1910.

Swift, Jonathan, *Swift: Poetical Works*. H. Davis, ed. London, 1967.

THESES

Donaldson, Alfred Gaston, 'The Application in Ireland of English and British Legislation Made Before 1801.' PhD thesis, Queen's University, Belfast, 1952.

McGrath, Charles Ivar Vincent, 'The Irish Revenue System: Government and Administration.' PhD thesis, University of London, 1997.

Rogers, Patrick, 'The policy of Henry VIII regarding the Religious Houses in Ireland.' PhD thesis, Queen's University, Belfast, 1928.

SECONDARY SOURCES

Anon, *A General Abridgement of Cases in Equity, argued and adjudged in the High Court of Chancery, &c*. By a gentleman of the Middle Temple. [Attributed variously to M. Bacon, Sir Geoffrey Gilbert, R. Foley and H. Pooley.] London, In the Savoy, printed by E. and R. Nutt, and R. Gosling, (assigns of E. Sayer, Esq;) for Henry Lintot, 3rd edition, 1739.

Ashley, Sir William James, *Surveys Historic and Economic*. London, Longmans, Green, 1900.

Bacon, Francis, Baron of Verulam, Viscount St Alban, *Works*. London, R. Gosling, 1730.

Baker, John Hamilton, *An Introduction to English Legal History*. London, Butterworths, 4th ed. 2002.

Baker, John Hamilton, *Manual of Law French*. 2nd ed. Aldershot, Scolar Press, 1990.

Baker, John Hamilton, *The Order of Serjeants at Law: a Chronicle of Creations, With Related Texts and a Historical Introduction*. Publications of the Selden Society. Supplementary Series, vol. 5, London, Selden Society, 1984.

Baker, Sir John, *Oxford History of the Laws of England*. vol 6. 1483–1558. Oxford, Oxford University Press, 2003.

Ball, F. Elrington, *The Judges in Ireland, 1221–1921*. London, Murray, 1926. reprint by Round Hall, 1993.

Ball, R.M., 'Exchequer of Pleas, Bills and Writs' (1988) *Journal of Legal History* 308.

Barton, Charles, *An Historical Treatise of a Suit in Equity*. W. Clarke & Son, 1796.

Beckett, J. C., *Protestant Dissent in Ireland 1687–1780*. London, Faber, 1948.

Birks, P., ed., *Life of the Law: Proceedings of the Tenth British Legal History Conference*. London, Hambledon, 1993.

Blackstone, William, *Commentaries on the Laws of England*. Oxford, Clarendon Press, 1765–69, reprinted New York, Legal Classics Library, 1983.

Bonfield, Lloyd, *Marriage Settlements, 1601–1740: the Adoption of the Strict Settlement*. Cambridge Studies in English Legal History. Cambridge, Cambridge University Press, 1983.

Bracton, *De Legibus et Consuetudinibus Angliæ: On the Law and Customs of England*. 4 vols. George Woodbine, ed. Translated with notes by Samuel E. Thorne. Cambridge, Mass., Belknap Press of Harvard University in association with the Selden Society, 1968–1977. See also Bracton Online, <http://hlsl5.law.harvard.edu/bracton/>, accessed 17 July 2008.

Breslin, John, *Banking Law in the Republic of Ireland*. 1st ed. Dublin, Gill & MacMillan, 1998.

Brooke, Robert, *La Graunde Abridgement*. London, In ædibus R. Tottell, 1573.

Brown, Archibald, *A New Law Dictionary and Institute of the Whole Law, for the Use of the Legal Profession, and the Public*. London, Stevens & Haynes, 1874.

Brown, W. *Practice in the Court of Exchequer, at Westminster, in its several branches, viz. 1. His Majesty's Revenue. 2. Proceedings by English Bill. 3. Actions at Law brought in the Office of Pleas*. 2nd ed. London, 1725.

Bryson, William Hamilton, *Dictionary of Sigla and Abbreviations to and in Law Books Before 1607*. Virginia Legal Studies Series. Charlottesville, University Press of Virginia, 1975.

Bryson, William Hamilton, *The Equity Side of the Exchequer: Its Jurisdiction, Administration, Procedures and Records*. Cambridge, Cambridge University Press, 1975.

Burroughs, Edward H. and Henry B. Gresson, *The Irish Equity Pleader: being a Collection of Forms of Bills in Equity Suits in Ireland, with Preliminary Dissertations and Practical Notes.* Dublin, Hodges & Smith, 1850.

Burton, Philip, *Practice of the Office of Pleas, in the Court of Exchequer.* London, A. Strahan and W. Woodfall, 1791. 2 vols.

Calvinus, Johannes, *Lexicon Iuridicum Ivris Cæsarei Simvl, Et Canonici: Fevdalis Item, Civilis, Criminalis: Theoretici, Ac Practici, Et in Schola and in Foro Vsitatarvm.* Coloniæ, apud Franciscvm Helvidivm, 1622.

Coghill, Sir Marmaduke, *Letters of Marmaduke Coghill 1722–1738.* D.W. Hayton, ed., Dublin, Irish Manuscripts Commission, 2005.

Cokayne, G. E., *The Complete Peerage of England, Scotland, Ireland, Great Britain and the United Kingdom Extant, Extinct, or Dormant.* 2nd ed. London, St Catherine Press, 1926.

Coke, Sir Edward, *The First Part of the Institutes of the Laws of England; or a Commentary Upon Littleton.* 18th Edition ed. with notes by Francis Hargrave and Charles Butler. London, J. & W.T. Clarke, 1823. Reprint, Legal Classics Library, 1985.

Coke, Sir Edward, *The Fourth Part of the Institutes of the Laws of England; Concerning the Jurisdiction of Courts.* 1817 ed. London, for W. Clarke and Sons. Reprint, Lawbook Exchange, 2002.

Connolly, Philomena, *Irish Exchequer Payments, 1270–1446.* IMC, 1998.

Cowell, John and Thomas Manley, *Nomothetes the Interpreter, Containing the Genuine Signification of Such Obscure Words and Terms Used Either in the Common or Statute Lawes of This Realm.* 2nd ed. London, Printed by the Assigns of R. Atkins and E. Atkins for H. Twyford, T. Basset, J. Place, and H. Sawbridge, 1684.

Craig, Maurice, *Dublin, 1660–1860.* New ed. London, Penguin, 1992.

Crawford, Jon G. *A Star Chamber Court in Ireland: the Court of Castle Chamber 1571–1641.* Dublin, Four Courts, 2005.

Cusack, Mary Francis, *A History of the City and County of Cork.* Cork; Dublin, Francis Guy, McGlashan and Gill, 1875.

D'Anvers, Knightley, *A General Abridgment of the Common Law.* 2nd ed. 2 vols. London, printed by E. and R. Nutt, and R. Gosling, for J. Walthoe, 1722–1725.

Dudley Edwards, R., '*Magna Carta Hiberniæ*' in Ryan ed., *Essays and Studies Presented to Professor Eoin MacNeill.* Dublin, At the Sign of the Three Candles, 1940.

Edie, Carolyn A., *The Irish Cattle Bills: A Study in Restoration Politics.* Philadelphia, The American Philosophical Society, 1970.

Ferguson, James F., 'A Calendar of the Contents of the Red Book of the Irish Exchequer' in (1854–55) 3 *Proceedings and Transactions of the Kilkenny and South-East of Ireland Archæological Society* 35–52.

Ferguson, William Dwyer, *A Treatise on the Practice of the Queen's Bench, Common Pleas, and Exchequer of Pleas, in Ireland, in Personal Actions and Ejectments.* Dublin, Milliken, 1841.

Finlay, John, *A Treatise on the Law of Tithes in Ireland, and Ecclesiastical Law Connected Therewith.* Dublin, J. Cumming, 1828.

Foss, Edward, *The Judges of England: With Sketches of Their Lives and Miscellaneous Notices Connected With the Courts at Westminster From the Time of the Conquest.* London, Longman, Brown, Green and Longmans, 1857.

Gadd, R. P., *Peerage Law.* Bristol, ISCA Publishing, 1985.

Gilbert, Geoffrey, *The History and Practice of the High Court of Chancery: in Which Is Introduced, an Account of the Institution and Various Regulations of the Said Court: Shewing Likewise, the Ancient and Present Practice Thereof in an Easy and Familiar Method.* London In the Savoy, Printed by Henry Lintot . . . for J. Worrall . . . and W. Owen, 1758.

Gilbert, Geoffrey, *A Treatise on the Court of Exchequer: in Which the Revenues of the Crown, the Manner of Receiving and Accounting for the Several Branches of Them, the Duty of the Several Officers Employed in the Collection and Receipt, the Nature of the Processes for the Recovery of Debts Due to the Crown, Are Clearly Explained: As Also Occasionally, the Nature of the Feudal and Other Antient Tenures, the Origin of Parliaments, Convocations, the Several Courts of Justice, and Many Other Curious and Useful Particulars Are Shewn.* London In the Savoy: Printed by Henry Lintot . . . for J. Nourse, 1758.

Gilbert, Geoffrey, *Two Treatises on the Proceedings in Equity: and the Jurisdiction of That Court. In Two Volumes: the First Entitled, Forum Romanum: or, the Roman Tribunal . . . The Second Entitled, Lex Prætoria: or, the Prætorian Law; . . . by a Late Learned Judge.* Dublin, printed for Richard Watts, 1756–1758.

Gilbert, Sir John Thomas, *A History of the City of Dublin.* The Sackville Library. Dublin, Gill and Macmillan, 1978.

Gilbert, Sir John Thomas, ed., *Facsimiles of National Manuscripts of Ireland.* London, HMSO; Dublin, A. Thom, 1879.

Gwynn, Aubrey and Neville R. Hadcock, *Medieval Religious Houses: Ireland: With an Appendix to Early Sites.* Dublin: Irish Academic Press, 1988.

Hall, Hubert, *The Antiquities and Curiosities of the Exchequer.* London, Elliot Stock, 1891.

Hand, G. J., *English Law in Ireland, 1290–1324.* Cambridge Studies in English Legal History. Cambridge, Cambridge University Press, 1967.

Hart, A. R., *A History of the King's Serjeants at Law in Ireland: Honour Rather Than Advantage?* Dublin, Four Courts Press for Irish Legal History Society, 2000.

Hervey, Revd S. H. A., *The Wedmore Chronicle.* Parish magazine, *c.* 1800. 2 vols.

Hill, J. R., *From Patriots to Unionists: Dublin civic politics and Irish protestant patriotism, 1660–1840.* Oxford, 1997.

Holdsworth, William Searle, Sir, *A History of English Law* (continued under the general editorship of A. L. Goodhart and H. G. Hanbury. vol. 17, General Index, by John Burke.) (Seventh edition. With an introductory essay and editions by S. B. Chrimes.) 17 vols. London, Methuen, Sweet and Maxwell, 1903–72.

Holdsworth, William Searle, *Charles Dickens as a Legal Historian.* New Haven, Yale University Press, 1929. Reprint, Law Book Exchange, 1996.

Howard, Gorges Edmond, *A Compendious Treatise of the Rules and Practice of the Pleas Side of the Exchequer in Ireland As It Now Stands Between Party and Party, With the Rules of the Said Court, and an Abridgment Under Each Head of Practice, of the Several*

Acts of Parliament Now in Force Relating Thereto. Dublin, 1759. 2nd ed., Dublin, Printed by Elizabeth Lynch, 1793.

Howard, Gorges Edmond, *A Treatise of the Exchequer and Revenue of Ireland.* Dublin, Printed by J.A. Husband, for E. Lynch, 1776.

Howard, Gorges Edmond, *A Treatise on the rules and practice of the Equity Side of the Exchequer in Ireland.* Dublin, printed by Oli. Nelson, 1760.

Howard, Gorges Edmond, *The rules and practice of the High Court of Chancery in Ireland, with the several statutes relative thereto.* Dublin: printed for Elizabeth Lynch, 1772.

Howard, Gorges Edmond, *A supplement to the rules and practice of the High Court of Chancery in Ireland, lately published.* Dublin, 1774.

Irish Records Commission, *Reports, 8th Report, 1819, Supplement.*

Jackson, E. Hilton and Herbert Broom, *Latin for Lawyers: Containing I. A Course in Latin, With Legal Maxims and Phrases As a Basis of Instruction, II. A Collection of Over One Thousand Latin Maxims, With English Translations, Explanatory Notes, and Cross-References, III. A Vocabulary of Latin Words.* 2nd ed. London, Toronto, Canada, Sweet and Maxwell; Carswell, 1937.

Jacob, Giles and Thomas Edlyne Tomlins, *The Law-Dictionary Explaining the Rise, Progress, and Present State, of the English Law, in Theory and Practice; Defining and Interpreting the Terms or Words of Art; and Comprising Copious Information, Historical, Political, and Commercial, on the Subjects of Our Law, Trade, and Government.* London, Printed by A. Strahan, for T. Longman, 1797.

James, Francis G., *Lords of the Ascendancy: the Irish House of Lords and its Members, 1600–1800.* Dublin, Irish Academic Press, 1995.

Johnston-Liik, Edith Mary, ed., *History of the Irish Parliament 1692–1800.* Belfast, Ulster Historical Foundation, 2002. 6 vols.

Kelly, James, *Henry Flood.* Dublin, Four Courts, 1998.

Kelly, James, *Poynings' law and the Making of Law in Ireland, 1660–1800.* Dublin, Four Courts and Irish Legal History Society, 2007.

Kenny, C. S., *Outlines of Criminal Law,* 18th ed. by J. W. C. Turner. Cambridge, Cambridge University. 1962.

Kenny, Colum, *King's Inns and the Kingdom of Ireland, The Irish 'Inn of Court' 1541–1800.* Dublin, Irish Academic Press in association with the Irish Legal History Society, 1992.

Kiernan, Thomas Joseph, *History of the financial administration of Ireland to 1817.* Studies in economics and political science No. 105. London, P. S. King & Son, 1930.

Lang, Andrew. ed., *The Annesley Case.* [Notable British Trials.] Edinburgh & London, W. Hodge & Co., 1913, reprint, Gaunt, 1995.

Lefroy, Thomas, *Observations on the proceedings by Elegit, for recovery of Judgment debts.* Dublin, 1802, KI Law Tracts.

Lyall, Andrew. *Land Law in Ireland.* 2nd ed. Dublin, Round Hall Sweet & Maxwell, 2000.

McEldowney, John F. and Paul O'Higgins. eds., *The Common Law Tradition: Essays in Irish Legal History.* Dublin, Irish Academic Press, 1990.

McGrath, Charles Ivar, *The Making of the Eighteenth-Century Irish Constitution: Government, Parliament and the Revenue, 1692–1714*. Dublin, Four Courts Press, 2000.

MacLysaght, E., *Seventeenth Century Hearth Money Rolls with Full Transcript for County Sligo*. Dublin, IMC, 1967.

Macnair, Michael, 'Sir Jeffrey Gilbert and his Treatises.' (1994) 15 *J. Leg. Hist.* 252–268.

Macnair, Michael R. T., *The Law of Proof in Early Modern Equity*. Berlin, Duncker & Humblot, 1999.

Madox, Thomas, Richard Fitzneale, and Gervasius, *The History and Antiquities of the Exchequer of the Kings of England, in Two Periods: to Wit, From the Norman Conquest to the End of the Reign of K. John: and From the End of the Reign of K. John to the End of the Reign of K. Edward II*. London, Printed by John Matthews and sold by Robert Knaplock, 1711. 2nd ed. New York, Rothman Reprints, 1969.

Malcomson, A. P. W., *John Foster: The Politics of the Anglo-Irish Ascendancy*. Oxford, Oxford University Press, 1978.

Mathew, T., 'Bardell v. Pickwick' (1918) 34 *Law Quarterly Review* 320.

May, Allyson N., *The Bar and the Old Bailey, 1750–1850*. University of North Carolina, 2003.

Megarry, R. E., *Miscellany at Law: A Diversion for Lawyers and Others*. London, Stevens, 1955.

Megarry, Sir Robert and H. W. R. Wade, *The Law of Real Property*. 3rd ed. London, Stevens, 1966; 4th ed. London, Stevens, 1975.

Milsom, S. F. C., *Historical Foundations of the Common Law*. 2nd ed. London, Butterworths, 1981.

Monck Mason, H. J., 'A Description of an Ancient Drawing in the Red Book of the Exchequer in Ireland' in (1820) *Transactions of the Royal Irish Academy: Polite Literature* p. 181.

Moody, T. W. and W. E. Vaughan eds., *A New History of Ireland: IV Eighteenth-Century Ireland 1691–1800*. Oxford, Clarendon, 1986.

Murray, Alice Effie, *A History of the Commercial and Financial Relations between England and Ireland from the period of the Restoration*. New York, Franklin, 1903, reprinted 1970.

O'Flanagan, J. R., *Lives of the Lord Chancellors and Keepers of the Great Seal of Ireland*. 2 vols. London, Longmans, 1870.

Oldham, James, *Trial by Jury: The Seventh Amendment and Anglo-American Special Juries*. New York, New York University, 2006.

Osborough, W. N., *Studies in Irish Legal History*. Dublin, Four Courts, 1999.

Parker, Henry, *Here endith a compendiouse treetise dyalogue of Diues [and] paup[er], that is to say, the riche [and] the pore fructuously tretyng vpon the x. co[m]manmentes . . .*, London, printed by Richard Pynson, 1493.

Parnell, Henry, Baron Congleton, *A History of the Penal Laws against the Irish Catholics: from the Treaty of Limerick to the Union*. Dublin, H. Fitzpatrick, 1808. Reprinted Clark, NJ, Lawbook Exchange, 2003.

Pawlisch, H. S., *Sir John Davies and the conquest of Ireland: a study in legal imperialism.* Cambridge, Cambridge University Press, 1985.

Phair, P. B., 'Sir William Betham's Manuscripts' (1972) 27 *Analectica Hibernica* 1.

Plucknett, Theodore F. T., *A Concise History of the Common Law.* 5th ed. London, Butterworth, 1956.

Pollard, M., *A Dictionary of Members of the Dublin Book Trade 1550–1800.* London, Bibliographical Society, 2000.

Pollock, Sir Frederick, and Maitland, F.W., *The History of English Law Before the Time of Edward I.* 2nd ed., Cambridge, Cambridge University Press, 1898.

Prior, Thomas, *A list of the absentees of Ireland, and the yearly value of their estates and incomes spent abroad...* 3rd ed. London, 1730.

Reeves, John, *History of the English Law From the Time of the Saxons to the End of the Reign of Philip and Mary.* London, E. Brooke, 1787. 2nd ed., Dublin, Luke White, 1787. Reprinted 1969 Augustus M. Kelley, Rothman reprints, inc.

Sanders, Francis William, *An Essay on Uses and Trusts, and on the Nature and Operation of Conveyances at Common Law, and those deriving their Effect from the Statute of Uses.* 2nd ed. London, E. and R. Brooke and J. Rider, 1799.

Selden, John, *The Table Talk of John Selden, Esq, with a Biographical Preface and Notes by S.W. Singer Esq.* London, William Pickering, 1847. Reprint Legal Classics Library, 1989.

Simms, J. G., *Jacobite Ireland, 1685–91.* London, Routledge & K. Paul, 1969.

Simms, J. G., *The Williamite Confiscation in Ireland, 1690–1703.* London, Faber and Faber, 1956.

Simpson, A. W. B., *Biographical Dictionary of the Common Law.* London, Butterworths, 1984.

Simpson, A. W. B., *A History of the Common Law of Contract: The Rise of the Action of Assumpsit.* Oxford, Clarendon, 1975.

Smyth, Constantine. J., *Chronicle of the Law Officers of Ireland, Containing Lists of the Lord Chancellors, and Keepers of the Great Seal, Masters of the Rolls, Chief Justices and Judges of the Courts of King's Bench, Common Pleas, and Exchequer, Attorneys and Solicitors General, With the Sergeants at Law, From the Earliest Period; Dates and Abstracts of Their Patents; Fees and Allowances From the Crown, Tenures of Offices, References to the Records, and Patents of Precedence.* London, Henry Butterworth, 1839.

Stephen, H. J., *A treatise on the principles of Pleading in Civil Actions.* London, 1824.

Surrebutter, John [John Anstey], *The Pleader's Guide, A Didactic Poem.* 1796. American edition, Chicago, 1870, reprinted New Jersey, Lawbook Exchange, 2000 (published with *The Comic Blackstone*).

Swinburn, Henry, *A Treatise of Testaments and Last Wills, Compiled Out of the Laws Ecclesiastical, Civil and Canon, As Also Out of the Common Laws, Customs and Statutes of This Realm.* 5th ed. London, printed by E. and R. Nutt, and R. Gosling (assigns of Edw. Sayer) etc., 1728.

Swinburne, Henry, *A Briefe Treatise of Testaments and Last Willes Very Profitable to Be Vnderstoode of All the Subjects of This Realme of England, ...* London, Printed by Iohn Windet, 1590.

Tidd, William, *The Practice of the Courts of King's Bench and Common Pleas in Personal Actions.* 6th ed. London, 1817.

Tidd, William, *The Practice of the Courts of King's Bench and Common Pleas in Personal Actions, to which are added the Law and Practice of Extents; and the Rules of Court, and Modern Decisions of the Exchequer of Pleas.* 7th ed., London, 1821.

Treitel, G. H., *The Law of Contract.* 11th ed., London, Thomson, 2003.

United Kingdom Government, *Chronological Table of the Statutes, Covering the Period From 1235 to the End of 1971.* London, HMSO, 1972.

Wallace, John William, *The Reporters: Arranged and Characterized With Incidental Remarks.* 4th ed., Buffalo, New York, William S. Hein, 1995.

Wallace, John William and Franklin Fiske Heard, *The Reporters: Arranged and Characterized With Incidental Remarks.* 4th, rev. and enlarged. Published under the superintendence of Franklin Fiske Heard ed. Edinburgh, Carswell, 1882.

Watson, William, *The Clergy-Man's Law or, The Complete Incumbent, Collected From the 39 Articles, Canons, Proclamations, Decrees in Chancery and Exchequer, As Also From All Acts of Parliament, and Common-Law Cases, Relating to the Church and Clergy of England, ...* London, Printed by the assigns of Richard and Edward Atkins, for John Place, 1701.

Williams, Joshua and T. Cyprian Williams, *Principles of the Law of Real Property.* 23rd ed. London, Toronto, Sweet & Maxwell; Carswell, 1920.

Wurzel, Harold, 'The Origin and Development of Quo Minus' (1939) 49 *Yale Law Journal* 39–64.

INDEX OF PEOPLE, PLACES AND THINGS

Roman numbers refer to pages in the Introduction.
Arabic numbers refer to pages in the Reports.
Barristers: where the first name has not been identified, only the surname is given.

INDEX OF SUBJECTS